Modern Iran since 1797

Modern Iran since 1797 offers a comprehensive analysis of political, social and economic developments in Iran since the end of the eighteenth century. Spanning two centuries, the book provides historical context for Iran's international relationships and its internal struggle to reconcile itself and its traditions with the modern world.

The book presents an overview of this crucial period in Iran's history, its emergence from the political turmoil of the eighteenth century through to its initial encounter with the industrial powers of Europe and its attempts to navigate the turbulent waters of European imperialism. It assesses the impact of European ideas on the triumph and tragedy of the Constitutional Revolution, which established the political template for the country going forward and against which all other political developments have been measured. This new edition has been updated to incorporate new scholarship and research to make a rounded assessment of recent developments and bring the text fully up to date. A substantive new prequel has also been added, covering the long nineteenth century from 1797 through to 1921, including a fuller and more detailed treatment both of the Constitutional Revolution and the events and ideology that underpinned it.

Written in a clear, engaging style and highlighting Iran as a state and society grappling with the realities of the modern age, *Modern Iran since 1797* remains the perfect guide for all those studying the history of modern Iran.

Ali M. Ansari is Professor of Iranian History at the University of St Andrews. His most recent publications include *The Politics of Nationalism in Modern Iran* (2012) and *Iran: A Very Short Introduction* (2014).

Modern Iran since 1797

Reform and Revolution

3rd edition

Ali M. Ansari

Routledge
Taylor & Francis Group

LONDON AND NEW YORK

Third edition published 2019
by Routledge
2 Park Square, Milton Park, Abingdon, Oxon, OX14 4RN

and by Routledge
52 Vanderbilt Avenue, New York, NY 10017

Routledge is an imprint of the Taylor & Francis Group, an informa business

First edition published by Pearson Education Limited 2003
Second edition published by Pearson Education Limited 2007
Second edition published by Routledge 2014

British Library Cataloguing-in-Publication Data
A catalogue record for this book is available from the British Library

Library of Congress Cataloging-in-Publication Data
Names: Ansari, Ali M., author. | Ansari, Ali M. Modern Iran.
Title: Modern Iran since 1797 : reform and revolution / Ali M. Ansari.
Description: 3rd edition. | Milton Park, Abingdon, Oxon ; New York,
     NY : Routledge, 2019. | Revised edition of: Modern Iran : the
     Pahlavis and after. Harlow, England : Pearson Education, 2007. |
     Includes bibliographical references and index. |
Identifiers: LCCN 2018046942 (print) | LCCN 2018049217 (ebook) |
Subjects: LCSH: Iran—History.
Classification: LCC DS272 (ebook) | LCC DS272 .A58 2019 (print) |
     DDC 955—dc23
LC record available at https://lccn.loc.gov/2018046942

ISBN: 978-1-138-28184-4 (hbk)
ISBN: 978-1-138-28185-1 (pbk)
ISBN: 978-0-429-39987-9 (ebk)

Typeset in Galliard
by Swales & Willis Ltd, Exeter, Devon, UK

For Marjon

Men make their own history, but they do not make
it just as they please; they do not make it under
circumstances chosen by themselves, but under
circumstances directly found, given and transmitted
from the past. The tradition of all the dead
generations weighs like a nightmare on the brain
of the living. And just when they seem engaged in
revolutionising themselves and things, in creating
something entirely new, precisely in such epochs of
revolutionary crisis they anxiously conjure up the
spirits of the past to their service and borrow from
them names, battle slogans and costumes in order to
present the new scene of world history in this time
honoured disguise.

Karl Marx, *The Eighteenth Brumaire of*
Louis Bonaparte

Contents

Preface to the 3rd edition

It seems remarkable to me now that the first edition of this text was completed in 2002 sitting with my mother and stepfather in their somewhat ramshackle villa in Kelarabad in Mazandaran on Iran's Caspian littoral. The world appeared an altogether more optimistic place then. The tragedy of 9/11 had of course by then occurred and President Khatami was facing severe pressure at home not least from yet another downturn in US–Iran relations. Yet despite membership of the 'Axis of Evil', there were still grounds for hope in the future. The international situation might yet still yield opportunities for a rapprochement with Iran, while the Reform movement in Iran, although stalled had not yet been fully derailed. The following decade was to put paid to such optimism and on both fronts, domestic and foreign, developments took a decided turn for the worse. Iran did benefit from the turbulence of the Global War on Terror, but not in the manner its political reformists might have hoped. Time of course offers the benefit of greater perspective and context. An assessment of a revolution after 20 years – especially when ten of those years were wracked by war – is quite different to one after 40 years, when it had reached its proverbial 'middle age', and the optimism of youth gives way to a somewhat cynical weariness. The reader will not be surprised to see such sentiments reflected at times in the pages of this book, not least the conclusion.

This new perspective has been enhanced by the period under review. This new 3rd edition, is most obviously distinguished from the previous two by having a substantive prequel added to cover the long nineteenth century from 1797 through to 1921. Not only has this allowed a fuller and more detailed treatment of perhaps the most significant development in modern Iran – the Constitutional Revolution – but also an assessment of the intellectual awakening that underpinned it and the political and social developments that in turn catalysed what I have described here and elsewhere as an Iranian enlightenment. This context of course changes the balance of the book. Whereas earlier editions juxtaposed the Pahlavis with the Islamic Republic and suggested the former to be anomalous – if in their own way revolutionary – to the natural trajectory of development, this broader context allows us to situate the Pahlavis more securely within the framework of the late Qajar era. Just as students of Turkish history have become increasingly aware of the debt Ataturk owed to the Young Turks, the Young

Ottomans and the Tanzimat, so too I hope it will become apparent that Reza Shah was himself a product of the Constitutional Revolution, and that many of the ideas he institutionalised had echoes in the Qajar period. We may (I hope) finally lay to rest the frequently attested assertion that Reza Shah 'changed' the name of the country to Iran, or indeed, reinvented the title *Shahanshah*. Even the tendency to archaism, and an association with the glories of pre-Islamic Iran were not a preoccupation peculiar to the Pahlavis. Both the Qajars and latterly the Islamic Republic showed a predilection in this regard, and certainly Ahmadinejad's affection for Cyrus the Great and the Achaemenids is almost on a par with Mohammad Reza Shah. The reader will see, that for all the change that has taken place, there are some interesting continuities, and the more a political order seeks to distance itself from its predecessor, the more it in fact resembles it.

Similarly, time and new research has allowed to make a fuller more rounded assessment of developments. The uprising of 2009, and the Arab Spring that has followed, has allowed us to better contextualise the revolution of 1979. Not only in terms of size, but in the violence that enabled it. Gone are the more exaggerated figures for casualties, and research conducted in the Islamic Republic now suggests that total casualties never exceeded 3,000 for the period until the arrival of Ayatollah Khomeini in February 1979. Indeed, the evidence now suggests that the official assessments for casualties in the notorious Jaleh Square massacre were actually accurate. Similarly, the casualties for the Iran–Iraq War have been revised downwards to reflect new research. Perhaps the most significant shift however has been in the assessment of the intellectual inheritance which now leans much more towards Britain than France, and Reza Shah's own debt to the template for change established by the Constitutionalists. While the first two editions always made clear that Reza Khan could not initially have succeeded without the support of intellectuals, this association is now made much clearer and reflects more recent research on this period, including my own. I have nonetheless endeavoured to minimise any changes to the original text, limiting myself to ironing out inconsistencies and factual errors. Where new research has raised questions, I have tended to place these in the endnotes and students are encouraged to review those as well as the additional literature in the bibliography. The reader will I hope, be forgiving of those parts of the text where the stitching together of the new and old texts, their tone and interpretation, are more apparent than intended.

It goes without saying that no text is definitive, and no text is without its errors. Every effort has been made to eradicate the latter, and new sources, research and perspective will see new interpretations emerge in due course. This, like any text should be regarded as a snapshot of the state of the field, an interpretation, and a platform to encourage the inquisitive to delve further into the history of this fascinating political culture. I am grateful for the support of colleagues in St Andrews and further afield, for their comments and often vigorous debates which have helped shape and refine my own views. Particular thanks to my colleague at St Andrews, Siavush Randjbar-Daemi for his help in locating digital Persian sources and for his invaluable suggestions in updating the Guide to

Further Research. I am especially grateful to Paul Luft and David Morgan (whose own excellent *Medieval Persia 1040–1797* in the same series, segues nicely into this volume and provides even more historical context) for reading through and commenting on the first draft of the 'prequel'. Thanks are also due to my editor at Taylor and Francis, Zoe Thomson, for allowing me to insert an extensive prequel and for her patience in awaiting its arrival. I am also grateful to Larry Potter, from Columbia University, a seasoned and loyal user of the earlier editions, who kindly offered me his thoughts on aspects of style. While I have retained many block quotes – in large part because I think it is important for students to hear the historical voices as far as possible first hand – I have moved to eliminate those unfortunate British understatements and most egregiously my overuse of 'arguably'. This might be considered a hangover from my doctoral dissertation when it was deemed prudent to 'qualify' everything, and have been duly, and somewhat refreshingly excised from the main text. I am extremely grateful to my copyeditor Jonathan Hoare, for ironing out the many inconsistencies that inevitably work their way into a text of this length. Thanks are also due to Bonita Glanville-Morris at Taylor & Francis and Julian Webb at Swales & Willis. Last, but by no means least, I would like to thank the National Archives for permission to use extracts from their files. Needless to say, any remaining errors or stylistic *faux pas* are mine and mine alone.

Ali M. Ansari
University of St Andrews – June 2018

Glossary

Ayan Notables, traditional term ascribed to the (landed) aristocracy.

Ayatollah Literally 'sign of God', honorific title given to the most senior religious jurists. Emerges into usage in the twentieth century, and its proliferation has led to further qualification to distinguish those of the highest religious authority as 'Grand Ayatollahs'.

Basij Often translated as 'popular militia'. Under the Islamic Republic, this is often rephrased as 'Islamic militia'.

Bazaaris The traditional merchant classes, operating informally, through extended family networks. Most cities and towns have their 'bazaar'.

Hojjat-ol Islam Literally, 'proof of God'; honorific title afforded to those religious jurists below the rank of Ayatollah.

Ijtehad The use of independent judgement, usually through analogical reasoning, to derive new legal rulings from the existing body of law.

Imam This has two distinct meanings. More commonly, this is the title given to the leader of the Islamic community by Shi'a Muslims, who believe that leadership devolved upon the heirs of the Prophet through his son-in-law Ali, the first Imam. Iran's Shi'as are predominantly 'Twelver', believing that there were Twelve Imams in total, the last of which disappeared into occultation, and who will return at the end of time.

Majlis Literally, 'Assembly', more commonly translated as 'Parliament'; the Constitutional Revolution witnessed the establishment of a 'National Consultative Assembly', replaced after the Islamic Revolution with the 'Islamic Consultative Assembly'.

Marja-e Taqlid Literally, 'source of emulation'; term applied to those Ayatollahs worthy of emulation by a distinct group of followers.

Mujtahid Shi'a *ulema* whose education and training in jurisprudence and Islamic legal texts allow them to practice *ijtehad*. The qualification, in the modern period, is reserved for those of the rank of Ayatollah and above, although not all Ayatollahs are recognised *mujtahids*.

Shah Persian term for 'King'; *Shahanshah*: literally 'King of Kings', sometimes, though not accurately, translated as 'Emperor'.

Ulema   The plural of 'alim', a learned individual, more commonly associated with religious scholars, and generally utilised with reference to the
clerical class.

Velayat-i Faqih   Literally, Guardianship of the Jurisconsult; political concept
developed by Ayatollah Khomeini institutionalising the supremacy of the religious jurist in political affairs. The jurist so appointed is termed the *vali-e faqih*.

Chronology of modern Iran

1797	Death of Agha Mohammad Khan; accession of Fath Ali Shah
1804	Outbreak of First Russo-Persian War
1807	Treaty of Finkenstein
1813	Treaty of Golestan
1826	Outbreak of Second Russo-Persian War
1828	Treaty of Turkmenchai
1833	Death of Abbas Mirza
1834	Accession of Mohammad Shah
1848	Accession of Nasir al Din Shah
1850	Execution of the Bab
1851	Death of Amir Kabir
1856/7	Anglo-Persian War
1857	Treaty of Paris
1872	Reuters Concession
1891/2	The Tobacco Revolt
1896	Assassination of Nasir al Din Shah
1906	Constitutional Revolution
1908	Discovery of oil, foundation of the Anglo-Persian Oil Company (APOC)
1914	Outbreak of the Great War
1919	Paris Peace Conference; attempted imposition of Anglo-Persian Agreement
1921	Coup, led by Seyyed Zia Tabatabaie and Reza Khan, overthrows government
	Reza Khan appointed Army Commander, and subsequently Minister of War
1923	Reza Khan appointed Prime Minister
1924	Debate on Republicanism/Fifth Majlis
1925	Majlis deposes Qajar dynasty, elects Reza Shah as first king of new Pahlavi dynasty
1926	Coronation of Reza Shah
1927	Dress codes imposed; inauguration of Trans-Iranian Railway project
1928	Foundation of the National Bank of Iran

1933	Death of Teymourtache
1934	Law for the foundation of Tehran University ratified
1935	Foreigners informed they must desist from using the name 'Persia' and instead use 'Iran'
1936	Abolition of the veil
1939	Outbreak of Second World War
1941	Allied invasion and occupation of Iran; abdication of Reza Shah; succession of Mohammad Reza Shah
1946	Azerbaijan Crisis; beginning of Cold War
1949	Assassination attempt on the Shah while visiting Tehran University
1950	General Razmara becomes Prime Minister
1951	General Razmara assassinated; Dr Mosaddeq becomes Prime Minister
	Oil Nationalisation bill ratified
	Britain boycotts Iranian oil
1952	Diplomatic relations with Britain severed
1953	Coup '28th Mordad'; overthrow of Dr Mosaddeq and National Front government
1955	Iran joins Baghdad Pact; Baha'i pogrom launched
1956	Suez Crisis
1957	Foundation of SAVAK
1958	Qarani plot; Iraqi Revolution
1960	*Coup d'état* in Turkey; Dr Ali Amini appointed Prime Minister
1962	Resignation of Amini
1963	Shah launches the White Revolution
	Riots in various cities protesting reforms
1964	American government personnel granted immunity from prosecution in Iranian Courts
	US loan to Iran approved
	Ayatollah Khomeini exiled
1965	Prime Minister Mansur assassinated, replaced by Hoveida
1967	Coronation of the Shah
1968	Britain announces 'East of Suez' policy
1971	Shah celebrates 2,500 years of Persian Monarchy
1973	Shah engineers quadrupling of oil price
1975	Foundation of Rastakhiz
1976	Change to Imperial calendar
1977	Jimmy Carter begins presidency
1978	Article critical of Ayatollah Khomeini published in *Etelaat* newspaper
	Cycle of riots begin unwinding of Pahlavi regime
	Jaleh Square massacre
	Muslim month of Moharram witnesses massive demonstrations against the Shah
1979	Shah leaves Iran; Ayatollah Khomeini returns
	Monarchy abolished; Islamic Republic founded
	US Embassy occupied and diplomats taken hostage

1980	Iraq invades Iran
1982	Iran recaptures occupied territory, symbolised by reconquest of Khorramshahr
1988	Ceasefire in Iran–Iraq War
1989	Imam Khomeini dies; Ali Akbar Hashemi Rafsanjani becomes President
1997	Election of Seyyed Mohammad Khatami to the Presidency
1998	Revelations about the 'chain murders'
1999	Attack on student dormitories by Islamic vigilantes leads to nationwide demonstrations
2000	Reformists seize control of Parliament
	Hardline reaction begins
2001	Khatami elected in second landslide election victory
	9/11 and war in Afghanistan
2002	George W. Bush describes Iran as part of 'Axis of Evil' in State of the Union address
	Details of Iran's nuclear programme revealed
2003	Invasion and occupation of Iraq
2004	Hardline conservatives seize control of Parliament in what is widely seen as a fraudulent election
2005	Hardline Mayor of Tehran, Mahmoud Ahmadinejad, elected President
2009	Presidential election crisis
2013	Election of Hasan Rouhani
2015	Joint Comprehensive Plan of Action (JCPOA) agreed between the P5+1 and Iran
2018	The United States withdraws from the JCPOA

Iran in the twentieth century (showing territorial changes from the 19th century)

Iran in the twentieth century (showing territorial changes from the 19th century)

Contemporary Iran ▬▬ Boundaries of modern Iran ▬▬ Current international boundaries

1   Introduction

All ranks in Persia are brought up to admire show and parade; and they are more likely to act from the dictates of imagination and vanity, than of reason and judgment. The character was well drawn by Muhammad Nubbee Khan, the late ambassador to India. 'If you wish my countrymen to understand you, speak to their eyes, not their ears'.

(Sir John Malcolm, *Sketches of Persia*, 1827)

Few countries have proved so persistently incomprehensible to Western analyses as Iran. Seemingly determined to obstruct and frustrate understanding, Iran has come to occupy a particular position in the Western world view,[1] which in many ways mirrors Iran's multifaceted attitude to the West. At once fascinated and enamoured by the exotic luxuries and sophisticated manners of the civilised *Persians* (the 'Frenchmen of the East', as Curzon described them), they are also regarded as strangely resistant to the onward march of 'modernity', and prone to a destructive fanaticism which belies rational comprehension. Such interpretations are not new and are a reflection of the West's encounter with Iran in the nineteenth century, which coincided not only with the political ascendancy of the West, but with the development of the discipline of history. Indeed, the study of history, as we know it today, is a product of modern Western society, and many of the first histories written reflected the aspirations, prejudices and demands of a Western readership. Indeed, many of the primary documents were products of Western bureaucracies and consulates. When Iranians encountered their 'history' therefore, it tended to be mediated through the pens of Western historians, while their own, largely oral traditions were dismissed as fable and at best as literary artefacts, skilfully written, but of little historical value.[2]

This tendency has been increasingly challenged in the twentieth century, in part as a result of the changing nature and importance of the Iranian state, but more importantly, because of the growth in education and the determination of 'Iranians' to write their own history. Ironically, the moment of real historical growth in the aftermath of the Islamic Revolution coincided with the deepest failure of understanding. Just as some Iranian historians were seeking to explain the Islamic Revolution in terms of the Iranian historical experience in the twentieth century, some foreign scholars and commentators (including émigrés) were determined to wrench the political upheaval of 1979 away from its historical roots and towards a comparative framework which sought to resituate Iran within a distinctly 'Islamic' setting. To some extent the West successfully re-appropriated Iranian history, and the narrative which dominates the Western perception of Iran is that of the early revolution, almost as if little happened beforehand, or indeed subsequently. Whether 'History' had stood still or not in the East, the West seemed determined to bring it to a standstill.[3]

The reality is, however, one of dynamic change rooted in Iran's determination to successfully confront and harness the challenge of modernisation and 'modernity'. This change was all the more traumatic because of the innate and profound conservatism of a society that proved at first highly resistant to the change that was being imposed. Yet after decades of apparent stupor, as the Qajar era came to a close with the triumphant rupture of the Constitutional Revolution, Iran embarked on a period of radical modernisation, understood as the appropriation, absorption and application of Western achievements to an Iranian environment. This apparently wholesale process of imitation provoked uncertainty and reaction, which began to challenge the particular conception of modernity imposed most vigorously by Reza Shah. A window of political opportunity, prior to the *coup d'état* which overthrew Dr Mosaddeq, witnessed the bitter debates and often violent contest over the development and identity of an Iranian state, which was then succeeded by another period of sustained autocracy. By the end of this period, even Western definitions of modernisation were beginning to be redefined. The most dramatic change, of course, occurred during the Islamic Revolution of 1979, when Iran appeared on the face of it at least, to definitively break with its Western patrons.

This book seeks to chart Iran's engagement with the challenge posed by the West and Western modernity, from the foundations of the Qajar state in 1797 to the ongoing contest in pursuit of an 'Islamic Democracy' in contemporary Iran, and to situate current developments within their proper historical framework, a narrative frame of reference that is frequently cited and referred to by Iranians. A pivotal moment in the history of modern Iran, as will be detailed later, was the Constitutional Revolution of 1905–11, even if many of its ideas were not realised until the advent of Reza Khan and the subsequent establishment of his dynasty. This crucial period in the history of the country established the political template against which much else is measured. But the Constitutional Revolution did not emerge from a vacuum but was itself rooted in the encounter with European 'modernity' which confronted Iranian statesmen from the early years of the nineteenth century. Military power was swiftly followed by economic penetration and intellectual engagement on a scale that would profoundly affect the development of the country. Yet by anchoring our understanding of modern Iran in the broader context of two centuries of development we are better able to judge the degrees of continuity and change that have affected the country and see the Pahlavi period as an acceleration of a trend that was established decades before their emergence: as much a consequence as a cause of change.

Needless to say, in a country which continues to be politically volatile, history remains contested as rival interpretations of determining events are vigorously debated and refined. The narrative is still being woven. As perspectives change, and new sources emerge, our understanding of modern Iranian history will necessarily be further refined, and even if archives are proving more difficult to access, published sources are on the increase and provide historians with new, and far more accessible avenues for research. (See the Guide to Further Research p. 346.)

Recognising these limitations, there are nevertheless a number of discernible themes and tensions which may be said to inform Iranian history since 1797.[4]

Reform and reaction

This is fundamentally a book about change and the politics of managing that change, as successive governments and political elites sought, and continue to seek, to navigate a stable and sustainable route from a perception of tradition to a particular conception of modernity.[5] This change has occasionally been sudden, violent and explicitly political, but on other occasions, arguably of greater durability, the transformation has been a gradual (if still comparatively rapid) social and economic one which in the space of a century has fundamentally altered the political landscape of Iran. On occasion, the process of change has been indigenously engendered, but foreign influence has been strong, especially within the framework of ideas. For most of the period covered by this book the management of change has been the responsibility of elites. It was a succession of elites which performed the function, sometimes well, at other times ineffectually, of the 'revolutionary' vanguard, bringing new ideas about social organisation, and political and economic development, and adapting them (with varying degrees of efficacy) to Iranian circumstances. Reform, even revolutionary reform, has been imposed on a largely unwilling and conservative society by elites convinced of the truth of their policies. The applicability of borrowed policies and the efficacy of implementation in relation to the social reality confronted often dictated the success of a given policy. At the same time, it would be wrong to suggest that the elites who dictated the pace and direction of change were oblivious to the consequences for society and to social forces they could neither control nor dictate. As will be seen, elites were regularly confounded by the consequences of policies that they initiated, or that had been the result of broader unforeseen trends in the international economy during the nineteenth and twentieth centuries. Similarly, while elites by and large functioned as the means through which the Western model of development, however that was defined in its specifics, was adapted and transferred to Iran, it has only really been from the 1990s that the process of synthesis has gathered pace and wider society, empowered by education and social media, has played an increasing role in shaping the wider debate. In this sense society was becoming more democratic even if politics was proving resistant to the idea. Meanwhile, the intelligentsia, one of the distinctive social groups of twentieth-century Iran, alternated between a conscientious and almost dutiful critique of the establishment, and a very occasional co-option into the political elite.

These problems, which have been faced by Iranian statesmen since at least the Treaty of Turkmenchai in 1828, and which were brought into sharp focus during the Constitutional Revolution (1906–11), revolve, on one level, around the need for political and economic reform and the nature and form it should take, while, at a deeper level, they have focused on the cultural and intellectual contradictions that require some form of resolution. Just as the growth of the modern state and the international order forced the implementation of well defined and delineated international boundaries, and encouraged the development of rational bureaucratic structures, so too it has rendered obsolete and ineffectual the convenient and essential ambiguity which has allowed the co-existence of contradictory ideas about identity both domestically and internationally to continue.[6] The rationalisation of ideas has forced Iranian intellectuals to reconsider the ambiguous relationship between 'Iran' and 'Islam', and, crucially for our purposes, Iran and the West. At times, crude attempts were made to impose cultural homogeneity, to develop a singular 'idea' of Iran to the exclusion of all others. But the impracticality of this led gradually and tentatively to the adoption of a more sophisticated, inclusive model, one which sought to redefine relationships to facilitate a pluralistic model in which identities were complementary rather than antagonistic. Indeed, it may be argued that the single most important theme of this book is the continuing contest over the right to define the identity of Iran and its relationship with the outside world.

Ideas over which direction Iran should take in response to the challenge posed by the West emerged in the aftermath of Iran's defeats at the hands of Tsarist Russia in the early nineteenth century and gradually came to dominate the thinking of Iranian statesmen. By the end of the nineteenth century ideas of nationalism were increasingly prevalent among the political elite, and while there was a broad range of opinion as to what exactly nationalism entailed, and to what extent it was antagonistic to religion (and Islam in particular), there was a broad consensus that reform was an increasingly urgent necessity. Arguments raged among the intellectual and political elite as to the precise nature of national revitalisation and the utility or otherwise of nationalism, be it secular or religious in character. Some rejected such ideas wholesale as a Western invention, others felt it could be usefully adapted to Iran, while still others, such as Kermani, espoused an increasingly chauvinistic secular nationalism, which viewed Islam as an alien religion imposed by force on the Iranian people. Diverse, often contradictory, views emerged which were to develop throughout the twentieth century and while the central *raison d'être* of national revival united all of them, thereby emphasising a broad nationalist consensus, differences in detail prevented a workable and durable synthesis. The consequence was that it often took a political or economic crisis to bring these disparate groups together to practical political effect. Thus it was that the economic crisis of the late nineteenth century compounded the developing political disenchantment with the Qajar state to unite different factions from a cross-section of society, including the *ulema*, the intelligentsia, the aristocracy and the *bazaaris* (an inter-related if ideologically disparate group of individuals), to mobilise themselves against the Qajar state in the Constitutional

Revolution of 1906. Its rapid success, while indicative of the weakness of the Qajar state which opposed it and its limited popular impact, must not detract from the profound consequences of the movement, which effectively succeeded in permanently altering the political culture of the country by introducing the lexicon of constitutionalism, frequently ignored but always acknowledged by successive regimes.

The Constitutional Revolution: the pivot of modern Iranian history

Many of the problems implicit in developing and imposing a practical programme for change became very apparent during the Constitutional Revolution and Movement, and were a major cause of the collapse and perceived failure of the movement. The Constitutional Revolution also highlighted a number of characteristics of political movements and social change in Iran. These problems and characteristics were to recur frequently throughout the period covered by this book, and in many ways constitute the central themes and issues. For instance, a critical political problem faced by the leaders of the Constitutional Revolution was the limited level of popular political awareness and the desirability of extending it. The Constitutional Revolution was led and dominated by elites, and while urban groups participated in the final stages particularly through the encouragement of leading members of the Shi'a *ulema*, its popular appeal, while spontaneous and often decisive, was not profound. Popular grievances were much more immediate and were not a reflection of the liberal democratic values espoused by members of the elite who had access to foreign ideas, or indeed had lived abroad. This meant that, while some members of the political opposition had a clear idea of the sort of constitutional monarchy they wanted, along with an elected parliament, the notion of 'popular sovereignty' that they also encouraged was incomprehensible to the majority of Iranians, while more traditionally minded members of the elite thought the concept blasphemous. Furthermore, it should be remembered that popular participation remained an urban phenomenon and, given that in 1906 it is estimated that only 10 per cent of the population lived in cities and towns, the general pool can be seen as somewhat limited. At the same time, it is worth stressing that the Constitutional Movement was in a very real sense a child of the European Enlightenment from which it drew its ideas and vocabulary. These tended to emphasise the 'republic', in other words the rule of law, over any concept of 'democracy' and implicitly supported the idea of an elite vanguard.

This lack of a popular base, or indeed the mechanism of government, was to severely hinder any chance of immediate practical success for the revolutionaries, who found the social and practical foundations for their political aspirations to be weak. It also allowed their opponents within the state to challenge their authority and confront their limited power with increasing confidence. At the same time, this lack of social penetration should not lead to the conclusion (suggested by some historians) that the Constitutional Revolution was little more than a political curiosity, a storm in a teacup, idealistic in the extreme, and a practical catastrophe for the Iranian state. While its practical consequences were in the short term to render government impotent, this was not entirely the responsibility of the leaders of the movement, although it may be ascribed to their general political weakness and lack of a profound political base. On the other hand, as noted above, its intellectual legacy was immense, perpetuated as it was in the recollections of both victors and vanquished, the intellectual vanguard who left a highly charged and emotive reference for successive generations of political leaders. The myth of the Constitutional Revolution and its high ideals, destroyed by a reactionary king encouraged by his foreign allies, was delivered with great passion by veterans of the movement to a new generation of political leaders who were only too eager to emulate the achievements of their illustrious if tragic predecessors. In time the myth would be spread, by the growth in literacy and the emergence of mass forms of communication and media, to a far wider audience, but the fact that the movement enjoyed an urban focus ensured that the seed of this myth was planted at the political heart of the country. For it is important to emphasise that, small as the urban centres were, they were the focus of political activity and the political centre of gravity from which political awareness would consolidate itself and spread. While it would be several decades before the foundation of the University of Tehran, the capital city, for all its poverty, had established itself as the pre-eminent political centre in the country. Tabriz may have been the gateway for ideas. Tehran was where these ideas were to be exploited. Throughout the twentieth century Tehran never lost this political status and indeed, as rural–urban migration accelerated in the middle of the century, this status was simply exaggerated.

Another major theme highlighted by the Constitutional Revolution was the clash between those who held to secular nationalism and popular sovereignty, and those whose religious allegiances made the unequivocal support for such concepts problematic. It is important to recognise that in the mutual antagonism which existed and continues to exist between the doctrines of Islam and those of nationalist ideologies, especially the secular varieties of nationalism, we are dealing in essence with ideas that are open to interpretation and change, and a degree of fluidity has always existed between them. Islam and nationalism, according to individual interpretations and understandings, sometimes opposed each other, at other times made curiously convenient bedfellows. What is certainly true is that Iranians were forced increasingly to confront the contradiction they had previously relegated to comfortable and convenient ambiguity. As the Constitutional Revolution was to show, this was not simply a theological debate, but an intellectual and ideological exercise of immense practical consequence. Not only were the *ulema* as a social class immensely influential in Iranian political life, but given that a major aspect of popular culture was permeated throughout with myths and symbols of Islamic derivation, the *ulema* effectively possessed the language of communication which could most easily access large tracts of the population. Islam, its symbols and cultural constructs, was quintessentially the language of popular mobilisation and this social strength has probably only begun to significantly dissipate in the last two decades. This is not to denigrate the symbols of a distinctly national identity that Iranians may have had not least through the varied myths derived from the *Shahnameh*, but as these traditional myths were being gradually replaced in the twentieth century with a new 'national' historiography, which was for much of this period in the process of rediscovery or construction,[7] it was natural that the average Iranian would turn to stories and personalities that were familiar. While this nationalist mythology was relatively underdeveloped in popular political culture (in stark contrast to elite culture), Islamic mythology was correspondingly more profound and had established deep roots. It was a reality which was not only accepted but approved of by the political elite, who firmly held to the belief that religion was the best tool for the maintenance of social order. It inadvertently delegated to those who could aspire to religious authority priority access to the masses, and as such it became a prominent ideological and practical obstruction to those who increasingly felt nationalism was the tool of popular mobilisation *par excellence*.

Social structures

Antagonism between these two ideological trends was exacerbated by the tendency to extremism and polarisation among factions. This was itself a reflection and consequence of the limited political base these elites enjoyed. On the one hand, it eliminated the need for compromise which a broader base would necessitate, while on the other, the absence of such a base meant that practical achievements could only be accomplished by those collections of individuals whose convictions were so profound and so passionately held that they could function effectively as a vanguard, albeit at the expense of the exclusion of others. In short, the politics of individual rather than collective pluralism accentuated competition within the political elite to a high intensity. This encouraged ambiguity, compromise and the maintenance of the status quo, but paradoxically forced those desirous of change to take up increasingly extreme positions to signify both their political dedication to change and also their intention, born of frustration, to get things done. As a political process it was a curious reflection of a traditional patrimonial structure struggling to break free of itself, and more often than not, as the sociologist Max Weber argued, it was the function of charisma, real or created, to break the mould. Iran in the twentieth century threw up a succession of 'charismatic' leaders whose function it was to break out of the gravitational constraints of patrimonial stagnation which, in the eyes of many observers, both Iranian and foreign, was the main cause of Iran's failure to keep up with the Western world.

According to Weber, charismatic authority, as an ideal type, seeks no authority but itself. It is as a consequence 'revolutionary' in relation to the tradition from which it has emerged; the espousal of 'revolution' is often a badge of legitimacy. However, as the case of Iran shows only too well, none of the revolutionary leaders entirely escape the tradition from which they have emerged and to a greater or lesser extent the consequences of their leadership are mixed. But if patrimonial and revolutionary politics are the domain of the elite and the vanguards, they have been gradually supported in increasing measure by social changes and the growth in political awareness – at times a consequence of their reforms, but at others a result of technological changes and ideological influences beyond their direct control. Throughout the twentieth century therefore we see added to the Iranian political spectrum not only a more active religiously inspired mass participation in politics, but an increasingly emphatic Marxist influence, especially in urban centres but, with the advent of the wireless radio, also extending into rural areas. Increasing rural–urban migration assisted this process. Throughout the century the new and increasingly potent factor of Marxism was being added to the equation of Iranian politics, a factor which the practitioners of traditional patrimonial politics viewed with ambivalence and distrust. Some sought to harness it to their cause with varying degrees of success, none were able to entirely control it, while others rejected it altogether as a dangerous consequence of reform and revolution. The growth of mass politics in Iran also highlights the nature of revolutionary change in Iran in the twentieth century, emphasising that, while some changes were engineered by the elites, others were the unforeseen consequences of their actions, or indeed were the result of broader trends in global political competition and economic development.

International integration

This is another major theme of this book – the emergent integration of Iran into the international order. Iran has never been isolated from the international order. From the sixteenth century onwards, Iran had played a distinctive role in the politics of the Islamic world and from the seventeenth century the cultural and economic influence of Safavid Iran on the wider world was significant. European embassies and trade missions established themselves at the court of the Great Sophy in Isfahan, while Iranian goods and fashion began to have an impact on the courts of Europe. By the eighteenth century there was a growing literary interest in 'Persia' and, as Britain expanded into India, so interest in Persian literature and language grew. At the same time Russian power expanded in the north and for the first time Iranians became aware, as the Ottomans had done, of the threat posed by European military power. However, it was not until the beginning of the nineteenth century that this military power began to make itself felt. At the treaties of Golestan (1813) and Turkmenchai (1828), Iran felt the full brunt of Russian military and political power as her Caucasian dependencies were stripped from her and Russia gained extraterritorial rights within the country. This was the first time that the Iranian state felt the consequences of her weakness, although society as a whole remained unaffected. Throughout the nineteenth century as Britain and Russia competed for influence it was first the state, and later the commercial classes, which felt the impact of European penetration. Ideas also began to emerge, but it was still very much an elite preoccupation. The importance of Russia and Britain to the politics of Iran was made explicit in the Constitutional Revolution, when first British support facilitated its success, and then Russian antipathy encouraged its failure.

While idealism and imperial expansion occasionally motivated British and Russian policy towards Iran, their fundamental strategic interest in Iran was a desire to ensure that it did not fall completely under the control of either power. More often than not, the Russians sought to extend their dominance while the British sought to limit it. Iranian politicians often skilfully played each against the other. However, the discovery of oil by William Knox-D'Arcy in 1908, after having been sold the exploitation rights by the Iranian government in 1901, altered the equation dramatically. Prior to the discovery of oil, Britain's interest in Iran revolved around the defence of her Indian empire, but with the Royal Navy move towards oil in 1913, Iran became a strategic interest of great importance to Britain, and European penetration into both state and society was accelerated. Oil lubricated the wheels of integration. Not only did it bring new wealth to the country, allowing the implementation and financing of many of the reforms imagined by Qajar statesmen, it made it possible for Iranians to travel abroad. Crucially, it brought Europe to Iran, in the shape of the Anglo-Persian Oil Company and its enormous refinery in Abadan. British interests expanded and diversified throughout the country bringing more Iranians into contact with the outside world. This contact was multiplied during the Second World War when Iranian geopolitics, along with oil, encouraged the Allies to occupy her and use her as a transit route to supply the beleaguered Red Army from 1941 to 1946 when the last Red Army troops left the country. The Allied occupation had an immense impact on Iranian society, while the emergence of the Cold War, arguably begun in Iran in 1946, saw Iran entangled in a superpower rivalry of much greater intensity than anything she had experienced in the previous century. The second Pahlavi Shah indeed saw it as essential for Iran to fully integrate the country within America's Cold War interests, in order to access the capital required to finance his own 'revolution'. The patron–client relationship allowed successive Iranian statesmen, as their predecessors had done, to occasionally 'wag the dog', sometimes to an extent that the division between patron and client seemed to contemporaries to be distinctly blurred. Iran offers an interesting case study of a country able to use its international relationships (a consequence of its ability to maintain at least a nominal independence) to play a role far above its military and political strength.[8]

Weapons of the weak

In dealing with the outside world, Iranian politicians have been, by and large, excellent practitioners of the weapons of the weak to confound, confuse and frustrate the ambitions of greater powers in Iran. Acutely aware of their own military weakness but driven by ambitions of imperial stature inherited from an earlier age, Iranian statesmen have substituted diplomatic for military power, and have shown a diplomatic sophistication which has often confounded both partners and opponents whose impressions of Iran have too often been dictated by one-dimensional statistical analyses of the country. Western powers, confident in their own achievements and imperial in their ambitions, were consistently outmanoeuvred and frustrated by the activities of their Iranian counterparts, a result too often credited to the inadequacies, immorality, dishonesty and downright ineptitude of Iranians. While this was on occasion a true reflection, as is the case with any nation, it more often than not reflected the prejudices of Europeans who found their ambitions frustrated by a political system, by which I mean language as well as structure, which they could not fully comprehend.[9]

This continuing miscomprehension has plagued Iran's relations with the outside world and the West in particular for much of the period under review. This lack of cultural empathy and communication was of course bilateral, and, in so far as the Iranians were concerned, was often deliberate. Both sides recognised the important relationship between knowledge and power, and, while the West sought clear lines of demarcation to facilitate control, so Iranian statesmen counteracted this threat by the use of persistent dissimulation. This was often extended to all things 'modern', thereby accentuating the cultural impasse between Westerners, who could not understand why Iranians should be opposed to developments that would add to their material well-being, and Iranians, who construed such developments as merely extending the tentacles of Western penetration and domination of Iran. Just as in the nineteenth century Iranian politicians opposed the construction of roads on account of the fear that it would allow foreign troops to overrun the country more quickly, so in the twentieth they argued against the institutionalisation of processes and in favour of ambiguity, lest foreigners 'understand' and as a consequence 'control'.[10] Arguably, it is only in recent years that this fear has been systematically addressed by Iranian intellectuals and a dialogue begun, though it is clearly far too early to say where this intellectual exercise will lead.

Analysing Iranian political structures

As noted above, this conscious desire to prevent foreign comprehension of the political and social processes has been compounded by an almost irrational desire on behalf of foreign observers to force Iran to fit a particular model of development witnessed, theoretically at least, in the Western world. Most striking perhaps, is the implicit (and occasionally explicit) determination to impose the 'secularisation thesis' – in which 'secularisation' (inadequately defined) is regarded as an essential precursor to 'modernisation' (again inadequately defined, but more often than not seen as synonymous with 'Westernisation') – even though the Western experience is neither as seamless or uniform as the various high priests of modernisation would have us believe. The secularisation thesis has frequently been accompanied by a 'modernisation' thesis that sees all change as being driven by economic development which will in turn, by processes that are inevitable, trigger political and social change. These ideas, which came to prominence in the social sciences after 1945, are not without their critics (Huntington was a prominent early critic[11]) but they remain pervasive enough to warrant consideration and, where it affects policy and attitudes, genuine concern. Thus, for instance, it is not uncommon to find some frustrated commentators relegating Iran to the category of anomaly, the exception which proves the rule. Unfortunately, Iran is too big an exception not to encourage some reflection as to the reconstruction of the rules. Yet this has been a sadly neglected exercise, and foreign observers have been too quick to selectively analyse a particular event in favour of their particular theory.[12] Thus the British were quick to conclude, in the aftermath of the fall of Dr Mosaddeq, that Iranian nationalism was hollow and ineffective, while in the aftermath of the Islamic Revolution, views alternated between the sheer unpredictability of revolutions and its anomalous nature as a revolution that was apparently regressive rather than progressive in character.[13] While the reality is often complex, unusual and occasionally surprising, one should resist the temptation to dismiss as anomalous that which does not conform to our preconceptions. Any given narrative is constructed from 'historical facts' selected and inherited by the historian, and as such remains an interpretative exercise. This is not to deny the historicity of events, simply to point out that method as well as indigenous complexity may be responsible for difficulties in comprehension.[14] In the case of the Islamic Revolution, for instance, many earlier accounts were provided by intellectuals steeped in the Western tradition – fed in large part by the many Western-educated émigrés who fled the Revolution. Far from history being written by the victors, in this case it was overwhelmingly the *victims* who determined its direction.

The political structure of Iran remains complex because it represents an intricate tapestry of social and political classes in the process of dynamic change, reflecting the conflicting tendencies inherent in the transformation of traditional structures into 'modern' ones. Its very fluidity means that any analysis that does not take into account this dynamism is limited to being a mere snapshot, a one-dimensional static representation of a three-dimensional model in the process of continuous formation. Fluidity and dynamism exist not only in the construction and composition of social groups, but also in the ideas that drive them. In analysing the social groups that have shaped modern Iranian history we are faced with the prospect of charting the changes within social groups as well as with the ideas they purport to espouse. But just as continuity does not preclude change, so change is predicated on a measure of continuity. The fundamental question is not, therefore, whether structural analysis is possible, but how we approach it. Clearly the wholesale adoption and transfer of European constructs to Iran is unsatisfactory. At the same time, certain key developments in European historical and social theory can and must be applied, and there is no suggestion here that they must be rejected. This would be an equally unsatisfactory solution and in many ways an unrealistic exercise. Again it is the approach taken that is essential, if any systematic analysis is to enjoy some success.

Just as the environment under scrutiny is dynamic, so the approach must reflect this dynamism and accommodate it. To quote Karl Mannheim, 'In a realm in which everything is in the process of becoming, the only adequate synthesis would be a dynamic one, which is reformulated from time to time'.[15] Furthermore, the complexity of the environment must also be reflected in the theories which we bring to its study, avoiding the tendency to reductionism and generalisation. Above all, we must restore imagination to our understanding of Iranian history and that of the Middle East in general; avoid the tendency to objectify our subjects, denying them thought processes independent (or autonomous) of grand structures; and restore agency to a political process which is after all highly dependent, as noted above, on individual actors. While social and economic forces have played a role in shaping development, this must not blind us to the importance of imported ideas carried by the intellectual and political elite into a reluctant society. As has been noted above, this vanguard has on occasion been extremely small.

In light of these considerations, what social groups can be discerned? In the Constitution of 1906, six categories of the population were delineated: princes and the Qajar tribe; doctors of divinity and students; nobles and notables; merchants; landed proprietors and peasants; trade guilds. From these we can discern three main groups: the landed aristocracy, the *ulema* and the *bazaaris*. These three broad groups formed the main pillars of the Iranian state, and above them the monarch, whose traditional role was to mediate among them. In time, the Pahlavis would add another pillar, that of the army. But the army, for reasons which will become apparent, was the coercive arm of the state (monarchy); its institutional links with society were limited. The aristocracy, the *ulema* and the *bazaaris* had profound roots in society, and with each other, in kinship associations as well as commercial and social relations. The relative longevity of the Qajar dynasty had allowed an uncharacteristic continuity and stability to emerge among these groups, and some bureaucratic families could certainly lay claim to generations of service, but in comparison with European societies there remained a considerable amount of social mobility – in both directions.[16]

These three groups formed the governing elite of Iran, and their limited numbers belied their social influence in both financial and ideological terms. While not a middle class, they formed the intermediary group between the lower classes and the Shah, with whom they were not always in agreement. While many of the landed aristocracy in particular provided the personnel to staff the court and the administration, as a social group they were by no means uniformly in support of the monarch, although it would be fair to say they all supported the institution of the monarchy, albeit with some changes. What really distinguished the individuals in these groups was the ideas they espoused, and it is here that complexity sets in because, far from representing a monolithic class interest, it is clear that many had different opinions on what their class interest happened to be. Thus to take the example of the Constitutional Revolution, supporters of the movement came from all three groups, as did opponents. For instance, the prominent Tehran *mujtahid*, Tabatabaie, agitated in favour of the movement, while Sheikh Fazlollah Nuri declared it blasphemous. Such rifts were apparent in the other groups. Furthermore, affiliation to a particular ideological group depended very much on circumstance, and on occasion it was not unknown for people to switch loyalties when they felt particular interests were under threat. Such flexibility has been the hallmark of Iranian political activity throughout the century, and has, as noted above, inadvertently assisted the rigorous polarisation of views partly as a result of trying to force individual decisions and positions.

The emergence of social forces

Beyond this elite group, social groups of political importance were negligible for much of this period. But by the 1930s an embryonic professional 'middle' class outside the old elites began to emerge, and by the following decade, as a result of communist influences from the Soviet Union, a greater section of the urban lower classes and to some extent the rural peasantry were beginning to matter in political terms. Indeed in the Oil Nationalisation Crisis, Dr Mosaddeq was faced with a politically organised urban workforce that was viewed, not only by him, as increasingly outside his control. Fear of what this represented eventually turned the other traditional elite groups against Dr Mosaddeq, and indeed the crisis was a watershed in Iranian politics, because it signified that politics was no longer the preserve of the elite. Nationalism, and the mass mobilisation which accompanied it, was coming of age. Henceforth, political leaders would need to take account of the crowd in Iranian politics and greater efforts were expended seeking to manipulate it.[17]

In time Mohammad Reza Shah would use the land reform programme to remove one of the main pillars of the Iranian state, the landed aristocracy, and in turn would seek to weaken the *ulema* and the *bazaaris*. His intention was to replace them with a combination of the army and a new 'middle class' which would be dependent on him. Yet it is one of the curiosities of late Pahlavi Iran that a professional middle class rooted in society never emerged. Instead the new professionals were either co-opted into the elite or left on the margins. Indeed in the Pahlavi period this process of bifurcation applied to all classes with the consequence that the two-tier social model of elites and the rest was maintained, albeit with a different composition. This division between the 'haves' and the 'have-nots' was keenly expressed by a British diplomat in 1957 in his description of southern Tehran:

> Here the mullahs preach every evening to packed audiences. Most of the sermons are revivalist stuff of a high emotional and low intellectual standard. But certain well known preachers attract the intelligentsia of the town with reasoned historical exposés of considerable merits . . . The Tehran that we saw on the tenth of Moharram is a different world, centuries and civilisations apart from the gaudy superficial botch of Cadillacs, hotels, antique shops, villas, tourists and diplomats where we run our daily round . . . But it is not only poverty, ignorance and dirt that distinguish the old south of the city from the parvenu north. The slums have a compact self-conscious unity and communal sense that is totally lacking in the smart districts of chlorinated water, macadamed roads and (fitful) street lighting. The bourgeois does not know his neighbour: the slum-dweller is intensely conscious of his. And in the slums the spurious blessings of Pepsi Cola civilisation have not yet destroyed the old way of life, where every man's comfort and security depend on the spontaneous, un-policed observation of a traditional code. Down in the southern part of the city manners and morals are better and stricter than in the villas of Tajrish: an injury to a neighbour, a pass at another man's wife, a brutality to a child evoke spontaneous retribution without benefit of bar or bench.[18]

Nationalism[19]

Nationalism was the driving force of mass mobilisation in twentieth-century Iran. But nationalism remained an essentially contested concept in both theory and practice in Iran, and secular nationalism found itself competing with religious and dynastic forms of nationalism, each appealing to particular sections of Iranian society. While secular forms of nationalism informed by the West ignited the spark, and the Pahlavis adapted it to their own needs by refocusing attention on the importance of the dynasty to Iranian nationalism, it took religious nationalism to free Iranian nationalism from its elite pretensions and make it popular. Indeed, religious nationalism, the politicisation of Iranian identity as it had formed in the nineteenth century, reflected the successful synthesis of an elite-imposed ideology and the realities of popular politics.[20] It also reflected the fact that a distinctly 'national' identity was not an entirely alien concept to the mass of ordinary Iranians familiar with the *Shahnameh* of Ferdowsi.[21] Religious nationalism was a composite identity of tremendous political force, as was to be seen in the Islamic Revolution of 1979. It sanctified the nation. This is not as unusual a phenomenon as we are often led to believe in the West, where the suspicion of religion in some areas of scholarship has reached almost epidemic proportions.

The truth of course is that secularism, as opposed to laicism in the French model, has never disavowed religion. Indeed for many Iranians, even those who espoused and advocated a distinctly secular nationalism, Shi'ism remained an integral component of their 'national' identity. The real debate between secular and religious nationalists was the precise role of religion in society. Few secularists would have argued that religion had no function at all. On the contrary, while secular intellectuals in the West have been characterised as tending towards atheism or agnosticism, this has not been nor is the case in Iran. While some secular intellectuals, notably Mirza Agha Khan Kermani,[22] or later Ahmad Kasravi, may have been hostile to the *ulema* and their application of Islam, it did not follow automatically that they were necessarily anti-Islamic or irreligious. Their main criticism was targeted against organised religion and its function, in their eyes, as a pillar of the establishment and a constraint on meaningful reform. There were many in the *ulema* who were equally critical of their own function and organisation (one of the most notable being Ayatollah Khomeini) while others such as Kasravi were themselves the products of the very religious institutions they rejected.[23] Some of the most notable nationalists of the Constitutional period were members of the *ulema*, including Tabatabaie and, of course, Muddaris. While most of the early ideologues had received their primary if not secondary education in religious seminaries – the absence of alternatives in the nineteenth century made this inevitable. The consequence was that support for nationalism in its various forms cut across all the major classes.

Nationalism as a viable tool of political action was born in the Constitutional Revolution, came of age during the Oil Nationalisation Crisis and began its social maturation in the Islamic Revolution of 1979. It was shaped by the struggle against perceived imperial powers, but its resources were much deeper than other emergent nationalisms in the Third World. The rich, complex tapestry of historical experience and myth which constituted the idea and the identity of Iran, and ultimately produced Iranian nationalism, provided Iranians with coherent if ambiguous self-consciousness prior to the arrival of the Europeans. In this respect Iran had much more in common with China than it did with other countries in the Middle East. Therefore, while Iran at the turn of the century may have been an 'imagined community', it was a community bound together by an increasingly fertile and convinced imagination. With the growth of the media and the spread of literacy throughout the century it was an imagination which was to grow. While some conception of 'Iran' had undoubtedly existed prior to the modern era, the increasing centralisation of the state and the growth of communications was to encourage the erosion of local loyalties and identities and replace them emphatically with the notion of a singular, if not homogenous, Iranian national identity. Nationalism thus joined religion and constitutionalism as a major, if not predominant, term of reference in modern Iran. It defined people's loyalties, and leaders competed to be more nationalist than each other and to acquire the authority and legitimacy nationalism bestowed. While religion sanctified the nation, it was the concept of the nation which drew disparate groups together. There was no greater epithet than 'patriot' and no greater slur than 'traitor'. Similarly it was the fear of national disintegration and dismemberment which crystallised nationalist politicians and subsumed differences. It was an innate fear which was to be exploited regularly throughout the twentieth century by successive governments.

While in the West nationalism has increasingly been seen as the child of modernity, an unfortunate progeny, in Iran modernisation was the handmaiden of nationalism. Nationalism allowed modernisation and modernisation strengthened the nation. Thus Reza Khan used nationalist sentiment to forge a modern army through conscription and enforce Iran's national integrity by eliminating those forces which appeared to harm the power and authority of the state. New methods and new technologies allowed the state to be strengthened vis-à-vis the periphery and as a consequence, it was felt, the nation. Under Reza Shah the notion that a centralised, modernised state was beneficial to the nation, which was itself homogenous and singular, gained wide credence, but as a result it also came under increasing criticism. Just as there was growing criticism of what modernisation meant in practice, so there were questions as to how compatible nationalism and modernisation actually were. This tension over the compatibility of a nationalism which preached self-sufficiency and national honour with the needs of economic and social development – which frequently required the appropriation of foreign technology and personnel – continued throughout the century. More often than not, it was nationalism that won over the demands of modernisation, either because national honour dictated that developmental plans were too modest, or because in the absence of indigenous expertise, developmental plans could wait.

The other major tension which persisted was the nature of modernisation itself and whether the centralisation of the state was the policy which had to be pursued. Arguing that Qajar weakness was a consequence, in part, of the impotence of the Qajar state, reformers sought to rectify the problem by concentrating on the strengthening of the central organs of the state. Indeed the Pahlavi state created by Reza Shah and his supporters, while flawed, marked the first time that the Iranian state consistently and regularly affected the lives of ordinary Iranians. But as the state began to dictate to society, so people increasingly queried previous assumptions and argued for decentralisation as a way of strengthening the nation with the state. There was and continues to be a debate and at times confusion between the centralisation of (sovereign) authority and the centralisation of power.

These arguments about the nature of the state, and the aims of modernisation are a consistent theme in modern Iranian history and the contradictions they contain help explain the erratic nature of development. Indeed it may help to see the process of development in Iran as a dialectical one in which a sequence of contradictions emerges and needs resolution, either intellectually, practically or coercively, before the next stage can be reached.[24] Sometimes these resolutions are violent in nature, at other times relatively peaceful, but on all occasions the atmosphere of tension is palpable. This often gives the impression of instability, and certainly the closer one is in spatial and temporal terms, the more confused, erratic and unstable the situation seems. However, the advantage of history is that it allows us to view change from a distance of relative comfort and to create a more complete picture from the various strands that are revealed. Even these advantages are, in the Iranian case, relative and, in a society in the throes of revolutionary change, certain precautions need to be taken into consideration before any definitive conclusions can be drawn.

Continuity and change

Lambton famously noted in reference to Medieval Iran that 'continuity did not preclude change'. One might of course add that by extension, change does not preclude continuity and as Iranian Constitutionalists and their later intellectual heirs concluded, successful change was often predicated on knowing how to preserve that which was valuable to the cohesion of society at large. In this respect Iranian intellectuals drew on and undoubtedly echoed the writings of Edmund Burke in arguing that knowing what to preserve, allowed one to face the future of change with a good deal more confidence. This debt to what we might term a British Enlightenment tradition naturally conflicted with other more revolutionary traditions that were drawn from French thought and later in the twentieth century from the Russian experience, from where it might be added many Enlightenment ideas were first mediated. But the dominance of Burkean ideas reflected the social and political realities faced by many Iranian reformers and revolutionaries who appreciated that durable revolutionary change paradoxically relied on a measure of conservatism. Too sudden or dramatic a change, as France, and the Soviet Union would suggest, only encouraged a reaction to the old order albeit in new clothes, and real change had to be built on foundations of continuity. The political trick was to understand the relationship between these two poles and to harmonise them such that change could be managed towards sustainable progress. It should come as no surprise that for those in power in Iran, Britain and later the United States provided models of emulation and admiration, even if there were regular disagreements about policies, and the less than ideal way in which Britain and the United States applied their policies.

For much of the period under review Iranian society remained intensely conservative in its outlook, and with two centuries to survey, it is remarkable just how much continuity exists in social mores and attitudes, to say nothing of the linguistic continuities that exist in vernacular (as opposed to bureaucratic and court) Persian over several centuries. Malcolm's discussions on a range of social and religious issues with his Iranian companions in the early 1800s would not appear entirely out of place in contemporary Iran. The state, inasmuch as it existed, in the nineteenth century, saw its role as managing this conservatism, rather than seeking to change it, and it was only with the onset of the Constitutional Revolution that this attitude changed. Here on in, the Iranian state shed its early modern perspective to promote an Enlightenment doctrine of the state as an agent of change and a means of promoting the welfare of its citizens. Henceforth, and certainly with the rise and rule of Reza Shah, the state imposed change and promoted the welfare of its citizens often despite themselves and against their wishes. This was accelerated in different ways under Mohammad Reza Shah, but certainly did not end under the Islamic Republic. Indeed the Islamic Revolution may have changed the substance but it was quite definitely Iranian in form, and in its determination to impose change upon its erstwhile citizens, the Islamic Republic owed a far greater debt to its republican pretensions than its Islamic ones. Over time, the roles would reverse. An increasingly educated public, empowered and connected by technology, sought both to engage and to emulate the outside world. Their 'imagined community' now spanned the globe. The children of the Constitutional Revolution had come of age, shaken off their innate conservatism to embrace a more progressive politics. Enlightened despotism, as in Europe, had achieved its purpose and was now viewed as surplus to requirements – a position unsurprisingly not held by those in power, who have sought to resist the tide of change by entrenching their power in a divine authority to which their monarchical predecessors could only aspire. Just as society eventually responded to the demands of politics, so too in time will politics have to respond to the real revolutionary change of a society on the move.

Notes

1 Epitomised in January 2002 by being accorded membership of the 'Axis of Evil' by the United States, although subsequent US announcements have sought to soften the impact.

2 For an attempt to reconcile these conflicting traditions, see Sir John Malcolm's much neglected *History of Persia* in two volumes, London: printed for John Murray and Longman and Co. by James Moyes, 1815.

3 The notion that the 'East' is 'unhistorical', where change does not occur, is Hegelian. See G.W.F. Hegel, *The Philosophy of History*. New York, NY: Dover, 1956, pp. 11–223.

4 Akbar Ganji has defined these 'tensions' as between nation v state, left v right, theocracy v secularism, tradition v modernity, repressive autocracy v freedom and democracy. See A. Ganji, *Ali-jenab sorkh poosh va ali-jenab khakestari* (The Red Eminence and the Grey Eminence). Tehran: Tar-e no, 2000, pp. 11–12.

5 J.S. Coleman, 'The Development Syndrome: Differentiation-Equality-Capacity', in J.S. Coleman and L. Binder (eds), *Crises and Consequences in Political Development.* Princeton, NJ: Princeton University Press, 1971, pp. 73–100.

6 See R. Mottahedeh, *The Mantle of the Prophet: Religion and Politics in Iran.* New York, NY: Simon and Schuster, 1985.

7 Ironically, it is under the Islamic Republic that this process is beginning to reach fruition.

8 See for instance Y. Mazandi, *Iran – Abar Ghodrat-e Qarn?* (Iran – Superpower of the Century?). Tehran: Alborz, 1373/1994.

9 In essence the problem of 'Orientalism' as highlighted by Edward Said, a critique which has itself come under considerable scrutiny. See also V. Martin, *Creating an Islamic State: Khomeini and the Making of a New Iran.* London: I.B. Tauris, 2000, pp. 174–87.

10 This critique of 'modernity' may be characterised as distinctly Foucauldian, and it should come as no surprise that Michel Foucault is widely read among Iranian intellectuals, both religious and lay, in the post-revolutionary era.

11 S.P. Huntington, *Political Order in Changing Societies.* New Haven, CT: Yale University Press, 1968.

12 As Alexis de Tocqueville noted, revolutions tend to be not only politically isolated but intellectually quarantined; see *The Ancien Régime and the French Revolution.* Manchester: Fontana, 1966, Part 1, Chapter 1, p. 34.

13 See for instance Keddie's discussion 'Can Revolutions Be Predicted? Can Their Causes Be Understood?', in N. Keddie, *Iran and the Muslim World: Resistance and Revolution.* London: Macmillan, 1995, pp. 13–34. Also G. Watson, 'How Radical Is Revolution?', *History Today,* November 1988, pp. 42–9.

14 This debate on the nature and selection of the 'historical fact' is of course extensive. See for example E.H. Carr, *What Is History?* London: Pelican, pp. 7–30. See also H. White, 'The Historical Text as Literary Artifact', in B. Fay, P. Pomper and R.T. Vann (eds), *History and Theory: Contemporary Readings.* London: Blackwell, 1998, pp. 15–33.

15 K. Mannheim, *Ideology and Utopia.* London: Routledge & Kegan Paul, 1960, p. 135.

16 A social mobility noted by Lord Curzon.

17 See E. Abrahamian, 'The Crowd in Iranian Politics, 1906–1953', *Past and Present* 41, 1968, pp. 184–210.

18 FO 371 127139 EP 1781/3 dated 7 September 1957.

19 Nationalism has been discussed in greater detail in my *The Politics of Nationalism in Modern Iran.* Cambridge: Cambridge University Press, 2012.

20 For our purposes, 'nationalism' will be defined as the politicisation of the cultural identity which bound together the various ethnicities constituting the Iranian state under the Qajars.

21 For example, see Sir John Malcolm, *History of Persia* and Vita Sackville-West, *Passenger to Tehran.* London: Hogarth Press, 1926, pp. 105, 121 (see also fn. 49).

22 Kermani is recognised as one of the first Iranian nationalist ideologues.

23 Another key thinker in this regard, though outside the scope of this book, is Jamal al Din al Afghani, increasingly referred to by Iranians as 'Asaadabadi'.

24 For an interesting discussion see J.A. Bill and R. Springborg, *Politics in the Middle East.* New York, NY: HarperCollins, 1994, pp. 5–8.

2 The legacy of the eighteenth century

In 1800, Sir John Malcolm, then serving as an officer in the army of the East India Company, was dispatched to Iran to establish diplomatic and commercial relations. Having left his native Scotland at the tender age of 12, Malcolm had grown up in the Persianate world of post-Mughal India, and was well versed in the Persian language, but above all and perhaps more importantly, possessed a profound cultural appreciation of the Iranian world.[1] He recognised the importance of presentation and image, the subtleties, bordering on tedium, of the various idiosyncrasies that defined Persian etiquette that regulated both society and politics. On arrival in Iran he took care to ensure that his embassy remained disciplined and where necessary on display, providing a careful coordinated theatrical presentation to the Iranians he was sure had been sent to observe him. His first encounter with officialdom at a regional court proved the first contest of wills which Malcolm won with a degree of aplomb that attested to his political acuity.[2] He was rewarded with an audience with the monarch himself, Fath Ali Shah, the nephew of the founder of the Qajar dynasty whose regal bearing, and portrait, has become emblematic of the entire dynasty.

The encounter was to prove revealing and the conversation in many ways provided a valuable vignette and template, not only for Iran's relations with the newly empowered 'West', but in the monarch's appreciation of his own kingdom. The Iranians were not oblivious to European power, but in the 80 years since the fall of the Safavid dynasty in 1722, there was a tentative if reluctant realisation that the balance of power had shifted. For a people who were notoriously uninterested in the world beyond their own horizon, they had acquired a curiosity about the establishment of European interests in India, both French and British; a development, which along with the expansion of Russian power in the north, ensured that 'Europe' and Iran were to be effective neighbours for more than a century. Fath Ali Shah began by inquiring about the strength of the French, notably commending Malcolm for an honest answer that he felt was remiss from his own courtiers, who he pointedly noted, tended to exaggerate.

But it was when he inquired about the nature of government in Britain that the yawning gap between East and West became apparent and Iran's problems were laid bare for all those who cared to see. On being informed of the role of George III within the British constitution, Fath Ali Shah remarked that he appeared to be little more than a chief magistrate. His comments, as related by Malcolm, were revealing: "'Such a condition of power", said he, smiling, "has permanence but it has no enjoyment. There you see Suliman Khan Kajir, and several other of the first chiefs of the kingdom – I can cut all their heads off: can I not?" said he addressing them. "Assuredly, 'Point of adoration of the world', if it is your pleasure". "That is real power", said the king; "but then it has no permanence . . ."'.[3] Fath Ali Shah added that the one consolation was that his sons, of which there were many, would fight for the inheritance and Iran would consequently be ruled by a soldier. None of this needless to say augured well for the future stability of the kingdom and the contrast with Britain, and Europe in general, was increasingly clear as was the challenge faced by an Iranian state that had emerged from a century of political turmoil. Ultimately, British observers would conclude that Iran's problems were neither innate nor predetermined but a function of inadequate and unstable politics. Reform the political system (as indeed the British had done) and benefits would flow. This simple exchange in many ways exposed the central challenge that faced Iranian statesmen for the next century, and indeed, beyond.

The Safavid inheritance

The modern Iranian state is naturally the product of multiple factors, influences and experiences but for our purposes the foundations and cultural parameters of the state were established under the Safavids, the dynasty that ruled Iran between 1501 and 1722. It was the Safavids who established the territorial boundaries of the modern state and while these may have retracted on all fronts, the border with the Ottoman Empire, demarcated by treaty in 1639, remains one of the oldest fixed borders anywhere in the world. As the Huguenot merchant and writer, Sir John Chardin, who was resident in Isfahan in the latter half of the seventeenth century, noted caustically, 'Persia is the greatest empire in the world, if you consider it according to the geographical description given by the Persians'.[4] Indeed the Iranian imagination extended far further than the realities of their imperium. Chardin, a keen observer of the Iranian worldview, noted that Iranian geographers retained the ancient boundaries, 'alledging, that they are still in right and fact, the bounds of their country', and should not be adjusted on account of transient political events that only required a leader of quality – such as the late Shah Abbas, known to posterity as 'the Great' – to reverse.

This complacent attitude was borne of a keen sense of cultural superiority cultivated through historical experience, which suggested that for all the turmoil that might occur, 'Iran' – for that was the name in common usage at the time – would somehow still remain, Iran.[5] All travellers to the country in the early modern period note this nomenclature and it is worth reiterating here to remove once and for all the impression that the appellation 'Iran' is a twentieth-century exercise in archaism. This idea of Iran was drawn from both literary and historical experience, though the distinction between the two was not at all clear at least until the end of the nineteenth century. It was encapsulated and largely though not exclusively drawn from the *Shahnameh*, the poetic epic which charted the ascent and descent of 'Iran' through to the Islamic conquest in the seventh century. It was this text that framed a distinctly Iranian world view, and it was the concept of *Iranshahr* (later transcribed as *Iranzamin*), the land or empire of Iran, far more than any classical depiction of Imperial Persia, that was being reflected in Chardin's writing. The ideas and the stories behind them formed a good part of the cultural and folkloric heritage of the peoples of the Safavid empire, but they were perhaps most actively promoted by the bureaucratic elites that were to serve a series of dynasties and were to provide, in stark contrast to the rulers, an unusually robust and continuous narrative thread.

The success of the Safavids as a dynasty – to date the longest lasting of Iran's 'modern' dynasties – depended in large part on their being able to draw on and exploit a number of sources of legitimation, including a 'Turkic' inheritance and most obviously as the guardians of Twelver Shi'ism, which the founder of the dynasty, Shah Ismail forcibly introduced on his accession in 1501. So prominent and consequential has Shi'ism been in the subsequent history of the country, that earlier historians have tended to emphasise this characteristic above all others, a trend that was unsurprisingly reinforced by the onset of the Islamic Revolution in 1979 (when for a brief period at least, almost all Iranian history was interpreted through an Islamic lens). Subsequent research has suggested that despite claims of descent from the Prophet and links with the Imamate, Safavid Shi'ism was a good deal more eclectic, and even cosmopolitan in approach than had initially been thought.[6] This is certainly reflected in the nature of the empire itself, which incorporated and indeed tolerated a number of different faiths. Later Safavid monarchs, scions of Circassian concubines who emanated from the Christian heartlands of the empire in the Caucasus, appeared to have been quite open-minded about the religious beliefs of their subjects.[7] This was by no means a sectarian empire with totalitarian intent, even if it inflicted the occasional pogrom.

The seventeenth-century Safavid state, the product of Shah Abbas' reforms, thus drew on Persian, Islamic and perhaps to a decreasing extent Turkic sources of legitimacy – a cosmopolitan inheritance for a cosmopolitan empire. Shah Soleiman I, the penultimate monarch was emblematic of this complex inheritance. The son of a Circassian mother he was described by Chardin as blond and blue eyed (although he dyed his hair black),[8] his first language was effectively Turkish, and his birth-name was Sam, the grandfather of the Persian (mythological) hero, Rostam, and while his throne name was decidedly Muslim, his adherence to scripture was not.[9]

Of the three ostensibly Muslim empires of the period, the Ottoman, Safavid and Mughal empires, the Safavid was neither the richest nor the most powerful, but it certainly managed to hold its own, despite territorial losses to the Ottomans, and what it lacked in material power it made up for with cultural depth and reach. Both the Ottomans and the Mughals had connections to the Persianate world. The language of government in Mughal India was Persian providing in many ways for a fluid cultural zone in which men of letters moved and settled relatively freely.[10] While to the West the Turco-Iranian culture of the Ottoman Empire remained relatively accessible to the Turco-Iranians of the Safavid empire. Perhaps most strikingly for the better part of a century following Shah Abbas' death in 1629, Iran enjoyed a period of prolonged peace almost unprecedented in its recent history. This cannot but have increased the affluence of its society as trade increased and merchants were protected, even if the state became as a consequence even more complacent, and the government in the shape of the king and his court, indulgent to the point of decadence.

The failure of the dynasty to produce a ruler with the energy of Shah Abbas I has traditionally been blamed in the latter's policy of ensuring that all heirs be raised within the confines of the harem, thereby depriving them of any meaningful political experience prior to their accession. There is little doubt that such a policy cannot have helped matters but it is just as likely that the lack of a serious challenge – either internal or external – had resulted in an administration that proved highly resistant to change and overconfident in its own abilities. To this complacency we must add the impact of what was to prove the last of the reigning Safavid kings, Shah Sultan Hossein (1694–1722), whose inadequacies were a salutary reminder that the Shah remained the lynchpin of the Iranian state.

Shah Abbas the Great had begun his reign as an exponent of piety and ended his rule as a cynic, given to bouts of melancholy and a perceived religious cosmopolitanism that led some Christian missionaries to convince themselves that he might actually convert.[11] Shah Sultan Hossein's journey appears to have been the reverse of this. Possessed of striking blue eyes like his father, the new king appeared to combine the decadence of Shah Soleiman with a meekness and excessive piety that drew the derision of his courtiers. Although they would seem to have been partly responsible for the succession insofar as the heir apparent had reportedly warned them to choose another if they wanted glory, and only him if they wanted peace and tranquillity. Under Shah Soltan Hossein, indulgence and piety appeared to increase in equal measure though guilt about the former ensured that the latter increasingly took precedence, and while government fell into a stupor, it was to prove dangerously inadequate to any challenges that might emerge.

This challenge was to emerge from the eastern margins of the empire, from an unexpected quarter that was unsurprisingly viewed with typical complacency. Following persistent raids by Baluchi tribesmen, Shah Soltan Hossein decided to dispatch a Georgian prince and vassal, Gorgin Khan, to restore order. This he duly achieved but at the cost of antagonising and provoking into rebellion the Afghan warlord Mir Wais. Gorgin was assassinated in 1709, and the situation was left to fester for several years until Mir Wais' death in 1717. It was then decided to use tried and tested diplomatic and financial means to bring the rebellious Afghans back into the fold. Unfortunately for Shah Soltan Hossein, Mir Wais' son, Mahmud was to prove considerably less amenable to any form of financially induced charm and instead launched a raid into the heartlands of the empire, occupying Kerman in 1720.

The Safavid administration appeared incapable of taking the threat seriously and were reassured when after six months Mahmud withdrew, only to find that he returned with more energy in 1722, this time coming to within 20 km of the capital Isfahan. Even now the response was incoherent and lacklustre, with the Safavid administration hamstrung by a mixture of Shah Soltan Hossein's fatalism and superstition. It was not that the state was materially incapable of mobilising a force to repel the Afghan marauders, but more that the political will and moral fibre to evince a coherent strategy and mobilisation were lacking. Having approached the threat with a barely disguised sense of contempt, the sudden and somewhat shocking defeat of a larger and better equipped Safavid army by the Afghans resulted in near panic as the capital found itself under siege. So began one of the more catastrophic periods in modern Iranian history, the trauma of which would be felt long after the siege ended.

The siege of Isfahan lasted from March through to October 1722, when faced with the starvation of the city, Shah Soltan Hossein finally relented and surrendered to an Afghan warlord who was just if not more surprised by the turn of events. With typical fatalism Shah Soltan Hossein had concluded that Mahmud's triumph had been ordained by divine providence and consequently he had no choice but to hand him the crown. The man who had come to plunder the empire found himself instead inheriting it and it is worth bearing in mind that Mahmud and his cousin Ashraf, who overthrew him in 1725, both regarded themselves as rulers of the 'imperial kingdom' of Iran.[12] Not that the kingdom itself was content with the change of dynasty. The authority of the Safavids survived the immediate shock of defeat and pretenders continued to lay claim to the throne. The Afghan 'interregnum' was to prove a highly disruptive and bloody period, as both Afghan rulers sought against the odds to consolidate their gains. The hapless former Shah Soltan Hossein was finally executed in 1726, when an Ottoman army threatened to restore him to the throne.

These developments raise an important and distinguishing point with respect to the Safavid state which is often forgotten by historians who seek to draw parallels with both the Ottoman and Mughal empires. While the dynasty was central to the idea of Iran, it did not necessarily supplant it in the popular and perhaps more importantly, the bureaucratic imagination, that intellectual elite who were bound by the idea and who acted as a vehicle for its transmission. Mahmud did not seek to overthrow the empire or necessarily redraw its boundaries around his own distinct patrimony, but to inherit the throne and kingdom intact. Similarly the collapse of the dynasty, did not immediately imply the disintegration of the state, still less of the cultural frame of reference that was Iran. Government, in terms of the central administration, had failed, and regional governance was experiencing the consequences, but it was striking that the authority of the Safavids long outlived their political demise. Part of this no doubt reflected their religious legitimacy, and their longevity. But it also reflected their broad appeal to, and close association with what remained a cosmopolitan empire.

Warlords and saviours

While Iran's new rulers settled into a life considerably more destructive and debauched than the political order they had just overthrown, Shah Soltan Hossein's only remaining son, Tahmasp (in this case a throne name drawn from the *Shahnameh*), sought to gather loyal supporters in the north. Among these supporters was the erstwhile chief of the Afsharid clan from north-eastern Iran, Nader, who took the honorific title, Tahmasp Quli Khan (the slave of Tahmasp), as he formally entered the service of the young pretender. His impact in material and cultural terms was to be profound. Here was the saviour who would restore Iran's fortunes just as it appeared that dynastic misfortune would lead to a political fragmentation of the empire.

It is difficult to overestimate the impact that the loss of Isfahan had on public perceptions. Indeed, the impact was felt as far afield as Europe, even provoking what may be the first academic dissertation on Iranian history, at a European University, that of Uppsala.[13] More immediately, the dramatic weakening of the state convinced neighbours that now was the time for some choice territorial acquisitions. The Ottomans moved in from the west, ostensibly in support of a Safavid restoration, while to the north a new emerging power was making itself felt in the form of Russia. Iran's Caspian provinces were soon being occupied, as Peter the Great sought to turn the Caspian into a Russian lake. The Afghan inheritance was proving to be a shadow of its former self. The origins of Nader Afshar are difficult to ascertain and in later life he took pride in effectively being self-made without an aristocratic lineage. He seems nonetheless to have made himself by dint of birth and more importantly, military prowess, the chief of the 'Turkic' Afsharid 'clan'.

While the term 'tribe' has often been used to describe these vast kinship networks (though these groups did not necessarily signify consanguinity of any other than an invented sort), the term is avoided here as being too loaded with negative connotations to be of use within the Iranian context. These extensive networks varied in size and did not necessarily imply a nomadic lifestyle. What did distinguish them was that they drew their strength from a rural rather than an urban base, and that these rural settings were often peripheral to the centres of power, which were usually located in cities and towns. This does not mean that they came from the margins of empire in a geographic sense – as indeed Mahmud's Afghans had done – but that they were located on the peripheries of power that were largely urban based.

Similarly I have used 'Turkic' rather than 'Turkish' throughout to avoid confusion with modern concepts of Turkish identity, or indeed the nationalist tendency to appropriate backwards into history, meanings and associations that do not apply. That the Afsharids were Turkic implies that their bases were rural and that they tended to communicate primarily in a Turkic dialect. It has no bearing on religious belief, which in Nader's case appears to have been pragmatic rather than pious, and bore no relation to their identification or otherwise (as we shall see) with the Iranian state and worldview. This of course reflected the mytho-historical inheritance of the *Shahnameh*. 'Iran' and 'Turan' – terms which reflected the rural–urban dynamic and tensions of the Iranian oecumene, rather than any intrinsic ethnic division – may have grown to be distinct but they were born of a common inheritance and Turkic roots by no means precluded or prevented an adherence to a broader idea of Iran.[14]

There is some evidence that Nader visited Isfahan as a youth and was suitably unimpressed by the excess and indulgence which he witnessed.[15] If so it is likely to have had an impact on his own attitudes to life and politics that were reflected in an austere lifestyle that naturally endeared him to those of a military inclination. Nader's rise to prominence was as dramatic as it was ultimately to prove tragic. His mercurial career possessed a good deal more calculation than posterity has bestowed on him and he was careful to position himself as the military arm of the Safavid heir apparent. It was in the service of Tahmasp that he began the re-conquest of the kingdom from the Afghans, Ottomans and Russians. It says much of the nature of the Safavid state and its dynastic collapse, that Nader was able to turn things round with alacrity raising a force to contend with the various challenges. It also says much of the continuing authority of the Safavid state reinvigorated by Nader's military achievements, that the Russian withdrawal from the Caspian provinces was concluded by negotiation and overseen by observers.

Indeed by 1730 much of Iranian territorial sovereignty had been restored, the Afghan interregnum was effectively at an end, and Nader had incorporated many of the remaining elements into his own forces. Confronted by the duplicity of Tahmasp he had him deposed in 1732, formally assuming the title of regent, for Tahmasp's infant son, now enthroned as Abbas III. In marrying his son to Tahmasp's sister, it was increasingly apparent that Nader had dynastic ambitions of his own, and by 1735, having eliminated any outspoken supporters of the Safavids, he took the fateful decision to seize the throne. In 1739 he launched his invasion of India, defeating and debilitating the Mughals before returning with a haul of gems and jewels that allowed him to announce the waiving of all taxes for a period of three years. India, however, was to prove to be his undoing.[16] If Nader eschewed the decadence of the Safavids, he was to prove no less avaricious when it came to men and money for his continuing campaigns, and the following years to his assassination in 1747, were not only to witness even greater exactions on the fragile Iranian economy (the much vaunted period of tax relief was soon forgotten), but crucially what appears to have been his own moral breakdown following the blinding of his son and heir in what amounted to a fit of jealousy. Nader never appears to have recovered from this, becoming more violent, vengeful and ruthless with every day that passed, such that in 1747 he was murdered by his lieutenants. The empire he reconstituted and substantially extended soon collapsed to be fought over by his successors, with one of his Afghan generals moving swiftly to establish a distinct Afghan kingdom.

The failure of Nader Shah's dynastic ambitions have made him little more than a footnote in Iranian history, albeit one that has etched itself in Iranian memory. His legacy in material terms was not a positive one. He left the country far poorer in men and materials than he found it, and morally and spiritually unprepared for the challenges that it would soon face. But the moral of the tale, of usurpation and decadence tends to disguise some important lessons of the period. Far from simply a reckless warlord Nader was careful and calculated about his projected ascent to the throne. He cultivated the three great pillars of legitimacy, drawing on his Turkic associations and lineage by seeking on one level to emulate the achievements of Tamerlane, while at the same time stressing his Persian legitimacy by defining himself as '*Nader-e Iranzamin va khusrau-e giti setan*' (Nader of *Iranzamin* and world conquering *khusrau*), an epigraph that was to be found on the coin minted for the occasion of his coronation[17], later adding the title *Shah-e Shahan* (king of kings). Warriors and merchants initially found much that appealing in the new order.

He even sought to reshape the religious environment in his favour. Aware of the continuing affection and loyalty to the Safavids through their association with Shi'ism, Nader Shah sought from an early stage to diminish that appeal by re-situating Shi'ism as a distinct yet inclusive school within the orthodox 'Sunni' tradition. Some have argued that he sought to do this to enable further conquests within the broader Muslim world, but the cosmopolitan nature of the Safavid 'imperial' state does not suggest that religion was a barrier to conquest. More likely it reflected the extensive inclusion of Sunnis within Nader Shah's army, as well as his own distaste for what he considered to be the excesses of the Safavid court and their religious enablers. Indeed in many ways Nader Shah's pragmatic approach to religion reflected a wider reaction to the ineffectual piety of Shah Soltan Hossein, and a sense that the state had been weakened by a decadence facilitated by an excess of faith. It is often assumed that such charges of decadence emanated principally from European observers, but Iranian contemporaries were no more forgiving of the excesses that characterised the late Safavid court.[18]

Nader Shah's failure cannot therefore necessarily be attributed to a misguided religious policy, though his studied neglect of the religious classes meant that he had to compensate in other areas. His victories brought undoubted lustre to his name – not least his descent on Delhi – and his broader policies, most obviously his determination to build a navy, could well have set Iran on a quite different political trajectory, but his failure to ground his ambition in any institutional and administrative foundation meant that his continuous campaigns extorted but never adequately invested in the structures of the state. A militarisation of the state that might have been a catalyst for a systematic reform of the administration only served to weaken the structures he had inherited, and in the absence of a clear, competent and above all charismatic succession, Nader Shah's imperial legacy fell victim to its vulnerabilities and was fought over by his successors. Merchants and bureaucrats who he had initially cultivated found themselves impoverished and terrorised; his soldiers grew tired of endless campaigns and an increasingly arbitrary and unpredictable master, while those religious classes – the *ulema* – so frequently scorned, proved themselves only too keen to take revenge.

For European observers, the collapse and fragmentation of the empire in the hands of rival dynasts, confirmed a narrative of decadence they had only too enthusiastically dismissed a few years earlier, as Nader Shah had been characterised as the new Alexander. Now as *his* successors fought over his legacy, Nader Shah was once again reduced to the caricature of the Oriental despot, a salutary lesson to all of the depredations of arbitrary rule. The lessons drawn by Iranians were decidedly more mixed, and reflective of the reality that history and historical memory is as much what we choose to forget, as what we choose to remember. In popular political mythology, especially as successive dynasties failed to match his military prowess, it was these achievements above all that came to shape memory and narrative. Nader Shah's rise was evidence that Iran's greatness was only a charismatic leader away, and that however bad things might be, fortunes could be reversed in quick order. Leadership mattered, and an effective leader with a hard apprenticeship could transform Iran's position in the world. It was this sentiment that was reflected in Fath Ali Shah's comment to Malcolm. Instability had its faults and his sons would fight over their inheritance but fortunately Iran would be governed by a soldier.

Agha Mohammad Khan and the establishment of the Qajar dynasty

Agha Mohammad Khan ranks as one of the most remarkable figures ever to have sat on the throne of Iran. He shared much with his predecessor but one, Nader Shah, in both vices and virtues. Austere, disciplined and unforgiving, he could be ruthless and avaricious beyond reason. Like Nader Shah he was to prove far more calculated in his ascension to power than his popular image portrayed, but unlike him, he learnt from his predecessor's mistakes and proved both shrewd, if brutal, in his pursuit of dynastic stability. When Hajee Ibrahim, his first minister, was asked whether Agha Mohammad was personally brave, he is reported to have replied, 'No doubt; but I can hardly recollect an occasion where he had an opportunity of displaying courage. His head never left work for his hand'.[19]

According to the official histories produced by the Qajars, their family had been the natural and designated successors to the Safavids, following the fall of

Isfahan in 1722. But this legitimate right had been usurped, first by Nader Shah and the Afsharids and subsequently by his successors, most notably the Zand under Karim Khan. Consequently the entire history of Iran from the fall of the Safavids to the establishment of the Qajars under Agha Mohammad Khan was one of political turmoil born of the usurpation of power. In this reading stability returned to the kingdom when the rightful dynasty took its place, although as we will see there was more than providence at work in the establishment of the Qajars. The Qajars traced their own lineage back to one of the Turkic 'tribes' – though in their case confederacy might work even better than 'clan' – that accompanied the Mongol invasion of Iran in the thirteenth century. This military genealogy and pedigree was to also serve them well as one of the military backbones of the Safavid state, a position that was to provide much of their justification as dynastic successors. Unfortunately this military pedigree was found wanting when faced with the superior military and political acumen of Tahmasp Quli Khan, and later Karim Khan Zand, as one pretender followed by another was quickly disabused of any regal pretensions.

The young Mohammad Khan, the heir to what was proving to be Qajar misfortunes, found himself the hostage of Adil Shah, one of Nader Shah's nephews, then ruling in the Caspian province of Mazandaran. Tradition dictated that any aspirant to the throne had to be in possession of all his senses, with deprivation of one or more rendering the claimant ineligible. In most cases this involved blinding the hapless individual whether they made any claim to the throne at all. In Mohammad Khan's case, despite his young age (he was thought at the time to be between five and six years of age), it was considered better to be safe than sorry, although Adil Shah took mercy on his hostage and decreed that he should be castrated instead, thereby depriving him of any possibility of founding a dynasty. Malcolm was of the view that this singular act of cruelty had a profound effect on Mohammad Khan's outlook on life, now provided with the title 'Agha' on account of his predicament rather than his rank. Whatever the psychological impact, it did little to dampen his political determination and arguably drove him to succeed where his father and grandfather had failed.

If his grandfather fell victim to Nader Shah, his father was to find himself on the losing side of a contest with Karim Khan Zand, another of Nader Shah's lieutenants, who established his own primacy in western Iran, basing his capital in Shiraz. Agha Mohammad Khan, who had fled the court of Adil Shah to fight alongside his father, now found himself the prisoner of a new court, albeit one that was by all accounts kinder. It may have been that Karim Khan perceived no threat from the eunuch prince, or indeed that Karim Khan himself was of a much more sympathetic disposition. Certainly posterity remembers Karim Khan as a kindlier and more sympathetic ruler than either Nader Shah or Agha Mohammad Khan; a virtuous oasis of tranquillity – at least in the south and west of the country – in an otherwise turbulent century. What he lacked in pomp and conquest he made up for in a judicious administration. His behaviour certainly appeared to reflect a general yearning for calm and his treatment of Agha Mohammad Khan, whom he considered more an advisor than prisoner, was by all accounts exceedingly lenient. Agha Mohammad Khan for his part was not someone who was quick to forgive and retained a keen sense of his own patrimony. According to Malcolm,

> Aga Mahomed did not withhold his counsel, though he cherished a most implacable hatred to the whole Zend family. He often related an anecdote, which displays his feelings at this period and gives an insight into his extraordinary character. 'I had no power', he said, 'of declaring openly that revenge which I always harboured against the murderers of my father, and the despoilers of my inheritance; but while I sat with Kerreem Khan in his hall of public assembly, I often employed myself in cutting his fine carpets with a penknife which I concealed under my cloak, and my mind felt some relief in doing him thus secretly all the injury I could'. When Aga Mahomed Khan mentioned this, the carpets that he had tried to destroy were become his own; and he used to add, 'I am now sorry for what I did: it was foolish, and showed a want of foresight'.[20]

Be that as it may, it would appear that Agha Mohammad Khan did acquire some knowledge of government and administration from being at Karim Khan's court, if such proximity did little to enhance his sense of compassion though it should be stressed that Karim Khan's reputation was relative and by no means absolute. His refusal to adopt the title Shah, and opt instead for 'Vakil' or representative, has been interpreted by some to suggest some yearning for a popular mandate, but it is more likely to indicate his somewhat stoic deference to the waning authority of the Safavids.[21] Indeed Karim Khan's restoration of Shi'ism to its central status in the life of the state was no doubt encouraged by the need to engender the comfort of the familiar for a society fatigued by war, and it will have done no harm to his posthumous reputation among an *ulema* anxious for redemption after the trials of Nader Shah.

Nevertheless, in practice Karim Khan could exercise violence, even if he chose to outsource this to his half-brother Zaki Khan. Even an oasis had to occasionally confront the reality of politics. A Persian historian records that Zaki Khan took particular pleasure in punishing rebels by making 'a garden of his enemies', and having them tied to large branches and buried head first as if to create an avenue of 'human' trees.[22] This rather innovative and distinct method of suffocation may have been inspired by an account of Khusrau I's execution of the Mazdakite rebels, recorded in the *Shahnameh*.

Unsurprisingly when Karim Khan died in 1779, neither his subjects nor the members of his extended family were thrilled at the prospect of Zaki Khan's accession. The comparative calm of Karim Khan's rule was swiftly replaced by a return to political intrigue and infighting initiated by, but soon not limited to the Zand family. It soon became apparent that Karim Khan was the exception that proved the rule. But the dynamic was to change with the escape of Agha Mohammad Khan who rode with alacrity – a three-day ride – from Shiraz to the northern temperate lands that remained the power base of the Qajar confederacy. There his first task was to consolidate his control over his family, not all of whom were immediately convinced of Agha Mohammad Khan's legitimacy, still less his ability to lead. This proved to be a painstaking struggle over four years in which Agha Mohammad Khan cultivated an impression – all too regularly apparent – of ruthless violence while at the same time being sure to develop a network of alliances that would serve him well as he progressed towards the crown that had evaded his father and grandfather. It was a difficult balance that was not always achieved but he proved himself a more successful political manipulator than any of his rivals.

The consolidation of control over the extended family, and the defeat of the rival Develu clan of the Qajar confederacy, provided him with the foundations of an army that grew with every victory and political manoeuvre however minor. This was not an army on a par with that wielded by Nader Shah, in either size or professionalism, but it would prove sufficient to subdue the country. He also took care to cultivate links with both the merchant classes, whose money he needed, and the *ulema*, whose blessing he craved. The Qajars, unlike the Safavids, could claim no charismatic legitimacy in terms of a direct connection to the Shia Imamate, but they could present themselves as the guardians and pro-tectors of the true faith. The Shia clerical establishment that had been ostracised by Nader Shah, and who had suffered in the general political turmoil, were wel-comed back by Karim Khan, and now found themselves effectively re-established as part of the institutional apparatus of the emerging Qajar political settlement. The settlement was all the more interesting because the balance of power was quite different to that which had existed under the Safavids. The *ulema*, who had institutionally redefined themselves in the absence of a strong central state, were no longer servants of the state, but increasingly saw themselves in a rela-tionship of mutual dependence.

This nevertheless was a development that would take time to realise its full potential, but the structures were being put into place. Far more immediate in terms of Agha Mohammad Khan's rise to power was his handling of the elites, and for all his cultivation of networks he betrayed a ruthlessness and strategic focus that shocked even his closest supporters and beneficiaries. Unable to pro-duce an heir, he had decided that the succession would fall on his nephew, Baba Khan (the future Fath Ali Shah), whose character and approach was in many ways the mirror image of his uncle. Agha Mohammad Khan saw no reason to engage in battle when an assassination would suffice but the means by which he would achieve this often required a protracted charm offensive to lull the hapless victim into a false sense of security. The victim was more often than not a relative on the basis that these were the only individuals who could pose a legitimate threat to the succession. Agha Mohammad Khan therefore pursued a policy of exten-sive and diverse marriages for his nephew, thereby binding all parts of the Qajar confederacy (most obviously the two significant branches of the Quyunlu and the Develu), as well as other families of significance to the succession, with a policy of what we might term targeted assassination.

In one particularly notorious case, Agha Mohammad Khan used his nephew as bait to lure his brother into an ambush. Jafar Quli had been instrumental in ensuring Agha Mohammad Khan's rise to pre-eminence but had fatally balked at the rewards he was offered which he considered to be beneath him. Concerned that his loyalty might fail, Agha Mohammad Khan invited his brother to one of his palaces, providing Baba Khan as his guide. As they wandered round the palace, Jafar Quli was set upon and murdered, much to the consternation and shock of Baba Khan, who was probably even further confused by the grief with which Agha Mohammad Khan greeted the body of his slain brother. He then berated his nephew for his lack of composure and focus!

> It is for you I have done this! The gallant spirit that lately animated that body would never have permitted my crown to rest upon your head! Persia would have been distracted with internal wars. To avert these consequences, I have acted with shameful ingratitude, and have sinned deeply against God and man![23]

According to Malcolm, the perception, or the willingness to accept, that Agha Mohammad Khan conducted himself for the benefit of the common good, helped to mitigate some of the genuine horror that his actions generated. There can certainly be few better expressions of ruthless realpolitik.

One might also add that these acts of violence were in large part limited to aristocratic rivals and rarely affected the wider population for whom such struggles were a normal consequence of political contests. However, there were times when Agha Mohammad Khan was determined to make an example well beyond the pale of even the most accepting of his subjects, and where his emotions overran and subsumed his most rational of calculations. It is these excesses that have come to characterise his entire rule and which have cast a long shadow on his rise to power. The first and most damning indictment revolves around his treatment of the Zand family and in particular the heir to their fortunes, Lutf Ali Khan. His treatment of Lutf Ali Khan is all the more galling when compared to the beneficent manner in which he was accepted into the Zand court, and is contrasted unfavourably with the chivalry with which the young Zand prince was associated. Lutf Ali Khan had proved an implacable foe and such was Agha Mohammad Khan's frustration at his failure to capture him at Kerman, that he put the city to the sword, looting and pillaging for three days. When Lutf Ali Khan was finally betrayed into Agha Mohammad Khan's hands, the Qajar prince proved merciless in his treatment such that Malcolm refuses to provide the details to English readership, noting only that 'The page of history would be stained by the recital of the indignities offered to the royal captive'.[24] As if this was not enough Agha Mohammad Khan then had the bones of Karim Khan dug up and reburied under the staircase of his palace in his new capital Tehran, so that he might every day trample on the remains of his enemy.

The second act of wanton violence and massacre was perpetrated against the Georgians who had rebelled and sought sanctuary with the Russians. Agha Mohammad Khan decided that measures needed to be taken and in the absence of any Russian military assistance, the Georgians found themselves vulnerable to a punitive expedition of some force. Tiflis was sacked and some 15,000 Georgians were taken into captivity. The memory of this assault lingers still in the Caucasus. On his return, Agha Mohammad Khan was finally persuaded and felt confident enough to have himself crowned. Thus in 1796, some 17 years after Karim Khan's death, Agha Mohammad Khan 'conditionally' accepted the crown announcing, 'Recollect . . . if I do, your toils are only commencing; for I cannot consent to wear the Persian crown, without as much power as has been enjoyed by the greatest sovereigns of Persia'.[25]

It is a matter of debate which sovereigns he had in mind, but the crown he had designed for himself was called the Kayanid Crown, after the largely mythical pre-Islamic dynasty that ruled Iran up to and including the Sassanians. It was a very clear statement of intent and ambition and was indicative of a tendency among Iranian dynasts to reflect the glories of the pre-Islamic imperial era.[26] Indeed the assumption that this was primarily a preoccupation of the Pahlavi dynasty (1925–79) is incorrect. The chief difference being that the focus of imperial nostalgia was firmly located within the compass of the *Shahnameh*, and was not drawn from the texts of Classical Greek historians.

For all his efforts and plans for the future, Agha Mohammad Shah's formal reign was to prove brief. Unlike Nader Shah he had planned carefully and to the last detail for the succession, but like his predecessor he ultimately bore his power with an air of dangerous complacency. Irritated by the noise being made by servants outside his tent, Agha Mohammad Shah was persuaded to postpone their execution until the Sabbath (Friday) was over, so as to not despoil that holy day with blood. He however failed to take care to ensure that the condemned were safely guarded and over-night they decided not to meekly await their fate but to slip into the king's tent and murder him in his sleep. It was an inauspicious end to what for many must have been a terrifying reign.

Agha Mohammad Shah's justification, if it must be sought, was the longevity of the dynasty which he founded and the relative stability that this bequeathed to a country torn by decades of political strife. Indeed Malcolm, whose first visit to Iran came within three years of Agha Mohammad Shah's death, argued with an admirable air of objectivity, that his actions could only be understood in the context of a country whose absence of laws as might be comprehended in the West had been compounded by a century in which all convention and tradition had been overturned.

> The extraordinary rise of Nader Shah and of Kerreem Khan had destroyed that sacred regard for the royal family which had protected the weakest of

the Seffavean monarchs . . . the usurpation of the kingly name was so common, that it was no longer held in respect . . . the kingdom was in a state of complete anarchy . . . Never was a character better formed to remedy these evils than Aga Mahomed Khan.[27]

In effect Agha Mohammad Khan was the price Iran had to pay for the restoration of stability. This was echoed in the remarkable reflection of Hajji Ibrahim, Agha Mohammad Shah's First Minister, who oversaw what was to prove to be a highly smooth succession, when he commented to Malcolm that, 'My object has been to give my country one king; I cared not whether he was a Zend or a Kajir, so that there was an end of internal distraction. I have seen enough of these scenes of blood'.[28]

Notes

1   R. Pasley, *Send Malcolm! The Life of Major General Sir John Malcolm 1769–1833*. London: British Association of Cemeteries in South Asia, 1982, p. 31. See also J. Malcolm, *Sketches of Persia*. Elibron Classics reprint, 2005 [first published London: John Murray, 1827], p. 204.

2   Malcolm, *Sketches of Persia*, pp. 65–6.

3   Malcolm, *Sketches of Persia*, p. 215. See also Mirza Abul Hassan Khan, *A Persian at the Court of King George, 1809–10: The Journal of Abul Hassan Khan*. London, Barrie Jenkins, 1988, p. 253; 'the King's power is strictly limited by the law'.

4   J. Chardin, *A New and Accurate Description of Persia and Other Eastern Nations*, Vol II. London: Argonaut Press, 1971 [first published London: A. Bettesworth and J. Batley, 1724], p. 125.

5   See Chardin, p. 126. Sir William Ouseley for example makes this clear in the introduction to his *Travels in Various Countries of the East: More Particularly Persia*, Vol I. Elibron Classics reprint, 2004 [first published London: Rodwell and Martin, 1819], p. xii.

6   A. Newman, *Safavid Iran: Rebirth of a Persian Empire*. London: I.B. Tauris, 2008, pp. 117–25.

7   See in this respect, R. Matthee, *Persia in Crisis: Safavid Decline and the Fall of Isfahan*. London: I.B. Tauris, 2012, pp. 177–82.

8   Chardin, p. 511.

9   R. Matthee, 'Solaymān I', *Encyclopædia Iranica*, www.iranicaonline.org/articles/ solayman-1.

10 See for example, M. Tavakoli Targhi, 'Contested Memories: Narrative Structure and Allegorical Meanings of Iran's Pre-Islamic History', *Iranian Studies* 29(1/2), Winter–Spring 1996, pp. 149–75.

11 Matthee, *Persia in Crisis*, p. 178.

12 On this terminology, see discussion on p.

13 The somewhat short dissertation (by modern standards), by Isaac Isaacson and entitled, 'On the Current Revolutions in Persia', was nonetheless submitted in 1725, less than three years after the fall of Isfahan and a clear testament to the speed with which the news travelled and the interest it garnered in Europe.

14 In the Iranian myth of descent as outlined in the *Shahnameh*, the king of the world, Fereidoon, divides his empire among his three sons, giving the choice part, Iran to his youngest son Iraj. Salm tales the west (Rum) and Touraj takes Turan in the east. In

time 'Turan' becomes identified with the Turks who come to occupy Central Asia, but in the mythology, these are fraternal divisions and rivalries.

15 M. Axworthy, *The Sword of Persia: Nader Shah, from Tribal Warrior to Conquering Tyrant*. London: I.B. Tauris, 2009, pp. 21–2.

16 Axworthy estimates this sum to have been in the region of £87.5m, equivalent to the cost of the entire French war effort in the Seven Years War. Axworthy, *The Sword of Persia*, p. 211.

17 James Fraser, *The History of Nadir Shah*. London: A. Millar, 1742, pp. 119–20.

18 Axworthy, *The Sword of Persia*, pp. 30–31.

19 John Malcolm, *History of Persia*, Vol II. London: John Murray, 1829, p. 204.

20 Malcolm, *History of Persia*, Vol II , pp. 176–7.

21 John Perry, 'Karim Khan Zand', EI Online, www.iranicaonline.org/articles/karim-khan-zand.

22 Malcolm, *History of Persia*, Vol II, p. 77.

23 Malcolm, *History of Persia*, Vol II, p. 186.

24 Malcolm, *History of Persia*, Vol II, p. 126.

25 Malcolm, *History of Persia*, Vol II, p, 193.

26 A. Amanat, *Pivot of the Universe*. London: I.B. Tauris, 1997, p. 7.

27 Malcolm, *History of Persia*, Vol II, pp. 182–3.

28 Malcolm, *Sketches of Persia*, p. 222.

3 Fath Ali Shah and the challenge of Europe

Iran in 1800

That the succession proved to be relatively smooth was a reflection of Agha Mohammad Shah's effective establishment of royal hegemony invested in this case in his family. Not only had he eliminated rivals from other clans, he had shown impressive ruthlessness in dealing with any potential threats (real or otherwise) from within the extended Qajar family. What threats might now exist chiefly lay abroad, and in this Agha Mohammad Shah, upon his coronation, had proclaimed that he intended to enjoy as much power as any previous sovereign. His decision to launch a punitive expedition into Georgia was a clear indication that his imperial ambitions were as important to him as his royal and dynastic ones. As befits a monarch whose worldview was shaped by the *Shahnameh*, Agha Mohammad Shah was known to encourage his troops into battle with recitations from the epic. But as already indicated, the image he presented to the world was underpinned by a realism that would sadly evade his successors.

The world inherited by the Qajars differed in significant respects from that bequeathed by the Safavids. Nader Shah had inherited a state, that for all its flaws and failures, remained structurally sound and morally coherent. Only these foundations allowed him within a matter of years to turn round the fortunes of the Iranian state and put into the field an army comparable to if not in excess of – both professionally and in terms of size – anything his rivals could achieve. Moreover, his enemies remained familiar, and the focus of his attentions were the Ottoman Empire to the west and the Mughals to the east. The Russian incursion was an indicator of the challenge to come but at the time was all too brief and not considered serious. Nader Shah even contemplated a dynastic 'union' with Russia, one which remarkably envisaged 'the two states becoming one'.[1]

But in the 30 years since Nader Shah's death, as Iran turned inwards to resolve its own political contradictions, the international order had changed in dramatic ways that had escaped all but the most astute Iranian observers. In the first place, the military balance had tilted significantly towards Europe where the 'military revolution' had transformed both the military capacity and the political structure of the European state. While Nader Shah had put significant forces into the field he had neither the time nor perhaps the inclination to reorganise the state – and its finances – to support this. The consequence being that the financial and economic resources of the Iranian state were exhausted. Agha Mohammad Shah found himself reliant on a force that was both professionally and in terms of size, considerably less effective, and what was crucial was his awareness of this new reality.

Agha Mohammad Khan had shown himself to be resistant to the excessive flattery that had come to characterise Iranian political and court life. As with Nader Shah he reacted viscerally against the decadence of Safavid tradition and was known to upbraid officials for lyrical panegyrics that failed to get to the point sufficiently quickly.[2] Identifying with the warrior class, he tended to show contempt for the traditional bureaucratic elite who were inured neither to hardship nor to clarity in communication. There were of course exceptions, and Hajji Ibrahim's determination to speak 'truth to power' without fear or favour won him the admiration of his master.

Not that the Hajji was immune to the occasional lapse, a notable exception to this rule being Hajji Ibrahim's apparent under-estimation of Russian military power. Encouraging his troops into war against the Russians, Agha Mohammad Shah turned to Hajji Ibrahim for his opinion only to find his chief vizier to have become uncharacteristically caught up in the rhetoric. Enthusiastic about the prospects for victory, Hajji Ibrahim was swiftly rebuked by his king, who then privately revealed his true assessment:

> have I been mistaken? Are you a fool? Can a man of your wisdom believe I will ever run my head against their walls of steel, or expose my irregular army to be destroyed by their cannon and disciplined troops. I know better. Their shot shall never reach me; but they shall possess no country beyond its range. They shall not sleep; and let them march where they choose, I will surround them with a desert.[3]

Agha Mohammad Shah's assessment and proposed strategy for dealing with the new Russian threat was to prove all too accurate. But this appreciation was neither conveyed to his nephew and heir, the newly enthroned Fath Ali Shah, nor was it a sentiment widely held by Iranian officials whose prejudices against Russia remained firmly fixed within the Safavid era. Indeed if the world around them had changed in dramatic ways, with Russian power encroaching from the north and the British establishing themselves in India – a projection of European power which genuinely seemed to puzzle the Iranians – these changes seem barely to have impacted on the Iranian imagination. When Malcolm first approached the Qajar court in 1800, he was confronted by a request to emulate the Elizabethan dress of the Shirley brothers who had visited the court of Shah Abbas the Great, on account of the fact that Fath Ali Shah expected to be accorded the same dignity as that given to his illustrious predecessor.[4] The Iranians it would seem had a keen sense of history, if not an acute conception of progress, and this anecdote encapsulated the notion that the developments of the previous century had effectively by-passed them altogether. It also reflected a wider social conservatism, seen in the continuity of language and idioms, that sought to preserve the formalities of the past.[5]

Iran in 1800 was a brief oasis of calm before the European storm. The calm was of course deceptive and was a reflection of the comparative stability, dynastic and by consequence domestic that had followed the turbulence of the previous 80 years. There were to be sure anxieties over the succession, but in the event Baba Khan's transition into Fath Ali Shah proved comparatively uneventful, and Agha Mohammad Shah's meticulous strategy of conciliation and elimination appeared to have borne fruit. The authority of the monarchy had been re-established even if its power remained fragile.

Agha Mohammad Shah had been a peripatetic monarch, self-disciplined, austere and driven. He projected his power through relentless activity, patronage and raw fear. Reflecting in the authority recreated by his uncle, Fath Ali Shah was to prove his antithesis in almost every respect. His was to be a more settled monarchy, with a court established in the capital Tehran, drawing on the elaborate court etiquette, rules and regulations that had come to characterise a distinctly Persian royal tradition. Out went austerity, and in came indulgence, not only in presentation but also in tone. Where Agha Mohammad Shah eschewed flattery, Fath Ali Shah positively cultivated it, with a new literary-historical 'return' (*bazgasht*) movement intended to glorify the dynasty in a historical, even pre-Islamic context.[6] While the uncle drew encouragement from the martial verses of the *Shahnameh*, the nephew went further and commissioned a sequel – the *shahanshah-nameh* (the book of the king of kings) to extol the achievements of the Qajars.

Above all Fath Ali Shah compensated for his uncle's shortcomings by marrying and producing children on a scale rarely witnessed in Iranian history and certainly not since equalled or surpassed. Marriage was of course a deliberate act of policy and Agha Mohammad Shah ensured that his nephew was connected by marriage to all the important families of the Qajar confederacy and in some cases beyond. The bonds were not only intended to cement political alliances, they also served to replenish a political stock decimated by years of warfare, and not least Agha Mohammad Shah's own reign of terror. Fath Ali Shah's household (*haram*) was possessed of no less than around one thousand spouses of various ranks, siring an estimated 300 daughters and 60 sons, of which around 100 survived their father (according to one source he was survived by 'some sixty sons and more than forty daughters'),[7] but whose progeny further added to the extended royal family and the surfeit of 'princes' that would come to characterise nineteenth-century Iranian politics. This was patriarchal government at its best, government through the extended household,[8] with Fath Ali Shah creating his own quite specific kinship network which would bind not only the political wounds of the country but its political fabric in a patchwork of loyalty to the crown. Eschewing the peripatetic monarchy of his uncle, Fath Ali Shah did not principally transform the nature of the monarchy through the development of the bureaucracy (which remained modest), but rather through a dramatic expansion of the family who were dispatched as governors to various provinces albeit aided, abetted and occasionally mentored by a bureaucracy that was finding its feet after decades of political turmoil. Fath Ali Shah's government, for all its Persian royal regalia, was thus effectively government by apanage – through a reinvigorated aristocracy – and while familial relations remained close, the new Shah could lay claim to running a reasonably coherent and well-coordinated government. As the generations wore on however, the system was to be pregnant with potential discord for the future.

In the meantime however, Fath Ali Shah's most serious threats and challenges were to come from abroad. Unlike many of his compatriots, the new Shah showed himself to be moderately inquisitive about developments abroad, even if the questions remained more superficial than useful. The threat from Russia was all too real, though not as yet taken with any sense of immediate foreboding. It could be dealt with in time even if the realisation was dawning that some assistance might be sought from friendly powers. Malcolm's arrival in 1800 allowed some enquiries to be made, not only of the British and their activities in India, but of their relative strength to the other power of interest, the French. Malcolm was suitably complimentary about French power, an answer that drew plaudits from Fath Ali Shah who lamented that his own officials had a tendency to exaggerate and flattered to deceive, unlike Malcolm whose honest answer had done him credit.[9]

Malcolm's mission not only signalled a change in the geopolitics of the region but also the moment when European politics and the concerns of Europe began to impinge on Iran. The Ottoman Empire had long been part of the European dynamic and had engaged and often exploited the rivalries that had shaped it. The Safavids had been invited to engage in this broader struggle in a putative if somewhat ambitious alliance against the Ottoman Empire. But Iran's enemies had traditionally been located either on its eastern or western borders, with the Ottoman Empire being the most serious and frequent military competitor. The eastern frontiers, as with the northern territories, had been more a matter of control and subjugation rather than an existential military threat, and as far as India was concerned, more often than not it was the Iranians that posed the threat, as Nader Shah had shown only too well. Russian expansion southwards however, indicated a change in the dynamic insofar as the Russian state was now the subjugating power which in its move southward was posing a direct threat to the territorial integrity of Iran. And not only Iran. There were many in Calcutta, then the administrative centre of the East India Company, who feared that Russian ambitions extended to British holdings in India. In this, British India and Iran shared a concern which they might be able to act upon, and Malcolm's mission was not only to investigate the possibilities of collaboration but to assess the military capabilities of the Iranian state, which only 50 years earlier had proved so effective that the Russians could be 'negotiated' out of their territorial ambitions.

But the political and diplomatic situation, as the Iranians were to discover, was not quite so simple. European politics were to prove not only more complicated but to add layers to what otherwise might be considered a straightforward coincidence of interests. The French Revolution had overturned the traditional balance of power in Europe, most of whose powers viewed the revolution as a threat to the natural political order. Britain, France's traditional foe on the continent, found itself financing a series of coalitions with a range of partners it might have considered rivals elsewhere. This emerging global conflict found itself trying to reconcile a number of conflicting interests which ultimately were to find themselves subservient to European priorities. Britain and Russia were to find themselves imperial rivals but European allies, and it was the latter position that would ultimately dictate policy and effectively complicate Malcolm's mission. It was to be further complicated by the situation he found on the ground in Iran. If Iran remained to all intents and purposes a Great Power, with a military potential, it could be expected to hold its own against Russia and at the very least deter any further Russian expansion southwards. In this context British Indian policy would be directed towards containing any potential Iranian aggression towards the south and east. Barring that, the objective was to bolster and support the Iranian state such that the Russians would be deterred and contained. There was, however, little stomach to support Iranian ambitions to reclaim sovereignty over the Caucasus – as Agha Mohammad Shah had putatively achieved some years earlier – and by extension to divert and/or weaken the Russian position in general. The British position was therefore a delicate balancing act that required a status quo that neither the Russians nor the Iranians appeared willing to sustain.

Indeed Malcolm's assessment of the situation of Fath Ali Shah's realm was not altogether encouraging. The stability induced by Agha Mohammad Shah's calculated brutality had clearly come at some cost to the moral fibre of the state, and while the authority of the monarchy had been re-established, the Qajars themselves could lay no claim to popularity. These were not charismatic monarchs in any traditional understanding of the term and while Fath Ali Shah himself was regarded as congenial – and a welcome contrast to his uncle – the acceptance of the new dynasty was probably as much a result of sheer exhaustion, as the consequence of Agha Mohammad Khan's policy. Malcolm noted that one veteran of the wars who had been witness to Agha Mohammad Shah's rise had remarked ruefully that the Qajars 'are a sad set, and we shall never have good times again while they keep the throne'.[10] The monarchy remained the lynchpin of the state and was in theory at least, absolute in all matters, although even Malcolm noted that the Shah was bound by custom, convention and ritual, which Fath Ali Shah observed diligently. The political system would have been considered by the European categories of the day an 'oriental' despotism, quite unlike the enlightened versions that had populated much of continental Europe, but a despotism, that, as Abrahamian has noted succinctly, lacked 'the instruments of despotism'.[11] Power was an exercise in negotiation, not only between the Shah and his relatives but indeed between them, their officials and their subjects, ensuring that absolute power was only exercised with a degree of consensus.[12] This process made despotism tolerable but it also made it functional in an informal manner which often placed the power of personality and the practice of effective communication beyond any rules, regulations or indeed any conception of the rule of law.

The informality of administration and the power of personality resulted in an enormous degree of flexibility and malleability in the application of justice, where much depended on the competence of the individuals and the relations they maintained.[13] It resulted in a degree of fluidity in Iranian society, and in its hierarchy that compared favourably with the somewhat rigid social distinctions Malcolm considered a necessity for the regulation of British society.[14] Lord Curzon famously described Iran as among the most 'democratic' countries in the world for this very reason, though he did not intend it as a compliment.[15] When Malcolm questioned his Iranian companions, as to how they might regulate their society, they simply responded that they possessed the moral tales of Saadi – the great thirteenth-century Persian poet, to which even Malcolm conceded that, 'these stories and maxims, which are known to all, from the king to the peasant, have fully as great an effect, in restraining the arbitrary and unjust exercise of power as the laws of the Prophet'.[16] In contrast to the rigidities of court etiquette, this was a society regulated by a code of ethics rather than a code of laws, still less the rule of law.

Fath Ali Shah was, in a very real and traditional sense, the *Shahanshah*, or King of Kings; not in the sense that would come to characterise its use in the twentieth century, but as a king *over* other kings. This was not a centralised state but a plural imperial system in which the many 'Guarded Domains of Iran' (as the Qajar state was officially known),[17] came under the purview of the supreme arbiter. It might indeed be better described as an imperial kingdom, such was its hybrid nature and pretentions. As if to emphasise this plurality and its various constituent elements he also adopted the Turko-Mongolian title of *Kakhan* (Khan of Khans). He was not a magistrate like the British monarch, but certainly a Leviathan-like figure, who bestrode the political system, balancing it and above all managing it. It was the very fractiousness of Iranian political society – divisions and rivalries no doubt encouraged by the Shah – which in large part enabled any pretensions to 'absolute' power.[18]

This was enhanced and compensated for in the deliberate cultivation of authority, and in particular in the majesty that imbued and enhanced that authority. Fath Ali Shah even went so far as to have rock reliefs carved in apparent emulation of the Sassanian reliefs that could be seen throughout the country but most obviously in the environs of Shiraz.[19] Similarly, the titles of the Iranian monarch increased, arguably in inverse proportion to the real power being wielded, and often as a direct result of that diminishing power, as if to stress and reiterate the authority being represented. But it also reflected deeper cultural prejudices and anxieties, as well as a dangerous political vanity, which as Chardin had noted earlier, convinced and reassured Iranians that their kingdom was among the, if not indeed *the* greatest kingdoms in the world. When Malcolm came to sign a treaty of friendship between Britain and Iran, he was struck by the extensive preamble to the document written in excessively colourful prose whose flattery was careful to ensure that while King George might have dominion over the seas, Fath Ali Shah, 'the mighty Khusrau', retained dominion over the earth.[20]

Such vanities were not the preserve of the crown, but just as Fath Ali Shah revealed moments of acute and realistic observation, so too Malcolm, in his discussions found a people less haughty than their public protestations of greatness might suggest. There was undoubtedly a pride in 'Iran' and a dislike of what were considered slights against the dignity of the people.[21] Malcolm was especially critical for example of the secluded position of women and was not shy in stating that, 'by making slaves on one half of the creation you make tyrants of the other'. One of his companions, Jafar Khan, interjected with a barely disguised indignation:

> Really sir, you form a very erroneous judgment of the condition of our women. In this, as in many other instances, where our religion or our customs are concerned vulgar errors pass from one to another till they are believed by all. Many person in England imagine that a pigeon was taught to pick peas from the ear of the Prophet, who thought he might succeed by this device in persuading the ignorant that the pigeon was a celestial messenger. They also say that his tomb at Mecca is supported between heaven and earth by means of a loadstone. If true, it would be a miracle; but it is not true: nevertheless people believe it, and the more readily, because it is wonderful. Now, it is the same with half the stories about our women. Why, I am told, it is a common belief with you that Mahomed has declared women have no souls![22]

Jafar Khan then proceeded to enumerate the various rights and privileges accorded to women, including rights of inheritance and the protection of their dignity, which he argued could not be impugned unless four witnesses could be brought to testify to any guilt, a standard so high that it was barely possible that such testimony could be found. Even if it was, the wife takes an oath to God to the contrary, her punishment is avoided. If she is divorced she is entitled to her entire dowry, a sum, Jafar Khan argued, which would frequently leave her husband in ruin. 'What protection can be more effectual than this?'[23] Moreover, not only were women much more influential and politically connected than one might imagine, they became mistresses of their households upon marriage, and if yes, these marriages were arranged by their parents, they were arranged with the best of intentions not with the worst of material gain, though this did, Jafar Khan conceded, occasionally happen, in Iran as, he understood, it did in Britain – a point that Malcolm did not contest.

In defending their faith as well as their 'national' dignity, the discussion on the position of women in Iranian society also revealed interpretations and justifications, not as unfamiliar to contemporary ears as one might expect, that sought to distinguish the Iranian experience from other Muslim societies. This was especially apparent when it came to the question of polygamy and the example, Malcolm pointedly noted, provided by the Prophet Mohammad. Here, another of Malcolm's companions, who happened to be a Seyyed, felt the need to intervene.

> The reasons of Mahomed (on whom be the blessing of God), are inscrutable; but as far as his acts can be judged by erring mortals, or considered otherwise than as proceeding from Divine authority, we may believe that in permitting polygamy, he only followed the custom of the Jews; in whose Prophet, Moses, you Christians as well as we Musselmans, believe. The limitation to four legitimate wives was intended as a check, no doubt, upon those habits of sensual indulgence, into which not only the affluent Jews but the Pagan Arabs, had fallen; and it was the enormity of their vices which led our Prophet to denounce such severe punishment now and hereafter upon those who continued to follow wicked courses.[24]

The question of polygamy had more immediate and practical causes insofar as Fath Ali Shah's household stood out as an obvious example of excess in this regard. But here too, there was a familiar riposte about the cost of such households, their impracticability in terms of harmony, and as a consequence their rarity. Western prurience in this regard, it was suggested, resulted from a weakness for sensationalism and, as Jafar Khan argued, a lack of context and perspective.

> You English take your ideas of the situation of females in Asia from what you hear and read of the harem of kings, rulers and chiefs, who being absolute over both men and women of their territories, indulge in a plurality of wives and mistresses. These, undoubtedly, are immured within high walls, and are kept during life like slaves; but you ought to recollect, that the great and the powerful, who have such establishments, are not in proportion of one to ten thousand of the population of the country.[25]

The Seyyed went further,

> the number who take advantage of the licence to have a plurality of wives is not as near as you imagine. Take a thousand Persians and you will not find ten with more than two wives and not thirty with more than one. Who can afford it?[26]

This particular discussion, as revealing as it was, characteristically ended as it might where no actual women were involved, on a jocular note of self pity for the hapless and harassed menfolk of Iran,

If you have any doubts respecting the equality of condition of their partners, do but listen now and then near their houses, and you will hear a shrill and sharp voice rating the supposed lord and master in a manner which will instantly relieve your mind from any anxiety you may now feel for the rights of the softer sex in Persia.[27]

This discussion, which has been reproduced here at some length, remains important for the light it sheds on the perception of gender relations in Iran both from those foreign observers who regarded it as oppressive and counter-productive to the general well-being of society (Malcolm considered that the 'society of women', by which he meant social interactions, were vital in mod-erating masculine excess and in the general civilising of society), and Iranians themselves, who were at once defensive in their reaction to criticism, but also more nuanced and self-critical in that defence. More intriguingly perhaps was the contextual and at times cynical reading of religion and its influences. Polygamy for example was justified on historical grounds and in its restrictions, as a measure of the way in which Islam had curtailed the excesses of the (pagan) Arab society of the time.

But there were other distinctions that became apparent in discussion with regard both to history and to the artefacts of that history. In discussion on the origins of Persepolis for example, speculation ranged over whether the monu-mental platform and its accoutrements had been built by Solomon, or indeed, as another interjected by Jamshid, the 'first and most wonderful man of Persia'. Still another noted that the Europeans believed it had been burned to the ground by Alexander in order to 'please a beautiful lady', before adding with an air of mis-chief that clearly irritated his more pious companions,

> we Mahomedans have the consolation to think this proud abode of unbeliev-ers was destroyed when one of our first caliphs conquered Persia, through a spirit of holiness. It was a rule . . . of the first pious propagators of our reli-gion, always to give the infidels an earnest in this world of what they might expect in the next; so they and their profane works were included in one common sentence of destruction.[28]

Islam in Iran, even in 1800 was thus heavily affected by the *Persian* context within which it found itself. These were *Iranian* Muslims for whom their faith came adorned with Iranian distinctions and historical narratives that clearly set them apart. That is not to suggest that they did not complement each other, but where tensions existed, Iranian traditions often triumphed, even if the triumph was facilitated through the adoption of some religious motif. The traditional Persian New Year festival – No-Ruz – was by Malcolm's reckoning celebrated with as much joy and festivity as by the 'ancient Persians'.

> This single institution of former days has triumphed over the intolerant big-otry which destroyed the religion it was grounded on: and the Mahomedans

of Persia have chosen rather to be upbraided with the impious observance of what their enemies term a usage of infidels, than to abolish a feast so cherished by their ancestors.[29]

The new year, which coincided with and celebrated the vernal equinox, was commemorated throughout the kingdom for an entire week though the first day was the most important, when 'all ranks appear in their newest apparel; they send presents and sweetmeats[30] to each other; and every man kisses his friend on the auspicious morning of the Nou Roze'.[31]

If the festival coincided with a particularly important commemoration in the Muslim lunar calendar, for example the martyrdom of Hussein at Ashura, the festivities would be postponed so that the mourning could be completed before the festivities could then begin. But by and large, any conflicts of interest and sentiment were masked by ensuring that some religious festival could be celebrated at the same time, such as the anniversary of the elevation of Imam Ali to the position of Caliph. A similar marriage of convenience could be witnessed in the formal banners and symbols adopted by the monarchy. One popular banner contained a representation of the sword of Ali, *Zulfikar*. But another popular motif was the Lion and the Sun, which was used extensively in flags, palaces and had now been converted into an Order, much sought after by officers in the regular army. Indeed each new 'regiment' was presented with a banner emblazoned with the Lion and the Sun, in a great ceremony presided over by a mullah who would bless the flag.[32] By the end of the nineteenth century these two banners would merge, and a once reclining lion would stand upright clutching the sword of Ali.[33]

The pride with which Iranians held their kingdom and its apparent historical precedence in esteem was palpable to Malcolm, even if this pride was tempered with a degree of melancholy about the misfortunes that had befallen them. It was apparent that an air of fatalism was never far from their minds as officials pondered the feckless and inefficient manner in which the country was run. As one governor who could barely disguise his excitement on coming across an especially beautiful valley – '*Iran hameen est! Iran hameen est!*' (This is Iran! This is Iran!) – added in a note of despondency to Malcolm, that for all the bounties conferred by God on the peoples of Iran, this richness in materials was balanced by a woeful deficiency in administration, 'God is just', as Sadee says: he gives fertile fields, roses and nightingales, with wicked men to one country, and deserts and screech-owls with righteous men, to another.[34]

The Great Game begins

This inefficient, if functional administration extended itself to the army which remained at core, an irregular army raised periodically through what amounted to a 'feudal' levy which might be effective under dynamic leadership but which even Agha Mohammad Shah understood had its limitations when confronted by a disciplined European army. What Agha Mohammad Shah was quick to appreciate others took time to absorb and when the initial *modus vivendi* was shattered by the accession of Alexander I in 1801, and a renewed Russian push southwards, the crown prince, Abbas Mirza, based in Tabriz, was tasked with the defence of the realm and the reclamation of those Caucasian territories that had once again lapsed into the Russian orbit. The new Russian commander in the Caucasus, Prince Tsitsianov, a Georgian convert to the Russian cause, proved to be a particularly aggressive exponent of Russian imperialism, and his dislike for 'Persians' and 'Asiatics' (who were in his eyes degenerates of a singular kind) was well known. In 1803 he launched an attack on Ganja, storming the citadel and massacring between 1,500 and 3,000 of its inhabitants, before incorporating the region into Georgia. Abbas Mirza had headed a relief column but was too late for the hapless inhabitants of Ganja, and the first salvo in the new Russo-Persian war would take place a year later in 1804, when Tsitsianov launched his attack on Erivan. On this occasion, Abbas Mirza reached the city in good time, with a preponderance of troops (some 18,000) forcing the much smaller Russian force (3,000) to withdraw. It was in many ways an auspicious start to what was to prove a war of profound consequence for Iran's status in the world.

The Russians then found themselves preoccupied with matters further afield in Europe, lending a respite to this particular front. Defeat at the hands of the French and Napoleon at Austerlitz in 1805 was to prove a further distraction and their continued struggle in Europe through to 1807 provided an extended period of relief in the Caucasus. Not that Abbas Mirza remained complacent during the interlude. Despite the apparent victory at Erivan it was increasingly clear to him that military reforms would be needed if Russia was to be effectively confronted and defeated, and in light of the news from Europe there was really only one country that could provide this. In 1807, an Iranian diplomatic mission was dispatched to the small east Polish town of Finkenstein where they were received by the Emperor Napoleon looking for allies in his continuing war against Russia. The eponymous Treaty which swiftly followed resulted in the sending of a military mission to Tehran under the leadership of General Gardane, with the express intention of reforming the Iranian army with a view to its use on Russia's southern flank.

The Treaty marked Iran's formal entrance into European Great Power politics, and a diplomatic system it was to find at times bewildering and frustrating. The Treaty was succinct, and absent of legalisms that were soon to become a hallmark of European diplomacy, laying out the broad parameters of a new relationship without convoluted caveats or qualifications.[35] It was in sum an arrangement between dynasts, and Napoleon at least, seems to have understood that simplicity had its own merits when dealing with non-European potentates. There was, at least, less that could be lost in translation. The vagaries of European politics was, however, to prove more complicated. No sooner had Gardane begun his work (indeed before he had actually arrived in Tehran), Napoleon had decisively defeated the Russians at the battle of Friedland, leading to the Treaty of Tilsit between the French and Russian empires, peace for continental Europe and a tentative alliance between the two Great Powers.[36] Napoleon had no need of his Iranian alliance, and Fath Ali Shah discovered to his cost that European emperors could be no less fickle than

Iranian ones. It was to be a rude awakening and introduction to the dynamics of a Great Power politics whose priorities were clearly European.

Unsurprisingly the country that leapt at the opportunity afforded by the sudden French vacancy was Britain, and soon two new embassies were dispatched, from India and, as a measure of the importance with which securing Iran was now regarded, from London itself. If the Iranians were flattered by the rebounding attention, there was a degree of confusion over which mission had priority in the ensuing negotiations, and Malcolm, who had come from India, found himself relegated to second place, behind Sir Harford Jones' mission.[37] Quite apart from this initial complication, by the time the embassies had arrived in 1808, the situation in Europe had shifted again. Britain continued to be actively engaged against France, but her relations with Russia proved more ambivalent. British Indian interests might be anxious about Russian expansion, but London was more interested in cultivating Russia and forcing a wedge into the fragile Franco-Russian alliance. Britain therefore found itself in the delicate position of wanting to support Iranian ambitions, but not to the extent that they might actually be successful.[38]

It was an awkward position that the Iranians were never fully able to fathom, and was reflected both in the series of increasingly convoluted treaties signed between Britain and Iran between 1809 and 1814, and perhaps most personally, in the experience of Iran's first resident ambassador in a European country, Abol Hasan Khan.[39] Abol Hasan Khan departed for Britain in 1809, accompanied by James Morier. Morier reportedly drew on the ambassador for much of the satire that would in time emerge in his *Adventures of Haji Baba of Isfahan*, one of the first bestsellers of English literature and a book that was to have a profound effect on the way in which the British were to perceive Iran.[40] Its popular impact was to distress other British travellers to Iran, including Malcolm, who were swift to bring out their own memoirs as a consequence.[41]

Be that as it may, Morier's pen portrait of Abol Hasan Khan also provides us with a valuable insight into the attitudes and mores of the Iranian bureaucratic elite at this time. British travellers brought up on the classics were always keen to observe traits – such as imitativeness – that they had been taught to believe were characteristics of the 'Persians'. Morier was not be disappointed. Abol Hasan Khan proved to be an engaging and inquiring companion, if given to vanity and an occasional air of childlike wonderment. While he was openly contemptuous of the Ottomans, qualifying Morier's appreciation of the Anatolian landscape with an aside about the poor quality of the inhabitants – 'What a pity this charming country is in the hands of these people! If we had it, (and God grant we shall) what a paradise it would be' – he was also open to new ideas and conventions, and intellectually curious and considerably more accommodating to European practices than the Ottomans.

I went to visit the *Mirza*, where one of his servants took off his cap and saluted me by a bow in our fashion: again, at a ball, several of his attendants took off their caps and sat bald headed, from the supposition that this was disrespectful in European company to keep the head covered, whilst they see everyone uncovered. There were many other accommodations to our usages which would never have been yielded by the Turk; such as eating with knives and forks, sitting at table, drinking wine, etc. The Mirza himself told me that when in Calcutta, he wore leather breeches and boots.

Morier concluded that to his mind had the Iranians enjoyed the same proximity to Europe as the Ottomans had done they would not only have surpassed the Ottomans in their adoption of European civilisation, but 'with their natural quickness [they] would have rivaled us in our own arts and sciences'.[42] This was undoubtedly an exaggeration but it did reflect a growing British view that Iran's problems were at root political rather than social, and given the correct political environment and system, there was little they might not achieve. The 'wicked' nature of Iranians in sum, was more nurture than nature.

Similarly, when Abol Hasan Khan arrived in England, he surprised his Ottoman colleague by determining soon after his arrival, to learn English, an achievement he never really mastered, but the effort being enough to enamour him to his British hosts.[43] Indeed the Persian ambassador proved such a success with London society that according to Morier,

> Everybody is extremely pleased with the Meerza . . . His ability is conspicuous not only in his public transactions, but also in every private party. The women in particular are quite mad about him and make as much interest to get an introduction to him as if he were the Shah in person'.[44]

His frustration came from the protracted nature of his mission and the delay with which he felt he had been received by court and king, though as Abol Hasan Khan's diaries reveal, for all the slight he purported to have suffered, he returned to Iran impressed with what he had seen.[45]

The outcome of these diplomatic exchanges was, as noted, a series of treaties, which bound Britain, with decreasing certitude to the military support and assistance of Iran, should the latter be attacked. The treaties were amended as the political realities shifted, and certainly once France and Russia found themselves once again at war, Britain was keen not to be seen to place any further undue pressure on her new Russian ally. Consequently the Treaties were written in such a manner as to avoid specifying any particular country and to ensure that Britain's support would only be forthcoming in Iran's defence, not in the case of an Iranian aggression. This distinction would be lost on the Iranians who considered themselves the aggrieved and defensive power on the basis that they had initially been subject to a Russian aggression. Nonetheless the legal nuances of treaties aside, the political and military realities were changing fast, as Napoleon's defeat in Russia in 1812 freed up Russian resources for the Caucasus. Indeed in late 1812, Abbas Mirza's substantially larger forces were decisively defeated at the battle of Aslanduz and subsequently Lankaran, resulting in the loss of many of his vaunted 'new army' (modelled on European lines) and opening up the route to Azerbaijan.

In 1813 Iran acceded to the Treaty of Golestan, signed on behalf of the crown by Abol Hasan Khan.[46] The Treaty with Britain was revised once again in 1814 to reflect the new realities.[47] Between them, these treaties, confirmed in the Treaty of Turkmenchai some 14 years later, established the pattern and parameters of Iran's international relations for the better part of a century. They confirmed Iran's diminished status and defined Iran's position as a disputed territory between the empires of Russia and Britain. Iran became part of a broader Eastern Question, with 'Persian' particularities of its own, but the question remained essentially about the management of decline and the containment of any egregious fallout for either of the main parties. The Iranians for their part had to learn to navigate dangerous waters, whose dangers they were slow to appreciate. Later national-ists, such as Taqizadeh, would argue that Iran's awakening began in 1828 with the Treaty of Turkmenchai and the rude realisation of decline. But this realisa-tion was slow to take hold and many within the Iranian political establishment remained fixated on the past and consequently far too relaxed about the future. Ironically, the treaties themselves, and the provision they made for the succes-sion in the line of Abbas Mirza – a provision which the crown prince sought with the aim of providing stability – ensured that Iran was trapped in a succession of ineffectual monarchs, both unwilling and unable to effect any sort of meaningful change in the government of the country.

The Treaty of Golestan agreed to the cession of the Caucasian territories to Russia – albeit from an Iranian perspective this was regarded as temporary rather than permanent – an acceptance that only the Russians would be allowed to deploy naval warships in the Caspian Sea – a provision that by all accounts was unproblematic given that Iran did not possess a navy – and finally, and perhaps most importantly, a clause, apparently requested by Abbas Mirza, that the Russians recognise and if necessary support the legitimate heir to the throne. This was obviously an invitation to interfere in the domestic politics of the country which the British could not ignore, and ensured a maximalist reading of Article 11 of the 1812 Anglo-Persian Treaty which had included Abbas Mirza as a party to the agreement.[48] On one level, Abbas Mirza could be pleased with the assurances received and the political stability this promised, but it was a dangerous precedent.

The new Treaty of 1814 incorporated the earlier elements and mutual obli-gations, reflecting the new imbalance in power but perhaps more acutely the comparative absence of professional expertise, and any understanding of how European treaty negotiations and the legalisms that were now being incorpo-rated. Quite unlike the relatively straightforward and unambiguous Treaty of Finkenstein, the Anglo-Persian treaties were increasingly qualified with caveats and small-print, much of which appears to have been lost on the Iranian officials who must have been relatively few in number given the absence of any bureaucratic apparatus. It goes without saying that the longer the treaty, the more open to interpretative disagreement not least from the incongruities of Persian–English translation. Despite being described by the British as the '(Definitive) Treaty of Defensive Alliance', the Iranians simply referred to it as a treaty viewing the 1812 rendition as the basis.[49] To this 1814 version was added an appendix which further clarified the assistance that might be afforded to Iran should she be attacked, but also it would seem to remove any prior obligation Britain may have had in the lead up to Golestan.

Be that as it may, it is probably fair to say that the British were better versed in Persian than their counterparts were in English, and the Treaty obligations contained oddities that arguably point to agreements being lost in translation. As noted above the British were keen not to antagonise the Russians, and consequently this defensive pact did not specify a potential aggressor beyond them being 'European', which could have of course included France, but clearly after the Treaty of Golestan the political dynamics had changed. The revised Treaty consequently discussed at some length the precise condition in which Britain might come to Iran's assistance and the means by which it would do so, indicating that in the absence of material assistance (presumably troops), an annual subsidy would be provided instead. Most curious were the obligations with respect to any Afghan incursion. Here the Iranians were obligated to assist the British should the Afghans attack British India but the British were only obliged not to interfere in any Afghan assault on Iran.[50] In 1814, in addition to a general clause about not interfering in the domestic politics of the country, the British also specified the subsidy that would be afforded – a sum of 200,000 tomans – only to be delivered once a number conditions, assessed and approved by Britain, had been reached.[51] This was not a straightforward treaty of alliance, and by a clear margin, served British rather than Iranian interests, although the Iranians certainly appear to have interpreted the collective treaties of 1812/1814 as an expression of support.

The Iranians certainly appear to have approached the Treaty of Golestan as a truce rather than a perpetual treaty.[52] Indeed, even a passing knowledge of European history would have suggested to them that for all the preambles about eternal peace, treaties have been viewed as pauses before the next conflict, although even in this respect they misjudged the mood leading up to the Congress of Vienna (1814–15) and the changes that were being addressed to the emerging system of international law. That said, assuming that they did view the Treaty as a temporary truce, one might have expected the shock of defeat to have induced a review and reform of their military establishment with a view of re-entering the fray in a better state of preparation. In reality the reforms that were affected with the help of British advisors were partial and inefficient insofar as they were targeted to one aspect of a complex equation. Malcolm summarised the problem with admirable clarity:

> An army cannot be maintained in a state of discipline and efficiency for any length of time, unless its pay be regular, and its equipments complete: and this can never be the case, except in a state where the succession to the throne is settled, where the majority of the population are of peaceable habits, and administered, and not liable to be altered at the will of the sovereign, and of his delegates. That a regular army, by influence of its example, and

habits of order, may be instrumental in promoting civilisation, there can be no doubt; but this change must coincide, with many other reforms, or every effort to render it effectual to the great end of national defence will prove abortive, and terminate in disappointment. The reigning king of Persia has been disposed to try this system, by observing advantages the Russians derived from their discipline, and believing that his subjects if clothed, armed and trained in the same manner, would be more equal to a contest with that nation; and he has probably seen with satisfaction the growth of a force, calculated, from its formation, to increase his power over the most turbulent part of his subjects.[53]

In sum for Iran to effect a military revolution which might in turn catalyse and encourage reforms elsewhere, particularly in the administration and politics of the kingdom, those other aspects had to respond. Abbas Mirza might aspire to a 'modern' European style army, but to achieve this he had to encourage the adoption of other facets of modernisation, most obviously a more regular and reliable system for raising revenue, and these it seemed neither his father nor his senior courtiers were willing to countenance. It was not that Fath Ali Shah had not reflected on such a development though, as he revealed to Harford Jones he did not consider a parliamentary system remotely suitable, or indeed feasible, for his kingdom:

> Supposing I was to call a Parliament at Teheran, and deliver up to it the whole power of taxation, I should then never get a penny – for no Persian parts with money, unless he is obliged to do it . . . [it would take] a very long time to make such a Government, and such a people, as yours. Our Government is simple, and the people know all about it in a day. Our laws are much simpler than yours, – and so far they are better; and I know the experience, that, under these laws, and under this Government, Persia has improved very much since I came to the throne.[54]

Indeed the government of the kingdom seemed resolutely wedded to its patriarchal ways with courtiers flattering to deceive a monarch who for all his charm was only too susceptible to intrigue. An early, tragic example was the fate of Hajji Ibrahim: Agha Mohammad Shah's pragmatic chief minister who successfully managed the succession was to be undone by the intrigue of rivals who persuaded Fath Ali Shah to rid himself of his 'over-mighty' minister. Hajji Ibrahim was not only executed along with other family members (the Haji having reportedly been thrown into a cauldron of boiling oil) and his wealth confiscated, but his son was also blinded.[55] Such instability of tenure was never calculated to develop a bureaucracy that might speak truth to power. Fath Ali Shah, needless to say, came to regret his act of ingratitude lamenting that only Hajji Ibrahim 'was fit to give counsel to a monarch'.[56]

Consequently, there was very little change in the government and administration of the kingdom, and much that could be said to have become worse given the quality of the officials that surrounded the king. As for the army, while improvements were made, the Iranians protested that the support from Britain, in terms of the subsidy if not troops, was not forthcoming. Britain's position of course was that the stated subsidy would only be paid out if Iran was attacked. In the event, Abbas Mirza, who had a better appreciation of the military balance of power than others in government, found himself forced into a renewed conflict with Russia, at a time which was not of his choosing, even if most people expected the conflict to be renewed sooner or later. All the indications were indeed there and since 1813 there were ample provocations and opportunities for the war to flare up. The Treaty of Golestan itself begged further questions about the precise demarcation of the borders, and subsequent attempts by the Russians, flush with victory over Napoleon, to settle this matter, were hindered in no small part by their haughty approach to the whole matter. British attempts to mediate were also not considered helpful, and certainly the Russians did not find their assistance with respect to the border demarcations remotely objective.

But the real catalyst for renewed conflict appears to have been the appointment of General Ermelov as commander of the Caucasus region with a view to achieving consensus on the border even if this involved some concession to Iran. In the event Ermelov, much like his predecessor Tsitsianov, took a much more provocative approach, concluding that no concessions could be made and instead did his best to offend his Iranian interlocutors. Abbas Mirza concluded that conflict was at some stage inevitable and was encouraged by the positive results of Iranian agitation in the Caucasus and reports of rebellions against Russian rule. In the event he was pre-empted into open conflict by a declaration of *jihad* by members of the Iranian *ulema*, resulting a precipitate conflict with yet another decisive military defeat. Faced with the prospect of Russian troops marching into the Iranian heartland, Fath Ali Shah hastened to sign a new treaty, that of Turkmenchai, in February 1828.[57]

The Treaty of Turkmenchai marks a definitive point in Iran's modern history and her encounter with European civilisation. It has been singled out by posterity and certainly nationalist historians and commentators as the moment in which Iran's 'Great Power' status was effectively and definitively, removed.[58] One should of course not exaggerate the contemporary impact, and the Treaty did in large part simply confirm a process that had been apparent before and certainly after Golestan in 1813. But in both confirming and in important ways extending the obligations of Golestan, Turkmenchai reinforced a sense of permanence that would prove difficult to absorb. Iranians were used to setbacks. Tragedy was in many ways part of the national narrative. But so was redemption, usually in the guise of the man on horseback who would come to the rescue of the kingdom. Nader Shah had after all rescued the kingdom and restored imperial pride after the cataclysm of the fall of Isfahan. Agha Mohammad Shah – for all his brutality – had likewise restored the rightful frontiers of the state and stability. Abbas Mirza, the dynamic, open-minded heir apparent, would likewise right the wrongs of Golestan. Turkmenchai would in short order come to puncture this narrative of redemption, not least because the salvation of Iran, Abbas Mirza predeceased his father by one year in 1833.

Not only was the border issue settled very much in Russia's favour and the other elements of the Treaty of Golestan confirmed but now Iran was faced with punitive reparations to the tune of some 20 million silver roubles. This was an extraordinary sum even for the time (more-so for a state that had just lost some of its most lucrative tax-yielding provinces) and rubbed the salt of humiliation into the wound of defeat. Moreover, a supplementary commercial agreement provided special rights to Russian merchants and Iran also had to accept the establishment of a permanent Russian embassy in Tehran. Both these concessions were in time to be mirrored by similar concessions to the British. Iran's introduction to the norms of European diplomacy was thus the result not of mutual recognition and interest, but as part of a treaty obligation, and the Russians treated the mission less as a diplomatic outpost and more as a means of ensuring compliance. The British, for their part refused to pay the subsidy on the obvious grounds that Iran had been the aggressor on this occasion, and indeed while British officers had been brought in to help train the Iranian army, and arms and munitions appear to have been supplied, British support remained limited. According to the records of the East India Company no subsidy was paid until 1828–29 – in other words until the conclusion of the war. The subsidy was paid towards the reparations on condition that other obligations of the 1812/14 Treaty were waived.[59]

If the introduction to European diplomacy was less than auspicious, the first engagements were to prove nothing short of disastrous. The Russians had dispatched as their first ambassador the novelist Griboedov, with the express task of ensuring that all the terms of the Treaty were implemented. Griboedov approached this with all the zeal of a civilising mission, much on the lines of previous Russian officials, and proceeded in short order to cause offence to his hosts. One aspect of the Treaty dealt with the repatriation of prisoners of war, which by all accounts should have been relatively straightforward, but broadly interpreted this gave Griboedov apparent licence to scour the land for any and all Russian 'subjects', including a number that might have settled, deserted and converted. Matters swiftly took a turn for the worse when it was reported, and widely believed, that Armenian and Georgian women, who had been married and/or converted, had been seized and taken to the embassy, where it was suggested, they had been forced to renounce their conversion. This, needless to say, raised the ire of the population of Tehran, who in February 1829, only a year after Turkmenchai, stormed the embassy at the instigation and encouragement of a leading cleric and *mujtahid* (one who was able to exercise *ijtehad*, interpret and pronounce on scripture), killing everyone, including Griboedov, with the exception of one Russian official.

This astonishing development was perhaps only surpassed by the official Russian reaction. Fath Ali Shah was understandably nervous about the consequences and swiftly dispatched his grandson, Khusrau Mirza to St Petersburg bearing gifts for Tsar Nicholas, along with the most sincere of apologies. Tsar Nicholas, who was at the time preoccupied with a war against the Ottomans, appears by all accounts to have dismissed the outrage as little more than a local difficulty, from which all parties could swiftly move on. This calm and somewhat calculated reaction has led some to speculate that there was more afoot and that at the very least, the Tsar was not unhappy about Griboedov's fate. In other circumstances it would have served as an ideal pretext for a further military confrontation, or indeed a further extension of the terms of Turkmenchai, but fortuitously for Iran the mind of the Russian autocrat was elsewhere.

For all his failures in the realm of foreign policy, Fath Ali Shah was effectively able to end his reign in comparative peace. The politics of the country had been stabilised, the authority of the monarch restored. Economic life was regenerating, even if the pace of progress remained slow. At the same time, Turkmenchai was a humiliation that was deeply felt on both a personal and a political level. The imperial pretensions of the kingdom had been dealt a severe blow. The reparations were extensive and for all the British assistance with its payment, it took considerable persuasion by the British for Fath Ali Shah to part with some of his personal wealth, in order to satisfy the terms. The one compensation of the Treaty was the dynastic stability that was assured through the guarantee of the succession. Regrettably for him, and perhaps for the dynasty as a whole, his son and heir Abbas Mirza, predeceased Fath Ali Shah by a year. Biological accident therefore robbed the Treaty of any advantage that might accrue to the dynasty and the country as a whole. Abbas Mirza had represented the promise of the Qajar dynasty, another emphatic move away from the brutality of Agha Mohammad Shah towards a more 'modern', daresay *Europeanised* conception of monarchy, through a prince whose martial experience at the frontiers of the kingdom had exposed him to both new methods and realities.

Notes

1 Maryam Ekhtiar, 'An Encounter with the Russian Czar: The Image of Peter the Great in Early Qajar Historical Writings', *Iranian Studies* 29(1/2), Winter-Spring 1996, p. 60.
2 Malcolm, *Sketches of Persia*, p. 82. Also, *History of Persia*, Vol II, p. 209.
3 Malcolm, *History of Persia*, Vol II, p. 201. Also Harford Jones Brydges, *An Account of the Transactions of His Majesty's Mission to the Court of Persia in the Years 1807–11*, Vol I. Elibron Classics reprint, 2005 [first published London: James Bohn, 1834].
4 Malcolm, *Sketches of Persia*, p. 208.
5 On this see both Chardin, p. 187 and Ouseley, pp. xiv–xvi. There is a remarkable continuity and familiarity with expressions.
6 P. Luft, 'Qajar Iran in the Early 19th Century: Tradition and Modernity' (unpublished), p. 14.
7 Amanat, *Pivot of the Universe*, pp. 19–20.
8 For these distinctions see M. Weber, *Economy and Society*, Vol II. Berkeley, CA: University of California Press, 1978, pp. 1006–69.
9 Malcolm, *Sketches of Persia*, p. 213.
10 Malcolm, *Sketches of Persia*, pp. 127–9.
11 E. Abrahamian, 'Oriental Despotism: The Case of Qajar Iran', *International Journal of Middle East Studies* 5(1), 1974, p. 13.

12 V. Martin discusses this in, *The Qajar Pact: Bargaining, Protest and the State in 19th Century Persia*. London: I.B. Tauris, 2005, p. 214.

13 Malcolm, *History of Persia*, Vol II, p. 351.

14 Malcolm, *Sketches of Persia*, p. 239.

15 G.N. Curzon, *Persia and the Persian Question* (2 Vols). London: Frank Cass, 1966 [first published 1892], Vol I, p. 444. For the classically educated Curzon, 'democracy' was a more vulgar and less desirable form of the republican ideal.

16 Malcolm, *Sketches of Persia*, p. 69.

17 Amanat, *Pivot of the Universe*, p. 13; for the range of titles enjoyed by the Qajar monarchs see, p. 10.

18 Abrahamian, 'Oriental Despotism', p. 8.

19 Luft, 'Qajar Iran', p. 14.

20 Malcolm, *Sketches of Persia*, pp. 80–82; for the English version see, J.C. Hurewitz, *Diplomacy in the Near and Middle East: A Documentary Record*. Princeton, NJ: Princeton University Press, 1956, pp. 69–70. While comparatively brief even in English translation, the effect of the Persian prose is all too apparent with a concomitant lack of clarity.

21 Malcolm, *Sketches of Persia*, pp. 110–11.

22 Malcolm, *Sketches of Persia*, pp. 162–3.

23 Malcolm, *Sketches of Persia*, p. 163.

24 Malcolm, *Sketches of Persia*, pp. 165–6.

25 Malcolm, *Sketches of Persia*, p. 164.

26 Malcolm, *Sketches of Persia*, p. 166.

27 Malcolm, *Sketches of Persia*, p. 166.

28 Malcolm, *Sketches of Persia*, pp. 110–11.

29 Malcolm, *History of Persia*, Vol. II, p. 404.

30 These sweetmeats are described by Malcolm as *guzangabeen*, whose description approximates to our modern *gaz*. *History of Persia*, Vol. II, p. 406, note c.

31 Malcolm, *History of Persia*, Vol. II, p. 406.

32 Malcolm, *History of Persia*, Vol. II, pp. 406–7.

33 See for example the frontispiece to C.J. Wills, *In the Land of the Lion and the Sun*. London and New York: Mage, 2004, originally published in 1893.

34 Malcolm, *Sketches of Persia*, p. 143.

35 For details of the treaty (in Persian) see, Gholamreza Tabatabai Majd, *Moahadat va gharardadha-ye tarikhi dar doreh-ye Qajariye* (Historical Treaties and Agreements of the Qajar Era). Tehran, 1373/1994, 'Treaty of Finkenstein', pp. 42–7. For the English translation see Hurewitz, *Diplomacy*, pp. 77–8.

36 For further detail, see Iradj Amini, *Napoleon and Persia*. London: I.B. Tauris, 1999.

37 P. Sykes, *The History of Persia*, Vol II. London: Routledge and Kegan Paul, 1969 (first published 1915), p. 307.

38 See for example M.E. Yapp, *Strategies of British India*. Oxford: Oxford University Press, 1980, p. 83.

39 Abol Hasan Khan was a nephew of Haji Ibrahim. See Yapp, *Strategies*, p. 63.

40 See for example Wills, *In the Land of the Lion and the Sun*, p. 3.

41 See for example the 'avant-propos' of Brydges, *An Account of the Transactions*, and the preface to Malcolm's *Sketches of Persia*.

42 J. Morier, *A Journey through Persia, Armenia, and Asia Minor to Constantinople, in the Years 1808 and 1809*. Elibron Classics reprint, 2008 [first published London: Longman, Hurst, Rees, Orme and Brown, 1812], pp. 364–6.

43 His English was passable if not fluent, see D. Wright, *The Persians amongst the English*. London: I.B. Tauris, 1985, p. 59.

44 Wright, *The Persians*, p. 57.

45 See his diary, Abol Hasan Khan, *A Persian at the Court of King George*. London: Barrie Jenkins, 1988. The Persian title was *The Book of Wonders*. On the Treaty negotiations

see, pp. 118–19. Also Wright, *The Persians*, pp. 60–61. Morier notes that Abol Hasan Khan was careful to note down all the things he had seen in Britain, *A Journey through Persia*, p. 367.

46 Majd, *Moahadat*, pp. 72–86; also Hurewitz, *Diplomacy*, pp. 84–6.

47 See Wright, *The Persians*, p. 65.

48 See Yapp, *Strategies*, p. 83, Abbas Mirza was made party to the 1812 Treaty in order to ensure a continuation of the alliance being envisaged. This naturally entailed some support for his succession. For the 1809 Treaty in Persian (defined as 'summary' – *mojamal*) see Majd, *Moahadat*, pp. 49–61; for the 1812 revised Treaty, see pp. 59–71, this is described as 'comprehensive'. It is worth noting that the British guarantees for the succession and therefore facility for intervention are never as explicit as those listed in Golestan and subsequently Turkmenchai.

49 Majd, *Moahadat*, pp. 87–98; also Hurewitz, *Diplomacy*, pp. 86–8.

50 Majd, *Moahadat*, p. 65. This is stated in the 1812 Treaty and repeated in the 1814 revision.

51 Majd, *Moahadat*, pp. 99–105. Sykes asserts that the subsidy was paid annually unless Iran engaged in aggressive war but this appears to misread the terms of the Treaty and in any case records suggest no subsidy was actually paid, see below; Sykes, *History of Persia*, Vol II, p. 309. Yapp by contrast notes that the subsidy would only be paid if she had been attacked by a European power, see *Strategies*, p. 89. Yapp gives a detailed assessment of the negotiations from the British perspective.

52 Sykes, *History of Persia*, Vol II, p. 314, argues that all sides regarded it as interim though the Russians did not envisage its reversal, rather its confirmation and clarification.

53 Malcolm, *History of Persia*, Vol II, pp. 361–2. See also the revealing discussion in Brydges, *An Account of the Transactions*, pp. 80–81.

54 Brydges, *An Account of the Transactions*, pp. 300–301. Fath Ali Shah revealed insights into British history – referring to *Lizbat dil sheer* – Elizabeth the lion-hearted (i.e. Elizabeth I), and even suggesting that Abbas Mirza could marry the daughter of the Prince of Wales; 'where would all the kings of the earth be compared to such a King and Queen!', pp. 327–8.

55 See Sykes, *History of Persia*, Vol II, p. 302.

56 Malcolm, *Sketches of Persia*, p. 224.

57 See Hurewitz, *Diplomacy*, pp. 96–102; Majd, *Moahadat*, pp. 122–39.

58 See also Sykes, *History of Persia*, Vol II, p. 320.

59 'Affairs of the East India Company: Appendix C No. 21', *Journal of the House of Lords* 62, 1830, pp. 1368–71.

4   Resistance, revolt and reaction

Despite his failures on the field of battle, Abbas Mirza remained a popular prince with a progressive countenance. Indeed, those who had encountered Abbas Mirza, regarded him as an impressive and intellectually curious personality.[1] His premature death was to prove a major setback for the dynasty if not for the new diplomatic framework which had guaranteed the succession in his line. Fath Ali Shah ensured that Article 7 of the Treaty of Turkmenchai would now be transferred and applied immediately to Abbas Mirza's descendants, in this case Mohammad Mirza. Fath Ali Shah's death a year later in 1834 therefore witnessed another relatively smooth succession – not entirely without its difficulties because of challenges that had emerged from a number of Abbas Mirza's brothers, but these were to prove neither insurmountable nor unduly disruptive. Unfortunately for Iran just as Fath Ali Shah proved the antithesis of his uncle, so too did Mohammad Shah stand in stark contrast to his father.

Disinterested, pious and indolent, Mohammad Shah's 14-year reign was dominated by his spiritual mentor and 'Sufi' guide, Haji Abbas Iravani, known to posterity by his official title, Aqasi (first officer of the household). Aqasi had been brought in as a tutor to the young prince by Abbas Mirza and he worked diligently to ensure his protégé would in time succeed to the throne. The portraits of Mohammad Shah by both Iranian and European observers are on the whole sympathetic, reflecting perhaps the more austere lifestyle, and certainly drastic reduction in the household, compared to that of his grandfather. He was furthermore the first Qajar monarch to adopt, in style and dress at least, some of the accoutrements of European culture and learning. But his almost complete deference to Aqasi in matters of state was to bring nothing but ruin to the fragile political system he had inherited. The stubbornly patriarchal nature of the government meant that there was heavy reliance on the quality of both the king and the senior officials for the efficient management of the state. It says much of Fath Ali Shah's personal political skills that he was ultimately able to navigate the state through the turmoil of military defeat, but the absence of any institutional development combined with the shock of defeat in 1828 undoubtedly served to weaken the fabric of the state. Abbas Mirza might have been able to make amends, but his son and chief minister were to prove singularly unsuited to the task at hand.

Aqasi's qualifications for any of the positions that he held or indeed aspired to (his religious pretensions were not grounded in any formal training), and his rise to prominence were a result of patronage rather than talent. He certainly had no previous experience of administration and it showed in his complete mismanagement of the government finances. Already weak, Aqasi's projects, both in seeking to develop the army and to further irrigation throughout the country – both ostensibly noble aims – only served to bring the government to the brink of bankruptcy. He had no conception of how the financial administration worked and as one Iranian satirist put it, 'Not a farthing did Ḥājjī (Āqāsī) leave in the Shah's coffers; all was spent on guns and the irrigation of *qanāt*s. Neither did the friend's crop see a drop of that water, nor was the enemy bothered by that gun'.[2] A generous interpretation would argue that Aqasi faced unprecedented challenges from the political and economic encroachments of the Russian and British empires, and contemporary Iranian commentators have suggested that Aqasi was in some ways a forerunner of the resistance to European power and the stranglehold they would likely have on the country. But Aqasi's reaction was not likely to stem this inexorable pressure, nor immunise Iran against it.

Following Turkmenchai, the Russians had persuaded Iran that a more fruitful direction for this martial ambition would be eastwards towards Afghanistan, and Mohammad Shah duly turned his attention towards the reclamation of Herat, a city that had long been considered part of the imperium. But this of course would bring Iran into direct conflict with Britain, who viewed the emerging state of Afghanistan as an important buffer state against potential Russian incursions southwards. Britain might have considered Iranian expansion eastwards compatible with their own strategies for the defence of British India had they felt that Iran could hold its own against Russia. But Golestan and Turkmenchai had proved otherwise and more worrying was the growing belief that Iran might in time become a Russian satellite. The fact that Aqasi hailed from Iravan (Yerevan) and could thus claim Russian citizenship did nothing to allay these fears. As a result repeated Iranian attempts to seize Herat were rebuffed by the British with the most serious repulse occurring in 1838.

These military adventures proved a further drain on a treasury whose mismanagement was driving the country to ruin. Aqasi's response to these failures was to double down on tried, tested and clearly ineffective procedures, with further emphases on military reforms that for all intents and purposes remained ill suited to the temperament and political culture of the country. In one area, however, he did show some foresight and that was with the dispatch of the first Iranian students abroad to France in order to acquire the technical skills of European civilisation. Paradoxical as it may seem, Aqasi did show a relatively tolerant and open-minded attitude to new ventures that did not appear to be a threat to his own position, supporting for example the launch of the first Persian newspaper (*kaghaz-e akhbar*) by one such student (Mirza Saleh Shirazi) who had returned from Europe in 1837.

The first students had been dispatched to Europe by Abbas Mirza returning with Harford Jones to Britain in 1811 and throughout the next two decades a steady trickle of students were sent to learn the secrets of Western success.[3] By the 1830s returning students and their often detailed travelogues ensured that Iranians were becoming increasingly acquainted with developments in Europe and while the number of travellers remained few and were largely drawn from the political elite, their curiosity revealed a fascination with the political culture of the West and the ideas that shaped it.[4] Mirza Saleh Shirazi, who travelled to Britain between 1815 and 1819 was keen to provide his readers with an account of the distinct aspects of British history.[5] Among other travellers who were to keep diaries were three princes who had in actual fact fled the country following the tensions that had followed the succession to Fath Ali Shah. Their account, which was subsequently translated into English suggested a shift in attitudes from those that had affected Abol Hasan Khan some 25 years earlier. While wonderment remained a feature of the recollections, they were now written less for entertainment and more in an attempt to absorb and acquire knowledge. The political sophistication of Britain for example, and the affectation for the idea of 'liberty' were on a par with the industrial and engineering achievements, and the building of bridges and tunnels under the Thames for example, were no more extraordinary than the ubiquity of newspapers,[6] the general education of the populace (viewed in exaggerated terms) and the wealth that abounded in London in particular, as well as the governance of the East India Company.[7] The princes became well versed in the politics of Britain, with details about the composition of Parliament, the constituent nations of the United Kingdom, as well as the political ideologies of the 'Whigs' and the 'Tories', which could only have come from first-hand sources. They even found time to become initiated into Freemasonry.[8]

But perhaps the most important lesson they learnt from their British excursion was this: that political development was a matter of self-discipline, education and above all the application of the rule of law. It was not unique to any particular people or nation, and could be acquired and applied.

In fine, in former times, the Franks, especially those of England, were like animals an quadrupeds, and had no arts of any description. They dwelt in forest, mountains, and the extreme coasts of the sea, dressed in the skins of animals, eating the natural productions of the earth, and if they had a king they sometimes killed him; and likewise their kings killed many of the people. These oppressions, outrages and violations caused always quarrels between the kings and their subjects. Many people, during the height of oppression, had no rest, and were obliged to abandon the country, and go to the New World and other parts. It appears that at different times, according to the wisdom of the Lord the Omnipotent, oppression falls upon the people in different kingdoms, according to the state of their hearts. These horrible outrages which at this time are practised in their extreme in the Asiatic kingdoms, are entirely banished from Europe, where there is no oppression, and cannot be. In all parts and cities of England which we visited, the inhabitants are a very high minded people, and conduct their affairs with perfect prudence, so much so, that they have no governors, nor do they require civil power. All of them know the law, and what is justice: they obey their laws, which are founded on liberty. Every person enjoys this liberty and acts according to its laws.[9]

'Civilisation', even in its European form, was a process to be learnt and acquired. In the 1830s these were not ideas that had gained traction beyond a very small number of the elite, those that had been able to travel or indeed enjoyed regular contact with the Ottoman and Russian polities. Even among those, it is not at all clear how many were receptive to these ideas beyond curiosity or indeed had any inclination to adopt them. But as Morier's pen portrait of Abol Hasan Khan suggested, some of the members of the Iranian elite proved remarkably open-minded to new ideas and influences and were not instinctively reactionary. Their ability, and indeed enthusiasm to engage with new networks, not least the Freemasons, provided avenues for intellectual engagement and exchange that would in time bear fruit in the agitation for political reform. The fundamental idea that the roots of their problems were political and not social (or biological as later race theorists would argue) was to prove an enormously attractive one for Iranian ideologues of change. This central lesson of the Enlightenment was to prove far more potent in the transfer and translation of ideas than any expression of military or indeed industrial power. To even come close to achieving these, other lessons had to be absorbed.

Mohammad Shah's reign and Aqasi's 'rule' were to prove little more than a political interval between the military and later political and ideological impact of Europe. Aqasi's inaction had deferred and perhaps delayed this charge of ideas, although one might also argue that he inadvertently prepared the ground, with his dispatch of students. But challenges were also coming from elsewhere, with the emergence of what can be characterised as a 'progressive' millenarian movement under the religious leadership of Mohammad Ali Shirazi, known to his followers as the 'Bab' – the Gate. Far from being a throwback to the past, the Babi Revolt, as it came to be known, can fairly lay claim to being the harbinger of Iran's 'modern' revolutions.

The Babi Revolt

On Mohammad Shah's deathbed in 1848, Aqasi reportedly assured his ailing monarch that he should die content in the knowledge that his kingdom was more tranquil than those European kingdoms now engulfed in revolution.[10] As assurances went, not only was this wholly misrepresentative of the reality on the ground but it very much summed up the detached nature of the crown and Aqasi's management of the court. Within two months of the Mohammad Shah's death, the new king, Nasir al Din Shah faced a series of revolts the most serious of which emerged from a hitherto unseen quarter, a millenarian movement led by a charismatic religious leader who sought to overturn the entire religious and ultimately political order of the state. The 'Babi Revolt', which developed from the eventual repression of a religious movement with revolutionary intent, revolved around the emergence of Mohammad Ali Shirazi, known to his followers as the 'Bab' or the 'Gate'. The title signified his pre-eminent status as the interlocutor with the Hidden Imam, the twelfth and last of the Shi'a Imams who would return and reveal himself at the end of time and inaugurate a new era of universal justice and peace. By 1848, the Bab had thrown all caution to the wind and declared himself to be the Hidden Imam, instantly transforming what had been seen as primarily a religious movement into a revolution of enormous political significance. Unsurprisingly the state was forced to respond.

The movement and the revolt it spawned fascinated Western observers, not least Edward Browne who wrote extensively on the movement and documented its rise as a new religion born in the full light of history. Iranian views were more mixed. The movement had gained considerable traction and support among the elite and their extensive connections helped both to protect the movement and to ensure its ideas enjoyed a more sympathetic hearing than might have otherwise been the case. Intellectuals who aspired to the more secular ideals of the West were at once appalled that a millenarian movement of this nature could arise in Iran, regarding it as symptomatic of Iran's educational backwardness, while at the same time condemning the government and the *ulema* for their brutal repression of the movement. It left a lasting scar on the body politic of Iran, which has yet to heal. But in crucial ways it also forced Iranians to think beyond the orthodoxies that had framed their lives.

The rise of Babism cannot be understood outside the transformations in 'orthodox' Shi'ism that had taken place following the fall of the Safavid Empire in 1722. Safavid Shi'ism had always been something of an eclectic affair and scholars have become increasingly aware that both theory and practice were often at odds with what we might understand today as Twelver Shi'ism, that branch of Shi'ism that accepted 12 Imams beginning with the Prophet's son-in-law and cousin, Imam Ali. The Safavids had claimed a genealogical connection with the Imams, a heredity which appears to have been applied retrospectively as the dynasty moved away from the more overtly millenarian, and possibly messianic claims of the its founder, Shah Ismail. This gave them a religious legitimacy to complement their other sources of monarchical legitimacy, and the clerics that were invited in to encourage and secure the gradual if emphatic conversion of the country from Sunnism to Shi'ism were unsurprisingly especially indebted to the Safavids. Indeed the early Shi'a *ulema* were very clearly servants of the state, even if by the end of the seventeenth century, and certainly by the reign of the hapless Shah Sultan Hussein, clerical leaders were aspiring to more political authority, in the face of the wayward attitudes of the Safavid monarchs themselves.

The collapse of the Safavids however, dramatically altered this dynamic, and as noted above, Nader Shah was to prove considerably less sympathetic to the *ulema*, viewing their excessive influence as part of the cause of Safavid decadence and decline. Nader Shah's attempt to diminish the distinctive status of Shi'ism by having it accepted as one of the main schools of Sunni orthodoxy was in part driven by his desire to sabotage Safavid religious legitimacy, but it was also driven and supported by a wider distaste for the excesses of the *ulema*, many of whom were regarded as little more than purveyors of superstition and uncompromising zeal. Half a century later, Malcolm would recount some of this cynicism both in his memoirs and his larger survey of Persian history, noting for example that a popular saying to the effect that a man might 'hate like a mullah', 'is to assert that he cherishes the most inveterate hostility'.[11] He further noted:

> Religion is a favorite topic of conversation, particularly when a stranger of an opposite faith is of the party. It is not unusual to hear the subject treated in a manner which proves at least that there is the utmost latitude of speech. I have frequently listened to these discussions with some surprise. I heard a person of high rank one day exclaim, in mixed company, where some priests were maintaining the sacred claims of the descendants of the Prophet – 'This is all very well for superstitious fools who know no better: but I have travelled and read and have more than once met with a dog of a Syud [*sic*], and an angel of a Jew!' This speech produced a hearty laugh at the expense of the holy man.[12]

Nevertheless, Nader Shah's attempts were to fail with the demise of his own dynasty and subsequent, less effective empire builders found it more prudent to develop a mutually supportive relationship with a Shi'a *ulema* that, while bruised, remained an important component of the social fabric of the country. This not only reflected the reality that two centuries of Safavid rule had effectively rooted the *ulema* within Iranian society, but the fact that the political turmoil of the eighteenth century and the absence of coherent political structures, had elevated the *ulema* in importance to society in general. In the general absence and weakness of government, it was the *ulema* that stepped in to fill the vacuum when disputes needed resolving or a matter adjudicated. As the authority of the crown was restored under Agha Mohammad Khan and a new relationship developed with the *ulema*, their role as intermediaries between the people and state became more pronounced. As Malcolm notes,

> The ecclesiastical class, including the priests who officiate in the offices of religion, and those who expound the law as laid down in the Koran and the books of traditions, are deemed by the defenceless part of the community the principal shield between them and the absolute authority of their monarch. The superiors of this class are free from those personal apprehensions to which almost all others are subject. The people have a right to appeal to them in all ordinary cases, where there appears an outrage against law and justice.[13]

They were enabled in this role by the resolution to a methodological dispute over the nature and extent of scriptural interpretation known as the *Akhbari–Usuli* dispute. Those espousing the *akhbari* method enjoined a more abstract and philosophical approach, and argued for a more limited role bound strictly by the traditions of the Imams. Those promoting the *usuli* method argued for a more practical approach in which scriptural interpretation could be used to provide solutions to people's problems. The corollary of this was the level of power that might be accrued by a senior cleric practising *ijtehad* (exegesis) such that he might in turn become a source of emulation (*taqlid*). Indeed for all the practical benefits, the *usuli* approach encouraged a science of interpretation (hermeneutics, if you will) that could cross over into esotericism, as the development of exegesis demanded increasingly profound insights and knowledge. It was an epistemological distinction therefore that harboured within it the seeds of great religious authority and not coincidentally it was in the early nineteenth century that the great *usuli* scholar, Mullah Ahmad Naraqi, expounded on the dominance of the 'jurist' (*faqih*):

> It is so obvious that any common or learned man understands and admits that if a prophet on the verge of a trip or his death had said of a certain person that: 'so and so is my inheritor, and he is exactly like me, and has the same position as I do, and is my vice-regent, and is my trusted person' . . . then undoubtedly to him belongs whatever belonged to the prophet in matters of the common subjects and whatever pertains to his community of believers . . . [the *fuqaha*] are the best of God's creatures after the Imams, and superior to all men after the prophets, and their superiority over the people is like the superiority of God over everything, and [it is also] like the superiority of the Prophet over the subordinate subjects.[14]

One should be careful, from our current perspective, not to exaggerate the significance and impact of such ideas. In the early nineteenth century, both the *ulema* and Shi'a doctrine remained far more fluid and dynamic. Orthodoxies we may be familiar with today had yet to be agreed upon, and there was certainly no explicit hierarchy as we have today, with *hojjat-ol Islams* (proofs of Islam) and *ayatollahs* (signs of God). What was developing, as a consequence of the triumph of the *usuli* method, was the concept of the *marja*, the 'source' of emulation. But this combined with the fluidity of structures enabled great religious authority to devolve upon individuals who could through learning (and a measure of charisma) claim some deeper knowledge of the meaning of the sacred texts. Indeed there is a strong case to be made that the Babi Movement was not a reaction of Shi'a orthodoxies but enabled by the fluidity of the religious environment, and that the consolidation of doctrine was a consequence and not a cause of the revolt.

The Babi Movement emerged from what came to be known as the Sheikhi movement, named after its eponymous founder, Sheikh Ahmad al Ahsai, a Shi'a cleric from eastern Arabia who moved to Iran in 1806, where he stayed until 1822. The Sheikh gained a reputation for his learning and soon came to the attention of the governor of Kermanshah and indeed the Shah himself, further benefiting from such esteemed political patronage, to extend his following. Unsurprisingly this growing network of support raised the ire and irritation of more mainstream members of the *ulema*, who in time-honoured fashion sought to distinguish, define and effectively place beyond the pale the Sheikh's ideas by identifying them as 'Sheikhi', and therefore not strictly speaking with the Shi'a canon. Given the cynicism which many of the elite harboured against the mainstream clergy, such criticism probably garnered him even more support. Al Ahsai was succeeded by Seyyed Kazem Rashti, who lacked much of the charisma of his predecessor, or indeed the political protection. So while he sought to emphasise that the Sheikh's ideas were very much 'mainstream', prudence dictated that he seek refuge in Ottoman Iraq where he would be less vulnerable to attack.

The Sheikh's ideas would be familiar to those intellectual movements that seek renewal and regeneration through an apparent return to the basics shorn of years of accumulated innovation. The complexities and contradictions of contemporary Shi'a thought had to be stripped away by a return to the infallible sources of guidance, to whit, the Qur'an, the hadith and the Imams. This could be achieved through a (re-)interpretation of the texts, the final arbiter of which would, needless to say, be the Sheikh himself. As Naraqi (quoted above) might have agreed, in the absence of the Hidden Imam, an intermediary would be required both to provide guidance – through the exercise of reason – and to understand the Hidden Imam's wishes – through an esoteric and spiritual connection. Having established his particular credentials, the Sheikh then began to propound ideas that certainly pushed the boundaries of Shi'a exegesis. Not only did he allude to the divine qualities of the Imams – an attribution that would clearly enhance his own position as the intermediary – but he defined God as the 'Primal Will' – a term that would not have been out of place in the Enlightenment (itself of course not immune to ideas drawn from Eastern mysticism). Moreover he argued that the resurrection was not physical but could only be understood in spiritual terms. Critics accused him of harbouring heterodox 'Sufi' ideas; a term used to imply heresy. (The irony of this charge given the origins of Safavid 'Shi'ism' should not be lost.).

Rashti's term as the leader of the Sheikhi community and his prudent move to Iraq served to incubate these ideas, and the community of followers continued to grow, until in 1843/44, when Rashti's death threw the community into confusion with the urgent search for a new leader. They were to discover their new leader in the person of Seyyed Ali Mohammad Shirazi, who came from a mercantile family in Shiraz. Much to his family's distress the young Ali Mohammad had shown little interest in the family business and had left Shiraz to go and study with Rashti in Iraq, where according to Babi tradition, he impressed Rashti with his erudition, learning and pietism. In 1840, much to his family's relief, Ali Mohammad returned to Shiraz but before long he was experiencing esoteric moments of revelation, such that visiting Sheikhis became convinced of the young man's charismatic qualities. He soon adopted the title, the Bab, with increasingly explicit claims to have an association with if not direct connection to the Hidden Imam – a proposition that simply served to excite his followers further, while raising the charge of heresy from critics.

When he finally revealed that he was actually the Hidden Imam's representative on earth, the *ulema* decided that it was time to take action, and a *fatwa* was issued in 1845, condemning the Bab to death. Interestingly, and reflective of the somewhat distant relationship between the crown and the *ulema* at this stage, Mohammad Shah was not moved to do much about the *fatwa*, and he was certainly not going to implement it. Instead he decided that it may be time to interview this self-proclaimed religious leader and see for himself just how serious a development this was. As it happened, Mohammad Shah, persuaded perhaps by more nervous courtiers, decided that discretion would be the better part of valour, and had the Bab arrested prior to his arrival in Tehran and diverted to a fortress in Azerbaijan. This single act of political duplicity began the transformation of a religious movement into a decidedly political one, though the Bab's subsequent claims would accelerate this transition and make it inevitable. Frustrated by his impromptu incarceration, the Bab began to issue increasingly virulent condemnations of the Shah, while his followers grew more militant, leading, it was alleged, to the murder of a prominent notable in Qazvin in 1847. Finally in July 1848, he made the fatal proclamation that he was no longer the representative of the Hidden Imam but the Hidden Imam returned[15] – an extraordinary leap of faith with monumental consequences for the political and religious fabric of the Iranian state, to say nothing of the broader Shi'a and by extension Islamic world.

This was a Shi'a revolution, born of a particularly febrile religious environment which nonetheless contained within it some kernels of what we could come to understand as 'modernity'. The Bab, in his 'explication' or *bayan*, which he had drawn up while in prison, appeared to draw on a number of ideas, some of which were indebted to Persian philosophical ideas of self-improvement, which themselves coincided with and drew on Enlightenment concepts of the power of education. But he also drew on quite specifically Persian – indeed Zoroastrian – ideas of cyclical renewal. His revelation did not signify the end of time, but the inauguration of a new era, when humankind would evolve further towards the sublime. He instituted a new calendar beginning with his revelation, with the new year coinciding with the traditional Persian new year at the vernal equinox, and he wrote many of his works, including his *bayan*, in Persian. The Baha'is who would later emerge from the Babi Movement under the leadership of Baha-ollah, would make this Zoroastrian connection explicit, and it was no coincidence that Zoroastrians featured prominently among converts.

Nonetheless, perhaps the most dramatic immediate expression of the revolutionary mood came from one of the prominent female followers of the Bab, Qurrat al Ayn, also known by her Babi title, 'Tahereh' (the pure). Attending a meeting of leading Babis to discuss the future of the movement, Tahereh revealed herself as both courageous and an advocate of a radical break with the past. As Amanat recounts,

> Tahereh's public appearance at the . . . gathering without a facial veil (*neqab*) during her public speech from the pulpit shocked her fellow Babis as a symbolic breach of one of the most sacred Islamic mores. This was probably the first instance in the history of Islamic Iran than an urban Muslim woman had intentionally removed her facial veil in public, an act that remained

unrepeated for at least another half a century. Echoing the Bab, she argued that the Babi movement was an independent revelation that abrogated the Islamic cycle and that in the post-Sharia interregnum, religious obligations were no longer binding.[16]

It was at this propitious moment, with a sense of timing that would perhaps only be matched by his grandson some 58 years later, that Mohammad Shah died.

Amir Kabir

Mohammad Shah's illness and eventual death in September 1848 temporarily diverted the public excitement away from the proclamations of the Bab, towards the succession. Nasir al Din Mirza had encountered the Bab during his incarceration in Azerbaijan where he had presided over his putative trial and interrogation. Although accounts of the meeting vary, they all agree on the singular point of the Bab's momentous proclamation – a proclamation that was met with incredulity and an attempt to declare Ali Mohammad Shirazi insane. It was striking that even at this late stage, with the Bab compounding his 'heretical' utterances, the Qajar state was still willing to find a legal way out of a solution that his clerical critics were demanding, reflecting perhaps the sympathies he enjoyed among broad swathes of the Qajar elite. The crown prince instead decided that the Bab should be administered a beating in an effort to get him to recant. He was then dispatched back into custody to await political developments.[17]

Aqasi's claim to the dying Mohammad Shah that he could die in the comforting knowledge that his kingdom was at peace was clearly belied by the challenge posed by Babism and even Nasir al Din Mirza could surmise that something was afoot in the realm. His relatively smooth transition to the throne, facilitated by his chief minister and advisor, Mirza Taqi Khan, known to posterity as Amir Kabir (the great commander), was met with open rebellion in Khorasan, led by a rival Qajar claimant, Hasan Khan Salar (who actually proclaimed in favour of a rival prince Bahman Mirza, Nasir al Din Shah's uncle, who at the time was exiled in Russia), the mutiny of the Tehran garrison, and the impending Babi uprisings in Mazandaran and Zanjan. These had all been simmering prior to Mohammad Shah's death, but his demise triggered renewed revolts most obviously in Khorasan, which was effectively lost to central government control for two years. The revolts served to make a financial crisis worse as the ability to raise the money required to quell the mutinies was being hampered by the absence of any meaningful administration. That Amir Kabir was able to restore order was a testament to his considerable political skills, his ability to balance both Russian and British demands, as well as curtail the excesses of domestic politics. Above all he sought to restore the majesty of the monarchy for he understood that it was only in the restoration of monarchical authority that the power to effect change could be wielded.

As the *atabek*, or the 'father of the prince', Amir Kabir was in a unique position to influence and educate his ward, and on Nasir al Din Shah's accession to the throne, Amir Kabir swiftly took on the responsibilities of government. His rise, and ultimately his fall, would be precipitous, reflecting what observers noted was the real fluidity of politics and political power in Iran. Indeed Amir Kabir, the man who now controlled the reins of administration, had been born the son of the court cook. This prompted Lord Curzon to later comment that, 'from one point of view, Persia is the most democratic country in the world'[18] – a conclusion that reflected his classical education, and was not intended to be a compliment. Amir Kabir's rise to prominence and his determination to restore some order to the court and the wider administration no doubt engendered a good deal of political jealousy from those whose positions were threatened by this new approach. And Amir Kabir, like viziers before him, was to remain wholly dependent on the whims of the monarch he sought to serve and strengthen.

For him, one had to start with the education of the prince, and this as tradition dictated, did not simply relate to knowledge of politics and history, but in the inculcation of manners, as befit the holder of the Peacock throne and the Kayanid crown. Discipline, punctuality and a regal demeanour were all requisites of monarchy and Amir Kabir lamented the indolence that appeared to affect the new king:

> With these excuses and postponements from duties it is absolutely impossible to rule over such an unruly [country] as Iran. Suppose I was ill or dying . . . do you intend to rule or not? If you must rule, then carry on with it. Why are you evading? It was not a universal principle for all kings of the past to reach the throne at the age of thirty or forty. Some ascended at the age of ten and ruled with utmost fortitude for thirty to forty years.[19]

In order to stimulate his interest in matters of government, Amir Kabir endeavoured to inspire him with the historical figures of the past, most notably successful monarchs such as Shah Ismail, and to some extent Nader Shah, even though the latter had met an ignominious end. Similarly he encouraged the young Shah's interest in Napoleon with a two-volume translation of the French emperor's life, even if much like Nader Shah, triumph on the battlefield had ultimately ended in defeat. The fact that Napoleon had created a new social order and had fought both the Russians and the British held a certain attraction for the Qajar court.[20] Meanwhile, despite his initial sympathies towards the British,[21] Amir Kabir considered a translation of Sir John Malcolm's two-volume history of Persia to be unsuitable on account of its somewhat dispiriting conclusions. Far better to encourage an interest in the tales of the *Shahnameh*.

Amir Kabir's education of his prince was to have mixed results insofar as he was never able to rid Nasir al Din Shah of his persistent indolence and inattention to detail, while at the same time ensuring that by urging the young king to act with authority and determination, history suggested he, the Amir Kabir, would likely be the first casualty. The question remained whether Nasir al Din Shah would ultimately emulate the founder of his dynasty, Agha Mohammad Khan, or indeed, as it seemed more likely, his great-grandfather. Time in any case was of the essence, given the many enemies that Amir Kabir was incurring through his policy of strict austerity, beginning where it mattered – at court. As the British diplomat Sheil was to observe, Amir Kabir was clearly a 'man of talent' who desired the 'good of the country', but because of his 'pride and overbearing and most injurious manner', he 'scarcely possesses [a] single friend or supporter'. Beyond the court the merchants likewise complained that, 'Not only is there no amelioration, but [there is the sense] that Persia is in a much worse condition than when the Ameer assumed the government'.[22]

Aqasi's legacy was never going to be easy to overturn, but methodically, if brusquely, Amir Kabir brought the country to heal. Khorasan was restored to central government control through a mixture of coercion and persuasion. The Babi Revolt on the other hand was crushed with perhaps the most famous struggle occurring at the fort of Tabarsi where Babis resisted a siege for several months. The Bab himself was eventually executed by firing squad in 1850, not that this served to quell the movement. On the contrary, in 1852 an assassination attempt on the Shah resulted in a whole-scale nation-wide pogrom. The movement in any case split between two contenders to the Bab's mantle. Those who followed Sobh-e Azal, became known in due course as the Azali Babi's of which less is known on account of the secrecy with which they now had to pursue their beliefs. A far greater number gave their allegiance to Baha-ollah, who reformed the now renamed 'Baha'i' religion as explicitly pacifist, and an international reach with a new base in Haifa, in the Ottoman Empire. This order was achieved in large part because of the administrative organisation implemented by Amir Kabir with a reduction in expenses, as well as the size of the army, which by 1852 mustered around 70,000 men. Billeting was henceforth forbidden and the army was provided with new strict regulations for drill and discipline, as in European armies. Perhaps the most important development of this period was the establishment of Iran's first college of higher or advanced education in the *Dar al Fonun* (polytechnic) for the purposes of teaching the military sciences and providing Iran's new army with a professional officer cadre. It was to be staffed by European instructors drawn largely from the Austrian Habsburg Empire, including a Czech, an Austrian, a Swiss and an Italian, who arrived in Tehran on 24 November 1851, only to find that Amir Kabir himself had just been removed from office.[23]

Amir Kabir's all too brief tenure in office was to have a profound effect on the political history of Iran, not least on the mythology of decline, renewal and reaction that has become emblematic of the modern history of the country. Popularly seen as having been undone and deposed by the machinations of the Russian and British legations who opposed his attempts to divest Iran of undue foreign interference, the reality of his fall is more sanguine and traditional. Like Hajji Ibrahim before him, Amir Kabir was not one for the rituals of court etiquette and the many enemies he affronted with his manner made him all the more dependent on the whims of his master. In this respect the control he appeared to exude only excited the jealousy of far more senior members of the court, most obviously the Shah's mother who grew to resent the hold that Amir

Kabir appeared to have on her son and worked diligently to undermine him. Ultimately Amir Kabir's own *raison d'être* worked against him. Having urged his protégé to be a king, it was not surprising if sooner or later Nasir al Din Shah sought to prove himself by dismissing the 'atabek' himself. This might have been the moment of course for Nasir al Din Shah to break with tradition and to endorse his mentor much as the feckless Louis XIII had chosen to support Cardinal Richelieu. But tradition prevailed much to the initial satisfaction of the Russian and British legations, until that is, it became apparent that Nasir al Din Shah intended to pursue this particular tradition to its logical conclusion and have Amir Kabir executed.

Amir Kabir's posthumous status as Iran's first 'national' martyr was cemented by the tragedy that unfolded towards his untimely death. Unable to secure the protection of either the British or Russian embassies, both of which seemed determined to facilitate rather than hinder the dismissal, the apparent threat of such extraterritorial protection paradoxically convinced Nasir al Din Shah, that the 'over-mighty' minister had to go. Meanwhile Amir Kabir never appeared to give up hope of a reprieve, apparently anticipating that a visit from the Shah's men signalled his restoration to favour. The visit (in early 1852), however, was to ensure the termination of his life not just his career, and Amir Kabir, visiting the baths to prepare himself for the visit, found himself 'encouraged' to open his veins. His end was not as gruesome as those who had preceded him but it did cause considerable consternation among the European delegations, not least the British and the Russians, who had not anticipated such an end, and whose indignant response may have reflected the guilt they felt from their studied inactivity. Indeed, far from asserting the royal prerogative and impressing foreign dignitaries with his power, Nasir al Din Shah succeeded in earning their opprobrium, reinforcing the conviction that Iran was straying far from acceptable – and civilised – norms of behaviour. Indeed if the execution of Amir Kabir revealed anything, it was growing divergence between the political cultures of Europe and Iran. Malcolm was no less distressed by the execution of Hajji Ibrahim, but he was a good deal less judgemental, and general policy was less affected. Now, with the tangible divergence in relative power, Europeans increasingly viewed the Qajar state with a mixture of disdain and contempt.[24]

The Anglo-Persian War and the Treaty of Paris 1857

Few events encapsulated this new relationship better than the causes and consequences of the Anglo-Persian War of 1856/57. Ever since the Treaty of Turkmenchai in 1828, the Russians had persuaded the Iranians that territorial compensations could be found in the east, and whenever Russian influence was in the ascendancy, Iranian ambitions tended to be tested. Thus Mohammad Shah had been persuaded to attempt to seize Herat, and now Nasir al Din Shah appeared to be following suit. For the Russians the added bonus of course was the irritation this would cause the British in their defence of India. The British had long con-cluded that any Iranian expansion eastwards would simply serve as a vehicle for the expansion of Russian influence. The Afghan 'state', insofar as it was recognised, was to remain a buffer state, a 'no man's land' between the Russian and the British empires. Iran's renewed turn east at this stage was all the more curious to the British because Amir Kabir's replacement, Mirza Agha Khan Nuri was regarded as sympathetic to their cause, though this, in light of the Shah's determination to act resolutely on his own authority, probably worked against them.

At the same time the British did not help matters by dispatching Charles Murray as their new minister in Tehran. Murray's sense of imperial and civilisa-tional superiority can be compared to that of Griboedov, and his attitude towards the Iranians was no less dismissive. Part of the British problem lay in their dislike of what were considered extraneous and by extension expensive political commit-ments. This had been apparent in their extensive rewrites of the Anglo-Persian treaties from 1809 to 1814, and since then, Iranian attempts to secure a more formal relationship were continually rebuffed. The British wanted to maintain the status quo. They sought to prevent any Russian expansion southwards but likewise were not interested in encouraging Iranian attempts to retake the Caucasus – a military adventure it was surmised that would end in defeat, cost (British) money and ultimately deliver to Russia the influence and control that Britain most wanted to avoid. British reluctance of course played into Russian hands. And while the Iranians sought to take advantage of what they perceived to be British weakness in the Crimean War, the Russians were only too keen to take advantage of a breakdown in British–Iranian relations that were now exacerbated by Murray's diplomatic incompetence, expressed not only in his haughtiness but in his willingness (like his Russian predecessor) to engage in domestic political intrigue. Lacking any expertise in the Persianate world (he was unusual in not having had experience in India), the consequence of Murray's behaviour was to heap offence upon offence, such that relations approached breaking point.[25] Matters were compounded by the Shah's own superstitious mentality in which a dream had convinced him that a break with Britain had been ordained,[26] and astrologers had assured him that Herat would indeed fall.[27]

Herat did indeed fall as the astrologers had predicted, but war with Britain also followed. In the event the conflict proved short lived with a brief British incursion into southern Iran, convincing Nasir al Din Shah that negotiations had to be reopened. The resulting Treaty of Paris in 1857 was to prove, much to the relief of the Iranians, remarkably lenient, certainly when contrasted with the punitive measures inflicted by the Treaty of Turkmenchai. Britain reinforced her position as a 'most favoured foreign government' and a joint commission was to be established to 'decide upon all pecuniary claims of all British subjects upon the government of Persia'. But there were no punitive reparations, nor were territorial losses imposed on Iran other than a formal recognition of the new state of Afghanistan, and the 'independence' of Herat. Moreover, in one significant concession:

In case of violation of the Persian frontier by any of the States referred to above, the Persian government shall have the right, if due satisfaction is not given, to undertake military operations for the repression and punishment of the aggressors but it is distinctly understood and agreed to, that any military force of the Shah which may cross the frontier for the above-mentioned purpose, shall retire within its own territory, as soon as its object is accomplished, and that the exercise of the above-mentioned right is not to be made a pretext for the permanent occupation by Persia, or for the annexation to the Persian dominions, of any town or portion of the said States.[28]

The Treaty also incorporated an earlier Agreement, signed in August 1851, for the abolition of the Slave Trade in the Persian Gulf, noting that the Treaty would extend the agreement by a further ten years after its initial conclusion in 1862, 'and for so long afterwards as neither of the High Contracting Parties shall, by a formal declaration, annul it; such a declaration not to take effect until one year after it is made'.[29] The inclusion of this article, which had little to do with the war in Afghanistan, reflected a significant shift in international diplomacy, incorporating an ethical and humanitarian principle into an international treaty. It was at the very least an exercise in soft power and the Iranian negotiators cannot have missed the moral point being made, even if British moral aspirations were on occasion to be found wanting.

Edward Eastwick, who served in Iran between 1860 and 1863 was in many ways the antithesis of Murray. A classical Orientalist by training, he had lived in India, taught at Haileybury College for the Indian Civil Service, and had written among other things, a 'Life of Zoroaster'. He was as such well versed in the travails of the East and approached Iran more sympathetically than Murray had done. His account of a visit to Khorasan, where the governor protested the weakness of Iran's territorial defences and Britain's moral failure after 1857, was revealing:

'For my own part', continued the prince, 'placed as I am here to defend a province which ought to be the brightest jewel in the Persian crown, and seeing, as I do, the waste and desolation caused by the merciless hordes of the Turkumens in what was formerly one of the most populous and flourishing countries in the East, I am at a loss to understand the behaviour of the English. England professes herself to be the ally of Persia, and yet she pertinaciously opposes measures which are absolutely requisite to secure the Persian frontier. England assumes to be the determined enemy of the slave trade, and has gone to enormous expense to liberate the African races, to whom she is in no way bound save by the tie of common humanity. It is surely then, inexplicable, that England should have never lifted a finger to save or rescue the hundreds of thousands of Persians who are carried off into slavery by the Turkumens. So far from that, England shackles and impedes every effort that the Persian government makes for the protection of its own subjects, and, by expelling Persia from Herat, and even discouraging a friendly alliance between the two countries, renders the tranquility of Khorasan impossible'. I must confess I thought there was a great deal of truth in the remarks of the prince.[30]

Notes

1 For a character sketch see, P. Jaubert, *Voyage en Armenie et en Perse*, Elibron Classics reprint, 2005 [first published Paris: E. Ducrocq, 1860], pp. 151–72.

2 Abbās Mīrzā Molkārā, *Šarḥ-e ḥāl*, p. 83, quoted in A. Amanat, 'Āqāsī', *Encyclopædia Iranica*, www.iranicaonline.org/articles/aqasff-ujuli-mnsz-adras-ivxni-ca.

3 Wright, *The Persians*, pp. 70–86. Abbas Mirza had initially determined to send them to France but the failure of the French alliance ensured their diversion to Britain.

4 See the letter from Jaafar Hewsainy [sic] in Wright, *The Persians*, pp. 78–80.

5 See C. de Bellaigue, *The Islamic Enlightenment: The Modern Struggle between Faith and Reason*. London: The Bodley Head, 2017, pp. 123–6. For the text itself see, *Safarnameh-ye Mirza Saleh-ye Shirazi* (The Travelogue of Mirza Saleh of Shiraz). Tehran: Sahami, 1347/1968. For a detailed account of the visit see N. Green, *The Love of Strangers*. Princeton, NJ: Princeton University Press, 2016.

6 Najaf Koolee Meerza, *Journal of a Residence in England*, Elibron Classics reprint [first published London, 1839], p. 52.

7 Meerza, *Journal*, pp. 80–81.

8 Meerza, *Journal*, pp. 123–4. The first Iranian to be inducted into the Masons was in 1807 in France; Abol Hasan Khan, the first ambassador to Britain became a Freemason in 1810 at the instigation of Sir Gore Ouseley, see Abol Hasan Khan, *A Persian at the Court of King George*, p. 17. For more detail see H. Algar, 'Freemasonry ii. In the Qajar Period', *Encyclopædia Iranica*, www.iranicaonline.org/articles/freemasonry-ii-in-the-qajar-period. See also H. Algar 'An Introduction to the History of Freemansonry [sic] in Iran', *Middle Eastern Studies* 6(3), 1970, pp. 276–96. Wright, in a brief chapter dedicated to the question of Freemasonry in his *Persians amongst the English*, pp. 167–71, argues that membership was never used as a tool of policy and that the interest was usually initiated by the Iranians. The latter point is most likely true but it seems unlikely that the British were unaware of the merits of membership.

9 Meerza, *Journal*, pp. 28–9, later the princes recount the nature of the fall of the House of Stuart and the Hanoverian succession with some accuracy, pp. 91–2.

10 Amanat, *Pivot of the Universe*, p. 103.

11 Malcolm, *History of Persia*, Vol II, p. 457.

12 Malcolm, *History of Persia*, Vol II, p. 462, note e.

13 Malcolm, *History of Persia*, Vol II, p. 304.

14 S.H. Nasr, H. Dabashi and S.V.R. Nasr, *Expectation of the Millenium: Shiism in History*. New York: University of New York Press, 1989, p. 296.

15 D.M. MacEoin, 'Babism', *Encyclopædia Iranica*, www.iranicaonline.org/articles/babism-index. See also E.G. Browne, 'Babiism', in *Selections from the Writings of E G Browne and the Babi and Bahai Religions* (ed. M. Momen). Oxford: George Ronald, 1987, pp. 412–13.

16 A. Amanat, *Modern Iran*. New Haven, CT: Yale University Press, 2017, p. 242. See also Browne, 'Babiism', pp. 414–15.

17 Amanat, *Pivot of the Universe*, pp. 84–8.

18 Curzon, *Persia and the Persian Question*, Vol I, p. 444.

19 Quoted in Amanat, *Pivot of the Universe*, p. 119.

20 Amanat, *Pivot of the Universe*, p. 130.

21 Amanat, *Pivot of the Universe*, p. 109.

22 Quoted in Amanat, *Pivot of the Universe*, pp. 116–17.

23 J. Gurney and N. Nabavi, 'Dār al-fonūn', *Encyclopædia Iranica*, www.iranicaonline. org/articles/dar-al-fonun-lit.

24 On the death of Amir Kabir and the European reaction see, Amanat, *Pivot of the Universe*, pp. 157–68.

25 On the Shah's indignation see the translation of his letter to the Sadr Azam regarding Murray's behaviour, appended to the Treaty of Paris, 1857, in which he describes Murray as 'impertinent', 'stupid, ignorant and insane'. House of Commons Parliamentary Papers Online.

26 Amanat, *Pivot of the Universe*, p. 265.

27 Amanat, *Pivot of the Universe*, p. 289.

28 Treaty of Peace between Her Majesty the Queen of the United Kingdom of Great Britain and Ireland, and his Majesty the Shah of Persia, signed in the English and Persian Languages, at Paris, March 4, 1857, Article VII. Interestingly the Treaty begins with the prayer, 'In the name of God the Almighty, the All-Merciful'.

29 Treaty of Peace, 1857, Article XIII.

30 E. Eastwick, *Journal of a Diplomate's Three Years Residence in Persia*. London: Smith and Elder, 1864, pp. 253–4. It should be noted that the prince's assessment of the numbers taken into slavery are undoubtedly exaggerated, or indeed Eastwick has inserted an 'of' instead of 'and', as in 'hundreds *and* thousands'.

5 'Enlightenment' and the Iranian awakening

Iranian nationalist historiography is divided as to the origins of the 'Iranian awakening'. The consensus leans towards the narrative presented most eloquently by the British Persianist, Edward Browne, which sees its origins in the Tobacco Revolt at the end of the nineteenth century.[1] The noted nationalist ideologue and activist, Hasan Taqizadeh on the other hand, argued for 1828, and the Treaty of Turkmenchai.[2] But a better case may be made for 1857 and the Treaty of Paris, which marked the period of British ascendancy in political and certainly ideological terms.[3] Coinciding with the continuing fallout over the Babi Revolt, which had shaken the orthodoxies of Iranian political culture, along with a second significant military defeat in just over a generation, it confirmed to all but the most idealistic Iranian politicians that something had to be done. Even Nasir al Din Shah, like Fath Ali Shah, began to openly lament the loss of his great vizier.

In this intellectually febrile environment, there was, it seemed, a window of opportunity for new ideas to be seriously considered, and British soft power, in the aftermath of the surprisingly lenient Treaty of Paris, now had a receptive audience upon which to work. In time this would have a profound impact on the political development of the country. It was in this period that Iranian identity began to be defined in terms of a 'nation', a cohesive political identity which bound the many peoples of Iran together. For all the disappointments of British policy, British politics and the plural construction that was the United Kingdom of Great Britain and Ireland provided a useful template for Iran's emerging nationalists who sought to reimagine the imperial 'Guarded Domains' as a reinvigorated, inclusive, 'national' state, in contradistinction to the 'nation-state' model that would dominate among those who sought to emulate the Francophone model. In practice of course, the tensions between these two models would make themselves felt for much of the next century and beyond. The idea of the nation became central to Iranian political discourse, but it remained contested.

The politics of economic regeneration

Significantly in the initial stages of the response to defeat, the desire for reform took on an economic hue, in the belief, not for the last time, that change could be catalysed through economic engagement which would in time encourage a gradual political transformation. This was not a view that was wholly endorsed by objective observers of the Iranian predicament, as testified to by Malcolm's comments noted above, but in policy terms, for a British government – especially that of British India – which remained anxious about Russian opportunism, any approach that minimised political disruption was to be encouraged. Indeed British policy, even at this stage remained essentially one of strategic defence in deference to British Indian priorities – much to the chagrin of many officials, not least Curzon. Iranian officials had in any case, for their part, concluded that the best way to ensure the country's revitalisation was to restore its economy. Within its own internal dynamics, the Iranian economy had grown steadily throughout the nineteenth century, but for anyone appraised of the international situation, or indeed who had travelled to Europe, the yawning gap in economic achievement was all too apparent. The best way to re-energise and reshape the economy was to draw in foreign investors who would bring both capital and crucially expertise (a trade agreement had in fact been signed with the United States in 1856). But foreign investors had be attracted to an environment that was not only massively underdeveloped as far as infrastructure was concerned (both the Ottoman Empire and Egypt could boast of more, though in neither case was it extensive and Egypt enjoyed distinct geographic advantages), but lacked the political and more importantly, legal framework that would be considered necessary.[4] The solution was to offer contractual terms so generous that the prospective investor would find it difficult to refuse.

Such 'concessions' were not a new idea. Trading concessions with favoured status for particular merchant companies and states had been part of the canvas of economic relations for centuries, with foreign parties paying for economic privileges afforded over a number of years. States often regarded them as a useful means of extra revenue. But they were initially offered in a different political environment where the balance of power often favoured the host state and these were reflected in the terms. Indeed the balance of dependence favoured the state and in any dispute it was the merchant company that was the supplicant, pleading its case.[5] By the second half of the nineteenth century this balance of power had changed dramatically, companies were now backed by their own increasingly powerful states (in India of course the 'company' had become the state), while the host states had weakened immeasurably. They were now the supplicants. In the Iranian case the situation was further complicated by the need to find a balance between the various competing powers most obviously Great Britain and Russia, and British ambivalence – the scourge of more bullish statesmen like Lord Curzon[6] – was driven in the main by a determination neither to provoke Russia nor to provide it with further opportunities to extend its influence.[7] The Russians for their part sought to maintain influence at court through the provision of loans, a keen eye on parity with the British and as a last resort, a determination to disrupt any concession that might extend British influence.

The first substantive concession to be offered was a relatively straightforward affair in that it related to British imperial communications with India through the establishment of the Indo-European Telegraph Department. Founded in 1862, the 'department' oversaw the establishment of a telegraphic network which traversed parts of Iran through to India. It soon became the single most important British investment in Iran till the early part of the twentieth century. It was swiftly followed by the establishment of the Indo-European Telegraph Company contracted to the German company Siemans for the construction of a telegraph between Tehran and Russia.[8] The construction of the telegraph was to have important consequences for political cohesion and awareness but through the 1860s its development suggested that the system of concessions might bear fruit even if in economic terms there was little immediate benefit.

It also marked the first time that non-diplomatic European personnel began to take up residence in Iran, albeit in small numbers but broadening the range of engagement between Iranians – most obviously those directly employed by the department, many of whom were drawn from the religious and ethnic minorities, including Babis and Baha'is - and Europeans. Not that this was necessarily a positive development insofar as these new professionals rarely came with any meaningful understanding of the culture. One indeed boasted of the importance of James Morier's Haji Baba of Isfahan in shaping his appreciation:

> Colonel G . . . taking me out to lunch with him, bought me Morier's 'Hadji Baba', saying, 'When you read this you will know more of Persia and the Persians than you will had you lived there with your eyes open for twenty years'. This is going a long way; it is seventeen years since I went to Persia, and I read 'Hadji Baba' now, and still learn something new from it; and, though one sees plenty of decay, there is very little change.[9]

The irony of a work of fiction being used as a cultural reference would have distressed earlier British commentators, though its pervasiveness was a good indication of how bad relations had become, even in the space of a decade. The repugnance at the execution of Amir Kabir had long since turned to contempt and in some quarters, pity. Just how pitiful the situation had become was revealed during the debacle over one of the most dramatic concessions to be offered, that awarded to Baron Julius de Reuter in 1872.

Peter Julius Reuter had made his money selling financial intelligence in Europe, taking advantage of the developments in telegraphy to trade business intelligence between London and Paris. Naturalised as a British subject in 1857 he was created a Baron in 1871, before moving to explore investment opportunities in Iran. Nasir al Din Shah's new prime minister, Mirza Hussein Khan Moshir al Dawla, an admirer of Amir Kabir had concluded that Iran's interests could be best served if he secured a broad economic agreement with Britain and bound her as closely as possible to Iran, such that in Henry Rawlinson's terms Iran could be regenerated, 'through the identification of her interests with those of Great Britain'. The resulting agreement, signed for the princely sum of £40,000, was in the words of Lord Curzon:

the most complete and extraordinary surrender of the entire industrial resources of a kingdom into foreign hands that has probably ever been dreamed of, much less accomplished in history . . . The concession also handed over to him the exclusive working for the same period of all Persian mines, except those of gold, silver and precious stones; the monopoly of the government forests, all uncultivated land being embraced under that designation; the exclusive construction of canals, kanats, and irrigation works of every description; the first refusal of a national bank, and of all future enterprises connected with the introduction of roads, telegraphs, mills, factories, workshops and public works of every description; and a farm of the entire customs of the empire for a period of twenty five years from March 1st 1874, upon payment to the Shah of a stipulated sum for the first five years, and of an additional sixty percent of the net revenue for the remaining twenty. With respect to the other profits, twenty percent of those accruing from the railways, and fifteen percent of the those derived from all other sources, were reserved for the Persian Government. Such was the amazing document that fell like a bombshell upon Europe.[10]

Far from rejoicing at the triumph of this British entrepreneur, the Foreign Office reacted with unerring anxiety faced as it was with international criticism from those powers who found themselves cut out of opportunities by the avaricious opportunism of 'British imperialism', as well as the fear of the reaction from Russia who might well demand a similar style concession in the north. Moreover the whiff of anti-Semitism coloured some opinions in London as it was noted that it was unhealthy for so much of Iran's resources to be placed under the control of an individual of 'Jewish extraction'.[11] In Iran itself, for all the apparent good intentions, the concession was viewed with a measure of despair not least because of the growing belief that the concessions were being issued largely to raise money for the Shah's personal entertainment and travels, rather than for the good of the country. In the end an unholy alliance of otherwise disparate parties, including the Foreign Office, international agitators and Iranian opposition (both progressive and reactionary) ensured that the concession, much to Reuter's understandable irritation, was never to be realised. Instead the Foreign Office supported compensation for the agreement and injury to a British subject which eventually resulted, more than a decade later, in Reuter's acquiring a new concession, including some limited mineral rights but importantly, for the foundation of the British Imperial Bank of Persia, founded in 1889. This was to prove an enormously influential concession, which

included the monopoly for issuing banknotes, control of the borrowing market and regulation of the interest rates, privileges that eventually drove out of the market local moneylenders unable to compete with the bank's larger capital and efficiency. By the end of the Qajar era the Imperial Bank, which operated with little competition from its Russian counterpart, held a near total sway over Persian finances, both public and private.[12]

One should be careful at this stage not to ascribe too popular an opposition to the Shah and his government. The country was vast and communications, for all of the development of the telegraph, remained rudimentary. While there existed a coherent 'imagined community' of Iranians, such an identity could not yet be described as motivated by a nationalist ideology and the extent of the politically engaged remained limited. Literacy remained the preserve of the elite and governmental or bureaucratic Persian remained as florid and intentionally incomprehensible as its practitioners could make it. Be that as it may, among the elites, frustration was growing at the seeming unwillingness of the Shah to engage in any serious reform, and to seek concessions as a means of supplementing his own income. As the Persianist, Edward Granville Browne cogently argued:

> I think the jealousy with which the Persian people are prone to regard these railways, tramways, monopolies, concessions, and companies, of which so much has been heard lately, is both natural and reasonable. These things, so far as they are sources of wealth at all, are so, not to the Persian people, but the Shah and his ministers on the one hand, and to the European promoters of the scheme on the other. People who reason about them in Europe too often suppose that the interests of the Shah and of his subjects are identical, when they are in fact generally diametrically opposed; and that the Shah is an enlightened monarch, eager for the welfare and the progress of a stubborn and refractory people who delight in thwarting his benevolent schemes, when in reality he is a selfish despot, devoid of public spirit, careful only of his own personal comfort and advantage, and most averse to the introduction of liberal ideas amongst a people whose natural quickness, intelligence and aptitude to learn cause him nothing but anxiety. He does everything in his power to prevent the diffusion of those ideas which conduce to true progress, and his supposed admiration for civilization amounts to little more than the languid amusement which he derives from the contemplation and possession of mechanical playthings and ingenious toys.[13]

What Browne, the first and perhaps most significant of British 'dissidents' against official policy, was effectively alluding to, was a reversion to the position held by the earlier British Orientalists: that attempts at economic reform in the absence of political change was meaningless. Critical of those British statesmen (by which he was referring to Lord Curzon, whose own monumental study of Iran, *Persia and the Persian Question*, had been published a year earlier in 1892[14]) who had tended to praise the Shah, largely for diplomatic reasons, Browne laboured under no such constraints. For Browne, Nasir al Din Shah was a reactionary whose brutal suppression of the Babis had revealed his inner barbarous nature beneath the veneer of civilisation.[15] Uninterested in 'liberal' ideas which might redound to the benefit and welfare of his subjects, he on the contrary did everything to obstruct the spread of new ideas and by extension political reform. Given Browne's intimacy with members of the political elite, it would be realistic to conclude that his views reflected their own frustrations with the monarch. Iran's problems were fundamentally political and would only be solved once the lynchpin of the political system, the monarch, was contained, controlled and directed by a constitution, defined by law.

An Iranian awakening

As noted above the Babi Revolt shattered the religious and by extension political orthodoxies that had hitherto defined Iran. Not for the first time, nor indeed perhaps the last, a religious movement had moved dramatically from the margins of political life to pose a direct challenge to the centres of authority. In a previous age, they may even have succeeded in seizing power. On this occasion the Qajar state proved sufficiently resilient even if it did not emerge from the encounter unscathed. The paranoia with which the orthodox *ulema* continue to treat the Babi Revolt and its Baha'i offspring is a reflection of the very real threat it felt, and continues to feel. It was indeed one of the paradoxes of the *Usuli* triumph that legalism and scholastic exegesis might periodically find itself challenged by those who claimed a more mystical and esoteric connection to the Hidden Imam.

For followers of the Bab, his teachings provided the means and the legitimacy to think differently, as the actions of Tahereh showed only too well and if repression forced many of them underground, the ideas continued to permeate through society.[16] This was undoubtedly a boon to the intellectual life of the country, even if contemporaries such as the noted thinker, Akhundzadeh voiced embarrassment at the notion that an individual could make such messianic claims. For him,

> If someone today appeared among the people of Europe in the manner of a prophet or *imam* and . . . issued a public call and assumed upon himself claims of miracle working and super-natural acts and blessings, he would instantly be considered insane and sent for recovery to an asylum.[17]

This embarrassment was, however, matched by the horror evinced by the pogrom against the Babis in 1852, which likewise did not reflect well on Iranian society, or indeed on the Qajar state which had simply responded to 'superstition' with a barbaric reaction.[18] Neither had much to commend it.

The solution was to be found in the philosophy of the Enlightenment. Mirza Fath Ali Akhundzadeh (1812–78), born in the Caucasian territories which in his lifetime had been ceded (if not in his own mind irrevocably[19]) to the Russian Empire, found himself acquiring the accoutrements of Russian culture, such that he gained access to European philosophy, albeit via the Russian language.[20] At the same time his exile and distance from the country and above all culture of his birth enabled him, as with many other members of a diaspora, to harbour idealistic and somewhat romanticised perceptions of his country's past, a return to which would facilitate a recovery from the present malaise. Such historical romanticism was of course routine in Iranian political culture, but Akhundzadeh's was able to use a Russian window to apply what he understood to be the philosophy of Europe. Affected by the writings of Voltaire, Akhundzadeh drew parallels between the French philosopher's horror of religious violence in France – in this case the massacre of Protestants on St Bartholomew's day in 1572 – and the massacre of the Babis, taking inspiration for Voltaire's argument on the importance of tolerance.

For Akhundzadeh the solution to Babism was not violent suppression but intellectual engagement and the education of the public. Babism had emerged from a religious milieu that was oppressive and reactionary so the solution to this problem was to tackle the source and not the symptom, otherwise,

> So long as such absurd beliefs are entrenched in people's minds, either a shrewd Bab will appear or a cunning religious master (*sahib-i mazhab*) will come and, in the space of an hour, will lure all these unenlightened people (who believe in jinn and satan and angels and miracles and blessings) and will overthrow the despot.[21]

In order to avert this possibility, not only must religion be challenged but the system of rule reformed such that the people would be free to debate ideas.

However such a situation was not possible in a despotic political system in which the monarch operated beyond the bounds of the law in an arbitrary manner and, 'The people under his rule are base and bond slaves and are deprived of their freedom and human rights'. Once again drawing inspiration from Voltaire, Akhundzadeh contrasted the despotism of Iran with the 'Enlightened' despotism that had developed in Europe – the powerful monarchs who had used their powers to enhance their 'civilisation' and above all enact laws. For Akhundzadeh, what Iran needed was a Peter the Great, or indeed Frederick the Great.[22] These were, in his mind, and it must be said in conformity with the intellectual views of the time, progressive monarchs who had catapulted their people from ignorance towards enlightenment. That their methods might not have always been 'liberal' was secondary to the ends achieved. His aggressive promotion of liberalism owed something to his familiarity with John Stuart Mill whose argument that 'truths' could only be realised through a critical engagement with ideas, found a receptive audience in Akhundzadeh. Education, and European education at that, was paramount. The people had to, 'accept European ideas. In the Iranians' minds European ideas must have priority over European commerce and manufacturing'.[23] In a remarkable call to arms to the Iranian people, Akhundzadeh pronounced:

> O People of Iran! Had you been aware of the spirit of freedom and human rights, you would not have submitted to such servitude and wretchedness. Instead you would have acquired [political] awareness, opened *faramush-khanehs*[24] . . . created [political] parties, and provided the means for solidarity. In number and capability you are far stronger than the despot; you need only concord and unanimity. If you had such a spirit of unity, you would

have been able to find a way out and deliver yourselves from the bonds of absurd beliefs and the oppression of the despot. Alas that such spirit cannot be achieved except with awareness, awareness cannot exist without progress, progress cannot materialise without being a liberal (*liberal*), and being a liberal cannot happen without emancipation from religious beliefs. Alas, your religion and your beliefs are obstacles in the way of your liberty.[25]

Much as with the European experience, sectarian violence had resulted in an intellectual response that ultimately served to challenge the political settlement and its religious foundations. Just as the French state was found wanting in its brutal support for Catholicism, so too was the Qajar state in its alliance with the orthodox Shi'a *ulema*. Both required reform, and Akhundzadeh and his later contemporary, and to some extent follower, Mirza Agha Khan Kermani (1854–96), sought to provide a template for the development of a secular state freed from what they perceived to be the shackles of religious obscurantism. One consequence of this development was (as in Europe) a move away from religious history towards a more secular interpretation which highlighted and idealised the pre-Islamic inheritance. This was not an especially novel experience within the Iranian context which had after all retained some remembrance of its pre-Islamic history through the *Shahnameh*, and as noted above the early Qajars were not beyond a 'return' (*bazgasht*) movement of their own. Iranians had long become habituated to a dual history, reflected in many ways in their retention of multiple calendars and of course the celebration of the new year at the vernal equinox. But what Akhundzadeh and Kermani were pursuing was something more explicit. Not the toleration of parallel structures but the emphatic domination of one over the other. This was of course the paradox of the liberal project as extolled by Mill, but in the context of the time, it was regarded by reformers as a necessary tonic for the revolution of the Iranian mind.

Faced with the 'fierce urgency of now',[26] the tone of some of the texts, admonishments and proscriptions became increasingly radical. Akhundzadeh argued, for a time at least, for the replacement of the Arabic script, while Kermani became increasingly vocal in his advocacy for the resurrection of the 'Aryan nation' (*mellat-e aryana*) – a phrase more jarring to our modern sensibilities than it would have been in the nineteenth century when the idea of the Aryan peoples and 'race' were becoming more prominent in intellectual circles.[27] Kermani may have encountered such ideas in his collaboration with the noted French racial theorist, Count Joseph Arthur de Gobineau, who had gone to Iran as part of the French legation in 1855. Deeply cynical about contemporary Iranians, Gobineau was in contrast entranced by an idealised image of the Ancient Persians, whom he considered pure-bred, and it was principally to these Ancient Persians that Gobineau's racial romanticism was directed. Some of these ideas may have influenced Kermani's own outlook,[28] and he certainly proved to be much more vocally anti-Arab in his writings than other writers, complaining that,

The root of each of the branches of the tree of ugly character of Persia that we touch was planted by the Arabs and its fruit [sprang from] the seed sown from the Arabs. All the despicable habits and customs of the Persians are either the legacy and testament of the Arab nation or the fruit and influence of the invasions that have occurred in Persia.[29]

One should take care nonetheless not to ascribe modern sensibilities and definitions to previous ages. Anti-Arab sentiment was not unknown in Iran, and cultural prejudice of this nature was commonplace, not least between 'Persian' and 'Turkic' communities within Iran itself. Criticism of the 'Arabs' in a historical sense, and by extension the *ulema*, was also common among the elites who found the strictures of the latter suffocating and hypocritical, and the historical legacy of the former was in many ways shaped by their reading of the *Shahnameh*. Kermani's views therefore would have found a receptive audience and were not a wholesale appropriation of European racial ideas. He may have taken them in hitherto more vulgar directions but to describe him as a promoter of racial theories is to likewise assume that he both understood and absorbed these ideas and that when he produced his polemics, he was applying this precise meaning to the notion of 'race' (*nejad*).[30] The truth is likely to be far more ambiguous, especially when we consider that Kermani's views quite clearly changed. Initially a convert to Babism and a later follower of Azali Babism, he subsequently turned his back on Babism and religion altogether, before returning once again, to pursue, in a somewhat instrumentalist manner, the goal of a cosmopolitan Islamic polity.[31] One should in sum be careful not to ascribe too much order and clarity to ideas which were intended to be provocative, polemical and as a consequence, frequently contradictory.[32]

Moreover one should also take care not to ascribe too great an influence to both Akhundzadeh and Kermani, the impact of whose writings would have been limited by the low levels of literacy and the absence of print culture in Iran. Most political thinkers would have at one stage or another moved abroad and accessed printing in India, Istanbul or indeed further afield in Europe but the circulation of these ideas within Iran would have, by necessity and practicality, been limited. What nonetheless was emerging in this period was a distinctly Iranian 'republic of letters', among a limited number of educated elites, in contact with like-minded individuals in the Ottoman Empire and Europe, often through membership of Masonic lodges,[33] which served as an international intellectual brotherhood, and a means by which ideas could be disseminated. Indeed the evidence suggests that was a far greater engagement with European thinkers than previously appreciated.[34] While Akhundzadeh was limited to Russian, Kermani seems to have acquired a knowledge of various languages, including English and French, and as Iranian intellectuals travelled beyond the Persian hinterland, they acquired increasing proficiency in European languages.[35]

Given that these were secret societies – *faramush-khanehs*[36] – as Akhundzadeh described them, and the term by which these lodges became known in Iran, it is naturally difficult to assess their impact. But one way of detecting their influence and the way in which ideas were translated into different cultures is through a review of the terms used. And in this respect, Kermani very helpfully provided a lexicon of terms, acquired from French and applied to Iran. Interestingly, of the 19 French terms he introduces, race is not one of them. Instead we have words and definitions for 'despote', 'civilization', 'progrès', 'philosophe' and 'patriote', among others. The definition provided for 'civilisation' – 'consists of saving a nation from envy, avarice and state of savagery . . . barbarism and ignorance; of acquiring full knowledge necessary for progress in life, science and technology; and of improving and spreading humanitarian mores and customs among the people' – is drawn directly from Enlightenment ideas and distinctly understands civilisation to be a process that can be acquired.[37]

Another 'free-thinker' whose ideas were also inspired by the Enlightenment was Jamal al Din al Afghani. Afghani, who is known to posterity as a vigorous anti-imperialist and advocate for pan-Islamism, promoted a much broader range of ideas than some of his disciples and followers would suggest. Having spent a formative period in British India, he then travelled widely in the Middle East and visited both London and Paris. Afghani gained a popularity and in some cases notoriety as a 'rebel with a cause', and his tendency to tailor his polemics to his audience ensured that particular groups came way with a distinctly partial view. His Arab and Ottoman followers, consequently, gave greater credence to his tracts on the revival of Islam. His Iranian followers, who also knew him by his birthplace, Asaadabad, tended to see him less as a pan-Islamist and more as a philosopher in the progressive tradition of the Enlightenment, albeit one with a religious leaning. Afghani, who despite the moniker he chose, was born and raised in a thoroughly Iranian and Shi'a milieu, and had no illusions about the nature and qualities of the *ulema* he encountered, and his promotion of Islam as a means of revival was definitely a reformed Islam and by no means a defence of the status quo. Far from it. Afghani, who like Kermani, became a Freemason – and appears by some accounts to have become a member of two lodges, after having been expelled from the first for being too politically active – was a keen promoter of Enlightenment philosophy as an antidote to obscurantist and reactionary religion.

These ideas are most explicitly voiced in a lengthy response to the French philosopher Ernest Renan, who pronouncements on the failings of Islam as indicative of the moral and intellectual weakness of the 'Semitic' Arabs, clearly and justifiably irritated Afghani.[38] But his response is intriguing for far more than his rejection of racial stereotyping. The piece is replete with Enlightenment ideas, not least towards religion, the importance of education and the vitality of reason. Thus:

> I will say no nation at its origin is capable of letting itself be guided by pre reason . . . since humanity, at its origin did not know the causes of events . . . it was perforce led to follow the advice of its teachers and the orders they gave. This obedience was imposed in the name of the supreme Being to whom educators attributed all events, without permitting men to discuss its utility or its disadvantages. This is no doubt for man one of the heaviest

and most humiliating yokes, as I recognise; but one cannot deny that it is by this religious education, whether it be Muslim, Christian, or pagan, that all nations have emerged from barbarism and marched toward a more advanced civilisation.[39]

Afghani's defence of religion is heavily qualified as a means of advancing civilisation and nor does he privilege one over the other, including for good effect the paganism of the ancients. He added that if it were true that the Muslim religion had indeed obstructed science, was this not true of all religions and might we not expect that such an approach would disappear one day, as indeed it had done with Christianity? What Islam is doing, he suggests, is no different to that which occurred in Christendom. 'I know all the difficulties that the Muslims will have to surmount to achieve the same degree of civilisation, access to the truth with the help of philosophic and scientific methods being forbidden them'.[40] While admitting that the Arabs rushed 'while in a state of barbarism' to acquire the sciences of the Greeks and the Persians, he noted that the Arabs did promote them as indeed Renan himself is good enough to concede. He objected, however, to Renan's determination to show that the cultivation of these sciences was left to the non-Arab peoples of the caliphate (a view that Renan may have himself acquired from Ibn Khaldun), and makes the following important point with regard to the identification of an Arab race or peoples: 'if one is willing to consider that human races are only distinguished by their languages and that if this distinction should disappear, nations would not take long to forget their diverse origins'.[41] He concludes nonetheless with the following clarion call for the superiority of, and lament for, philosophy:

> Religions by whatever names they are called, all resemble each other. No agreement and no reconciliation are possible between these religions and philosophy . . . Whenever religion will have the upper hand, it will eliminate philosophy; and the contrary happens when it is philosophy that reigns as sovereign mistress. So long as humanity exists, the struggle will not cease between dogma and free investigation, between religion and philosophy; a desperate struggle for which I fear, the triumph will not be for free thought, because the masses dislike reason, and its teaching are only understood by some intelligences of the elite, and because, also, science, however beautiful it is, does not completely satisfy humanity, which thirsts for the ideal and which likes to exist in dark and distant regions that the philosophers and scholars can neither perceive nor explore.[42]

Ironically Renan's response to this was to applaud Afghani's intellect emblematic of his Iranian ethnicity. But it is remarkable nonetheless how this response mirrors Enlightenment arguments and perhaps more interestingly, for all his eloquence, how similar Afghani's views in religion, and the rise of the Arabs on the back of Greek and Persian science, echo comments made by Kermani and Akhundzadeh. There is little doubt that Afghani was more nuanced and certainly more cosmopolitan in his approach – both characteristics that endeared him to the salons of Paris and London, where he achieved a near celebrity status – confirmed posthumously by Browne in his evocative study of *The Persian Revolution*, published in 1910. Indeed, this 'Oriental statesman', of 'cosmopolitan sympathies and encyclopaedic learning', for all his reputation as a proponent of Islamic revival, was a keen advocate of constitutionalism and the rule of law, 'A patriarchal government without a written code is tolerable; but neither law nor government, only cruel, rapacious, unscrupulous and sleepless tyranny, that is not tolerable; yet that is our lot'.[43] The Iranian people, thundered Afghani, demand a code of law, an idea which Afghani argued had first been systematically proposed by the Iranian Armenian diplomat and bureaucrat, Malkom Khan.

Malkom Khan had enjoyed a number of official posts before being sent to head the Iranian mission in London in 1872, a post he held till 1888, eventually falling out with the government altogether over a financial scandal with which he had become embroiled.[44] Just as Afghani's travels to the West had provided him with a valuable platform with which to reach out to dissident opinion in Europe, so too Malkom Khan's position gave him unusual access to European intellectual (and to an extent, policy) circles. There is much that one can be critical of in Malkom Khan's behaviour, not least his dubious financial dealings,[45] and his tendency to exaggerate his influence, but he was sufficiently eloquent in his arguments for the noted Arabist Wilfrid Blunt to come away from an encounter with the impression that 'he was the most remarkable man I have ever met, and more convinced than ever of the superior intelligence of the Eastern mind'.[46]

Malkom Khan's real influence, however, came with the establishment of the first effective dissident 'newspaper' (though it might be better described a series of political pamphlets), which enabled the wider dissemination of the political ideas then circulating. The newspaper, called *Qanun* (to which Afghani contributed) or 'The Law', which began publication in 1890, sought to articulate an argument for the revolution of the 'mind', encouraging its readers to strive to acquire both knowledge and manners, but above all for the establishment of a 'constitutional' system, by which he meant a legal order and the rule of law, rather than a democratic political system. Indeed it is worth stressing that the leitmotif of constitutionalism was the 'rule of law' not the establishment of 'democracy', which was generally viewed with some disdain by thinkers. 'Republicanism' was identified with the rule of law, and not considered a contradiction to a constitutional monarchical system.

> A State without law means the destruction of the world. A state without law means the enemy of the rights of the people. Curses upon a state without law. Shame on those ignorant and dishonourable people who pay taxes to a state without law.[47]

Malkom Khan had no illusions about the problems facing Iran and argued forcefully for the establishment of what might best be termed, an 'enlightened' despotism. Iran needed an autocrat, albeit one with a council composed of a supportive elite, with both the authority and power to get things done, who could catapult the country forward, and his model for this was none other than Peter the Great. The Russians, having been treated with traditional disdain in Iranian political culture, now provided the example of a state that had managed to grasp the nettle of progress and civilisation, and they had achieved this through the will of an individual. Iran too, needed such an individual. Moreover, in an exhortation that would echo down the years and be reiterated more dramatically by later nationalist thinkers, Malkom Khan warned his compatriots that they had neither the luxury of time nor choice, 'In matters of government we cannot and must not invent anything ourselves. Either we must take the knowledge and experience of Europe as our model, or we cannot take a single step to rise out of our barbaric state'.[48]

These intellectuals shared a desire not simply to think about the state of affairs but to find ways to change it. Their involvement in the Freemasons, far from suggesting pernicious foreign influence, was indicative of a political iconoclasm and activism in pursuit of ideals that can broadly be identified with the European Enlightenment,[49] albeit adapted to their own context and particular problems. All had become increasingly frustrated with what they considered to be the single greatest obstacle to change – the Shah, and the necessity to move towards a constitutional system bound by the rule of law. In these aspirations they found a receptive and in many ways, supportive audience in dissident opinion, most obviously in, though not limited to, Britain.[50] Indeed if the British government, in coordination with the Government of India, sought to maintain the political status quo and to cultivate – in public at least – the friendship of the Shah, who Curzon had argued, somewhat incredulously, was considered by Iranians to be, 'the most competent man in the country, and the best ruler it can produce',[51] it was quite clear, to the limited circle of intellectuals at least, that any reliance on Nasir al Din Shah to actually promote any reform was misguided and that on the contrary some form of political agitation would be required. Britain fortunately provided the political template by both enabling dissident opinion, *and* in delivering the political environment against which they could successfully agitate. It was through such a process that they were able to transform themselves from a 'republic of letters' into an effective political movement.

The Tobacco Revolt

British policy was not unsympathetic to the Iranian predicament. The fear of Russia was shared by Britain, not least the government of British India whose priority was the retention of Iran as a buffer state against Russian encroachments southwards. The anxiety, expressed by the British minister Sir Henry Drummond Wolff to the Prime Minister, the Marquis of Salisbury, in the spring of 1888, was that Russia would use every pretext to cajole, pressure and forcibly seize territory from Iran in Khorasan, and that Iran, finding any practical British support wanting, would be forced in turn to compromise further with the Tsar, leading inexorably to the Russian occupation of Herat and the rest of Afghanistan. Moreover, impressed by the 'general demeanour' of the Persians, and 'their aptitude for civilisation', Drummond Wolff was concerned 'that a people so much in advance as are the Persians of their own government might view with indifference their transfer to another allegiance, giving them more material comfort'.

Drummond Wolff suggested to Salisbury that a satisfactory solution could be found in encouraging the economic regeneration of Iran, with the support and agreement of the Russians with a view to persuading the Shah himself to overcome his 'fear of progress', in the interests of the stability of his dynasty. In order to achieve this and to give the Iranians themselves a stake in the economic development of their country, it was important to ensure that any wealth accrued would be protected and not subject to the avaricious whims of the Shah.

> I have been told by more than one authority . . . that the one thing necessary for the development of Persia is a Decree securing to everyone his life, liberty and property so long as he conforms to the law and leads the life of a peaceable citizen.

Securing such an agreement, if the Shah, and more importantly Russia were amenable, 'would present many advantages, the principal being the certainty, as far as can be anticipated, of tranquillity for some years, and of relief from the watchfulness and alarms which constantly recur to disturb our Indian policy'.[52]

The convention or 'Understanding' reached with Russia (and the Shah) was brief, (a total of five Articles) dealing in the main with the formation of joint commission to investigate the ways in which communications (railways and canals) might be constructed to facilitate the development of Iran's resources. The last article (V) was directed towards the Shah:

> His Majesty the Shah, being deeply impressed with the necessity of securing peace and tranquillity within his dominions voluntarily undertakes to publish an Edict securing in perpetuity the civil and religious liberty of his subjects, whatever their creed, and further securing to his subjects their lives liberties, and property so long as they obey the laws of the land and are not condemned by competent Judges and Tribunals.

Drummond Wolff's relative optimism was, however, to be undone by the Shah's clear lack of interest in any development that might affect his apparent power, including anything that might diminish his financial position. The assets of the Qajar dynasty were not insignificant,[53] but the Shah was reluctant to spend from his own pocket what might be secured through the disposal of various concessions. Far from regarding the concessions as a strategic necessity born of Iran's economic weakness with a view to restructuring Iran's economy, the Shah appeared to view them as a temporary fix for his financial shortcomings and a useful way, as Browne noted, of paying for various indulgences, not least several expensive trips abroad. These included three visits to Britain, in 1873 (when he was awarded the Order of the Garter), 1878 and 1889, when the British sought to impress him with the technological advances of the Industrial Revolution, including a visit to view the new Forth Rail Bridge in Scotland.[54] He was by all accounts duly impressed. But it was soon apparent to all and sundry that he was no latter day Peter the Great, and the impressions made upon him were more superficial than serious. Thus while he might have been persuaded to issue the 'Edict' or *farman*, in order to impress his British friends, their cultivation and flattery of him seems to have assured him that such statements need only be honoured in the breach. When for example Afghani returned to Iran in 1889,[55] ostensibly on the back of the edict for which he claimed some credit, he found the welcome less than warm. What especially enraged him, interestingly enough, was the failure of the British to act in defence of the edict on which they had insisted.

> What made the Persian believe that England meant to help them? I pray you, did not your Ministers a year or two ago urge upon the Shah a fir-man granting security of life and property to his subjects. Did not the Shah issue such a firman, and, after considerable pressure and long debate and hesitation, frankly communicate to the Powers? Did not her Majesty [Queen Victoria] upon hearing this express to Malcom Khan her profound satisfac-tion, and was not your Minister at Teheran regarded as a party to the trans-action? All Persians believed that a firman thus issued and *communicated* to the European Powers gave the Powers, England first and foremost, the diplomatic right to insist upon its due observance, or at least to demand the explanation for any gross violation of it. Well, what followed? I, Sheikh Djemal ed Din, soon after became the natural and respectful mouthpiece of the people's joyful aspirations. I am received with favour by His Majesty, my words are approved, the regeneration of Persia is at hand; law is to be given, life and property are to be safe, our wives and daughters protected from out-rage, our bread winners from cruel and ruinous exactions – all is going well. Suddenly I am seized, banished, imprisoned: my friends were imprisoned and tortured, without explanation, without trial . . . the people's eyes were opened; they felt they could place no reliance on the Shah . . . But their eyes were then to the Powers, to England first and foremost. Now would the British minister, at least, certainly speak one little word at Teheran, if only to ask for some explanation of so gross a violation of the blessed firman. But no not a word!'[56]

Quite apart from reflecting poorly on the continuing clash between principle and practical politics, Afghani's outburst was also indicative of both the intellectual debt and expectations that were made of Britain. Britain's failure to live up to those expectations was to be a cause of repeated disappointment among Iran's intellectuals, and one might add a source of embarrassment to many of its offi-cials, especially those serving in Iran.[57] As for the Shah, political exigencies aside, these trips simply added to his financial woes and therefore encouraged him fur-ther down the path of seeking quick and easy sources of revenue.

Having finally resolved the outstanding issue of the Reuter's conces-sion with the granting of a concession to Reuter for the establishment of the

Imperial Bank, the Shah now used the opportunity of his 1889 trip to agree to another concession for the monopoly over the sale of tobacco throughout Iran. Merchants who had just discovered that their ability to trade in currencies, local or otherwise, had been suddenly curtailed, now found that another lucrative product had been summarily handed to a foreign company. Such a 'trading' concession was as far removed from Drummond's original idea as could be imagined. Rather than find the means to invest in Iran's long-term economic viability, this was simply a means for a number of select individuals – not least the Shah – to become rich at the expense of many whose livelihoods depended on the trade. Matters were not helped by the fact that the British subject involved, a Major Talbot, was by all accounts a man on the make with little interest in the development of Iran. Indeed a dispatch from Tehran noted in a somewhat biting account of the agreement that while the Foreign Office had supported the establishment of the Imperial Bank and Reuter's application for a Royal Charter, the concession granted to Major Talbot 'on the 8th March 1890', was achieved 'without any intervention on the part of Her Majesty's Legation at Tehran'.[58] The concession provided for a 50-year monopoly in return for an annual payment to the Iranian government of £15,000, 'and after provision for a dividend of 5% for the shareholders, the Persian Government were further to receive one quarter of the net profits'. The Foreign Office noted that it was not clear how much Talbot had paid for the concession, 'nor what he received for it from the London Syndicate who in their turn made it over for £300,000 to the Tobacco Corporation'. The entire scheme appeared to suffer from a distinct lack of scruples.

Despite protestations from the Russians, the Shah proceeded to announce the establishment of the new 'Tobacco Regie' in March 1891. This proved to be the catalyst that opponents and reformers were looking for (indeed given the fallout over the 'edict' and Malkom Khan's establishment of the newspaper *Qanun*, the timing could not have been more opportune), and no doubt with some encouragement from the Russian legation, a movement to abolish the Regie, and more importantly, send a message to the Shah, began to take shape. The agitation of the likes of Afghani and Malkom Khan coalesced with opposition for the merchants who in turn appealed to the senior *mujtahids* to take decisive action. The Shah, who had already begun to waver over the summer, found the real limitations on his power, and even one might add his authority, exposed in December 1891, when the *mujtahid* Seyyed Hasan Shirazi issued a *fatwa* (legal opinion) decreeing (somewhat ahead of his time) that tobacco was unclean and smoking was henceforth to be forbidden. It was reported that once Nasir al Din Shah observed that even the ladies of his household were adhering to the *fatwa*, he realised that the only solution was to abrogate the concession, though no doubt the demonstration outside his palace provided added urgency. It was agreed that the *fatwa* would be rescinded once the concession was terminated and a notice to this effect issued by the Tobacco Corporation itself. 'This their local representative only consented to do under pressure from Her Majesty's Minister, who thought such a notice requisite with a view to allay disturbances likely to lead to the abolition of all foreign enterprises, and to endanger British lives'.[59]

The discomfort felt by the local diplomats did not extend to their duties to British subjects who faced losses as a result of the Shah's volte face. Though by all accounts the Iranian government also sought mediation through the British Legation, rather than seek arbitration which they feared would be ruinous to the economy. The corporation claimed £600,000 to account for their purchase of the concession and the various assets acquired in order to administer it. In the end they settled for £500,000 in return for handing all the infrastructure to the Iranian government. This was a modest reduction in the claim but it was supposed that the Shah, having been the chief beneficiary of what amounted to a glorified tax farming exercise, might delve into his own not inconsiderable financial resources to meet the claim, and it might be added, restore some of the personal lustre that had been lost. The Shah, however, 'pleaded penury', and the government was forced to find alternative sources. The British Imperial Bank fortunately came to the rescue though the initial terms were deemed so harsh the Iranian government threatened to seek the assistance of the Russians – the classic diplomatic ploy which rang the required alarm bells in the British Legation and ensured a compromise solution would be reached. Not that the Iranians possessed or played a strong hand in the entire debacle. Having turned to the Russians to frighten the British they now found the British more accommodating though not magnanimous. The Imperial Bank agreed to loan £500,000 to the Iranian government for payment of outstanding commitments to the Tobacco Corporation which would be secured through the assigning of some £30,000 of customs duties annually from Iran's southern ports. The loan itself would be repaid 'within forty years by equal monthly instalments of £12,500 paying interest at 6 per cent on the outstanding capital'.[60]

Few events exposed the ineptitude of the Qajar court and state as the Tobacco Revolt of 1891/92. It was generally acknowledged that the monarchy was a cipher buffeted between the rival powers of Russia and Great Britain. But the revolt exposed its very real weakness to domestic pressures, when those domestic forces could act in concert. Intellectual agitation, mercantile money and clerical authority proved to be a potent force in unnerving a king whose stability on the throne depended as much on his perceived authority, as on his ability to keep his foes divided. For all these players in this increasingly febrile political environment the Qajar state appeared to be heading into terminal decline and British and Russians at least began to draw up contingency plans as the 'Persian Question' appeared to be entering its denouement.[61] For Browne, writing with some benefit of hindsight, there was a ray of light in the otherwise depressing spectacle:

Only one great and good thing came out of all this wretched business. The Persian people, led by their spiritual guides, and led, moreover, on the whole with wonderful wisdom and restraint, had shown that there was a limit to what they would endure, that they were not spiritless creatures which they had been supposed to be, and that henceforth they would have to be reckoned with. From that time especially, as I believe, dates the national awakening of which we are still watching the development.[62]

Notes

1 E. Browne, *The Persian Revolution*. Cambridge, Cambridge University Press, 1909, p. 57.
2 S.H. Taqizadeh, *Opera Minor: Unpublished Writings in European Languages* (ed. I Afshar). Tehran: Shekufan, 1979, p. 203. Kasravi similarly begins his narrative with the failures of the defeats of Fath Ali Shah though his narrative starts significantly by contrasting the failures of the Qajars with the triumphs of Nader Shah and the stability of Karim Khan, see A. Kasravi, *Tarikh Mashruteh-ye Iran* (History of the Constitution in Iran). Tehran: Amir Kabir, 1378/1999 [first published 1940].
3 Sykes in fact argues that it was the development of the 'Telegraph' in the aftermath of the Indian Mutiny, see Sykes, *History of Persia*, Vol II, pp. 367–9.
4 On the political and geographic difficulties faced by Iran see, Curzon, *Persia and the Persian Question*, Vol I, pp. 613–39.
5 Chardin contains an interesting example of English merchants seeking privileges apparently promised to the Sherley brothers some 50 years earlier only to be dismissed by an irritable vizier. See Chardin, *A New and Accurate Description*, pp. 100–104.
6 The British Orientalist, Henry Rawlinson was also an advocate of a robust British policy. Rawlinson is quoted in Curzon, *Persia and the Persian Question*, Vol I, p. 480.
7 For details on British policy in this period, see A. Amanat, 'Great Britain iii. British Influence in Persia in the 19th Century', *Encyclopædia Iranica*, www.iranicaonline.org/articles/great-britain-iii.
8 M. Rubin, 'Indo-European Telegraph Company', *Encyclopædia Iranica*, www.iranicaonline.org/articles/indo-european-telegraph-company.
9 Wills, *In the Land of the Lion and the Sun*, p. 3.
10 Curzon, *Persia and the Persian Question*, pp. 480–81.
11 Geoffrey Jones, *Banking and Empire in Iran: The History of the British Bank of the Middle East*. Cambridge: Cambridge University Press, 1986, Vol I, p. 13. Jones also notes that the Foreign Office were sceptical of a north–south railway, 'as it could only increase the danger of Russia getting closer to a warm water port'.
12 Amanat, 'Great Britain iii. British Influence in Persia in the 19th Century'.
13 E.G. Browne, *A Year amongst the Persians*. London: Century Publishing, 1984 [first published 1893], p. 99.
14 Curzon, *Persia and the Persian Question*, pp. 400–401.
15 Browne, *A Year amongst the Persians*, p. 110.
16 On the impact of the Azali Babis see, A. Amanat 'Memory and Amnesia in the Historiography of the Constitutional Revolution', in T. Atabaki (ed.), *Iran in the Twentieth Century*. London: I.B. Tauris, 2009, pp. 23–54.
17 Maryam B. Sanjabi 'Rereading the Enlightenment: Akhundzada and His Voltaire', *Iranian Studies* 28(1/2), Winter–Spring 1995, p. 51.
18 The cruel punishments inflicted on transgressors was graphically documented by Curzon in his, *Persia and the Persian Question*, Vol I , pp. 456–7.
19 Sanjabi, 'Rereading the Enlightenment', p. 41.
20 Sanjabi, 'Rereading the Enlightenment', p. 39, note 2.
21 Sanjabi, 'Rereading the Enlightenment', p. 57.
22 Sanjabi, 'Rereading the Enlightenment', p 56. Akhundzadeh used both the French word '*despote*' and its Persian equivalent, *mustabidd*.
23 Cyrus Masroori, 'European Thought in Nineteenth Century Iran: David Hume and Others', *Journal of the History of Ideas* 61(4), October 2000, pp. 666–8.
24 The Persian word used for Masonic lodges.
25 Sanjabi, 'Rereading the Enlightenment', pp. 56–7.
26 A phrase attributed to Martin Luther King Jr.
27 For a discussion of Kermani's political views and his adoption of a European discourse on race see, M. Bayat Philipp, 'Mīrzā Āqā Khān Kirmānī: A Nineteenth

Century Persian Nationalist', *International Journal of Middle East Studies* 10(1), 1974, pp. 44–7.

28 According to M. Bayat, he also assisted in the translation of Morier's *Haji Baba of Isfahan*, 'Āqā Khan Kermānī', *Encyclopædia Iranica*, www.iranicaonline.org/articles/aqa-khan-kermani. The Persian translation is said to have been popular until it was discovered that the original had been written by an Englishman.

29 Quoted in S. Bakhash, *Iran: Monarchy, Bureaucracy and Reform under the Qajars: 1858–1896*. London: Ithaca Press, 1978, p. 345. See also Bayat Philipp, 'Mīrzā Āqā Khān Kirmānī, p. 49.

30 On the changing meaning of 'race' see A.M. Ansari, 'Iranian Nationalism and the Question of Race', in M. Litvak (ed.), *Constructing Nationalism in Iran: From the Qajars to the Islamic Republic*. Oxford: Routledge, 2017, pp. 101–16. See also in this respect, Sorour Soroudi, 'Mirza Aqa Khan Kermani and the Jewish Question', in *Persian Literature and Judeo-Persian Culture: Collected Writings of Sorour S. Soroudi* (ed. H. Chehabi). Cambridge, MA: Harvard University Press, 2010, pp. 338–57.

31 See in this regard, P. Abdolmohammadi, 'The Iranian Constitutional Revolution and the Influence of Mirza Aqa Khan Kermani's Political Thought', in A.M. Ansari (ed.), *Iran's Constitutional Revolution of 1906: Narratives of Enlightenment*. London: Gingko Library, 2016, pp. 120–21.

32 Bayat Philipp, 'Mīrzā Āqā Khān Kirmānī, p. 50.

33 Bayat Philipp, 'Mīrzā Āqā Khān Kirmānī, p. 39. Kermani later assisted Malkom Khan in the establishment of a lodge, named '*Adamiyyat*' in Istanbul, and with the distribution of his newspaper *Qanun*. More work needs to be done with respect to Ottoman–Iranian intellectual networks, and clearly Iranian intellectuals were aware and influenced by developments leading to the Ottoman Constitution of 1876. See also in this respect, N. Sohrabi, *Revolution and Constitutionalism in the Ottoman Empire and Iran*. Cambridge: Cambridge University Press, 2011, pp. 301–13.

34 Masroori, 'European Thought', p. 659.

35 Bayat Philipp, 'Mīrzā Āqā Khān Kirmānī, p. 37.

36 Literally 'houses of forgetfulness'. The tendency by some writers to translate this as 'houses of oblivion' seems somewhat over-defined.

37 Bayat Philipp, 'Mīrzā Āqā Khān Kirmānī, p. 51.

38 Jamal al Din al Afghani, 'Answer of Jamal al Din to Renan', *Journal des Debats*, 18 May 1883 (trans, N. Keddie) in *An Islamic Response to Imperialism* (Berkeley, CA: University of California Press, 1986), pp. 181–7.

39 Afghani, 'Answer of Jamal al Din to Renan', pp.182–3.

40 Afghani, 'Answer of Jamal al Din to Renan', p. 183.

41 Afghani, 'Answer of Jamal al Din to Renan', p. 186.

42 Afghani, 'Answer of Jamal al Din to Renan', p. 187.

43 Jamal al Din al Afghani, 'The Reign of Terror in Persia', *The Contemporary Review*, 61, 1892, pp. 238–48, reprinted in L. Ridgeon (ed.), *Religion and Politics in Modern Iran*. London: I.B. Tauris, 2005, p. 5.

44 Browne notes this but does not name Malkom Khan, referring instead to 'a Persian subject (of whose identity I am ignorant)', see *The Persian Revolution*, p. 31. For details of the 'Lottery' scandal and its broader context see, Wright, *The Persians*, pp. 157–9.

45 The standard, if somewhat unsympathetic biography of Malkom Khan in English was written by Hamid Algar, who was clearly not well disposed to his subject. See H. Algar, *Mirza Malkum Khan: A Biographical Study in Iranian Modernism*. Berkeley, CA: University of California Press, 1973.

46 Browne, *The Persian Revolution*, p. 38. See also M. Bonakdarian, 'Iranian Constitutional Exiles and British Foreign-Policy Dissenters, 1908–9', *International Journal of Middle East Studies* 27(2), 1995, p. 183. See also Wright, *The Persians*, p. 154.

47 *Qanun* 15 (undated), p. 1 (translation my own). For more detail see A.M. Ansari, 'Taqizadeh and European Civilisation', *Iran* 54(1), 2016, pp. 51–2.

48 *Qanun* 15 (undated), pp. 12–13. Browne implies in *The Persian Revolution*, that Malkom Khan had argued for a parliament, see p. 37. This may be Browne's extrapolation of Malkom Khan's demand for a 'council'.

49 On these diverse narratives see, A.M. Ansari, 'Introduction: Developing Iranian Intellectual History', in Ansari (ed.), *Iran's Constitutional Revolution of 1906*, pp. 1–14.

50 Two prominent members being Edward Browne and Wilfrid Blunt.

51 Curzon, *Persia and the Persian Question*, Vol I, p. 401. This was of course Curzon at his diplomatic best. His description of 'government' was not so generous, and he was particularly scathing about the continued application of violence as punishment, see pp. 456–7.

52 Sir H. Drummond Wolff to the Marquis of Salisbury, 21 April 1888, reprinted in *Iran: Political Diaries, 1881–1965*, Archive Editions. Cambridge: Cambridge University Press, 1997, Vol I, pp. 45–8.

53 See Eastwick, *Journal*, pp. 115–20, on the extensive crown jewels.

54 On Nasir al Din Shah's visits to Imperial Germany see, D. Motadel, 'Qajar Shahs in Imperial Germany', *Past and Present* 213, November 2011, pp. 191–235. It is striking how much of the formalities were made up on the spot, with the German bands playing Strauss' 'Persian March' in the absence of an obvious national anthem. Nasir al Din Shah reportedly found much of the decoration bewildering and 'Arabian', p. 232. According to Wright, when Mozaffar al Din Shah visited Britain in 1902, a 'Persian Anthem' was played, which according to his host, Prince Arthur, was 'simply excruciating'. See Wright, *The Persians*, p. 176.

55 Browne, *The Persian Revolution*, p. 42; see also Curzon, *Persia and the Persian Question*, Vol I, pp. 460–61, on the 'Edict' and its application.

56 Afghani, 'The Reign of Terror in Persia', p. 12.

57 John Darwin, the noted historian of the British Empire, describes this (in relation to rule in India) as the 'awkward compromise between principle and practice', see J. Darwin, *The Empire Project*. Cambridge: Cambridge University Press, 2009, p. 180.

58 Memorandum on Questions Pending in the Eastern Department, August 1892, p. 19, reprinted in *Iran: Political Diaries*, Vol I, p. 67.

59 Memorandum on Questions Pending in the Eastern Department, August 1892, p. 20, reprinted in *Iran: Political Diaries*, Vol I, p. 68.

60 Memorandum on Questions Pending in the Eastern Department, August 1892, pp. 21–2, reprinted in *Iran: Political Diaries*, Vol I, p. 69–70.

61 See Amanat, 'Great Britain iii: British Influence in Persian in the 19th Century'.

62 Browne, *The Persian Revolution*, p. 57.

6 The Constitutional Revolution and its aftermath

Browne's seminal study of the Constitutional Revolution of 1906 established the narrative template which has largely survived to this day.[1] It was an intensely intimate portrait written while the revolution was itself unfolding, targeted at a British readership whose interest in such matters was at best marginal. Browne himself had not visited Iran for the better part of a generation but he had maintained close ties and communications with a number of Iranian ideologues and activists, an engagement that both enriched his study but also made it vulnerable to charges of romanticism. Browne sought to trace a narrative of national awakening, with a cast of heroes and villains, from the Tobacco Revolt through the Revolution in 1906. In painting his 'national' canvas, Browne drew on tropes that would have been familiar to students of European nationalisms, most obviously the Italian Risorgimento, a subject Browne had studied, with its own tobacco boycott.[2] The tendency therefore was to apply some of these ideas, images and concepts to the Iranian experience and provide a dramatic narrative that would appeal both to public opinion, and perhaps to policy makers themselves.

His contemporary, Lord Curzon was similarly having considerable difficulty in interesting his countrymen in the fate of 'Persia', though his aims, aspirations and target audience were somewhat different. Curzon's diplomatic description of Nasir al Din Shah aside, his was a much more sober assessment of the realities of late Qajar Iran, and as a consequence, a much greater anxiety about the probabilities of Russian aggrandisement. Curzon's romanticism related much more to the ideals of British imperialism though he too was to frequently find it wanting and a cause of great disillusion. His assessment of the Iranian people and their capacity for change was perhaps nearer to the truth in the 1890s than Browne's uplifting portrait suggested. In the first place, while the revolt was undoubtedly a nationwide protest, to some extent enabled by the new means of telegraphic communication which now existed, this could not be described as a 'mass movement' – in the common-sense understanding of the term – nor was it especially spontaneous. The Tobacco Regie was announced in March 1891, and it was the better part of nine months before it was rescinded, following what was to prove a decisive, if somewhat belated intervention, by the *ulema*. The demonstrations that were organised were neither especially large nor widespread, limited as they were to the major cities such as Tabriz and Tehran (Isfahan and Shiraz also experienced protests), a city whose population in 1891 was estimated to be 210,000.[3] Nor should one underestimate the role of Russian agitation in encouraging the protest and the subsequent climb-down.[4]

Indeed, the immediate aftermath of the revolt did not prove auspicious for any aspiring political movement for change. Afghani, in discussions with Browne in London, made clear his utter contempt for the Shah and his government, noting somewhat bitterly that six or seven heads would have to be cut off before any progress could be made, the first of which needed to be that of the Shah. Browne noted dryly 'that it was curious to note' that the Shah was indeed eventually assassinated in 1896.[5] But the Qajar state showed no evidence of wanting to respond to the anger being expressed seemingly unwillingly to treat it any differently to the set-backs experienced with earlier attempts at securing concessions, most obviously the original Reuter's concession of 1872. Indeed following the assassination of the Shah, the government ruthlessly pursued its opponents with the extradition and execution of Mirza Agha Khan Kermani and two of his fellow travellers, in July 1896. Afghani, who was complicit in the assassination – the assassin, Mirza Reza Kirmani, a disciple of Afghani had been encouraged to return to Iran and do the deed – avoided extradition and died of cancer in Istanbul in 1897.[6]

Moreover, Nasir al Din Shah's son and successor, Mozaffar al Din Shah was to prove no more disposed to political reform than his father, nor indeed any more diligent in the allocation and award of concessions. Iran became a veritable menagerie of diverse concessions to a variety of European powers who took on responsibilities for the management and administration of a range of government activities from customs collection to the Gendarmerie. The most significant was that awarded to an Australian entrepreneur, William Knox D'Arcy in 1901, for the exploration, exploitation and marketing of oil, natural gas, asphalt and ozocerite.[7] The terms of this concession suggest that little or nothing had been learnt from previous experience, with the Shah offering an extensive concession on an asset for which he had little understanding or appreciation, and whose pursuit he felt was somewhat nonsensical. The 60-year concession, for which the Shah was paid a fixed sum of £20,000 plus a further £20,000 in stocks, granted D'Arcy rights over the entire country other than the five northern provinces of Khorasan, Astarabad, Gilan, Mazandaran and Azerbaijan, following objections from the Russians. In return the Iranian government would be paid 16 per cent royalties on the annual 'net' profits, an arrangement which suggested that the Iranian negotiators had a poor understanding of the concept of profit.[8] Given the scale of the investments required, it was quite possible that any company might not turn a profit for some time. Be that as it may, as noted above, it appears that the Shah considered the entire operation as something of a waste of time for which he had procured a handsome payment.

Rarely have such momentous decisions for the future of the country – and the future of Anglo-Iranian relations – turned on such a grotesque under-appreciation of the country's assets. But then Mozaffar al Din had soon achieved what no one had anticipated, and that was a worse reputation than his father, for indolence and lack of interest in the affairs of state. Even Iranian observers considered the new Shah 'simple minded, easily persuaded, undecided, changeable, fond of buffoonery, and entirely in the hands of corrupt courtiers . . . utterly ignorant and illiterate, knowing nothing of history and politics, and utterly devoid of prudence, judgement and foresight'.[9] These characteristics, and his general ill health and reported hypochondria led the French papers to label him 'Mauvaise affaire ud Din Shah',[10] a term that might have well applied to the state of the country as a whole, which appeared to be entering a phase of terminal, irrevocable decline.

Indeed the prognosis of the British minister in Tehran, Arthur Edward Hardinge to the Foreign Secretary, Sir Edward Grey in December 1905, was decidedly grim, suggesting that there was a very real possibility that the state might collapse under the weight of its own incompetence and insolvency.[11] Mozaffar al Din Shah had inherited a government machinery that was heavily in debt and proceeded to make matters worse by seeking to play off the Russians and British, to secure the loans he required to fund an unsustainable lifestyle, not least expensive trips to Europe. In a little under ten years Mozaffar al Din Shah matched his father's three trips to Europe causing consternation in Britain in 1902, when he insisted on being awarded – as his father had been – the Order of the Garter. A diplomatic incident ensued when Edward VII, in contrast to his mother, demurred from offering such a 'Christian' honour to a non-Christian king, and it was only under considerable pressure from Hardinge that Edward VII relented and Mozaffar al Din Shah was duly invested with the Order the following year in Tehran.[12]

Hardinge's efforts were made despite the fact he considered the Shah the least capable of any of the monarchs of the Qajar dynasty, surrounded by courtiers whose principal aim appeared to be to 'kill and cut up the goose with the golden eggs'. Facing impending bankruptcy – Hardinge assessed that the 'evil day' cannot be deferred indefinitely, and certainly no more than three years – there would be a real problem in maintaining, or indeed retaining an administration and army that simply could not be paid. The 'so called Persian army' was in reality 'an ill-armed and undisciplined mob', adding that

> when Lord Downe came to Tehran a few years ago to confer the Garter on the Shah, his military instincts were outraged by the spectacle of the sentry at the Palace, who, in the absence of a musket, presented arms to him with the broken leg of a table.[13]

The only military unit worth its name was the Russia-sponsored Cossack brigade of some 1,500 men, though it was noted, even these men were unlikely to obey their Russian officers 'in the event of disorders inspired by Mahommedan [*sic*] fanaticism'.[14]

In a remarkably acute analysis of the position of the Shi'a clergy (much of which stands the test of time), Hardinge drew attention to their power and influence – the good relations which Britain by and large maintained with them through Britain's control over the 'Oudh bequest'[15] – and the fact that their general disunity on matters of theology represented both a strength (it was difficult to know who to negotiate with) and a weakness insofar as they were unable to put up a united front against the Shah. Be that as it may, Hardinge noted,

> if any man of real capacity or statesman-like qualities were to arise at Nejef, the great Shiah university in Turkey, who were to be recognized, like the late Mirza Hassan Ashtiyani, the destroyer of the Regie, as their undisputed head, it is conceivable that he might, in the present state of Persia, effect a revolution and even hurl the Shah from his throne.[16]

Hardinge noted other threats to the dynasty and state from the Babis, 'and a small revolutionary party' which he said had been founded and inspired by Afghani and appeared to contain a range of views from those who sought some sort of Muslim Union to those who sought to emulate the 'Young Turkey' movement in the Ottoman Empire.

> These anti-dynastic groups are on the whole anti-Russian, as is generally speaking the larger, so called Young Persian, which, without desiring the fall of the dynasty, seeks its ideals in the liberal West. The late commander of the Cossack Brigade, Colonel-Kosokofski, who knew Persian well, often told me that one of the most dangerous factors, from a Russian point of view, was 'la jeune Perse', and though I am inclined to suspect that he exaggerated this danger, there is, I believe, a good deal to be said for his view. I am certainly of the opinion that it is in our interest that the younger generation of Persians should learn French and become imbued with the spirit of Liberalism, and I have always from this point of view done my best to encourage the 'Alliance Francaise', the Persian 'Ecole des Sciences Politiques', and other similar institutions existing at Tehran for the diffusion of western culture under the French form in which alone it has much chance of spreading in Persia.[17]

The fatigue that pervaded Hardinge's analysis of the situation was palpable. A succession of British ministers had sought to present some measure of optimism for the future, and, within the framework of what was broadly understood to be British interests, to provide possible solutions for the economic and political regeneration of the Iranian state. A stable sympathetic state was considered to be in the best interests of British policy in the East and certainly for the defence of British India. Moreover for all the conflict of interests that might emerge with the Government of India and Whitehall, British ministers on the ground in Tehran, from Malcolm to Hardinge, all betrayed a degree of empathy with the plight of the Iranians. The Russians, from the British perspective, were encouraging profligacy and bankruptcy with a view to penetrating and eventually taking over the Iranian state; and the incompetence of the Iranian court was accelerating this process. Hardinge noted that such was the unpopularity and ineffectiveness of the Qajar dynasty, that in any previous age they would have by now been overthrown and that ironically, any insurrection had been forestalled in the general knowledge that 'it would have brought about the armed intervention of Russia or Great Britain, or both, for the preservation of the *status quo* in Persia'.[18] The depressing result of this policy was to ensure that Iranians laboured under a dynasty that had effectively lost its way, and that Britain's best interests would now be served through an accommodation with Russia for 'spheres of influence'. By this he did not mean partition, but specific spheres in which Britain and Russia agreed to suspend diplomatic rivalries, on the lines of the Austro-Russian agreement in the Balkans. It was only this type of limited agreement that he felt would be acceptable to the Russians, who would be reluctant to abandon their aspirations to reach 'the open ocean'.[19]

What was remarkable about this report was at once its astute assessment of the balance of forces within Iran, the weaknesses of the monarchy and the challenges that it faced from its own maladministration, the position of the Russians as well as the domestic forces arrayed against it, and at the same time the ultimately dispiriting conclusion it reached about the future of the country. The 13 years that had elapsed since the abrogation of the Tobacco Regie had, barring the assassination of Nasir al Din Shah, been years of relative inactivity. The country had by all accounts entered a period of inert stupor, from which, as far as foreign observers were concerned, there appeared to be little chance of relief. Monthly reports from 1905 painted a picture of a country in increasing turmoil, with a central government that had effectively ceased to function. But the simmering discontent had been interpreted as localised and largely ineffectual. Yet within months of Hardinge's report, a latent 'constitutional movement' had developed, in stages into a fully-fledged revolution which would transform the political landscape of the country. In the words of his successor Sir Cecil Spring Rice, 'The year 1906 has been a very important epoch in Persian history. For it has brought with it the introduction of parliamentary institutions'.[20]

The Constitutional Revolution of 1906 was *the* defining moment in modern Iranian history, the reference point against which all subsequent political contests would be measured. It marked the high-water point of British influence in Iran, and yet Hardinge (or for that matter the Russians), for all the intelligence he had access to, from a variety of diplomatic and corporate sources, was none the wiser to this possible development. Part of this undoubtedly reflected the disposition of the observer for whom years of political frustration had resulted in understandable cynicism. But it is also a salutary and humbling reminder that 'revolutions' are by their very nature, unpredictable.

The revolution unfolds

In many ways, one of the most remarkable aspects of the Constitutional Revolution is how it was driven and led by a relatively small number of individuals drawn essentially from the educated elites of the population and funded by disillusioned members of the aristocracy and the bazaar. It was by no means a class-based action insofar as all sections of society were divided in their loyalties, and one suspects that if Mozaffar al Din Shah had not been the kindly and somewhat ineffectual person that he was, that the gathering momentum behind the movement could have been forestalled and indeed prevented. As it happened, Mozaffar al Din Shah's haphazard and incoherent response ensured a far greater unity of purpose than might have otherwise been the case. Nonetheless, that the intellectual and political leaders of the movement were a relatively small group of individuals, most of whom appeared to be members of a single Masonic lodge in Tehran – the Iran Awakening Lodge[21] – stands testament to the enormity of their achievement, in the face of a political environment that remained inherently hostile, and which placed natural limitations on that immediate achievement.

Mohammad Ali Foroughi, Zoka ol Mulk, who would in time become a leading figure in the constitutional project and prime minister twice under Reza Shah, recollected in later life, just how vast the challenges were at the turn of the twentieth century. A scion of a junior bureaucratic family, Foroughi had been instrumental in the establishment of the School of Political Science (noted above by Hardinge) in 1899 and had promoted the teaching of the social sciences most obviously law and politics, and he reflected on just how difficult it had been to establish a syllabus. Indeed it had only been possible to get a 'secular' syllabus approved by assuring the *ulema* that students would have to take compulsory courses in Shari'a law. But perhaps more problematic was the stubborn conservatism of Iranian society and their suspicion of all things new and alien. He noted that being short-sighted he had taken to wearing spectacles, but in the dim light still found himself moving with caution so as to avoid falling, when a boy seeing his trepidation, urged him, 'Sir, take off your glasses in order to see'.[22] This advice, no doubt delivered in some jest, was emblematic for Foroughi of that gulf that continued to exist between a small yet increasingly cosmopolitan elite and the mass of the population, whose horizons remained strictly limited.[23] That this elite was nonetheless able to transform the political fortunes of the country within the space of a year, taking both themselves and foreign observers by surprise, depended in large measure on a fortuitous conjunction of events.

The financial and economic situation of the country has already been noted but by the latter quarter of the nineteenth century, the financial malaise that had grown to affect the court and government was beginning to affect the wider economy. Iran's economic situation had shrunk considerably in international terms throughout the nineteenth century, even if from a domestic perspective it had shown some recovery from the devastation of the eighteenth century. But from the 1870s even this relative recovery was fading, and as the gulf with the industrial might of Europe became even more stark, concessions to Western powers that stripped even more economic power from local merchants made the situation all the more acute. The first indications of this looming crisis were felt during the Tobacco Revolt. The relative unity between the merchants (*bazaar*), members of the *ulema* and the emerging intelligentsia, seemed by all accounts to be a harbinger of political developments to come and certainly Nasir al Din Shah's abrogation of the Regie gave some cause for encouragement, even if the immediate aftermath appeared to settle back into regular patterns of inactivity.

The elimination of key members of the agitating intelligentsia in the following decade through natural and unnatural causes proved to a be temporary respite insofar as they were replaced, as noted above, by a far more energised and engaged group of thinkers and activists. Moreover senior members of the *ulema* were also becoming increasingly frustrated with the state of affairs, and alliances were being forged – alliances that were facilitated by the reality that most members of what we might term the 'secular' intelligentsia had themselves emanated from seminaries (aside from foreign, largely missionary schools[24]). Indeed it is worth bearing in mind that the 'secular' orientation of these thinkers related to both their criticism of reactionary elements of the *ulema* as well as their perception of the correct relationship between 'church' and 'state'. This was not the *laicism* that would come to characterise the later Turkish Republic but a perspective much more akin to the Anglo-American tradition, and not an approach that would have been alien to Jamal al Din al Afghani, who many later activists, including most notably Hasan Taqizadeh, regarded as an inspiration. These were in sum not distinct bodies of thought who had coalesced through a sudden coincidence of mutual interest: there was a good deal more intellectual symbiosis between the intelligentsia and the reform-minded *ulema*.

Added to this simmering discontent was the sudden and unexpected pre-occupation of Russia with its own domestic problems. Mozaffar al Din Shah, faced as he was with a collapse of his authority both in the wider country and among principal members of the court, some of whom appeared to be conspiring to remove him, now also faced the prospect of an absentee sponsor, as Tsar Nicholas II had to cope with the shocking defeat of Russian forces by the Japanese and a subsequently revolutionary challenge of his own. Indeed the impact of the defeat of Russia in the Russo–Japanese War of 1905 can scarcely be overestimated. As Hardinge himself noted,

> The spectacle of the fall of the most powerful of autocracies [Russia] is being watched with keen interest in Persia, not merely, I think because of its possible effect on the future relations of the two countries, but also because of the feeling that what has taken place in Russia might take place in Persia likewise, and because of the overthrow of the autocratic power at St Petersburgh [*sic*] the Kajar dynasty really loses its most powerful temporary prop against an attack from within.[25]

The Tsar's ruthless response to the revolutionary uprising at home also had the inadvertent effect of sending many aspiring revolutionaries – especially those from Armenia – southwards in to Iran.[26]

In the event, the spark which ignited the 'revolution' proved to be something characteristically trivial: the arrest and beating of a number of merchants who had been protesting what they considered to be the excessive exactions of the new customs regime that had been imposed. It had not helped that the customs duties had been outsourced to a Belgian official by the name of Joseph Naus, who proved somewhat too effective and efficient in his task, much to the satisfaction of a government in desperate need of money, but considerably less enamoured of the merchants who had to provide the money. It did not help that Naus was culturally insensitive enough not to realise that being photographed dressed as a cleric would offend some sensibilities. A number of other merchants in support of their colleagues decided to take sanctuary (*bast*) in the Royal Mosque where they were joined by leading clerics including the *mujtahids*, Seyyed Abdullah Behbehani and Seyyed Mohammad Tabatabai, the first real indication that matters might be taking a turn for the worse as far as the government was concerned.

They were joined by a more vocal and spirited Agha Seyyed Jamal al Din, who proceeded to preach against the 'tyranny' afflicting the country, rhetoric which prompted the authorities to react by gathering a few well-armed followers to forcibly evict them. The resultant beating inflicted on the 'elderly' Seyyed Jamal al Din in Tehran (in December 1905) prompted a determined and somewhat unexpected protest by the leading clerics, who resisted attempts at mollification by the government and departed for a further *bast* in the shrine of Shah Abdol Azim, south of the city. Their withdrawal from the city of Tehran encouraged the Shah to attend to their complaints by agreeing to address shortcomings in his government and to grant some form of unspecified popular representation. Further prevarication from the Shah brought forth more clarity from the protestors who insisted that the Shah send them a signed letter assuring them that the chief minister would be dismissed, and to promise to convene an '*adalat khaneh*' or House of Justice, which according to Browne, 'was to consist of representatives elected by the clergy, merchants and landed proprietors, and presided over by the Shah himself; to abolish favouritism; and to make all Persian subjects equal in the eyes of the law'.[27]

Quite what the assorted protestors sought at this early stage is unclear and other sources are less equivocal than Browne. The coalition taking shape had different ideas what the House of Justice might be, though given the intellectual context of the movement it is likely that some if not all the protestors were agitating for a 'parliament' or legislative assembly of some sort. The Shah, on the other hand, had no enthusiasm for such a development and once the clerics had come out of *bast*, Mozaffar al Din Shah resorted to the tried and tested method of establishing a council to look into the idea of reform, as a means of quietening things down. The Persian Legation in London meanwhile took the opportunity to dampen down any enthusiasm, to point out that there had been a misunderstanding with regard to the House of Justice, 'and that it was intended to be a purely judicial court, not a legislative assembly'.[28]

Calm nevertheless appeared to have been restored to Tehran, though protests did erupt in other cities including Shiraz and Rasht, and preachers in the capital continued to rail against the corruption of the government. As an indication of the change in mood, Spring Rice quoted one revolutionary as noting that, 'what we hardly dared to think a year ago was openly spoken'.[29] The convening of a council did not yield the result the government sought in large measure because one official had the temerity to actually speak out, which resulted in his being sent off to a 'distant mission'. But the culture of deference appeared to have been shattered, even at the highest levels of government, and the authority on which the increasingly powerless government depended was eroding daily. At the instigation of the Russians, another outspoken official, the minister of commerce was also dismissed, leading to another lull in the hostilities. This was reinforced in May 1906 by the ailing Mozaffar al Din Shah succumbing to a paralytic stroke, incapacitating him, ensuring an extension to the political ceasefire, but also fatally weakening the machinery of government at a crucial time. Indeed government now effectively devolved on the reactionary minister of court and his confederate the chief minister, both of whom sought to shield the Shah from unnecessarily bad news. None of this augured well for the government, insofar as any hint of accommodation was now shelved, and protestors likewise felt they were confronting corrupt ministers rather than the person of the Shah himself.

The lull was extended to July when the government decided to arrest another well-known preacher for fomenting dissent. As soldiers came to arrest him, a scuffle broke out as the crowd sought to prevent the incarceration. As matters became heated the officer in command ordered the soldiers to fire into the crowd, which they refused to do, leading the officer to take his pistol and shoot dead a young student activist. The death of this poor unfortunate, who happened also to be a Seyyed, marked a serious escalation in the confrontation. A major melee ensued and the troops were routed. The preacher himself, the original cause of the confrontation, was rescued. This initial bloodletting was soon, however, to be followed by more tension as the Tehran bazaar was closed and individuals began to wear white sheets to denote their willingness to die for their cause. While protestors were determined to honour the death of the young Seyyed, the chief minister likewise was even more determined to put an end to the entire movement and troops were sent in again to disrupt the process resulting in further shooting and bloodshed. By this stage, clearly outraged at the government's behaviour, Behbehani held up the Shah's letter and denounced the fact that the people's demands had been met by bullets. Following a further standoff, in which the mosque where they were located was effectively besieged, it was agreed that the senior clerics could leave the mosque where they had been held up, as long as they left alone without followers in tow. On 15 July they duly left (Browne's account, sourced to Taqizadeh, suggests that they were in fact accompanied by a huge number of supporters[30]), but noted that if the people's demands were not met, if the chief minister was not dismissed and reforms not introduced, they would proceed to Qom and deprive the capital of any religious guidance or indeed legal transactions[31] – a form of excommunication.

The developments which followed were among the most extraordinary in modern Iranian history and shed light on the complexity of the relationship with Britain, but also the difficulties encountered by British officials on the ground in Tehran in their own attempts to reconcile government policy with their own convictions. Faced with a government that was not only willing to use force, but seemed to have no compunction in disrespecting the traditional *bast* – while they did not enter the mosque, government forces had surrounded it and occupied the bazaar – the revolutionaries decided on a dramatic alternative strategy, by seeking to exercise an 'expedient' which since the establishment of the foreign legations had become an extension of the traditional '*bast*'. Behbehani had apparently already on 9 July (prior to the death of the Seyyed) written to the senior British diplomat at the embassy, Evelyn Grant Duff requesting British assistance and support in the continuing political struggle.[32] Grant Duff, who was at the time effectively the Charge d'affaires holding the fort after Hardinge's departure and before Cecil Spring Rice's arrival, was by all accounts somewhat nonplussed by the request and simply responded that there was no way the British government could support a movement directed against the Iranian government. On 16 July, following the decision to depart to Qom, Behbehani wrote again, expressing the desire and hope that the British government would nonetheless be supportive.

The next development suggests that Grant Duff approached the situation with a much more emollient tone. On 18 July two individuals approached the British Legation summer compound at Golhak (at that time some seven miles outside the city), to ask whether if the people decided to take refuge or *bast* in the Legation compound, Britain would seek military assistance in removing them. Given Grant Duff's unequivocal answer the previous time about non-interference in in internal political matters, his response this time round was decidedly vague, noting that he hoped he would not have 'recourse to such an expedient . . . but that it was not in his power, in view of the acknowledged custom in Persia and the immemorial right of 'bast', to use, or cause to be used, force to expel them if they came'.[33] This diplomatic ambiguity unsurprisingly was interpreted by the individual concerned as a green light and on the following day, some 50 'mullahs and merchants' took up residence in Golhak, rapidly rising over the next week.[34]

> Their numbers soon increased, and [by 2 August] there were about 14,000 persons in the Legation garden. Their conduct was most orderly. The crowd of refugees was organised by the heads of the guilds, who took measures to prevent any unauthorized person from entering the Legation grounds. Tents were put up and regular feeding places and times of feeding were provided for. The expense was borne by the principal merchants. No damage of a wilful character was done to the garden, although, of course every semblance of a bed was trampled out of existence, and the trees still bear pious inscriptions cut into the bark. Colonel Douglas, the Military Attaché, kept watch over the Legation buildings, but no watch was needed. Discipline and order were maintained by the refugees themselves.[35]

It was in this tense febrile political environment that negotiations began in earnest, firstly among those in the Legation itself, to outline and refine their demands and secondly with the Shah's government. Later critics of the Constitutional Revolution have argued that it was at this stage that the British took advantage and basically transformed what was a religious uprising in favour of the implementation of the Shari'a, into a fully-fledged constitutional movement with a legislative assembly and 'man-made' laws. For all the ambiguity of the original demands, this charge lacks credibility and ignores the intellectual discussions of the previous half century. What seems more likely is that repeated government intransigence, prevarication and backtracking had persuaded the revolutionaries that their demands had to be clear, precise and emphatic. Moreover, the *bast* itself provided an unprecedented opportunity for the movement to work together and concentrate on the matter at hand. The *bast*, which if the figure of 14,000 is to be believed, included, by any reasonable estimate, approximately 7 per cent of the entire population of the city.[36] This was in effect a unique concentration of intellectual talent resolutely determined to stay in place until their demands had been defined and then met. It should not be surprising therefore that the *bast* provided a unique opportunity for intellectual clarity. These demands were then articulated, at their request, by Grant Duff, reflecting the awkward reality, 'that the people had entirely lost confidence in their own Government and declined to treat with them, except through the British representative'.[37]

The government was persuaded to explore a settlement when it transpired that the commander of several Tehran regiments served notice that they would not fire against the people and that on the contrary 'they were on the point of themselves taking refuge in the British Legation'. Extensive negotiations continued with the revolutionaries insisting that the British Legation act as guarantor of the Shah's assurances, once they were finally delivered. This, Grant Duff naturally refused to do, not wanting to be responsible for the Shah's commitments, though he did agree to attend the meetings as an observer, and to answer questions when asked. Finally the Shah relented and agreed to the formation of a National Consultative Assembly, with legislative powers. By 5 August agreement was reached, a Royal proclamation made to the effect of establishing an elected Assembly of Delegates.[38] The *bast* was concluded a few days later on 9 August, much to the elation of the revolutionaries.

The *ulema* ended their self-imposed exile in Qom a week later and a preliminary 'assembly' was held in the palace precincts presided over by the Shah on 19 August when he expressed his desire that those gathered would 'continue to serve him', to which the senior *ulema* responded, 'that they did not serve him but themselves and the nation'.[39] This needless to say was not the end of the tribulations, and a number of court officials sought yet again to water down the proposals, while governors refused to organise the necessary elections. The government was then threatened with the prospect of further *basts* throughout the country in the British consulates in Rasht, Tabriz and Mashhad. Fortunately the government relented and an Electoral Law was ratified on 9 September 1906, designating six categories of electors: princes and the Qajar tribe; doctors of divinity and students; nobles and notables; merchants; landed proprietors and peasants; trade guilds. This male franchise was furthermore limited to those of property or professional association.

The urgency with which the elections were held and the first Parliament, or Majlis, convened on the 7 October was indicative of the general anxiety that the government might yet again seek to dilute the arrangements, so it was seen as imperative to maintain momentum. Equally the Shah's health, despite optimistic pronouncement from the court, was not held to be good and there may have been some further concern that the crown prince might not in time be as amenable or malleable as his father. (Indeed the delegates took care to ensure that the crown prince undertook not to dissolve the Majlis for the first two years).[40] Nonetheless the speed with which the delegates moved came at the cost of a certain amount of general credibility. Not only was the balance of deputies heavily weighted towards Tehran – of the 162 members a full 64 were designated from Tehran – but it was decided to convene the Majlis before the provincial members had actually arrived, thereby ensuring that the delegates from Tehran enjoyed a highly privileged position as discussions proceeded towards the formulation of a constitution.

The Constitution itself, modelled on that of the Belgian Constitution – itself derived from the unwritten British constitution – was drawn up into two Fundamental Laws, the first of which was promulgated on 30 December 1906 and signed into law by the Shah on 1 January 1907.[41] The preamble noted the auspicious command for the establishment of a National Council on 5 August 1906, 'to promote the progress and happiness of our Kingdom and people',[42] before moving on to outline the constitution of the Assembly, its rights and its duties. The Fundamental Law stipulated a bicameral system on the British model, with a lower house (*majlis*) of some 162 delegates (which could in due course be increased to 200 delegates) and an upper house, or Senate, of 60 members, 30 of which would be appointed by the Shah. Both houses were required to approve legislation though financial matters remained the prerogative of the lower house, and in cases of disagreement a third body may be formed of elected delegates from both houses to consider the issue. Failing agreement at this stage, matters could then be sent to the Shah who might urge further consideration and if still no agreement could be reached, then the Majlis could be dissolved and new elections called following a two-thirds majority in favour of dissolution in the Senate. What was perhaps most striking about the balance of power between the two chambers was the dominance of the Majlis and its determination to keep control of all financial aspects of the state. Barring a vote for dissolution the Assembly would sit for two-year terms.

The Supplementary Fundamental Law was ratified in October 1907, adding further important layers to the Constitution including the official religion (Twelver Shi'ism), the frontiers of the Empire, the designation of the capital (Tehran) and the national flag – 'green, white and red, with the emblem of the Lion and Sun'. The Supplementary Law also stipulated the establishment of an 'Ecclesiastical Committee' composed of five *mujtahids* or clerics of similar standing to assess the compatibility of all proposed legislation with Islamic Law. The five members of the committee would be elected by the Majlis from a shortlist nominated by the *ulema*. The Supplementary Fundamental Laws also went to some lengths to enumerate the rights of the Iranian nation in Articles 8 through 25 including the stipulation that all the people of the empire were to enjoy equal rights under the law, and that no one could be arrested, unless they were in the act of committing a crime, except on the express orders of the judicial authorities and even then the individual had the right to know within 24 hours on what charge they had been held under arrest. Article 26 made clear that 'The powers of the realm are derived from the people; and the Fundamental Law regulates the employment of those Powers'.[43]

Mozaffar al Din Shah did not live long enough to see the Supplementary Fundamental Law ratified. An otherwise unimpressive reign ended on the auspicious note that the Shah lived long enough to enact into law (after some further encouragement) the most profound political change to affect Iran in recent memory and to expire before he could do any further damage. As Spring Rice eloquently expressed it,

> The Shah lingered on, and finally sank into a state of lethargy, from which he only revived at intervals. His medical attendants expressed their astonishment at his extraordinary vitality. His death was announced on several occasions. At last he consented to appoint his son Regent and agreed, though with some demur, after a grave and earnest remonstrance from the Chief Mujtahids, to sign the Constitution. He finally expired on the 8th January.[44]

What is perhaps most striking about this achievement, which took most observers, not least the British, by surprise, was the collective nature of the effort. Even the Iranian intelligentsia, the *rowshanfekr*,[45] or enlightened thinkers, could barely hide their excitement at the fact that the senior members of the *ulema* had been enthusiastic participants in securing political change.[46] But this alliance of mutual convenience was soon to find itself under serious strain, not least because there was little agreement on what precisely had been achieved and the balance between what we might term the religious and secular forces. The speed at which the first Majlis had been convened gave undue prominence to the deputies from Tehran and it was soon apparent that even this limited number of individuals were not entirely in agreement as to how to proceed, or indeed what precisely their role was to be.[47]

Fortunately Foroughi was on hand to produce a handbook for all newly elected delegates to explain to them the basic functions of the constitutions, the role of a 'national' monarchy (by which he means the crown in parliament in the service of the people), the concept of 'rights' (translated from the French *droit*), and the role and function of deputies in developing and scrutinising legislation.[48] Drawing on both French and British examples, the political system outlined, as suited to Iran itself, is essentially that of Great Britain, with an extended discussion of rights and the function of the law to protect citizens and facilitate freedom, within the law.

> Freedom consists of this that an individual has the right to do anything they desire on the condition that it harms no one else. Thus, one should not confuse freedom with stubbornness (*khod-sari*)[49] since freedom does not mean that an individual can do whatever they want, and an individual's rights has limits and those limits include the obligations an individual has towards other people. And lastly those obligations required for the harmony of society.[50]

The enthusiasm with which the delegates proceeded was shaped in part, as noted above, by the need to maintain momentum, but it is also likely that overcome by their own success they failed to fully appreciate the daunting nature of the task ahead of them. Securing a constitution and establishing a Majlis was in many ways, the easy part of the process. The more difficult part would be to translate many of the diverse and ambitious ideas about the regeneration of the Iranian state into practice and in the absence of a coherent government machinery would soon make the limitations of the constitutional project apparent. All the more so because it was soon quite clear that those elements at the sharp end of the 'revolution' were not likely to accept defeat without a fight. The new Shah, Mohammad Ali, who felt that his father had been prematurely 'killed' by the political situation, was distinctly unenthusiastic about the new restrictions on his powers and was especially resistant to the idea that the new Majlis should enjoy some sort of oversight over his finances.[51] Indeed one of the major obstacles to any progress was the belief among some delegates that the financial resources could be secured from the crown and not necessarily through general taxation, which needless to say would have involved financial exactions on themselves and their constituents. Mohammad Ali Shah for his part found unsurprisingly, that he could exploit divisions between the revolutionaries themselves, most obviously between those *ulema* who found the secular aspects of the Constitution problematic and for whom the implementation of the Shari'a outweighed the desire for a constitution, and the more enthusiastic activists who wanted to push the boundaries further than tradition might initially permit. Their position was not helped by the fact that neither the proposed Senate, nor the Ecclesiastical Committee were convened (the Senate was not actually convened until the reign of Mohammad Reza Shah in 1949; the Ecclesiastical Committee appears to have been ignored altogether).

Of more immediate concern, however, was the changing international situation. The sudden triumph of the revolution had occurred in extremely auspicious international circumstances, with the Russians preoccupied with their own local difficulties. Meanwhile, a more junior British official was holding the fort in Tehran after the departure of Hardinge and before the arrival of Cecil Spring Rice. Given the realities of communications between Tehran and London in 1906, Grant Duff enjoyed a remarkable degree of latitude to take decisions as he saw fit within what might be understood to be the broad parameters of British policy. But British policy was changing with the change in government in 1906 from a Conservative to a Liberal government and Sir Edward Grey, appointed Foreign Secretary from 1906 was not especially interested in a robust policy against the Russians. On the contrary, the defence of India could be assured by an accommodation with Russia and the mood in Britain certainly leaned in that direction. He was therefore somewhat perturbed to find that Grant Duff had involved Britain in the Constitutional Revolution, and could not hide his irritation that a British diplomat had become so central to the process that he had effectively mediated its successful conclusion. In stark contrast to those on the ground, there was little faith in London in the abilities of the Iranian revolutionaries and a genuine fear that the ensuing chaos would simply be an invitation to the Russians – once they could turn their attention southwards once again – to take advantage of the situation and seize control.

Sir Cecil Spring Rice's apologetic missive to Grey in January 1907 sought to emphasise the very real advantages gained by Grant Duff's initiative

> forced upon him by the circumstances of the case . . . His action as peace-maker, which was marked by vigour and impartiality, and which was crowned with complete success, resulted in a very great increase in influence and prestige of the British Government in Persia, and a corresponding diminution in the influence of Russia.[52]

Grey, however, was more focused on the European situation and under pressure from the French appears to have been persuaded that some accommodation with Russia was essential if the European balance of power was to be maintained and most importantly, Germany contained. The result was the Anglo-Russian convention of 1907, which harking back to Drummond Wolff, resuscitated the idea of spheres of influence in which Britain and Russia would exercise influence absent of interference of the other, with a 'neutral' zone spanning the middle of the country in which both empires could continue to contest influence.

The division agreed by Grey very much favoured the Russians, who seemed to gain exclusive access to much of the northern and most populous parts of the country, while Britain retained what amounted to a buffer zone in Iranian Baluchestan in the apparent interests of defending India.[53] Significantly, the Government of India was not particularly impressed by this division of the spoils, and unsurprisingly conservative politicians, most notably Lord Curzon, spoke out against it in Parliament. Spring Rice was shocked and protested to Grey that 'we are regarded as having betrayed the Persian people'.[54] Few diplomatic choices can have had such serious ramifications not least because Grey had effectively committed Britain to the sort of European entanglement to which its statesmen were normally averse. The long-term consequences would become all too apparent in 1914, but in the meantime European priorities meant that once again British policy in Iran suffered and any advantage secured was wilfully thrown away. The short-sightedness of the convention was made all too apparent when a year later D'Arcy struck oil in Masjed-e Soleiman, in south-west Iran, an area not in the initial British sphere of influence. The discovery of oil and the formation of the Anglo-Persian Oil Company would in short measure transform Britain's relationship with Iran from one dominated by geopolitics and the defence of India, to one of immediate and direct strategic importance: a transformation confirmed by Churchill's decision, as First Lord of the Admiralty, to buy a controlling share in the company in 1913, as the Royal Navy began the process of moving from coal-powered to oil-powered ships.

A revolution contested

For the Constitutionalists themselves, this change in international relations meant that what protective cover they might have had, was now gone. The awkwardness felt by British officials on the ground was palpable as they noted in reports to London that while the formal policy of Russia was non-intervention, their diplomats on the ground were aggressively supporting the Shah and undermining the Constitutionalist cause. This while British officials were dissuading the Constitutionalists from seeking help on the basis that it would only encourage Russian intervention.[55] The Shah decided that the best strategy to undermine the Majlis would be to show its ineffectiveness in maintaining order throughout the country and consequently he did everything he possibly could to create a sense of anarchy, a goal which according to Marling he only partially seems to have achieved.

> The government has done its best to maintain order, but being without money and without forces, and with its good intentions constantly thwarted by the Shah's unscrupulous intrigues to discredit the new regime, its efforts have been of little avail, and if the condition of the country has hardly got beyond one of peaceful anarchy, it is really due to the pacific character of the nation.[56]

Mohammad Ali Shah, reinvigorated by Russian support, nevertheless felt confident enough to attempt to close the Majlis in December 1907. But he found himself facing stiff resistance and, fearing for his life from a revolutionary movement that was turning decidedly radical, hesitated and pulled back. He proved more successful some six months later, even bringing guns to bear on the Majlis, closing it down and re-establishing, for a brief period at least, Qajar despotism. The focus of revolutionary activity moved elsewhere, most obviously Tabriz, where Baqer Khan and Sattar Khan seized control of the city becoming the locus of resistance to royalist forces.[57] Other noted revolutionaries, such as Hasan Taqizadeh, fled to Britain in an attempt to rouse popular opinion in their favour and excoriating Britain for having abandoned a movement which 'was in an especial sense the spiritual child of Great Britain'. In a 'Manifesto' printed in *The Times* (15 October 1908) and in a subsequent 'Appeal to England', Taqizadeh protested that the revolutionaries did not seek British intervention for the sake of it but sought British help to prevent the Russians from intervening. It was Russian support for the Shah that was suffocating the Constitutional movement and Britain's failure to act to restrain the Russians was inexplicable to the Iranians:

> For, we repeat once more, with confidence and certainty, the interests of the Persian people and of England are identical, and if the reactionaries triumph, all England's influence in Persia, both political and commercial, is at an end, and the Russian spirit in a Persian body will be the autocrat of Persia . . . The Persian Constitution came into being under the auspices of England, and is England's spiritual child. For a century the Persians have regarded England as their friend, and today their hopes are fixed on her alone. And so we, a little while ago like yourselves Members of a National Assembly (now alas! destroyed by violence), but now exiles who can only hope to help our country by arousing your sympathy, to seek which we have come so

long a journey, make our appeal to you on behalf of our beloved land, and on behalf of the liberties and laws whereby alone her welfare and even her independent existence can be secured, in this place, whither for so long the oppressed have turned for help, and which is the fulcrum of all free institutions and the ancient home of Liberty.[58]

It is unclear whether Taqizadeh's exertions had the desired effect. Browne was full of encouragement but likewise increasingly frustrated with British government policy, and the Foreign Office in any case made clear to Browne that his association with 'revolutionaries' was to be discouraged.[59] Nevertheless, neither the British nor the Russians found the possibility of extended Qajar despotism any more attractive than the alternative as Mohammad Ali Shah could not offer any solutions to the political turmoil affecting the country. For all the vaunted order he would establish, he had no more access to funds than the revolutionaries and soon found himself falling out of favour with the citizens of Tehran who had initially welcomed what they thought would be a return to a semblance of normality. Instead, opposition persisted, the Shah prevaricated and the foreign legations agitated for compromise. Mohammad Ali Shah's occasional utterance in favour of the Constitution was soon revealed to be a cosmetic attempt to placate the opposition, and what paltry trust had existed soon dissipated. By the middle of 1909, two armed forces, the Bakhtiaris from the south, and a force led by a leading northern magnate, Sipahdar (who had recently switched to the Constitutionalist cause despite continued reservations), began to converge on Tehran, causing much panic in the court. Despairing of any Russian assistance, by July, the latest attempt at autocracy was over. Mohammad Ali Shah was persuaded to abdicate, and his son, Ahmad, was proclaimed Shah on 17 July 1909.[60]

The restoration of the Constitutional order was the occasion of some celebration but also retribution. Mohammad Ali Shah had not been clement on his own seizure of power, now the Constitutionalists sought revenge and perhaps the most high profile was the prominent cleric Sheikh Fazlollah Nuri. Nuri had initially supported the protests against the Shah but soon found himself at odds with his co-conspirators, not least Behbehani and Tabatabai, in his disdain for what he considered to be the secular direction of the revolution. Taking the fateful step to proclaim his support for the autocracy of Mohammad Ali Shah, when the latter abdicated and went into exile, Nuri found himself at the mercy of his opponents and was executed for treason. At the same time, prior to his departure, Mohammad Ali Shah was persuaded to ratify a new Electoral Law (1 July 1909) which sought to clarify some of the anomalies in the earlier laws with respect to representation, ensuring that Tehran was no longer over-represented, and that now the religious minorities – Armenians, Chaldeans, Zoroastrians and Jews – each enjoy a single delegate. Perhaps even more significant was to be the reduction by 75 per cent in the property requirement for the franchise, from 1,000 tomans to 250 tomans.[61]

This progress aside, the Constitutionalists remained in practical terms paralysed in a downward spiral of insolvency. Not short of good ideas for the reform of the state, the Constitutionalists were increasingly frustrated by an acute absence of means to get anything done – most obviously a functioning government machinery. With no systematic means of raising funds they sought in vain to mediate a line between drawing further loans from the Russians and the British, and extorting funds from royalists now exposed by the change in political circumstances. All this of course simply raised political tensions not least between the Constitutionalists themselves, as ideals about the rule of law fell victim to political expediency and the urgent need for money. Frustrated with the continued Russian military presence on Iranian soil, to say nothing of the somewhat haughty demeanour of various Russian diplomats whose attitude towards the revolution was never better than lukewarm, the Constitutionalists sought salvation elsewhere.

Britain was no longer an option, not least because even had she the political inclination it would have been met by resistance from the Russians. An ambitious proposal 'for the engagement of seven Frenchmen for the Finance Department, four Italians for the Gendarmerie, two Swedes for the police, and two other foreigners for the Ministry of Justice', was swiftly shelved.[62] The solution was therefore sought with a new relatively young emerging power, the United States, to help reorganise and administer Iran's chaotic and largely non-existent financial system.

Neither Britain nor Russia were enthusiastic about an official relationship and it was finally agreed that the United States would not be formally engaged by Iran but that it would provide experts on a private basis who could then be directly employed by the Iranian government. The nominated candidate for this daunting task was the banker Morgan Shuster, who arrived in Iran in May 1911 to find a country seemingly on the brink of collapse. Shuster, who wrote a damning account of his short tenure in Iran – he barely lasted a year – was unequivocal about the pernicious effects of Anglo-Russian rivalry, though they were by no means the only countries taking advantage of this peculiarly Persian bazaar:

> Imagine if you will, a fast decaying government amid whose tottering ruins a heterogeneous collection of Belgian customs officers, Italian Gendarmes, German artillery sergeants, French savants, doctors, professors, and councillors of state, Austrian military instructors, English bank clerks, Turkish and Armenian courtiers, and last, but not least, a goodly sprinkling of Russian Cossack officers, tutors, and drill instructors all go through their daily task of giving the Imperial Persian Government a strong shove toward bankruptcy, with a sly side push in the direction of their own particular political or personal interests. In this pleasant diversion, the gentlemen and even the ladies of the foreign legations were somewhat peacefully engaged, when several unfortunate Americans landed on Persian soil with the truly extraordinary idea that they were to be employed under the orders of the Persian Government.[63]

Shuster quickly discovered, 'that the Persian finances were tangled – very tangled – had there been any to tangle. There were no Persian finances in any ordinary sense of the word',[64] and that the Europeans he encountered considered Shuster's task to be so tragic as to be comical:

> the jest of the diplomatic corps at Teheran [was] that the Americans would not remain in Persia three months; the wife of one distinguished foreign service minister said that a month would see them back on the road to Enzeli; and the idea that any serious attempt would be made to straighten out Persian financial affairs only called forth laughter.[65]

Shuster nevertheless attended to his task with a keen determination that unsurprisingly resulted in a good deal of resistance. The British remained ambivalent but unsupportive for fear of antagonising the Russians, while the Russians became increasingly obstructive as Shuster began to make modest progress with the development of a central treasury and a paid Gendarmerie tasked with collecting taxes. Indeed the modest progress made in the relatively short period of time suggested that with a measure of political will and administrative integrity, a good deal might be achieved. But Shuster faced, as he admitted, not only the violent reaction of Russia and her Iranian allies, but also the political obtuseness of Iranian politicians whose fluid political loyalties he found bewildering. Ultimately, as might have been expected, the Russians perturbed by the fact that Shuster had selected a British official to run the Gendarmerie, demanded the government remove Shuster. When this was refused, the Russians resorted to the one measure that assured them of immediate results: military force.

Russian troops began to systematically suppress the constitutional movement throughout the north of Iran – in their designated sphere of influence. The second Majlis was closed in December 1911, and Shuster's contract was abruptly terminated a few weeks later. With the closure of the Majlis, the first phase of the revolution effectively came to a stuttering halt. By 1912 the Russians had bombarded the Shrine of Imam Reza in Mashhad killing some 50 unarmed pilgrims and exacted a bloody retribution in Tabriz:

> On New Year's day, which was the 10th of Muharram, a day of great mourning held sacred in the Persian religious calendar, the Russian Military Governor, who had hoisted Russian flags over government buildings at Tabriz, hung the Sikutu'l Islam, who was the chief priest of Tabriz, two other priests and five others, among them several high officials of the Provincial government. As one British journalist put it, the effect of this outrage on the Persians was that which would be produced on the English people by the hanging of the Archbishop of Canterbury on Good Friday. From this time on the Russians at Tabriz continued to hang or shoot any Persian whom they chose to consider guilty of the crime of being a 'Constitutionalist'. When the fighting there was first reported, a prominent official of the Foreign Office at St Petersburg, in an interview to the press, made the statement that Russia would take vengeance into her own hands until the 'revolutionary dregs' had been exterminated.[66]

This first, dramatic phase in the Constitutional Revolution had witnessed profound changes to the body politic and political culture of the country. Within the space of a year, a state that had appeared to otherwise keen observers to be on the brink of collapse, through insolvency if nothing else, rebounded with an intellectual and political vigour that took everyone, not least the revolutionaries themselves by surprise. The shock of success, enabled by a weak king, a divided elite and favourable international circumstances was translated into a fierce sense of urgency to consolidate gains that in many ways undermined the achievement by not providing a firm foundation upon which to build for the future. The struggle that ensued was both 'national' and local, both geographically widespread and demographically focused. This in many ways was the natural consequence of the urban character of the political context in a country that remained largely rural. But that should not imply that large swathes of the country were untouched by developments. The breakdown in central government, the civil war that followed Mohammad Ali Shah's accession, as well as the intervention of the Bakhtiaris, to say nothing of the Russians, all ensured that the consequences were felt far and wide.

The political achievements of the revolution were likewise real and durable, if tragically incomplete. The Majlis was convened, and a constitutional order established. There was a lively debate in both parliaments about the way forward, and there was indeed no shortage of ideas on the need for nationwide education, a national 'central' bank,[67] and even discussion for the construction of a railway (notably, given later controversies, traversing the country from east to west, which was considered both better for trade, and certainly of more value to the British).[68] Political 'parties' and 'newspapers' flourished even if they lacked a wide social basis and were more factional and individual than broad based. A new distinctly political discourse (the names of the various factions and 'parties' were emblematic: 'democrats', 'freedom-seekers') was injected into the political culture of the country, a consequence not only of the intellectual context but of the deliberate and determined work of the Constitutionalists such as Foroughi and Dehkhoda who worked diligently to appropriate and adapt for Persian, the language of constitutional politics, now aided in their traditional dissemination by the new medium of newspapers.[69]

But what these Constitutionalists lacked to realise their ambitions were the institutional means and above all the money. This perennial shortage of money and an inability to address the structural issues behind it led to expedient measures that resulted in greater tension and factionalism. One group, the 'Democrats' sought more dramatic changes with a radical agenda for change, while the aptly named 'Moderates' advocated for a slower more managed transition with greater sensitivity for the religious sensibilities of the country. Frictions between these two factions broke into violence by 1910 with assassinations of rivals, including dramatically the murder of the leading Constitutionalist cleric, Seyyed Abdullah Behbehani. Taqizadeh, among the more radical voices in the Democrat party, judiciously went into exile.[70]

Matters were further complicated by the sudden return of Mohammad Ali Shah in 1911, in a failed attempt to seize back the throne he had ostensibly abdicated in favour of his son.

War

With the failure of Shuster and the Russian occupation, the political situation became untenable. Indeed the Russian repression, appalling as it was, elicited little coherent response, as if the country had reached the limits of political exhaustion. Central authority was crumbling and power was devolving onto local princes, magnates and tribes. In response to the Russian military intervention, the British moved to protect their interests in the south, most obviously in the oil-rich province of Khuzestan where specific arrangements were made with the local Sheikh of Mohammerah. It was in this unenviable position that Iran drifted rudderless towards the impending cataclysm of the Great War. A third Majlis was convened at the end of 1914 but it lasted barely a year, and in the absence of a credible government, Iran's professed neutrality was studiously ignored, not only by the belligerents but by many of its own politicians. With the Russians refusing to vacate Iran, their presence persuaded the Ottomans to defend their eastern frontier by sending troops into Iran, while the British likewise responded by dispatching forces from India and forming the South Persia Rifles. Allied anxiety only increased when Iranian politicians were suspected of conspiring with the Germans and indeed for a time, the German 'Lawrence', Wilhelm Wassmus, proved to be a source of some difficulty in southern Iran.[71]

Meanwhile in the north, one of the more charismatic individuals to emerge was Mirza Kuchik Khan who had been among the Sipahdar's followers in 1909, and now established his 'Union of Islam' in Gilan in 1915, with a following estimated at around 3,000, acquiring the name *Jangalis*, for their habit of living in the forests. According to Sykes (who served in Iran during the war),

> Kuchik Khan was undoubtedly inspired by patriotic feelings. He would frankly state that he could lay claim to the 'best of the good', but thought that he might be classed among the 'worst of the good'. He had no hesitation in branding the Persian Government as being the worst of the bad. He observed his plighted word in dealing with the British, whom he impressed favourably.[72]

It is easy to exaggerate the chaos that emerged, and one should not conflate the collapse of central government with the collapse of order in general, but it is likewise difficult to overestimate the social, political and economic dislocation that affected the country as foreign armies fought over its territory, and where the welfare of the general population came a poor second to the needs of those armies.[73] In this context it is not surprising that the population of Iran suffered extensively in the war and its immediate aftermath, especially with the onset of famine and influenza, but in the absence of nationwide data it is difficult to come to firm conclusions. Sir Percy Sykes suggested that influenza in Fars Province killed some 20 per cent of the population.[74] Nevertheless, one must guard against extrapolating from particular areas to the entire country given the diversity of the experience and the differences in geography. For example, one scholar estimates the population in 1921 to have been just over 11.3 million, which suggests, if accurate, that the impact of the war on the demographics of the country was less than generally believed though still by no means insignificant at between 5 and 10 per cent of the estimated population prior to the war.[75]

What, however, remains most striking is that despite the dire domestic situation, the political elite of the country remained remarkably confident in its own abilities to project Iranian ambitions and demands. There were to be sure changes afoot among the Constitutionalists about how they might constructively tackle the problem of political reform and progress the country away from the failure in central authority that afflicted them. But there seems to have been little sense that the sovereignty and political integrity of the Iranian state might be under serious threat. On the contrary, Iranian statesmen emerged from the Great War reinvigorated by the possibilities that the new international environment presented. The war after all had seen the collapse of Tsarist Russia through revolution and the dissolution of the Ottoman Empire through military defeat. Iran on the other hand had survived, and despite the depredations of the Constitutional Revolution, the advent of the Paris Peace Conference and the new discourse on national self-determination, seemed the apposite time to address the injustice of the Treaty of Turkmenchai. Indeed with a self confidence that belied the political realities of the day, Iran dispatched a well briefed delegation to Paris, ostensibly to join the victors in dividing up the spoils of victory.

The British, now the dominant foreign power in Iran, were unsurprisingly dismissive of Iranian claims to have a seat at the table and ultimately the Iranian delegation enjoyed little more than observer status on the margins. The Iranian claims for territorial restitution were certainly extraordinary. According to Sykes,

> Oblivious of the fact that chronic anarchy and corruption reign within her own border, Persia demanded that her boundaries should be restored to the spaciousness of ancient days, when the Oxus was the eastern limit of the empire. In other words, to the east she claimed Transcaspia, Merv, and Khiva. To the north-west, she claimed the Caucasus up to Derbent, including Erivan, the chief centre of the Armenians and Baku. On the west she wished to annex Asia Minor to the Euphrates, thereby including the entire province of Kurdistan and the important centres of Diarbekr and Mosul.[76]

What was perhaps most striking about these claims, other than their territorial reach, was the omission of the Shi'a heartlands in southern Mesopotamia. Indeed Najaf and Karbala were mentioned only in terms of the Iranian state desirous of having 'her important interests safeguarded', but far short of political control.[77] There were similar omissions to the east of course, reflecting the continued dominance of British power. There was no mention for example of Herat, nor any attempt to overturn the 1857 Treaty of Paris. An appreciation of British interests in what was to become southern Iraq may have reflected this hesitation but it certainly did not explain the enthusiasm for territorial restitution of 'Kurdistan', described in the claim as 'a territory inhabited by a people Persian in race and language'.[78] There can be no clearer indication of the growing dominance of nationalist ideology within a political discourse that was framed within an imperial legacy and inheritance. The transition from the 'Guarded Domains' of the Qajar era, the 'imperial kingdom', to the imperial nation of the Pahlavis, was well underway, and one might well conclude that the Pahlavis were less a cause and more a symptom of the intellectual changes that were already taking root.

The language of the 'nation' was certainly one that would gain more traction with the delegates in Paris, and even Sykes could admit that Iran's other claims for self-determination, sovereignty and some measure of reparation were not entirely unwarranted.[79] The language of 'national' self-determination was perhaps most forcefully articulated by Taqizadeh in a Memorandum drafted for the delegates in which he pleaded in explicitly nationalistic terms for Iran to be welcomed as an equal partner into the community of nations and indeed to become a member of the new League of Nations. Iran, argued Taqizadeh, should be entitled to this on account of its long history of nationhood, its progressive character and its adherence to its international agreements and humanitarian conventions.[80] However much one might justifiably criticise the flamboyant nationalist overtones of the text, it was clearly aimed at a particular audience with a view to having Iran formally recognised within the new international order. There was in this sense some sound method to the apparent diplomatic madness.

Sykes of course did conclude, that for all the regrettable treatment of the Iranian delegation they did nonetheless lack a sense of proportion of where the possible ended. Quite apart from the territorial claims, the Iranians were also looking for some international assistance to help them get out of the political and economic morass in which they had found themselves. Their vision seemed by all accounts to be another attempt to revisit the international assistance they had sought during the early days of the Constitutional Revolution. Lord Curzon, newly appointed as Foreign Secretary, whose keen interest in Iran held a patrician affection that brooked no compromise, saw an opportunity which had long evaded him of tying Iran more firmly to the British camp. He saw no reason for an international team, which would to his mind only confuse matters, and given that Britain was now, by dint of the Russian Revolution, the paramount foreign power, no particular reason to share this responsibility. The Anglo-Persian Agreement that followed in 1919, drew on the requests the Iranians had made but substituted Britain for the coalition of partners requested.[81] Along with a £2 million loan to finance the various reforms, it included provision to reform the army, aspects of the administration as well as the communications (including railway construction) and trade policy.

It was the product, in a very singular sense, of Curzon's ambitions for British–Iranian relations going forward, and arguably reflected an uncharacteristic enthusiasm on his part, as if having been confronted with an opportunity to unfold his life's goal, he was not going to relinquish it. The agreement itself was not unreasonable given Iranian demands and the realities of her political situation, but presentationally it would have benefitted from diplomatic support. As Sir Edward Grey, now Lord Grey of Fallodon noted, 'Here was a case of helping a weak country where the League of Nations ought to have been brought into the matter, and it was a great pity that the league had not been brought in'.[82] The consequence of this was that the Agreement was regarded by the United States and France in particular, as an exercise in political aggrandisement. More serious was the fact that the Agreement was viewed with deep suspicion among the political elite in Iran, and an unhelpful degree of apathy among the British civil servants tasked with getting it implemented.

Curzon's passion was certainly not shared. In order to get the Agreement implemented, Curzon insisted that it be ratified in the Majlis, and, somewhat reluctantly convinced by Sir Percy Cox, he duly set aside substantial funds – £131,000 – to grease the palms of the deputies, working on the not unreasonable assumption that money would be required to 'persuade' the deputies to vote the right way. Vosuq al Dowleh, the Prime Minister was, however, not keen to call a new parliament and his prevarication, as well as, it would seem, his failure to make the necessary financial disbursements, ensured that opposition to the Agreement became more vocal, forcing Vosuq's resignation in 1920. (The view that Vosuq al Dowleh had been in receipt of a bribe became widespread though interestingly he sued and won against a British writer who alleged this resulting in the withdrawal of the book.) Add to this the general lack of enthusiasm among British officials – to say nothing of the Treasury in London, who viewed further Middle Eastern entanglements with dread – the Agreement, much to Curzon's frustration, remained stillborn.[83]

A despondent Curzon complained to the new British minister in Tehran, Sir Percy Loraine, that the failure of the Agreement was a collective one for which the British government shared a substantive part of the blame noting with barely disguised contempt that the Chief of the General Staff had told him, 'the sooner you are out of these places altogether the better'. By the time Loraine had arrived in Tehran in October 1921 he was not only dealing with the fallout of the Anglo-Persian Agreement but with an entirely new political situation. Iran's Constitutionalists, reeling from the failure of their revolution, and the devastation caused by the Great War, had taken a new turn and decided on a radical new solution for the long overdue regeneration of the Iranian state.

Notes

1 For a discussion of Browne's importance see Mansour Bonakdarian, *Britain and the Constitutional Revolution of 1906–1911*. New York: Syracuse University Press, 2006, pp. 91–6.

2 Browne describes the Constitutional movement as the 'Persian Risorgimento' in the opening pages of *The Persian Revolution*, p. 2. See also Mansour Bonakdarian, 'Edward G. Browne and the Iranian Constitutional Struggle: From Academic Orientalism to Political Activism', *Iranian Studies* 26(1/2) Winter–Spring 1993, pp. 7–31.

3 There are few if any statistical sources until the twentieth century. Amanat assesses that by 1850 the population was no more than 80,000, see *Pivot of the Universe*,

p. 12. The population of the country as a whole fluctuated throughout the century as a result of periodic famines and epidemics. Estimates at the turn of the nineteenth century vary from between 6 million and 9 million. A British report dated to 1868 posited a lower figure of 4–5 million with 85,000 for Tehran, see C. Issawi (ed.), *The Economic History of Iran, 1800–1914.* Chicago, IL: University of Chicago Press, 1971, pp. 27–9. Lambton considers that by 1873 it was no more than 8–8.5 million, see A.K.S. Lambton, 'Land Tenure and Land Revenue', in P. Avery, G.R.G. Hambly and C. Melville (eds.), *The Cambridge History of Iran*, Vol VII. Cambridge: Cambridge University Press, 1991, p. 469. In terms of the rural–urban divide, see G. Hambly in the same volume, pp. 544–9. Based on Hambly's estimates we can conclude that around 10 per cent of the population could be considered urban.

4 Browne, *The Persian Revolution*, p. 55.
5 Browne, *The Persian Revolution*, p. 45.
6 N. Keddie, 'Afğānī, Jamāl-Al-Dīn', *Encyclopædia Iranica*, www.iranicaonline.org/articles/afgani-jamal-al-din.
7 F. Kazemi, 'Anglo-Persian Oil Company', *Encyclopædia Iranica*, www.iranicaonline.org/articles/anglo-persian-oil-company.
8 R. Ferrier, *The History of the British Petroleum Company*, Vol I. Cambridge: Cambridge University Press, 1982, p. 641. The concession was written in French and Persian, with the French version being definitive in case of dispute.
9 Browne, *The Persian Revolution*, p. 416.
10 Wright, *The Persians*, p. 172.
11 A. Hardinge to Sir Edward Grey, dated 23 December 1905, pp. 1–22, reprinted in *Iran: Political Diaries*, Vol II, pp. 485–506.
12 D. Wright, 'Hardinge, Arthur', *Encyclopædia Iranica*, www.iranicaonline.org/articles/hardinge-arthur; for detail of the Shah's visit to London and the 'The Garter Nightmare', see Wright, *The Persians*, pp. 172–84. For an account of the Shah's first European tour, see G.M. Wickens, 'Shah Muzaffar al Din European Tour, AD 1900', in E. Bosworth and C. Hillenbrand (eds.), *Qajar Iran.* Costa Mesa, CA: Mazda, 1983, pp. 34–47.
13 Hardinge to Sir Edward Grey, p. 7.
14 Hardinge to Sir Edward Grey, p. 7.
15 This was a bequest from the King of Oudh to be used for religious purposes at Najaf and Karbala, and was administered by the British Residency in Baghdad.
16 Hardinge to Sir Edward Grey, p. 8.
17 Hardinge to Sir Edward Grey, p. 10.
18 Hardinge to Sir Edward Grey, p. 12.
19 Hardinge to Sir Edward Grey, p. 12.
20 Sir Cecil Spring Rice to Sir Edward Grey, 'General Report on Persia for the Year 1906', dated 29 January 1907, p. 3, reprinted in *Iran: Political Diaries*, Vol III.
21 Mangol Bayat, 'The *Rowshanfekr* in the Constitutional Period', in H.E. Chehabi and Vanessa Martin (eds.), *Iran's Constitutional Revolution: Popular Politics, Cultural Transformations and Transnational Connections.* London: I.B. Tauris, 2010, p. 179. As Bayat notes, 'By 1910 the list would read like a Who's Who of prominent Constitutional figures, ideologically disparate, ranging from radical through moderate to conservative'.
22 Mohammad Ali Foroughi, 'The Modernization of Law', *Journal of Persianate Studies* 3(1), 2010, p. 40.
23 A similar anecdote is provided almost a century earlier by Malcolm, *Sketches of Persia*, p. 88.
24 On the state of schooling in this period see D. Menashri, *Education and the Making of Modern Iran.* London: Cornell University Press, 1992, pp. 46–65.
25 Hardinge to Sir Edward Grey, p. 10; see also the first-hand account of events as cited by Browne, *The Persian Revolution*, p. 122.

26 On the role of the 'Russian' Armenians, see Houri Berberian, *Armenians in the Constitutional Revolution of 1905–1911*. Oxford: Westview Press, 2001, pp. 226.

27 Browne, *The Persian Revolution*, p. 114.

28 Browne, *The Persian Revolution*, p. 114.

29 Spring Rice, 'General Report on Persia for the Year 1906', p. 4.

30 Browne, *The Persian Revolution*, p. 118.

31 Spring Rice, 'General Report on Persia for the Year 1906', p. 5.

32 Spring Rice describes Behbehani as the most energetic 'but not the most incorruptible of the Mujtahids', see 'General Report on Persia for the Year 1906', p. 5.

33 Spring Rice, 'General Report on Persia for the Year 1906', p. 5.

34 Browne, *The Persian Revolution*, p. 118.

35 Spring Rice, 'General Report on Persia for the Year 1906', p. 5. It is worth noting some discrepancy in dates in the British report. In the first place the report notes that the Legation was occupied on 9 July, which would appear to be a straight typographic error, and is corrected in the continuation of the report from Cecil Spring Rice to Sir Edward Grey, 'The General Report for Persia', dated 28 February 1907, p. 5. Similarly this later report corrects the date for maximum occupancy from 2 September to 2 August, and has been duly noted and corrected in the quote here.

36 Lambton, 'Land Tenure and Land Revenue', p. 470, puts the population of Tehran in 1900 at 250,000, almost twice the size of Tabriz. Abrahamian estimates the total population in this period to be circa 12 million with 20 per cent 'urban' in a broad understanding of that term, see E. Abrahamian, *A History of Modern Iran*. Cambridge: Cambridge University Press, 2008, p. 6. A Russian assessment from 1913 on the other hand suggests a lower overall population of 7.5 million with a higher proportion in towns (25 per cent) and a population in Tehran and Tabriz of 350,000 and 300,000 respectively, see Issawi, *The Economic History of Iran*, pp. 33–4.

37 Spring Rice, 'General Report on Persia for the Year 1906', p. 6.

38 Browne, *The Persian Revolution*, pp. 353–4.

39 Spring Rice, 'General Report on Persia for the Year 1906', p. 6.

40 Spring Rice, 'The General Report for Persia', dated 28 February 1907, p. 7.

41 For the Persian text see, Nazem al Islam Kermani, *Tarikh-e Bidari Iranian* (The History of the Iranian Awakening). Tehran: Farhang, 1349/1970, pp. 38–45.

42 The Fundamental Laws of 30 December 1906, reprinted and translated in Browne, *The Persian Revolution*, p. 362; the specific reference to 'happiness' here also suggests an awareness of the US Constitution.

43 The Supplementary Fundamental Laws of 7 October 1907, reprinted and translated in Browne, *The Persian Revolution*, pp. 372–84. See also A. Gheissari, 'Constitutional Rights and the Development of Civil Law in Iran, 1907–41', in Chehabi and Martin (eds.), *Iran's Constitutional Revolution*, pp. 74–6.

44 Spring Rice, 'General Report on Persia for the Year 1906', p. 13.

45 On the definition of these terms see N. Nabavi, 'The Changing Concept of the Intellectual in Iran of the 1960s', *Iranian Studies* 32(3), 1999, pp. 333–50. The term *rowshanfekr* did not become popular until the 1940s, as a direct translation of the Arabic, *monavver al fekr*.

46 Browne, *The Persian Revolution*, p. 123.

47 On the general inexperience of delegates see V. Martin, 'Constitutional Revolution ii, Events', *Encyclopædia Iranica*, www.iranicaonline.org/articles/constitutional-revolution-ii.

48 Mohammad Ali Foroughi, *Hoquq-e Asasi: ya adab-e mashruteat-e dol* (Fundamental Laws or the Rules of Constitutionalism of States). Tehran, 1325/6 (lunar) / 1907/8, reprinted in I. Afshar and H. Homayunpur (eds.), *Siyasatnameh-ye zoka-ol-molk, maqale-ha, nameh-ha, va sokhanrani-ha-ye siyasi-ye Mohammad Ali Foroughi* (The Book of Politics of Zoka ol Molk, the Political Articles, Letters and Speeches of Mohammad Ali Foroughi). Tehran: Ketab-e Roshan, 1389/2010, pp. 5–62.

49 Foroughi, *Hoquq-e Asasi*, pp. 51.

50 Foroughi, *Hoquq-e Asasi*, pp. 51–2.

51 Nazem al Islam Kermani, *Tarikh-e Bidari Iranian*, p. 57.

52 Spring Rice, 'General Report on Persia for the Year 1906', p. 1.

53 Bonakdarian, *Britain and the Constitutional Revolution of 1906–1911*, p. 81.

54 Quoted in Wright, *The English amongst the Persians*. London: I.B. Tauris, 2001, p. 30. See also the reference to the questions raised in the House of Commons in Kermani, *Tarikh-e Bidari Iranian*, p. 22. For a detailed discussion of Grey's policy and the dissent this caused see Bonakdarian, *Britain and the Constitutional Revolution of 1906–1911*, pp. 71–91.

55 Charles Marling to Sir Edward Grey, 'Annual Report, 1907', dated 29 January 1908, p. 11.

56 Charles Marling to Sir Edward Grey, 'Annual Report, 1907', dated 29 January 1908, p. 10.

57 Sir G. Barclay to Sir Edward Grey, 'Annual Report, 1908', dated 10 February 1910 [NB this would appear to be a typographic error and should read 1909], p. 5. Barclay notes that the role of Tabriz at this stage cannot be underestimated.

58 Hasan Taqizadeh, 'Manifesto from Refugees', and 'Persia's Appeal to England (1908)', in *Maqallat Taqizadeh*, Vol VII. Tehran: Shokufan, 1356/1977, pp. 445–62. The documents are signed by both Taqizadeh and Moazed ed Saltana.

59 See Bonakdarian, 'Edward G Browne and the Iranian Constitutional Struggle', p 13, note 17. See also Bonakdarian, *Britain and the Constitutional Revolution of 1906–1911*, p. 220.

60 Sir G. Barclay to Sir Edward Grey, 'Annual Report, 1909', dated 10 February 1910, p. 9, reprinted in *Iran: Political Diaries, 1881–1965*, Vol IV, p. 403.

61 See Browne, *The Persian Revolution*, p. 386.

62 Sir G. Barclay to Sir Edward Grey, 'Annual Report, 1911', dated 28 January 1912, pp. 1–2, reprinted in *Iran: Political Diaries, 1881–1965*, Vol V, pp. 353–4.

63 W. Morgan Shuster, *The Strangling of Persia: Story of the European Diplomacy and Oriental Intrigue That Resulted in the Denationalization of Twelve Million Mohammedans*. Washington, DC: Mage Publishers, 1987 [first published 1912], pp. 37–8.

64 Shuster, *The Strangling of Persia*, p. 38.

65 Shuster, *The Strangling of Persia*, p. 35.

66 Shuster, *The Strangling of Persia*, pp. 219–20. See also Sir W. Townley to Sir Edward Grey, 'Annual Report, 1912', dated 18 March 1913, p. 6, reprinted in *Iran: Political Diaries, 1881–1965*, Vol V, p. 466.

67 Kermani, *Tarikh-e Bidari Iranian*, pp. 17–19; the intention to establish a national bank was announced on 12 December 1906.

68 Sir G. Barclay to Sir Edward Grey, 'Annual Report, 1911', dated 28 January 1912, p. 27, reprinted in *Iran: Political Diaries, 1881–1965*, Vol V, p. 379. See also in this regard O. Bast, '"Sheer Madness" or "Railway Politics" Iranian Style? The Controversy over Railway Development Priorities within the Persian Government in 1919–1920 and British Railway Imperialism', *Iran* 55(1), 2017, pp. 65–6. Railways development was hindered in many ways by all parties involved. While the British and the Russians both provided plans for development the anxiety always remained that the railways would be used for the economic penetration of Iran by rivals. For rival plans see Issawi, *The Economic History of Iran*, pp. 184–99.

69 Nahid Mozaffari, 'An Iranian Modernist Project: Ali Akbar Dehkhoda's Writings in the Constitutional Period', in Chehabi and Martin (eds), *Iran's Constitutional Revolution*, p. 197.

70 Sir G. Barclay to Sir Edward Grey, 'Annual Report, 1910', dated 28 February 1911, p. 7.

71 Percy Sykes, *History of Persia*, Vol II, pp. 443–6. For German efforts, see G. Lenczowski, 'Foreign Powers' Intervention in Iran during World War I', in Bosworth and Hillenbrand (eds.), *Qajar Iran*, pp. 78–87.

72 Sykes, *A History of Persia*, Vol II, pp. 489–90.
73 On this debate see, O. Bast, 'Disintegrating the "Discourse of Disintegration": Some Reflections on the Historiography of the Late Qajar Period and Iranian Cultural Memory', in Touraj Atabaki, *Iran in the 20th Century: Historiography and Political Culture*. London: I.B. Tauris, 2009, pp. 60–63.
74 Sykes, *A History of Persia*, Vol II, p. 515, see also p. 519 with reference to a famine in Western Persia.
75 K.S. MacLachlan, 'Economic Development, 1921–79', in Avery, Hambly and Melville (eds.), *The Cambridge History of Iran*, Vol VII, p. 609.
76 Sykes, *A History of Persia*, Vol II, p. 519.
77 See, 'Claims of Persia before the Conference of the Preliminaries of Peace at Paris, Paris, March 1919', Part II, point 4. I am grateful to Philip Grobien for having brought this document to my attention. For a detailed analysis of these discussions, see Philip Grobien's thesis, 'Resurrecting Empire: Iranian Irredentism in 1919', forthcoming.
78 'Claims of Persia before the Conference', Part II, point 3.
79 Sykes *A History of Persia*, Vol II, p. 520.
80 H. Taqizadeh, 'Memorandum on Persia's Wishes and Aspirations Addressed to the Peace Conference of Paris', The Hague, April 1919, reprinted in S.H. Taqizadeh's *Articles and Essays*, Vol VII. Tehran: Shokufan, 1977, pp. 722–8.
81 Sykes, *A History of Persia*, Vol II, pp. 520–22.
82 Quoted in Sykes, *A History of Persia*, Vol II, p. 522.
83 G. Waterfield, *Professional Diplomat: Sir Percy Loraine*. London: John Murray, 1973, pp. 61–5.

7 Reza Khan and the establishment of the Pahlavi state

On the night of 21 February 1921, Reza Khan, the commander of the Cossack Brigade based in Qazvin, entered Tehran and arrested some 60 prominent politicians, assured the Qajar king that he had come to save the monarchy from certain revolution, and then demanded the appointment of his co-conspirator, a liberal journalist from a prominent religious family, Seyyed Zia Tabatabaie, as Prime Minister. The Shah swiftly conceded. By virtue of this 'coup', Reza Khan, a hitherto unknown figure, was thrust into the political limelight and at the age of 42 gained a seat in the cabinet with the newly created title of Army Commander. By May 1921, he had ousted Seyyed Zia and acquired the portfolio of Minister of War, spending the rest of the year consolidating his grip on the coercive machinery of the state. Bringing various organisations such as the Gendarmerie under the auspices of the Ministry of War, he replaced foreign officers with his own appointees from the Cossack Brigade and then pursued a systematic campaign against his military rivals. By December 1921, the head of the rebel leader Kuchik Khan was displayed in Tehran in a visible, if brutal, signal that a new order had arrived and was in the process of construction. In the following year he moved against those elements which he felt were destructive to the integrity of the state and the centralisation of power, using his newly constructed and expanding army to great effect. By 1923 he had been appointed Prime Minister, and by 1925 so complete was his apparent hegemony that a grateful Majlis deposed the now redundant dynasty and bestowed the royal dignity on Reza Shah Pahlavi, thereby establishing the Pahlavi dynasty.

> It was the disillusioned public opinion and, in particular, that of the middle class, starving for the establishment of a strong, centralized government, which encouraged and prepared Reza Khan's rise to power. The middle class saw in the person of Reza Khan the realisation of its goal.[1]

Reza Khan's emergence and dramatic rise was predicated not only on the new army which he created and nourished, but on the initially unwavering support of key elements of the intelligentsia who, despairing of the political impotence of their country in the aftermath of the Constitutional Revolution and the apparent failure of that revolution to yield the results they had hoped for, turned to a 'saviour'. Or, to paraphrase Tulard, faced with internal and external threats to its interests, the Iranian intellectual elites invented a 'saviour'.[2] Indeed the rise and consolidation of the Pahlavi dynasty and the state it supported cannot be understood in the absence of the civilian element which was crucial to the construction of the modern state in Iran and the establishment of the dynasty as fundamental to the survival of that state. Reza Pahlavi provided the coercive arm and drive, but the ideological and practical administrative details were developed by others, working behind his protective shield and ultimately subsumed by him. Reza Khan was a man of his time, as much a product of the exigencies of his age as a consequence of his own ambition. He was the man on horseback, the saviour the secular intelligentsia craved and moulded to their desires. Like all myths, he was to prove all too human.

The man on horseback

As befits a figure of great controversy, Reza Khan's background, as well as his rise to power, have been and remain the source of enormous debate. His supporters have constructed an elaborate military lineage for the brusque commander of the Iranian Cossack Brigade, emphasising his 'Iranian', as opposed to 'Turkish', pedigree, his vigorous nationalism and, according to his son at least, a genealogy which stretches far into the distant mists of Iranian historical mythology. Whatever links to royalty he may have had, Reza Khan was nevertheless, like the founders of previous Iranian dynasties (most notably Nader Shah whom he appears to have admired), a 'prince' in waiting, with a manifest destiny known to only a few and many years of hard schooling in the harsh Iranian countryside, before he heard the call of duty and, of course, destiny. While few would doubt his nationalist credentials (although many would query what he understood by nationalism), much of the rest of the description is completely unverifiable and in all probability nonsense. While we know that he came from a family hailing from Mazandaran in the Caspian littoral, we know little of his immediate family, nor can we be certain of his date of birth, although it has been placed at around 1878.[3] Our lack of verifiable information about his background is, of course, a boon to myth-makers of all shades and his detractors have not been slow to exploit this gap to their own advantage, painting a very negative picture of an illiterate, ruthlessly self-serving man, placed in power by the British and emblematic of the worst type of Iranian tyrant. As far as the British were concerned, their views also varied widely, and while Sir Percy Loraine was an admirer and earnest supporter, his successor Sir Harold Nicolson made no secret of his dislike for the man. They may of course have reflected the two different periods in which they encountered Reza Khan. Loraine met him during his rise to power, when he was consolidating his grip and centralising government at a time when most British observers viewed such a possibility with incredulity. Nicolson, on the other hand, became acquainted with Reza Shah in full flight, seeking to implement somewhat grandiose schemes and intolerant of the British from whom he was anxious to distance himself. What we *can* say about Reza Khan is that he had physical presence and considerable drive. He was not a sophisticated man, for which he drew considerable criticism from those who were undoubtedly better educated, though much like previous dynastic founders, the condescension went both ways. Reza Khan was certainly not as ignorant as his opponents tried to portray him, nor indeed in any practical sense illiterate, and if he eschewed the flowery prose of the Qajar establishment, he possessed, as Loraine noted admiringly, a keen sense of the political culture within which he operated.[4] As such he had an unusual capacity to get things done, and in the aftermath of the political inertia of the Constitutional era, this was an asset worth its weight in gold to the many Iranian Constitutionalists who backed him. He was in the Rousseauian sense, the Iranian 'noble savage', a 'cossack' whose simple birth and harsh upbringing had moulded a fundamental purity of soul which would inject new life into the staid and corrupt nobilities of the present.[5] If he proved to be a little less noble and a little too savage for some, the cost was worth bearing, and, in any case, it was argued, such rough edges would be smoothed in time.

In 1921, in the aftermath of the fall of Vosuq al Dawleh's government and the failure of the Anglo-Persian Agreement, many within the political establishment grew increasingly anxious at the continued impotence of the Iranian state and the consequences this might have for the current order. The Constitutionalists in particular were concerned that no programme of reform had actually been implemented and that the aspirations of the revolution of 1906 remained unfulfilled. The problem they had concluded had been a lack of means as opposed to a lack of ambition, which at times had been so excessive as to both overwhelm and undermine the integrity of the Constitutional Revolution. The Constitutionalists had in reality sought to limit a government that in terms of basic machinery, did not as yet exist. The solution lay not only in a return to the earlier ideas of Akhundzadeh and Malkom Khan, but to a review of European history itself, where it became apparent that first one had to create the state machinery before one could limit it. Good governance had to precede constitutional government and good governance required centralised and forceful authority. As in Europe in the eighteenth century, Iran was in need of its own 'Enlightened' despot, a 'Persian' Peter the Great, who could drag Iran kicking and screaming into the modern world if need be, impose dress codes and outlaw beards. This may not be ideal but it was a necessity if the promise of the Constitutional Revolution was to have a chance of fulfilment. Hasan Taqizadeh was perhaps the most forceful advocate of the revolutionary application of European ideas to the Iranian experience outlining a 23-point blueprint for radical change.[6]

The British for their part, frustrated by the failure of the Agreement, wanted a solution to the 'Persian Question' which would minimise their own costs and protect their strategic interests, principally in India. All three viewed the threat posed by Soviet Bolshevism with growing anxiety. In this atmosphere of heightened tension, Reza Khan, the commander of the Cossack Brigade stationed in Qazvin, in alliance with the liberal journalist Seyyed Zia Tabatabaie, marched some 2,500 troops to Tehran, which he entered without opposition on 21 February. Arresting several dozen politicians, he demanded the appointment of Seyyed Zia as Prime

Minister. The Shah acquiesced, and the bloodless, almost uneventful coup was a fait accompli. Reza Khan was himself appointed Commander of the Army, a new post, and at the age of 42 took his place in the new cabinet. At this stage, it was by no means certain that the coup would lead to anything other than another cycle of political negotiation, machination and very probably collapse. Indeed, so great was the popular conviction that this was a British coup that the Foreign Office resisted calls from their diplomats in Tehran to recognise the Zia regime, for fear that the government's fall was simply a matter of time.

Britain and the coup of 1921

At this stage it is worth reflecting on the precise role played by Britain in the coup. Critics of the Pahlavi state and Reza Khan in particular argue that he was the solution to Britain's problems in Iran after the failure of the Anglo-Persian Agreement and Britain's need for strong government in Iran. This was a charge that Reza Khan was aware of and later during his rule he commented to his aides that while people might allege such a connection, that Britain might have facilitated his rise, he would prove his independence from them. If Harold Nicolson's comments are anything to go by, Reza Shah achieved this by some considerable measure. The popular view that the British were involved in the 1921 coup was noted as early as March 1921 by the American embassy and relayed to the Iran desk at the Foreign Office,[7] and Reza Khan was sufficiently concerned to issue a proclamation emphasising his authorship of the coup:

> [I]f you have any complaints to make to the author of the coup you can refer to me without fear, instead of searching here and there and resorting to the newspapers . . . I am not at all ashamed of my deeds in the eyes of the public, and it is again with honour that I announce myself to be the actual author of the coup d'état.[8]

Indeed supporters of Reza Khan and the Pahlavis in general have sought to diminish the British role and to argue that, on the contrary, the rise of Reza Khan and the establishment of the Pahlavi dynasty was against British interests. In later years every effort was expended in emphasising this point, and Nicolson's comments, if not Loraine's, were used to support it. It is certainly true that since the Great War there had been much discussion of possible coups, the Germans having investigated the possibility and Reza Khan himself having approached the German embassy in 1917 for support.[9]

Be that as it may, given the paramountcy of Britain's position in Iran after the First World War, it seems likely that she would have played some sort of unde-fined role in the politics of the country. The debate thus must revolve around the nature and scope of this intervention. The degree of direct involvement from Whitehall, as opposed to the energetic responses of local British military and diplomatic officials (as in 1906), was probably not as great as opponents of the Pahlavi regime have maintained. As Zirinsky argues cogently, 'Britain did less than is believed by those who accept the myth, but more than London thought at the time'.[10] It certainly seems true that General Ironside was suitably impressed by what he felt were Reza Khan's martial qualities, and diplomatic officials such as Cox and Loraine were sympathetic, and in the latter's case visibly impressed, by what they saw. It may be fair to say that British personnel facilitated a coup that had been long in the thoughts of a select band of Iranian conspirators (including a number of individuals who would go on to serve in Reza Shah's government), by providing logistical support on the ground, and discouraging any doubts that may have lingered in Whitehall.

However, the continued popular belief in British involvement in the establishment of the Pahlavi dynasty was to haunt Reza Shah and his son as much if not more than the 1953 coup was to cause problems of credibility for Mohammad Reza Shah. Indeed, in retrospect, the coup of 1921 was more problematic because it underpinned the whole edifice of the Pahlavi state and as a result has come to be seen as a turning point in the modern history of Iran. There was a lingering question of legitimacy which cast a shadow on the Pahlavi dynasty from its inception.

The consolidation of power and the imposition of a new order

As has been noted, few, least of all the British, predicted a long life for the new government. In many ways such predictions proved correct. Seyyed Zia lasted barely three months before a series of proposed reforms alienated sufficient numbers of the establishment to have him deposed. Lacking allies and offered a convenient refuge in Palestine by the British, Seyyed Zia left, and Qavam al Saltana, a landed aristocrat, was persuaded to replace him. The real victor in this apparent counter-coup was Reza Khan, who had used his position to curry favour with members of the political elite, convincing them that he represented a force for stability in marked contrast to the avowed radicalism of Seyyed Zia. In portraying himself as a champion of the traditional order, Reza Khan showed an instinctive political acumen that many of his initial supporters had not foreseen. Far from being simply the military arm of Seyyed Zia's coup, Reza Khan clearly had ambitions of his own and he actively courted key members of the establishment in order to consolidate his own position. For some this was confirmation that the saviour had arrived, for others fears were aroused concerning the extent of the new Army Commander's ambitions, but for many others this emergent power on the Iranian political stage was simply not taken seriously. This more than anything else gave Reza Khan an enormous advantage over his potential rivals. Qavam rewarded him with the post of Minister of War in May 1921 and in the following nine months he established his grip on the armed forces, reconstructing them under his unified command.

While in retrospect Reza Khan's rise to dominance in Iran may appear rapid, it certainly was not smooth, and indeed it might be considered a testament to his political skill that he was able to surmount these obstacles in a methodical campaign of consolidation and conquest. For Reza Khan, like his autocratic precursors, had to conquer Iran from the inside out before he could even contemplate ruling it. Indeed in many ways his was a very traditional route to supreme power based as it was on an army created by and loyal to his person. Reza Khan did not have a tribe, so he set out to forge one. He brought the Gendarmerie, previously administered by the Ministry of the Interior, under his control in the Ministry of War, and replaced its foreign officers with his own men from the Cossack Brigade. This new amalgamated army was divided into five army divisions of some 8,000 men each, ultimately providing Reza Khan with a mobile force of some 40,000. To finance this army, Reza Khan encouraged the Majlis and the Shah to allocate him funds, and where necessary he acquired the authority to appropriate local funds, whether customs duties or other forms of taxation. His principal sources in this period were indirect taxes and funds diverted from various state lands. For Reza Khan, the army was the 'soul' of the nation[11] and he lavished considerable funds and praise on it. He was acutely aware that loyalty would not be retained by the force of his personality alone, but that financial rewards had also to be distributed. His pressing need for more funds and his avowed intention to use such funds to expand the army was clearly attested to in a discussion he had with an American traveller, Powell, who encountered Reza Khan in 1923.

> In the course of a long and very candid conversation with Reza Khan I asked him what, in his opinion, was the most pressing need of Persia. 'A foreign loan', he answered promptly. 'And what would you do with it?' I asked him. 'Treble the size of the army'.[12]

Loraine, the British minister in Tehran, noted with no little admiration Reza Khan's enthusiasm for and inculcation of the 'military spirit', also noting that it was dependent upon the force of character of the Minister of War. 'One could hardly imagine a country less disposed than Persia to the growth of a military spirit, but we are already in the presence of the apparition of that spirit'.[13] Needless to say this enthusiasm for the military, its primacy over all other organs of government and the general trend towards the militarisation of society which it presaged did not bode well for civil–military relations in the Pahlavi era.

The construction of this new army was not an easy task, and it would be fair to say that it was very much forged on campaign. While not always successful in the field, it proved successful enough to provide itself and its commander with a momentum which was increasingly irresistible. Reza Khan first had to suppress the Gendarmerie revolts in Tabriz and Mashhad led by rival contenders for the mantle of military saviour, Major Lahuti and Colonel Muhammad Taqi Khan Paysan. Lahuti's uprising in Tabriz was swiftly dispersed by the better-armed Cossacks and the aspiring revolutionary fled to the Soviet Union where he developed a new career as a revolutionary poet. Paysan was more unfortunate, in that he was prematurely killed in a skirmish with Kurds near Astarabad. Had he survived, he may have posed a serious challenge to Reza Khan's military ascendancy.[14] Somewhat fortuitously therefore, opposition from key elements in the Gendarmerie were swiftly dispensed with, although friction between the two branches of the new 'model' army continued.[15] These relatively easy victories were followed by the collapse of the hitherto threatening *Jangali* movement in the Caspian littoral province of Gilan.

The *Jangali* movement (Forest Movement), as has been noted above, was the name given to the Committee of Islamic Unity led by one Mirza Kuchik Khan, whose disgust at the actions of the central government in Tehran had encouraged him to lead an uprising in the northern province of Gilan. The movement had since been tarnished by its association with the Bolsheviks who had landed troops in Enzeli in 1920, ostensibly to recover equipment left behind by the White Russians, despite the fact that Mirza Kuchik Khan's rising predated the Bolshevik Revolution in Russia. Indeed there is little evidence to suggest that Mirza Kuchik Khan was an avowed socialist, but his decision to ally himself with Haydar Khan, a socialist revolutionary from Tabriz and to avail himself of the logistical support of the Soviet Union, caused consternation among the traditional elites in Tehran. The proclamation of the Gilan Republic and the formation of the Communist Party of Iran in July 1920 only served to accentuate fears. The government in Tehran quickly sought to come to terms with the Soviet Union and negotiations were held leading to the Perso-Russian Treaty of 1921, which saw the removal of Russian troops and the convenient declaration by the Communist Party of Iran that the Iranian revolution had to wait until the full development of a 'bourgeois' society.[16] The actual signing of this agreement came several days after the coup in Tehran, leaving a much more aggressive government to reap the fruits of the negotiations. The movement, having thus been deprived of both military support and ideological conviction, was ripe for an assault by the new central government. But to make matters worse, Reza Khan's careful cultivation of the Russians (to ensure their departure) convinced Mirza Kuchik Khan that he had been betrayed by his erstwhile socialist allies. As a result, he turned on Haydar Khan thus engaging in a divisive internal conflict at the very moment when unity was essential. As a result, the army division sent to bring Kuchik Khan to heel found the occupation of Rasht, the provincial capital, a relatively uneventful affair. Kuchik Khan fled the government's forces and suffered an ignominious end, freezing to death in the wilderness, while the other leaders either capitulated or fled to the Soviet Union. Kuchik Khan's frozen body was discovered, unceremoniously decapitated and his head displayed for all to see in Tehran. This 'victory' more than the others earned Reza Khan the gratitude of the traditional elites as the threat not only of separatism but Bolshevism seemed to vanish in the face of the determination of the Minister of War. Subsequent campaigns were not as easy, but they were relatively successful and earned Reza Khan the praise of the literati and the gratitude of the ruling classes. Between 1922 and 1925 successive campaigns were launched against the Kurds, Shahsavans, Lurs, Baluchis, Turcomans and, most significantly, a British protégé, the Sheikh of Mohammerah in the oil-rich province of 'Arabistan'.

Ever since the discovery of oil by William Knox-D'Arcy in south-west Iran in 1908 and the acquisition by the British government of a 'golden share' in the newly formed Anglo-Persian Oil Company (APOC), Britain had had a strategic interest in the political security of the province of Arabistan/Khuzestan. In the absence of central government forces, Britain had found it prudent to cultivate links with the local rulers, in this case the Arab Sheikh of Mohammerah. Rumours mounted, particularly in Tehran, that Britain intended ultimately to detach the province from the rest of Iran and invest sovereign powers in the Sheikh. In light of the break up of the Ottoman Empire and the creation of myriad new states under British protection in the Persian Gulf in the 1920s, this rumour could not easily be dismissed as mere fiction. Reza Khan moved cautiously against Sheikh Khazal, probably anxious about the position of the British but also aware that serious resistance would make any campaign, at such a distance from Tehran, potentially hazardous. A previous detachment which had advanced on Khuzestan in 1922 had been routed by Bakhtiari tribesmen. It was probably correct to assess the British position as crucial to any successful outcome, and it may be said that Reza Khan's greatest triumph in this campaign was won not against Sheikh Khazal but with Sir Percy Loraine, whose responsibility it was to formulate the British position. Loraine was increasingly of the view that Sheikh Khazal's position was untenable and that some form of submission to the central government and Reza Khan in particular was inevitable. The decision was taken to abandon their protégé and concentrate their efforts on Reza Khan. Indeed Loraine's assessment in May 1923 that full submission to the army would be no more than 18 months away proved highly prophetic, and it was perhaps this decision more than the events of 1921 which consolidated Reza Khan's power.[17] Demands by the central government, encouraged by Millspaugh (see below), that the Sheikh, as an Iranian subject, should pay his taxes to Tehran, brought matters to a head, and on 6 November 1924 Reza Khan personally led an expeditionary force to the south. Faced with overwhelming force, and lacking any form of British support, the Sheikh quickly submitted and placed himself at the mercy of his new overlord.

News of the triumph reverberated around Tehran and only further confirmed Reza Khan's dominance of the political process. Indeed the submission of Khazal was more a political than a military triumph and, while the image being constructed of Reza Khan was that of a military leader triumphantly leading his troops against rebels and separatists, as Khazal's submission indicates the actual level of fighting was not extensive. This is not to detract from Reza Khan's achievement, but only to emphasise a distinctive quality of politics in Iran which Reza Khan, initially at least, clearly understood. War in Iran was as much about the threat of force as the use of force; it was in a very intimate way a 'continuation of politics by an admixture of other means'. For many of the tribal groups suppressed in the first instance by Reza Khan, it was enough to be faced by overwhelming force for them to submit, for submission could now take place with honour. The central government they had previously dismissed, with justification, as ineffectual had been replaced by one which clearly exuded power – in particular personal power – and that is why it was essential for Reza Khan to go personally to Khuzestan and receive the submission of the Sheikh. In this respect, Reza Khan was following a traditional form of tribal politics, reflected also in the governmental politics of the capital. Where he differed from tradition was in his subsequent treatment of those who had submitted.

Cultivating the myth of the saviour

It says much of the Constitutional Revolution and the intellectual foundations that underpinned it that nationalism – in all its diverse varieties – soon became the lingua franca of Iranian political discourse. It remained of course an elite discourse but this did not make nationalism an insignificant force. The vast patron–client networks which characterised traditional Iranian society meant that the elites were not alienated from society as a whole; on the contrary, they extended deep roots throughout society. The new mood of nationalism was not lost upon foreign observers, not least Loraine, who noted on his return to Iran in 1921 that 'it seems to me that there is a far more effective and coherent public opinion than when I formerly knew this country and it is intensely nationalistic'.[18]

With the emergence of Reza Khan, the nationalists, especially the secular variety, were provided with manifest proof of their salvation. In 1921, Reza Khan was but one possible contender for this mantle, but with the demise of potential rivals such as Paysan, the field was clear, and Reza Khan cultivated the myth of the saviour. As noted above, he would be the 'Enlightened Despot' rescuing the floundering Iranian revolution, providing the necessary force to implement the policies of centralisation and modernisation. As one historian has noted,

> In the early years of Reza Khan's rise to power, he was seen as a modernising reformer who could give Iran national unity and restore the country's pride and independence. The reformist intelligentsia rallied behind Reza Khan, perceiving him as a stabilising, nationalist force.[19]

As Reza Khan brought a succession of rebels and provincial autocrats to heel, the sympathetic views of many of the intelligentsia melded into eulogy – all of which served to magnify the importance of Reza Khan to the nationalist programme of revitalisation. The famous revolutionary poet Arif Qazvini, who had formerly been a supporter of Paysan, wrote:

> The winds of the Sardar Sepah [one of the titles of Reza Khan] will revive this country from the verge of destruction. As long as the mullahs and the Qajars remain, who knows what dishonour will befall the country of Cyrus? . . . If the crown and throne of Anushiravan and Jam had any honour, this beggar king [Ahmad Shah] has destroyed it . . . Always the people were the arbiters of the nation's destiny; it was the people who made Fereydoun and Ghobad their kings.[20]

Such allusions to Iran's pre-Islamic greatness were also made by other poets, such as Ishqri, who composed a nationalistic operetta entitled *Resurrection* in which the great kings of the past and Zoroaster returned, horrified that the great nation they had left had become so destitute.[21] Appeals to a sense of Aryan ethnicity and a pre-Islamic Zoroastrian heritage were echoed in the sentiments and actions of Reza Khan. Thus in the aftermath of the coup, Reza Khan addressed his embryonic army with the words: 'Gentlemen! Our dear homeland stands in urgent need of its brave sons . . . Be alert and diligent: the dust of Ardashir is watching over you'.[22] For many Iranian intellectuals, desperate for some form of progress, Reza Khan seemed to epitomise all that they were looking for. Loraine of course was equally impressed, although other British observers were more cautious in their enthusiasm. While Loraine felt that Reza Khan was 'undoubt-edly the most striking character on the Persian political stage today',[23] Oliphant commented that Reza Khan, 'is patriotically minded and . . . may consolidate [Iran] to a degree not hitherto attained'.[24] There were of course critics both in the Majlis and in the press; these were gradually suppressed so that eventually the chorus sang with one voice. While Reza Khan sought to manipulate the Majlis elections in order to get an obedient chamber, his first task was to circumscribe the press, a relatively easier task given the continued existence of martial law. Recalcitrant and obstreperous newspaper editors were punished by floggings, or their newspapers were closed down. Such treatment soon reached the ears of Majlis deputies who protested the unlawful actions of the Minister of War. Sayyid Mudarris was perhaps too hasty when he replied,

> We have no fear of Reza Khan. Why should we speak with reserve? We must speak frankly. We have the power to dismiss and to change the government, the Shah and everyone else. We can also dismiss Reza Khan if we so desire, and nothing is easier . . . The authority of the Majlis is supreme . . . However, the good qualities of the Minister of War outweigh his bad ones . . . He is a mere fly on the face of our nation. In my opinion the Minister of War has major merits and minor defects.[25]

For the nationalists, Reza Khan was the vehicle through which their agenda would be implemented. He was a tool of political action, undoubtedly more important than 'a mere fly on the face of [the] nation', but dispensable all the same. The Minister of War did not see things in quite the same way. By 1923 he had become Prime Minister and was pushing through fundamental social and political reforms to the fabric of the country, the success of which, he emphasised, was dependent on him. Far from being a cipher, Reza Khan was redefining Iranian nationalism around his person and making it dependent on his continued existence. This was the start of a 'dynastic nationalism' which would propel Reza Khan towards the throne and provide the ideological umbrella under which other varieties of nationalism would hopefully coalesce. But first the civilian administration had to be reformed and dominated.

Domination of the Majlis and civilian reforms

Reza Khan grew increasingly intolerant and distrustful of the traditional elites whom he felt were too engrossed in their personal feuds and interests to either recognise or understand the wider issues at hand. There was also, undoubtedly, some bitterness at the way in which he felt they treated him, complaining more than once that they were constantly ungrateful. At one stage he even offered to resign, telling his officers at the Ministry of War: 'Certain objections were made lately against my person. If my painstaking labours are not known to all, at least my own conscience is aware of their sincerity of purpose'.[26] However, Reza Khan was a shrewd political operator and, while later during his reign he showed a brashness and insensitivity which made him many enemies, during his ascendancy he revealed a nuanced understanding of the various factions and social groups which permeated the political landscape. He chose his allies carefully and according to circumstance, so that during Seyyed Zia's brief premiership he cast himself as the protector of tradition against those who would pursue radical reform. Within a year, as he felt more secure in his position as Minister of War, Reza Khan was manoeuvring to establish a firm grip on the civilian levers of power, in particular the legislature. While pacifying the Majlis with an offer to lift martial law and transfer all financial matters to the Ministry of Finance, as well as offering his resignation (which was rejected), he worked on securing allies among the deputies. He was supported in this strategy by two very able lieutenants who in every way epitomised the liberal, radical intelligentsia, and who put their full weight behind the aspiring strong man of Iran. Ali Akbar Davar, a Swiss-educated lawyer, and Mirza Abdul Hussein Khan Teymourtache, one of the largest landowners in Khorasan, provided the intellectual muscle behind Reza Khan's brute force. Along with Prince Firuz Farmanfarmaian, a scion of the Qajar royal house, they formed the potent triumvirate which effectively moulded modern Iran behind the protective shield provided by Reza Khan.

In 1922, the government sought the services of an American to organise and administer governmental finances. Attempts to bring Morgan Shuster back failed and in his place a delegation of 11 men arrived headed by Arthur Millspaugh. Millspaugh demanded and received considerable powers with which to reorganise the finances of the country. Reza Khan cultivated his friendship and both men developed an initially amicable rapport, with Reza Khan transferring much of his financial responsibilities to Millspaugh in return for a generous monthly grant which he would use for the upkeep of the army. This reorganisation of the finances brought him the gratitude of the traditional merchant classes (*bazaaris*), and some 200 signed an open letter to the Minister of War praising his achievements for the country:

> Before our beloved commander saved us, the Islamic Empire of Iran was fast disintegrating. The army had collapsed, the tribes were looting, the country was the laughing-stock of the world. Thanks to the army commander, we now travel without fear, admire our country and enjoy the fruits of law and order.[27]

By the end of 1923 he had so successfully undermined his opponents that Ahmad Shah reluctantly appointed him Prime Minister.

Increasingly dominant in the domestic politics of the country, Reza Khan gradually moved towards the new 'Reformist' Party, headed by Davar and

Teymourtache. In 1923, Davar issued a manifesto with a programme of changes which the party would pursue should it achieve a majority in the Majlis. Among the policies to be pursued were a reorganisation of the provincial administration on a 'rational' basis, the settlement of the tribes, separation of politics from religion, full constitutionalism, the implementation of a welfare system, universal free education and the propagation of the Persian language both within the country and abroad.[28] It was a bold programme, and the Prime Minister was not in a hurry to pin his colours to Davar's party. Instead he continued to maintain his alliance of convenience with the conservative factions, upholding traditional values in return for their continued support. This relationship of mutual convenience came to a head by the end of the Fourth Majlis, when Reza Khan introduced a bill implementing universal conscription for a period of two years. As he saw it, conscription would produce the national army he craved. It would also substantially increase the reserves of manpower at his disposal. The traditional elites in the Majlis, the landowners and the *ulema* were not impressed. For many landowners conscription would not only deprive them of labour, it would also erode their local power by taking youths away to be 'indoctrinated' elsewhere. For the *ulema*, the thought of youths being taken away from their traditional environment, with everything that entailed, was anathema. For the secular nationalists allied with Reza Khan, conscription was the vehicle through which a *unified* nation would be built and Reza Khan was the 'revolutionary leader' who would implement it.

The Fourth Majlis had taken measures to rationalise the civil service, with competitive entrance examinations and a table of ranks. The Fifth Majlis ratified a reform package far bolder and with far more profound consequences for the social fabric of the country. In order to get the measures passed, Reza Khan ensured that only supportive deputies were elected. Election manipulation was assisted by the fact that the Minister of Interior was a general, but local detachments also made sure that votes went to the right candidates. The result was a triumph for the Reformists and their allies the Socialists, who together provided the legislative muscle for the Prime Minister's programme. The Fifth Majlis convened on 11 February 1924 and promptly passed the following package of reforms:[29]

- Compulsory two-year military service;
- A cut in the court budget;
- The abolition of decorative court titles, which had become the hallmark of the Qajar Court;
- A statutory obligation on all citizens to obtain birth certificates and to register a family name;
- Taxes levied on tea, sugar and income in order to finance the proposed trans-Iranian railway;
- Standardised weights and measures;
- Reform of the country's calendar replacing the lunar *hegri* year with the older Iranian solar year as the official calendar (still dated from the Prophet's Hegira to Medina) and replacing the Muslim names of the months with Persian ones.[30]

While some date the beginning of the 'new order' in Iran to the coup of 1921, that is probably only true in terms of the state and elite politics, and it remains very much a retrospective judgement. However, the reforms ratified by the Fifth Majlis served notice in no uncertain terms to society as a whole that a new order had arrived and that the revolution promised in 1906 was beginning to take effect. Not only were communities to be dislocated and a nation constructed through conscription, but traditional methods of kinship recognition and the way societies related to each other, were being transformed by the statutory obligation to register a surname. This was to have profound consequences often overlooked by historians. Surnames were an alien concept to most Iranians, who identified themselves either by their locality or through paternal lineage, and, if senior enough, by titular rank (although these had just been abolished).[31] The adoption of surnames resulted in a great deal of confusion as traditional reference points were eliminated overnight. But it had another effect: it allowed for better, more efficient administration and, arguably, control of the population. State and society, which had hitherto enjoyed an ambiguous and amorphous relationship, mediated by numerous tiers of government, were being rationalised. And as the state became more focused, defined and rationalised, so it began the process of defining and rationalising society. 'Modernity' had arrived.

Reza Khan took for himself the surname 'Pahlavi' in an explicit bid to associate himself and his family with the glories of pre-Islamic Iran. 'Pahlavi' was the name given to Middle Persian, the language of Sassanian Iran, though there is evidence he was unaware of the origins of the name.[32] A publication carrying the date July–August 1924 (Dhu al Hijja 1342) entitled *Shahanshah Pahlavi* (itself an indication of the presence of dynastic nationalism and ambition prior to the deposition of the Qajar dynasty) argues that the name means 'civilised', 'free' and was accorded to the best of people during the Sassanian period. Indeed it argues that it was the family name of the Sassanian 'tribe' (*ta'efeh*) and this remarkable lineage represented the purest of Iranians – a formidable claim which would seek to provide Reza Khan with a royal pedigree without comparison.[33] By associating himself with this name, Reza Khan made the first tentative, if profound, step in reinventing his past in order to suit present (imperial) pretensions. For the time being, however, imperial ambitions were set aside, as Reza Khan and the country sought to debate the merits of the last proposed reform of the Fifth Majlis – the decision to declare a republic.

The 'republican' intermezzo

Republicanism had been gaining ground among certain members of the intelligentsia and had even divided loyalties within the army.[34] There is little doubt that Reza Khan was influenced by developments in Turkey, and although the British legation notes that he had dismissed notions of a republic as early as 1923 following a trip to Qom,[35] there is evidence that he toyed with the idea a little while longer, encouraging the media to publish articles in favour of republicanism while at the same time attacking the decadent Qajars.[36] Such ridicule of the

Qajars of course served to elevate the person of Reza Khan, who was perceived as everything the Qajars were not.

The journal *Iranshahr*, in an editorial entitled 'Republicanism and Social Revolution', argued that, 'Today almost all of Europe, including Russia, has adopted the republican system of government. There is no doubt in our minds that in the modern age the republican form of government is the best system of government'.[37] Poets and writers were also reported to have been paid to ridicule the Qajar, Ahmad Shah, and write favourably about the republican movement. The poet Arif wrote a poem entitled 'The Republican March' which included the following lines: 'From the Angel Gabriel, afar, hear the soul stirring soul of Pahlavi, Arif, may Sardar Sepah [Reza Khan] live long in Iran, for he will lead the country facing extinction to its survival'.[38] When the Fifth Majlis eventually decided to draw up a bill for the abolition of the monarchy, the deputies avidly scrutinised the American Constitution.[39]

However, while important and indeed significant sections of the secular intelligentsia and professionals such as army officers supported the idea of a republic, often with some vigour, they miscalculated the popular response. In this respect they echoed the assumptions and mistakes of their forebears who, during the Constitutional Revolution, sought to lead the popular will without necessarily connecting to it. This connection still remained very much a monopoly of the *ulema*, although reservations about republicanism were not exclusively their preserve. This growing concern over the consequences of a republic provoked a strong traditionalist surge, led by the most important members of the *ulema*, against such a development, and even some members of the liberal intelligentsia, fearful of possible dictatorship, sought refuge in tradition. Indeed, this fear was very real and it bound hitherto unsuspecting allies together to prevent the unchecked rise of what remained an unknown quantity. Mudarris, a staunch opponent of Reza Khan, was also known to be working against the establishment of a republic.[40] Refuge was sought in tradition and ironically a move intended to rid the country of 'royal and clerical despotism' instead resulted in a consolidation of royal and clerical tradition, a consequence Reza Khan could not ignore nor was he indeed inclined to. On 4 March 1924 it was noted that the *ulema* in Qom had declared a republic to be contrary to Islam, and indeed would mean the end of Islam.[41] In the face of such opposition, Reza Khan 'bowed' to establishment pressure and, as he had detached himself from Seyyed Zia Tabatabaie in 1921, now he moved again to position himself firmly with the traditionalists.[42] Indeed, according to one recent interpretation of events, Reza Khan actively cultivated *ulema* support in order to restore some of his battered prestige following the apparent unpopularity of republicanism.[43] Although he dominated the organisations and institutions of power, Reza Khan found himself curiously out of touch with popular opinion beyond the fringes of the media. Reza Khan's hegemony was in many ways a fragile beast.[44]

On 1 April 1924, Reza Khan had decided emphatically against the institution of a republic, issuing a declaration which made clear his alliance with the traditionalists:

[F]rom the very first both I and, indeed, the whole army have considered the care and the preservation of the glory of Islam as one of the greatest of our duties and objectives, and have always striven that Islam might advance daily in the path of progress and exaltation, and that the honour owed to sanctity might be completely observed and respected, therefore at the time when I went to Kum [sic] to bid farewell to the ulema, I took the opportunity of exchanging views with them, and finally we decided that it was expedient to proclaim to the whole people that the question of the republic be dropped.[45]

The fact that he publicly acknowledged his discussion with the *ulema*, and that the decision was made after consultation, undoubtedly strengthened his position with the traditionalists and the *ulema* in particular. Here, apparently, was a man who would compromise with the traditional sources of authority and whose reformist zeal was tempered by respect for tradition.

Arguably, political weakness forced such a compromise by Reza Khan, and the traditionalist fear of an Ataturkist dictatorship was to a considerable extent assuaged by the alternative trajectory of a dynastic change rather than an abolition of the monarchy.[46] However, this was by no means a smooth process and although the Majlis began discussions for the deposition of the Qajars in 1924, the actual deposition was not ratified by the Majlis until 31 October 1925, when the government was temporarily entrusted to Reza Khan Pahlavi 'pending the establishment of a final form of government'.[47] This delay reflected the divisions between deputies and within the political elites, many of whom remained resistant to the idea of a dynastic change.[48] Within a month it was becoming apparent that Reza Khan would soon become Reza Shah, though it was still not clear whether he would be a transitional monarch 'for life' or would actually found a new dynasty, reflecting perhaps the simmering hopes of republicanism.[49] This last debate was itself resolved, with no little reluctance, in the next month, when the Majlis invested dynastic sovereignty in Reza Shah Pahlavi. The popular reaction was not positive, and while this may reflect the general detachment of many people from the political process, it is peculiar that such a significant development should have such a muted response throughout the country. The clearest recorded reaction was one of 'amazement at the audacity of Reza Khan in aspiring to kingship'.[50]

Reza Shah became king on the twin pillars of tradition and nationalism while at the same time purporting to be a force for modernisation. His first edicts acknowledged his debt to the forces of tradition by stressing the importance of Islam. He also adopted largely symbolic policies which emphasised the traditional patriarchal role of the monarch. He reduced the price of bread, urged women to be 'moral' in their everyday conduct and, in an act echoing the behaviour of the most 'just' of Iran's past rulers, he instituted a series of 'complaints boxes' through which the ordinary man could make direct appeals to the Shah.[51] Nationalism was served by the fact that the deposed dynasty was 'Turkish' as against the 'Persian' character of the Pahlavis, as noted by *The Times*,

Under the Qajars, who were Turks, the mothers of princes in the line of succession had to be members of the Royal tribe, consequently no son of a Persian mother could sit on the throne of Persia. In future this will be reversed.[52]

Notes

1 Bahar, *Brief History of Political Parties in Iran*, 2: 265, quoted in M.R. Ghods, 'Iranian Nationalism and Reza Shah', *Middle Eastern Studies* 27(1), 1991, p. 43. Bahar was a contemporary intellectual of Reza Khan and had initially supported him but later became disillusioned. His use of the term 'middle class' probably reflects his own ideological convictions. It might be more accurate to use the term 'traditional classes'.

2 J. Tulard, *Napoleon: The Myth of the Saviour* (trans. Waugh). London: Methuen, 1984, p. 350.

3 British diplomatic sources, however, date it earlier to 1873; see FO 371 E3366/3366/34 dated 2 August 1927, *Leading Personalities in Persia*.

4 Complaining bitterly about his inability to make Iranian parliamentarians 'understand' Loraine noted that he 'completely disarmed him' with reference to a Persian colloquialism that totally belied his lack of formal education: 'When a wise man argues with a fool', he told Loraine, 'the greater part of the blame lies with the wise man'. FO 371 11481 E397 dated 18 January 1926, Loraine's assessment of Reza Shah.

5 The idea of an injection of 'new blood' remains a common trope in Iranian history. Some needless to say had their initial enthusiasm tempered by the reality of the 'Cossack' in Reza Khan, see Malek ol Shoara Bahar's reflections in S. Meskoob, 'Nationalism, Centralisation of Power and Culture in the Twilight of the Qajars and the Dawn of the Pahlavis', *Iran-Nameh* 12(3), Summer 1994, pp. 483, 496–7.

6 See *Kaveh* 4 September 1921, p. 3. For further details of Taqizadeh's views see 'Taqizadeh and European Civilisation', *Iran*, 54(1), 2016, pp. 47–57. For details of the 23 points see A.M. Ansari, *The Politics of Nationalism in Modern Iran*. Cambridge: Cambridge University Press, 2012, pp. 62–3.

7 M.P. Zirinsky, 'Imperial Power and Dictatorship: Britain and the Rise of Reza Shah, 1921–1926', *International Journal of Middle Eastern Studies* 24, 1992, p. 646.

8 D. Wilbur, *Reza Shah Pahlavi: The Resurrection and Reconstruction of Iran*. New York: Mazda, 1975, pp. 62–3.

9 See A. Ashraf, 'Conspiracy Theories', *Encyclopædia Iranica*, www.iranicaonline.org/articles/conspiracy-theories.

10 See Zirinsky, 'Imperial Power and Dictatorship', p. 639. Later British views were less circumspect. For instance, a British Embassy report from 1932 concedes that the British put Reza Shah 'on the throne', FO 371 16077 E2844 dated 8 June 1932. Antony Eden's memoirs are also explicit about Britain's role in putting Reza Khan in power.

11 Wilbur, *Reza Shah Pahlavi*, p. 95.

12 A.E. Powell, *By Camel and Car to the Peacock Throne*. Garden City, NY: Garden City Publishing, 1923, p. 298.

13 Loraine, FO 371 9024 E4612 dated 7 May 1923.

14 This is certainly a view argued by S. Cronin, *The Army and the Creation of the Pahlavi State in Iran, 1910–1926*. London: I.B. Tauris, 1997, pp. 11–12. See also S. Cronin, 'Opposition to Reza Khan within the Iranian Army, 1921–26', *Middle Eastern Studies* 30(4), October 1994, pp. 724–50.

15 For a detailed analysis of the construction of the new army and the frictions which persisted see Cronin, *The Army*.

16 See H. Katouzian, 'Nationalist Trends in Iran, 1921–1926', *International Journal of Middle Eastern Studies* 10, 1979, p. 535.

17 Loraine, FO 371 9024 E4612 dated 7 May 1923.
18 Loraine, FO 371 6408 E14290 dated 23 December 1921.
19 Ghods, 'Iranian Nationalism and Reza Shah', p. 37.
20 Quoted in Ghods, 'Iranian Nationalism and Reza Shah', p. 42.
21 S.R. Shafaq, 'Patriotic Poetry in Modern Iran', *Middle East Journal* 6(4), 1952, pp. 417–28.
22 Quoted in Wilbur, *Reza Shah Pahlavi*, p. 61.
23 Loraine, FO 371 7804 E102 dated 31 January 1922.
24 Quoted in Zirinsky, 'Imperial Power and Dictatorship', p. 653.
25 From Hussein Makki, *Tarikh-e Bist Saleh*, quoted in Wilbur, *Reza Shah Pahlavi*, p. 67.
26 Quoted in Wilbur, *Reza Shah Pahlavi*, p. 67.
27 Makki, *Tarikh-e Bist Saleh* II, 36–7, quoted in Abrahamian, *Iran between Two Revolutions*. Princeton, NJ: Princeton University Press, 1982, p. 131.
28 Davar's political party, FO 371 9024 E6348 dated 14 May 1923.
29 FO 371 [. . .] E2431/455/34 dated 16 February 1924.
30 Iran essentially utilised three forms of dating with the Muslim lunar calendar taking pride of place alongside the solar calendar and the Turkic calendar. This reform ensured that the solar calendar became the official calendar although both the lunar and Turkic calendars remained in use despite government protestations. See M. Roostai, *Tarikh nokhostin farhangestan-e iran beh ravayet asnad* (A Documentary History of the First Farhangestan). Tehran: Nashreney, 1385/2006, pp. 84–5.
31 I owe this insight to Professor Farhang Rajaee.
32 Wilbur, *Reza Shah Pahlavi*, p. 229 notes that Reza Shah asked Ernst Herzfield what the name actually meant. Recent commentators have suggested that the 'Pahlavis' were one of the seven great aristocratic clans of the Achaemenian period.
33 It is possible that the date 1342 alludes to the solar calendar dating it at May 1963, yet the history recorded certainly does not carry on further than 1925 (suggesting perhaps that the actual publication date post-dated the author's dated introduction). The fact that it uses Islamic months seems to indicate that it predates the reform of the calendar. Furthermore, there are none of the characteristic references to his son that would have appeared on official publications of this date.
34 For a comprehensive discussion see Vanessa Martin, 'Mudarris, Republicanism and the Rise to Power of Reza Khan, Sardar Sipah', *British Journal of Middle Eastern Studies* 21(2), 1994, pp. 199–210.
35 FO 371 10145 E3748 proclamation dated 29 April 1923.
36 FO 371 [. . .] E3512/255/34 Intelligence summary dated 1 March 1924. Money was also allocated to sympathetic members of the clergy. See also FO 371 [. . .] E3944/255/34. See also FO 371 [. . .] E3743/455/34, a useful diary of events on the republican movement, dated 1 April 1924 which notes, 'The abuse of the Kajars was accompanied by the most flattering remarks and praise of the Serdar Sepah, whom the papers proposed to elect President of the future republic'.
37 H. Kazemzadeh, 'Republicanism and the Social Revolution, *Iranshahr* 2, February 1924, pp. 257–8. Quoted in Abrahamian, *Iran between Two Revolutions*, p. 133.
38 Quoted in Wilbur, *Reza Shah Pahlavi*, p. 76.
39 See Martin, 'Mudarris', p. 203; Wilbur, *Reza Shah Pahlavi*, p. 77.
40 FO 371 [. . .] E3945/255/34 Intelligence summary dated 15 March 1924.
41 FO 371 [. . .] E3944/255/34 Intelligence summary dated 8 March 1924.
42 The apparent confusion over the popular status of republicanism can be witnessed in the pages of *The Times* which carried two differing reports dated 19 March 1924.
43 Martin, 'Mudarris', p. 210. See also FO 371 [. . .] E3743/455/34 dated 1 April 1924, reports Reza Khan's indecision and uncertainty over the popular response to republicanism.
44 An interesting example of the rebellious nature of Iranian society is recounted by Katouzian in 'Nationalist Trends in Iran', p. 539, where the unfavourable popular

response to Reza Khan's authoritarian edict in the aftermath of the coup was recorded in no uncertain terms by a member of the Tehran populace.

45 FO 371 [. . .] E3748/455/34 enclosure, Prime Minister's proclamation from *Sitareh Iran* dated 1 April 1924.

46 FO 371/Persia 1926/34–11500 Annual report for 1925.

47 *The Times*, 31 October 1925. Although there was apparently little general interest in the deposition of the Qajars, there were reports that members of the clergy and merchants had 'expressed amazement at the audacity of Reza Khan in aspiring to kingship'. See FO 371 [. . .] E7529/18/34 dated 19 November 1925.

48 Among the prominent opponents of the dynastic change were Mohammad Mosaddeq and Hasan Taqizadeh, for details of the debate see Ansari, *The Politics of Nationalism in Modern Iran*, pp. 80–82.

49 FO 371 10840 E7540 dated 21 November 1925. Republicanism remained a strong sentiment among certain sections of the elite and professional classes.

50 Loraine to Chamberlain, FO 371 [. . .] E7529/18/34 dated 19 November 1925.

51 FO 371 10840 E7219/E7532 dated 23 November, 8 December 1925.

52 *The Times*, 13 December 1925. This was also commented upon by the British Embassy; see FO 371 10840 E7677.

8 Reza Shah
Modernisation and tradition, 1926–41

It is often considered that Reza Shah was the quintessential moderniser. The Shah who dragged Iran 'kicking and screaming' into the modern age, whose faults are surpassed by his monumental achievements, was possessed of a determination misunderstood and unappreciated by many of his countrymen. Much like Ataturk, argued his supporters, Reza Shah's achievements would only be fully recognised long after he had gone. There is much to be commended in this argument, though the more fulsome praise awarded by royalists – especially their conviction that Reza Shah was Iran's man of destiny, favoured by providence to save the country – is clearly the product of an ideological interpretation of the historical record and one, like all such interpretations, which tends to obscure the complex reality behind the myth. The panegyrics for Reza Shah had begun during his rise to power and while he was still Prime Minister. Praise continued after his accession to the throne, actively encouraged by Reza Shah, with increasing emphasis on his importance to the development of a modern Iran.

While the intelligentsia craved a saviour who would implement the national project for rejuvenation, Reza Shah increasingly encouraged a different interpretation, one which realigned the focus of attention away from the nation and onto himself and his dynasty. While the Court Minister, Teymourtache, could privately argue that Reza Shah was a necessary transition towards a republic, with himself as the first Iranian president, Reza Shah's agenda was entirely different. Having overcome his earlier dilemma as to whether to choose a republic or a monarchy, Reza Shah now emphatically pursued the monarchical route, developing a thesis which would later be extended by his son that, without the dynasty, the nation would cease to exist. It was a subtle shift in the doctrine of nationalism which placed the dynasty on a par with if not superior to the nation. Far from being the first servant of the state, Reza Shah was becoming a prerequisite for its continued existence. The inherent contradiction implicit in the juxtaposition of a traditional monarchy with the institutions of the modern state, and the desire to implement a legal-rational model of government, would be resolved through loyalty to the dynasty and the development of a dynastic nationalism which would incorporate these diverse trends.

For royalists this synthesis was achieved, but for the vast majority of the population the myth was too large to swallow. Many accepted his not insubstantial achievements along with his faults; others were increasingly alienated by his tendency towards what was seen as dictatorship, an altogether modern autocracy distinct from traditional Iranian monarchy; still others emphasised the traditional institution Reza Shah represented, the method of his rise to power and his creation of a tribe (the Pahlavi army) in the absence of one. As one historian has argued, 'Traditionalism and patrimonialism, and not any ideological blueprint guided his rule'.[1] There is much indeed to commend all three interpretations, and in truth they reflected different aspects of his rule. The modern Iranian state is very much that which was created and developed during the rule of Reza Shah, though it would be incorrect to accord him the credit for its design which he inherited from the Constitutionalists. Indeed, while he was probably a more instinctive than ideological ruler, his instincts were undoubtedly shaped by the ideas that framed the age within which he operated and which were mediated through the officials (largely Constitutionalists) whom he employed.[2] He ruled with distinctly modern tools of government, an army and a bureaucracy, and he sought to change society not manage it. At the same time, he acquired enough land to make him the largest landowner in the country with accumulated interests that led him to have much in common with the traditional landed aristocracy. His pursuit of change was constrained by this interest. His government was a personal one, which on the one hand allowed his energy and drive to permeate different aspects of government, but on the other exposed him as a patrimonial ruler – traditionalist, nationalist and modernist – as traditional as his predecessors. Reza Shah, as we shall see, was an amalgam of all three, an incomplete synthesis whose inherent contradictions created as many problems for the Iranian state as his zealous determination solved.

The invention of tradition

As the first 'truly' Iranian monarch in living memory, Reza Shah was anxious to have a coronation ceremony which would reflect his pedigree. The coronation ceremony, whose organisation was by all accounts haphazard, was the first event in which this aspect of the monarchy could be advertised both to a domestic audience and to those international dignitaries who would be present. It was important therefore to emphasise nationalistic symbols, but also to stress their deep historic roots. Thus the coronation ceremony, although replete with nationalist imagery, paid considerable heed to tradition, both authentic and invented, more than may have been expected from a modernising monarch. Although, as Loraine noted, difficulties arose when officials failed to discover the correct procedure of previous coronations. The only real guideline was that the crown had to be placed on the head of the Shah by the eldest member of the Imperial family, a possibility made less likely for a 'dynasty of humble origin and recent creation'. In the event, the corona-tion ceremony was modelled upon the non-religious portions of the British coronation ceremony, while the act of crowning would be performed by the Shah himself.[3] The *ulema* were present and there was no music in deference to religious sensibilities.

As the Shah sat on the throne, the *Imam-Jomeh* of Tehran proceeded with a speech sprinkled with verses from the Qur'an. Following this, the Minister of Court, Teymourtache, proceeded towards the throne with the 'Pahlavi crown' which, according to Loraine, combined, 'the forms and *motifs* of European regalia with those of the tiaras of the Achaemenid and Sassanian dynasties'. The crown was delivered to the Shah by both the Minister of Court and the 'aged mullah of Khoi', another symbolic gesture to the *ulema*, and was promptly placed by the Shah upon his head, thus associating himself not only with modernisation, but with Iran's ancient dynasties. Additional regalia included the sword of Nader Shah and a royal sceptre, which the Shah wore, while other artefacts of royalty not worn by the Shah included the swords of Shah Abbas the Great and Shah Ismail, Nader Shah's bow and Shah Ismail's armour.

The twin themes of tradition and nationalism were evident in the Shah's coro-nation speech in which he stressed that

> the object to which my special attention has been and will be directed is the safeguarding of religion and the strengthening of its basis, because I deem this as a measure which is beneficial for national unity and to the social mor-als of Persia.[4]

This was followed by a speech from the Prime Minister, in which he encouraged the Shah to live up to the standards set by his illustrious predecessors, liber-ally quoting from the *Shahnameh*, and alluding to both Iran's real and mythical inheritance, after which the Shah left the palace in a glass coach flanked by out-riders, although the presence of detachments of tribal levies in national costumes provided a more 'authentic' national and traditional flavour. Indeed the cere-mony was a curious mixture of the traditional and modern. Crowds gathered to watch the passing state procession and while, according to Loraine, 'His Imperial Majesty was greeted by the populace with spasmodic hand-clapping', there was 'no exuberance of enthusiasm'.[5] The whole ceremony has been captured evoca-tively by Vita Sackville-West, who wrote that despite all the imperfections, Reza Shah was possessed of a certain majesty. Indeed her description of the new dynast is worth quoting:

> In appearance Reza was an alarming man, six foot three in height, with a sullen manner, huge nose, grizzled hair, and a brutal jowl; he looked, in fact, what he was, a Cossack trooper; but there was no denying that he had a kingly presence.[6]

The continuation of reform: nationalism and modernisation

For at least the first half of his rule, Reza Shah was aided by a handful of extremely competent officials, one of whom was undoubtedly a key driver of many of the reforms.[7] As the British embassy noted in 1929,

> When in February 1927 the then Persian government was reconstituted it was very soon realised that apart from questions connected with the army, the control of the whole machinery of government was centred in three men, Teymourtache, the Minister of Court, who was outside the Cabinet but yet dominated it; Prince Firuz, the Minister of Finance; and Davar, the Minister of Justice. These three men were intimate friends and for more than two years completely controlled the situation; it was an open secret.[8]

Teymourtache was probably the most influential member of this triumvirate and he knew it. Clive later added,

> The present arrangement whereby the Minister of Court is a grand vizier in all but name would appear to be a temporary expedient, due to the personality of Teymourtache and the idiosyncrasies of the Shah. It is unconstitutional and no-one expects it to last.[9]

Mirza Abdul Hussein Khan Teymourtache was a major Khorasani landowner. Educated at a military school in St Petersburg, he spoke French and Russian well, and understood English. He had travelled throughout Europe, including Germany, France and Switzerland, and was recognised as an ardent nationalist and the main architect of the repeal of the capitulations. Prince Firuz Mirza GCMG, a great-great-grandson of Fath Ali Shah, had been educated in law at Beirut and Paris, and was a member of the Paris Bar. He was fluent in French and understood English. Ali Akbar Davar, the true technocrat, was the son of a minor court official. He studied law at Geneva University and served in a number of ministries. These three men were critical to the creation of the modern Iranian state, and while later official histories did their utmost to diminish their role in order to elevate the importance of Reza Shah, contemporaries were aware of their importance. The British legation noted that 'Taimourtache [sic] is of course the prime mover in the present Nationalist policy of the Persian government'.[10] The alliance which operated between Reza Shah and his three ministers was one of shared interest rather than mutual affection. It worked because each side saw the value of the other, and recognised each other's importance to the general cause of an Iranian national renaissance.

Reza Shah was too politically astute, however, to place his new dynasty at the mercy of three able men, in particular his aristocratic Minister of Court, whose view of the new Shah as a valuable tool of nationalist policy differed from his own perceptions. He recognised that his value lay in being the coercive wing of the new reforming government, and it was essential that he maintained a firm grip on the army, nurturing it, protecting it and cultivating its loyalty. The army was central to the survival of the dynasty and in time would make its mark on the character of the state. By extending the conscription law, Reza Shah ensured the growth of the army from 40,000 to a total of 127,000 in 1941; there was also a parallel five-fold increase in the military budget. In addition, he began the development of a small air force and a navy based in the Persian Gulf. To ensure the loyalty of this army, Reza Shah emphasised its status in society, providing career officers with a better standard of living than other state employees through higher salaries and access to cheap land. Loyalty was never automatic, however, and Reza Shah was careful to ensure that all senior generals were kept under tight control. Divisional structures were also in time abolished and replaced by regimental and brigade structures to make sure that units were small enough not to pose a challenge to the Pahlavi state. Nevertheless, despite these precautions, a British diplomatic assessment in 1930 noted that,

> Never since the Shah ascended the throne of Persia, has he been more popular than today, and if the Pahlavi regime is to fall in the near future it will be by the hand of the assassin, not by mutiny of his troops.[11]

Reza Shah and his government were intensely nationalistic.[12] They also made it rapidly clear that they would support the social pillars of tradition, in so far as they did not challenge the authority and power of the new order and its nationalist ambitions. Despite all the pretensions of the coronation, Reza Shah was not overly enamoured of the old aristocracy, nor with the *ulema*, both of which he regarded as 'reactionary' and constraints upon reform, but also, importantly, as social intermediaries, who could, and traditionally did, mediate the state's penetration of society. His disdain for the vast majority of the aristocracy was notorious and, along with his sequestration of land, it made him few friends among the members of this traditionally important social group. His treatment of the *ulema* was similarly insensitive and often, as will be seen later, brutish. A visit to Shiraz in 1929 was typical.

> The Shah ignored, or was rude to the notables, mollahs and merchants who were presented to him, and spent most time with the foreign diplomats. Indeed most Shirazis commented that he only talked to the British consul! When the group of notables were presented, 'Notables' (Ayyan!), ejaculated the Shah, that is to say muft-khur (drones living without working).[13]

At the same time, it is prudent not to over-generalise Reza Shah's relationship with the traditional pillars of the establishment. While in Abrahamian's words, life for the old upper classes 'could easily turn nasty, brutish and short',[14] there was also considerable co-option of the old elite into the establishment of the new order; the Minister of Court was one obvious example. This was an incomplete hegemony and, while the traditional elites were suppressed, they were not eliminated. Indeed, later in the reign, in line with his own position as the largest landowner in the country, considerable concessions were afforded to landlords with respect to their tenants.

However, for the present, expectations that Reza Shah would 'routinise his own charisma' and support the traditional status quo, managing but not changing society, were soon discovered to have been misplaced. The predominance of an ambitious nationalist agenda over all other aspirations was conveniently summarised by the programme of Teymourtache's Iran-i No (New Iran) Party which called for: 'The independence of Iran under the banner of Pahlavi; the progress of Iran through the power of Reza Shah to civilisation and modernity; resistance to foreign influence; opposition to all reactionary and subversive ideas'.

The party significantly pledged itself to support the Shah in a complete reform of the Iranian character, from 'lethargy to energy, from individualism to altruism, from prevarication to simple truth, from corruption to rugged honesty'.[15] The centrality of the person of the Shah and the dynasty was evident. In addition, this was to be an exclusive party in that the mullahs were a particular social group who were expressly forbidden to join, a reality which, combined with the apparently anti-Islamic flavour of the party rhetoric, drew considerable criticism and a concessionary statement from the Prime Minister that Islam would be safeguarded.[16] But it was the totality of the Pahlavi project as expressed in the *Iran-i No* manifesto which was the most audacious aspect of the reform programme. The idea that 'character' could be reformed or that at the very least the 'pure Persian' could be separated from the chaff that had accumulated around him, was one that owed more to the French Revolution than to the Constitutional Revolution. Reza Shah's government was about to embark on an exercise in social engineering, limited only by technological and administrative weakness, but nevertheless seeking to reach beyond the public sphere into the private domain of Iranian existence. Such a hegemonic project required, in so far as possible, total control. Not only were potential aristocratic rivals removed, exiled or eliminated, but other parties, such as the Socialist and Communist parties, were summarily banned in 1927. In the same year Mudarris was encouraged to take early retirement and, following the Mashhad riots of 1935, suddenly died in suspicious circumstances.

The administration of this particular programme of modernisation would be facilitated by the rationalisation of the country's cumbersome and complex bureaucracy. Ultimately, ten new ministries were established (Interior, Foreign Affairs, Justice, Finance, Education, Trade, Post and Telegraph, Agriculture, Roads and Industry), employing 90,000 civil servants drawing government salaries. The Interior Ministry in particular was thoroughly reorganised to cope with its new responsibilities for law and order, 'elections' and military conscription, while provincial administration was rationalised on the lines envisaged by Davar's Reformist Party manifesto of 1923. This rationalisation was a gradual process which eventually led in 1937 to the country being divided into six *ostans* (provinces), subdivided into *shahrestans* (counties) and further into *bakhshs* and *dehestans*.[17] These were subsequently amended, replacing the original six *ostans* with ten.[18]

Among the most serious structural changes to be addressed was the continuing existence of 'capitulatory rights' which had been offered to foreign governments throughout the previous century and which provided for extra-judicial privileges for foreign citizens. Nationalist opinion viewed them as an affront to national dignity and sovereignty and wanted their abolition. For this to be achieved, Iran needed a domestic judicial system comparable to those operating in the West, and this in turn entailed removing judicial authority from the *ulema*. The decision to abolish the 'capitulations' was announced at the opening of the new Courts of Justice on 26 April 1927[19] and the British diplomat, Clive, with a view to the position of the Anglo-Persian Oil Company, expressed concern over the possibility of implementing a new judicial system complete with laws and a trained legal profession within a year.[20] The rapidity with which the new Minister of Justice, Davar, was expected to implement the overhaul reflected a nationalist determination which superseded considerations of practicality and also revealed how concepts of modernisation took second place to the nationalist agenda. As Reza Shah noted at the opening of the Courts of Justice, 'It is not necessary for me to mention the effect of judicial reforms on the progress of the national welfare and how these reforms contribute to the national prestige'.[21] National prestige was also evident in the implementation of a number of minor reforms in which Iranians were increasingly separated and distinguished from foreigners, ranging initially from the justifiable – Iranians were no longer permitted to be hired as agents for foreign legations[22] – to (one year later) the increasingly sensitive, which required that the flags of foreign legations be flown only on special days, and that the term 'oriental' be dropped since it suggested inferiority.[23]

The traditionalists, represented in the main by the *ulema* but also containing members of the traditional middle classes (*bazaaris*), were not prepared to accept the changes without a measure of resistance. The *ulema* began to agitate against the changes in the dress code which promoted the wearing of the Pahlavi hat and short jacket, especially among government employees, as well as the reforms in the judiciary which resulted in an eight-day strike in Isfahan.[24] Although the government had not made it compulsory, there was evidence that the police and army were encouraging members of the public to make the change.[25] The other cause of discontent was the implementation of conscription which again found widespread opposition among the traditional middle class who were concerned for the social and economic consequences of losing an adult male for two years to a state organisation. The main disturbances occurred in Isfahan and Shiraz where the bazaar closed down, prompting the Shah to comment that 'the foreigners were still at work and had now succeeded in making trouble down there'. The opposition was so strong that the Shah was persuaded to compromise with the *ulema* – although the choice of Teymourtache as negotiator was undoubtedly misplaced given *ulema* misgivings – arguing that the law would not be applied rigorously for many years, and that importantly there would be an option to buy oneself out of military service.[26] There was a limit to the Shah's tolerance, however, and when the Queen was allegedly insulted by a mullah in Qom for apparently 'revealing' too much while visiting a shrine, Reza Shah reacted ferociously, reportedly entering the shrine with his boots on and beating the chief of police as well as the mullah in question.[27] While some applauded his actions, many more were scandalised by his behaviour, particularly within the confines of a shrine.[28] Later in the year, following a visit by the King and Queen of Afghanistan, when the latter had appeared unveiled, Reza Shah used the opportunity to relax the strict dress code for women.

Indeed, any compromise represented only a temporary respite for the traditionalists as the emphasis shifted towards revisions in the dress code for men. The imposition of the new dress code, although incremental, was probably the most explicitly ideologically driven policy implemented by Reza Shah. It also revealed the somewhat schizophrenic nature of government policy, at once antagonistic to all things foreign, while, at the same time, seeking to imitate them. This apparent contradiction was justified by the government and its supporters by an appeal to ancient Iran, arguing that since, as Western historians had discovered, Iran and the West shared common historical origins, Iranians in imitating the West were simply returning to their roots.[29] The aims of this policy were explicit: to change attitudes through imitating the fashion of the West – by dressing like Europeans, it was hoped Iranians would begin to think like them. It was the quintessential act of social engineering and has come to characterise Reza Shah's reign – the parallels with the policies of Peter the Great of Russia should be obvious. European style of dress was continually being encouraged and when a deputation of merchants all suitably attired in Pahlavi caps and frock coats went to see him, Reza Shah was 'enormously pleased and made them a little speech about uniformity in dress and manners, which, he said, [would] lead to uniformity in life and politics, and would finally weld Persia into a unified whole'.[30] As one historian succinctly put it, 'In sum, Iranians would be more willing to imagine themselves as a community, to paraphrase Benedict Anderson, if they all looked alike'.[31]

The dress code, as a symbol of 'modern' Iran, not only served the interests of national unity but in its uniformity it also reflected the Shah's affection for all things military. Some Iranians indeed suggested that the Pahlavi cap appealed to the soldier in Reza Shah. As Clive noted when the dress code finally passed into legislation, the Pahlavi cap and frock coat had the unfortunate quality of making

> the wearer look like a railway porter . . . Many believe that the Pahlavi cap is but a stage on the road to the adoption of the European hat and many would wish that it were so, but others believe that the somewhat vague military conception of the head-wear delights the heart of the Shah, and that it is likely to remain at least during his lifetime as the universal head-gear of his subjects.[32]

The cap was particularly unpopular with the devout, since it made it difficult if not impossible for the wearer to touch the ground with his forehead during prayer. A consequence of the reform was that it led many to believe that its chief purpose was to encourage irreligiousness and also encouraged many (somewhat ahead of their time) to wear the cap back to front!

The law that was introduced to the Majlis at the end of 1928 instituted a series of fines and terms of imprisonment for those who failed to comply and, although the *ulema* and the priests of other faiths were exempted, there is evidence that the police and army were not especially discerning when it came to enforcement. The law was further added to when in 1930 the government ordered all school children to wear clothing made from Iranian cloth, extending the regulation a month later to all government employees.[33] One unforeseen consequence of the general exemption given to the *ulema* was that they now remained the one social group permitted to wear the turban and gown, thereby distinguishing them from the rest of society. Far from ensuring their marginalisation in Iranian society as a relic of the past, it ironically became a major factor in forging their distinct identity and as the social group most antagonistic to the Pahlavi project. Reza Shah had inadvertently created a formidable opposition complete with an identifiable social marker.

However, in the immediate term, the sum total of these unpopular conscription and dress laws, along with a rigorous policy of enforcement, was to aggravate the population and make the Shah increasingly unpopular. People were increasingly offended at being told what to wear and while evidence suggests that townspeople were more affected than rural dwellers, the latter were forced to don the cap when they came to market – only of course to dispose of it on leaving. In fact some villagers possessed a collective cap which was worn by whichever hapless soul was charged with going to town. During his visit to Shiraz at the end of 1929, every attempt to whip up some genuine enthusiasm for the visit through the press fell largely on deaf ears. The crowds that did turn up were organised by the local governor-general, Abul Hasan Khan Pirnia, who, according to the local British consular official, 'had worked like a Trojan in the past month to stir up enthusiasm for the visit', but in the event such was the security that few managed a glimpse of the Shah as he sped away in his car. This simply encouraged Shirazis in the view that the Shah was afraid.[34]

Fear was not a prudent image to project, especially when combined with a series of imposing reforms which had penetrated deep into Iranian society and provoked anger and resentment among those sections most dismissive of central authority, the tribes. In 1926–27 disturbances had broken out in towns throughout the country as the traditional middle classes protested the imposition of conscription, but far more serious were the tribal uprisings which began in 1928 and continued sporadically until 1934. While Reza Shah's treatment of the tribes continued to be ruthless and often brutal, it is important not to become carried away with the romantic view of the tribes frequently painted by European (often aristocratic) travellers enamoured of concepts of the 'noble savage' liberated from the vagaries of industrialisation. Reza Shah and most reformers (not all his supporters) would have found these views patronising and, in their opinion, an excellent example of European desires to keep Iran backward, if charming.[35] For many Iranians the tribes, with their autonomous function within the state, posed a threat to the very fabric of the state and to the security of society. They were an anachronism. They had to be settled and brought not only under central authority, but under central control. That Reza Shah was able to do this systematically both before and after his accession to the throne was in part a consequence of the creation of the new army, but also of the particular role of the tribes within the political process, of which their leaders were an integral part. Indeed, it is important to remember that the term 'tribe' in relation to the vast confederacies which inhabited parts of Iran may in some senses be considered a misnomer. While the tribes were essentially pastoral nomads, they operated within recognised pastures. Furthermore, their leaders, far from being alienated from the urban, settled political elite, were more often than not part of it.[36] They thus straddled both the rural and urban aspects of society, and were representative of both central authority (often occupying key ministerial posts) and, when it suited them, centrifugal forces. This proved a double-edged sword, because while the tribal leaders possessed a refuge beyond the reach of central government, their presence at the heart of government made them, paradoxically, accessible to the very intrigue that would be their undoing. Reza Shah possessed an instinctive ability for traditional Iranian politics, and tribal politics was the most traditional available. Manipulating tribal leaders to suit government purposes required astute political management – a prudent mixture of persuasion and co-option, coercive force and, critically, the projection of authority to which submission was no dishonour.[37] What differed under Reza Shah was his insistence on breaking the social fabric of tribal life and integrating it into a sedentary culture. For many Iranians familiar with Iranian history who believed that national decline had begun with the nomadisation of economic and social life in the Middle Ages, Reza Shah's policy was the correct one, even if the method of its implementation was often regarded as crude and brutal.

Reza Shah's 'pacification' of the two major tribal confederacies, the Bakhtiaris and the Qashqais, was representative of this policy. The Bakhtiaris were a tribal confederation of immense political importance and influence, whose traditional pasturelands were located in central Iran around Isfahan. They had played an important role in the Constitutional Revolution, helping to defeat the royalists in 1909. Aware of their political importance and strength, Reza Shah appointed one of their leading Khans, Sardar Asad, as Minister of Post and Telegraph, and later as Minister of War, receiving in return Bakhtiari help in crushing the Arabs, Lurs and other lesser tribal groups in the West. Although Sardar Asad was cultivated as a trusted ally, Reza Shah also recognised that he possessed a power base beyond central government control. This not only offended his 'modern' sensibilities and desire to monopolise the legitimate use of coercion,[38] but from another perspective it raised instinctive patrimonial fears of the 'paradox of sultanism'.[39] In other words, just as the Bakhtiaris had turned against the Qajar Mohammad Shah in 1909, could they not too turn against Reza Shah? Arguably as a result of this fear, Reza Shah moved to emasculate the Bakhtiaris, first by restricting the right of tribal Khans to maintain armed retainers, and then in 1928 by curtailing their ability to lease land directly to the Anglo-Persian Oil Company. Indeed, their association with the British was emphasised in order to delegitimise them in the eyes of the majority of Iranians. The Qashqai leadership was not as well integrated as the Bakhtiaris, and consequently proved a harder nut to crack. Nevertheless the strategy was similar. In 1926, Reza Shah engineered the arrival in Tehran of the Qashqai Il-Khan, Saulat al Daula, and his eldest son, Nasir Khan, ostensibly as Majlis deputies, but in reality prisoners. With the leadership removed, the government began the disarming of the tribe with considerable, if not excessive, zeal. The addition of fiscal exactions and conscription eventually led to a mass revolt in the spring of 1929, joined by other tribes but not initially the Bakhtiaris. Caught unprepared, and concerned that the uprising might in actual fact spread to the cities, Reza Shah played for time, conceding on some of the demands, sending Sardar Asad to mollify the agitating Bakhtiaris, and allowing Saulat al Daula and Nasir Khan to return to the Qashqais. Consolidating his forces and making good use of the new road network, Reza Shah then moved swiftly to crush the tribal revolt, which was effectively terminated by the end of August. The Bakhtiaris' punishment was systematic and swift. Three Khans were executed and, in 1934, three further Khans were imprisoned (and subsequently 'disappeared'), Sardar Asad dying of 'unnatural' causes soon after his arrest. In 1936, in line with the administrative changes already mentioned, Bakhtiari was divided and brought under the jurisdiction of the governors of Khuzestan and Isfahan. For the Qashqais, largely as a result of their obstreperousness, punishment was systematic, swift and brutal. Another revolt in 1932 was rapidly suppressed and more leaders were either executed or exiled, while forcible settlement of the nomadic elements of the tribe created social and economic problems.[40]

One of the most significant consequences of the Qashqai revolt was its use as a pretext to move against Firuz. It marked the first stage in the dismantling of the triumvirate which had done so much to shape modern Iran and maintain the new king on the throne. Reza Shah had retained suspicions about Firuz's ambitions because of his Qajar lineage and his large estates in the south in the environs of Shiraz, where the tribal revolt had taken place.[41] He was encouraged to act not only because Firuz was seen as an Anglophile, which won him few friends among the majority of nationalists, but importantly because his brother, Mohammad Huseyn Firuz (who was army commander in the south during the revolt) was seen to have failed. Given these links and the fact that some were convinced that the British had been behind the uprising, having, it was argued, dispatched the ubiquitous T.E. Lawrence to stir up the tribes,[42] it is not difficult to see how a case against Firuz could have been constructed. Following the arrest of his brother, Prince Firuz was arrested on charges of embezzlement. While probably manufactured, they were not implausible given Firuz's popular reputation for unscrupulousness and gambling. Ultimately, however, the catalyst for Prince Firuz's dismissal and arrest may have been Reza Shah's calculation that he was no longer useful nor necessary to his own survival.

The ideological distaste which Reza Shah and his supporters showed for tribalism, and all that they felt it implied, was mirrored by an overzealous admiration for urban life. But while traditionally Iranian urban life was closely connected to the rural within an integrated economic system, Reza Shah was more in favour of a modern industrial urban identity, which for him was epitomised by European cities. Just as he sought to reinvent rural life, so too did Reza Shah seek to reinvent urban life in an image of his own liking.[43] This growing *irrationality* of ration-alisation and modernisation, and the concomitant resentment and resistance of Iranian society, were very obvious in the ambitious government programme of town planning. The results at times impressed foreign observers, who remarked on the progress that had been made on road construction and maintenance, though others considered the developments to be superficial. Forbes, writing in 1931, described Tehran as 'slightly Hollywoodesque, for the new streets looked as if they had not quite settled where they were going, and the rows of new houses, one room deep, were all frontage'.[44] Favourable impressions aside, even the British embassy had to concede that 'houses that might impede the municipal schemes [were] being ruthlessly swept away with little or no compensation to the owners'.[45] Under such circumstances it is not surprising that resistance to change mounted and in some cases new towns were simply left uninhabited, as one visit to a new town in Sistan revealed:

> This 'town', which had been constructed within the year by Sarhang Murteza Khan in anticipation of His Majesty's visit, is commonly known as 'the town of walls'. It is distinguished by the fact that it has no inhabitants, although giving the illusion of fine streets and sumptuous houses. There are some eight wide, straight avenues, brilliantly illuminated at night by electricity, bounded on either side by high whitewashed walls and with quite magnifi-cent porches at regular intervals, apparently the entrances of the houses of the wealthy. To those 'in the know' that is 'the sum and total' of the town, with the exception of the house, situated in a garden which the Shah occu-pied. Behind the walls and within the fine entrances are plots of waste land, on which there are not and never likely to be, any buildings. The inhabitants continue to live in the ancient part of the town which His Majesty did not see. Sarhang Murteza informed me that His Majesty was well pleased with the 'new' town. He also complimented Hisam ud Dawla on his garish, mod-ern dwelling and told Shaukat ul Mulk to learn from his nephew and bring his fine old Persian house at Birjand 'up to date'.[46]

Much as in Shiraz in 1929, the visit to Sistan in 1931 did not have the desired effect, as noted in the same dispatch:

> Whatever may have been the object of the Shah's visit, it certainly has not achieved what must be the principle object . . . increase of popularity of the occupant of the throne. Everywhere, at least everywhere where such state-ments can be prudently made, one heard expressions of disappointment. The more enlightened were shocked at the Shah's lack of graciousness – the common people said, 'He is Teryaki', and with that expression vanished all respect for the Shah's person. Sarhang Murteza Khan – reputed to have great influence with the Shah – is himself not a little dejected since His Majesty's visit. I asked if the Shah had been pleased with his visit. He replied, 'I don't know – I expect so. He would have told me alright if he were not'.

Indeed, popular discontent with Reza Shah's methods and the willingness of the 'common people' to voice it, belie the notion of the state domination of society and instead reinforces the view that social tensions within the emergent modern state persisted. At the same time, this willingness also reflected increasing state penetration and intervention in society, encroaching upon a private domain that had hitherto been left to its own devices. The reforms which were implemented in the first ten years on Reza Pahlavi's increasing domination of the Iranian state (1921–31) were dramatic in their breadth and had a profound impact on Iranian society. Questions remain as to how far the central government was able to pen-etrate the rural areas where the majority of the population still lived. But it seems clear that, at the very least, the impact, however unsavoury, was growing. As one British official noted with obvious enthusiasm, 'After 6 months' absence I have been struck by the progress that has been made, especially in the matter of trans-port, road construction and upkeep, and in municipal activity', adding almost as an afterthought that 'In every town I passed through street widening was the order of the day, houses that might impede the municipal schemes being ruth-lessly swept away with little or no compensation to the owners. This is especially noticeable in Tehran itself'.[47]

During this first decade, while economic policy was developed and imple-mented, attention was focused on establishing political domination and, in effect, preparing the ground for the more ambitious economic programmes which were to follow. Infrastructural projects were initiated, particularly in the development of the roads essential for the rapid mobilisation and dispatch of armed forces throughout the country. In 1925, there were some 2,000 miles of roads, often in a poor state of repair. This figure had multiplied to 14,000 miles of road, in relatively good condition, by the end of Reza Shah's reign. In addi-tion, he began in earnest the planning and construction of the Trans-Iranian Railway, an expensive project for which funds had been allocated in the Fourth Majlis. On 16 October 1927, Reza Shah formally inaugurated the project with considerable enthusiasm, 'I can scarcely express my joy as I take part in this celebration and inaugurate the construction'.[48] While ostensibly 'Iranian' in its conception and funding, the engineers actually building the railroad were by and large of foreign extraction, emanating principally from the United States (the initial team consisted of 34 American engineers), but also from Greece, Germany, Italy and Belgium. It took 11 years to build and in connecting north central Iran to the south-west, it fulfilled a national ambition despite its expense. It was in many ways a triumph of nationalism over economic common sense and its real utility was in connecting the Shah's estates in Mazandaran to the main population centres. In winding its way to the south-west it may have also been driven by military considerations, in particular the suppression and control of the tribes.

The year 1927 also witnessed the first concrete measures to control and regu-late the activities of the country's doctors, reflecting, as with the later education reforms, some of the more positive and uncontroversial aspects of social reform in this period. At the same time, many of these social reforms were the result of programmes and policies developed by the technocrats and statesmen who surrounded the monarch. In 1923, a Pasteur Institute, modelled on the institute of the same name in Paris, was founded in Tehran, under the instigation of the then Foreign Minister, Prince Firuz. Headed by the Frenchman Dr Joseph Mesnard, for an initial period of seven years, the Institute was directed towards researching and developing programmes which would improve public health. An additional bureau for animal vaccinations was added in 1925 and in 1929 all slaughter of livestock outside the municipal slaughterhouses was banned. By 1930, an adequate medical school existed in Iran, although it was run effectively by French staff, requiring knowledge of the French language of any aspiring candidates. Most Iranian doctors were still trained abroad, but as a result of these measures, the number of doctors per person began to rise, although by the end of the 1930s there were still only 2.5 doctors to every 100,000 people.[49] Further measures legislating for vaccination against a variety of diseases were ratified by the Majlis throughout the reign, culminating in 1941 with a law for the prevention and combat of infectious diseases. It required:

- Compulsory treatment for venereal diseases;
- Free medication for needy patients;
- Wilful or negligent transfer of diseases became a criminal offence;
- Periodic inspection and certification of brothels;
- Compulsory vaccination against smallpox at the ages of 2 months, 7, 13 and 21 years;
- Additional vaccinations in times of epidemics;
- Vaccination certificates required of all children entering school and of all job applicants;
- Doctors were required to report all cases of infectious diseases to the Ministry of Health;
- All public places were to be inspected regularly.

A vigorous hospital-building programme was also inaugurated, often manned by foreign doctors and administrators; non-governmental organisations, such as the Red Lion and Sun Society (the Iranian equivalent of the Red Cross), were founded, with the press encouraged to print articles dealing with public health and hygiene. One of the few areas not dealt with by 1941 was the question of water supply and sewage. By and large however, it was an impressive programme, comprehensively implemented, although incomplete and, crucially, dependent on consistent European aid and assistance. The Reza Shahi Hospital in Mashhad, for instance, was established and operated by German doctors.[50] It is also important to remember that while the motives for public health policy were often altruistic, the spectre of nationalism was never far away. The concept of a healthy nation, purified of essentially 'foreign' malignancies, was not far from the minds of some administrators. It must be said, however, that such attitudes were not unique to Iranians, and indeed may have reflected the large input of European doctors and medical administrators in Iran at this time.

With the establishment of the National Bank of Iran (Bank Melli) in 1928, the government made the first tentative steps towards dismantling British economic dominance in Iran and providing Iran with the financial muscle to push through more ambitious economic reforms. In the previous year, the resignation of Millspaugh was contrived, with the Shah reportedly commenting that, 'There can't be two shahs in this country, and I am going to be *the* Shah'.[51] The financial administration of the country would now reside with Iranians. The new Bank Melli was intended to take over the government accounts and to be responsible for note issue, a responsibility hitherto left to the many foreign banks operating in Iran, principally the Imperial Bank of Persia, a British-owned entity. The desire to establish a national bank had been voiced by the Constitutionalists in 1906, but in the following years, as government disintegrated, foreign banks gained in importance as the only stable and reliable financial institutions in the country. Following the Russian Revolution, the Russian-operated bank ceased operations, while the Ottoman Bank operated only a few branches, leaving the Imperial Bank in a dominant position. By default, therefore, it effectively became the state bank of Iran, a position which the nationalists and Reza Shah found intolerable. However, it was one thing to establish a bank but another to run it efficiently and gain the confidence of the general public. Indeed many merchants continued to run the informal network of currency exchanges throughout the country, a system which had served them well for centuries and to a large extent continues to function and serve them well today.[52] Far more problematic than the local merchants was the attitude of the Board of the Imperial Bank who found it difficult to take the new 'upstart' bank seriously. When the German Dr Kurt Lindenblatt arrived in Tehran in 1928 to take up his new post as manager of Bank Melli, the Board of the Imperial Bank advised the general manager in Iran, Wilkinson, that, 'It is no part of your duty to assist them, and I hope your conversations with them will be as nebulous as you can make them'.[53] Indeed it was not until 1931 that the Imperial Bank relinquished its control over note issuing, and it took almost another 20 years of painful wrangling before the Imperial Bank's financial stranglehold on Iran was broken (see Chapter 9).[54]

Of far more immediate concern for the government, however, was the Anglo-Persian Oil Company (APOC), another British concession, whose control of Iranian oil made it one of the chief sources of revenue for the Iranian government. Along with the cancellation of the foreign capitulations, Reza Shah had wanted to revoke the generous agreement signed with the company by his dynastic predecessors and have it comprehensively renegotiated. With access to more oil revenue, the ambitious projects for economic development could be fully financed. The challenge to APOC was, of course, far more than simply a financial matter. With the British government in possession of a 'golden share' in the company, it was increasingly viewed in Iranian circles as yet another branch of the British government in Iran. With its discriminatory attitude to Iranian employees (a feature which it shared with the Imperial Bank), and the fact that it paid considerably more to the British exchequer in taxes than it did to the Iranian government in royalty payments, it was obvious that a state of antagonism would develop between the conflicting camps. When the Minister of Court, Teymourtache, paid a visit to the refinery in Abadan and commented on what a fine asset it was, alarm bells began ringing in Whitehall.[55] It was in fact one of Britain's largest and most valuable overseas assets and when the original concession was cancelled in 1932, the British government exercised its 'right' to send additional Royal Navy ships to patrol the Persian Gulf as well as taking the opportunity to point out that Iran's foreign assets might themselves be at risk. Any doubt as to the strategic importance of APOC to the British government and, as a consequence, Britain's interest in political developments within Iran, were dispelled by the following secret dispatch of Knatchbull-Hugessen some three years after the signing of the supplementary agreement:

> In long periods of disorder and weakness in the past we have had to adopt direct methods to protect our vital interests . . . if the regime is suddenly overturned a republican form of government would never last in Persia, for Iran will never be blessed with an organised form of government unless it has a strong man at the centre . . . our course would not appear difficult – as soon as we are satisfied that the new Sovereign or President was in full control we should presumably open relations with him and things would go on as before. In the event of [chaos] it might become necessary to take precautionary measures to protect the oilfields but the oil royalties would give us an important hold. None of the aspirants to power would wish to risk prejudicing the prospects of abundant payments and, on our side, we should, I presume, be able to have the last word as to whom the recipient of the royalties should be. In such circumstances it would be most important that a clear understanding should exist between His Majesty's Government and the Anglo-Iranian Oil Company that the royalties should only be paid to the candidate or conqueror approved by His Majesty's Government. I presume this is already assured.[56]

The message was loud and clear, and in 1933, after what the British considered to be protracted and tedious negotiations, a compromise was reached.[57] In return for a modest increase in the royalty payments from 16 per cent to 20 per cent of the annual profits, and the promise to train more Iranians to take on administrative positions, Iran agreed to extend the term of the original concession by another 32 years, from 1961 to 1993. While the British settled down contentedly to another 60 years of Iranian oil, reaction within the country was less than cheerful. Indeed the agreement only convinced Iranian nationalists of their country's continued international impotence and the need for more extreme measures. For the time being, however, the nationalist volcano subsided into dormancy.

However, just as the Qashqai revolt served as a pretext for the removal of Firuz, so the dispute with APOC laid the groundwork for the fall of the second and probably most important member of the triumvirate. Teymourtache, the Minister of Court, was taken aback by Firuz's fall, and complained bitterly about Reza Shah's growing paranoia and lack of trust in his most loyal supporters.

Not for the first time, he confided, probably imprudently, to a British diplomat that should the Shah die, then a republic would be the only route available.[58] Such language, should it have reached the ears of the Shah, would of course have done little to assuage his growing suspicions. While Firuz was regarded as an Anglophile, Teymourtache was popularly regarded as too pro-Russian and something of an Anglophobe. Educated in Russia and imbued with Russian culture, there is little doubt that Teymourtache felt an affinity with all things Russian, but while rumours and apparent revelations appeared to link him more concretely to the Russian/Soviet cause, there is little evidence, even in the Russian sources, that this was indeed the case. But as with Firuz, the mud stuck. What made Teymourtache's position increasingly untenable was not his closeness to the Russians, but the undoubted antipathy of the British and the growing suspicions and paranoia of the Shah. It was this volatile mixture which was ultimately to be Teymourtache's undoing.

British antipathy was a direct consequence of their reading of the Minister of Court's aspirations with respect to APOC, and his relations with the new Soviet government. He did little to assuage British fears in either respect. Tensions had been increased in 1927 with the break in Anglo-Soviet diplomatic relations. The Russians had never been satisfied with the British oil concession in the south, especially in the absence of one of their own in the north, and they used the renewed antagonism with Britain to encourage Iranian seizure of the oilfields and the cancellation of the concession.[59] In August 1928, Teymourtache wrote to the president of APOC, Sir John Cadman, pointing out that as the original concession had been agreed and granted by a deposed and defunct dynasty, and long before the existence of any representative institutions in the country, it could no longer be considered valid. It had to be renegotiated with more favourable terms for Iran. Negotiations came to a head in 1931, when Cadman refuted any Iranian claims as unrealistic and eventually Reza Shah unilaterally cancelled the concession in 1932, resulting in a British appeal to the League of Nations. The Soviets were understandably delighted and began to push for their own oil concession. Teymourtache seems to have encouraged this desire, as one historian has argued, to increase Iranian leverage against the British in the ongoing negotiations.[60] Instead it succeeded in raising British fears of Soviet penetration, a fear shared by many Anglophiles within Iran as well as nationalists who viewed both Soviet and British political penetration with equitable distaste.

This fear had earlier been nourished in 1930 with the publication of a series of articles in a French newspaper based on the memoirs of a Soviet agent, Agabekov. The articles revealed Soviet espionage in Iran and appeared to implicate the Minister of Court (although the original Russian edition made no mention of Teymourtache). Reza Shah expanded his police network in 1931 with the appointment of General Ayrom as Tehran police chief. Within two months, 32 suspects were arrested on the basis of the Agabekov disclosures and 27 were convicted. Given the predominant fear of communist subversion among members of the political and economic establishment, the atmosphere in political circles was not conducive to Russophiles, alleged or otherwise.

But arguably more damaging to Teymourtache's political survival were rumours, encouraged by his enemies, of his own political ambitions and the widespread view that he was the real force behind the creation of modern Iran.[61] Both of these allegations were offensive to Reza Shah, who increasingly came to view his Minister of Court as a threat to himself and his dynasty. Indeed as late as 1933, press articles credited 'to Teymourtache every manifestation or intensification of political or social development in Persia down to, or up to, the Shah's social and hygienic education'.[62] Fearful of Russian penetration, acutely aware of British pressure and imbued with a deep sense of suspicion, Reza Shah decided to take the opportunity to move against his 'Grand Vizier' in a manner befitting his imperial predecessors. Avoiding the contentious and controversial charge of treason, Reza Shah decided instead to arrest Teymourtache on suspicion of corruption and embezzlement. Much like Firuz, given his extensive gambling and the debts he had reportedly accumulated, it was a charge that could be plausibly constructed. Nevertheless the prison sentence was heavy: five years' solitary confinement with an extensive fine. With Teymourtache in prison, Sir John Cadman arrived in Tehran in April 1933 to begin final negotiations on the oil agreement, aware that a major obstacle had been removed. Following direct negotiations with the Shah the new agreement was ratified by the Majlis on 28 May.

Teymourtache's fate, however, was to be less satisfactory and, in retrospect, a source of some regret to the British. Forbidden family visits, and locked in a cell devoid of any furniture, the flamboyant former Minister of Court was pronounced dead from 'heart failure' and 'pneumonia' on 4 October 1933. While never substantiated, it was generally believed that Teymourtache was murdered, probably through the slow ingestion of poison. The British Minister Mallet evinced some regret and no little shock at the manner of Teymourtache's departure when he wrote, 'Thus, the man whose brilliant talents had placed him on a pinnacle of power far above all the Shah's subjects was left by an ungrateful master without even a bed to die upon'.[63] Firuz survived until 1938, a few months after the energetic Davar committed suicide rather than face humiliation at the hands of his monarch.[64] Without the triumvirate to coordinate and check developments, policies were administered with even more haste and the cult of personality was emphasised with increased vigour.[65]

Institutionalising the dynasty: the politics of dynastic nationalism

The dismantling of the triumvirate did not signal the end of modernisation. On the contrary, significant steps were yet to be taken, especially in the realm of education and the economy. But it did signify the beginning of the intense personalisation of politics around the person of Reza Shah, and by extension the dynasty he wished to institutionalise within the body politic. In seeking to leave his personal stamp on the development and shape of the country, Reza Shah, paradoxically, also began the process of alienation as the country divided into a small influential elite devoted to the Shah, and the rest, from various social backgrounds, who were increasingly divorced from the political process. In moving from nationalism to 'dynastic nationalism', the Shah consolidated his position within an unnaturally narrow social base which combined localised strength with foundational fragility. This was an exclusive nationalism in which 'patriotism' was defined as much by one's loyalty to the dynasty as to the nation. To his followers he personified the charismatic saviour they yearned for. But to the growing throng of critics he was little more than a traditional patrimonial ruler with the additional benefit of modern institutions of government to support him. Modernisation, they argued, was increasingly subservient to the needs of the dynasty. As a consequence of his increasing centrality, militarism grew, in part because it pleased the Shah, but also because it consolidated the loyalty of a grateful army. The cult of personality developed as the Shah became increasingly convinced of his identification with the principles of progress and national independence, prompting competing courtiers to reassure him of this and to reinvent his past in light of his brilliant present.

The importance of the army for the succession ensured that the Crown Prince became involved and identified with it from an early stage, and the Shah continued to give preferential treatment to soldiers, in particular the officer corps, ensuring that ample funds were always allocated from the budget.[66] In his final dispatch Clive noted:

> the artificial growth of militarism in what is essentially an unmilitary country. The arrogance and indiscipline towards the civil population of the officers and men of this new army are growing more marked. The Persian soldier today carrying his rifle does not hesitate to level it at any civilian on the slightest provocation, real or imagined . . . The newly enrolled conscripts are the worst offenders . . . The danger which 10 years ago existed from banditry is today tending to increase from the forces called into being to suppress it.[67]

Reza Shah's 'tribe' was becoming increasingly unruly! As one diplomat noted,

> The Shah has not forgotten the instrument by which he rose to power, and continues to take a deep and personal interest . . . They profit by their importance in the eyes of their royal master and, though naturally timid, adopt a swashbuckling attitude and strut about the streets of the capital shouldering their civilian brethren into the gutter.

At the end of 1931 the Shah ordered an amendment to the conscription law requiring all students of theology to perform military service after the completion of their studies, thereby eroding the concessions he had previously granted the *ulema* and extending the military institution over the entirety of society.[68]

The fear, distrust and disdain which he engendered in the general populace, and the traditional middle classes in particular, contrasted markedly with the steady stream of eulogies which emanated from government officials.[69] The closing session of the Eighth Majlis saw a number of deputies compete to praise the Shah. The President of the Majlis, Mirza Hussein Khan Dadgar, argued that the Eighth Majlis had been successful

> owing entirely to the wisdom and firmness of His Imperial Majesty the Shah
> . . . Mirza Khalil Khan Fahimi then eulogised the President for his self denial,
> his calm temper and his impartiality, and went on to allude to the happy
> results obtained and reforms realised under the aegis of His Majesty. Another
> speaker . . . observed that the people of Persia ought to thank God for giving
> them such a sovereign as Riza Shah Pahlavi.[70]

As Hoare summarised,

> the sum and substance of the matter . . . is that nothing has any existence in
> this country but for the grace and creative will of the supreme mind and no
> man has any personality or authority but by the imperial inspiration. In fact
> the Lord *he* is God.[71]

To complement the rhetoric, lavish festivals were organised in commemoration of the Shah's birthday, in a clear example of the naturalising tendency of political myth to embed a particular concept within popular culture. In some cases, nevertheless, the effect was counterproductive: 'The first chariot, in the form of a large head, was supposed to be a "div" (devil) announcing the arrival of the procession. The irreverent saw in this head a likeness to Reza Shah Pahlavi'.[72] In addition, the government began to insist on the 'proper' use of 'authentic' titles, and, having abolished the more elaborate Qajar titles which many felt had proliferated in the nineteenth century, turned to ancient Persian terminology, retaining those that had been used by the Qajars such as *Shahanshah*. Of course as with much else, the interpretation of nomenclature reflected the prevailing political mood of the day. If under the Qajars, the term tended to denote a 'king among kings' albeit a distinct primes inter pares who aspired to a supreme authority, under Reza Shah the *Shahanshah* was in a very real sense, 'king over kings' and now had the power to exercise that authority. Despite the precedent of its use in the Qajar period, some British diplomats, through an unusual degree of ignorance, or more likely, an irritation at the pretentious means at which the Iranian court had insisted on its use, were less than complementary at the new etiquette they were being forced to adopt.

> The insistence on the word 'Shahinshahi' [sic] is probably an attempt to
> magnify the importance of the Persian government through the re-adoption
> of an ancient appellation. The Persian Government presumably resent the
> use of the word 'aliyyeh' [elevated] as not being sufficiently respectful . . . If
> we want to be obstructive, or pull their legs, we might ask them which kings
> is Reza king over.[73]

The Persianisation of the state was a major aspect of government policy in this period, not only titles, but military ranks and, in 1933, shop signs. The Municipality of Tehran warned shopkeepers in January that

> as everybody must agree that this practice is in opposition to national prestige and national dignity, all shop proprietors are warned that from 21 March next all shop signs must be inscribed in large Persian letters with the foreign characters in smaller type below.[74]

Indeed national prestige continued to take increasing precedence over modernisation to the extent that any conflict was often resolved in favour of national prestige. Moreover, in this period it was not simply the nation which dominated the agenda, but the increasingly forced symbiosis between the nation and its dynasty, which helps explain the imperial sensitivity over the use of correct titles. The dynasty took precedence. Thus in the most dramatic and arguably successful of reforms during this period, those of education, the devil in the detail which hindered its coherent development was the preoccupation with the 'correct' form and nature of education which would support rather than undermine the state. Education would provide the new national state of Iran with its greatest vehicle for ideological dissemination but in limiting the depth (if not the breadth) of that dissemination and focusing on the importance of monarchy, it subjected the process of education to a narrow political agenda and thereby handicapped it from the start.

At the opening of the Ninth Majlis the Shah announced that one of the major aims of the session was to prepare for the 'moral purification and the education of the public'.[75] The reform of education and the founding of Tehran University was to be one of the greatest if flawed achievements of Reza Shah. He made it clear that he wanted Iranians to study in Iran rather than be faced with having to go abroad, but integral to this was the desire to control education and to avoid having to send Iranians abroad where they might be confronted with political ideas contrary to the security and stability of the dynasty. Educational reforms had been initiated in the mid-1920s, but had only really gathered pace by the end of the decade. In 1928, a standardised textbook was imposed on all secondary schools together with a standardised Persian (a significant impetus for reform and simplification of the language). Local dialects were avoided and history teaching emphasised the Achaemenid period, while geography stressed the unity of the nation.[76] With the Persianisation of elementary schools proceeding vigorously, the government turned its attention to foreign schools, preventing Iranians who had not completed elementary school in Persian from attending them and insisting that they teach at least some classes in the Persian language. Initial reforms concentrated on the primary and secondary school system, with subsequent attention in the following decade given to higher education. In 1934, the six higher education institutions were amalgamated to form Tehran University, and new colleges in dentistry, fine arts, and science and technology, among others, were subsequently added. In 1936, elementary adult education was inaugurated, with secondary education implemented the following year, the same year in which the Ministry of Education was formed to coordinate activities. As a result of these reforms, the number of students increased dramatically, from 55,960 children in primary education in 1925 to 287,245 in 1941. They would in turn feed into secondary and higher education. The number of secondary students doubled from 14,488 in 1925 to 28,194 in 1941, and higher education witnessed an increase from fewer than 600 students to over 3,300. There was, unsurprisingly, a corresponding decrease in the number of students attending the traditional religious *maktabs*.

The law for the foundation of Tehran University, which was passed on 29 May 1934, also revealed the determination to maintain state control. The principal of the university was to be appointed by royal decree.[77] Indeed the foundation of the university had in large part been encouraged by the desire to restrict education abroad, which Reza Shah worried would unnecessarily inflict dangerous ideas upon Iranian students. Having encouraged students on their departure to benefit from the moral education they could gain in Europe, he cautioned officials to 'select the countries which pay proper attention to moral education and you should send the students there. Certain foreign countries are poor in this respect'.[78] The foundation of Tehran University would obviate the need to send so many students abroad, although a consistently high demand for higher education, and the promise of secure government jobs, meant that students who could afford to still went abroad. State control over the management of the university was matched by a desire to monitor students' progress and imbue them with a sense of 'authority' from an early age. Students, certainly in secondary school, were expected to parade once a week under the aegis of an officer from the army.[79] Furthermore Reza Shah was at pains to inform students being sent abroad that 'You will render full service to your country only when you have served in the army. Military service is one of the essential duties of every patriot, especially the student class'.[80]

The militarisation of education, exemplified by the imposition of drill, was indicative of the central philosophy behind education reform, which was to produce competent loyal citizens – supportive of the state as defined by Reza Shah and able to operate the new industry which was being developed. Industrialisation had begun in earnest in the 1930s, largely because the worldwide depression inaugurated by the 1929 stock market crash had made commodities cheap and therefore affordable. High tariffs were introduced to protect domestic industry, which despite modest incentives remained the preserve of the state. Indeed most of the factories established in this period were at the behest of the state, and we might describe the economic system as one of 'state capitalism'. Limited rights were provided for workers, but in return they were prohibited from striking or from any other form of political activism. The scale of industrial development was impressive, rising from 20 modern plants in 1925 to 346 by 1941. Some 146 of these represented major industrial plants such as textile mills, sugar refineries and chemical enterprises. However, while this was impressive in quantitative terms, even a sympathetic writer has described the policy as 'an appetite for industrialisation far beyond the bounds of economic rationale, not for the sake of efficiency and welfare but as a symbol of prestige and status'.[81] Nevertheless, with the growth in industry came the growth of an industrial workforce. From fewer than 1,000 workers in 1925, the number rose to over 50,000 in 1941. If we add the rise in employment in other industries (such as the oil sector, fisheries and railways), then the total industrial labour force by the end of the 1930s had risen to some 170,000 people. It represented, as one historian has argued, the birth of the 'modern working class'.[82] Combined with a growing student population, it provided both the popular reservoir and ideological vanguard for the growth of one of the major ideological and political movements in twentieth-century Iran – socialism.

In the aftermath of the Russian Revolution, 'communism' and its association with a foreign power was a central concern of both the traditional elites and the nationalists. The landowners and *ulema* considered it both irreligious and a threat to their economic way of life. Nationalists saw it as a foreign import, the old Russian enemy with added ideological vigour. Kuchik Khan and the *Jangalis* had suffered because of their association with the Soviets, and Reza Shah had been quick to abandon his socialist allies after his coronation. The Communist Party of Iran had been banned in 1927 and a number of activists arrested. Ironically, through Teymourtache's connections with the Soviet government, relations between Iran and the Soviet Union remained amicable, and Iranian communists were left in an ambiguous situation, condemning an Iranian state which their fellow communists were content to approve. Government suppression meant that the new generation of activists had to go underground or abroad. The first signs of dissent came from Germany, where a special congress was held in Cologne demanding the release of political prisoners, the establishment of a republic and the denunciation of Reza Shah as a British stooge. In 1931, a group of Iranian students, working with members of the Iranian Communist Party, established a new periodical, *Paykar* (Battle). Following an article in which Reza Shah was derided as having previously worked as a bouncer and as a guard outside the German embassy (where he had acquired his taste for uniforms), German–Iranian relations became extremely tense.[83] Eventually the German government was persuaded to close down the newspaper and Iran enacted a more draconian law safeguarding national security. With the foundation of Tehran University, trouble moved closer to home. In 1936, the Teachers' College witnessed a successful strike by students complaining about poor wages, while in 1937 the students at the College of Law closed down the campus in protest at the lavish sums spent to prepare the university for a visit of the Crown Prince, when, they complained, the vast majority of villagers had no access as yet to educational facilities (despite educational reforms, rural illiteracy remained extremely high). In the same year students were arrested on charges of fascism and plotting against the Shah. The leader, an army conscript, was secretly executed. However, the most significant arrests came in May 1937 when 53 Marxists were detained by the police. Most were young and drawn from the Persian-speaking Tehran intelligentsia. Whatever the state of their radicalism at the time of their arrest, the harsh sentences meted to many of them (five were released, three acquitted) must have simply confirmed to them the injustice of the system. Many were to later form the nucleus of the Tudeh (Toilers) Party, the principal left-wing political movement in twentieth-century Iranian history.[84] Reza Shah soon lamented what many consider his greatest civilian achievement.

> Look at this group of young people whom we sent abroad with a heart full of hope, and whom we supported for years, so that they would return to their home land and serve it. Now that they are back . . . they brought us Bolshevism in their saddlebags.[85]

Distinct from its function as a hotbed of political activism, the university also served as the chief vehicle for the dissemination of state ideology. Its first task was to define the linguistics parameters of its activities and to this end the first steps were taken to replace what were considered foreign loan words (in the main appropriated from French) with more authentic Persian words, or indeed more simple constructions better suited to the development of mass education.[86] Responsibility for this was subsequently granted to the Persian Language Academy whose principal function was to weed out unnecessary and superfluous words many of which had emerged as a result of the verbosity of Qajar bureaucrats but also including more recent invented archaisms that many, including the Shah himself, found meaningless.[87] It was to find its task more difficult when it came to loan words from Arabic, and unlike in Turkey there was never any serious attempt to dispense with the Arabic script. The attempt to define ideology through a definition of discourse and nomenclature had been continuing throughout Reza Shah's reign, while his adoption of the surname 'Pahlavi' was a significant attempt to shape public opinion prior to his accession to the throne. The replacement of place names and other terms similarly reflected the nature of nationalist ideology and its increasing dynastic imperatives. While nationalists (and educationalists) were only too keen to adopt the word *danesh-gah* for university, the replacement of the name 'Bandar Anzali' with 'Bandar Pahlavi' for a port on the Caspian clearly had more to do with the institutionalisation of the dynasty, as did the replacement of 'Aliabad' by 'Shahabad'.[88] Probably the most significant and interesting change in practice was the insistence that foreigners desist from using the term 'Persia' and replace it with 'Iran'.[89]

The Iranian government had in fact initially insisted on this protocol in an exchange of letters with the new Turkish Republic in 1924.[90] Now a decade later and perhaps with more confidence this instruction had been sent to European powers. In this new move in 1935, the government of Iran was, at one level, simply insisting on a uniformity of usage across international frontiers. As the Iranian Foreign Ministry rather laboriously explained in a circulated memorandum:

> As the members of the Legation are aware, the words 'Iran' and 'Irani' are rendered in most foreign languages, following ancient Greek historians, by the words 'Persia', 'Persian', 'Persien', 'Perser', etc. Nevertheless, these

appellations, as is shown by historical, geographical and racial evidence, do not correspond with the real significance of the words, 'Iran' and 'Irani'; and the proper course is to translate 'mamlikati-Iran' (the country of Iran) into the various foreign languages simply by 'Iran', and to represent the word 'Iraniha' (people of Iran) by 'Iraniens' or the like in the other European languages. For this reason the authorities of the Imperial government are proposing to remedy this etymological and historical inexactitude. Therefore the Ministry of Foreign Affairs will be exceedingly obliged if, from the first day of Farvardin, 1314 (21 March 1935) the Legation will cease to employ the words 'Perse' and 'Persian' in conversation and correspondence, and will employ in their place the words 'Iran' and 'Iraniens'.[91]

However, at another level, the aim of the request was to disassociate the new *modern* Iran from the old decadent 'Persia' of the Qajars and as such represented the rebranding of the nation in international eyes. It was a move widely supported by nationalists who regarded the term 'Persia' as too exclusive and not inclusive of ethnic groups who could legitimately be termed Iranian but not (strictly speaking) Persian. This was not, of course, how foreigners tended to use the word and a certain amount of confusion ensued as at one stage it was suggested that the 'Persian' Gulf be renamed the 'Iranian' Gulf.[92] But further, it represented the essential contest to define the meaning and identity of Iran, since the 'Iran' defined by the Pahlavis – centralised, industrial, secular and loyal to the Shah as the linchpin of the entire system – was not one appreciated nor accepted by all its citizens. Certainly, the emphasis on the 'Aryan' roots of the term, and its association with racial theories rising to prominence in Germany, sat uncomfortably with many Iranians who defined their collective nationhood in cultural rather than racial terms.[93] That the recent impetus had emanated from the Iranian legation in Berlin only confirmed these suspicions.

Indeed, Germany had been playing an increasingly important role in Iran since the end of the 1920s, in particular with the dismissal of Millspaugh and the arrival of Lindenblatt as First Director of the Bank Melli. Many Iranians had viewed Germany as a potential partner in the development of the country. She had no colonial history in Iran, and as a European power antithetical to both the Soviet Union and Great Britain, she would be only too happy to assist Iran in her bid to break free from her traditional foes. The coincidence of interest represented by the existence of common foes would be transformed with the rise of the Nazis into a commonality of interest via the developing myth of Aryanism, although this was to prove more aspirational than practical.[94] Nevertheless, the utility of this myth for future Iranian–German relations was not lost on the Iranian legation in Berlin when it urged the government to be more proactive about the use of the word 'Iran'. There was also much about the politics of Nazi Germany which appealed to Reza Shah – nationalism, self-sufficiency, the collective will to rebuild a shattered nation – but there was also much to offend the monarch's traditional disposition and, as noted above, fascists were as much a target of the security forces as communists. While there is little doubt that Reza Shah drew some international legitimacy from the fact that his methods were little different from those of many dictators in Europe, too much has subsequently been made of his affinity with the Nazis, or indeed his affection for Aryanism: he did after all marry his son and heir to an Egyptian princess. More important was the change in perception in European intellectual circles following the rise of the Nazis, which was not appreciated in Iran and cannot have been beneficial for the Pahlavi monarch. Remarking on the Shah's increasingly intolerant suppression of his critics, and in particular the formation of a 'Political Department' within the police to monitor dissidents and the press, one British diplomat wrote, 'In his ruthless suppression of carpers and critics the Shah had no need, however, to follow a foreign example; indeed, the "Fuhrer" of Iran may rather be regarded as the prototype of the Aryan Hitler'.[95]

It has similarly been often argued that Reza Shah drew much inspiration for his reforms from Mustapha Kemal in Turkey, with whom Iran, along with Afghanistan and Iraq, entered into the Saadabad Pact in 1937. While once again there was a clear commonality of interest and sympathy between the two Middle Eastern heads of state as well as with members of their respective intelligentsias, the often overstated and clearly perceived imitative relationship does not bear careful scrutiny.[96] Ataturk was starting from a base considerably more advanced in terms of 'modernisation' than that of Reza Shah (and as a result was an obvious example Iranian intellectuals could look to), but even so, Ataturk was more prudent in the application of his policies. The respective attitudes towards the *ulema* stand out, as do other civil reforms. While surnames were introduced in Iran in 1924, it was another ten years before they were introduced in the Turkish Republic. Furthermore, while Reza Shah was clearly impressed by what he saw during his state visit to Turkey, encouraging him to make further changes to the dress code, his subsequent decision to ban the veil altogether has no comparison in Turkey.

The decision to enforce the use of the European hat, or 'international hat', while relieving Iranians of the burden of the Pahlavi cap, was not greeted with enthusiasm.[97] Once again, its adoption was justified by the government and establishment on the grounds that it had been the headdress of the Sassanians – a peculiar image indeed.[98] This was either meaningless or completely unconvincing to most Iranians, especially given that it was actually called the 'international hat', and so great was the discontent that some felt it would simply fuel the radicalisation of the populace:

> The introduction of European hats is not as popular as the press, by its frequent and almost frenzied zeal for them, would have us believe. A friend told a member of staff that the bazaar quarter of Tehran is seething with discontent and latent fanaticism . . . The peasants, among whom there is still a strong religious superstition, are said to be murmuring a good deal . . . One or two Iranians have recently remarked to members of the Legation that they fear the ultimate conversion to Bolshevism of the working class when/once religion has been eliminated from their system.[99]

The Shah was clearly elated with the new dress code and the uniformity, and apparent discipline, it imparted:

> On the 12th June the Shah asked me if I had been present at the opening of the Majlis. When I replied in the affirmative, His Majesty expressed pleasure and remarked that if I had been there some years ago I should have noticed a great difference. Then all were attired in various garbs, there was no cohesion, no corporate feeling. On the 6th June last the members were all dressed alike, there was uniformity and discipline; that was what a Parliament should be.[100]

Protests that did emerge from these increasingly heavy-handed social policies were often brutally suppressed, the most notorious having occurred in Mashhad in July 1935. Opinions differ as to the precise sequence of events, but unrest had been mounting against the Shah's dress codes and its seems that a senior member of the *ulema*, Hajj Aqa Hussein Qummi, decided to seek an audience with the Shah to air popular grievances, in particular the adoption of the new hat and the concern that the government intended shortly to enforce the unveiling of women.[101] Once in Tehran, not only was he not permitted to see the Shah, but he was effectively placed under house arrest. When news of his predicament arrived in Mashhad a large crowd gathered to protest at the shrine of Imam Reza, the holiest shrine in Iran. Other accounts relate that the crowd had gathered to protest the Shah's policies on the occasion of the anniversary of the Russian bombardment during the Constitutional era. What the local garrison did next is also a moot point. Some argue that the troops entered the shrine guns blazing, while others suggest that the Governor-General of Khorasan was in fact reluctant to enter the shrine. In any case, two days later a larger crowd gathered and this time, following direct instructions from the Shah, the troops, using machine guns, indiscriminately fired into the crowd resulting in a massacre of several hundred people. Equally seriously, it severely damaged the prestige and image of the Shah among the people, but in particular among the *ulema*, many of whom could not forgive the blatant violation of the sanctity of the shrine which they had witnessed. As the British Consul in Mashhad reported,

> Such is the simplicity of the humble Khorassanis that, even after this demonstration of cruelty, they still held to their belief that the Shah would punish the officials responsible for bloodshed and desecration of the shrine. When some nights later, troops surrounded the building and mowed down men, women and children with machine guns, they were disillusioned.[102]

One inadvertent consequence of this was the elevation of Qom as the centre of Shi'a scholarship at the expense of Mashhad.

Despite the subsequent execution of the administrator of the shrine, Mohammad Vali Asad, ostensibly the cause of the massacre, insult was soon heaped upon injury when Reza Shah decided to launch, as had been suspected, his most striking assault on tradition – the forced abolition of the veil for women, given visible manifestation when the Queen attended a ceremony in European dress. Guidelines on social etiquette were made available in order to instruct ladies as to the best way to behave in public, for the purpose was not only to unveil women but to integrate them into general society. The notion that women should interact socially with men they might not know and not be segregated at public functions was just as shocking to Iran's patriarchal society as the act of unveiling itself. The following extract from the magazine *Setareye Jahan* was typical:

> In these days of progress of women, it is well for us to give some instruction in the social etiquette of women, and hints on conduct at both public and private assemblies. Women on entering public meetings must on no account remove their hats. They are not compelled to take off their hats and gloves. Umbrellas of course are an exception and should not be brought into the room. Ladies should allow precedence to those of higher rank and older and should not stare at other lady guests to observe their toilet, nor should they primp with the aid of their own hand-bag mirrors in such a way as to attract attention. Those who have the habit of putting their handkerchiefs, cigarette cases or other articles in their breasts or up their sleeves must quit and use their bags for such things. Loud laughter and talking which attracts attention are forbidden. Many matters and events relating especially to women must not be narrated to men. As to blowing the nose, it should be done without noise yet without too obvious an attempt at concealment. Conversation about the dress and age of other ladies present is displeasing. To take fruit or sweets with gloves on is forbidden.

These continuous changes in the dress code proved frustrating for the populace, as a report from Khuzestan conveys.

> The first far reaching reform was the abolition of the Pahlavi hat . . . It was then announced that all persons working in the sun might wear a sun helmet. The next effort was on motor drivers, who were instructed to procure peaked caps of a European model. Towards the end of 1934 the wearing of hats inside offices was forbidden. It was not until the summer of 1935 that all officials adopted European hats and received instructions not to deal with the public if wearing Pahlavi hats. Regulations were also published as to how to wear and when to remove one's hat. Various forms of persuasion were used by the Governor-General, the police and the military – but little force was used except in isolated instances of remonstrance. Special hats of quaint design were ordered for tribesmen, and it was found that a Pahlavi hat with the stiffening removed made a graceful 'God blimey' object, which for a time satisfied the authorities . . . After three months of quiet persuasion a few arrests were made, and from then onwards no more Pahlavi hats were seen. On the whole the public accepted these changes without much fuss, as it was

realised that a hat with a brim is a more practical article, except for religious observance, which is of importance to a very small minority, at any rate of town-dwellers . . . The women's turn came in 1935, when school mistresses and girl students were invited to remove their veils. The wives of all officials were next instructed to conform, but no general attempt was made to coerce the public. Agents and spies were sent to guide and report on public opinion . . . The necessity to provide new hats and clothing in replacement of the chaddur has been a severe financial strain on many of the population. Resistance has mostly been on these grounds.

Interestingly, the British were in this case seen as the prime motivators rather than any admiration for Ataturk, the assessment continues:

No sooner was the women's emancipation movement well launched than instructions came through that all officials must immediately obtain correct regulation dress for official occasions and evening wear. Those who had not conformed were excluded from the receptions on the Shah's birthday and at the Nowruz, and note was taken of the names of those who failed to attend. The local notables were advised that they were expected to follow suit and to obtain morning coats, silk hats and evening dress. This has probably caused more hardship and discontent than the previous changes. Local tailors, amongst whom are many Indians, have reaped a golden harvest. It is perhaps partly of this that it is popularly supposed that His Majesty's Government is the instigator of the dress reforms.[103]

The reaction to this policy, even among the professional and propertied middle classes, varied from satisfaction at seeing the members of the *ulema* 'dying of grief and strain', to a sense of the ridiculous born of the knowledge that unaccustomed as they were to European dress, their appearance might be regarded as ludicrous. As noted above, many women simply refused to leave their homes, while the poorer elements in society found they couldn't afford the new clothing. At a soirée given for the Shah's birthday by the Governor-General of Kerman, the demand that men appear in 'tails' resulted in 150 of the 200 invited guests not turning up. As one British diplomat noted,

What, I think, has hurt the richer classes most is that they know themselves to be ludicrous in their Europeanised roles, and ridicule is notoriously hard for an Iranian to bear . . . one feels that many wrongs will have been forgotten before people forgive the Shah for the offence which he has given to nearly all classes.[104]

In his increasingly zealous bid to construct a unified nation in both body and soul, Reza Shah grew correspondingly intolerant of those who did not adhere to his vision of Iran. In this respect, ethnic, political and religious 'deviants' were all targeted. As his coercive power grew, so the battle shifted from the temporal to the ideological plane, from the realm of action to the realm of thought. And it was not only the Shi'a *ulema* that were persecuted, but Zoroastrian, Christian, Jewish and Baha'i Iranians all came under attack, principally through the restriction or banning of their right to educate their children in specific schools. But in other cases worse was to follow. The Jewish Deputy was arrested, tried and executed in 1931 for ostensibly, 'causing, by false promises, a number of unfortunate Jews to leave their beloved fatherland of Persia and suffer untold agonies as emigrants to Palestine'.[105] Protected by the army, and promoted by comprehensive censorship which prevented news of protests or dissent from being published,[106] the Shah's identification of himself with his particular conception of Iran continued to be emphasised. By 1939 the attempted ideological monopolisation of the state was reaching fever pitch.

> The Persian press . . . is under strict government control. It confines itself almost entirely to the reporting of events. Editorials and original articles are more often concerned with the discussion in quite general terms of social objects which the government wishes to encourage than with internal events. Editorials on foreign and international affairs would involve the expression of opinions on these topics, a thing most carefully avoided except where Iran itself is directly concerned . . . and extremely venomous articles on the press of any country whose most insignificant journal happens to make a reference to Iran or its Royal Family that the Shah considers uncomplimentary. Pride of place in all papers is given to reports of activities of the Shah and the Royal Family . . . All material of whatever nature is censored. Censorship is exercised by a Department situated in the Ministry of the Interior, on which the police, educational authorities and the Ministry of Foreign Affairs are represented. Foreign news reports are controlled by a special organisation known as Agence Pars, which is a department of the Ministry of Foreign Affairs. The Ministry of Post and Telegraph record foreign wireless news bulletins and send these to Agence Pars . . . The recently formed Institute for the Orientation of Public Opinion, on which sit representatives of the Ministry of Foreign Affairs, Ministry of the Interior, Educational and Police Authorities, has contact with the press. The proceedings of the Institute, which chiefly takes the form of public lectures, are reported in detail, and the press is utilised by them to put before the public particular points of view. These however are usually concerned with internal rather than foreign affairs. Lastly, there is a Department of the Police which reads articles appearing in the press. It draws the attention of editors to any points, requiring rectification, or any tendencies to be suppressed, etc. It also summarises articles appearing in the press and submits these summaries to the Shah.[107]

As one commentator noted, almost all nationalist outbursts were state controlled and press articles frequently extolled 'the Shah as the father of his people', concluding pessimistically that 'In his policy of centralisation and unification the

Shah has created enemies and in destroying the power of the mullahs he has forgotten Napoleon's adage that the chief purpose of religion is to prevent the poor from murdering the rich'.[108] But other problems also lay on the horizon, not least from the Shah's own policies in encouraging 'Westernisation' and raising expectations among the young, who were increasingly asking questions about the political direction of the country.

> It is anticipated that the rising generation of Iranians will shortly provide a problem which, unless great economic changes take place, must ultimately prove a source of embarrassment to the Government . . . With the outward trappings of westernisation there is springing up among these young men an inquisitiveness as to social and political conditions in other countries . . . Some time in the not very distant future this body of youth will prove an unruly element, which, unlike ignorant masses demonstrating in a shrine, cannot be dispersed with machineguns, and may well prove dangerous to an Administration founded exclusively on the fear of a single individual.[109]

The fall

In the event, the fall came quickly. Not from within, but from an almost irresistible challenge posed by the Allies in the Second World War. It was an exercise in realpolitik in which Reza Shah Pahlavi became expendable in the interests of the wider international imperatives. The fact that it happened so easily, with so little domestic opposition, is testament to the hollowness of the regime that had been constructed: solid in appearance but devoid of the broad social base with the moral fibre or nationalist fervour necessary for its sustenance. With the advent of war in Europe in 1939, and in particular the German invasion of the Soviet Union in 1941, Iran's position became precarious. The rise of Hitler, as we have seen, had already provided British diplomats with a model with which to view developments in Reza Shah's Iran. As the dominant power, Britain was increasingly concerned by German industrial and commercial influence in the country, and worried about the prospects of political influence. It was, in all probability, a misplaced concern. While Reza Shah may have had more affinity with the fascist dictators and was certainly keen to foster the bond of Aryanism, in strictly political terms he was equally averse to all those who might pose a challenge to his power, whatever their political affiliation. The Zoroastrian Deputy, Sharokh Arbab Keykhosrow, for instance, was gunned down in the street in 1940 because his son had broadcast a series of pro-Nazi speeches in Germany.[110] Indeed, it would appear that Reza Shah frowned on attempts to start a 'Nazi' party in Iran.[111] It may be fair to conclude that allegations of German sympathies, while plausible, were largely a mechanism of justification for the Allied policy of occupation, following Hitler's drive towards Moscow and Baku, and the urgent need to supply the beleaguered Red Army with essential equipment.

The strategy for occupation was twofold. First, a comprehensive propaganda campaign to malign the Shah, for which the BBC Persian Service was founded, would be followed by a military invasion from two directions. The Red Army would occupy the north, while the British and the Americans would enter from the south, in a plan reminiscent of the 1907 partition agreement between Great Britain and Tsarist Russia. In the event, such was the unpopularity of the Shah that little effort was actually needed from either front. Few needed convincing that the Shah was surplus to requirements, while the much-vaunted army crumbled in less than a week. For those who had invested time, money and emotion in the regime, it was a severe humiliation. For much of the population, however, the Allied invasion was like a breath of fresh air releasing them from a state of political suffocation. The Shah, bitter at the turn of events, abdicated in favour of his son and departed into exile in South Africa. The degree of alienation which he felt, but for which he was undoubtedly in part responsible, is reflected in his last statement to his cabinet:

> Gentlemen! I am leaving the country soon, and must say something that you should know. No one has ever had any appreciation from me for his services and no one was ever thanked or rewarded by me, although some excellent services were rendered. Do you know why? The reason is because this country has no opposition. My decisions were all made and carried out without you . . . With regard to my plans and ideas, the secret of my success was that I never consulted anyone. I studied the problems quietly, and without showing why I was interested. But last year for the first time in my life I tried to change this way, and consulted the Higher War Council . . . If I had not done so, I would not now find myself in this situation.[112]

An assessment

> He had no personal charm, and did not seek popularity. He considered it his mission to work for the Iranian nation not by courting her, but by administering to her the medicines he considered useful for her health even if they were bitter, without taking the trouble to enclose them in sugar-covered capsules. He knew what Iran needed, and had no intention of consulting anybody on the subject.[113]

On the occasion of the demise of our late king, Major Campbell, our vice consul in Zahedan, heard a well informed Iranian say, 'If the Shah of Iran should die, his subjects would be so happy that they would forget to bury him'. On the same occasion, a person of some importance said to a member of staff at Zabol: 'King George was not our king, but we mourn his death as a just ruler. Iranians would have rejoiced if their king had been taken instead'.[114]

This movement for Westernisation and modernisation answered, or seemed to answer, the desire and need of the intellectuals. By thus conforming to the temper of a potentially influential section of the population of the country, Reza Shah was able to persuade the people to furnish him with such force as was necessary to impose his will. Realising that he could control the mass only by acting through the minds of the people, he used the force . . . to create instruments to reach and influence the public mind, and in this his efforts were accompanied by a considerable measure of success. As time went on, however, the dictatorship became more and more severe and more and more cramping to the freedom of the individual. On the one hand, the citizen was finally deprived of all opportunity for effective and creative social action, while, on the other hand, the force which the dictator had acquired was used more and more to indulge his own lust for power and material possessions . . . Reza Shah was the price Persia had to pay for undue delay in making the political and social adjustments which were implied in her incorporation as a national state into Western society.[115]

Opinions will continue to remain divided over the character, personality and achievements of Reza Shah. His supporters attribute to him all the achievements of his age and more. His detractors attribute to him all the ills of his age and more. An appreciation of Reza Shah is important not only for the purposes of history but because his reign and his legacy continue to inform political values and judgements today. Many of the leaders of Iran in subsequent periods, not least the Ayatollah Khomeini, lived through their formative experiences during this period. Indeed it is not inaccurate to argue that an understanding of modern Iran is not possible without an appreciation of Reza Shah, his methods and the flawed legacy which he left his countrymen. As Chehabi asks, 'If the gradual discarding of the veil observed in the 1920s and 1930s had been left to take its course, might the violence to which ill veiled (*bad hejab*) women are subjected in contemporary Iran not have been avoided?'[116] His was an incomplete achievement which left most of his countrymen teetering between ambivalence and dislike. As Lambton noted in late 1940,

> There is . . . a general feeling that the Shah has done a great deal for the country. On the other hand there is a widespread opinion that the Crown Prince in the event of the Shah's death may not succeed in establishing himself on the throne, but it is of course not openly voiced.[117]

For many who were willing to tolerate Reza Shah, he was indeed viewed as a transitional figure, necessary but most definitely transient. Others were less forgiving, viewing him as a modern version of the despots of old, harnessing all the tools and institutions of the modern age to his dynastic ambitions. As Lambton noted in an assessment shortly after his fall,

> It was unfortunate for Persia that by the 1920s when Reza Shah rose to power the better had learned to control the worse, and thus it was that Reza Shah, by acting through the worse, was able to maintain himself in power.[118]

Reza Shah sat astride a period of transition from tradition to modernity but which ultimately yielded less modernity and more tradition. He oversaw the establishment of the framework of the modern state, using the able talents of Teymourtache, Firuz and Davar, but subjected its growth and development to his own dynasty. To Reza Shah must be accredited the blueprint for modern Iran, an achievement which even Ayatollah Khomeini could cautiously acknowledge. However, it would be left to his successors to build upon the very rough edifice he had erected, refining it and imbuing it with the one vital ingredient it lacked – conviction.

Notes

1 M.R. Ghods, 'Government and Society in Iran, 1926–34', *Middle Eastern Studies* 27(2), 1991, p. 219.

2 There was no shortage of templates and programmes for Reza Khan to follow, see Ansari, *The Politics of Nationalism in Modern Iran*, pp. 61–5, particularly p. 104. See also, Meskoob, 'Nationalism, Centralisation of Power and Culture', p. 499, and p. 507, note 50. See also the highly influential essays by M.A. Jamalzadeh, *Yeki Bud Yeki Nabud* (Once upon a Time), Berlin: Kavyani, 1340/1960 [first published 1922].

3 FO 371 [. . .] T 6376/191/379, Loraine to Austen Chamberlain, dated 1 May 1926.

4 FO 371 [. . .] T 6376/191/379, enclosure document 87, dated 1 May 1926, translation of Shah's speech from throne.

5 FO 371 [. . .] T 6376/191/379, Loraine to Austen Chamberlain, dated 1 May 1926.

6 Sackville-West, *Passenger to Tehran*, p. 142.

7 After Teymourtache's fall, the foreign press attributed much of the reforms to him, 'down to, or up to, the Shah's social and hygienic education', much to the annoyance of Foroughi, FO 371 16941 E879 dated 28 January 1933. For a long overdue reassessment of Teymourtache see M. Rezun, 'Reza Shah's Court Minister: Teymourtache', *International Journal of Middle Eastern Studies* 12, 1980, pp. 119–37.

8 FO 371 13782 E4703 dated 16 September 1929. See also J.R. Forbes, *Conflict: Angora to Afghanistan*. London: Cassell, 1931, p. 185.

9 FO 371 13782 E6245 dated 2 December 1929. Also FO 371 15341 E3611 dated 11 July 1931.

10 FO 371 [. . .] E2316/526/34 dated 5 May 1927. See also Rezun, 'Reza Shah's Court Minister', pp. 119–37.

11 FO 371 13542 E6707 dated 3 December 1930.

12 As Haas wrote in 1945, 'Far from talking of a deified nation as Mussolini did, he did assign to the nation a place in the scale of values that came very near to such a conception'. R. Haas, *Iran*. New York: Columbia University Press, 1945, p. 169.

13 FO 371 13781 E95, dated 7 December 1929.

14 Abrahamian, *Iran between Two Revolutions*, p. 150.

15 FO 371 12286 E4109 Intelligence Summary, dated 10 September 1927.

16 FO 371 12293 E3909 dated 13 September 1927. Clive described the party as 'Fascist'.

17 FO 371 20833 E7456/560/34 dated 4 December 1937.

18 FO 371 21895 E672/167/34, Intelligence report/amended Administrative Division, dated 15 January 1938.

19 The decision to reform the judiciary had been revealed earlier, see FO 371 12293 E1225 dated 14 March 1927.

20 FO 371 [. . .] E2316/526/34 dated 5 May 1927.
21 FO 371 [. . .] E2316/526/34, enclosure document 7, the royal speech at the opening of the newly formed Justice Courts, dated 26 April 1927.
22 FO 371 12286 E4109, Intelligence Summary, dated 10 September 1927.
23 FO 371 13071 E4672 dated 24 September 1928.
24 FO 371 12286 E4109, Intelligence Summary, dated 10 September 1927.
25 FO 371 [. . .] E353/95/34 dated 31 December 1928.
26 FO 371 [. . .] E4979/520/34 dated 5 November 1927.
27 FO 371 13064 E2128 dated 23 April 1928.
28 The interpretation of this incident has changed over time reflecting the political mood of the country. Originally regarded as indicative of Reza Shah's insensitivities, 40 years of the Islamic Republic have altered perceptions in Reza Shah's favour and a dramatisation of the incident for Iranian television (*Emarat-e Farangi*) did not necessarily elicit the 'correct' popular response.
29 Of course cultural cross-fertilisation is now more accepted; for instance the 'Persian coat' was adopted by European monarchs in the 1660s following a craze for all things 'Persian'.
30 FO 371 13071 E4672 dated 24 September 1928.
31 H. Chehabi, 'Staging the Emperor's New Clothes: Dress Codes and Nation Building under Reza Shah', *Iranian Studies* 26(3–4), 1993, p. 225.
32 FO 371 13781 E353 dated 31 December 1928.
33 FO 371 14538 E1804 dated 7 April 1930, and FO 371 13542 E2447 dated 14 May 1930.
34 FO 371 13781 E95 dated 7 December 1929 notes that in Tabriz the police and army regularly tear 'off the hats of aged sheikhs, trampling on them and otherwise destroying them'.
35 For an interesting discussion on the British view of the 'tribe' see M. Yapp, 'Tribes and States in the Khyber, 1838–42', in R. Tapper (ed.), *The Conflict of Tribe and State in Iran and Afghanistan*. London: Croom Helm, 1983, in particular pp. 154–6.

> In its final form the British view of the tribes was stood on its head and there developed the cult of the redeemed savage or laundered tribe, a neo-Rousseauesque view in which the tribesman, purged of those base practices which he had developed in the past, was to be insulated by British officers from contact with the corruption of Indian civil society and kept in a state of perfect childhood innocence.

Some Iranians felt that British sentiment towards Iranian society as a whole was of this ilk.
36 This reflected the very 'personal' nature of traditional politics in Iran. In seeking to settle the tribes, Reza Shah was in effect implementing a modern and essentially alien concept that territory, not people, mattered. One may say that it was indicative and symbolic of the depersonalisation of the state. Although in this case it was to be increasingly re-personalised and refocused within the leader, Reza Shah.
37 See R. Tapper, *Frontier Nomads of Iran*. Cambridge: Cambridge University Press, 1997, p. 284.
38 One Weberian argument propounded in S. Arjomand, *The Turban for the Crown*. Oxford: Oxford University Press, 1988, p. 63.
39 B. Turner, *Weber and Islam*. London: Routledge & Kegan Paul, 1974, pp. 80–81.
40 It was of course, as with much else, an incomplete achievement. The tribes were down but not necessarily out! Ironically, in the absence of a strong central state, the destruction of the tribes as an autonomous, decentralised social force, may have resulted in the weakening of the state as a whole, as was to become apparent in 1941. The Allies would probably not have been able to occupy Iran so rapidly had the tribes still been a potent force, a reality which was not lost on some Iranians.

41 FO 371 15341 E3611 dated 11 July 1931.

42 FO 371 15341 E3611 dated 11 July 1931, Clive's last dispatch.

43 For a useful discussion of the rural–urban relations in Iranian society, see H. Katouzian, *The Political Economy of Modern Iran*. London: Macmillan, 1981, pp. 14–17. The entire introductory chapter will be of interest to students of Iran.

44 Forbes, *Conflict*, p. 105.

45 FO 371 13071 E5964 dated 17 December 1928.

46 FO 371 15341 E606 dated 21 January 1931; see also FO 371 13781 E95 dated 7 December 1929, street widening in Tabriz; FO 371 16076 E1458 dated 23 March 1932, Shiraz; FO 371 16953 E1101 dated 27 February 1933, new town of Tol-e Khosrow; H. Filmer, *The Pageant of Persia*. Indianapolis, IN: Bobs-Merrill, 1927, describes the development of Malayer. See also *The Times*, 8 April 1931.

47 FO 371 13071 E5964 dated 17 December 1928.

48 Quoted in Wilbur, *Reza Shah Pahlavi*, p. 125.

49 L.P. Elwell-Sutton, *Modern Iran*. London: Routledge, 1941, p. 129.

50 A. Banani, *The Modernisation of Iran*. Stanford, CA: Stanford University Press, 1961, p. 66.

51 A.C. Millspaugh, *Americans in Persia*. Washington, DC: The Brookings Institution, 1946, p. 26.

52 J. Bharier, *Economic Development in Iran, 1900–1970*. Oxford: Oxford University Press, 1971, p. 239. See also Katouzian's criticisms of this policy in his *Political Economy*, p. 113.

53 Quoted in Jones, *Banking and Empire in Iran*, pp. 217–18.

54 In the event it was not until September 1932 that all Imperial Bank banknotes were withdrawn after the Iranian government asked for an additional delay to allow them to organise their own currency distribution.

55 See FO 371 13071 E5964, dated 17 December 1928. The British diplomat minuted of the Minister of Court that 'His general attitude was one of paternal pride in the Oil Company, as though it was a Persian institution'. To which a Whitehall official noted, 'One hopes that the pride of the MoC in the oilfields will not become too paternal'.

56 FO 371 E906/239/34 nr 279, dated January 1936, p. 7, quoted in Rezun, 'Reza Shah's Court Minister', p. 122.

57 FO 371 16076 E3927 dated 23 July 1932, dispatch by Hoare on the Anglo-Persian Treaty negotiations.

58 FO 371 14542 E1804 dated 7 April 1930; Rezun, 'Reza Shah's Court Minister'.

59 Rezun, 'Reza Shah's Court Minister', p. 123.

60 Rezun, 'Reza Shah's Court Minister', p. 129.

61 See Rezun, 'Reza Shah's Court Minister', p. 127. He argues that it was popularly held that Teymourtache would succeed Reza Shah as the first president of a Persian Republic.

62 FO 371 16941 E879/47/34 dated 28 January 1933, Foroughi in conversation with Hoare.

63 FO 371/E6345/47/34 dated 24 October 1933; quoted in Rezun, 'Reza Shah's Court Minister' p. 133. The parallels with the death of Amir Kabir are striking, not least the British reaction.

64 According to one author, Davar left a forthright letter for the Shah to read criticising the implementation of policies. See B. Aqoli, *Davar va adleyeh* (Davar and the Administration of Justice). Tehran: Elmi Publishers, 1369/1990. Other evidence, however, suggests that Reza Shah valued Davar even if he over-worked him and very much regretted his loss, see Hussein Makki, *Tarikh-e Bist Sale ye Iran* (A Twenty Year History of Iran). Tehran: Amir Kabir, 1982, Vol VI, p. 324.

65 FO 371 16951 E610 dated 14 January 1933. Laments that with Teymourtache gone no one will stand up to the Shah.

66 FO 371 13542 E6707 dated 3 December 1930.
67 FO 371 15341 E3611 dated 11 July 1931. Also FO 371 17907 E1133 dated 31 January 1934. A notorious case of favouritism was recorded in *The Times*, 28 November 1933.
68 FO 371 15359 E5619 dated 12 November 1931.
69 FO 371 16953 E1101/1101/34 dated 27 February 1933.
70 FO 371 16941 E878/47/34 dated 28 January 1933.
71 FO 371 16941 E878/47/34 dated 28 January 1933.
72 FO 371 17907 E2251 dated 24 March 1934. See also FO 371 17907 E3490/940/34 dated 24 May 1934. The army was often heavily involved in such festivals.
73 FO 371 17890 E56 dated 6 December 1933. In this respect they had moved some distance for the cultural awareness represented by Sir John Malcolm, see Chapter 3.
74 FO 371 16951 E610/610/34 dated 14 January 1933.
75 FO 371 16941 E1878/47/34 dated 25 March 1933.
76 See Menashri, *Education and the Making of Modern Iran*, pp. 93–8.
77 FO 371 [. . .] E4642/2960/34 dated 23 June 1934.
78 Quoted in Wilbur, *Reza Shah Pahlavi*, p. 135.
79 FO 371 18988 E616 dated 12 January 1935. See also Haas, *Iran*, p. 169.
80 Quoted in Wilbur, *Reza Shah Pahlavi*, p. 143.
81 Banani, *The Modernisation of Iran*, p. 147.
82 Abrahamian, *Iran between Two Revolutions*, p. 147.
83 FO 371 15352 E5662 dated 4 November 1931.
84 For substantially more detail see Abrahamian, *Iran between Two Revolutions*, pp. 154–62.
85 Quoted in Menashri, *Education and the Making of Modern Iran*, p. 141.
86 FO 371 18992 E4041/608/34 dated 14 June 1935. On the origins of the movement see, M. Kia, 'Persian Nationalism and the Campaign for Language Purification', *Middle Eastern Studies* 34(2), 1998, pp. 11–18. On the role of the language academy see M.A. Jazayeri, 'Farhangestān', *Encyclopædia Iranica*, www.iranicaonline.org/articles/farhangestan.
87 Makki, *Tarikh-e Bist Sale ye Iran*, p. 208. For more details see Ansari, *The Politics of Nationalism in Modern Iran*, pp. 97–109.
88 FO 371 16065 E50/E2522 dated 16 December 1931. A whole range of words were replaced with what was considered to be their Persian equivalents, including *Shahpur* for prince, and *Shahdukht* for princess, in a clear appeal to pre-Islamic Sassanian norms.
89 FO 371 18988 E3505/305/34 dated 29 December 1934; FO 371 18988 E952/305/34 dated 23 January 1935.
90 Roostai, *Tarikh nokhostin farhangestan-e iran beh ravayet asnad*, p. 83.
91 FO 371 18988 E305/305/34 dated 29 December 1934.
92 Mohammad Reza Shah decided that foreigners could use both terms, and indeed the English *Daily Telegraph* newspaper continued to use the term 'Persia' until 1979.
93 On the debate over race see Ansari, 'Iranian Nationalism and the Question of Race', pp. 101–16.
94 See in this respect, D. Motadel, 'Iran and the Aryan Myth', in A.M. Ansari (ed.), *Perceptions of Iran: History, Myths and Nationalism from Medieval Persia to the Islamic Republic*. London: I.B. Tauris, 2014, pp. 119–46.
95 FO 371 20052 E1147/1147/34 dated 28 January 1936.
96 See for instance H. Arfa, *Under Five Shahs*. London: Murray, 1964, p. 246.
97 FO 371 18992 E4628/608/34 dated 12 July 1935.
98 Wilbur, *Reza Shah Pahlavi*, p. 166.
99 FO 371 18992 E5443/608/34 dated 28 August 1935.
100 FO 371 18992 E4041/608/34 dated 14 June 1935.
101 FO 371 [. . .] E4628/608/34 dated 29 July 1935.
102 FO 371 20048 E4788/405/34 dated 10 July 1936.

103 FO 371 20048 E3515/405/34 dated 28 May 1936, New dress regulations.
104 FO 371 20048 E476/E994/E1155/E1565/E2325/E3172/E4515/405/34 dated 11 January 1936. Provides a comprehensive survey of the consequences of this reform.
105 FO 371 16065 E300 dated 19 January 1932.
106 FO 371 20052 E1147/1147/34, Annual report dated 28 January 1936.
107 FO 371 23263 E7945/1281/34 dated 18 October 1939.
108 FO 371 18992 E794/794/34 dated 5 January 1935, views of Mr Busk.
109 FO 371 20048 E4788/405/34 dated 10 July 1936.
110 Abrahamian, *Iran between Two Revolutions*, p. 163.
111 FO 371 20835 E3685/904/34 dated 5 July 1937.
112 Wilbur, *Reza Shah Pahlavi*, pp. 207–8.
113 Arfa, *Under Five Shahs*, p. 280.
114 FO 371 20048 E4788/405/34 dated 10 July 1936.
115 A.K.S. Lambton, 'Persia', *Journal of the Royal Central Asian Society* 31, 8 September 1943, p. 13.
116 Chehabi, 'Staging the Emperor's New Clothes', p. 229.
117 FO 371 24570 E139/2/34 dated 21 December 1940.
118 Lambton, 'Persia', pp. 13–14.

9   Political pluralism and the ascendancy of nationalism, 1941–53

The 12 years following the abdication of Reza Shah, between 1941 and 1953, were witness to a dynamic period of political activity in Iran. Situated after the political repression of the preceding 16 years and the developing autocracy of Mohammad Reza Shah, the period provides a valuable window on the social dynamics of power in modern Iran. During the reign of Reza Shah it may be argued that the foundations and basic architecture of a modern state were constructed on the remains, not altogether removed nor eliminated, of the traditional state. This modern state sought to create a new society in its own image, appropriating from and to some extent accommodating the traditional structures of Iranian society, in a bid ultimately to transplant it. Reza Shah succeeded to some extent in suppressing, through sheer force, traditional structures and attitudes, but failed to replace them with anything substantive or profound, in part because of his own ambiguous attitude towards them. He was, after all, a curious amalgam of 'moderniser' and traditional patrimonial monarch. Reza Shah's legacy was therefore both complex and dynamic, with a momentum of its own but not altogether focused. In his absence, power once again became diffuse and plural, emanating from diverse localities, all competing to capture his ambiguous inheritance, and divert and direct it to their own ambitions.

We may say, therefore, that Iran was at this stage possessed of two states and two societies, two 'modern' and two 'traditional'. An awkward Pahlavi state and society overlaid a traditional social base with its own integrated power structures (essentially the landlords, *ulema* and *bazaaris*) threatening to subsume it, while the latter reacted in its own defence against a state and embryonic society it often viewed with suspicion. Each laid claim to authenticity and legitimacy. Yet in 1941, the distinction between these two 'Irans' was neither clear nor apparent, in part a reflection of the incompleteness and ambiguity of Reza Shah's policies. The chasm was not yet so wide as to prevent a complex web of inter-relationships emerging. While the state created under the auspices of Reza Shah might dominate, the society he sought to form in his own image was as yet too exclusive to compete with the multitude who were either excluded from or disinterested in the new project. Neither was it, in its subservience to a patrimonial monarch, an especially 'modern' society, despite appearances. Indeed in seeking to disenfranchise and depoliticise *his* modern society, he constrained its political development, leaving that process to its traditional counterpart. In this way, it was *traditional* society which provided the counterbalance to the modern state and, with an emerging critical awareness, and subjected to a dialectical dynamic, it gradually began to 'modernise' itself.[1]

This process of integration between old and new was encouraged by re-emergent statesmen who straddled the traditional and the modern, and who were anxious to replace Pahlavi exclusivity with Iranian inclusivity. But it was also reflected in the growth of socialism as a political philosophy among many young people. They combined traditional social values with distinctly modern methods and ambitions, and they were an increasingly vocal and influential force in Iranian politics. As a result the monarchy no longer enjoyed the primary position it had held in the Iranian political arena. Though it remained in many ways the linchpin of the Iranian state, around which others sought to manoeuvre, its ability to operate unhindered was at times severely curtailed. Certainly during the premiership of Mosaddeq, the young Shah was effectively powerless, although the institution of the monarchy remained a focus for political loyalties and activity. This diffusion of power was accelerated and encouraged by the emergence of mass communications and the advent of the modern media, not only in terms of newspapers, which proliferated certainly in urban centres (in particular Tehran), but more crucially with the widespread use of the wireless radio. Literacy and proximity to the centre were no longer prerequisites to political action, although it must be stressed that the emergent political consciousness which it engendered only began to make itself felt at the end of this period. While the popularisation of politics, especially in the towns, was growing, political agency remained essentially the preserve of the elites. Politics was in essence elite-driven, even if some members of the elite found themselves increasingly held hostage by the crowds they had helped mobilise, in a peculiar case of the 'paradox of sultanism'. The radio was crucial to the integration of social and political activity in this period, which may for ease of discussion be divided into two parts: the first to 1946, essentially the period of the Allied Occupation, witnessed the breakdown and fragmentation of the artificial social consensus imposed by Reza Shah; from 1947 onwards we see the new Shah's first attempts to reinvigorate the dynastic nationalism of his father, in light of his mixed inheritance. Ironically, this attempt to seize the initiative was definitively appropriated by Dr Mohammad Mosaddeq who became the supreme icon of the nationalist movement displacing, temporarily at least, the young Shah, and transcending the division between the Pahlavi state and the resurgent traditional society. Indeed the failure of 'nationalism' to provide a cohesive bond by which Iran could resist the Allied invasion of 1941 reflected more the weaknesses of dynastic nationalism as conceived by Reza Shah. His 'modern' society was as yet too diffuse, weak and small to be the ideological engine of social cohesion. But this weakness did not translate automatically, as some foreign observers concluded, to the traditional structures, including all those who had been excluded or alienated by Reza Shah, and who had little sympathy for or empathy with the state which was in the process of collapsing. For many of them, the Allied Occupation liberated Iranian nationalism from the grip of the Pahlavi dynasty and gave it new life,[2] which would in time explode onto the international stage during the Oil Nationalisation Crisis of 1951–53, marking the emergence of another important dimension of Iranian development in the twentieth century – her emphatic integration into the international political and economic system.

The levels of political awareness

Much to Reza Shah's irritation, his industrial and educational reforms, as we have seen, provided the framework and catalyst for the growth of political awareness. His tendency to increase the institutions of social and political control by the end of his reign may be an indication of the growth of this tendency, which undoubtedly would have developed rapidly once these restrictions were lifted. Assessing the level or extent of such awareness, in the absence of widespread polling or surveys (which themselves may be inaccurate), is notoriously difficult. However, we may start with a self-assessment provided by 'progressive elements in Iranian society' in an anonymous letter to the British embassy in 1946. The writers note:

> About two thirds of the population of Iran is composed of peasants and tribesmen who are illiterate . . . In recent years the Tudeh Party has conducted a campaign against their exploitation, which has made them conscious of this aim, which is for them their only interest in politics. Otherwise their apathy is unbounded. The other third of the population live in towns and nearby villages; more than half being illiterate labourers . . . with slightly more political consciousness resulting from their contact with town life . . . There remains one sixth of the population with degrees of political consciousness varying according to their standard of education and intelligence. They include government employees and other people in receipt of salaries, artisans, shopkeepers . . . Over this stratum sits a class estimated to be a mere one per cent of the whole population which possesses and controls nearly all the wealth of the country and rules its people . . . They are the real rulers of the country.[3]

Though the writers lament the 'unbounded apathy' of the rural masses, they do nevertheless point to the fact that this was the period when their political consciousness was being awakened, largely through the systematic efforts of the communist Tudeh Party, ably assisted by the occupying Soviet forces. For the Tudeh, the rural peasantry were an untapped political resource, and they expended much effort in seeking to cultivate their loyalty. It is true that the rural population were as yet not as relatively important in a political sense as their urban cousins (elections, for instance, while profligate, were not conducted in a manner approximating democratic norms; people were often told how to vote and ballots were regularly 'pre-written'), and their political awareness remained very much second-hand, but they were never entirely ignorant of developments, and as the period progressed, could not realistically be ignored.

As one *Times* columnist wrote, 'this illiterate peasant is no fool. The poets are his companions and he knows his Ferdowsi and Hafiz and Saadi. Given incentive, he is quick and apt'.[4] Similarly, the British embassy noted in 1941 that the Iranian public was a good deal more sceptical about Allied war aims than at first expected: 'British propaganda . . . suffers, however, from one grave handicap. References to the objects for which the war is being fought – democracy, freedom, liberty, the security of the smaller nations – have a cynical sound in Persian ears'.[5]

The low level of literacy attested to in this letter is reinforced by an industrial survey conducted for the Seven Year Plan published in 1326 (1947–48), which reveals that among industrial workers literacy levels were no higher than 10–20 per cent. In chemical factories, of 4,548 workers some 1,331 were registered as literate, whereas among 4,501 workers in the sugar factories only 297 were noted as literate.[6] This tends to support the view that politics remained the preserve of the political elite and was focused almost exclusively in Tehran. Indeed Tehran's primacy in domestic politics and the consequent dubious legitimacy of many 'national' parties was criticised in an article entitled 'Parties of Iran' in the newspaper *Rahbar* in April 1943: 'Do not wonder that instead of parties of Iran we speak of the parties of Tehran. All the parties arise in Tehran and consist of some interested persons staying in the capital'.[7] However, so intense was the level of political activity among the intellectuals and professional classes, and such was the integration of the traditional social structures prevalent at that time, that even the illiterate were drawn in some measure towards political awareness and participation. This was encouraged by the mushrooming of the popular media.

The mass media

Some idea of the level of political activity can be ascertained by the propensity for political parties and the proliferation of newspapers. That both these organs often lacked structure and durability should not detract from the fact that they existed because of tremendous political enthusiasm. One scholar has recorded 22 significant parties active between 1941 and 1946, each with a comprehensive political programme.[8] Parties mushroomed in the run-up to elections, and branches or associate parties were established in provincial centres; student groups were actively cultivated.[9] Trade unions and 'Workers' Committees' also developed and invariably produced lists of demands which contained political rhetoric. In the case of the Azerbaijan Workers' Committee, the Soviet influence is clear – the first article of its 35-point programme of action stresses that it has been established 'To fight energetically against *despotism, dictatorship* and *fascism* [my italics], and to establish complete liberty: of the nation, of association, of the individual, of language, and of the press'.[10]

Press activity was if anything even more energetic, and every political grouping had at least one newspaper, usually a weekly, with which to voice its views. The number of newspapers often surprised Western observers. Bullard noted in 1943, 'There are 47 newspapers in Tehran, a city of only 750,000 inhabitants, the large majority of whom are illiterate'.[11] By 1951, in the lead-up to oil nationalisation, this figure had risen to some 700 papers in Tehran alone.[12] Cuyler-Young noted astutely in 1948:

> In few countries of the literacy percentage of Iran are journalists more numerous, facile, superficial and irresponsible. Yet for all the spawning and specious nature of the Iranian press, it can be said that a considerable section of it is substantial and serious, and influential beyond what literacy statistics might lead one to expect, since papers are read in groups, and news and opinions passed on by readers to illiterate friends and acquaintances.[13]

Indeed the awareness of widespread illiteracy ensured that many pamphleteers would ask readers to inform others who were unable to read of the contents of a particular pamphlet.[14]

The one party that actively sought the support of the illiterate, be they in cities or in rural areas, was the communist Tudeh Party. A thorough organisational framework and a seductive programme of action, along with a measure of support from the Soviet authorities, resulted in a positive and broadly successful attempt to mobilise the otherwise politically apathetic masses. The other parties and political groupings, often suspicious of the 'masses' were forced to react to the Tudeh challenge. The British Consul in Tabriz noted the development of Tudeh tactics as early as December 1941 along with the concern of the traditional political elite:

> It is not that the 'proletariat' here are communist minded so far, but the authorities fear that the demagogues . . . will gradually work upon them to cause unrest and later revolt against the established order. One of the new 'parties' is called Tudeh Azerbaijan . . . and its aim seems to be to interest the lower classes, who so far have never been touched by political ideas. Its newspaper 'Azerbaijan' . . . prints twice weekly cartoons of wretched peasants and farmers being beaten and bullied by hard faced landlords, or drawings of rich capitalists cheating poor ragged workers of a halfpenny while handing out large banknotes to dancing girls at cabarets, and so on.[15]

Almost ten years later, Lawford noted of the Tudeh paper *Mardom* that 'the paper is clearly designed less as a medium for educating Persians in the theory of dialectical materialism than as a weapon in the Tudeh Party's campaign to achieve political power in this country'.[16] There was a clear, conscious effort on the part of political groups to extend their influence into society which they increasingly viewed as a reservoir of potential support. The most aggressive in this regard was the Tudeh Party, but others, anxious not to be outmanoeuvred, also cautiously dabbled in populism.

The radio

With Soviet finance and support the Tudeh also had a spectacular new tool of dissemination which required no literacy, allowed immediate reception of political news and propaganda, and was dependent upon no one: the radio. The Allied Occupation as well as political interest ensured a relatively wide ownership of radios which meant that rousing speeches were no longer limited by space. As Pyman noted of the relatively remote town of Arak in central Iran:

> A member of the Qajar family who owns a good deal of land near Arak told me the other day that there are many wireless sets in the villages in that area to which all the peasants listen. The effect of this and of the bundles of Tehran newspapers which periodically reach the village is to give people an interest in politics which they never had before and a critical attitude towards their landlords.[17]

Governments of the day were quick to acknowledge the power of radio and would broadcast programmes to repudiate Tudeh views, stress their own commitment to reform and of course trumpet their achievements.[18]

The limits of plurality

Nevertheless, there were limits to this emergent political awareness. As Abrahamian points out,

> of the 12 premiers, 9 came from the 19th century titled families, 2 from Reza Shah's bureaucracy, and one from his military elite. Similarly, of the 148 cabinet ministers, 81 were sons of the titled and wealthy families, 13 were technocrats representing the court, 11 were army officers, and eight were prosperous entrepreneurs outside the bazaar.

He adds,

> Of the 148 ministers, only 15 were salaried personnel and modern educated professionals with roots in the middle class and without links to the palace. What is more, of the 50 ministers who held three or more cabinet posts, 39 came from titled and landed families, seven from the upper echelons of the bureaucracy, two from prominent military households, and only two from the salaried middle class.[19]

As if to emphasise the venality of the system, Elwell-Sutton commented in 1949 that, 'The 300 odd vacancies in some 24 cabinets between August 1941 and

November 1948 were filled with few exceptions from a clique of 70 to 80 politicians, all over 50 years of age, and many over 60'.[20] Even the Majlis, which so frequently argued with the executive, remained the preserve of the traditional elite. Of 128 deputies elected in 1943, 44 had sat in the previous Majlis, 65 were landowners, 13 were connected with commerce and industry, 4 were mullahs and another 46 were dependent on various forms of political activity including a number who were elected to serve traditional interests.[21]

Despite the existence of various competing political 'factions' and parties, this group remained essentially fluid, choosing to revolve around personalities. Mohammad Reza Shah in this period was but one personality attempting to reinvent himself as the saviour of Iran. Few parties could develop coherent durable structures which would outlive the founder. The only real contender was, ironically, the Tudeh Party (and its offshoots), which, despite solid social foundations, suffered the stigma of foreign support. Qavam enjoyed modest success with the establishment of the authoritarian Democrat Party. The National Front, a broad coalition of parties, was the most successful of all the political groupings, but this was more because of a unique combination of talents and circumstances (ironically a well-defined 'enemy') rather than coherent structure and organisation. Indeed Mosaddeq argued against any such organisation, saying that the country was not ready for such a body.[22] The dominance of personalities is indicative not only of the limits of political awareness and consciousness, but of the importance of traditional political structures. Reza Shah had sought to refocus the personalisation of the state onto himself, defining himself as a traditional patrimonial ruler with modern tools of government to subsume and suppress other competing political personalities. Now these were re-emerging, traditional institutions coated in the discourse of modern democracy and plural government. That is not to say that this process did not affect these traditional structures, for in time they would; it was simply that at this change in Iran's political development, the 'traditional' outweighed the 'modern'.

The dominance of nationalism

Developments confirm that this was by far the most potent ideology of the period. Groups of all political persuasions attempted to appear more nationalistic than their rivals and the most stinging criticism of a political opponent remained the charge of 'traitor'. Each competing group sought to cloak itself in the mantle of nationalism, which proved a fluid and adaptable concept. Its fundamental credentials as the ultimate arbiter of legitimacy were not challenged. So pervasive was this concept that divisions between factions were defined by the types of nationalism they ostensibly espoused. As a result the concept of nationalism and the definition of patriotism were hotly contested. For the first time since Reza Shah's coercive hegemony, intellectuals publicly challenged the assumptions of dynastic nationalism, refuting the notion that loyalty to the nation and the crown were one and the same. At the same time they challenged the vision of 'Iran' as defined by the Pahlavi state. These were often subtle but important differences.

Thus Reza Shah's use of 'Iran' emphasised a particular historical narrative which would connect the modern state to its pre-Islamic 'Aryan' past imagined as a homogenous whole, defined by a strong centralised state: a 'nation-state' in every sense. Now nationalist politicians, reflecting perhaps the new political realities moved away from this reading and returned to the more inclusive and pluralistic interpretation that had dominated the Constitutionalist movement. An inclusive reading that would serve better as a means of fostering unity. Thus as noted earlier, one could be a Kurd or Azerbaijani and still be fundamentally 'Iranian'. Iran was therefore culturally inclusive and while predominantly Persian, was not exclusively so. For these nationalists the whole was not greater than the sum of its parts, although tensions between these two readings would continue to exist with political exigencies often resulting in a reversion to centralised conception identified with Reza Shah. Nonetheless, in the changed political environment, it was not surprising that the exclusive dynastic nationalism of the Shah would be vulnerable to a political leader who might embody a more inclusive broad-based nationalism.

Fragmentation: challenges to the Pahlavi state – the Allied Occupation

The rapidity of the collapse of Reza Shah's state reflected not only the imperfection of his programme of centralisation, and the personal nature of the state, but also the fragility of the cement holding it together. Few people were interested in its maintenance. But perhaps the most damning personal indictment was inflicted by the apparent collapse of the army. The institution that symbolised Reza Shah's state and power, the institution that had been favoured over all other organs of government, had proved almost ridiculously inadequate to the challenge posed by the Allied invasion. The invasion, which had been launched on 25 August 1941, was effectively concluded by the end of the month. The Iranian government turned over control of the greater part of the country to the Allies by 9 September; a week later, Reza Shah abdicated, and went into exile on 28 September. After some prevarication, in which consideration was given to a restoration of the Qajar dynasty,[23] the Allies settled on Reza Shah's son, the young and somewhat traumatised Mohammad Reza Pahlavi, who was sworn in as the new Shah in the Majlis on 17 September. It was a precarious start to what would turn out to be a turbulent reign. Stripped of many of the powers enjoyed by his father, the young Shah looked on as intellectuals and resurgent politicians emerged to dissect the collapse of the Pahlavi state and allocate blame.

Unsurprisingly, the first targets for national scrutiny and recrimination were the institution of the monarchy and the army, along with the cult of militarism fostered by the deposed Shah. Having been trumpeted as the very soul of the nation by Reza Shah, the undignified rapidity of the armed forces' apparent disintegration in the face of the Allied attack brought the military into popular disrepute. Similarly, the particularly aloof and dictatorial style of monarchy espoused by Reza Shah was seen as a prime reason why the Iranian state failed to respond effectively to the Allied invasion. The close, personal association between army and monarchy was regarded as detrimental to the security of the state. Traditionalist politicians, most of whose formative years revolved around the events of the Constitutional Revolution, sought to divest the crown of its author-ity over the armed forces and bring the military under civilian control.[24] Almost immediately, the young Shah was deprived of his responsibilities as commander-in-chief of the armed forces, as well as the Gendarmerie, previously amalgamated and centralised by Reza Shah.[25]

This attack upon the army and the monarchy was supported by the new young socialists, born of traditional society (some indeed emanated from aristocratic families) but shaped and nurtured by the industrial and educa-tional policies of the previous 20 years. Imbued with a strong sense of social responsibility, they represented the unforeseen consequence of Reza Shah's modernisation and reflected one of the first dialectical syntheses of traditional society and modern state. Young, idealistic and determined, they, along with the traditional notables, viewed the 'military state' as developed by Reza Shah to be detrimental to the welfare of the country. Though these two ideologi-cal camps differed strongly on the specifics of political reform (most young socialists had little time for the old elite), the Allied invasion offered them the opportunity to challenge the centralised militarist-monarchical autocracy, which they both had reason to despise.

Not surprisingly the army and the monarchy sought to defend their positions and rallied to each other.[26] The Shah was weaker and was encouraged to distance himself from the person of his father.[27] This clearly was not a credible position to take especially when it became apparent that the new Shah was in reality in awe of his father,[28] as he was later to indicate; but in the immediate aftermath of the invasion, it was deemed prudent to publicly argue against 'dictatorship',[29] to emphasise a willingness to reign rather than rule, and to acknowledge the excesses of the father.

In contrast to his father, he became more accommodating, stressing to the Majlis that he 'had no powers', in an effort to disguise, retain and if possible add to what power he had left.[30] However, his real weakness meant that tradi-tionalists, eager to maintain the social status quo in an increasingly destabilised situation, were much less eager than their socialist allies to eliminate the insti-tution of the monarchy itself. They encouraged its representation as a symbol of unity. Thus as early as late 1942, the Prime Minister broadcast an effusive speech praising the 'beloved Shah who is the source of the nation's happiness'.[31] The Shah was assisted in this belief in himself by a characteristically sycophantic court,[32] as well as the general adulation of the provincial populace who frequently expressed genuine enthusiasm on meeting the Shah.[33] Ironically therefore, his real weakness was compensated for by a restitution of a modified form of the ideology of dynastic nationalism.

The army sought refuge with the crown,[34] though initially it sought to disas-sociate itself from such an exclusive relationship. Eager to deflect criticism, it first sought to relegitimise its social and political status in Iranian society by divesting itself of responsibility through rationalisation of its defeat and by indicating the relatively common occurrence of such rapid defeats in modern warfare. Thus in 1942, the Minister of War claimed that the defeat of the army was due to poor mechanisation, noting that other armies had suffered similar reversals for just such technical weaknesses (presumably France in 1940 and the USSR in 1941).[35] Then it sought to distance itself as a tool of the monarchy and to stress its role as the ultimate symbol of national unity. As one Majlis deputy noted, 'people must not get into the habit of thinking of the army as something distinct from the nation; it was not'.[36] Nevertheless the relationship between the monarchy and the military remained intense, helped by the Shah's personal fascination with all things military.[37] The Shah always regarded the army as his chief pillar of support.[38]

The armed forces felt deeply humiliated by the defeat and their dislike for the Allied forces and desire for revenge[39] was both endemic and infectious among a population whose national pride was dented and whose relationship with the occupying powers rapidly turned sour. The popular cynicism towards Allied war aims and the ostensible reasons given for the invasion were initially outweighed by the general satisfaction at the abdication of Reza Shah. But the social reality of occupation, including food shortages and economic dislocation,[40] encouraged nationalist sentiment to the point of extreme chauvinism.[41] At one stage the outbreak of disease was blamed on Polish refugees and the Allies who brought them.[42] Many openly voiced their support for the Germans, and swastikas were daubed on pavements.[43] Despite the fact that the Americans had joined their Russian and British allies in occupying Iran, politicians sought to draw favourable comparisons between Iran and the United States. In one speech the Shah sought to draw comparisons between Iranian nationalism, fighting for 'independence', and American nationalism, subtly noting its distinction from the British.[44]

At the same time officials, such as the Shah and Prime Minister Soheili in their New Year messages, sought to alleviate the sense of hardship and humiliation by placing events within an intensely nationalist interpretation of history. Thus Soheili notes,

> Since the day when Iran was united under the banner of Cyrus the Great and in the centre of Asia achieved unprecedented power and became famous throughout the world, and the star of her prosperity rose daily towards its zenith, 2500 years have passed. During this time, this 2500 years, the people of this land have experienced repeatedly calamity, misfortune, scarcity and famine, but they have never lost their courage and they have resisted until they successfully overcame their afflictions and experienced once more the more prosperous and more glorious days of former eras. This *truth* [my emphasis] is one of the secrets which compelled our ancestors to treasure to this extent the coming of the New Year.[45]

Gradually the humiliation of defeat and occupation was transformed into praise for Iran's selfless assistance to the Allies. In effect, Iran became one of the Allies! Indeed, by the end of the war official disdain for the Allies was set aside, though popular anti-Allied sentiment remained strong. As one intelligence officer wryly noted in 1945, 'Persia celebrated the victory of herself and her Allies over Germany with restrained elation'.[46] The Shah was also aware that, in order to deflect criticism of the monarchy, he would have to address issues of immediate relevance and he began the process of realigning himself with the young socialist tendency and showing concern for popular welfare. Nevertheless, though his real political weakness brought some respite from the criticism, his failure to control the extravagances of the court, especially during a time of hardship, contrasted sharply with his purported image as the caring monarch. As a result, the monarchy, and in particular his conduct of it, came under renewed attack.[47] Traditionalists, naturally sympathetic to the institution of monarchy, frowned upon the loose morals exhibited by the court; however, criticism from the new socialists was stronger. The monarchy dealt with this challenge in two ways. By exaggerating the potential for social disruption and revolution, the Shah sought to manipulate the traditionalists' desire for a symbol of unity. At the same time he strove to become more revolutionary than the revolutionaries and to promote himself as the champion of youth and the lower classes. He cleverly sought to extend his appeal to these two disparate groups.[48]

The alliance between the traditionalists and the more radical 'national socialists' proved short-lived. The traditionalists became increasingly concerned about the growing strength of the socialist agenda, with ideas which would challenge the socio-economic status quo. For the socialists and communists, supported by the occupying Soviet forces in the north, restricting the power of the monarchy and divesting it of control of the military was but the first step towards a complete change of the social order. No clearer indication of this perceived threat and the impact it had on restoring the 'value' of a strong army (and by extension the monarchy), can be given than the reaction to the workers' revolt in Isfahan in 1944, couched, of course, in nationalist terms. As Abrahamian notes,

> Fatemi of the Patriots, who a few months earlier had demanded a drastic cut in the army, now declared, 'unless we immediately finance an effective army, such uprisings as occurred in Isfahan will spread and destroy the whole foundation of private property'.

Similarly, a Democrat, whose spokesman had been vocal in denouncing the chiefs of staff, exclaimed, 'now that our house is on fire, all citizens should be in favour of a strong military. Without a strong military, the fire will consume Iran'.[49] Characteristically, it was the construction of a 'social problem' which resulted in the gradual rehabilitation of the military autocracy. Not for the last time the political establishment rallied around the one available symbol of national unity and security when faced with the threat of social upheaval.

The tribal revolts

The tribal revolts, principally that led by Nasir Khan Qashqai in Fars, reflected another attempt to redefine the boundaries of nationalism and to present an alternative perspective. Indeed few events in this period better reflect the failure of Reza Shah to fulfil his plans than the resurgence of the tribes. The opponents of renewed tribalism attempted to delegitimise the movement by attacking it as anti-nationalist and as the source of all the economic troubles of the country. However, it is equally a measure of the changes that had occurred that Nasir Khan, aware of these attacks, stressed his nationalism and his loyalty to the concept of an Iranian state. To Nasir Khan, it was the Pahlavi state which was the source of all problems, and which by its very nature was contrary to nationalist interests. In a declaration to the people of Fars, he differentiated himself and his aims from those of the Pahlavi state:

> Today even the brigands of the glorious cycle of Pahlavi are attempting to accuse the true patriots of the country [*vatan-parast va mellat doost*] of being the cause of intrigue and disorder in the country . . . O Iranian nation! I have put everything I have, my life, my honour and my tribe for your sake and am prepared to make all sacrifice for my country. I pray to God to be able to stop all such disorder. But the Iranian nation should take a fundamental decision, and do not let the reins of the country into the hands of unqualified persons, and not allow such people to rob the country.[50]

There can be no better indication of the dominance of nationalism within the Iranian consciousness than its use by a tribal chief whose tribe undoubtedly suffered under a government driven by a particular interpretation of nationalism. It is also significant that Nasir Khan's objection to the centralised state did not extend to a rejection of European-style clothes, which had originally caused such irritation. As the British Consul in Isfahan records, 'He was quietly and extremely well dressed (without hat) in the European manner and in fact apart from a suggestion of sleekness and alertness not generally associated with the soil could easily pass as a young and prosperous English farmer'.[51]

In the initial popular reaction to the rule of Reza Shah, there was considerable sympathy for the views and grievances of the tribes. As one British diplomat noted,

> there has been much agitation in the press and among certain deputies in favour of Nasir and the Qashqai. Nasir, who is really a rebel, has been held up as a great patriot and the Qashqai as the potential backbone of the defence of Persia's independence. The tribes, it is being argued, should be conciliated and preserved as fighting units.[52]

The newspaper *Etela'at* carried Nasir's plea for justice for the tribes.[53] Another paper, *Mehr-i Iran*, carried an article which noted that 'Persian history is full of great deeds of tribesmen in defence of the nation's soil'.[54] There was a clear attempt to rehabilitate the tribes by seeing them as a positive force in Iranian history, though it is significant that even those who sympathised with the tribes agreed with the principle of forced settlement. Nationalist concerns over territorial integrity, combined with a desire to protect private property, tended to outweigh any such sympathetic sentiments. Thus Majlis Deputy Nobakht's defence of the Qashqai position in the Majlis was shouted down with allegations that the Qashqais threatened internal security.[55] Ultimately, the fear of state disintegration, engendered by the separatist movements in Azerbaijan and among the Kurds, along with the simple social reality that many tribesmen were not upstanding citizens and prone to looting,[56] meant that the initial challenge to the centralist conception of modernisation failed.

The separatist movements in Azerbaijan and Kurdistan

In a period replete with crises and tension, the separatist movements in the Soviet-occupied provinces of Azerbaijan and Kurdistan marked the first serious challenge to the Pahlavi state and the popular self-conception of nationhood. It showed the disparities in the popular understanding of the meaning of 'Iran', and it harnessed far more intense feelings than any previous event. Once again the competing groups used the discourse of nationalism to support their cause, and one of the curiosities of the crisis was the similar way in which the central government in Tehran and the separatist movements espoused nationalist rhetoric. Thus, although the government in Tabriz berated Tehran for centralised government along with the exclusive use of Farsi, within the boundaries of Azerbaijan itself it tended to mimic those very policies. The movements in Azerbaijan and Kurdistan had arisen from a desire for local autonomy against the centralising and overtly 'Persian' policies of the previous government. They were supported and ultimately manipulated by the occupying Soviet forces who encouraged the transition from autonomy to separatism, a shift which challenged the integrity of the nation as understood by most nationalists of whatever political hue in Tehran. These movements are important not only because they allow us to see the variations in the concept and identity of 'Iran' but also because these essentially Soviet-sponsored movements in Azerbaijan and Kurdistan set the pace for the socialist policies which were to be adopted by most other political groups in Iran. But, crucially, their overt secularism was to encourage the emergence of 'religious nationalism' as a political force in the country. The crisis also witnessed the first concerted construction of a leadership cult beyond the confines of the monarchy. It centred on the person of the Prime Minister Ahmad Qavam, who had engineered the return of Azerbaijan. Ironically the very public entrance of the Shah and the army into Tabriz was to provide a substantial boost to the Pahlavi dynasty and the status of the military, both of whom sought to capitalise from new Cold War tensions. Indeed the Azerbaijan crisis, it has been argued, marked the beginning of the Cold War and signified Iran's entrance into the new global order.[57]

Nationalism dominated political rhetoric for both sides during the dispute. Initially, there was considerable caution on behalf of the new 'Azerbaijani National Government', and Pishevari, its leader, was anxious not to ignite the nationalist anger in Tehran. Talk first revolved around autonomy with specific statements rejecting any notion of violating Iranian integrity.[58] In Tehran, however, the reaction was not as conciliatory as that initially offered to the Qashqai. Talk of autonomy, along with obvious Russian support raised the spectre of another Treaty of Turkmenchai.[59] For many, Pishevari's claim for autonomy was an act of deception which did not concur with reality, such as the fact that the Tehran-appointed governor of Azerbaijan, Murteza Qulikhan Bayat, discovered that the Democratic Party of Azerbaijan treated him 'not as governor but as ambassador to the Azerbaijan Republic'.[60] On the other hand, there is also evidence to suggest that the allegations of separatism had been encouraged by Azerbaijani émigrés in Tehran (angered at the socialist bent of the new provincial administration) to promote nationalist sentiment in the capital as well as elicit support from supporters of traditionalism, the army and the monarchy against the spectre of Marxism.[61]

Whatever the reality of the situation, feelings rapidly polarised. The media along with popular writers such as Ahmad Kasravi were swift to raise the alarm through a particular interpretation of Iranian history, crude differentiation and exaggeration of the extent of the problem. Arguably, the paranoia over imminent national disintegration fuelled the growth of the problem. Thus Kasravi protested the existence of separate nations, arguing, 'If similar claims are to be advanced by other linguistic minorities – especially Armenians, Assyrians, Arabs, Gilanis and Mazandaranis – nothing will be left of Iran'. The newspaper *Etela'at*, in an editorial entitled 'Azerbaijan is the centre of Iranian patriotism', argued that Turkish was simply a tongue left behind by the Mongol and Tartar invaders.[62] Such rhetoric was not confined to radical nationalists, but was even voiced by papers close to the liberal Seyyed Zia. The paper *Kushesh* insisted that Persian must remain the language of education in Azerbaijan since Turkish was only an 'unfortunate deposit' left by the 'savage Mongols'. A Liberal Majlis deputy protested, 'this so-called democratic Party of Azerbaijan is striking terror among peace-loving citizens and is spreading the false notion that Persian is not the mother language of all Iranians'.[63]

That developments in Mahabad and Tabriz could cause such consternation among the political and intellectual elite in Tehran was probably less a result of genuine Azerbaijani nationalist sentiment and more to do with the organisational structure and political leanings of the leftist Democratic Party. Backed by the Soviet authorities, the separatist movements were able to exploit the socio-economic disparities of contemporary Iranian society and eventually suggest national independence. Ironically their methods bore a striking resemblance to those of Reza Shah, whom they obviously detested.

The initial stage of this policy was to inculcate a sense of distinctiveness through an emphasis on the use of the Azeri language in pamphlets and programmes of action.[64] Anxious not to be labelled as 'traitors', the leftist groups sought to exploit feelings of injustice among the Azeris and grievances against the central government.[65] Landlords were often portrayed as agents of central government, hence 'Persian' and foreign. Thus, the British Consul in Tabriz noted that the newspaper 'Azerbaijan . . . prints twice weekly cartoons of wretched peasants and farmers being beaten and bullied by hard-faced landlords, or drawings of rich capitalists cheating poor ragged workers of a half-penny while handing out large banknotes to dancing girls at a cabaret'.[66] The paper did not avoid more direct attacks upon the competency of central government and was not averse to the use of dissimulation in order to aggravate the sense of distinction. As the Tabriz Consulate noted,

> The newspaper 'Azerbaijan' overstepped itself last week in its usual anti-government tirades by printing an article accusing the local authorities of sending large quantities of wheat . . . to Tehran while there was only 40 days supply left here, so that in a few weeks Azerbaijan would be without bread. As a result the whole ignorant population of Tabriz rushed to the bakeries.[67]

Such policies were not always effective. As the British Consul in Tabriz noted,

> It was interesting to learn from one landowner at Rezaieh that the minority of good and humane proprietors who had not ill-used their peasants but had lent them money in times of need and taken an interest in their lives and welfare, were not being victimised now; on the contrary, the villagers in some cases stuck by them as an island in a surrounding sea of troubles.[68]

Apart from their attempts to encourage class differentiation and social problems, the leftist groups also aimed to present themselves as socially aware and part of the mainstream national socialist ideology. Thus Tudeh Azerbaijan was effectively renamed the Democratic Party of Azerbaijan. Political programmes talked of the fight against 'despotism', 'dictatorship' and 'fascism'. The first two slogans had good Iranian roots; the last, however, is a clear indication of Soviet influence.[69] On the whole the extreme left-wing groups had the most sophisticated political programmes and the organisation with which to disseminate them. It is a measure of their ideological strength that most other political factions adopted socialist policies and attempted to mimic organisational practices.[70] Probably the most effective political reaction to the Democratic Party of Azerbaijan was the Democratic Party of Qavam, which had developed a far more authoritarian structure than other parties. Additionally, as one of Qavam's advisers was later to admit, 'the situation forced us to adopt a radical image to compete with the revolutionaries'.[71] It is also an indication of the effectiveness of the secularising tendencies of the communist movement that Azerbaijan was witness to the first, albeit tentative, religious reaction, in the form of an Islamic Revolutionary Party.[72]

Once sentiment had been sufficiently aroused in this direction, it was but a simple step to push in practice for independence, allowing Pishevari to claim, with some justification, that such a demand was a natural outgrowth of years of social and economic neglect by central government. Thus, in justifying Azerbaijani independence, Pishevari argued,

> Azerbaijanis are Persians [Iranians] and wish to remain part of Persia [Iran] but they cannot surrender the liberties which they have won with so many sacrifices . . . I was ready to convert the national government into a provincial council and to recommend officials be appointed by the central government but the government would not agree.[73]

Despite remaining vague about the issue of national independence,[74] the new Azerbaijan government set about establishing the symbols of the new nation with a vigour and enthusiasm which would have made Reza Shah proud. The policy had been implemented from the beginning of the movement in order to make explicit differences with Tehran. Thus it was noted in 1941 that:

> The party held a large meeting at a theatre this week to pass a resolution whereby the wide main thoroughfare of Tabriz had its name solemnly changed from Khiaban Pahlavi (after the ex-Shah who created it) to 'Khiaban Sattar Khan' for one section and 'Khiaban Bagher Khan' for another after two local nationalist firebrands of the 1909 revolutionary days.[75]

By 1946 symbols of nationhood were far more explicit, including the over-writing of Iranian postage stamps, the issue of banknotes, the institution of new festivals and a new national flag. This flag was on show during the *NoRuz* (New Year) celebrations:

> The new Azerbaijan flag was conspicuous in the procession: it consists of the Persian tricolour, green, white and red, with a badge in the middle composed of ears of corn surrounding a conventional representation of mountains with the rising sun or some sort of beacon above them and the word 'Azerbaijan' inscribed between the tops of the ears of the corn.[76]

In addition a new curriculum was imposed, 'which not only endeavours to impart to the students a sound knowledge but also make them politically minded, by teaching them the history of Azerbaijan and enables them to judge for themselves where their real interests lie'.[77] Ironically, despite their own differences with monolithic Iranian nationalism, Azerbaijani nationalism was found to be no more tolerant towards minorities.[78] Two laws most similar to those of Reza Shah were those insisting on the use of 'domestic' textiles in manufacture, and the imposition of conscription, which was described as a 'national duty'. Conscription was no more appealing to Azeri nationals than it was to Iranian nationals, and the legislation caused much discontent.[79]

The movement based in Mahabad was not as well organised as that of Azerbaijan and initially at least it bore more similarity to the revolt of Nasir Khan, in that the Kurds sought more autonomy over their own affairs. Although there was little affection for the central government, especially in the guise of the armed forces who viewed Kurdistan as their special preserve, efforts were geared towards decentralisation rather than independence. However, agitation, and no little Soviet support, encouraged the development of a fledgling nationalist movement. Thus the British Consul noted that despite government incompetence, its position in Kurdistan remained relatively strong and that '[t]here is no genuine demand from Kurds . . . for independence'.[80] Indeed, in one of the first demands laid down by the Kurds for greater decentralisation, Soviet influence is apparent as it required that 'Arms held by Ajams [Iranians], who are the enemies of the Kurds and Fascists, must be collected and handed in to the Soviet authorities'. The Iranian government was aware of Soviet agitation and protested to the Allied powers that the Kurds involved were simply bandits. Indeed the Kurds admitted in their demands that they had looted.[81]

Soviet influence was most obvious in the use of narratives and euphemisms to extol the Kurdish national cause. For example, a Kurdish independence pageant was held in Mahabad which, according the British Consul in Tabriz, involved:

> A woman, with her hands chained, and carrying two babies on her arms, represented Kurdistan. She took her stand before three men representing Persia, Turkey and Iraq. A hand, bearing the Hammer and Sickle device, then came from behind the screen and unlocked her chains. Her veil fell and revealed on her bosom a Red Flag bearing the words: 'Long live Stalin, the liberator of small nations'. Durakhshani, the Commandant of Persian troops . . . said this new activity in the cause of Kurdish independence had begun immediately after the inauguration of the Mahabad branch of the Iran–Soviet Cultural Society, about three weeks ago.

Furthermore, when the Kurdish leader Qazi Mohammad appeared in Tabriz, 'he was greeted with the "Kurdish hymn to Stalin" in which Stalin is extolled as the supporter and the saviour of Kurdistan. Portraits of Stalin were carried in the procession'.[82] The Kurdish conception of what could be constituted as 'modern' also bore the hallmark of Soviet ideology:

> We desire to inform the whole world that the Kurdish nation, in solid unity, desire to adopt modern educational methods and to reject age old agricultural and other implements which have been in use since the days of Adam, and to adopt mechanistic implements.[83]

The separatist movements in Kurdistan and Azerbaijan failed because they did not enjoy as much popular support as they pretended to,[84] and did not anticipate the strength of Iranian national feeling, which effectively forced the government in Tehran to take action. There is little doubt that many of the political and intellectual elite were concerned about copycat movements, and indeed Nasir Khan had reacted to developments in Azerbaijan by starting his own 'Fars National Movement', which was in reality ineffectual. The movement to 'liberate' Azerbaijan gathered speed among Iranian nationalists who regarded it as a crucial test for the country. Not only did the movement radicalise nationalist thought, but it was also seen by both the Shah and the army as a vehicle which would ensure their popular rehabilitation.[85] The initiative, however, would come from elsewhere.

The idea that Iran was in need of a saviour, someone distinct from the young Shah, had been reverberating around elite circles since the abdication of Reza Shah. Many leading intellectuals and politicians sought to fill this vacuum in the national consciousness, including of course the young Shah, but he lacked credibility among the elite.[86] This preoccupation with a great leader is exemplified by the fact that most political parties were centred around individual politicians – the Tudeh was the one significant exception to this rule. Qavam was the first politician able to exploit this sentiment and give substance to this powerful myth. He spared no effort in cultivating this image of himself and even tested the idea with the British embassy.[87]

Qavam was a wily politician and one of the more constructive statesmen to have emerged in twentieth-century Iran. A member of the old aristocratic elite, he was described by Seyyed Hassan Mudarris as 'a sharp sabre indispensable for battles'.[88] The brother of the deeply unpopular Vosuq al Dawleh who had overseen the signing of the Anglo-Persian Agreement of 1919, Qavam was among the politicians arrested by Reza Khan following the coup in 1921. Soon, however, after the dismissal of Seyyed Zia, Qavam was released and asked to form the new government. He was Prime Minister again for a short while between 1922 and 1923, but with the rise to dominance of Reza Khan he went into exile, returning later to live quietly in retirement until the fall of Reza Shah by which stage he was in his sixties with considerable knowledge and experience of the political system. Indeed his background and age, and the fact that he had witnessed Reza Khan's rise and played with his infant son prior to the establishment of the Pahlavi dynasty, meant that he was considerably underwhelmed by the majesty of the Pahlavis and certainly regarded the new Shah as somewhat naive and ineffectual. As if to labour a point, his cabinet in 1946 included a number of individuals ill-disposed to the Pahlavis, including Muzaffar Firuz, the son of the murdered Prince Firuz. Qavam had become Prime Minister briefly in 1943, but much like Churchill in 1939, Qavam very much felt that finally his time had come in 1946 when he was once again called to the premiership during the Azerbaijan crisis. Qavam was an astute politician with a keen understanding of the processes at work. He cultivated friends and enemies alike in the knowledge that a fluid political process meant that one could never have too many friends. And he was not averse to talking to the 'enemy', if he felt it would serve his cause, in this case the liberation of Azerbaijan, which would bring its own rewards. He had, as noted above, created a political party around his person with strongly authoritarian structures. He also demanded and received control over a number of key ministries and brought in able administrators to help run the government. With this behind him he turned to deal with Azerbaijan, recognising that the linchpin in this process was in Moscow. An agreement with the Allies had concluded that all foreign forces would leave Iranian territory no more than six months after the end of the war. By January 1946, Soviet forces had still not left, providing a protective cordon around the separatist movements and causing great anxiety in Tehran. The new Prime Minister took the unconventional approach. While appealing to the Allies, and launching a protest at the United Nations Security Council (the first time the Security Council had been approached in this way), he took the decision to cultivate links with the left, and to begin negotiations with Pishevari. Granting the Azerbaijani government greater autonomy and freedom of action, Qavam effectively bought himself time as well as the growing antipathy of his enemies.

Among the many leaflets distributed in Tehran to mark the success of the government mission to Azerbaijan, was one which read: 'Freedom lovers of Iran guided by Qavam as Saltaneh, Iran's able statesman, are advancing towards new and greater triumphs and victories'.[89] Qavam's cultivation of this image not surprisingly drew criticism from his political foes who were at once jealous of his success and anxious about his authoritarian tendencies. Characteristically, the 'saviour' was charged with aspiring to 'dictatorship', and the dissimulation which had made him the 'guide' of 'freedom lovers' was used to equally good effect against Qavam. Far from being a friend of freedom, Qavam was now decried as its enemy; the newspaper *Atesh* headlined that 'Freedom Was in Danger'.[90] So suspicious were his critics of his intentions that a power cut which prevented the full broadcast of the Shah's *NoRuz* speech, but which was restored in time for Qavam's, was ascribed to a deliberate action by the Prime Minister![91]

Portraying himself as a friend of the left, Qavam also utilised his contacts in Moscow to investigate Soviet concerns and desires, and noted that their chief preoccupation was not the separation of Azerbaijan or Mahabad from Iran. Rather they were more interested in commercial concessions, particularly in the granting of an oil concession in the north to match the British oil concession in the south. Much to the horror of the nationalists in Tehran, Qavam agreed to this particular Soviet demand on the basis that it would result in the withdrawal of all Soviet troops. Noting that the agreement would need to be ratified by the Majlis, Qavam convinced his Soviet friends that this would be a mere formality. In this Qavam exemplified his intrinsic cunning, well aware that the Majlis was extremely unlikely to ratify any such agreement. In some ways, Qavam ensured this by pandering to Soviet sensitivities, for instance relaxing restrictions on the Tudeh Party. Such behaviour was bound to galvanise the establishment deputies in the Majlis. It was also bound to raise the ire of the British who began to draw up 'contingency plans' should Qavam 'drift into the position of a Russian puppet'.[92]

But Qavam's strategy was more complex. He recognised that the central government was militarily weak and therefore sought to achieve by political intrigue what he could not do by force. In cultivating the left, and appearing more revolutionary than the revolutionaries, Qavam sought to draw support away from the established socialist parties towards himself. He also wanted the support of some of the more sophisticated political organisations in the country, particularly in the Majlis, since the support of left-leaning deputies would be essential if he was to implement the many reforms, including constitutional reforms, he felt were essential to the welfare of the country. Similarly, in appearing friendly to the Soviet Union, he sought to undermine their support for Pishevari by arguing, successfully, that there was more to be gained by working with Tehran than by working with Tabriz. The *coup de grâce* would be the failure of Majlis deputies to ratify the agreement, thereby denying the Soviets their oil concession despite their having withdrawn their troops. Qavam would be hailed as the saviour of the nation and would possess a strong base in the Majlis as well as throughout the country to push through his domestic agenda. Like all complex political strategies it assumed too much and anticipated too little. The antipathy of his enemies developed into a fierce antagonism, especially when the Qashqai rebelled in the south demanding similar concessions to the Azerbaijanis, and the spectre of national disintegration emerged with a vengeance. Pressure from the nationalists in Tehran along with the British and Americans forced Qavam to change tack. With the Soviets out of Azerbaijan, government troops reoccupied the province almost unopposed – Azeris were no more disposed to Pishevari's state-imposed nationalism than they were to Reza Shah's. The Soviets may have been frustrated by their lack of an oil deal, but this was not regarded as Qavam's achievement. He was now anxiously rebuilding his links with the traditional establishment, having somewhat belatedly appreciated the strength of their opposition. The collapse of the separatist movements was, unsurprisingly, seen as a nationalist triumph. Popular sentiment was well expressed by chief of staff Razmara, who said,

> Today the population of Iran is celebrating the liberation of Azerbaijan but in fact we should be celebrating the liberation of Iran as a whole for, by deciding to intervene in Azerbaijan, we have dispelled a tremendous danger and serious menace to the entire territory of Iran.[93]

Qavam naturally sought to reap the harvest himself.

But this was not to be the case. In trying to be too clever, Qavam had undermined his own position, and in moving troops into Azerbaijan he forsook the support of the socialist groups he had so carefully cultivated. For the time being it was the military and the Shah who basked in the reflected glory of Qavam. For the military, the reoccupation of Azerbaijan ensured their rehabilitation in the national consciousness. They were once again perceived as a tool of national unity. In this respect the crisis had positive implications for the military. The Shah also gained credit but the net gain was probably not as substantial. The Shah and the dynasty had come in for substantial criticism in Azerbaijan; the Shah's birthday was not commemorated;[94] and Reza Shah was described as Reza Khan.[95] Furthermore, insiders were aware that the 'liberation' of Azerbaijan had more to do with Qavam's diplomacy than the Shah's leadership, or indeed any rumoured American ultimatum.[96] Nevertheless, the Shah gained because it was considered necessary to restore the political balance.[97] Such sentiments benefited from the increased popular appeal of the monarchy in times of national crisis. The chief of staff Razmara, in the French language newspaper *Journal de Tehran* emphasised that the Shah preceded Qavam in significance for the liberation of Azerbaijan: 'Celui qui fut le principal auteur de cette libération est sans aucun doute Sa Majesté Impériale le Chahinchah . . . Après Sa Majesté Impériale le Chahinchah, celui qui joua le plus grand rôle dans la libération de l'Azerbaijan, fut Ghavam Saltaneh'.[98] *The Times* reported that 'The troops were enthusiastically received in Tabriz by the crowds who lined the streets draped with the national colours and decorated with portraits of the Shah'. The monarchy and the army cannot but have benefited from the fact that, 'In Tehran the opinion is that this is one of the great days in the history of Persia'. They were both centre stage in the grand theatre of Iranian history. A national holiday was declared and a 'big military parade' was arranged.[99] It was also noted that the Kurds welcomed the arrival of the troops with patriotic demonstrations, although some of this enthusiasm was probably engineered.[100]

The Azerbaijan crisis effectively marked the beginning of the Cold War,[101] a development which the Shah and the army were quick to exploit. In an audience with Le Rougetel, the Shah was quick to situate Iran within the new Cold War tensions and to rationalise his desire for a large well-equipped army. Thus, 'The Shah also spoke of the re-equipment of the army which he is now inclined to think of as a first line of defence against a Soviet invasion of the Middle East'.[102] The communists, down though not out, reacted angrily to this new tendency. Their chief newspaper, *Mardum*, ridiculed the new Cold War environment, describing

America's declared interest in the integrity of Persia as blatant hypocrisy, the real purpose of the USA being firstly to prepare Persia as a battleground for a capitalist struggle against the USSR and secondly to use the country as a market for old clothes and military junk.[103]

The Shah, meanwhile, continued to capitalise on his new popularity with a three-week visit to Azerbaijan in 1947. By all accounts he was received enthusiastically: 'Bouquets of flowers were thrown into the train and in some villages cows and sheep were slaughtered in honour of the Shah . . . The royal visit is a symbol of the newly restored national unity'.[104] The popularity of the Shah at the conclusion of a tense national crisis, especially given his relative ineffectiveness throughout, is testament to the fact that the monarchy as an institution and symbol of nationhood remained strong in the eyes of many Iranians. The fact that there was very little talk of republicanism reflected the understanding of this fact by the political and intellectual elite. However, the Shah's interpretation differed. For him the sanctity of the institution was not distinct from the person; adulation for the institution (as expressed, for instance, by Razmara) was in his eyes adulation for his person. Rather than respect the institution to which he was born, the Shah was to draw increasing criticism for the 'uncharacteristic' behaviour of the court, a problem he would exacerbate as he turned his attention to institutionalising the monarchy through the further development of dynastic nationalism.

Contested 'nationalisms'

The period of the Allied Occupation was a traumatic if educational experience for many Iranians. It was also the first time many of them had encountered Westerners and Western culture; this impact is often under-appreciated. Hitherto, contact with the West had been limited to those who had travelled abroad, or been in contact with foreign institutions within Iran, in particular the various embassies and corporations such as the Anglo-Iranian Oil Company (AIOC – which had changed its name in 1935 following the insistence on the use of 'Iran' rather than 'Persia'). Any understanding of the West was therefore bound to be limited and particular, and aside from periodic contacts with officials from AIOC, to remain essentially an elite experience. The Allied Occupation broadened this experience, not only through the technological innovations which Allied soldiers introduced into Iranian society, but more emphatically, through individual contact. This contact was by and large not positive, in so far as it did not endear the local populace to the occupying forces. Economic dislocation and rampant inflation, a regrettable consequence of Allied military priorities, both served to frustrate the good intentions Allied forces may have had towards the populace. While compet-ing radio broadcasts facilitated the growth of political consciousness, other forms of Western material culture assisted in the process of shaping that consciousness. In the 1930s, the dominance of French films on Iranian cinema screens had prompted protests of imported immorality from Iranian journalists,[105] while, in the following decade, the introduction of American films was to have an unfore-seen if altogether more damaging social consequence.

> In 1943 the Minister of the Interior, a jurist and former prosecuting attor-ney, conducted an investigation which demonstrated that many cases of juvenile crime on record in Iran, and many of delinquency, had been inspired by American gangster films. It is perfectly true that these films end on a moral note, but this is a thin apology for the techniques taught and activities suggested to impressionable minds. Under the guise of 'crime doesn't pay', audiences and regions in Iran for the first time were being introduced to the existence of an organised underworld.[106]

This perceived corruption of traditional Iranian values both coincided with and encouraged the growth of a popular and distinctive 'national' consciousness. Ordinary Iranians began to identify themselves more clearly with a distinctive Iranian national culture, while elites who were already imbued with a strong sense of national mission were only further convinced of the need for protective measures. Yet the dynamic at work was, as always, more complex than a grow-ing mutual antagonism. In 1946, the noted nationalist intellectual Khalil Maliki, still then a member of the communist Tudeh Party, paid a visit to Great Britain. Having expected an extension of the British embassy in Tehran, Maliki was pleas-antly surprised to find a diversity of social and political views, many of which bore close proximity to his own. For Maliki, it was clearly a revelation that beneath the political exterior lay a social coincidence of interests. In light of the events which were to follow, his letter of thanks to the British authorities may be seen in retrospect as both prescient and indicative of an opportunity, not lost, but most certainly delayed.

> I have come to know their qualities and their love of freedom and democracy in a way I could never before. It is my belief that if British policy in Persia were interpreted according to the will of the people of this country and if the

democratic and human tendencies of the average Briton were to be the active agents of British policy in Persia then many of the present difficulties of my dear country would be resolved.[107]

The young Shah and the development of dynastic nationalism

The immediate political impact of the reoccupation of Azerbaijan was the re-emergence of the Shah as a central player in the Iranian political process. Far from willing to operate within strictly defined if highly constrained constitutional parameters, the young Shah was anxious to make his mark and to portray himself as a worthy successor to his father, with whom unfavourable comparisons were regularly being made. Indeed, monarchists determined to restore 'order' to the state were continually encouraging the young Shah to seize the reins of power. Mohammad Reza Shah nevertheless remained acutely aware of the unpopularity with which his father was viewed in many political circles, and with characteristic, if in this case prudent, hesitancy, he refused to be pushed into pursuing a policy which might result in further counterproductive reaction. For the first five years of his reign, therefore, he resigned himself to a strategy of political ambivalence, building on the widespread sympathy which remained for the institution of the monarchy, and successfully enhanced its social and political position. Only after his apparent triumph in the 'liberation of Azerbaijan' was the Shah emboldened to move more vigorously to reinstitutionalise the Pahlavi dynasty as the quintessential agent of national revitalisation. In echoes of 1979, it proved a flawed strategy which ultimately yielded the mantle of 'saviour' to another.

The institution of the monarchy, as the linchpin and moderator of Iranian society, tended to increase in popularity during periods of uncertainty and tension,[108] and its political influence among the rural masses, in one sense the 'politically unaware', remained strong. Even among the politically aware, talk of 'republicanism' in this period was relatively slight. This fact is even admitted by critics of the notion of monarchical mystique, such as Azimi, who notes that 'it appears that there had been no serious thinking towards such an end [republicanism]', adding that it was an indication of the strength of 'royalist subculture' within the Iranian body politic.[109] The British diplomat Lawford, who was able to become quite close to the Shah, noted:

> I was very much struck by the popularity of the Shah in all the countryside through which we passed on our various journeys. Every morning as we rode out of the gates of the palace and through the villages that are scattered over the valley there were groups of peasants, often in very ragged clothes, who shouted and cheered and applauded with what appeared to be sincere enthusiasm.[110]

This enthusiasm was facilitated by the fact that the Shah was apparently at ease when it came to dealing with the common people, and was not averse to walking among them unguarded and hearing their petitions.[111]

At the same time, the Pahlavi dynasty, especially in the immediate aftermath of the abdication of Reza Shah, was deeply unpopular, in particular with the political and intellectual elite.[112] Arguably, as more Iranians became politically aware and discerning, so the fascination with monarchy waned and criticism of the specific activities of the dynasty grew. The Shah was severely handicapped in this respect as his father's heir, and by the continuing antics of the court which clashed dramatically with the popular expectation of what an Iranian royal court should be like. Thus during his dispute with Qavam in the aftermath of the liberation of Azerbaijan, it was noted that Qavam still elicited respect and sympathy as a part of a noble and distinguished family while the Shah was disliked as the son of an upstart and a tyrant.[113] Court extravagance was a more serious problem since it was one the Shah was expected to manage. As early as 1943 members of the establishment criticised the excessive expenditure of the royal family and doubts were expressed as to the Shah's willingness to curb this expenditure.[114] There was continued criticism of lavish parties and Princess Ashraf, the Shah's twin sister, was increasingly viewed as the real power behind the throne.[115] Such behaviour was to carry social and political repercussions and it was noted that 'feeling now varies between mild dismay and violent indignation at His Majesty's failure to make himself master in his own house'.[116]

The Shah was, however, sufficiently moved by his reception in Azerbaijan, and by the general popularity of the monarchy as an institution, to effectively ignore the criticism and seek to redefine himself and his dynasty in the eyes of the Iranian people. As noted above, he was encouraged in this decision from an early stage by courtiers and other sycophants, as well as those who saw political advantage in manipulating the Shah. As the British embassy noted in 1942,

> The Shah . . . is gradually being got at by flatterers: in fact by just the sort of people who turned his papa in the wrong path. One of the major curses in Iran in the past has been the king-worship which dates from Darius or earlier.[117]

Men such as General Razmara sought to convince the Shah of his sense of mission and the need for 'action':

> He is continually filling the Shah's head with the type of advice most palatable, e.g. 'be the man your father was' – 'the country is in such a mess that only the personal rule of an absolute ruler can save her' – 'the Majlis: its rooted interests and internal jealousies is preventing the government from governing therefore you must shut it'.[118]

Others genuinely felt that the Shah had much to offer, including Alam and Seyyed Zia, who believed him to be a 'Man of Destiny'.[119]

In attempting to reinvent himself, the Shah sought to distance himself from the traditional social alliances of the monarchy and instead to be seen as the champion of the emergent young radical intelligentsia. He was a keen advocate of social reform and made it known that the plight of the average Iranian was a matter of great personal concern. Thus Bullard noted in 1943, 'I felt that the Shah now wishes to be regarded as the champion of youth and of the lower classes and the protagonist of social reform', adding significantly, 'that he greatly distrusts the class represented by the Prime Minister'.[120] Furthermore,

> The Shah said that the hope of the country lay in the hands of the young – in ideas and not necessarily only in age. He referred to a movement and what he described as 'le type des jeunes' which he said was growing, and encouragement must be given to them.[121]

Indications are that the Shah enjoyed some success in pursuing this new image, as the military attaché noted,

> The Shah was given a very enthusiastic reception by a crowd of about 10,000 spectators at a football match between British and Persian teams in Tehran, which may indicate that attempts that have recently been made to represent him as the champion of youth have not been without success.[122]

It is debatable how genuine the Shah was in his advocacy of social reform and his revolutionary credentials were always tempered by political realities, which dictated that his natural allies remained the conservative traditional elements in society. Furthermore, the failure of the court and to an increasing extent of the Shah, to curtail their often lavish expenditure drew criticism, especially from the most extreme left-wing groups.

In order to counter this challenge, the Shah attempted, unsuccessfully, to become even more radical, at one stage advocating a further decentralisation of power,[123] and shocking many of his traditional supporters, by announcing on a visit to the United States that he intended to redistribute crown lands to the peasants.[124] Needless to say,

> The impact on the political scene has been very great. Liberal and reformist elements see in the Shah's decision the beginning of a process which alters for the better the whole economic, social and political structure of Persia; the great landowners and those who depend on them are alarmed and are seeking to prevent and forestall the promulgation of analogous legislation applicable to their own estates.[125]

However, the Shah limited the favourable impact of this legislation by putting the funds received from the sale of lands at the disposal of a charity run by the ever unpopular Princess Ashraf.[126] It may be said that he succeeded in alienating both the radicals and the traditionalists.

However, contrary to the image which he tried to portray to the public at large, the Shah was neither sympathetic to greater decentralisation nor particularly enamoured with democracy. Indeed the evidence suggests that he favoured greater centralisation, with himself at the helm.[127] In many ways the militaristic vision continued to predominate. Indeed, it soon became apparent that far from wanting to distance himself from his father, he was anxious to encourage Reza Shah's political rehabilitation. However, for this to be possible, Mohammad Reza Shah was forced to recast the image of his father, to many Iranians the quintessential despot, in a new mould. As one personalities file reported, 'the present ruler retains a warm filial regard for his father and pays him the compliment of imitating him as much as possible; he also initiates propaganda in favour of Reza, but it is not taken seriously'.[128] This propaganda involved the careful reconstruction of the historical record stressing the achievements of Reza Shah, while ignoring the essential arbitrariness of his rule. For instance, in 1943 there was '[a] campaign for the whitewashing of the ex-Shah, representing him as a misunderstood and much maligned public servant, led astray by astute politicians'.[129] This reinterpretation also allowed the Shah to realign himself with the radicals by blaming the evils of Reza Shah on the traditional elite political class. Nevertheless, on Reza Shah's death the following year, few were overcome by grief. The Shah's decision to initiate a period of mourning was criticised, and many sections of the press analysed Reza Shah's reign unfavourably. The Tudeh Party even expelled a member who had attended a mourning ceremony.[130]

This, however, did not deter the Shah, and his strategy gained momentum in the aftermath of the triumph of Azerbaijan, as preparations were made to bring Reza Shah's body back to Iran. As Le Rougetel noted, 'Many laudatory articles on the late Shah's reign have recently been published urging that justice should at last be done to the memory of a great and patriotic sovereign'.[131] In seeking to achieve his father's rehabilitation into the national narrative he capitalised on growing nostalgia for the 'order' his father represented, in stark contrast to the apparent chaos of contemporary Iran.[132] He encouraged the Majlis to confer the title of 'the Great' on his father, in a deliberate attempt to sanctify the dynasty. The move was not welcomed, and many felt that the Majlis was 'usurping the functions of history'.[133] As Le Rougetel noted,

> the attempt to elevate the reputation of Reza Shah by conferring on him the title of 'the Great' has offended the Persian sense of propriety. Especially of late the Persians have been favourably inclined towards achievements of the late Shah, but they do not consider that this is the moment to honour him with the title which has so far been reserved for such venerated figures as Cyrus and Shah Abbas.[134]

Despite, or because of, this concerted campaign, the practicalities of returning the body of Reza Shah proved problematic and prolonged, not least because the Shi'a clergy were unsympathetic. The Shah had wanted to bury Reza Shah in the grounds of Saadabad Palace, but the mullahs argued that since he had been interred in non-Shi'a ground, he had to be reinterred within proximity of a shrine. The Shah's suggestion of either Mashhad or Qom was turned down by the local *ulema*.[135] With respect to the tomb itself, the Tudeh Party criticised the lavish expenditure, and protested that the money could have been better expended on the poor.[136] Probably the best and most favourable commentary on the whole affair was offered by a local gardener, who noted, 'Why do they not leave the old Shah where he is? Then there would be plenty of room in the new tomb for the present one'.[137]

Despite these simmering criticisms, the Shah had been greatly assisted in his attempt to reinvent both himself and his dynasty by a fortunate escape from assassination which had elicited widespread public sympathy.[138] On a visit to Tehran University to commemorate its foundation by his father, the Shah had been shot and hit several times at close range, but by dint of good fortune survived the attack despite being wounded in the face. The assassination attempt and its almost miraculous failure (one of several throughout his reign) was to have a profound impact on the Shah's perception of his own role and manifest destiny. Public sympathy, outraged at the attack on the institution, if not the person, of the monarch, nevertheless provided the Shah with further encouragement and provided the catalyst, despite some considered protests, for the government to outlaw the Tudeh Party.[139] Arguably, however, the Shah misinterpreted public sentiments when he decided to exploit this public sympathy to his benefit by pushing through constitutional reforms which would increase his direct political power through the establishment of a second representative house, the Senate. The reform which was pushed through in the face of concerted opposition, meant that the Shah would be able to nominate half the senators. In order to sell reform, particularly to foreign critics, the Shah unashamedly and somewhat disingenuously appealed to the ideological logic of the West. In an interview with a journalist from the United Press, which was reprinted in the French language *Journal de Tehran*, the Shah noted that the creation of a senate had restored balance to the constitution, and that now the Iranian monarchy better resembled the constitutional monarchies of Europe.[140]

The Shah, convinced of his own mission and supported by a carefully cultivated myth of his dynasty's role in the progressive narrative, had promised that his new powers would allow him to implement practically the social causes he had been championing. The reality was that he did little better than his predecessors. As Le Rougetel noted in a letter to Bevin,

> The Shah, who had promised a new deal, has failed to live up to his promise. Therefore it is generally felt he must be either a knave or a fool, or both. This is of course, a heaven sent opportunity for all adversaries of the Shah, his dynasty or his country, and they have not been slow to exploit it.[141]

It was indicative of the Shah's less than central role in Iranian politics at this time that, just as his pursuit of dynastic nationalism was gathering pace, he found himself marginalised by events and outmanoeuvred by his political rivals. Far from projecting himself as the leading character in the political theatre, the Shah found his influence waning rapidly. His wedding to Soraya Esfandiari, intended to solidify the dynasty by providing a male heir, was a haphazard affair. Efforts were made to capitalise on the fact that Soraya was Iranian, despite the fact that her mother was German, and this does seem to have flattered national pride, though it is a matter of debate how popular the wedding ceremony and festivities actually were.[142] Though the press dutifully trumpeted the occasion and new postage stamps were issued, there was some concern over inviting 'opium smoking' Bakhtiaris into the court, and the mullahs frowned on the European character and upbringing of the new queen.[143] Once again sensitive to charges of extravagance, the Shah limited the festivities, so much so that

> [w]hen . . . it became known that though the Agha Khan and Begum were coming for the wedding, they would not be accompanied by Rita Hayworth, the realisation struck home that glamour as well as pomp was to be absent: the issue of a special commemorative postage stamp and the reported arrival of a German circus were poor consolations.[144]

The Shah's first attempt to seize the political initiative had failed. His youthful enthusiasm for his father and the dynasty had resulted in the premature implementation of policies which he could not sustain nor the public genuinely support. By seeking to directly influence the political process he needlessly attracted criticism and was effectively outmanoeuvred by politicians who were more astute and more in tune with public sentiment. As a joint US–British assessment noted in 1951, 'The Shah . . . has thus far been unable to use nationalist elements to strengthen the crown or to effect much needed reforms in the face of the landowning–merchant oligarchy'.[145] The fact that, by late 1951, pamphlets protested the official commemoration of the Shah's birthday, is an indication of how low the esteem of the dynasty and indeed the institution of monarchy had fallen.[146] It was Dr Mosaddeq rather than the Shah who was to become the supreme icon of the nationalist movement.

Dr Mohammad Mosaddeq and the Oil Nationalisation Crisis

While Reza Shah and his acolytes forged the modern Iranian state, it was left to Dr Mohammad Mosaddeq and the movement he was identified with to define it and provide it with substance. While Reza Shah crafted the vessel, it was Mosaddeq who filled it. The legacy of Reza Shah was incomplete, as the events of 1941 were to prove. The social foundations of the new state had been found wanting, and few people had shed tears when the monarch was forced to abdicate and was then sent into exile. Such was the depth of the popular antipathy that when his son and heir sought his political rehabilitation nearly a decade later the most pervasive social response was one of ambivalence. Indeed, in some circles, the son's affection for his father was regarded as a political handicap. However genuine his aspirations for reform may have been, they were subsumed in the popular imagination by associations with dictatorship and repressions which had characterised the last decade of his father's rule. Thus it was that Mohammad Reza Shah's attempts to inherit the mantle of Iranian nationalism proved premature. Much to the young Shah's indignation, his role was somewhat abruptly 'usurped' by a politician and constitutionalist of the old school, from the very patrician class from which he had sought to disassociate himself. The frustration was palpable.

Dr Mohammad Mosaddeq was an aristocrat, a scion of the Qajar royal house, a French- and Swiss-educated lawyer, who had consistently opposed what he regarded as the incremental aggrandisement of power by the Pahlavi state and the monarch in particular. He had been one of the most vocal opponents of Reza Khan's elevation to kingship, arguing, somewhat disingenuously, that the constitutional limits on kingship would prevent the Prime Minister, as Reza Khan then was, from continuing his good work. Unsurprisingly, Reza Shah did not appreciate this argument, and Mosaddeq was to spend much of the next 15 years in the political wilderness, until Reza Shah's abdication and the Allied Occupation released the political ferment. Nevertheless, for much of the following decade, there were few indications that the ageing Mosaddeq would return with such vigour to the political fray. Indeed, much like Churchill in 1940, many in 1950 regarded Mosaddeq as a politician well past his prime. British diplomatic sources had for many years considered him a 'demagogue and a windbag',[147] and there is little evidence that his political peers and rivals in Iran felt otherwise.

However, this was not to be the first (or indeed last) time that the Iranian political establishment would be rocked by a shrewd political operator, who had been somewhat hastily and with no little arrogance dismissed and largely ignored by his opponents. Mosaddeq was able to capture a moment in Iranian history when nationalism emerged from its intellectual and elitist cocoon and became a force for political action. Where Reza Shah and his acolytes defined an increasingly exclusive ideology of 'Persian' nationalism, Mosaddeq successfully capitalised upon and extended its popularity. Between 1951 and 1953, Persian nationalism became truly Iranian – inclusive, broad-based and with an increasing mass appeal. As the supreme icon and symbolic leader of this Iranian nationalism, Mosaddeq's political legacy has far outweighed his practical achievements, which in essence were to end in failure. As the British embassy noted in 1951, 'Dr Musaddiq is personally popular and has succeeded in making himself a symbol of the Persian conception of nationalism'. He had achieved this quite simply by doing 'something which is always dear to Persian hearts: he has flouted the authority of a great power and a great foreign interest and he has gone a long way towards damaging the prestige of the first and the prosperity of the second'.[148]

In this respect, his premiership, seen by his supporters as a lost opportunity, paralleled that of another great icon of political reform, the nineteenth-century Qajar Prime Minister Amir Kabir, who was likewise undone by a suspicious monarch and the machinations of foreign powers. Mosaddeq was a popular Prime Minister, but the coup which ultimately overthrew him reflected the fragility of his power and his failure to maintain the support of key social groups. His subsequent canonisation within a broad band of the popular imagination had much to do with the intransigence of the Shah, who was increasingly anxious to eliminate him from the historical record, and the vociferous polemic of his supporters, who pursued the opposite agenda with equal zeal. But perhaps above all it had to do with the acute Iranian sensibility for political martyrs. For a nation of romantic fatalists, Mosaddeq's struggle and final failure epitomised a metanarrative which, with few exceptions, persists to this day. In short, much to the continued irritation of his opponents, his immediate failure ensured the sanctification of his memory within the growing political consciousness of Iran.

Towards oil nationalisation

Iranians of all political hues had long felt that the oil concession held by the Anglo-Iranian Oil Company in southern Iran was unjust and unfair, a remnant of a 'colonial' past which sat uneasily with the growing sense of national pride. Reza Shah and his Court Minister Teymourtache had sought a renegotiation in 1933, achieving a modest compromise but leaving much undone. The growth in political consciousness which had accompanied the Allied Occupation undoubtedly fostered greater resentment towards the AIOC, whose patronising attitude towards Iranians and overtly colonial lifestyle offended the sensibilities of many increasingly well-educated Iranians. Others commented on the importing of substitute Indian labour, as well as the enormous profits made by the company, which they compared unfavourably with the royalties paid to the Iranian government. British officials appear to have been remarkably diffident about such resentment, which cannot have been unknown, certain in their belief that it could not be translated into political action. They may have been assured in this by reports sent by company officials, as well as an innate prejudice depressingly prevalent in massive bureaucracies. Britain's investment was simply too large and important to contemplate the possibility of bad news. It may have been this prejudice which prevented officials from appreciating three stark road signs to nationalisation which emerged in the 1940s.

The first important signal was the struggle to curtail the activities of the British Imperial Bank of Persia, which had begun during Reza Shah's rule, but was now being completed by the brilliant technocrat and former employee of the bank, Abol-Hassan Ebtehaj. Ebtehaj's successes may be usefully compared to that of Mosaddeq. Both men challenged the tools of British hegemony in the country, but Ebtehaj was undoubtedly more successful in a practical sense, a reality which has ironically ensured his political marginalisation in the popular imagination. The initial steps to curtail the activities of the bank had begun in 1928 with the foundation of the Bank Melli (National Bank of Iran), and in the following decade the bank's ability to conduct business in Iran was increasingly restricted. In 1943, Abol-Hassan Ebtehaj had been appointed Governor of Bank Melli, an appointment British bank officials viewed with trepidation. Ebtehaj was determined that Bank Melli should function as the Central Bank in Iran and therefore any rival institution could not be tolerated: 'I consider this Bank as the State Central Bank, therefore it should be a dominating factor . . . and not parallel or in equal position with its competing and rival institutions'.[149] In his dealings with the British bank, Ebtehaj was to find many allies, not least among officials in the Bank of England, who likewise found the attitude of the officials of the British bank wholly unsuited to the new mood in Iran, and quite counterproductive to good business.[150] Ebtehaj proceeded first to challenge the British bank's dominant position over currency exchange resulting in a new agreement and limitations on the bank's activities by the end of 1943. He then went aggressively after the bank's business, suggesting, unsuccessfully, that the British army in Iran might wish to conduct its exchange business with Bank Melli. Far more significant, however, was Ebtehaj's successful procurement of the entire business of the US military in Iran which in 1942–43 had been conducted by the British bank. Having discovered that Bank Melli provided a better service, all accounts with the British bank were closed in 1944.

Following the conclusion of the war and the withdrawal of the Allies, the bank settled down to an expansion of its activities in Iran, fuelled as it was by the substantial profits it had nevertheless made during the occupation. Ebtehaj, however, had other ideas, and bank officials, like their counterparts in the AIOC, seemed completely oblivious to the new momentum of nationalism which was galvanising the country. As Jones argues succinctly, 'In retrospect, it can be seen that the Bank's judgement was characteristic of a wider British misunderstanding of the nature and strength of Iranian nationalism'.[151] Ebtehaj, in much the same way as Mosaddeq, was not blindly anti-British in his approach. He simply wanted to redefine roles and argued that the British bank's primary function should be to promote foreign trade rather than become involved in retail banking with branches throughout Iran. He was particularly incensed by the realisation that the bank restricted the use of Iranian deposits in Iran and suspected, with some justification, that these were being used to finance the bank's development outside Iran. In September 1945 he announced that he intended to cancel the 1943 agreement on foreign exchange and was not willing to replace it with anything new. Instead he served notice, much to the bank's frustration, that foreign exchange would forthwith be entirely under the control of Bank Melli. The bank's officials sought diplomatic protection in order to shield it from these pressures. However, despite a temporary respite, the pressures for change continued to mount, in part because the Foreign Office was unwilling to extend itself over the bank, which it considered of secondary importance when compared to the AIOC. Ultimately, it was the events surrounding the nationalisation of the oil company which were to lead to the bank's demise in Iran. Ebtehaj's determination to curtail the activities of the bank had itself been constrained by a series of political negotiations between the British and Iranian governments. Indeed the bank continued to operate after the lapse of its concession in 1949, but the collapse of Anglo-Iranian relations following the nationalisation of the AIOC meant that even the political avenue had been closed. Ebtehaj, who had left Bank Melli in 1950, was no longer a thorn in the Imperial Bank's side, but his determined assault, coupled with the expansion of business overseas, had convinced the bank's officials to reduce and eventually close down its activities in Iran. As Jones argues,

> Ebtehaj's campaign against the bank had proved a blessing in disguise, for in convincing it of the need to run down the Iranian operations, the bank was spared much greater losses when the oil crisis erupted . . . The bank's closure on 30 July seems to have passed almost unnoticed.[152]

Ebtehaj proved that British commercial and political power in Iran could be successfully challenged. His was a slow, systematic and methodical approach, but it had eventually worked. Oil nationalisation was undoubtedly of a different magnitude, and few British commentators were to be as objective in their approach as those in the Bank of England had been towards Ebtehaj. But Iranian politicians drew succour from two other catalysts, which were similarly seemingly ignored by British officials. On the one hand, Iranian politicians gazed with interest at the British Labour government's enthusiasm for nationalisation at home, while at the same time savouring the triumph at having denied an oil concession to the Soviets in the north. Indeed it is remarkable that the British did not appreciate the relevance of the Azerbaijan crisis for their own situation. While the Iranians regarded their relations with both the Soviets and the British in political terms, it seems that the British were intent on viewing it through legal terms. The AIOC remained *in situ* through an international agreement. Politics were an irrelevancy. It was to prove a fatal miscalculation.

Nevertheless, the AIOC had recognised, following considerable Iranian pressure, that some form of revision of the 1933 oil agreements had to be reached. The Supplemental Oil Agreement, the result of somewhat tortuous negotiations between the Iranian and British governments, envisaged an increase in revenues to the Iranian government. Iranians of all political hues had been consistently irritated, not only by the patronising attitude of the Company, but by the growing disparity in the revenue enjoyed by the Iranian and British governments from the exploitation of Iranian oil. According to BP figures, the British government had earned some £194,100,000 between 1932 and 1950, while the Iranian government had received £100,500,000 over the same period.[153] That the British government should earn more in tax than the Iranian government from royalties from the exploitation of Iranian oil offended the sensibilities of an increasingly nationalist populace. The explanation of the AIOC that the payment of taxes to the British Exchequer was a matter of British law fell very much on deaf ears. What the Company understood to be a legal issue outside its own control was regarded by the Iranians as a political issue which the British government should resolve. All the while the public mood was shifting towards outright nationalisation. While the AIOC gradually began to appreciate this changing mood, they were unwilling to countenance the notion of nationalisation and, supported by the British government, there was an air of disbelief at the 'ingratitude' of the Iranians. Similarly, Iranian activists lambasted the patronising pretensions of the British. This growing political and ideational gulf would be difficult to surmount in the absence of strong, visionary leadership.

On the Iranian side, there were few signs of such leadership after the resignation of the wily Qavam in 1947. The Shah, having appointed a series of pliant prime ministers, was singularly unable to either harness or curtail the public mood. The Prime Minister, Ali Mansur, had resigned in June 1950 rather than submit the Supplemental Oil Agreement to the Majlis. Faced with a political stalemate, and a growing crisis on the streets fanned by Tudeh Party activists and nationalists, the Shah decided to turn to his chief of staff, General Ali Razmara. Razmara's premiership is marred by controversy, regarded as he is by many nationalists as a traitor to his country. Yet in many ways his brief tenure as Prime Minister represented a lost opportunity. Razmara was not unaware of the public mood, but he also recognised that the consequences of nationalisation would in all likelihood be severe for Iran. A career soldier, whose rise through the ranks had been dramatic, Razmara possessed an instinctive dislike for what he considered the emotive and irrational dimensions of nationalist rhetoric. A rift with Britain might make for good politics, but it was bad statecraft. On his appointment he suffered from two stigmas which were to critically affect his ability for political manoeuvre. First was his somewhat arbitrary appointment to the premiership by the Shah without approval of the Majlis, while more damning was the general perception that his appointment had been approved by the British and American ambassadors. Despite these handicaps, Razmara sought to pursue an impressive agenda which coupled political reform with a solution to the oil crisis. Somewhat ahead of his time, Razmara argued for political decentralisation, with the formation of provincial assemblies, and land reform. These two projects offended both the landowners, who feared for their livelihoods, and the nationalists, who despite their dislike for the dictatorship of Reza Shah, fully approved of his policy of centralisation. Decentralisation, opponents argued, was simply 'a British plot to dismantle Iran'.[154]

More damning in the eyes of his critics, however, was his apparent failure to deal with the Anglo-Iranian Oil Company. Indeed, many argued that internal reform was of no consequence in the absence of a settlement of the oil issue, others that it was a pointless diversion. Razmara was well aware of the political mood in the country, but also recognised that a political conflict with Britain could have disastrous results. His aim was to come to some mutually acceptable agreement which would yield a 50 per cent share in the company's profits while accepting in principle the notion of privatisation. While British officials were willing to consider the possibility of profit-sharing, privatisation was a principle they were unwilling to countenance publicly. This left Razmara with little means of placating the nationalist masses, and in the absence of any public knowledge of the scheme for a 50 per cent share in the profits, Razmara was left with the unenviable task of arguing against nationalisation, and pointing to its myriad potential difficulties, confirming in the eyes of many his position as a British stooge. If he had hoped for any support from the king, Razmara was also to be disappointed. In fact relations between Razmara and the Shah had been tense, despite Razmara's previously unequivocal support for the royalist cause. Having earlier urged the Shah to emulate his father, Prime Minister Razmara found the constant interference of the court in the political affairs of the country a persistent nuisance, and consequently sought to curtail it. The Shah, for his part, was not overly enamoured with his military rival, and feared that his authority might be superseded.

His concern was misplaced. On 7 March 1951, while attending the funeral of an Ayatollah in Tehran's royal mosque, Razmara was assassinated by a member of the *Fedayin-e Islam*, following calls by Ayatollah Kashani for all 'sincere Muslims and patriotic citizens to fight against the enemies of Islam and Iran by joining the nationalisation struggle'.[155] The assassination, far from being denounced as an act of criminality, was hailed as a triumph against British imperialism by lawmakers and mob leaders alike. Even the court expressed a collective sigh of relief at the elimination of the hapless premier. Indeed the popular reaction to Razmara's murder remains astonishing, and can only be understood, if not justified, in the context of the tremendous upsurge in nationalist feeling throughout the country – a feeling which, as the assassination now indicated, had now been firmly wedded to religion. Nationalism, far from being inconsequential and ephemeral, as the British consistently argued, had become sanctified and was now to all intents and purposes part of a holy struggle. It was a potent marriage. Razmara was not only a traitor to his country but, by the same token, to his religion. The assassin, Khalil Tahmasibi, was hailed as a national hero and granted a parliamentary pardon. None of the *ulema* were willing to accept the invitation to deliver the sermon at Razmara's funeral, and on the very day of his assassination people in the bazaar openly rejoiced. The President of the Senate was hard pressed to describe the murder as an 'unexpected event'.[156] Dr Mosaddeq went on record to say that, 'The bullet which was fired by Khalil Tahmasibi not only saved Persia from a great danger but it also saved the whole of the East'.[157]

The premiership of Dr Mohammad Mosaddeq, 1951–53

Despite the popular air of euphoria, Razmara's assassination plunged the country into deeper political crisis. Not surprisingly, few elder statesmen were willing to fill his shoes in the absence of extraordinary measures. Faced with the determination of the National Front deputies on the one hand (with their domination of the street) and the intransigence of the British on the other, few were enthusiastic about seizing what many now viewed as a poisoned chalice. The Shah and the British increasingly discussed the possibility of dissolving the Majlis altogether, while the latter, seemingly oblivious to nationalist sentiment, cast around for a suitable strong man to seize the premiership and take firm control of the country. Ultimately, a compromise candidate was found in the person of Hussein Ala, a staunch royalist who was nevertheless widely recognised as a man of integrity. Ala was anxious not to accentuate the tensions which were building. Far from seeking extraordinary measures, he sought to cultivate links with the National Front and to pursue a satisfactory solution to the question of oil nationalisation. But events had moved on. Within weeks of accepting the premiership, Ala found himself hamstrung by the Majlis, which unanimously endorsed the principle of nationalisation. The British now sought a more drastic resolution either through the more royalist-inclined Senate (which nevertheless fully endorsed the decision of the Lower House), or indeed through a dissolution of the Majlis altogether. Having found that the Shah was unwilling to take this step, the British resolved to agree to the arrangement originally proposed by Razmara. This, it was felt, would at least provide Ala with a breathing space to appoint his cabinet and organise his administration. No sooner was this tacitly agreed, however, than events on the ground once again overtook the machinations of elite politics. The assassination of the former minister of education along with the initiation of strike action by oil workers in the south, pushed Ala into imposing martial law in the southern oil areas and in the capital. Caught between nationalist indignation and the British threat of military intervention, Ala was determined to restore order, while at the same time decrying the apparent British enthusiasm for gunboat diplomacy. Successfully settling the strike in the workers' favour by late April, Ala moved once again to establish his administration, only to find that the Majlis Oil Committee had unanimously approved a draft nine-point law for the nationalisation of the oil industry. Since he had not been consulted, Ala considered his position untenable, and after a turbulent 46-day tenure, he tendered his resignation. With Ala now out of the way, the British pinned their hopes on the appointment of Seyyed Zia, the journalist-cum-politician who had originally orchestrated the 1921 coup with Reza Khan, and who was known for his pro-British leanings.

Much to the surprise of the Shah and the British, however, a political miscalculation led to the appointment of Mosaddeq, who few had believed would accept the offer of the premiership. Mosaddeq, who had played the role of reluctant leader if not saviour with considerable skill, had rejected previous offers of the premiership on the basis that his appointment would prove too unpopular with the British. He cemented the popular view of his political autonomy. Now, however, faced with the prospect of Seyyed Zia's premiership, Mosaddeq seized the opportunity somewhat carelessly afforded to him and summarily approved by the Majlis. Binding himself to the principle of nationalisation, Mosaddeq insisted that his acceptance be predicated on the ratification of the nationalisation law, which the Majlis dutifully approved on 28 April 1951, followed by the Senate the following day. The Shah, much to the consternation of the British government, immediately signed the new law. The Cold War had now become hot. But the British reassured themselves with the view that Mosaddeq's premiership was a temporary if necessary interlude which would placate the crowd before normal business could be resumed. In short, faced with uncompromising realities, the British chose to dismiss them.[158]

Mosaddeq was to be a far more astute politician than his detractors realised. Crucially, he understood the Iranian crowd and, unlike other patrician politicians, was willing to use it. In many ways his premiership can be characterised as the first round in a continuing struggle between an emergent, increasingly politically conscious society, both traditional and modern, and the elites. The National Front was a broad movement composed of different parties including socialists and secular and religious nationalists, and driven less by a cohesive rigorous ideological platform and more by ambiguous if potent ideas of self-determination, nationhood and anti-imperialism. This inherent ambiguity was to draw much scorn from Mosaddeq's critics, but he recognised that the level of political consciousness required a simplification of the ideological agenda if it was to succeed in becoming truly popular. To his opponents, this was nothing less than a strategy of cheap demagoguery. For Mosaddeq it was a political necessity. That is not to say that the use of the crowd was not a dangerous political precedent to set, and from the beginning Mosaddeq was forced to try to curtail its excesses. In many ways, his ultimate failure to control the genie he had released was to prove his downfall as he increasingly reacted to rather than dictated the pace of events.

There is little doubt that by 1953, Mosaddeq had grown increasingly impatient with political processes which he felt were hindering the implementation of the nationalisation law and a resolution to the crisis. Supporters argue that, faced with continuing obstruction from the British, as well as from the Iranian political establishment who feared the consequences of social and political mobilisation, Mosaddeq was left with little choice but to accrue more and more powers to himself, and to effectively rule without the consent of the Majlis – a move which contradicted his own legal principles and offended his key supporters including Maliki and importantly Kashani. Yet there is little doubt that in forsaking the support of key social groups and relying increasingly on the Tehran mob, Mosaddeq fatally weakened his own position and essentially invited the possibility of a successful coup. His ultimate fate, however, should not detract from the fact that his original political position was much less robust and antagonistic. While he was unwilling to compromise on the issue of nationalisation, Mosaddeq was anxious not to translate popular dislike for the oil company into a general dislike of the British. Indeed Mosaddeq was acutely aware that nationalisation would not work without some measure of cooperation from the British, and was anxious to retain company workers and technicians albeit now under the auspices of the National Iranian Oil Company (NIOC). Mosaddeq reasoned that in the context of the nationalisations which the Labour government had pursued in Britain, the British people would come to understand and recognise the legitimacy of the Iranian move. In a speech following the nationalisation he argued that the British government had been unreasonable and 'would not accept this fair offer by you people of Persia'. When the crowd chanted, 'Death to Britain', Mosaddeq responded by saying, 'No, I will not have you say, "Death to Britain"; we want God to guide the British government to recognise our undoubted rights'.[159]

Unsurprisingly, the British were similarly unwilling to countenance what they regarded as a unilateral and illegal act of nationalisation, which if tolerated could lead to further problems in the Middle East. It did not escape their notice that Mosaddeq was rapidly becoming an icon of post-imperial change for many malcontents in the Middle East, not least the Egyptians, whose experience of British domination was much more direct. Mosaddeq himself cultivated this image, aware that economic austerity and hardship, as a result of an immediate British embargo on the purchase of Iranian oil, could only be sustained and tolerated if Iranians could be convinced of the historic and international importance of the movement. The degree of international importance grew in direct proportion to the level of domestic political difficulty. In 1951 Mosaddeq argued: 'Sometimes great opportunities arise for nations which, if exploited intelligently, will change the course of history to their advantage and will end centuries of privation, misery and despair'.[160] Again in the following year he emphasised 'No effort, no reward. History bears witness that no nation has ever achieved independence or gained freedom without undergoing toils and hardships'.[161] By 1953, the international importance of the anti-imperialist struggle, of which the Iranians were in the vanguard, had become explicit.

No nation has succeeded in shaking off a foreign yoke without struggle, as can be testified by ancient and modern histories of nations and freedom movements . . . Our movement served as inspiration to national risings of other peoples, and today peoples of North and South Africa anxiously await our success.[162]

In the face of such mounting rhetoric, it was difficult for either side to compromise, so resolutely had they become embedded in their respective principles – one legal, the other political. Negotiations continued, but the British were already considering a shift towards a political solution, albeit a covert one. This decision gathered momentum when the British discovered to their cost that the anticipated legal avenues open to them did not necessarily guarantee the solution they had been seeking. In taking their complaint to the United Nations, the British inadvertently provided Dr Mosaddeq with an international platform and access to US public opinion. For all their scorn, they were disturbed to find that the Americans found Mosaddeq endearing, if slightly odd. Mosaddeq for his part played the role of national liberation fighter to perfection, encouraging Americans to remember the spirit of '76 when they too had shaken off the yoke of British imperialism.[163] At the end of the day, however, the Americans were reluctant to commit to the Iranian cause and unwilling to abandon their British allies. Mosaddeq's subsequent disappointment was palpable:

We are very grateful to the American people for their very valuable moral support . . . but we expected the American government to pay more consideration to the rightful demands of the Iranian people, being cognizant of the fact that the American people have acquired their liberty and independence through their continued national struggle.[164]

For much of the first half of the century Iranians had grown accustomed to the belief that the United States offered the only serious avenue of release from the twin manacles of British and Russian imperialism. Now it was gradually dawning on Iran's politicians that American idealism all too easily fell victim to American national interest. This was not a revelation to the left-leaning activists in the National Front. But for many ardent secular nationalists (Mosaddeq included) who were eager to believe in the sincerity of the American dream, American apathy was a cause for concern. Still, the real villain of the piece remained Britain, and the United States, while sympathetic to British lobbying about the threat of communism in Iran, were reluctant to accept the British logic that military intervention was the best way forward. The Americans remained convinced that Mosaddeq was open to reason. The British, meanwhile, developed plans for the destabilisation and ultimate overthrow of his government. It is important to remember that these plans were by no means as efficient or indeed as covert as subsequent generations would like us to believe. Indeed documents of the period indicate that, far from being a well-planned covert operation, the view that Britain was machinating against Mosaddeq was popularly held, widely acknowledged and was in all likelihood exaggerated for political consumption. It was in fact inconceivable to many Iranians that the British would not be plotting, and there was a curious reciprocal need for a conspiracy. On the one hand the British did not want to appear impotent, on the other it was important for Mosaddeq that the British appear, if not omnipotent, a very real threat to the nation's existence. The British government, and the AIOC in particular, were after all the source of Iran's problems. This message was reiterated as problems mounted, 'that is our thesis, that all the poverty, confusion and calamity that now have befallen upon us are the results of the unjustified interferences by the former oil company and the British Government in our internal affairs'.[165] Oil company personnel had been formally expelled from Iran in October 1951, to be followed almost one year later by the diplomatic staff, signalling a formal rupture in diplomatic relations. The formal break came after months of mutual recrimination, in which the British were repeatedly (and not without some justification) accused of hatching plots and seeking to interfere in domestic affairs. So extensive did these fears become, however, that some, even among National Front supporters, doubted their veracity, and complained that it was all too easy to decry critics as agents of the British.[166] For instance, Dr Fatemi (the Foreign Minister) was quick to ascribe blame for his near assassination on the machinations of British Intelligence, and on his way to the hospital he was quoted as alleging, 'The British killed me'.[167]

The truth was, as always, more complex. The expulsion of the British denied the National Front the tangible enemy which was so essential to their cohesion, and revealed clear divisions of opinion and purpose. In the first place, the National Front depended in large measure on the input and support of Ayatollah Kashani and his ability to bring the religious and devout to the cause of oil nationalisation. Kashani's importance is often belittled by nationalist historians who tend nevertheless, somewhat paradoxically, to ascribe Mosaddeq's downfall to Kashani's withdrawal of support. More sympathetic voices are likewise eager to play down the implication that Kashani's withdrawal from the National Front facilitated the success of the subsequent coup. A better appreciation of Kashani's role would have prepared people for the torrent which was to follow a generation later. Ayatollah Kashani enjoyed a long pedigree of opposition to the British, having been expelled from Iraq in the early 1920s for having fomented and encouraged the Shi'a to eject the British. Highly articulate and intensely political, Kashani did not see himself as best supporting actor to Mosaddeq's 'saviour', but very much as an equal, if not a rival.[168]

As the British noted,

> This large segment of the populace in recent years has found a shrewd and willing leader and spokesman in Ayatollah Seyyid Abol Qasim Kashani, who in the present phase of the nationalist struggle is such a powerful symbol because of his lifelong opposition to the British and his persecution in imprisonment and exile at their hands.[169]

As to his methods, an intelligence report noted that

> Kashani has taken full advantage of his unusual theatrical talents, display-
> ing exceptional skill in exploiting his rural contacts and the self-interest of
> the Iranian clergy, and appealing to the piety of small merchants in urban
> centres. He has not hesitated to use his position as a member of the Moslem
> clergy to arouse latent suspicions of the Christian West.[170]

Kashani's support was essential in deflecting domestic criticism and in maintaining the momentum of the movement in the face of mounting pressure
from monarchists.

Prior to their expulsion at the end of 1952, the British had initially sought
to negotiate their way out of difficulty, but had rapidly come to the conclusion
that such an option, given the disparity of views, was unlikely to achieve the
desired result. Alternatives therefore revolved around the removal of Mosaddeq
either through constitutional or unconstitutional means. The preferred route
seemed to be that of constitutional means facilitated by illegal activities. They
sought to destabilise the government through economic pressures, and by giving
encouragement, financial and moral, to Mosaddeq's opponents. The key to their
plan was the determination of the Shah, whom they encouraged to exercise his
constitutional prerogative and dismiss Mosaddeq. The Shah, however, proved
singularly unwilling in this case to lead from the front and expose himself to
popular anger. Aware of Mosaddeq's popularity, and no doubt irritated by it, the
Shah was nevertheless unwilling to directly confront his Prime Minister, whom he
habitually referred to as 'Our Demosthenes'.[171] Mosaddeq, similarly, while anxious for the Shah to reign rather than rule, was not a republican, and recognised
that for all the Shah's personal failings and political ineffectuality, the institution
of the monarchy retained a substantial measure of respect and popularity, especially among traditional sectors of society.

Mosaddeq was also acutely aware that as economic problems mounted and
political rivalries intensified, the Shah would increasingly become the focus of
opposition activities, a focus that was not without its utility. As one diplomat noted,

> even the staunchest believer in the occult powers of the British Embassy
> cannot entirely escape the feeling that perhaps there are in Persian politics
> some forces which have some responsibility. A domestic scapegoat is there-
> fore essential and for this role the Shah is obviously cast.[172]

To be sure, Mosaddeq's enthusiasm for populist politics and his tendency to
play politics rather than adhere to constitutional legalities (despite his own legal
background) were bound to draw criticism. For instance, during the elections
for the Seventeenth Majlis which was to convene in February 1952, Mosaddeq
ensured voting was terminated as soon as a parliamentary quorum of deputies
had been elected, and before provincial and rural constituencies – where the
opposition vote was strong – could complete their ballots. Such dubious moves

were compounded by rhetoric which increasingly paid lip service to the socialists within the movement, causing growing concern among the traditional (landed) elites. Very much in this vein, Mosaddeq decided to take his challenge to the top by exercising his constitutional right to appoint the minister of war.

For all his prevarications, this was a provocation too far for the Shah who, like his father, felt he had a special relationship with all things military. Much to the satisfaction of the British and his supporters, the Shah finally decided to stand up to his Prime Minister, and rejected Mosaddeq's nomination. Mosaddeq tendered his resignation, effectively calling on the people to decide. It was a bold, calculated move, which nevertheless raised the political temperature considerably. No one had hitherto challenged the royal authority so explicitly. Moving to exploit the unexpected political vacuum, anti-Mosaddeq deputies voted in Qavam as Prime Minister. Qavam had been quietly if actively biding his time since the fall of his government in 1947. Now the opportunity for his return had presented itself and Qavam was keen to seize it. Yet even the wily Qavam had miscalculated the level of popular support Mosaddeq enjoyed, with the crucial backing of Ayatollah Kashani, who denounced Qavam as a 'secularist' and against religion.[173] Despite unleashing the army, five days of mass demonstrations forced the Shah and Qavam to back down, and led to the recall of Mosaddeq, this time considerably emboldened by his triumphant return. The day's events, which went down in the historical consciousness as the *Siyeh-e Tir* (Thirtieth of Tir, the date by the Iranian calendar), proved to be a major blow for both British and royalist aspirations, and was ultimately to lead to the breaking of diplomatic relations noted above.

Mosaddeq also took the opportunity to try to institutionalise the movement and to take revenge on those political groups who had resisted him, in particular the monarchy and the army. He announced that henceforth he would be acting Minister of War, and began stripping the Shah of many of the powers he had enjoyed under the Constitution, ensuring that henceforth he would be little more than a ceremonial monarch. Princess Ashraf, the Shah's very active twin sister, was sent into exile, while the Shah himself was prohibited from direct contact with foreign diplomats. It proved a massive humiliation. Meanwhile, the Thirtieth of Tir was to be established as an annual holiday, commemorating the 'national rising' which had restored him to the premiership. Next Mosaddeq turned his scrutiny to the army, curtailing its budget and setting up commissions to investigate corruption in arms procurement and the procedures for promotion. More controversially, he instigated a purge of the army resulting in the sacking of some 136 officers including 15 generals.[174] None of these acts was calculated to endear him to the military, and indicated the confidence with which he now governed the country.

At the same time, Kashani's support had come with a price and there was a notable shift towards the Islamisation of the movement. This use of the sacred was not new, but the emphasis was clear. 'Anyone who aims to belittle the holy struggle of our nation by assessing the achievements of the Iranian movement in economic terms and by comparing the independence of our country with a few million pounds, has undoubtedly perpetrated a blunder', announced Mosaddeq to the Majlis.[175] Not only was the struggle holy, but the Majlis also became 'sacred'.[176] In addition, Mosaddeq agreed to consider laws banning alcohol, which many of his deputies objected to on fiscal grounds, and to ban missionaries in Iran. Two Christian priests were in fact expelled on charges of spying for Britain.[177] There were nevertheless limits to this trend. Where religion served the nationalist cause its political utility and potency were clear. Where Kashani attempted to internationalise his appeal, the reaction in Iran (and elsewhere) was noticeably lukewarm. Iranians were attracted by the argument that their struggle against Britain was of international importance. They were less enamoured with Kashani's attempt to integrate the struggle within a wider Islamic context. He orchestrated demonstrations in favour of the struggle in Egypt against Suez, and in support of the people of Tunisia. With respect to the latter, it was noted, 'Practically nobody seems to have turned up and one newspaper report put the attendance at 17'.[178] He established a 'Movement of the East' (*Nezhat-e Sharg*), ostensibly to unify all Muslim peoples, though the reception abroad as well as at home was modest, and in some places hostile.[179] Most peculiarly, Seyyed Zia alleged that Kashani even suggested that he (Kashani) become the new Caliph, to which he had retorted that no Shi'a could become Caliph.[180] Such tendencies were not without their critics especially from the left in the National Front, who found the influx of religious terminology, and the concomitant influence on government policy, disconcerting. They conjectured that other plans were afoot:

> No one yet knows what the insincere and unfriendly Americans want to do with this country. The Yankees perhaps thought that as the Persians are Moslems and as Kashani has religious and spiritual influence over them it is impossible for them to become Communists. They therefore thought that they should be put under pressure in order that they may be reduced to destitution and then made into soldiers to fight the Communists.[181]

Such rationalisation was not entirely without foundation; as early as 1943 it was noted,

> While the priesthood has little influence with the so-called educated classes, it is still regarded with some respect by the lower classes, and the advances now being made to certain influential mullahs probably have their origin in the hope that their influence may be used against the spread of Communist ideas.[182]

Fear of the spread of communist ideas and the revolutionary destruction of the old order exacerbated the tension which was already growing. Fear of revolution, genuine or otherwise, had been cultivated by politicians of all hues to encourage a measure of incremental reform. Only in reform could communist ideas be contained and eliminated. Yet during the Oil Nationalisation Crisis this theory appeared to be backfiring. Despite being banned, the Tudeh Party continued to grow and, in conjunction with other socialist parties, formed the backbone of the

National Movement. They continued to publish their newspaper which predicted the inevitable destruction of imperialism; during marches, they openly defied and insulted the institution of the monarchy.[183] However, the Tudeh Party was never wholeheartedly behind Dr Mosaddeq and the National Front, and tended to criticise the Prime Minister with equal venom, despite the arguments of Mosaddeq's opponents that the two were close allies.[184] It is testament to the strength of the myth of the communist bogey that both sides, including Dr Mosaddeq, exploited this Cold War narrative to justify international support, especially American. It was reported in the *New York Herald Tribune* that 'Premier Musaddiq [sic] warned the Western world today that any right wing coup against his government would only pave the way for certain communist dictatorship'.[185]

Fear of a right-wing coup continued to preoccupy the Prime Minister's mind to a greater extent than concerns of a communist takeover, despite the detrimental effect Tudeh support was having on the attitude of the political establishment, including crucially the religious classes, who worried about the growth of an atheistic ideology. Even socialists within the National Front expressed concern at the Tudeh's dependency on the Soviet Union. Whatever the truth of these links, by 1953 Mosaddeq found himself increasingly exposed to the charge of being a Trojan horse for an inevitable communist takeover. This apparent inevitability finally catalysed the US into action. The new Republican administration in the White House under the leadership of President Eisenhower was far more sympathetic to British protestations than the Truman administration had been. Moreover, the British fully exploited the new mood of McCarthyism in the US to emphasise the imminence of a Soviet takeover. That Tudeh Party demonstrations regularly pilloried 'Uncle Sam' as well as 'John Bull' only fed these fears, and convinced US officials that 'saving Iran for the free world' required a proactive strategy rather than a policy of restraint. Following the diplomatic break with Britain, responsibility for the organisation of the impending coup against Mosaddeq fell on the US embassy.

The success of any coup was predicated, however, on the coincidence of interests at the domestic level. The debacle of Qavam's premiership in 1952 had indicated that, despite economic difficulties, Mosaddeq continued to dominate the political scene and that, while he retained the support of key sections of the political establishment (or indeed if they simply remained apathetic), his position was relatively secure. Time, however, was not on Mosaddeq's side, since there was a limit to how much economic dislocation the populace would tolerate, and a feeling that sooner or later a critical mass would be reached. More damning, however, were the methods he chose in pursuit of his domestic reforms, which succeeded, where his opponents could not, in alienating his own pillars of support. Enlightened though they were in relation to land, judicial and educational reform, his decision to seek emergency powers (initially for six months but then renewed for another six months), and to use martial law where necessary against recalcitrant opponents, caused widespread consternation. Both Kashani and Makki, representing differing wings of the movement, objected to what they considered to be Mosaddeq's 'dictatorial' tendencies.[186] Finally, in July 1953, faced with opposition from the Majlis itself, National Front deputies staged a boycott, denying the Lower House a quorum and forcing a constitutional crisis, which effectively resulted in the dissolution of the Majlis. To legitimise this move, Mosaddeq, with the explicit and increasingly visible backing of the Tudeh Party, decided to call a popular referendum.

By the summer of 1953, Mosaddeq appeared politically dominant with a popular appeal his critics could only envy. Yet the foundations of his power, in the absence of support from key social groups, were probably never weaker. Mosaddeq had become the 'demagogue' the British had always accused him of being, sacrificing his political astuteness on the altar of populism. Not only were the Left disillusioned with his unconstitutional behaviour, but Kashani and other religious parties objected to his apparent growing dependence on the Tudeh Party. The army, which had hitherto been generally apathetic as a result of austerity drives and purges, had become openly hostile. It was not uncommon for newspapers to call him the 'father of the nation' one day, and 'Hitler' the next.[187] Disenchanted officers formed a retired officers' association and were reported to be actively participating in anti-government sedition.[188] Mosaddeq was aware of the danger from the military and sought to cultivate loyalty by forming a new political party and encouraging senior officers to join it. It was undoubtedly counterproductive that party members had to take an oath of loyalty to the Prime Minister.[189] His plan failed dramatically, and the staunch vice-president of the Majlis, Razavi, was effectively heckled out of a speech to officers.[190] Furthermore, it was noted that there was growing clerical support for the Shah in Mashhad.[191] To some it appeared as if confusion reigned, and there are few things the Iranian political establishment abhorred more than the whiff of anarchy.

In such times, it was not unnatural for the institution of the monarchy to be seen as *the* anchor for social and political stability, and the focus of the political contest once again devolved upon the person of the Shah. As one diplomat noted, however,

> Although nominally the centre of the dispute the Shah appears in fact, to be a pawn in the game. The crowds which shouted for him on Saturday and Sunday were almost certainly doing so at the behest, to begin with, of Kashani and other elements opposed to Musaddiq, and later at the behest of Musaddiq's National Front supporters as well.[192]

Opponents of Mosaddeq alleged that he wished the Shah to leave Iran. They played on sentimental fears and loyalty, arguing that the departure of the Shah would result in the political fragmentation of Iran.[193] Mosaddeq found it prudent to refute this allegation publicly and also took measures to increase surveillance on the tribes who were known to have monarchist tendencies.[194] The Shah's continued prevarication simply added to the growing sense of uncertainty. As late as March 1953, 'The Shah continues to insist to all his advisers that it would be unwise for him openly to oppose Musaddiq until the myth of his greatness has been exploded'.[195] Just as the Americans had been persuaded to act by convincing them of the threat of communism, so too the British sought to convince the Shah of the threat Mosaddeq posed to the continuation of his own dynasty. As early as 1952, Falle noted that one method to catalyse the Shah into action might be to point out 'that a continuation of the present situation is dangerous for the dynasty'.[196] If the Shah was jealous of his military prerogatives, he was to prove even more anxious about his dynastic inheritance.

When the long-prophesied coup attempt finally came in August 1953, it was hardly the shock to the system that posterity has painted.[197] As noted above, Mosaddeq cultivated the popular belief in continuing foreign interference and the possibility of a foreign coup in order to maintain political awareness and give cohesion to a movement which was under serious strain. The British, and to some extent the Americans, were also publicly adamant that such an act of unilateral nationalisation would not be allowed to stand. The possibility, indeed probability, of a coup attempt was never really in doubt. Mosaddeq's fatalism arguably invited such a development, comfortable in the knowledge that either he would triumph as in 1952 against Qavam, or fall as the quintessential 'national martyr'. This image, while his most powerful political legacy, was not the route for which, as some would suggest, he was either destined, or indeed which he desired. When the Shah was finally persuaded to issue his *farman* (decree) dismissing Mosaddeq as Prime Minister and appointing General Zahedi in his place, Mosaddeq's reaction was measured, somewhat lackadaisical, and if anything too dismissive. Having received the *farman*, Mosaddeq peremptorily dismissed the messenger, Colonel Nasiri (who had approached the premier's residence with tanks), and stated that he would read it and answer in due course. In short, Mosaddeq did not behave like a politician who knew his time was up. Nasiri for his part returned empty-handed, and by all accounts this farcical attempt at a coup not only failed, but proved immensely counterproductive. As news emerged, supporters of the Prime Minister poured into the streets and attacked symbols of the monarchy. Newspapers vied to attack the Shah and in some cases the institution of the monarchy itself. *Bakhtar-e Emruz* argued for the establishment of a regency council; *Niruye Sevom* declared the Pahlavi dynasty to be at an end. Significantly, even the Pan-Iranist parties attacked the Shah. The Tudeh Central Committee issued a statement calling for the end of the monarchy and declared the Shah 'a treacherous man who has committed thousands of crimes in his kingship; he must be tried and sentenced to death'.[198]

For its Anglo-American architects, the coup attempt seemed to have gone disastrously wrong, a view confirmed by the Shah's sudden decision to take an extended holiday, first to Baghdad and then onwards to Rome. All the expensive financing and propaganda had apparently come to nothing. But this was not 1952, and this time Mosaddeq had miscalculated. Lacking support in either the *bazaar* or the *ulema*, he proved vulnerable. Pumping in more money and reassurance, the US and Britain convinced Mosaddeq's opponents to try again. This time they succeeded – Mosaddeq was overthrown. Zahedi became the man of the hour, determined to fulfil his role as the Iranian 'Nasser', while the Shah, on hearing the news in Rome, became convinced that his people really did 'love him'.

Mosaddeq was arrested and later put on trial where he began the reconstruction of his image as a national martyr and democrat toppled by the forces of reaction supported by foreign powers. It was a powerful narrative with sufficient truth to prove immensely problematic for the restored monarchy. Yet it was not the only truth. Mosaddeq finally succumbed through political miscalculations of his own doing, as much as by foreign intervention. Had he retained the firm social bases of his power, no amount of foreign interference (short of war) would have unseated him. But he relinquished them in favour of a crass populism which was ultimately vacuous. Faced with growing difficulties and the prospect of political anarchy, the establishment rallied around the institution of the monarchy determined to restore order. If in retrospect it has been judged a political mistake, if not a calamity, at the time many considered it a necessity. Subsequent events were to encourage the national reflection and remorse to which we are now accustomed (along with the political expediency of hiding behind foreign scapegoats), as it soon became apparent that the Shah was not the pawn his supporters had expected. Convinced of his people's affection, and failing to distinguish between the institution and the person of the monarchy, the Shah proved more vengeful and more determined to fulfil his own destiny than many had anticipated. Returning to Tehran, the Shah skirted over the question of his abrupt flight and reflected on Divine Providence, 'I myself on several occasions have been ready to lay down my life for your survival and will unhesitatingly continue to do so. In the February 15th incident [assassination attempt in 1949] God Willed that I should survive'.[199]

Notes

1 See Bill and Springborg, *Politics in the Middle East*, pp. 8–11.
2 It may be argued that Persian nationalism was defined by Reza Shah and popularised (Iranianised) by Mosaddeq.
3 FO 248 64/149a/46 dated 17 August 1946.
4 *The Times*, 'Persia Old and New: Younger Generation Groping for Reforms', 25 April 1946.
5 FO 371 27188, Intelligence Summaries 1941. It should be noted that in contemporary British sources 'Iran' was still referred to as 'Persia'. Whenever such sources are quoted, this usage is retained.
6 FO 371 75485 E6175 dated 13 May 1949, translation of report: Naficy, *Statistics for the Principal Industries of Iran for the Year 1326* [1947–48].
7 Quoted in F. Machalski, 'Political Parties in Iran in the Years 1941–1946', *Folia Orientalia* 3, 1961, p. 169.
8 Machalski, 'Political Parties in Iran in the Years 1941–1946'.
9 FO 248 1428, files relating to the Majlis elections of 1943, dated 14 July and 7 August 1943.
10 FO 248 1410, 'Programme and Desires of the Azerbaijan Workers Committee', dated 26 February 1942.
11 FO 248 1427 dated 24 April 1943.
12 FO 248 1514, file 10101/4/51, dated 5 January 1951.
13 T. Cuyler-Young, 'The Problem of Westernisation in Modern Iran', *Middle East Journal* 2, 1948, p. 130.
14 FO 248 1410, copy of a notice placed on a wall in Tabriz, dated 24 February 1942.
15 FO 248 1410, report of the British Consul in Tabriz, dated 29 December 1941.

16 FO 248 1494, Lawford to Bevin, 101/5/15/50, dated 18 February 1950.

17 FO 248 1531 10105/50, Memorandum by Pyman, dated 28 January 1950.

18 FO 248 1494 101/5/15/50 dated 18 February 1950, on government attempts to broadcast to minorities in their own language.

19 Abrahamian, *Iran between Two Revolutions*, p. 170 – one can contest his use of 'middle class'.

20 L.P. Elwell-Sutton, 'Political Parties in Iran', *Middle East Journal* 3(1), 1949, pp. 45–62.

21 FO 248 1435 22/181/44 dated 22 September 1944. For detailed backgrounds of Azerbaijani deputies see file 22/151/44 dated 18 May 1944; for Fars see file 22/38/44 dated 19 April 1944; Hamadan and Malayer file 22/126/44 dated 31 March 1944; and Khorasan file 22/103/44 dated 23 February 1944. For a not untypical character assessment of the foremost deputy from Kermanshah see FO 248 1428 dated 7 June 1943.

22 R. Ramazani, 'Intellectual Trends in the Politics and History of the Musaddiq Era', in J. Bill and W.R. Louis (eds), *Mosaddeq, Iranian Nationalism and Oil*. London: I.B. Tauris, 1988, p. 311.

23 This proved difficult, since the remaining Qajar heir was serving in the Royal Navy and had a poor command of Farsi.

24 FO 248 1407 dated 13 August 1942. See also Seyyed Zia's speech to the Fourteenth Majlis, quoted in Abrahamian, *Iran between Two Revolutions*, p. 205.

25 *The Times*, 14 October 1941.

26 FO 248 1407 file 1628, note 9/7/42, records quite clearly the relationship between the Shah and the army, noting that so uncertain was the Shah of his position that he stationed 600 soldiers round Saadabad Palace. Significantly, some older generals were reportedly less trustworthy.

27 *The Times*, 18 September 1941, notes the lacklustre reception given to the Shah as he was to be sworn in.

28 FO 248 1426, Interviews with the Shah, dated 21 August 1943.

29 FO 248 1426, Interviews with the Shah, dated 21 August 1943.

30 FO 248 1407 file 628, HM Minister's relations with the Shah, note no. 9/20/42 [1942; exact date unclear].

31 FO 248 1407 file 628, HM Minister's relations with the Shah, press summary, dated 17 September 1942.

32 FO 248 1407 dated 10 April 1942.

33 FO 248 1423, note from Bullard, dated 29 June 1943.

34 FO 248 1427, Persian Government and Internal Affairs, dated 8 May 1943, notes that Misbahzadeh, the former editor of *Keihan* was aware of the influence officers had on the Shah.

35 FO 248 1409 file 49, internal situation Fars; press summary dated 13 April 1942.

36 FO 248 1409 file 49, internal situation Fars; Deputy Anwar quoted in a press summary, dated 13 April 1942.

37 FO 248 1426, Interviews with the Shah, undated, noted 1943. Also memo dated 2 July 1943 notes that dull conversation revitalised by the mention of the 'war'.

38 FO 248 1407, HM Minister's relation with the Shah, file 628, dated 19 August 1942.

39 FO 248 1409 file 39, Internal situation Fars; report on the general situation, dated 10 June 1942.

40 FO 248 1427, Persian Govt and Internal Affairs; letter from Bishop of Isfahan to Bullard, dated 4 May 1943. See also FO 371 35109, Intelligence Summary 1943, file E1734, dated 23 February 1943, which notes that 'Tehran is on the verge of starvation'.

41 FO 248 1427, Persian Govt and Internal Affairs, file 544, dated 24 April 1943, notes that the press blame the British for everything. See also Bullard's report dated 6 April 1943.

42 FO 248 1410, Internal Situation Azerbaijan, file 144, dated 23 April 1942.

43 FO 248 1462, Persian Govt and Internal Situation 1946; letter from Arfa to Embassy dated 8 September 1946. See also FO 371 27188 E8305/268/34 dated 19 November 1941, which reveals that at the opening of the Thirteenth Majlis, crowds shouted 'Long Live Hitler!'

44 FO 248 1423, Interviews with the Shah, note from Bullard, dated 29 June 1943.

45 FO 248 1427 file 544, Persian Govt and Internal Affairs, text of Soheili's *NoRuz* (New Year) broadcast, dated 23 March 1943.

46 FO 371 45458, Intelligence Summaries 1945, E3434, dated 28 May 1945.

47 FO 248 1407 file 628 dated 19 August 1942. See also FO 248 1426 dated 18 March, 3 August 1943.

48 FO 248 1423, Talks with the Shah, dated 15 January 1943. See also FO 248 1426, Interviews with the Shah, dated 15 April 1943.

49 Abrahamian, *Iran between Two Revolutions*, p. 209.

50 FO 248 1409, Internal Situation: Fars file 39, dated 12 February 1942. See also letter from Nasir to Ghulam Hussein Muhazzab, dated 17 March 1942.

51 FO 248 1347/1348 file 64, Internal Situation in Fars; file no. 64/329/44, dated 9 October 1944.

52 FO 248 1409 file 39, dated 4 November 1942.

53 FO 248 1409 dated 17 January 1942.

54 FO 248 1409 dated 13 April 1942. See also letter to *Asr-i Azadi*, dated 20 April 1942.

55 FO 248 1409 dated 13 April 1942.

56 FO 248 1409, Letter from the Boir Ahmadis, dated 7 April 1944.

57 See, for example, L. Fawcett, *Iran and the Cold War: The Azerbaijan Crisis of 1946*. Cambridge: Cambridge University Press, 1992. This of course was an extension of the traditional rivalry between Russia and Britain over Iran, but the beginning of the Cold War gave the contest new meaning.

58 *The Times*, Text of the manifesto of the Azerbaijani Majlis, 17 December 1945.

59 *The Times*, 28 January 1946.

60 *The Times*, 12 December 1945. See also FO 248 1463, Internal Situation Azerbaijan; press attaché's report, dated 26 February 1946; also, conversation between Pishevari and Consul, dated 17 October 1946, and similar conclusion drawn from conversations with the Kurdish leader, dated 11 September 1946.

61 FO 248 1410, Internal Situation Azerbaijan, file 144, dated 20 February 1942.

62 Quoted in Abrahamian, *Iran between Two Revolutions*, p. 218.

63 Quoted in Abrahamian, *Iran between Two Revolutions*, p. 219.

64 FO 248 1410, Internal Situation in Azerbaijan, file 144, Programme and Desires of the Azerbaijan Workers Committee, dated 26 February 1942.

65 FO 248 1410 file 144, notice placed on Tabriz wall, dated 24 February 1942.

66 FO 248 1410, Internal Situation in Azerbaijan, file 144, dated 29 December 1941. See also memo dated 9 March 1942.

67 FO 248 1410 file 144, dated 8 April 1942.

68 FO 248 1410 file 144, dated 28 January 1942.

69 FO 248 1410 file 144, Article 1 of the Azerbaijan Workers' Committee, dated 26 February 1942. See also Tabriz consulate commentary dated 16 March 1942. Also Cuyler-Young, 'The Problem of Westernisation in Modern Iran'.

70 FO 248 1442, Persian Govt and Internal Situation, file 150, notes on Majlis proceedings, file 150/44/44, dated 6 April 1944.

71 Quoted in Abrahamian, *Iran between Two Revolutions*, p. 231. See also FO 248 1462, undated file 65/94/46, the Programme of the Democratic Party of Iran.

72 FO 248 1444, Internal Situation in Azerbaijan, file 439; report file 439/6/44, dated 6 April 1944. This, and the fact that Pishevari called on Azerbaijanis to join in *jihad* against the government in Tehran (see also R. Rossow, 'The Battle of Azerbaijan', *Middle East Journal* 10(1), 1956, pp. 17–32) were the first tentative

indications of 'religious nationalism', perhaps reflecting the growing politicisation of the masses.

73 FO 248 1463 file 69, Summary of Pishevari speech file 69/191/46, dated 17 May 1946.

74 FO 371 52680, Reactions to Azerbaijan; E9036, dated 11 September 1946, reveals that Pishevari still shied away from publicly declaring 'independence'.

75 FO 248 1410 file 144, Consular report, dated 29 December 1941.

76 FO 248 1463, Internal Situation, Azerbaijan; report on *NoRuz* (New Year) celebrations file 69/90/46, dated 23 March 1946.

77 FO 248 1462, Persian Govt and Internal Situation, file 65; summary of article from *Havanan* newspaper, dated 6 October 1946.

78 FO 371 52679 file 5; Consular tour of Azerbaijan, E7642 dated 8 August 1946.

79 FO 248 1463 file 69, Situation report 69/50/46, dated 23 February 1946. *The Times* records that Pishevari, on a visit to Tehran, took to wearing the uniform of the 'national' army, dated 28 April 1946.

80 FO 248 1410 file 144, reports, dated 22 May, 24 May 1942.

81 FO 248 1410, file 144, Kurdish Demands, dated 30 April 1942.

82 FO 371 45503, Kurdish Demonstrations, file 2495; E3660 dated 16 May 1945; E8663 dated 12 November 1945.

83 FO 248 1463 file 69, Kurdish declaration broadcast on Tabriz radio, file 69/120/46, dated 23 April 1946.

84 FO 248 1463, file 69, reveals that Azerbaijani forces were fighting the Turkish-speaking Afshar tribe, file 69/4/46 dated 2 January 1946. Also the reality of poor attendance at rallies, file 69/459/46, dated 4 December 1946.

85 *The Times*, 19 December 1946, notes that Turkish books were ritually and publicly burned in Tabriz.

86 FO 248 1427, Persian Govt and Internal Affairs, file 544; interview with Zarin Kafsh, dated 3 September 1943; also undated report of conference in favour of Seyyed Zia on 14 June 1943.

87 FO 248 1427, file 544; interview with Qavam, dated 25 November 1943.

88 Quoted in F. Azimi, *Iran: The Crisis of Democracy*. London: I.B. Tauris, 1989, p. 66.

89 FO 371 52678 file 5; E5994, dated 28 June 1946.

90 FO 248 1474, Persian Govt and Internal Situation, file 13, file no. 13/74/47, dated 14 July 1947.

91 FO 248 1474, file 13, file no. 13/26/47, dated 26 March 1947.

92 Abrahamian, *Iran between Two Revolutions*, p. 237.

93 FO 248 1463 file 69, file 69/467/46, dated 28 December 1946.

94 FO 248 1463 file 69, file no. 69/381/46, memo, dated 28 October 1946.

95 FO 248 1462 file 65, Article from *Azad Mellat*, dated 6 October 1946.

96 J.A. Thorpe, 'Truman's Ultimatum to Stalin on the 1946 Azerbaijan Crisis: The Making of a Myth', *Journal of Politics* 40(1), 1978, p. 188.

97 FO 248 1427 file 544, interview with members of the elite, dated 11 July 1943, in which they acknowledge the importance of royal mystique in maintaining the loyalty of the tribes.

98 FO 248 1463 file 69, file no. 69/467/46, dated 28 December 1946.

99 *The Times*, 14 December 1946. See also *The Times*, 27 October 1946, which indicates the popular reception received by the Shah and the army.

100 *The Times*, 19 December 1946.

101 Rossow, 'The Battle of Azerbaijan', p. 17.

102 FO 248 1474, Persian Govt and Internal Situation, file 13, Le Rougetel in audience with the Shah, file no. 13/124/47, dated 13 November 1947.

103 FO 248 1474 file 13, Creswell to Bevin, file no. 13/109/47, dated 23 September 1947.

104 *The Times*, 29 May 1947.

105 See *Ayandeh-e Iran* quoted by P. Chelkowski, 'Popular Entertainment, Media and Social Change in 20th Century Iran', in *The Cambridge History of Iran*, Vol VII. Cambridge: Cambridge University Press, p. 799.
106 N.C. Cook, 'The Theatre and Ballet Arts of Iran', *Middle East Journal* 3(4), October 1949, p. 408.
107 FO 371 52704, Khalil Maliki's visit to England, 1946, File 133.
108 FO 248 1474 file 13, Press Summary, file no. 13/76/47, dated 8 July 1947.
109 Azimi, *Iran: The Crisis of Democracy*, p. 344. See also FO 248 1493, file 101/2, Seyyed Zia's comments, file 101/2/248/50, dated 10 December 1950.
110 FO 248 1493, General Political Situation, file 101/2, conversations between Lawford and the Shah, file no. 101/2/196/50, dated 16 September 1950.
111 FO 248 1493, General Political Situation, file 101/2, conversations between Lawford and the Shah, file no. 101/2/196/50, dated 16 September 1950. See also file 101/2/185/50, Alam's comments on the Shah's trip to Kurdistan, dated 28 August 1950.
112 As early as 1944 Mosaddeq urged the Shah to distance himself from his father, FO 248 1442, Persian Govt., file 150, file no. 150/118/44, dated 17 October 1944.
113 FO 248 1474 file 13, Memo file no. 13/36/47 dated 26 April 1947.
114 FO 248 1426, Interviews with the Shah, files dated 13 July, 26 July 1943.
115 FO 248 1493 file 101/2, the clergy were similarly disenamoured of the affairs of the court, file no. 101/2/248/50, dated 10 December 1950.
116 FO 248 1485, Persian Govt and Internal Situation, file 21; file no. 21/13 49 Lambton's Assessment dated 27 January 1949, file no. 21/262/49 Le Rougetel to Bevin dated 18 November 1949.
117 FO 248 1407, HM Minister's relations with the Shah, file 628, memo, dated 10 April 1942.
118 FO 248 1442, Persian Govt and Internal Situation, file 150; report file no. 150/174/44, dated 2 December 1944.
119 FO 248 1485, file 21, conversation with Seyyed Zia, file no. 21/290/49, dated 12 December 1949. FO 248 1493, file 101/2, conversation with Alam, file no. 101/2/56/50, dated 25 March 1950. The Shah may have also drawn strength from the example of Napoleon, see FO 248 1442, file 150, file no. 150/18/44, dated 1 February 1944, which notes the prominent placement of a statuette of Napoleon in the Shah's study.
120 FO 248 1423, Interviews with the Shah, dated 15 January 1943.
121 FO 248 1426, Interviews with the Shah, dated 15 April 1943.
122 FO 371 35109, Intelligence Summary, file 110, E552/110/34, dated 27 January 1943.
123 FO 248 1493, General Political Situation, file 101/2/118/50, conversation with the Shah, dated 10 June 1950.
124 FO 248 1485, Persian Govt and Internal Situation, file 21, file no. 21/271/49, dated 24 November 1949.
125 FO 371 91519, The Shah's sale of Crown Lands, file 1461, E1461, dated 12 February 1951.
126 FO 371 75504, Royal Family Affairs, file 1944, no specific date or file no.; dated 1949.
127 See FO 248 1423, Interviews with the Shah, discussion with military attaché, dated 16 August 1943; general report undated; conversation with Misbahzadeh, dated 8 May 1943; FO 248 1442, Persian Govt . . ., conversation with Lascelles, file no. 150/85/44, dated 14 August 1944; FO 248 1493, General Political Situation, conversations with the Shah, file no. 101/2/119/50, dated 12 June 1950; conversation with Shepherd, file no. 101/2/104/50, dated 31 May 1950; FO 248 1514, Internal Situation, interview with the Shah, file no. 10101/12/51, dated 14 January 1951.

128   FO 371 40224, Personalities, file 2218, dated 14 March 1944. There is sufficient evidence to suggest that the Shah idolised his father; see FO 248 1442, Persian Govt, file 150, conversation between Trott and the Shah, file no. 150/81/44, dated 27 July 1944. Also FO 248 1493, file 101/2, conversation with Shepherd, file no. 101/2/211/50, dated 9 October 1950; conversations with Lawford, file 101/2/196/50, dated 16 September 1950.

129   FO 248 1427, Persian Govt, file 544, conversation with Minister of Interior Bahramy, dated 22 February 1943; see also FO 248 1426, Interviews with the Shah, memo dated February 1943.

130   FO 248 1442, file 150, file no. 150/144/44, dated 18 October 1944.

131   FO 248 1478, Royal Family Affairs, file 83, Le Rougetel, file no. 83/7/47, dated 2 February 1947.

132   FO 248 1442, file 150, file no 150/97/44, dated 5 September 1944. Also FO 248 1493 file 101/2, conversation with Shepherd, file no. 101/2/229/50, dated 20 November 1950; FO 248 1514 file 10101, Shepherd memo, file no. 10101/68/51, dated 12 March 1951.

133   *The Times*, 22 June 1949.

134   FO 371 75504, Royal Family Affairs, file 1944, Le Rougetel, date 1949.

135   FO 248 1478, Royal Family Affairs, file 83, Le Rougetel, file no. 83/19/47, dated 8 May 1947.

136   FO 248 1494, Tudeh Party activities, file 101/5, article from *Mardum*, file no. 101/5/50/50, dated 15 May 1950.

137   FO 248 1513, Royal Family Affairs, file 194/2, file no. 194/2/8/50, dated 19 April 1950.

138   FO 248 1485, Persian Govt and Internal Situation, file 21, file nos. 21/44/49, dated 14 February 1949, 21/36/49, dated 7 February 1949.

139   FO 248 1485, Persian Govt and Internal Situation, file 21, file no. 21/46/49, dated 11 February 1949.

140   FO 248 1485, file 21, file no. 21/143/49, dated 11 May 1949.

141   FO 248 1485, file 21, Le Rougetel to Bevin, file no. 21/262/49, dated 18 November 1949.

142   FO 371 91627, Wedding to Soraya, file 1941, E1941, dated 21 February 1951, and E1941, dated 26 February 1951. See also *The Times*, 12 February 1951.

143   FO 248 1513, Royal Family Affairs, file 194/2, file no. 194/2/24/50, dated 13 October 1950.

144   *The Times*, 11 February 51. FO 371 91627, E1941, dated 26 February 1951.

145   FO 248 1514, Internal Situation, file 10101, file no. 10101/452/52, dated 19 November 1951.

146   FO 248 1514, file 10101, pamphlet distributed at the Tehran sports stadium, file no. 10101/418/51, dated 29 October 1951. Some of the pamphlets were actually thrown into the royal box.

147   FO 371 E431/431/34, Biographies of Leading Personalities in Persia, 27 January 1931. See also Jones, *Banking and Empire in Iran*, p. 318, 'Mosaddeq . . . was regularly described by the British Ambassador of the time in his despatches to London as a "lunatic", and characterised as being "cunning and slippery", with "short and bandy legs" and "a slight reek of opium"'.

148   FO 248 1514, Internal Situation, file 10101, Situation report, file no. 10101/277/51, dated 4 September 1951.

149   Quoted in Jones, *Banking and Empire in Iran*, p. 306. For further details of Ebtehaj's achievements, see also the excellent account by F. Bostock and G. Jones, *Planning and Power in Iran: Ebtehaj and Economic Development under the Shah*. London: Cass, 1989.

150   See Bostock and Jones, *Planning and Power in Iran*, p. 73; also Jones, *Banking and Empire in Iran*, p. 319.

151 Jones, *Banking and Empire in Iran*, p. 318.

152 Jones, *Banking and Empire in Iran*, pp. 336–7.

153 Quoted in R. Ferrier, 'The Anglo-Iranian Oil Dispute: A Triangular Relationship', in Bill and Louis (eds) *Musaddiq, Iranian Nationalism and Oil*, p. 171.

154 Majlis Deputy Baqai, 6 July 1950, quoted in Abrahamian, *Iran between Two Revolutions*, p. 265.

155 Majlis Deputy Baqai, 6 July 1950, quoted in Abrahamian, *Iran between Two Revolutions*, pp. 265–6.

156 FO 248 1514, file 10101, file no. 10101/78/51, dated 11 March 1951.

157 FO 248 1531, file 10105, a pamphlet circulating in Tehran, file no. 10105/88, dated 3 March 1952. FO 248 1493, file 101/2, file no. 101/2/261/50, dated 31 December 1950, notes that the National Front hoisted pictures of the murderer of Hazhir in the Majlis with a caption praising him for having killed a 'traitor'.

158 See Shepherd's comments quoted in Azimi, *Iran: The Crisis of Democracy*, p. 257.

159 FO 248 1514, Internal Situation, summary of Dr Mosaddeq's speech, file no. 10101/368/51, dated 28 September 1951. See also 'Conversation with Dr Mosaddeq', by Kingsley Martin, in the *New Statesman and Nation*, 12 January 1952, in which he stresses several times that there is no quarrel with the British people.

160 FO 248 1514, file 10101, file no. 10101/517/51, dated 18 December 1951.

161 FO 248 1531, file 10105, speech to Seventeenth Majlis, file no. 1015/153A/52, dated 12 April 1952.

162 FO 371 104561, file 1015, text of Mosaddeq's speech, file no. 1015/26, dated 23 January 1953.

163 See for example, *The Times*, 22 October 1951; see also *The Times*, 8 and 23 October 1951.

164 FO 248 1531, file 10105, file no. 10105/124, dated 24 March 1952, not surprisingly, the word 'liberty' is used many times in his talk. FO 371 98633, file 11345, E11345, dated 20 March 1952 notes, 'This was beautifully stage-managed by Mosadeq who used his opportunity so skilfully that it contributed largely to the discomfiture of his enemies in the Senate'.

165 FO 248 1531, file 10105, file no. 10105/153A/52, dated 12 April 1952.

166 *The Times*, 27 September 1951.

167 FO 248 1531, file 10105, quoted from *Bakhtar-e Imruz*, file no. 10105/141, dated 31 March 1952. His impromptu remark was quoted in the newspaper *Shahid*, file no. 10105/88, dated 3 March 1952.

168 For an excellent assessment of Kashani, see Y. Richard, 'Ayatollah Kashani: Precursor of the Islamic Republic?', in N. Keddie (ed.) *Religion and Politics in Iran: Shi'ism from Quietism to Revolution*. New Haven, CT: Yale University Press, 1983, pp. 101–24.

169 Cuyler-Young, 'The Problem of Westernisation in Modern Iran', p. 139.

170 FO 371 104565, file 1015, Intelligence report, file no. 1015/126, dated 1 May 1953.

171 FO 248 1493, file 101/2, Shepherd's audience with the Shah, file no. 101/2/104/50, dated 31 May 1950.

172 FO 248 1541, The Shah and the Imperial Court, file 19401, dated 21 April 1952.

173 FO 248 1531, file 10105, Kashani's statement printed in *Shahid*, file no. 10105/268, dated 27 July 1952.

174 See Abrahamian, *Iran between Two Revolutions*, pp. 272–3.

175 Mosaddeq, Report to the Majlis, *Muzakirat-i Majlis*, 14 December 1952, quoted in Azimi, *Iran: The Crisis of Democracy*, p. 334. This is remarkably similar in sentiment to Ayatollah Khomeini's argument that the revolution was not orchestrated for the price of watermelons. See also FO 248 1514, file 10101, file no. 10101/476/51, dated 25 November 1951.

176 FO 371 104563, file 1015, Report to the Majlis, file no. 1015/79, dated 14 March 1953.

177 FO 371 98720, file 1782, file no. E17802, dated 3 May 1952. FO 371 104564, file 1015, file no. 1015/81, dated 20 March 1953.

178 FO 248 1531, file 10105, file no. 10105/76, dated 21 February 1952.

179 FO 248 1531, file 10105, Assessment by Middleton, file no. 10105/330, dated 30 September 1952.

180 FO 248 1531, file 10105, Note by Falle, file no. 10105/325, dated 28 August 1952.

181 FO 248 1531, file 10105, Pamphlet, file no. 10105/70, dated 18 February 1952. This very argument was used by opponents of the Islamic Revolution in 1979.

182 FO 371 35109, file 110, Military Attaché, E3588, dated 29 June 1943.

183 FO 248 1516, file 10105, Tudeh Party assessment, file no. 10105/?/51, dated 23 May 1951. FO 371 104561, file 1015, Azerbaijan Day Celebrations in Isfahan, file no. 1015/3, dated 31 December 1952.

184 FO 248 1516, file 10105, Excerpts from *Mardum*. In one Mosaddeq is compared to Attila, file no. 10105/29/51, dated 6 August 1951.

185 FO 371 104565, file 1015, file no. 1015/124, dated 30 April 1953.

186 FO 248 1531, file 10105, file no. 10105/296, dated 7 August 1952. See also Makki's interview in *Tarikh-e Iran-e Moaser* (Iranian Contemporary History) 1(1), 1997, pp. 178–216, where he notes growing dissatisfaction with Mosaddeq's methods after *Siyeh-e Tir*, p. 188, and argues explicitly that Mosaddeq was *not* seeking the establishment of a democratic government, p. 197.

187 FO 371 104561, file 1015, press reports, file no. 1015/18, dated 28 January 1953.

188 FO 371 104563, file 1015, report in *Etelaat*, file no. 1015/96, dated 13 March 1953.

189 FO 371 104566, file 1015, report in *Dad*, file no. 1015/33, dated 10 April 1953.

190 FO 371 104567, file 1015, file no. 1015/163, dated 21 May 1953. This reaction was in marked contrast to the previous year when it was recorded that many in the army were disillusioned with the Shah's inaction, see FO 248 1531, file 10105, file no. 10105/295, dated 2 August 1952.

191 FO 371 104566, file 1015, file no. 1015/143, dated 6 May 1953.

192 FO 371 104563, file 1015, file no. 1015/61, dated 2 March 1953.

193 FO 371 104564, file 1015, comments by Deputy Mir-Ashrafi, file no. 1015/95, dated 12 March 1953. See also FO 371 104562, file 1015, on Kashani's role in mobilising crowds in favour of the Shah, file no. 1015/51, dated 2 March 1953.

194 FO 371 104564, file 1015, file no. 1015/104, dated 6 April 1953. FO 371 104565, file 1015, file no. 1015/109, dated 10 April 1953. Makki, on the other hand argues that Mosaddeq did in fact wish to remove the Pahlavi dynasty and restore the Qajar dynasty; see Makki's interview in *Tarikh-e Iran-e Moaser*, p. 191.

195 FO 371 104564, file 1015, file no. 1015/82, dated 19 March 1953.

196 FO 248 1531, file 10105, file no. 10105/230, dated 12 June 1952.

197 For further details of the coup see K. Roosevelt, *Countercoup: The Struggle for the Control of Iran*. New York: McGraw-Hill, 1979; S. Dorril, *MI6: Fifty Years of Special Operations*. London: Fourth Estate, 2000, pp. 558–600. See also the Bibliography. For details of Anglo-American rivalry see J. Barr, *Lords of the Desert*. London: Simon & Schuster, 2018.

198 FO 371 104569, file 1015, file no. 1015/205, dated 16 August 1953.

199 *The Times*, 23 August 1953.

10 The consolidation of power, 1953–60

The *coup d'état* of 28 Mordad (19 August), which resulted in the overthrow of the Mosaddeq government, is often seen as one of the turning points in modern Iranian political history. It brought to an end a period of political pluralism and social dynamism, which, while occasionally chaotic, had undoubtedly left its mark on the political consciousness of the nation. It expanded and helped define the politicisation of society which had begun tentatively during the Constitutional Revolution. In this respect it complemented the development of the state which had occurred under Reza Shah. While in terms of international relations it did witness the replacement of Britain by America as the major power in Iran,[1] its immediate domestic impact remained unclear. It did not see the immediate return of the Pahlavi autocracy. British assessments of the Shah's attitude to his reversal of fortune pointedly referred to his failure to accurately read the political runes:

> After leaving Tehran last August with what must have been little hope of returning he [the Shah] suddenly found himself swept back on a wave of popular enthusiasm. Almost all experienced observers here, both Persian and foreign, are agreed that this enthusiasm was generated more by the Persians' deep rooted feelings for the institution of the monarchy than by any strong sentiments in favour of the person of the present Shah. Unfortunately His Majesty has, I understand, interpreted it largely as a demonstration of personal affection. This and the doubtful quality of much of the advice he receives from his court have not made it easy for him to make an accurate appraisal of the present state of the country.[2]

Yet, Mohammad Reza Shah, for all his enthusiasm about his perceived popularity, was acutely aware of his political weakness and, while he was anxious to institutionalise himself and his dynasty, he recognised that this would require time and considerable patience. On his return from Rome, the Shah was very much a first among equals, and even this position was under doubt. The Pahlavi state constructed by his father was intact, but the new society he had envisaged was very much in tatters. Traditional social structures, the pillars of the traditional state, were at the forefront of the political theatre. Even those sectors of society whose outlook could be described as 'modern', such as the landed aristocracy, represented the traditional elite, whose occasionally undisguised condescension continued to frustrate and irritate the Shah. That is not to say that the traditional pillars of Iranian state and society were incapable of 'revolutionising' themselves; as Mosaddeq (or indeed Kashani) had proved, many patricians were enthusiastic about reform, even if the motivation was principally that of preventing revolution. But they were not part of the Pahlavi project, and could claim social and political autonomy from the Pahlavi state. For their part, they saw the monarchy as the linchpin of the traditional social structure, whose function was to manage and oversee reform where necessary.

The monarch was a patrimonial ruler, traditional and stable. Charisma, and its associated vicissitudes, as witnessed under Mosaddeq, were not desired. The Shah, however, resented being part of this order, and struggled in the years following Mosaddeq's fall to break free from it. His authority might be traditional but his ambitions were revolutionary, and like his father he was determined to forge his own new order. Like his father he was haunted, and to a large extent driven, by the stigma of illegitimacy, made more acute in his case by the popular view that he had been restored to the throne by foreign powers. What this meant in practice was the Shah appeared politically ambiguous, courting the traditional pillars of society – landed aristocracy, *ulema, bazaar* – and seeking to consolidate his control over the armed forces, which remained less than complete. At the same time, and much to the bewilderment of these social groups, he sought to cultivate the young intellectuals and socialists who had been baying for his overthrow and execution in August 1953. For all its political utility, the Shah was also acutely aware that society was changing, and that the cultivation of such links was important. There is also little doubt that because of his own age he empathised more with the radical young than with the older patricians. Some were convinced by the Shah's overtures, most remained sceptical. They argued that for all his charismatic and revolutionary pretensions, the Shah remained a fundamental pillar of traditional society, whose main ambition was to centralise power in his person – to redefine the parameters of the patrimonial state, not to change it. To change the structure would make the monarchy redundant, and no one believed the Shah possessed such altruism.

A changing society

> In Reza Shah's Iran life was governed by tradition and custom. Poverty prevailed but ignorance and traditionalism formed a strong shield against discontent. Today, however, poverty remains but the shield has been pushed aside by changing conditions. The political ideas and new hopes which were disseminated up and down Iran by the outlawed Tudeh party will now be carried, either unwittingly or consciously, further afield by the new literates. Poverty and education, when allowed to meet, are an explosive mixture.[3]

The 1950s continued to be a period of social change. Social boundaries and political loyalties remained dynamic and fluid. Particular traditions and particular modernities regularly mixed, integrated and communicated with each other. A mullah might be well versed in radical theory, converse regularly with students and espouse liberal political views, while at the same time holding fast to a dogmatic social conservatism. Similarly, a Marxist student, eager to overthrow the established order, saw no contradiction in associating with the traditional merchants of the *bazaar*, from where indeed the student may have emerged. Radical students immersed in the traditions of southern Tehran might nevertheless consider themselves 'modern' and 'progressive', while mocking the radical chic of the wealthy north Tehranis, whose apparent enthusiasm for 'progress' was derided as little more than a crass materialism. The Tehranis, in turn, considered themselves the medium through which the benefits of modern society could be disseminated to the lower orders, not only via their servants, but also through regular contact with tenants on their estates. In short, it is important to remember that in the 1950s Iran retained a highly integrated and communicative social structure.

Iran enjoyed economic growth during this period but it remained erratic and uneven, with Tehran enjoying most of the development.[4] The professional educated classes grew as a proportion of the population, and it would be fair to say that the ranks of the politically conscious also increased, in part as a legacy of the Mosaddeq crisis, but also as a result of urbanisation[5] and the growth in communications. According to embassy official Carless, 'with better communications many peasants who formerly lived in blissful, isolated ignorance now know enviously about the comforts and dubious attractions of life in Tehran and other larger towns to which they are unfortunately attracted'. Furthermore, 'The political consciousness of the Iranian proletariat has developed quite rapidly during the past decade as the result of broadcasting, better communications (bus services are now quite highly developed), Tudeh propaganda and the stirring events of the Musaddiq era'.[6] Indeed so concerned was the government with the politicisation of society that it was decided as early as 1954 to establish a National Guidance Council, whose function was to control broadcasting and be 'an instrument of propaganda'.[7] Despite the government suppression of political activity, especially in the military government of Tehran, political activity continued, with many organisations active in the National Front re-emerging in the late 1950s. The British embassy counted some eight active parties, apart from the government-sponsored organisations which, despite restrictions, remained politically influential.[8] The government and foreign observers had to accept that a growing politically aware public had emerged and had to be managed.[9]

Criticisms of the Shah and his behaviour came from the politically active intelligentsia, those who provided the core support for the National Front, as well as members of the political elite (who were coming under increasing verbal attack from the Shah and were threatened with land reform), and the urban lower classes. It was also the case that most of this criticism was focused in Tehran while the citizens of other cities at times remained indifferent to the political irregularities of the government. Indeed many viewed an autocratic Shah as the natural and best form of government.[10]

In the countryside, many peasants retained an almost mystical reverence for the Shah, and it is not surprising that he saw them in many ways as his natural constituency. But these people, who often migrated to the cities, also retained a loyalty to Islam, a loyalty which the Shah along with most political activists failed to gauge accurately.

The return of the Shah

For all his euphoria at his return, and apparent belief in the affection of his people, Mohammad Reza Shah was justifiably suspicious of the ambitions and aims of the elites. As noted above, the political establishment that had played such a fundamental role in orchestrating his return expected a grateful Shah to fulfil his traditional function and essentially protect their interests. More specifically, and of more concern to the Shah, were the ambitions of his new Prime Minister General Zahedi, who revelled in his new role as saviour of the country, a role the Shah had previously mishandled and unwittingly delegated to Mosaddeq. Zahedi, who had during the war been arrested by the Allies because of his alleged Nazi sympathies, now found himself fêted by them, and vanity permitted him to believe that with Western support he would be the new strong man of Iran. He recognised the widespread belief that the Shah was personally incapable of being little more than a ceremonial monarch, and appreciated that both the traditional establishment and the West yearned for some 'strong', autocratic leadership. Indeed many among the traditional elites regarded the 12 years preceding Mosaddeq's fall as nothing less than a political disaster, and proof, if proof was needed, that democracy was not suited to Iran's political culture. With the Cold War gathering pace, the notion of firm leadership stabilising Iran and retaining her for the free world, was also popular in Washington, where popular participation in political processes was often interpreted as a euphemism for communist infiltration. In general, therefore, everyone agreed that democratisation, at this stage at least, was a 'bad thing'. Disagreements at this level only emerged when the debate turned to who should do the leading, and clearly the Shah and Zahedi were not of one voice. The Shah had no intention of playing Ahmad Shah Qajar to Zahedi's Reza Khan, and yet his position in 1954 was acute. Few people, including the Americans, had been impressed by his performance to date. They found his persistent hesitancy and indecision frustrating. Contempt had even extended to his immediate family. One diplomat in discussions with the new Minister of Court, Ala, discovered to his astonishment that:

> Abdul Reza was openly intriguing with Amini, the former Minister of Court, and others against his elder brother, the idea apparently being to depose the Shah one day, pass over Ali Reza and have the son of Abdul Reza declared Shah under a regency . . . The people behind this little plot apparently think that they can count on the support of Kashani and Makki and the advantage of bringing Abdul Reza's infant son to the throne was that he had in his veins the royal blood of the three families of Zand, Qajar and Pahlavi and, therefore, could be regarded as embodying all 'legitimist' claims.[11]

With the Shah's position weak, power devolved on a number of centrifugal forces, each of which sought to determine and define the future direction of the country. Traditionalists, including members of the aristocracy and the *ulema*, sought a return to the status quo. Zahedi sought centralisation in his own hands, while the remnants of the now officially banned National Front sought pluralism and democratic freedoms, as well as non-alignment. The Americans proved less interested in the domestic composition and structure of the government as long as communism and the Soviet Union could be contained. In this they frequently came into conflict with the other major political player of the period, Abol-Hassan Ebtehaj, who, as head of the Seven Year Plan Organisation, endeavoured to place Iran on a firm economic footing and minimise extraneous expenses. To give some idea of the fluidity of political relations in this period, it is worth noting that on the whole Ebtehaj enjoyed the support of the Shah against Zahedi, while the Shah supported Zahedi against the communists, and leaned towards the Americans in his enthusiasm for military expenditure, which Ebtehaj abhorred. The Americans for their part initially leaned towards Zahedi, were ambivalent but increasingly supportive of the Shah and, despite their major disagreements with Ebtehaj, tended to acknowledge that the latter was the only competent and honest administrator in the Iranian government.

The politics of consolidation

Following the re-establishment of diplomatic relations with Britain,[12] the first crisis that the new government had to solve was that of the oil dispute. An aristocratic technocrat by the name of Ali Amini was dispatched to negotiate a settlement with the Western oil companies, resulting in an overturning of the nationalisation law and an acceptance of the 50:50 profit-sharing agreement with a new oil consortium, which included the former AIOC, now British Petroleum, holding a 40 per cent share. The other 60 per cent share of the consortium was held by a number of American and European oil companies, and the agreement, which was reached after months of negotiation, essentially signalled the end of British commercial dominance in Iran and her replacement by the United States. American dominance was reflected in the growth of financial aid provided to the Iranian government, renewed pressures on the communist Tudeh Party, and the growing emphasis given to the military, much to satisfaction of the Shah. The US Point Four Program was implemented and for the first time American personnel began to arrive in substantial numbers throughout Iran. There was considerable debate as to the actual benefit of the aid and the American embassy eventually concluded in a report that the Iranians were unfortunately settling into the mindset that the US would bail out Iran financially, however badly they managed the economy.[13] American support was also reflected in Iran's international realignment and, much against the wishes of the Iranian intelligentsia, the Shah took Iran into the Baghdad Pact in 1955. Divisions of opinion were also clear in Iran's reaction to the Suez Crisis, with the government generally conceding the Western position, while intellectuals were openly critical.

Yet despite the ruthless suppression of Tudeh activities, the Shah proved himself far more lenient with the nationalists, anxious in part to fill the apparent vacuum left by Mosaddeq. To be sure, a strong stench of revenge was in the air, and any member of the National Front for whom a communist or Soviet link could be discovered or plausibly manufactured was pursued with vigour and imprisoned, and in the case of the former Foreign Minister Fatemi, eventually executed.[14] But on the whole, much to Zahedi's irritation and the puzzlement of many of his staunchest supporters,[15] the Shah opted for leniency even towards Mosaddeq himself, allowing him to effectively re-establish himself within the political consciousness. Nationalism, and Mosaddeq's personification of it, noted British diplomats, remained curiously resilient. One could have expected Dr Mosaddeq's popularity to have been low in the aftermath of the coup as peoples' memories of the chaotic conditions preceding his downfall were still fresh, but it is apparent that the government's decision to put him on trial revived much of his earlier popularity. Indeed as early as 12 November 1953, it was reported that widespread demonstrations had occurred in Tehran in favour of Mosaddeq and that the bazaar had closed as a mark of protest against his trial.[16] In fact, the public show trial was the perfect stage for Mosaddeq to make his theatrical comeback.[17]

The 'Mosaddeq myth'

As one British official noted,

> When he fell Dr Musaddiq was largely discredited . . . He might have remained so if he had not been brought to trial in the full glare of publicity. Although his performance in court was not very effective, the trial seems to have revived amongst the Persian people a great deal of the popularity which he had previously enjoyed . . . the majority of the people probably still favour Dr Musaddiq in spite of his policies or lack of them.[18]

Later that year it was noted:

> The articulate part of the Persian public has I believe realised that an oil settlement is desirable . . . Nevertheless, in their hearts they accept these hard facts reluctantly. The blow to their foolish hopes has left their nationalism still extremely sensitive. They were not as they see it on the wrong course, they were misled by Musaddiq slightly off the right one . . . Nationalistic principles remain sacred – better an oil-less economy than that these should be sacrificed.[19]

It is debatable how effective this policy of co-option was, though there is evidence that members of the National Front felt that his leniency was a reflection of his weakness. The release of Baqai and Ayatollah Kashani in 1956 caused consternation among his supporters, as Russell noted:

[T]heir release has tended to restore some heart to the nationalist rank and file (although 'rank and file' is perhaps an expression inappropriately applied to a movement which is primarily intellectual and bourgeois), encouraging them to believe that neither the government nor the Shah have any real teeth when it comes to a showdown. The 'Traditionalist' politicians are correspondingly depressed by this further example of the Shah's vacillation, and the military governor in particular is said to feel that much face has been lost.[20]

At the same time, and partly in recognition of the 'Mosaddeq myth', the Shah began the process, which would accelerate later, of seeking to appropriate the nationalist agenda. The first anniversary of Mosaddeq's fall, 19 August, was designated a national holiday, and as one British official noted, 'Celebrations on this scale have not been seen here for some years'.[21] At the same time, the Shah made known his displeasure after 12 university professors had commented that the coup of 28 Mordad (19 August) was 'regrettable'; they were duly dismissed.[22] However, with a 'magnanimity' which was to become a hallmark of the Shah's characterisation of himself, he allowed himself to be persuaded to have them reinstated. Not only that, he issued a *farman* that the children of those convicted of treason under Mosaddeq be given a proper education, and duly offered 500,000 rials for the purpose.[23] Indeed one British diplomat noted:

> There is reason to suspect that the Shah has been 'reinsuring' with the nationalists, but the most recent reports suggest that he may be having second thoughts. Although in a speech not long ago he declared that supporters of Musaddiq were today even more dangerous than the Tudeh Party, engineer Hasibi has been released and there is a possibility that Dr Baqai may be allowed freedom of movement, and even that new elections may be held in Kerman with Baqai allowed to participate.[24]

Later it was noted that 'the Shah's equivocal attitude towards some nationalist elements could develop into positive encouragement if he thought that support elsewhere for him was seriously weakened'.[25] At the same time, the Shah sought to denigrate Mosaddeq's personal role by emphasising, not entirely unreasonably, that current economic problems had their roots in the dislocation caused by nationalisation and Mosaddeq's mismanagement of the economy. In a press conference in 1956, Finance Minister Foruhar detailed the ills existing in the Iranian economy, especially the consistent failure to balance the country's budget. Avoiding the issue of military expenditure, which had drawn considerable criticism, he instead emphasised the increase in the money supply administered by Dr Mosaddeq arguing that 'it will be admitted that the country's budget deficit is nothing new. For several years now the country has been plagued by it'.[26] In a subsequent press conference, aware of US pressure not to bail out the Iranian economy and the need to enforce austerity measures, Foruhar reassured reporters that 'It should be remembered that before 1334 [1955] too the country faced a budget deficit. In the days of Dr Mosaddeq this was met by expending the country's reserves, borrowing from the International Monetary Fund and issuing banknotes'.[27]

Ebtehaj and economic development

Control over the future direction of the economy proved to be the central political battleground and Zahedi was to be the first casualty. Despite disagreements with Ebtehaj over expenditure, the Shah chose to place his confidence in the head of the Seven Year Plan Organisation, thereby effectively allowing Ebtehaj, a robust technocrat at the best of times, to continue running a government within a government. Zahedi, unsurprisingly and as the Shah must have anticipated, found this situation untenable and tendered his resignation in April 1955, hugely disillusioned with what he considered to be the ingratitude of the Shah. He was replaced as prime minister by the Minister of Court, the ageing Ala. With one potential rival out of the way, the Shah could turn his attention to controlling Ebtehaj himself, who was increasingly at odds with the Shah over the level of military expenditure being encouraged by the US and enthusiastically approved by the Shah. Convinced that Iran needed economic development above all else, Ebtehaj jealously guarded the revenues under his management and launched a number of long-term infrastructural projects. He was nevertheless hampered in his ambitions by his perceived arrogance, which alienated many colleagues, and the failure of the government to adhere to budget limits by embarking on, among other things, fanciful and grandiose schemes.[28] This resulted in the erosion of the oil revenues at his disposal as they were diverted to cover the continuing government deficit. He was a bitter opponent of the Shah's plans, supported by the Americans, to expand the military. According to Khodadad Farmanfarmayan, who worked under him, Ebtehaj was bitterly opposed to greater military expenditure:

> Once Admiral Radford had finished talking about his purpose to look into military need and military requirements, Ebtehaj made a fist and raised it and banged on the table so hard . . . and said, 'Admiral Radford, Iran needs development, not military expenditure'.[29]

Moreover, for all the Shah's magnanimity towards former members of the National Front, differences of opinion arose when Ebtehaj began employing former Iran Party members in the Seven Year Plan Organisation, on the justification that they were the only honest and efficient people available. The Shah is rumoured to have complained to Ebtehaj about 'those people who broke my statues'.[30]

Ultimately, the Shah was to win his battle with Ebtehaj, who resigned from the Planning and Budget Organisation in 1959, disgusted at the way in which the country's revenues had been diverted to what he considered non-essential expenditures. Ebtehaj was a driven individual, utterly convinced of the righteousness of his cause, and determined to push through the structural reforms he recognised were essential if Iran was to succeed in transforming its economy. In pursuing his goal, Ebtehaj proved abrasive and frequently contemptuous of what he believed to be the superficiality, pettiness and corruption of his compatriots. Not surprisingly, such views won him few allies within the political establishment. Ebtehaj, like a latter-day Richelieu, became increasingly dependent on the goodwill and support of the Shah. When the Shah found himself the target of Ebtehaj's wrath, his support soon vanished, though one suspects that by the end of the decade the Shah was less enthusiastic about allowing a parallel government under Ebtehaj to exist, especially since he had effectively succeeded in centralising power under himself. Ebtehaj was never to hold high office again, but found himself the target of a significant amount of foreign press inquiry, by virtue of the fact that he was known as the one man in Iran willing to speak his mind on controversial issues. This international interest, particularly in the United States and Britain, would have been sufficient to incur the Shah's jealousy, but Ebtehaj's outspokenness, and his frank criticism of the Shah, would eventually lead to his arrest. In a series of conference lectures, Ebtehaj criticised in no uncertain terms the haphazard and informal economic 'disorder' which continued to plague Iranian development, a theme which was appreciated by his foreign hosts if not his compatriots. At a conference in San Francisco in 1961, Ebtehaj scrutinised the problems of foreign aid, and argued that bilateral arrangements simply did not work:

> Under the present bilateral approach creditor governments are diverted from development projects by military and political considerations . . . Even if a recipient government became convinced in all good faith of the fairness of certain bilateral programs offered by another country, it would soon be condemned in the public mind. Opposition leaders will charge the government with selling out to the imperialists, and the public will believe those charges . . . Bilateral aid poisons the relationship between nations, frustrates the donor, and causes revulsion in the recipient. Donor nations are obliged to channel aid through the receiving country's officials whether they be qualified, honest, efficient or otherwise. Where the recipient government is corrupt, the donor government appears, in the judgement of the public, to support corruption . . . The bilateral approach cannot bring about reform. Furthermore, government-to-government aid delays internal pressure toward reform by providing considerable material resources to corrupt regimes and by unwittingly fostering the fear that development aid will be stopped if the old regime is overthrown. Under bilateral programs the lending government cannot impose a creditor's normal discipline for fear of jeopardizing the entire fabric of international relations. I can think of no better summary of all the disadvantages and weaknesses of the bilateral system than the modern history of my own country. Not so very many years ago in Iran, the United States was loved and respected as no other country, and without having given a penny of aid. Now, after more than \$1 billion of loans and grants, America is neither loved nor respected; she is distrusted by most people and hated by many.[31]

As accurate and prescient as his analysis was, rumours abounded of his impending arrest should he return to Iran, and in November 1961, one month after the conference, he was thrown into prison, although no charges were ever brought against him. Released after seven months, following an international campaign of support, Ebtehaj continued to work in Iran as a private citizen. Hugely respected, his reputation only grew as the Shah's diminished. Ebtehaj was in Europe when the Islamic Revolution broke out in Iran. He never returned to Iran, settling in London in 1984, where he died in 1999. Far more than Mosaddeq before him or Amini after him, Ebtehaj was the one great reformer who, had the Shah truly trusted and supported him, could have transformed the economic and ultimately political foundations of the country. A brusque technocrat, he was never comfortable with the extensive system of etiquette which dictated Iranian social and political relations, and which at the highest levels translated into empty sycophancy. But he understood the structural failings of the Iranian economy, dominated as it was by mercantile and landed interests networking through informal arrangements that were neither easily accountable nor transparent, and therefore open to abuse. In seeking to challenge and overturn this network of vested interests, over which the Shah presided, Ebtehaj needed the protection of a royal patron of at least the same moral fibre and determination as Reza Shah. This the son was unwilling to deliver, in part because he was as yet unready to challenge those vested interests, but also because, for all his revolutionary and progressive pretensions, the Shah was not prepared to (wittingly) undermine his own interests.

Cultivating the military: Iran and the Cold War

For the Shah, the security of his dynasty depended on the loyalty of the army, the one aspect of the modern state with which the Pahlavi dynasty was intimately connected.[32] In cultivating the army, the Shah found a willing ally in the United States and ultimately an enemy in Ebtehaj. Yet it is worth remembering that neither the army nor the United States harboured similar affection for the Shah. Not only did the army retain a significant number of Tudeh Party sympathisers and radicals who looked with interest at events in Egypt, but the United States remained singularly unconvinced that the Shah was the best person to lead the country. It occasionally gave the impression that it might look favourably on a strong man emerging from the armed forces. It was fear as much as affection which encouraged the Shah to cultivate these links. The strategy which the Shah adopted was not only, with the initial help of Zahedi, to root out communist sympathisers,[33] but to increase its budget and social prestige. The budget could only be realistically increased with the assistance of US military aid, which ultimately amounted to some $500 million in the decade after 1953. This aid could only be secured if the United States could be convinced of Iran's importance in the Cold War struggle. It was therefore important for the Shah to integrate Iran into this narrative and to define Iran as a front-line state whose strategic importance was paramount to Western security. A Western alliance was, in his eyes, 'positive nationalism' as opposed to the 'negative nationalism' espoused by the National Front. It was this desire to impress which encouraged the Shah to take Iran into the Baghdad Pact against the wishes of many of his advisers and, perhaps surprisingly, the British, who cautioned the Shah against joining a military pact before the Iranian economy had been placed on a firmer footing – an argument that mirrored that of Ebtehaj.[34] This did not prevent the Shah from occasionally raising the popular national issue of the sovereignty of Bahrain, much to the irritation of the British (a claim that was perhaps calculated as much to irritate the British as to rally the nationalists).[35]

The Shah never missed an opportunity to press his case. In a meeting with the new British Ambassador, Sir Roger Stevens, in February 1954, the Shah proved quick off the mark.

> When I presented my credentials . . . the Shah spoke to me cordially and at length about his desire to see Persia militarily strong. Persia, he said, was essential to the defence of the Middle East and any military understanding between Turkey and Pakistan must, in the long run, take her into account.[36]

During his subsequent trip to the United States, the Shah was even more emphatic:

> I am convinced that one of the essentials for preventing international communism from realising its ambitions with regard to Iran is for us, with the help of great free nations, particularly the US, to strengthen our armed forces to the extent that would render them capable of putting up an honourable defence if Iran is attacked.[37]

The Shah's protestations eventually allowed him, with US support, to increase the size of the army from 120,000 to nearly 200,000 in the decade to 1963,[38] though even the Americans grew perturbed at his constant demands for more arms and more money. Nevertheless, the US caution was far too enthusiastic for the British, who looked askance at the sequence of US military missions and the apparent determination of the Americans to play along with the Shah. By the end of the decade, the British military attaché noted that the Iranian military would be larger than that of Britain by 1962.[39]

Criticism of this military expansion was also increasingly heard at home. Tehran, which had been under military government and ruled with an iron fist by General Bakhtiar since Mosaddeq's fall, provided Iranians with a taste of what the further 'militarisation' of society might entail. When military government was finally ended in 1957, it was swiftly followed by the announcement of the creation of the state security service, known by its Persian acronym, SAVAK, under the stewardship of the very same General Bakhtiar.[40] Iranians viewed this development with suspicion and some openly complained that it indicated the extension of the military government to the rest of the country,[41] arguing that the military was little more than a tool of oppressive dictatorship and not an extension of national integrity.[42] The Shah was not immune to such criticism, and felt compelled on a number of occasions to answer his critics, even to the extent of detailing Iran's relatively low expenditure compared to comparable countries. In a speech to the Majlis in 1957, the Shah said, 'To strengthen our defensive and military power is not only in the interest of Iran, but also that of the Middle East and the free world'.[43] Furthermore,

In comparison with other countries our military expenditure is not great. It would be a good idea if we considered the military expenditure of countries like Switzerland and Sweden and found out what percentage of their revenues is spent on their armed forces. In 1948 when I was in Switzerland that country was spending 50 per cent of its budget on its armed forces . . . At the moment this country is trying to arm its forces with the latest weapons. We must note this fact: that if we had not joined the Baghdad Pact and, like any other independent country, had to secure equipment for our defence, our military expenditure would have been five, six, or even seven times more than it is now . . . By this calculation the money spent on our armed forces is about 17 per cent of the country's budget, and comparing this sum with the 50 per cent of Switzerland, the 75 per cent of Pakistan, or the nearly 50 per cent of India it is very little.[44]

For all his considerable efforts in this regard, the Shah was unable to feel secure with respect to his armed forces or indeed his Western allies. The British found his insistence on Iran's strategic importance repetitive and somewhat tedious. Harrison could hardly disguise his boredom in a report submitted in 1960:

The Shah then started talking about the future prospects of various Asian countries . . . and drew the conclusion that in contrast to Iran, the exploitation of natural resources and the increase in national production could not possibly keep up with the prospective increase in population in those countries. This of course led easily to the conclusion that the West should do more to support strategically placed, pro-Western Iran, etc., etc. To change the subject, I said I thought the Azerbaijan day military parade had gone off very well. The Shah agreed that the human material was quite good, but how pitifully inadequate and out of date the equipment was compared with that of countries like Afghanistan and even Iraq. Iran's friends and allies must give more material aid, etc., etc. In a further attempt to get away from this rather monotonous refrain, I asked the Shah whether he had met Dean Rusk. He said he thought not. But he was rather wondering about the triumvirate, Dean Rusk, Chester Bowles and Adlai Stevenson. Rusk was a Far Eastern expert, Bowles was interested in India and Stevenson in Africa. Was there not the risk of US foreign policy becoming rather distorted? Iran's allies must not forget their true friends, etc., etc.[45]

More damningly, the Americans themselves were having their doubts, disturbed by reports that their military largesse was not being appreciated by the Iranian public. 'According to their [US] own information, the general Iranian view is that the Americans are being "had for suckers", and that their aid has been poured out wastefully in support of a useless regime with little benefit to the country'.[46] Nevertheless, Iranian officials, including the Shah, recognised the advantages to be gained from playing along with this narrative, since 'the Americans will bail them out yet again to stop them falling prey to communism'.[47] US impatience with the Iranians' inability to get their house in order would ultimately lead to tighter controls under the Kennedy administration, with controversial results for Iranian economic and political development. But in the late 1950s it led to one of the more curious episodes in Iranian–US relations. In 1958, SAVAK uncovered an apparent coup plot within the army, with the alleged support of the United States, led by the respected and popular General Qarani. The Shah was convinced of US complicity in the affair and protested bitterly, despite repeated US denials.[48] Many other Iranians were also convinced that the US, having come to its senses, had grown weary of the Shah and, at the very least, hoped, with obvious British collusion (the British, after all, could not be innocent), to install a strong prime minister who could counterbalance the occasionally wayward monarch. In the absence of clear evidence one way or another, it is difficult to verify these allegations, although the coincidences are intriguing. It certainly appears as if some conspiracy was being hatched, although the level of direct US involvement, either in initiation or encouragement, is unclear.[49] What is known is that Qarani was in contact with the US embassy. Following his arrest and conviction, his sentence was relatively light, which convinced many of his US support, although he protested that he was in fact a mole. Of more interest, however, was the rumoured involvement of Ali Amini, then Iranian ambassador to Washington, and Hasan Arsanjani, then leader of the small *Azadi* (Freedom) political group, which was summarily disbanded.[50] Amini was subsequently to be forced upon the Shah as Prime Minister by the Kennedy administration in 1961, with the radical Arsanjani as his Minister of Agriculture charged with implementing land reform. (Amini was to be the last independent prime minister until 1979.) Arguably, the coup was hatched three years too early.

The Shah ascendant

By all external accounts, the Shah's position was in the ascendant by the late 1950s. He had successfully managed his relationship with the traditional classes, had terminated the military government in Tehran and established SAVAK. He had had a pliant prime minister in office since 1957, in the person of Manouchehr Eqbal, who constantly referred to himself as the Shah's 'household servant' (*chaker*).[51] The depoliticisation of society seemed so effective that the Qarani affair was soon superseded in the public consciousness by the Shah's imminent divorce from Soraya and his marriage to Farah Diba. So confident was the Shah of his new political settlement that he had allowed the establishment of two ostensibly rival political parties, modelled on the British system, in the shape of the National (*Melliun* – Conservative) Party, headed by Eqbal himself, and the People's (*Mardom* – Labour) Party, led by Asadollah Alam. Few were taken in by this democratic farce. Iranians joked that the parties would be better named the 'Yes' and 'Yes Sir' parties. That Alam was a close friend of the Shah's did not help, neither did Eqbal's very public exhibitions of obsequiousness.[52] Arguably Eqbal simply understood the personality of the Shah but, whatever his motives, many considered that he belittled the office of the prime minister. This aside, Eqbal's pronouncements on political participation left few people in any doubt of his patrician leanings. Commenting on his decision to restrict political activity by students, Eqbal curiously argued that, 'In my opinion the destruction wrought by these treacherous and illogical parties was worse than the Mongol invasion'.[53] The Shah nevertheless recognised that he had to maintain at least the façade of parliamentary government. He constantly stressed his constitutional credentials and repeatedly emphasised that freedom and democracy existed in Iran. In private he was far more forthcoming, even admitting to Sir Roger Stevens that his imposition of a two-party system was a farce.[54] That the Shah was able, until the end of the decade, to maintain this 'farce' and consolidate his own position was in part due to his own careful cultivation of his image as a progressive, modern and 'democratic' sovereign – open to new ideas and at the same time appealing to the traditional constituency (mainly outside Tehran), who saw nothing unusual in an autocratic Shah. Indeed this is what a 'Shah' was meant to be.[55]

Many of the ideas which were to become identified with the Shah during the 1960s and 1970s, the heyday of the 'White Revolution', were formulated and developed during the 1950s. Even before Mosaddeq's premiership, the Shah had toyed with ideas of land reform and had sought to position himself as a champion of the young and 'progressive' elements in society. He discovered to his cost that he was unable to convince this key constituency. Undeterred, although considerably more cautious, the Shah determined to pursue this course following Mosaddeq's overthrow. Arguably, it was an appreciation of Mosaddeq's ability to captivate the masses and a desire to emulate (and indeed surpass) this achievement that persuaded the Shah to try again. Now the Shah determined to show himself in tune with modern ideas, able to communicate with the left while at the same time emulating the kings of the past, in particular Cyrus the Great, and taking Iran towards what was initially described as a 'model country'. As noted above, the Shah, much to the irritation of his traditional constituents, treated his National Front opponents with some leniency. Less well known was his decision to converse and take advice from left-wing thinkers and sympathisers of the Tudeh Party, which had been officially banned and was subject to extensive repression. Lambton was surprised to discover in discussion with two Iranians in 1955 that some of the Shah's new advisers had Tudeh affiliations.[56] Such associations were to have a clear impact on the tone and tenor of his language, and he was not averse to attacking 'wealthy tax dodgers' and 'feudal' landlords – criticisms which sat uneasily with his own position as one of the wealthiest and most extensive landlords in the country.[57] His attempts to redistribute Crown Lands were regarded as disingenuous and more of a public relations exercise than a sincere attempt to reform tenure arrangements. After all, his critics argued, it was inconceivable that the Shah would undermine the financial pillars of his own power. Nevertheless the Shah persevered, outlining his vision in a booklet entitled 'The Pahlavi Estates Offices'.[58] The main themes of the Shah's thinking are articulated in this publication which notes that the main opposition to land reform came from two classes – those who told villagers that agricultural reform 'can only be carried out in the promised paradise' (in other words the *ulema*), 'and some large landlords' (also termed 'capitalists'). These were 'the red and the black' of later notoriety. There was also a third group, classified as the 'ignorant', who would be persuaded when it became apparent that property rights would be strengthened but more importantly that, with the ownership of land, Iran's tenant farmers would become proud yeomen, with a stake in their country and eager to defend their nation. To further convince the sceptical, it was argued that, 'An historical example is the action of Iran's ancient kings who, in order to safeguard the frontiers, granted arable land to wandering tribes who, becoming owners with pride in their property, defended the country'. While the Americans seemed to have been convinced of this vision, and may indeed have been the source, drawing as they would have done on their own historical experience, the British were less enthusiastic:

> The practical aim of land reform in Iran, quite apart from any considerations of social justice, must be to turn an indigent peasantry into an independent and self-reliant yeomanry, and if possible to increase production. The Government's American advisers (the United States Operations Mission) appear to be working on the assumption that anyone who owns his own land becomes ipso facto hard working, thrifty and enterprising in the Middle Western tradition; and they have succeeded in communicating something of their conviction to the Shah. Unhappily in Iran there is, or has been until recently at any rate, some substance in the more cynical landlord's contention that, if peasants had more money, they simply smoked more opium.[59]

The Shah decided to lead by example by establishing a 'model village' aptly named '*Shah-Abad*', and establishing 'model factories', increasingly emphasising that it was insufficient for Iran to be progressive, it had to be an example to the world:

> I am not content with seeing Iran a progressive country. I want my country to be a model country . . . I want Iran to become a model country, a model of justice and the administration of justice and a model of progress . . . We have the possibilities for making Iran a model country.[60]

As impressive as this rhetoric may have been, it increasingly drew criticism for its lack of pertinence to the reality of Iranian economic development. Indeed the more grandiose the Shah's language, the more he became hostage to fortune. As critics pointed out the growing disparity between vision and reality, the Shah's response seems on the one hand to dismiss his critics as carping pessimists, while reassuring himself with even greater utopian aspirations. It was the Shah's conviction that Iran was on the verge of a radical social and political transformation, which would allow it to 'catch up' with the West, that encouraged him to establish political parties on the Westminster model. The suspension of disbelief that this development required was matched by some of the Shah's remarkable observations on the economic transformation of the country: 'I am sure, however, that since the Iranian nation is progressing in every respect and our society is changing rapidly from medieval conditions to a progressive and modern society, this transformation' would take place shortly.[61] Earlier that year he suggested the construction of department stores, dismissing as unrealistic the complaint that it could lead to the unemployment of 20,000 shopkeepers.[62] Still later the Shah noted enthusiastically that, 'I have heard tell that the plain of Gurgan has been completely modernised. In a short time this region will resemble a centre of European or American activity'.[63]

Despite the absurdity of such comments, by the end of the decade the Shah spoke of his own role in shaping Iran's destiny at even greater length, expressing a belief that it was his own manifest destiny to 'save' Iran. This view had been shaped by his survival at the hands of an assassin in 1949, as well as his belief in the hand of 'Providence' in 1953.[64] Indeed in an interview for the *New York Post* in 1958, the Shah reinterpreted the events of 1953 in the following terms: 'Previously I was ready to die for my people, but the uprising demonstrated that my people were also ready to die for me'.[65] This wasn't simply his 'election', as the Shah frequently liked to say, but the crystallisation of a unique relationship. The Shah was the champion of the 'barefoot millions' against the avarice and greed of the 'Thousand Families'.[66] This message of the Shah as a tireless campaigner for the welfare of his people was being systematically disseminated throughout the country.

> At the end of December the Government initiated a propaganda campaign intended to demonstrate the extent of progress achieved during the last six years since the Shah's restoration. The Minister of State in charge of propaganda, Mr Nasratullah Mo'inian, claimed to be publishing 275,000 posters, 180,000 pamphlets and 750 illustrated articles, and to broadcast 120 radio talks and 800 commentaries.[67]

Harrison noted:

> The Iranian press and wireless afford an impression of a popular, active, earnest young monarch, now exhorting his Parliament to pass progressive legislation, now adjuring municipal authorities to care for the common people, now opening bridges and inaugurating new hospitals, now distributing title deeds to grateful peasants, now castigating corruption and reaction, now entertaining a procession of foreign rulers, now received by foreign princes with the honour due to the heir of Cyrus the Great; supported by a devoted prime minister and loyal government in indefatigable pursuit of the welfare of the people, upholding the national interest against the malevolence of threatening neighbours, and building a prosperous future upon a foundation of social justice, a developing industry and agrarian reform. An established and duly elected Parliament, a Lower Chamber comprising two respectable political parties and a handful of independent members, and a senate of venerable elder statesmen, senior soldiers and scholars, confirms this agreeable impression.[68]

This 'myth of the saviour', which the Shah clearly came to believe, was increasingly regarded as ridiculous by many of the people the Shah had sought to impress, such as the left-leaning intelligentsia. While Divine Providence might play well with traditional constituents, and there is evidence that the mystique of the monarchy remained stable in rural areas,[69] the left-wing intelligentsia found it absurd. At the same time the nationalists regarded the Shah's increasing association with Cyrus the Great pretentious at best, and enormously conceited at worst. In a letter to the US Ambassador, which Secretary of State Dulles later denied as fraudulent, Dulles' exasperation with the Shah's self-perception is apparent, 'You know, of course, that we have never cherished any illusions about the Iranian sovereign's qualifications as a statesman. The man tries to pose as the Cyrus of modern times. He has no grounds whatsoever for doing so'.[70] So enthusiastic did the Shah become with this association that he made clear his intention to celebrate the 2,500th anniversary of the Imperial Monarchy in 1959, a celebration which he expected to be international in scope. Unsurprisingly, the reception was less enthusiastic than he had hoped: 'The Iranians seemed to be in danger of over-estimating the general interest in foreign countries in a rather esoteric anniversary',[71] and plans were shelved.

A fragile royal dominance

In fact the last two years of the decade were to see much of the Shah's plans unravel, as first the Iraqi revolution in 1958 and then the coup against Menderes in Turkey in 1960 helped focus minds on the stability or otherwise of the regime in Iran. So concerned was the Shah with the loyalty of the army that, following the Iraqi revolution, he sought to reinsure himself with 'an unprecedented list of promotions' indicating 'that loyalty must in part be purchased'.[72] As with a decade earlier, the Shah discovered that his position was more vulnerable than he would have liked. One persistent source of criticism were the senior *ulema*, epitomised at this time by the Shah's tense relationship with Ayatollah Borujerdi, the generally acknowledged pre-eminent *alim* in Iran. The Shah was initially cautious in his relations with the *ulema*, seeking to redefine it away from the antagonism which had characterised his father's reign. He emphasised his wish to spread the faith of Islam,[73] and very publicly went on a pilgrimage to Mashhad.[74] In 1955 he notoriously turned a blind eye to the persecution of the Baha'is in an effort to heal his persistently tense relations with Ayatollah Borujerdi, who had declined to meet the Shah because of his 'wayward lifestyle' unbecoming of a Shi'a monarch.[75] Baha'is were officially banned from associating in groups, and the Baha'i temple in Tehran was publicly demolished. The Shah expressed public regret over the incident.[76] Privately, he agreed that the mullahs had to be removed from politics, but argued that the time was not yet ripe, and that it could take several years before he could move against them.[77] By 1957, one traveller to Mashhad (Russell) was moved to note,

> Reza Shah must have been spinning in his grave at Rey. To see the arrogance and effrontery of the mullahs once again rampant in the holy city! How the old tyrant must despise the weakness of his son, who has allowed these turbulent priests to regain so much of their reactionary influence.[78]

As late as 1959, the Shah was cultivating relations with Ayatollah Borujerdi in a bid to elicit his support against the Soviet Union.[79] Ayatollah Borujerdi responded to these overtures by issuing a *fatwa* declaring the proposed land reform to be against Islam,[80] much to the irritation of the Shah, who finally decided to throw caution to the wind:

> It may be worth reporting that Dr Eqbal has written to Ayatollah Borujerdi saying that if he did not come into line on the Bill, the Shah would carry out a 'white coup d'état', close up the two houses of parliament, and shear the clergy of their remaining privileges. Whether or not the Shah really has it in mind to carry out this apparent threat, the remarkable thing is that Eqbal has apparently gone on record in writing to this effect.[81]

Licentious behaviour aside, the Shah was also coming under increasing fire for the corruption of the court and the royal family. The Shah regularly protested that he was working selflessly for the welfare of his people: 'During these long years I have had to be at my work not only mornings, afternoons and evenings, but also at midnight or even two or three in the morning. I have had to defend the rights of the people during all these hours', suggesting for good measure that he considered the growing criticism to be a mark of ingratitude:

> I do not think it inappropriate to mention that when in other countries a man renders the public a service . . . people enthusiastically exalt him, they construct statues and memorials and mourn his death. In this connection I do not speak of myself because there is no need to.[82]

There is also some truth in the fact that Iranians instinctively distrusted their governments and were liberal in their criticisms and often too late in their praise.[83] However, in assuming the reins of power, the Shah was bound to attract criticism, and it would be fair to say that the politically conscious and active, who were concentrated in Tehran, were increasingly disenchanted with the Shah.[84] Many found it difficult to reconcile the traditional institution of the monarchy with the democratic sovereign the Shah wished to portray. In an effort to deflect criticism of his business activities, the Shah established the Pahlavi Foundation, but this again failed to convince his critics.[85]

The Shah's elaborate plans were eventually to collapse in the fiasco which surrounded the supposedly free elections in 1960. Having promised so much, expectations were dashed when it became apparent that the Shah intended to blatantly rig the vote. The daily *Sedaye Mardom* wrote on 14 August 1960, 'Indeed whilst on the one hand the rulers of the country maintain that these elections are free, 20m Iranians assert that they are not free, and since propaganda about freedom of election persists the dissatisfaction of public opinion increases'.[86] Kellas observed the air of ridicule in which people perceived the elections:

> It is claimed that many papers have been spoiled and many bogus or facetious votes cast for the Twelve Imams, Madame Delkash, the cabaret singer, and Mr Shamshiri, who runs the chelo-kabab house in the Bazaar . . . Personally I have found it hard to trace anybody, from my cook to the Minister of

Court, who has taken the trouble to vote at all; and the wry explanation for the most part is that 'it has no purpose'. Certainly a substantial proportion of the urban middle class have no intention of voting, a privilege which belongs to base mechanicals.[87]

The Shah sought to recover the situation by announcing that, if the people so wished it, he would cancel the elections; he would do this, he argued, because he was a true democrat.[88] Obviously concerned at the loss of credibility, the Shah reiterated his claim again at a press conference on 27 August:

> I have never acted contrary to the provisions of the Constitution and I am not prepared to do so now. I can act only within the framework of the law, unless the people – the real people, not two or three thousand people who stage demonstrations in the streets – show me that it is their inner wish and desire that the second alternative (annulling of the elections) be taken, in spite of the fact that this is outside the limits of the law. I am always willing to do anything for the sake of the country if I know that it is the real desire of the people.[89]

In ridiculing the elections and forcing the Shah to commit to a very public and humiliating U-turn, the intelligentsia and an increasingly aware political public served notice that the Pahlavi state was neither autonomous nor dominant – that the Shah himself had, yet again, singularly failed to convince as a plausible leader. The scene was now set for the launch of a comprehensive reform programme characterised as a 'White Revolution', though, as with a decade earlier, the Shah was forced to watch from the margins, as a new prime minister took the lead.

Notes

1 According to one commentator, the United States 'lost its virginity' in Iran through its widely acknowledged involvement in the coup.

2 FO 371 109986 EP 1015/14, Political and Economic Situation, dated 12 February 1954.

3 FO 371 127138 EP 1743/1 dated 30 May 1957; see also FO 371 133057 EP 1731/2 dated 15 August 1958, which details the advances in education.

4 FO 371 133006 EP 1015/38 dated 21 August 1958.

5 FO 371 133006 EP 1015/? dated 15 April 1958; see also FO 371 127142 EP 1822/1 dated 12 March 1957, which provides details of the 1956 census. Addenda to the overall census figures can be found in FO 371 140866 EP 1822/1 dated 1 December 1959.

6 FO 371 127074 EP 1015/3 dated 15 January 1957; FO 371 127138 EP 1743/1 dated 30 May 1957. FO 371 149761 EP 1015/143 dated 23 December 1960, includes a letter from the Iranian embassy in London which alleges that Tehran, a city of 2 million, possesses 40,000 television sets and 200,000 radios. See also FO 371 157600 EP 1015/36 dated 22 February 1961, which also includes a detailed class analysis.

7 FO 371 109985 EP 1013/2 dated 30 January 1954.

8 FO 371 127075 EP 1015/38 dated 16 August 1957.

9 FO 371 133006 EP 1015/38 dated 21 August 1958.

10 FO 371 157600 EP 1015/36 dated 22 February 1961.

11 FO 371 109986 EP 1015/18 dated 18 February 1954. Prince Ali Reza, widely viewed as a competent successor, was killed in an air crash in the autumn of 1954.
12 Denis Wright, who was later to serve as ambassador, was charged with this sensitive task, describing it with some accuracy as one of bringing together two 'estranged lovers'.
13 FO 371 120714 EP 1015/37 dated 29 October 1956. See also J.A. Bill, *The Eagle and the Lion: The Tragedy of American–Iranian Relations*. New Haven, CT: Yale University Press, 1988, pp. 125–6.
14 FO 371 127074 EP 1015/5 dated 4 February 1957. In an article by Elwell-Sutton for *The Scotsman*, the author notes that in the weeks following the coup one word dominated – *enteqam* – 'revenge'. See also, FO 371 109985 EP 1013/24 dated 17 November 1954.
15 FO 371 109986 EP 1015/4 dated 4 January 1954.
16 FO 371 109986 EP 1015/3 dated 29 December 1953.
17 According to Makki, the Shah confided to him that the trial and conviction of Mosaddeq were a mistake. See Makki's interview in *Tarikh-e Iran-e Moaser* (Iranian Contemporary History) 1(1), 1997, p. 198.
18 FO 371 109986 EP 1015/14 dated 12 February 1954.
19 FO 371 110060 EP 1534/49 dated 13 March 1954.
20 FO 371 120713 EP 1015/10 dated 23 April 1956.
21 FO 371 109985 EP 1013/17 dated 21 August 1954.
22 FO 371 109985 EP 1013/25 dated 1 December 1954.
23 FO 371 109985 EP 1013/26 dated 15 December 1954. See also FO 371 114807 EP 1013/2 dated 26 January 1955.
24 FO 371 114807 EP 1013/9 dated 3 May 1955.
25 FO 371 114811 EP 1018/33 dated 3 August 1955.
26 FO 371 120734 EP 1113/8 dated 20 April 1956.
27 FO 371 120734 EP 1113/14 dated 11 August 1956.
28 FO 371 110003 EP 1101/1 dated 14 May 1954.
29 See Bostock and Jones, *Planning and Power in Iran*, p. 153; the study is a detailed and valuable, if sympathetic, account of Ebtehaj's attempts at development to 1959.
30 FO 371 127074 EP 1015/4 dated 19 January 1957.
31 Quoted in Bostock and Jones, *Planning and Power*, pp. 160–61.
32 FO 371 120734 EP 1113/7 dated 10 March 1956, notes the Shah's favouritism for the army. FO 371 127111 EP 1201/1 dated 14 January 1957, notes that the armed services are indeed a privileged class. See also FO 371 133007 EP 1015/63 dated 17 December 1958.
33 See, FO 371 120714 EP 1015/35 dated 12 October 1956. The first major conspiracy was uncovered only a year after the overthrow of Mosaddeq and involved a large section of the officer corps.

> The communist organisation recently discovered in the defence and security forces ... had achieved a very serious degree of penetration. Many of the officers involved had a reputation for honesty and efficiency. The three services, the police and the Gendarmerie were all affected throughout the country and even the Military Intelligence Bureau had been heavily penetrated. So far about 600 suspects (nearly all officers to the rank of colonel) have been arrested and more are being sought or watched. One thousand NCOs are believed to have been connected with the organisation. Two special Courts Martial have been set up and hearings are about to start.

Still later it was rumoured that some 450 officers and NCOs with Tudeh affiliations had been discovered; this was kept quiet to avoid embarrassment.

34 FO 371 110060 EP 1534/32 dated 25 February 1954. Stevens argues that Iran should sort out her economy before joining a military pact. See also FO 371 114820 EP 1071/1 dated 31 January 1955, on British reservations. FO 371 114820 EP 1071/5 dated 11 February 1955, notes that the Shah's decision to take Iran into the Baghdad Pact followed a visit to the US. See also FO 371 114820 EP 1071/16 dated 12 March 1955, on the Shah's motives.

35 FO 371 133009 EP 1018/2 dated 17 January 1958.

36 FO 371 109985 EP 1013/4 dated 27 February 1954.

37 FO 371 114866 EP 1941/1 dated 5 January 1955.

38 Abrahamian, *Iran between Two Revolutions*, p. 420.

39 See FO 371 110035 EP 1202/1 dated 21 December 1954, which notes that the US planned to raise the strength of the Iranian army by 60 per cent in 15 months. FO 371 140841 EP 1201/1 dated 29 January 1959, British military attaché's report.

40 Bakhtiar, like Zahedi before him, was to find himself dismissed before too long (1961), eventually going into exile in Iraq, where he was assassinated.

41 FO 371 120714 EP 1015/33 dated 29 September 1956.

42 FO 371 140789 EP 1015/50 dated 9 July 1959, notes that although Iran is not a police state, SAVAK enjoys enormous powers.

43 FO 371 127095 EP 1104/2 dated 11 February 1957.

44 FO 371 133026 EP 1113/1 dated 13 February 1958. See also FO 371 140789 EP 1015/71 dated 26 September 1959; FO 371 149792 EP 1201/3 dated 2 February 1960.

45 FO 371 149761 EP 1015/142 dated 15 December 1960.

46 FO 371 120714 EP 1015/37 dated 29 October 1956.

47 FO 371 110060 EP 1534/49 dated 13 March 1954.

48 FO 371 133009 EP 1018/4 dated 28 February 1958, 1018/7 dated 4 March 1958. For a detailed analysis of the Qarani affair, see M.J. Gasiorowski, 'The Qarani Affair and Iranian Politics', *International Journal of Middle Eastern Studies* 25, 1993, pp. 625–44.

49 Gasiorowski, 'The Qarani Affair', pp. 625–44.

50 See the Quarterly Political Report submitted by Sir Roger Stevens, 10116/58 Despatch no. 51, dated 22 April 1958, reprinted in *Iran: Political Diaries 1952–1965* Vol. 14, Archive Editions, 1997, pp. 601–2.

51 See Abrahamian, *Iran between Two Revolutions*, p. 420.

52 FO 371 127075 EP 1015/45 dated 6 November 1957.

53 FO 371 127074 EP 1015/15 dated 14 April 1957.

54 FO 371 133006 EP 1015/37 dated 20 August 1958. Students in Isfahan noted that people could not tell the difference between *Mardom* and *Melliun*, see FO 371 149762 EP 1016/2 dated 23 February 1960. See also FO 371 149832 EP 1941/9 dated 12 July 1960.

55 FO 371 157600 EP 1015/36 dated 22 February 1961.

56 FO 371 114810 EP 1018/30 dated 18 July 1955.

57 FO 371 114810 EP 1018/14 dated 12 April 1955; also FO 371 109985 EP 1013/4 dated 27 February 1954; FO 371 109985 EP 1013/24 dated 17 November 1954. FO 371 109986 EP 1015/15 dated 20 February 1954.

58 FO 371 127095 EP 1104/3 dated 16 March 1957. The booklet contained in this file was published in 1956.

59 FO 371 140856 EP 1461/1 dated 15 January 1959. US intellectual support was no doubt predicated on the assumption that an independent peasant class was conducive to democracy. See also FO 371 140856 EP 1461/2 dated 15 January 1959:

> Critical observers argue also in general terms that the notion of the self-reliant Iranian yeomanry proudly working their own farms is an American pipe-dream, for the Iranian peasant's object in life is not hard work, bigger production and independence but to work as little as he can and if possible to get rich quick.

60 FO 371 133007 EP 1015/54 dated 31 October 1958.

61 FO 371 133007 EP 1015/59 dated 24 November 1958.

62 FO 371 133026 EP 1113/1 dated 13 February 1958. The extension of this, the suggested clearing of the bazaars entirely, was a major contributing factor to the revolution in 1979.

63 FO 371 157601 EP 1015/55 dated 28 March 1961. In an article for *The Spectator*, Michael Leapman noted the unevenness of development and emphasis on Westernisation, see FO 371 149761 EP 1015/143 dated 23 December 1960.

64 FO 371 110092 EP 1941/19 dated 18 October 1954. The Shah notes that the hand of 'Providence' had been at work in 1953, among other times.
65 FO 371 133007 EP 1015/62 dated 9 December 1958.
66 FO 371 133007 EP 1015/62 dated 9 December 1958.
67 FO 371 149755 EP 1015/20 dated 18 February 1960.
68 FO 371 149756 EP 1015/23 dated 8 March 1960.
69 FO 371 120714 EP 1015/31 dated 11 September 1956.
70 FO 371 133009 EP 1018/7 dated 4 March 1958. In a carefully calculated piece of flattery, when a crown prince was finally provided by his third wife, Farah Diba, the Israelis, in a gesture of goodwill which cannot have been without significance, offered the Shah a biblical parchment in praise of Cyrus the Great. Everyone, it seems, had expected the Shah to name the baby boy either Reza or Cyrus; in the event he was called 'Reza Cyrus'; see FO 371 149816 EP 1671/15 dated 8 November 1960.
71 FO 371 140887 EP 1961/4 dated 27 August 1959; FO 371 149835 EP 1961/1 dated 29 December 1959.
72 FO 371 140841 EP 1201/1 dated 29 January 1959. See also FO 371 149792 EP 1201/3 dated 2 February 1960.
73 FO 371 109986 EP 1015/22 dated 20 March 1954.
74 FO 371 114807 EP 1013/6 dated 23 March 1955.
75 FO 371 120714 EP 1015/35 dated 12 October 1956. It was rumoured that the members of the *ulema* had secured pictures of the Shah enjoying the nightlife in France, and they threatened to blackmail him.
76 FO 371 114863 EP 1781/1 dated 12 May 1955. See also FO 371 114863 EP 1781/6 dated 26 May 1955, FO 371 114863 EP 1781/9 dated 3 August 1955.
77 FO 371 114811 EP 1018/37 dated 9 August 1955; also FO 371 114811 EP 1018/46 dated 29 September 1955.
78 FO 371 127075 EP 1015/30 dated 27 June 1957.
79 FO 371 140789 EP 1015/61 dated 13 August 1959.
80 FO 371 149804 EP 1461/5 dated 1 March 1960.
81 FO 371 149804 EP 1461/7 dated 8 March 1960.
82 FO 371 140788 EP 1015/48 dated 30 June 1959. FO 371 149832 EP 1941/24 dated 10 November 1960. See also FO 140789 EP 1015/65 dated 27 August 1959. By this stage some questioners were urging the Shah to 'find solutions' to the constraints of government and bureaucracy.
83 FO 371 127135 EP 1671/4 dated 9 March 1957. The Shah asks the press for constructive as opposed to destructive criticism.
84 FO 371 140787 EP 1015/15 dated 18 February 1959. See also FO 371 149755 EP 1015/20 dated 18 February 1960, which notes that nevertheless, even among the less politically conscious, the birthday of the Twelfth Imam was celebrated with more enthusiasm than the anniversary of the assassination attempt on the Shah.
85 FO 371 133022 EP 1102/7 dated 2 June 1958; see also FO 371 140787 EP 1015/18 dated 23 February 1959, where Lambton notes that it is not corruption *per se* that is the problem but the fact that most people believe it has breached acceptable standards.
86 FO 371 149758 EP 1015/84 dated 16 August 1960.
87 FO 371 149758 EP 1015/87 dated 23 August 1960. See FO 371 149760 EP 1015/123 dated 19 October 1960. The Shah admits to Harrison that it was a mistake to say the elections would be free.
88 FO 371 149759 EP 1015/96 dated 29 August 1960.
89 FO 371 149759 EP 1015/105 dated 10 September 1960. The Shah also took the opportunity to point out that the 1951 elections (under Mosaddeq) were far worse in terms of vote-rigging.

11 The 'White Revolution'

By 1958, as has been noted, there was increasing concern about the stability of the monarchical regime, and whether it could contain, control and ideally channel the growth in political consciousness, which was sweeping not only Iranian society, but much of the Middle East. The Iraqi Revolution of 1958, with the massacre of the Iraqi royal family, had touched a nerve and came as a considerable shock to the political establishment. This was compounded by the coup against the Menderes regime in Turkey in 1960,[1] but also by the growing appreciation that the Shah had failed to emphatically suppress or redirect social and political discontent. The National Front, if less of a political threat, remained an ideological force, and Dr Mosaddeq, while under house arrest, remained the icon of nationalists throughout the country. Despite the suppression of the Tudeh communist movement, left-wing ideas featured prominently in intellectual discourse, with many writers continuing to be influenced by the radicalism of French political thought.[2] More significantly, there seemed to be a growing synthesis of socialist and Islamic discourse with the consequent 'revolutionising' of Islamic activism. Such was the potency of this popular brew that foreign observers became increasingly convinced that, 'This process will not be arrested until and unless there is a "popular" government, by which I mean a government that has established certain myths'.[3] Similarly, Russell noted, 'I fear that immediate methods are needed, perhaps even a dash of cheap economic demagoguery'.[4] A 'white revolution' was seen as the solution to the impending crisis – a bloodless revolution from above, led by a dynamic, populist, 'revolutionary monarch', which would anticipate and prevent the possibility of a red revolution, and ensure the stability and durability of the regime. The 'White Revolution', as it came to be known, was primarily an act of political rather than economic necessity, intended to serve and sustain 'a particular conception of relations of domination' centred around the Shah.[5] It was a revolutionary strategy aimed at sustaining a traditional system of authority. Its impact on Iranian society was profound, even if its consequences proved unforeseen.

The roots of the 'White Revolution'

The 'White Revolution', both in conception and implementation, has come to be associated with the Shah, and to epitomise an enlightened if flawed vision of rapid modernisation taking Iran towards a 'Great Civilisation'. In reality the Shah was less than enthusiastic about the idea of a 'white revolution'. He was concerned about the potential consequences and the problems inherent in reconciling monarchy with revolution.[6] Indeed in an interview in 1958, a journalist noted that, 'He [the Shah] often grew impatient when American diplomats urged him to modernise at a pace faster than his careful crawl. "I can start a revolution for you", he apparently told an American diplomat, "but you won't like the end result"'.[7] Moreover, his own understanding of recent events led him to argue that Iran had already had its 'revolution', witnessed in the 'popular uprising' against Mosaddeq, and, as he never tired of telling foreign observers, as a result Iran had now matured and was stable.[8] Indeed, Iran was nothing less than 'an island of stability'.[9] Yet if the Shah was himself initially unaware of the fragile foundations of his administration and dynasty, his acolytes proved more perceptive. With the foundation of the mock opposition party in the form of the Hezb-e Mardom in 1957 under the stewardship of his close friend Asadollah Alam, the Shah had intended to provide a vehicle by which he could mobilise the masses in his support. With the Prime Minister, Eqbal, in charge of the 'conservative' Melliun (Nation) Party, the idea was that Alam would gradually mobilise the people in a progressive agenda closely tied to the person of the Shah, and defined against the 'reactionary' Melliun. Unlike Melliun, Mardom was a meritocratic party which identified with its meritocratic Shah. It was, in Alam's words, 'truly the home of the people'.[10] This was by all accounts a tame experiment in political mobilisation which was highly controlled and limited in its ambitions. Few were convinced of any real opposition between Mardom and Melliun; still less were they able to reconcile the contradiction implicit in the organisation of a genuine 'people's party' by the Shah and one of his largest landowners. While the Shah was unenthusiastic about taking things further, and arguably saw no need, by contrast Alam was acutely aware of the need for a more radical programme. His discussion with the British diplomat Kellas in which he outlined his reasoning behind the foundation of Mardom is revealing and worth quoting in full [my emphasis]:

> Asadullah Alam went on to explain that what he had in mind was in fact a 'white revolution', which he hoped to bring about under the auspices of the Shah. He was working upon His Majesty's mind to this end. He confessed he had made little progress so far but he was confident that the Shah, for whose intelligence and good will he had the highest regard, would allow himself to be persuaded that he must take the lead of a popular and national crusade.
>
> Asadullah explained that to his mind the problem of the survival of the regime was a matter not so much of economics as of psychology and public relations. *Colonel Nasser had contrived to inspire the Egyptian people with new zeal by persuading them that his government was their own. Dr Musaddiq had elicited the same enthusiasm by the same means.* Asadullah had studied this phenomenon and concluded that the key to success was popularity based upon a measure of nationalistic fervour, which in turn must be founded in some patriotic aspiration, such as the recovery of Bahrain or a struggle against Arab expansion.

Asadullah added that the masses must also be shown that in the development programme of the Plan Organisation there was something for the peasant and the man in the street. The most popular man of the day was M. Moman, Mayor of Tehran, who was cleaning the streets and planting gardens which every man could see for himself and enjoy.

. . .

a progressive monarchy under a young ruler more popular than Colonel Nasser, Asadullah hoped to prevail upon the Shah to be rid of the present 'establishment', the existing ruling classes must give place to new and younger men. The old gang were not of course to be hurt; this was a white not a red revolution; but the Shah must sack them all. Asadullah proposed that the Shah should dissolve the Majlis, dismiss the government and liquidate the ruling classes on the grounds that they were obstructing the necessary reforms and inhibiting the realisation of national aspirations which were the object of Imperial policy.

The Mardom Party was to be the instrument of this new order. Asadullah confessed, however, that the Party's progress was not rapid. He found the younger intellectuals, whose support he courted, reluctant to join; they were suspicious and sceptical. To encourage them he was trying to persuade the Shah that the government should be encouraged to fight his Party, to persecute and be oppressive. He suggested that there might even be an election which his Party should lose; the loss would be attributed to the riches of the old order and the honest poverty of the peoples' own Mardom Party. Slowly, nevertheless, young nationalists were beginning to approach him. A young man had recently called upon him calling himself a 'pan-Iranian nationalist', and told him that he stood for 'nationalism without Shah. The Shah was an enemy of the people'. Alam tried to persuade him otherwise. 'Not only was he, Asadullah, a king's man, willing to listen to the young man but the king himself would hear him with sympathy, for His Majesty was the champion of the people'.

Asadullah confessed that he was experiencing difficulty with the Shah himself in promoting these ideas, and with Dr Eqbal. The Shah was wary, apprehending that Asadullah was a bit too impulsive and enthusiastic. He was afraid also that popular and nationalistic policies, however well controlled, might endanger stability.[11]

However, domestic and international pressures gradually convinced the Shah that if he did not lead the reform, he and his dynasty might be overcome by revolution from below.[12]

Social and economic developments

The decade of the 1960s continued to be turbulent for Iran, not least because of the tremendous growth in education within the country and also in the impact of Western student politics on Iranian students who travelled abroad in increasing numbers. Harrison noted the dramatic expansion of geographic mobility:

Forty thousand Iranians of the upper and middle classes now travel abroad year after year on private and official business, for pleasure, for medical treatment and for training. No less than 6000 Iranians apply to Her Majesty's Embassy here alone for visas for the United Kingdom annually. In reverse moreover, the country is invaded by foreigners; the European and American communities in Tehran numbered 700 in 1914 and today well over 10,000.

With respect to the student population he noted that 'there are now 17,000 students at six universities in the country and 15,000 more abroad; and between 20 and 30 thousand seek admission to the universities from secondary schools each year'.

Furthermore, many of the students of the previous two decades whose ideas had been shaped by developments in the post-war era were now in positions of considerable influence, not least Amini's ministers for agriculture and education. Put simply, a substantial 'middle class' or professional class, was finally coming of age.[13] According to Harrison, 'the development of a substantial middle class or middle classes, of professional, technical, clerical and managerial people, is the most notable feature of the last 35 years of Iranian social history'.[14] It is important in this respect to recognise that the political elite were also increasingly divided as to the need and nature of the reform. The fractures emergent among the 'ruling' class (both bureaucrats and landowners) contributed to an atmosphere of change and encouraged the view that radical reform was needed to secure and stabilise the country and the ruling establishment. Harrison's astute analysis of this development is worth quoting in full [my emphasis]:

Throughout the upper and middle classes, there are professional people, politicians, economists, planners, bankers, architects, journalists and writers who have been highly educated abroad; the elder, or pre-war, generation for the most part in France, the younger in the US, Germany, Switzerland and the United Kingdom. Although most of these people belong to privileged or prosperous families, whether of the upper or upper middle classes, they comprise a number of the real Iranian reformers and even revolutionaries. *Many indeed would readily connive at revolution, if they judged that it would serve to amputate the 'dead hand' of social and bureaucratic tradition and would offer a hope of more efficient administration and fulfilment of their own ideas whether political and economic aspirations or personal ambitions.* These people have seen what is going on in more highly developed societies. They are well read, they have been members of students' unions and debating clubs; and above all they have escaped for a few years from the autocratic system of domestic relations of Iranian family convention. They are acutely conscious, not so much of the absence of political freedoms in their own country, as of social injustice, nepotism, corruption and incompetence . . . The bulk of them are not more than 45 years old, and some of them together constitute virtually a corporate intellectual elite.[15]

Added to these factors must simply be the impact of the economic growth and land reform which affected Iran during this decade causing massive socio-economic dislocation and tension, all of which would have contributed to a certain ideological dynamism. The economic expansion and transformation is exemplified by the growth in telecommunications and mass media. Harrison noted that there were now some one million radio sets in the country, up tenfold from 1940, while a contemporary commentator was impressed by the rapid adoption of the television set, a whole new medium for the monarchy to reach the people. As Hambly noted, 'in 1962 it was estimated that there were 67,000 television sets in use reaching a potential audience of 670,000 . . . an audience far exceeding the total number of readers of newspapers and magazines'.[16] For all these reasons, the need for a clear programme of reform with a cohesive intellectual agenda, became a matter of urgency.

Amini and the launch of a 'white revolution'

By 1960, the Shah's second attempt to reinvent himself as a progressive monarch, this time with 'democratic' aspirations, had collapsed in the farce of the elections for the Twentieth Majlis. Despite the best efforts of the state media organisations, few believed in the sincerity of their Shah, and not for the first nor indeed for the last time, the Shah lost control of the political agenda. As Harrison noted,

> The Iranian press and wireless afford an impression of a popular, active, earnest young monarch . . . supported by a devoted prime minister and loyal government in indefatigable pursuit of the welfare of the people . . . building a prosperous future upon a foundation of social justice . . . Unhappily neither foreign observers nor most Iranians believe in this picture . . . the mass of people are indifferent to the regime. They simply do not believe that the government cares for the people or that the proceedings of Government have anything to do with themselves.[17]

In effect, a looming economic and political crisis precipitated by the cancellation of the elections of August 1960, combined with international pressure and a not untypical measure of procrastination by the Shah, resulted in the leadership of reform falling onto the shoulders of a respected Iranian aristocrat who had been ambassador to Washington, Dr Ali Amini. Amini and his zealous Minister of Agriculture, Dr Hasan Arsanjani, represented the highly educated and socially privileged 'revolutionaries' alluded to in Harrison's dispatch quoted above, though it would be fair to argue that Amini, was more reformer than revolutionary.[18] Ironically, despite his widely known liberal credentials, the fact that Amini's relatively brief premiership was conducted in the absence of a sitting Majlis incurred the wrath and enmity of National Front politicians who accused Amini of unconstitutional behaviour. Nevertheless, in his brief 18-month tenure, Amini and Arsanjani began the process of land reform in earnest, with the tacit approval of the Shah. They remained acutely aware of the sensitivities in being forced to take a political back seat.

Amini was well aware of the concern that land reform (the redistribution of large estates among tenant farmers) was causing among most landlords, many of whom resented the allusion to feudalism. Though most had accepted that some measure of land reform would be inevitable (after all even Dr Mosaddeq had proposed it), few were ready for the extent to which they would be stripped of their economic and, consequently, political power.[19] A previous attempt had been considerably modified by the sitting Majlis, but now Dr Amini, in the absence of a Majlis, was able to propose much tougher legislation and his enthusiastic Minister of Agriculture was keen to apply it. With customary vitriol Arsanjani attacked the backward and reactionary 'feudalists' and emphasised the 'progressive' nature of the reform which would pre-empt a red revolution. Since many *ulema* were also major landowners, and private property was considered inviolable in Islamic Law,[20] they too became the target of attack and, along with the landlords, were later to be characterised as *black reaction* by the Shah, while he would characterise the left as *red subversion*.[21] Indeed much of Arsanjani's rhetoric was seen as excessive and regarded by many as counterproductive: 'The Minister of Agriculture, by an intemperate campaign against "feudalism" in the name of land reform, has provoked disturbances amongst the peasantry and alarm amongst landowners'.[22] On another occasion on a trip to Maragheh in Azerbaijan, the site of the first land redistribution, the minister became embroiled in a bitter argument with a local landlord:

> The party then witnessed perhaps the most dramatic event of the day when Colonel Esfandiari appeared for an interview with the minister during a tea interval . . . It appears that the notorious Colonel had risen from the people to be the owner of 20 villages, 15 of which he had recently sold or donated to his children and relatives. He was offering four of the remainder for distribution and retaining one which had a population of 10,000 people. He pointed out that in doing so he was acting strictly within the terms of the law. Dr Arsanjani became very indignant and swore he would deprive the colonel of this village as it was iniquitous that he should remain in control of so many people. He added for good measure that he would strip him of his medals, to which Esfandiari responded that he could have the medals any time he cared to come for them.[23]

Like the Shah, Arsanjani was contemptuous of Iran's tribes and drew analogies with European history:

> [He] called the persistence of the tribes in living a nomadic life 'a vestige of the dark ages'. He said it was time for them 'to end this medieval practice of migration and living in tents', a practice useful for little except the opportunity it gave foreigners to take photographs of them. He envisaged the settlement of the tribes in agricultural areas where they could engage in farming.[24]

Arsanjani was convinced that the development of sedentary agriculture would be the salvation of Iran, and though in stark contrast to the Shah he frowned on industrialisation, he shared the latter's belief in the abilities of the Iranian peasant and actively promoted a conception of a liberated Iranian yeomanry:

> The Iranian peasant, who, although wholly illiterate, could recite his national epic by heart, was filled with resources of intelligence and character which had been untapped for centuries. The lamp and the bulb were there and only the liberation of a just social order was needed to supply the necessary connection and the electric current to light them. Every aspect of Persian life and initiative began in the village. The only real source of a potential resurrection of Iran was the Persian [sic] peasant.[25]

There was considerable resistance to the implementation of land reform from both the landlords and the *ulema*.[26] Landlords were particularly incensed by the notion that they were exploitative 'feudalists', and argued that the high estimation of the Iranian peasant was misplaced. More seriously, they argued that such a radical change in the socio-economic patterns of life could only harm agriculture and encourage migration to the cities. Ibrahim Mahdavi, in the newspaper *Nedaye Sepehr*, argued against the tendency to associate with the West:

> If this kind of ownership has a feudal root it has vanished since a long time ago to the establishment of constitution and law and relations between the villages and towns . . . Owing to the above factors feudalism in the shape as existed in Asiatic and Western countries never existed and cannot be coincident with land ownership in Iran.[27]

Amini, from a landowning family himself, was sensitive to the criticisms of the landlords and tried to soften Arsanjani's rhetoric.[28] Most landlords were not impressed by Amini's reassurances, and though they were increasingly prevented from airing their grievances publicly, they were privately scathing about the reform and particularly frustrated by what they considered to be an unconstitutional and illegal act in the absence of a sitting Majlis. Senior members of the *ulema*, including a hitherto unknown cleric by the name of Ruhollah Khomeini, condemned the reform as both unconstitutional and un-Islamic.[29]

Although some accepted land reform they were critical of its political aims.[30] One landowner, Malek Mansur, a bitter opponent of the reform, described the whole process of land reform as nothing more than a public relations exercise.

> In one case, after a quite bogus exposition of the activities of a rural cooperative society by the Minister of Agriculture, His Majesty had asked a peasant upon whom he was conferring title deeds whether he had found the cooperative useful; and the peasant replied 'What cooperative?' In another case His Majesty had asked a peasant, to whom he was about to give title deeds covering an allotment of 12 hectares, what was his annual income. The peasant replied, '30,000 tomans'. His Majesty asked that his question should be translated into Turkish and it was repeated in that language. The peasant

protested that he understood Persian very well, explained that he farmed in fact a hundred hectares and that his income was indeed 30,000 tomans. Whilst a third peasant was receiving his title deeds from the Imperial hand, it was known to all present that his house was being burned by Fazlullah Beg, Khan of the Shahsavan, who is the landlord in those parts.

Indeed according to Prince Malek Mansur, the peasants were reluctant to receive their deeds, knowing that having accepted them they could no more depend upon the indispensable assistance of Fazlullah Beg in hard times, and were earning his unlimited malevolence. Mr Malek Mansur observed that the error of land reform and of so many other government projects was that they represent an ill-conceived endeavour to help the people in spite of themselves. But it was socially and economically hopeless to try and work in spite of the people, instead of with the people. In any case, in his view, the Ministry of Agriculture were totally unequal to their task; if the doors of the Ministry were closed today, it would be two years before any farmer was aware of it.[31]

Other landlords ridiculed the notion, suggested by the Shah and Arsanjani among others, that the Iranian peasant could be transformed into a patriotic 'yeoman'.[32] According to Sultan Ali Soltani,

> The regime expected that the redistribution of land would produce a nation of patriots with a stake in the country, which they would be ready to defend against the Soviets. They were waiting for the camel's tail to reach the ground [the Persian equivalent of 'once in a blue moon']. On the contrary, they were promoting distrust, disorder and communism.[33]

Indeed it was the rumour becoming widespread that the land reform movement had been both designed and imposed by US development theorists at the instigation of the US government. As one British diplomat noted:

> Almost all critics of the bill are curiously united in blaming the 'Americans' for imposing it. Some argue that it has been thrust upon the Shah and the Government by the Americans, regardless of special conditions in Iran of which they have no experience, out of a misconceived notion that the existing system of land tenure is 'feudal' or reactionary. Others are persuaded that the Shah is promoting the bill in an inept endeavour to ingratiate himself to [sic] ill-informed American public opinion as a 'progressive' monarch. Some even believe that the Americans are dictating legislation in this sense in order to break the political power of the landowners, traditionally the friends of the British in Iran, regardless of the natural order of Iranian society.[34]

While suspicion of US motives remained ingrained, in immediate terms, critics directed their venom against Arsanjani whose enthusiasm for land reform at whatever cost was causing consternation. The British diplomat Makinson recounts a conversation with a certain Yusuf Akbar:

He said that strictly between ourselves he thought Arsanjani was going 'dotty'. He said that only the night before he, Arsanjani, had received an invitation, which he had publicly accepted, to attend a showing in Persian of a film about land reform in Mexico, called 'Viva Zapata'. Arsanjani had been scheduled to make a speech, but had apparently been dissuaded from such political foolishness. To do so would, according to Yusuf, have been public incitement to the peasants to riot.[35]

For all Arsanjani's enthusiasm, the implementation of land reform proved an erratic affair. But more serious were the objections being raised and the general sense that political anarchy was once again imminent. The Shah began to sense the possibility of a return from the political margins, and this time he would be ruthless in his seizure of the political initiative. As early as October 1961 the Shah was privately confiding that he might take direct control of the government, accusing Amini, somewhat unfairly, of 'dithering'.[36] Privately, he had made it clear to Harrison that 'he did not consider that Constitutional Monarchy, in our form, was applicable in this country. He also made it fairly clear that it was his present intention to rule for the next few years without a Parliament'.[37] By the beginning of 1962, the government was facing serious protests from students who rioted on the Tehran University campus. Police and paratroopers were sent in to disperse the students. Hundreds were injured.[38] That paratroopers should be sent onto the university campus was regarded by many as an act of sacrilege and a clear indication that the government was losing control. Amini, increasingly seen as a tool of the Americans, was also losing any sympathy he had enjoyed as a 'progressive' reformist landowner. The students, who had been shouting 'Long live Dr Mosaddeq', 'Down with Amini' and 'Down with the Shah', were accused by the government of having provoked the police, and of having been encouraged by an unholy alliance with the landlords – 'black reaction' as the Shah liked to label them. The British embassy was understandably dubious about Amini's assertions: 'An alliance of student agitators and "feudalists" against the programme of reform of a "progressive" government is . . . hard to believe'.[39] As with Mosaddeq seven years earlier, the turning point was to come in a confronta-tion with the military.[40] Amini, anxious to put Iran's financial house in order, had tried to cut the military budget, which had brought him into confrontation with the Shah and the military. He had also hoped for US aid to cover Iran's budget deficit; this was not forthcoming.[41] As a result, Amini resigned in July 1962 and the Shah appointed the loyal Alam in his place.[42] The scene was now set for the launch of *the* White Revolution.

The Shah and the 'White Revolution'

The White Revolution itself was launched by decree (the six points were first articulated in November 1961) and ratified by referendum in January 1963. It was composed of six principles: land reform, nationalisation of the forests, profit-sharing for industrial workers, sale of state factories, votes for women and the foundation of a Literacy Corps. Subsequently it was to be extended to 12 points and by the late 1970s to a total of 17 points. What distinguished this 'White Revolution' from what had preceded under Amini was that it represented a definite programme rather than a vague idea, and that its focus was the Shah as leader. Many of these ideas had been articulated prior to Amini, and had resurfaced during his brief premiership. They were, in many ways, simply revisions of earlier themes, but they were now increasingly identified with the person of the Shah. More importantly, the White Revolution and land reform had been the Shah's idea all along, a piece of historical revisionism which Arsanjani was only too happy to confirm.[43] Indeed according to Fereydoon Hoveida, the Shah was soon possessed of all the zeal of a convert:

> The Shah believed in his White Revolution. When I met him a few days after my arrival in Tehran in February 1965 he sounded convincing as he told me, 'We must forget all our past disagreements and close ranks to rescue the country from underdevelopment and ensure a bright future for future generations'. He was sitting on a marble table in his sister Princess Ashraf's villa, with his hands beneath his thighs and his legs dangling. 'I am going to go faster than the left', he promised. 'You are all going to have to run to keep up with me. All the old economic and political feudalism is over and done with. Everybody should benefit directly from the product of his own labour. That's the objective of my agrarian reforms. And for the workers we shall institute profit sharing . . . All young people must come back and take part in our great work'.[44]

The oratory of the period was to see further emphasis on the Shah's personal identification with 'progress', which by extension was 'anti-feudalist'. Indeed the Shah went much further than Amini in borrowing language which had first been expressed by the Tudeh Party, and agreeing that the term *ra'yat* (flock/serf) be eliminated from all official documents and discourse altogether.[45] Previously a 'democratic sovereign', the Shah increasingly sought to be a 'revolutionary monarch', at once egalitarian and autocratic. Many considered that the Shah, in trying to support two different constituencies, was attempting a difficult balancing act, one which in reality could not be reconciled with his ultimate priority, the long-term security of his dynasty.[46] For the Shah, on the other hand, it was the only way to provide the legitimacy he craved. It was in his eyes a strategy akin to 'Bonapartism' – peasants and the petit bourgeoisie would be drawn into a social and political alliance with their enlightened despot. His critics argued that it represented little more than patrimonial populism. In order to cement his vision the Shah developed a utopia towards which he would lead a grateful country. The roots of the 'Great Civilisation' were to be found in his description of a 'model' country, where spiritual fulfilment would be matched by material gains: 'Your income should be such that you and your family are full. That you will have smart clothes. That you will have a nice house'.[47] 'Before long', the Shah pointed out, 'our country will stand out as a rock of stability and security in this rough and stormy sea'.[48]

So caught up was the Shah with his utopian vision that his assessment of the success of land reform, as on previous occasions, bore little relation to reality. There was no doubt, as the Shah never tired of reiterating, that land reform and the forcible disenfranchisement of the aristocracy were having profound consequences for the social and political development of Iranian society, but the achievement was neither as clear nor as tidy as the Shah came to believe.[49] In the first place, land reform was not imposed on every landlord. Under Alam's premiership, a number of exceptions were introduced, including flexibility towards those landlords who showed a degree of mechanisation (how this was interpreted of course varied) or, more obviously, those who enjoyed a healthy politically useful relationship with the Shah. More seriously, the political imperative had resulted in redistributed plots being too small for efficient and economical cultivation. Whereas tenants had normally sought loans and assistance (for irrigation and mechanisation) from their landlords, the latter now felt released from any obligation or responsibility, and frequently made life difficult. Land reform ensured that a workable (if flawed) decentralised agricultural system was now being increasingly centralised. The new yeomen farmers had to ask central government for help. It was often unready, or technically incapable of filling the vacuum. Many farmers, both the smallholders and the landlords, were astonished at the arrogance of the newly formed 'Agricultural Corps', composed of young enthusiastic theoreticians dispatched to 'educate' farmers in the 'science' of cultivation. The immediate consequence was that many newly enfranchised smallholders simply sold their new farms to their old landlords and migrated to the burgeoning cities which were not prepared to welcome them.

The Shah was, however, convinced that the programme was working and that more importantly, by subjecting it to a referendum, in which he secured a suspicious 99 per cent of the popular vote, he was carrying out the will of the people.[50] Dismissive of his critics,[51] and increasingly reassured about his sense of mission,[52] the Shah seemed oblivious of his own recent comments about the use of manipulated referenda:

> Communist dictators resemble Fascist ones in that they enjoy holding elections. They hope to give the ordinary working man the idea that he has a voice in the Government of his country. But the Communist rulers allow only one political party; anybody who tries to start another, or who speaks against the ruling party, is likely to be liquidated. In the elections (if you can call them by that name), the voter has no choice, for the only candidates listed are those of the ruling party. *Purely as a matter of form, the citizen is urged or ordered to go and vote; the authorities then triumphantly announce that, let us say, 99.9 per cent of the votes cast were for the ruling party. I wonder how many intelligent people are fooled by that sort of thing.* [My emphasis.][53]

Many people, as it turned out, were not fooled. It soon became apparent that the Shah's protestations of enlightened altruism in his book *Mission for My Country*, in which he had stated that 'if ever I felt that Persia's monarchy had outlived its usefulness, I would be happy to resign as king and would even join in helping to abolish our monarchical institution', were largely for Western public consumption.[54] On the contrary, some suspected what the Shah admitted privately and had begun to hint at in public, that his own particular conception of 'democracy' bore few hallmarks of the Western variety. He was at pains to point out that civil freedoms had first been granted by Iran's ancient monarchs, and it was this role he sought to emulate.[55] In his message broadcast on Constitution Day in 1962, the Shah 'was at pains to point out that there is more to democracy than a couple of legislative chambers; nor was democracy a commodity to be imported from abroad, but every nation must find its own system of government by and for the people'.[56] Democratic pretensions, it seemed, were more of a public relations exercise, increasingly targeted at Western consumption. For the West, anxious to keep Iran out of Soviet hands, the image of a reforming monarch leading the revolution from above was exactly what the academic doctor had ordered. The Shah was the strong man required to dictate the transformation from the forces of tradition who, left to their own devices, would hand Iran to the communists. The praise was, therefore, necessarily and uncritically effusive.[57] Congratulatory messages from foreign governments, including that of the US, only served to convince the Shah of his own popularity. In responding to Kennedy's message of congratulation, the Shah somewhat haughtily replied, 'The result of the referendum does indeed reflect the wholehearted approval of my fundamental reforms by the well-nigh unanimous vote of the people of Iran'.[58] Within Iran, respect for the Shah's apparent public relations triumph was mixed with a palpable sense of concern. One notable weekly cautioned against the triumphalism in the air:

> It was not until January 13 that a serious weekly magazine (*Khandaniha*) asked outright the question in the minds of many people, 'Where is the Shah leading us?', and, in effect, gave warning that, unless kept under control, a revolution, whether started by the Tudeh or by the Shah, could be dangerous.[59]

Others also privately expressed their concerns at how the transformation of the Shah into a revolutionary leader could have dangerous consequences:

> while favouring reforms, they are apprehensive of the power which the Shah appears to be putting into the hands of ignorant country men and industrial workers . . . and fearful that forces may one day be unchained by demagogic leadership which could threaten both throne and constitution, particularly if disillusionment with the material benefits of the new land tenure sets in after the first flush of reform.[60]

One hint of this demagogic leadership came in June 1963, when Ayatollah Khomeini was arrested for speaking out against land reform and women's emancipation, leading to severe riots in Qom, Tehran and several other major cities. These riots were ruthlessly suppressed, though it was rumoured that much of the initiative for the 'law and order' operation came from Alam. Assessments of casualties varied, with the government claiming no more than several hundred and eyewitnesses stressing that the figure was nearer several thousand. Suffice to say that, for those opposed to the Shah and his methods, the clash marked the beginning of a prolonged uprising. For the Shah and his supporters it marked the end of 'tradition' and the reaction it represented. Not unusually, an event of evident historic significance yielded a multiplicity of interpretations. It is not known how much popular support Ayatollah Khomeini enjoyed, though some commentators noted extensive sympathy in the countryside. Outside this traditional constituency, it is likely that Khomeini's appeal was less theological and more political, in the sense that his outspokenness earned him the respect of opposition groups yearning for some real leadership. In this respect Khomeini was more a successor to Kashani than to Borujerdi, who had died in 1961 and whose death had left a vacuum in the Shi'a establishment. The Shah, who had always tried to maintain Borujerdi's support with very public shows of respect, had deliberately not formally acknowledged a successor, thereby leaving the field open to all comers. The emergence of Ayatollah Khomeini, a hitherto middle-level cleric whose position was transformed by political events, cannot have been the outcome the Shah desired. Certainly, Khomeini was one member of the *ulema* who was not convinced by the Shah's claims of a spiritual bond with the Imams.[61] Faced with his 'turbulent priest', the Shah initially placed Khomeini under house arrest and then released him six months later. It appeared as if the Shah had weathered the storm. Subsequent developments were to prove otherwise and show how easily the arrogance of power came to the Shah.

Rather than proceed with caution, the Shah moved swiftly to capitalise on what he perceived to be his triumph over 'black reaction'. With a certain amount of over-confidence the Shah dismissed Alam (who became Minister of Court) and replaced him with a technocrat, Hasan Ali Mansur, who would lead the *Hezb-e Iran-Novin* (The New Iran Party), the Shah's first experiment with a one-party system. The Mardom Party was retained for cosmetic purposes, but few doubted its impotence. Iran-Novin on the other hand was widely regarded as a US creation and yet another sign of the US infiltration of Iranian politics.[62] This apparently pervasive American connection was to resurface again within a year in what was to prove one of the most catastrophic decisions taken by the Shah. In 1964 it became apparent that the US State Department was seeking immunity from prosecution for all American personnel, diplomatic or otherwise, living in Iran. The State Department, anxious not to antagonise Iranian public opinion, had wanted the agreement to be informally ratified through an exchange of letters between the Iranian Foreign Ministry and the State Department. Mansur, however, was adamant that this was a constitutional matter which needed to be ratified by the Majlis, which having been packed with supporters could be expected to be a pushover. It is a testament to the strength of prevailing nationalist feeling that, despite this, of 130 deputies present, 60 deputies openly opposed the government. The American request had touched a raw nerve:

a situation which has brought to the surface the latent widespread criticism, in the press and among the public, of the grant of such privileges to foreigners – which is even talked of openly as a reversion to Capitulations . . . The Shah was extremely annoyed. Not only had Mansur's mishandling of the affair provided an opening for widespread criticism on an issue which can always be calculated to arouse public emotion.[63]

With the news that the Majlis had ratified a $200 million loan from the United States for the purchase of arms, the press, normally respectful, ventured to be critical, and it was noted that at least one local editor had suffered for his editorial. *The Echo of Iran* was closed down altogether.[64]

One of the most stinging criticisms came from the recently released Khomeini, who argued that the $200 million loan was a pay-off from the US government in return for capitulations. Few believed Mansur's argument that the two pieces of legislation were unconnected and, while nationalists might disagree with Khomeini on many issues, they could certainly empathise with his righteous indignation:

I cannot express the sorrow I feel in my heart. My heart is constricted . . . Iran no longer has any festival to celebrate; they have turned our festival into mourning . . . They have sold us, they have sold our independence; but still they light up the city and dance . . . If I were in their place, I would forbid all these lights; I would give orders that black flags be raised over the bazaars and houses, that black awnings be hung! Our dignity has been trampled underfoot; the dignity of Iran has been destroyed. The dignity of the Iranian army has been trampled underfoot! A law has been put before the Majlis according to which we are to accede to the Vienna Convention, and a provision has been added to it that all American military advisers, together with their families, technical and administrative officials, and servants – in short, anyone in any way connected to them – are to enjoy legal immunity with respect to any crime they may commit in Iran. If some American's servant, some American's cook, assassinates your marja in the middle of the bazaar, or runs over him, the Iranian police do not have the right to apprehend him! Iranian courts do not have the right to judge him! The dossier must be sent to America, so that our masters there can decide what is to be done! . . . They have reduced the Iranian people to a level lower than that of an American dog. If someone runs over a dog belonging to an American, he will be prosecuted. But if an American cook runs over the Shah, the head of state, no one will have the right to interfere with him. Why? Because they wanted a loan and America demanded this in return.[65]

Khomeini's diatribe was now sufficient for the Shah to have him exiled. As Wright noted, 'Khomeini's open hostility . . . expressed in terms, as you will see from the texts, [that] go far beyond anything we have heard from him in recent years'.[66] The ratification of the legislation was a monumental mistake, which effectively and emphatically witnessed the haemorrhaging of nationalist support from the Shah, and the gradual transformation of Khomeini from a recalcitrant cleric to a national leader. While some agreed with the premise that the Iranian legal system was flawed, few could tolerate the reintroduction of extra-legal rights for foreigners. They demanded, with justification, to know why the Shah did not take the opportunity to reform the legal system and complete the process begun by Davar. Instead short-termism triumphed, and within three months Mansur had been killed by an assassin.[67] The Shah, however, appeared oblivious to this, and simply had Mansur replaced by Hoveida, who was to serve in this capacity for the next 13 years. Increasingly determined to identify himself with the 'revolution', the Shah pressed ahead with his vision of the development of Iran and with his role clearly at its centre:

> Several years ago when we embarked upon the January 22 Revolution, despite the great enthusiasm of the nation . . . and despite the great joy, there were some who did not believe that the fruits of the revolution would appear so soon in the country. Our White Revolution and the implementation of the six points have brought about a great transformation in the economic and social condition of the country . . . Class privileges have disappeared. Superiority is now based only on qualifications . . . and the country has embarked on progress . . . Literacy Corpsmen, who first went to the villages to teach, have now gained so much confidence and trust of the local inhabitants that villagers consult them on all their affairs. In fact they have become representatives of the revolution . . . Of course this state of affairs is intolerable for the enemies of our homeland and the opponents of the revolution . . . These people are unaware of the will of God and the determination of the nation . . . poverty must gradually disappear from our midst. The word 'poverty' must be stricken from our dictionary . . . The Iran Novin Party, which was established at the time of our revolution, and which is the offspring and protector of the revolution, and also of all other parties which believe in the principles of the revolution, must spread the ideas of the revolution in such a way which it can become an un-penetrable political school of thought throughout the country.[68]

His confidence in his personal mission to deliver Iran from backwardness was further enhanced by yet another attempt to assassinate him, this time by a disgruntled guardsman in the Marble Palace. That a member of a unit expressly formed as a counterbalance to the dubious loyalty of the army should have tried to assassinate the Shah, should have been a cause for concern. But typically, a different understanding was gained, whereby, according to SAVAK, the soldier was either mad or a foreign agent (Soviet or British) determined to derail the reform programme of the 'Shah and People' by a scurrilous attack on the leader of the movement.[69] That he survived once again was an indication of Divine Providence, while the guards that died in defence of the Shah were described as 'martyrs'.[70] The Shah's growing dominance of the political arena was matched by a curious lack of attention to social detail. On the occasion of his silver jubilee in September 1965, the Majlis conferred upon him the lofty, and somewhat problematic title (in Western terms) of *Aryamehr* (Light of the Aryans). Yet the celebrations to mark his jubilee were greeted with indifference, despite the attempt on his life earlier in the year, which might have been expected, as in 1949, to result in a groundswell of sympathy. On the contrary, a British diplomat noted:

> Apart from the habitual eulogisers of the regime, the reaction of most sophisticated Iranians in Tehran seems to have ranged from unenthusiastic to openly critical. Politicians and officials were clearly feeling pretty exhausted after the first few days. Motorists became intensely irritated by the traffic jams, made worse than ever by the triumphal arches put up in places which are traffic bottlenecks at the best of times. They were not amused to find themselves stuck behind a procession of performing elephants on loan from a visiting Indian circus. The inadequate public transport system became even more inadequate when buses were taken off their routes to ferry 'celebrants' to mass functions. This cannot have been welcome to a lot of the poorer people; as one critic put it, a workman who earns 7/6 [37.5p] a day cannot afford to take taxis. Many people were critical of the lavish scale of the decorations and illuminations, on grounds of expense, of traffic congestion, and of the deleterious effect they had on Tehran's overstrained electricity supply. Others waxed sarcastic about the paeans of praise to the Shah put out by the government broadcasting network and the semi-controlled press. (To do the press justice there were also some mild criticism of the chaos caused by the celebrations, the blame being laid on the authorities responsible for administering them, not, of course, on the celebrations themselves.)[71]

Indeed:

> Uglier charges circulated by word of mouth. SAVAK . . . were widely accused of putting improper pressure on every form of organisation to contribute their quotas of money and men to the celebrations. (SAVAK are said to have been particularly busy dragooning people into attending a mass prayer rally in which an estimated 100,000 people participated, a few elderly reportedly dying of heart attacks.) Worse still, gangs of thugs were said to have gone round extracting money by threats of violence from merchants who were tardy in putting up decorations, while the authorities turned a blind eye.[72]

The Shah seemed less interested after 1965 in seeking advice, relying on a smaller and smaller circle of friends and sycophants, and stressing the main themes of *his* revolution. If fewer and fewer Iranians were bothering to listen, that mattered little, and in any case, the growth of the economy, which was largely the result of the maximisation of oil revenues in the late 1960s, allowed the Shah to disguise the anomalies and inconsistencies of the revolution he had inaugurated. Indeed by 1966 the Shah was feeling confident enough to issue a second book entitled *The White Revolution*, in which he referred to the 'Revolution of the Shah and the People' and expressed his interpretation of Iranian history and his role in it.[73] Soon this shift in emphasis was to go even further with the publication of *Pahlavism: A New Ideology* by a certain Manuchehr Honarmand.[74] This marked an altogether different departure for the Shah, who clearly had decided that the inherent contradictions of revolutionary monarchy could only be reconciled by the formulation of an entirely new ideology. It is unclear what the reaction to this somewhat intellectually feeble document was, but it did serve notice that the Shah no longer considered either himself or his dynasty expendable. On the contrary, as with his father before him, the dynasty did not serve the nation. The nation depended on the dynasty. But in an important distinction with his father, the Shah was not only revolutionary, he was Divinely Guided, and Divine Providence lay at the heart of this royal revolution:

> Premier Hoveida stated that the secret of Iran's economic and social success lay in the fact that it did not follow baseless schools of thought, nor was it inspired by East or West in its revolution – the revolution was inspired by national traditions and the Shah's revolutionary ideals.[75]

Notes

1 FO 371 149757 EP 1015/45 dated 7 June 1960.

> The coup has caused within the regime itself considerable anxiety . . . Only a few have taken comfort from the reflection that unpopular regimes have been swept away in neighbouring countries while Iran continues to confound the critics who have so long and so loudly proclaimed her to be the least stable element in the Western alliance in the Middle East.

2 In 1961, Jalal Ale Ahmad's highly influential if polemical *Gharbzadegi* (Westoxication) was published in Tehran. The other key thinker to emerge in this period was Ali Shariati.

3 FO 371 133006 EP 1015/38 dated 21 August 1958.

4 FO 371 133006 EP 1015/50 dated 30 September 1958.

5 FO 248 1580 dated 30 May 1960, Dr Ram in discussion with Kellas:

> Dr Ram claimed that the truth of course was that the Bill was a political measure. It was intended to show the world that Iran was not a feudal society, such as was supposed to be a liability in the struggle against Communism. It might indeed enjoy some success in this respect. But the proper way to resist Communism was economic, and the land reform law was not economic.

In an undated memo from 1960, Webster Johnson, USOM adviser in the Agricultural Bank, noted,

> In conversation generally I have said that we believe some form of agricultural revolution as regards techniques is necessary for Iran but that a technical revolution is quite different from re-distribution of land, which is a matter of politics and so largely outside our sphere.

6 FO 371 133006 EP 1015/37 dated 20 August 1958. Later Arfa would argue in conversation with Sir Roger Stevens that the whole notion was the Shah's idea in the first place, see FO 371 170374 EP 1015/33 dated 18 February 1963.

7 FO 371 133055 EP 1671/5 dated 3 October 1958. Article in *The Spectator*, written by Andrew Roth.

8 See for example: FO 371 140789 EP1015/57 dated 30 July 1959; FO 371 140789 EP 1015/64 dated 20 August 1959; FO 371 140789 EP 1015/65 dated 27 August 1959; FO 371 133006 EP 1015/37 dated 20 August 1958.

9 FO 371 149757 EP 1015/45 dated 7 June 1960.

10 FO 371 149756 EP 1015/39 dated 24 May 1960. In the government paper, Farman replied acidly to Alam's assertions: 'Mr Alam was one of the larger feudal barons in the country, more interested in dancing the rumba and grinding the faces of his peasants than in the welfare of the nation'.

11 FO 371 133006 EP 1015/34 dated 15 August 1958; FO 371 140790 EP 1015/78 dated 4 November 1959; see also FO 371 133006 EP 1015/37 dated 20 August 1958, on the Shah's initial reluctance towards a 'white revolution'.

12 In 1961, an article in the *Christian Science Monitor* made the following astute remark:

> Dr Musaddiq underestimated the attachment of Iranians to the institution of monarchy, although the present Shah, strictly speaking, is not of royal blood. If the Shah can identify himself with successful reform, radical changes in the present social and political system of his country would not automatically mean the establishment of a republic.

FO 371 157603 EP 1015/99 dated 15 May 1961. See also FO 371 157605 EP 1015/139 dated 1 June 1961, on the impending fear of revolution.

13 FO 248 1582 EP 1015/36 dated 1 March 1961.

14 See also FO 371 157599 EP 1015/7 dated 31 October 1961 for Lambton's assessment of growing middle-class 'political consciousness'.

15 FO 371 157610 EP 1015/229 1 August 1961.

16 See G. Hambly, 'Attitudes and Aspirations of the Contemporary Iranian Intellectual', *Journal of the Royal Central Asian Society* 51(2), 1964, p. 134. The Iranian embassy in London estimated that there were 40,000 television sets and 200,000 radio sets for a population of 2,000,000 in Tehran in 1960; see FO 371 149761 EP 1015/143 dated 23 December 1960.

17 See FO 371 149756 EP 1015/23 dated 8 March 1960. See also FO 371 149758 EP 1015/84 dated 16 August 1960.

18 In a private conversation Arsanjani is reported to have said, 'The monarchy is like a chair which stands on four legs, I have destroyed one of them' [i.e. the landed aristocracy]. Salvar notes that Arsanjani was determined to rid the country of the aristocracy; see Abbas Salvar, Interview in *Tarikh-e Moaser-e Iran* (Iranian Contemporary History) 1(4), 1998, p. 255. Amini distinguished between a 'white revolution' and a real revolution, implying that the former merely represented radical reform. See FO 371 164183 EP 1015/77, speech to the Ministry of Justice, dated 12 June 1962.

19 This view of inevitability, as well as a criticism of the 'feudalisation' of the debate is repeated by the former head of the Land Reform Organisation, Abbas Salvar, Interview, 1998, pp. 243–76.

20 FO 371 149804 EP 1461/5 dated 1 March 1960. Ayatollah Borujerdi issues a *fatwa* condemning land reform as against Islam. The Shah's reply to this move was unusually blunt, threatening the *ulema* with a 'white *coup d'état*'. See FO 371 149804 EP 1461/7 dated 8 March 1960.

21 Amini sought to pacify the *ulema* by appointing a religious adviser to the cabinet, going on pilgrimage to Mashhad and Qom, and visiting Kashani; FO 371 157611 EP 1015/241 dated 22 August 1961.

22 FO 371 157608 EP 1015/185 dated 22 June 1961.

23 FO 248 1589 dated 6 May 1962.

24 FO 248 1589, conversation with Phillips, dated 4 December 1962.

25 FO 248 1588, conversation with Kellas, dated 17 March 1962. In a subsequent conversation, Kellas unsuccessfully compared land reform in Iran with that of Egypt. Arsanjani 'went on to complain that I had a low opinion of the skilful Iranian farmers, while I magnified the ability of the degraded *fellahin* of Egypt'. FO 248 1589 dated 6 May 1962. See also M.R. Pahlavi, *Mission for My Country*. New York: McGraw-Hill, 1961, p. 10. Also the Shah's speech on 5 Dey 1341/25 December 1962 on the occasion of the anniversary of the murder of engineer Malek Ebadi in *Enghelab-e Sefid Shahanshah* (The White Revolution of the Shahanshah). Tehran, undated.

26 Salvar notes that some groups, including students, opposed land reform as an extension of their opposition to the Shah. Abbas Salvar, Interview, 1998, p. 265.

27 FO 248 1580, Ibrahim Mahdavi, dated 21 September 1960.

28 FO 248 1585 1461, *Keyhan International*, dated 20 July 1961, and letter dated 4 November 1961.

29 FO 371 157607 EP 1015/177 dated 20 June 1961. See also FO 248 1588, note by Kellas, dated 31 January 1962. FO 248 1589 dated 24 November 1962.

30 FO 248 1580, Kellas in conversation with Hussein Ali Qaraguzlu, dated 28 January 1960. See also FO 248 1588, Kellas in conversation with Mr Afshar, dated 10 April 1962.

31 FO 248 1585 1461, Kellas in conversation with Malek Mansur, dated 14 July 1961.

32 *Enghelab* speech on the occasion of the anniversary of the death of engineer Malek Ebadi, dated 5 Dey 1341/25 December 1962.

33 FO 248 1588, conversation with Kellas, dated 22 January 1962.

34 FO 371 149804 EP 1461/6 dated 8 March 1960. See also FO 248 1589 dated 10 September 1962, in which Lambton notes the dangerous repercussions for the regime of the prevalent idea of American imposition.

35 FO 248 1589 dated 29 October 1962.

36 FO 371 157611 EP 1015/253 dated 5 October 1961. See also EP 1015/255 dated 10 October 1961.

37 FO 371 157611 EP 1015/260 dated 5 October 1961. Alam, unusually, expressed concern at the possible outcome of direct rule, see FO 371 157612 EP 1015/267 dated 25 October 1961.

38 FO 371 164180 EP 1015/19 dated 23 January 1962; also FO 371 164181 EP 1015/23 dated 24 January 1962, and EP 1015/29 dated 24 January 1962.

39 FO 371 164181 EP 1015/32, Hiller, dated 31 January 1962. See also FO 371 164181 EP 1015/29, Hiller, dated 24 January 1962.

40 FO 371 157605 EP 1015/136 dated 26 May 1961, notes that the military had become increasingly dissatisfied with austerity measures and retirements (cf. Mosaddeq). FO 371 157606 EP 1015/156 dated 6 June 1961, notes that Amini's insistence that officers wear civilian clothes in non-military environments had caused discontent among the officer corps.

41 FO 371 164184 EP 1015/84 dated 18 July 1962.

42 FO 371 164184 EP 1015/85 dated 19 July 1962. Few were convinced by Alam's appointment and generally regarded it as the Shah concentrating power in his own hands. See FO 371 164185 EP 1015/110 dated 25 August 1962.

43 FO 248 1589, *Echo of Iran*, dated 9 September 1962.

44 F. Hoveyda, *The Fall of the Shah*. London: Weidenfeld and Nicolson, 1979, p. 134.

45 *Enghelab* dated 19 Dey 1341/8 January 1963.

46 See Jalal Ale Ahmad, *Plagued by the West* (trans. P. Sprachman). Delmar, NY: Caravan Books, 1982, p. 5: 'Nowadays even kings can appear revolutionary on the surface and use suspicious i.e. leftist language'.

47 *Enghelab* speech dated 13 Esfand 1341/3 March 1963; *Enghelab* address of the Shah to the heads of the Dehqan Congress, 7 Shahrivar 1341/28 August 1962.

48 FO 371 157599 EP 1015/19 dated 20 January 1961.

49 See, for example, *Enghelab* dated 1 Mehr 1341/22 September 1962.

50 The evidence of manipulation is clear, see: FO 371 170373 EP 1015/10 dated 24 January 1963. See also FO 371 170373 EP 1015/13 dated 28 January 1963; EP 1015/15 dated 25 January 1963; EP 1015/16 dated 25 January 1963. The Shah appears to have been impressed by the use of referenda by Charles de Gaulle.

51 *Enghelab* speech to farmers in Birjand dated 13 Farvardin 1342/2 April 1963.

52 *Enghelab* speech at Farmers' Cooperative Congress dated 19 Dey 1341/8 January 1963.

53 Pahlavi, *Mission for My Country*, p. 162.

54 Pahlavi, *Mission for My Country*, p. 327.

55 FO 371 157610 EP 1015/236 dated 10 August 1961.

56 FO 371 164185 EP 1015/108 dated 13 August 1962.

57 FO 371 170424 EP 1461/3 dated 6 February 1963.

58 FO 371 170424 EP 1461/2 dated 2 February 1963.

59 FO 371 170373 EP 1015/8 dated 15 January 1963.

60 FO 371 170373 EP 1015/18 dated 29 January 1963.

61 *Enghelab* speech to the people of Qom, dated 4 Bahman 1341/23 January 1963.

62 FO 371 175712 EP 1015/3 dated 8 February 1964, report by Sir Denis Wright.

63 FO 371 175712 EP 1015/27 dated 29 October 1964: Wright.

64 FO 371 175712 EP 1015/29 dated 30 October 1964.

65 R. Khomeini 'The Granting of Capitulatory Rights to the US', 27 October 1964, reproduced in H. Algar (trans. and ed.), *Islam and Revolution: Writings and Declarations of Imam Khomeini*. Berkeley, CA: Mizan Press, 1981, pp. 181–8.

66 FO 371 175712 EP 1015/31 dated 7 November 1964.

67 FO 371 189781 EP 1015/2 dated 21 January 1965, also EP 1015/6 dated 26 January 1965.

68 FO 371 189781 EP 1015/21 dated 27 April 1965.

69 FO 371 180804 EP 1942/31 dated 24 June 1965.

70 FO 371 180804 EP 1942/6 dated 12 April 1965.

71 FO 371 180804 EP 1942/49 dated 30 September 1965.

72 FO 371 180804 EP 1942/49 dated 30 September 1965.

73 M.R. Pahlavi, *The White Revolution*. Tehran: Kayhan Press, 1967.

74 M. Honarmand, *Pahlavism: Maktab-e No* (Pahlavism: A New Ideology). Tehran, Ordibehesht 1345/April/May 1966. This was the first of four volumes detailing the new 'revolutionary' ideology.

75 BBC SWB ME/3562/D/1 dated 17 December 1970, Hoveida's speech to the Central Committee of the Iran-Novin Party, dated 15 December 1970. See also BBC SWB ME/3568/D/1 dated 28 December 1970, Hoveida's statement to Iran-Novin Party meeting, dated 22 December 1970.

12 Towards the Great Civilisation

The last ten years of Mohammad Reza Shah's reign witnessed the consolidation, growth and extension of the Pahlavi state and the apogee of the Shah's personal power. The political and economic power of the state, exaggerated by a dramatic increase in oil revenues in the 1970s, masked the weakness of its social foundations. Despite having earlier criticised his father's methods and his failure to consult, the Shah now proceeded to construct a state organisation centred on his own person, which was increasingly insular in its orientation. Moreover, contrary to his own protestations, Mohammad Reza Shah was to prove more susceptible to flattery than his father had ever been.[1] Consequently, far from successfully penetrating society, the Pahlavi state sought to create an alternative 'modern' society in its own image and, cocooned within this social parody, was increasingly divorced from the growing discontent of a politically (and increasingly economically) marginalised and alienated society. That the Pahlavi state remained powerful despite these structural weaknesses reflected the relative autonomy of a state cushioned by substantial oil revenues and supported by an increasingly intimate military-industrial complex allied to the United States. Furthermore, both the Shah and his opponents recognised to varying degrees that the 'White Revolution' had effectively dismantled the structures of the traditional state, principally the patrician landowners, and as the Shah certainly believed, the *ulema*. The growing external strength of the state convinced the Shah that the remaining threat to his dynasty, that of 'red revolution' could be accommodated and co-opted within existing state structures. It is important to remember that whatever its weaknesses – and these were to be highlighted with the benefit of hindsight – the belief in the strength of the Pahlavi state and the Shah in particular was widespread and growing. While some groups certainly predicted its 'imminent' fall, there was nothing inevitable about the eventual collapse of the Pahlavi regime. The reasons for the Shah's fall, while varied, reflected the increasing centralisation of power in his hands. The economic and social problems resulting from the White Revolution were compounded by a series of politically inept decisions administered by the Shah; these served to further widen the gulf between him and his people, and fatally break the last vestiges of trust. That the latest and greatest crisis to hit the Pahlavi regime was transformed into revolution was the immediate consequence of the Shah's inability (or incapacity) to lead in a crisis, and the absence of anyone with political credibility to seize the initiative on his behalf. The revolution was in many ways an intensely personal failure, for while the 'Shah left', 'the Pahlavi state' founded by his father, to all intents and purposes survived.

The crest of the wave

Between 1967 and 1973, Mohammad Reza Shah reached the pinnacle of his personal power. If the institutionalisation of imperial authority was to prove irritatingly elusive, few doubted that the Shah had come of age and had settled into his self-defined role of enlightened autocrat with considerable skill. While critics persisted, and there remained much to criticise, successful economic growth in the ten years since the launch of the White Revolution, fuelled by the steady increase in oil revenues, helped to keep society by and large contented and the critics marginalised. The Shah could be forgiven his personal excesses, if social and economic improvements outweighed the political constraints which clearly existed. Between 1963 and 1973 economic growth in Iran averaged 10 per cent per year. It was steady if not dramatic growth which led some commentators, including those abroad, to argue that Iran was the new Japan, but in this case with substantial natural resources of her own. Oil revenues grew to feed this growth, but, by and large, they remained steady, and the growth reflected infrastructural and industrial development. If critics pointed to the flawed nature of this development and the harm done to agriculture through the social dislocation caused by the White Revolution, few were ready to listen, impressed instead by the myriad public works and grand infrastructural projects under way. For the believers these were the halcyon days, and those technocrats who had returned and placed their faith in the young idealistic and revolutionary Shah felt themselves vindicated. Soon, some argued, the Shah's economic miracle would be matched by a drive for further democratisation, as he himself had testified in various publications. This was transitional authoritarianism at its best and, faced with growing plaudits from abroad, some of his harshest critics began to come in from the cold and publicly acknowledge the Shah's obvious 'wisdom'.[2] For example, Parsa Nezhad, a former member of the Tudeh Party, acknowledged his mistakes in an interview in a manner which would be sure to endear him to the Shah: the reforms promoted by the left had been anticipated by the Shah (he was indeed a revolutionary) and the two farm corporations named after Darius the Great and the Shah emphasised to listeners the favourable comparison that ought to be drawn.[3]

> My studies on the country's economic growth led me to conclude that in fact some of our programmes on Iran's revolution and its economic, indus-trial, and social development were incongruous with Iran's realities, because the same government and regime had already implemented some of our programmes. Land reform has been carried out for example . . . We did not believe that anyone except us could implement land reform. We did not believe the bourgeoisie could implement land reforms . . . I saw that land

reform has actually been implemented in these areas – that is, the Iranian peasantry had received land, and the domination of feudalism had been abolished from the Iranian village.

I have seen an even more advanced phase of land reform, namely the farm corporations of Darius the Great and Aryamehr. These reflect a much higher phase of land reform . . . we thought that the abolition of feudalism and land reform implementation were empty propaganda. When I arrived here I saw for myself. The feelings of the peasants who talked to me were transferred to me. So I realised that the land reform we believed should take place following an armed uprising had been implemented without it.[4]

Other critics from the left, such as Dariush Homayun, were to be eventually co-opted into government, as the Shah increasingly sought to differentiate between those within the Pahlavi enterprise and those determined to be left outside. As the left-wing opposition *Radio Courier* noted in one of its broadcasts in 1967:

The current Iranian regime has taken various measures to enlist the services of intellectuals. These measures include establishing cultural centres such as the Pahlavi library, the Pahlavi cultural foundation and various cultural councils at the Royal Court, convening various congresses and conferences such as Poets' and Writers' Congress and the Arts festival held recently in which the Queen [Farah] took part, tight control of the Tehran, Tabriz, Shiraz, Meshed and Isfahan Universities through the trustees, control of the arts and culture ministry by Pahlbod, publishing newspapers and magazines, establishing a special transmitter for intellectuals, etc. . . . The regime has faced the Iranian intellectuals with two alternatives: either to capitulate and enjoy privileges such as a good position, wealth, fame and luxury, or to resist and suffer poverty, obscurity and privation. If you go beyond simple disobedience you have the SAVAK torturers, prison and execution waiting for you. Iranian intellectuals now ask themselves: should they join the current regime and try to justify its acts secretly and openly, or refuse to do so?[5]

The Shah's growing confidence was reflected in his decision to finally go ahead with a formal coronation in November 1967, the first in a series of spectacular pageants intended to 'stabilise monarchy in the Pahlavi dynasty'.[6] While there is little doubt that questions of political stability were paramount, the Shah explained the reason for his 27-year delay, with the observation that he had wanted to achieve some measure of socio-economic progress before agreeing to a coronation.[7] The coronation ceremony itself, which was watched by many for the first time on television, was a curious amalgam of invented 'Persian' tradition and European, specifically British, appropriation. While he, like his father, crowned himself with the Pahlavi crown modelled on what was believed to be the traditional Sassanian crown, much of the ceremony was derived from British practice, including a military escort of cuirassiers who looked strikingly like Life Guards and suitably attired liveried footmen. Indeed according to Sir Denis Wright, Sami'i from the Iranian Foreign Ministry was sent to London with express orders to discover how a coronation ceremony should be administered.[8] That a king who claimed to be the heir to 2,500 years of monarchy should seek to import royal traditions from abroad is a curious reflection on the Shah's attitude and the increasingly international dimension of his thinking. Other traditions and innovations appear to have been borrowed from Napoleonic France. His decision to crown himself, while echoing his father, was explained in terms lifted almost verbatim from Napoleon. According to the Empress, the Shah's justification for this procedure was that, since he represented the people of Iran, 'Through my hands, it is they who crown me'.[9] The *ulema* were relegated to the role of observers and, unlike his father, he did observe silence throughout the ceremony in deference to their religious sensitivities. The crowning of the Empress was an innovation, which also nevertheless had Napoleonic antecedents. It fitted with the Shah's notion that he had emancipated women during the initial stages of the White Revolution by giving them the vote, and Farah's coronation, along with the constitutional amendments adopted to make her regent in the event of the Shah's premature death,[10] were officially characterised as unique and progressive, despite the fact that the historical record notes that Iranian queens had ruled in Iran before.[11] Interestingly, this seemingly progressive move was rationalised by resorting to tradition. Farah was lauded as a *Seyyed*, a descendent of the Prophet through Imam Hasan, despite the fact that the title *Seyyed* cannot be transmitted through the female line. The tensions implicit in this symbolic act became increasingly apparent in interviews the Shah was to give in subsequent years, both to Oriana Fallaci and, importantly, to the American television anchor-woman Barbara Walters. It became apparent that there were stark contradictions between the Empress's role as potential 'regent' and the Shah's appreciation of the political aptitude of women.[12]

In many ways the coronation signalled the official beginning of the cult of personality. There was a dramatic upsurge in the number of statues of the Shah erected throughout the country. Prince Gholamreza unveiled a statue of the Shah in Twiserkan in September,[13] followed by Khoi (18 October), Kerman (23 October), Zahedan (26 October), Saveh (30 October) and Maku (11 November).[14] Other ceremonies also continued, with the senate holding a thanksgiving service on the occasion of the twentieth anniversary of the Shah's escape from assassination, coinciding with similar ceremonies held throughout the country.[15] While the Shah continued to be a revolutionary 'people's monarch', there was also something mystical about his persona. The Shah was increasingly described in messianic terms. In a speech to the Majlis, Hoveida declared, 'the Shah's constant missionary struggle to secure the Iranian people's rights is such that if revealed one day it will clearly show the extent to which the Shah's single-minded determination has been decisive'.[16] In the book *The White Revolution* published just before the coronation, the Shah explained his understanding of a king's all-encompassing responsibilities to his people:

Christensen, the Danish orientalist, has rightly said that a real king in Iran is not so much a political head of a nation as a teacher and leader. He is not only a person who builds roads, bridges, dams and canals, but one who leads them in spirit, thought and heart.[17]

This book was to be studied as a textbook in schools,[18] and in the following year seminars were inaugurated to study the text.[19]

Not everybody was impressed. For many in opposition, the idea that the White Revolution justified the Shah and the monarchy was treated with contempt:

> The propagandists also argue that the Shah's monarchy is unique in that it has launched a so-called white revolution and that it has enabled Iran to make maximum progress. They say that the world is amazed at the Shah's sagacity, that the 'entire world is studying and imitating what has been achieved through the Shah's genius, and that the Shah's era is the most brilliant era in Iran's history'. Shame![20]

Similarly, the central role that the Shah wished to claim for himself and the monarchy was also ridiculed. The Tudeh argued:

> The Shah and his propagandists claim that monarchy is a natural part of the Iranian culture. When a number of political prisoners were being tried, Masudi, the proprietor of *Etela'at* wrote: 'These people wanted to kill the Shah and began guerilla warfare in Iran. If the Shah were killed, there would be no Iran in which to conduct guerilla warfare'. Obviously this is incorrect. Many of the countries of the world have discarded monarchy. Even at its best – constitutional monarchy – this system of government is undemocratic. At its worst, the system is profoundly reactionary.

The article added that though many dictators throughout history have considered themselves indispensable to the universe, they usually proved to be inconsequential creatures. 'The idea of omniscient, omnipotent leaders can only appeal to the imbecile. It cannot deceive the wise'.[21] The government's tolerance of a new Pan-Iranist party (which sported insignia and uniforms reminiscent of Nazi Germany) did not help its public relations and opponents jeered at the new found cult of 'Aryanism' which the Shah encouraged.[22] At a student demonstration in 1970, participants decried the 'Fascist regime'.[23]

These criticisms, while occasionally voiced and undoubtedly present, nevertheless remained marginal. There were worrying signs by 1970 that the economic promise of the White Revolution was beginning to falter. Government statistics revealed inflationary pressures and a growing disparity in wealth. Yet these signs, ominous though they proved to be, were considered part of the grand scheme of things, and certainly would not deter the Shah from celebrating an event he had postponed several times before. These were the extensive ceremonies for the commemoration of 2,500 years of Persian monarchy. The idea had first been proposed in the 1950s, and had originally been regarded as a showcase in which modern Iran could be introduced to the world. It was initially envisaged as a cultural event in which the historical record would be put straight and the cultural contribution of Iran to world civilisation be truly recognised. Although the cultural aspects of the celebrations were extensive, the main theme of the entire spectacle was the centrality of the monarchy within the Iranian political system. The aim of the event was to identify the Shah not only with Cyrus the Great but to associate him with the great historical monuments of Iran's past. Iranians (and the world) would be reintroduced to their history in a narrative which centred on the monarchy and military might. As an exercise in the invention of tradition, there can have been few rivals. In the first place, historians were unsure of the precise date to be commemorated. Initial suggestions for the anniversary were first mooted in the 1950s. By 1964, it was announced that the celebrations would be held on 23 October 1965, which would coincide with the Shah's birthday and possibly, it was argued, his coronation. However, one month after this announcement the celebrations were postponed again, this time until 1967.[24]

By early 1971, preparations for the celebrations were in earnest and the person of Cyrus the Great emerged as less of an historical and cultural icon, and increasingly as a fundamental principle of government ideology. Indeed, before the Shah could effectively identify with Cyrus, the Achaemenid king had to be introduced and made familiar to a wider general public. Indeed, Cyrus was even evoked in the Prime Minister's budget speech:

> Since the beginning of its glorious history, our country has been famous for peace, friendship and humanity, and this can be clearly proved by studying the methods and measures of the great kings such as Cyrus the Great, whose efforts made possible our celebration next year of the 2500th anniversary of the Iranian monarchy.[25]

In his New Year message, the Shah was in buoyant mood, declaring the new Persian year to be the year of Cyrus the Great.[26] 'Cyrus the Great Year' was marked by special programmes on television and radio, and articles in the press: 'Schools, universities, factories, trade unions, women's and youth organisations have all prepared plans and set committees to ensure their playing a proper part in the festivities'.[27] Literary magazines and journals published widely on the ancient period and the symbol adopted for the ceremonies was the Cyrus cylinder.[28] It was during this year, while reflecting on past glories, that the model country of the future began to be described as the 'Great Civilisation'. Hoveida, in a policy statement to the Majlis, argued,

> It is an honour that Iran's revolution has put an end to backwardness and has placed us on the course of a bright change to the realms of a great civilisation, the principles of which were submitted to the Iranian nation by

the Shahanshah. It is natural that only through faith in the principles of the revolution and by depending on the firm idealistic and moral bases shall we be able to tread this road.[29]

However, it was the Shah who provided a definition (albeit ambiguous) for the concept. During a speech in the run-up to the celebrations, the Shah made clear his vision of the Great Civilisation, developing his new utopia on the back of his reconstructed historical narrative:

> I think that we can very firmly and with absolute certainty say that Iran will not only become an industrial nation but in my assessment in 12 years' time enter what we say is the era of the Great Civilisation. The era of the Great Civilisation for those interested to know means the kind of welfare state where everybody born, until he is dead, will enjoy every kind of social insurances to permit him to go into industry, to other jobs, to work and to die in peace and tranquillity. But also this welfare state doesn't mean that society will be completely undisciplined. It doesn't mean that our society will also sink into all the degradation that we can see in some places. Within the 12 year period illiteracy will be completely eradicated from this country.[30]

This speech was important not only for having introduced and elaborated upon the Great Civilisation, but significantly for having provided a timetable. The Shah was now proposing to lead his people to a tangible promised land of economic and technological progress within little more than a decade.

Of additional significance were the international dimensions and pretensions of the celebrations, which were intended to convey to the world the importance of the Iranian empire and monarchy. The official programme boasted that the ceremonies 'will be televised and transmitted throughout the world by Telstar satellite to allow millions all over the world to see it'.[31] Later it was to be claimed that some 2.4 billion people joined Iran in the celebrations.[32] Indeed, while there were numerous seminars and conferences held to highlight the achievements of Iranian culture and civilisation, the centrepiece of the celebrations, a military march past among the ruins of Persepolis left visitors in no doubt about the imperial driving force of this Persian cultural phenomenon. The immediate audience were to be visiting heads of state and the Shah's decision to follow nineteenth-century protocol when it came to seating guests made a subtle point with respect to the importance of monarchs over republican leaders. Thus Emperor Haile Selassie was second to himself in the official rankings, while presidents and vice-presidents came very near the bottom of the list. For this reason, President Georges Pompidou of France refused to attend, sending his prime minister instead.[33] It was in essence a celebration of 'monarchy', with the Iranian monarchy occupying its most senior ranks. European monarchs were heard to grumble about the unnecessary publicity given to this most traditional of institutions at a time when most considered discretion to be the better part of valour. One of the more esoteric and personal episodes in the official ceremonies was a eulogy delivered by the Shah at the tomb of Cyrus the Great at Pasargad:

Cyrus, great king, king of kings, Achaemenian king, king of the land of Iran, from me, King of kings of Iran and from my nation, I send greetings . . . you, the eternal hero of Iranian history, the founder of the oldest monarchy in the world, the great freedom giver of the world, the worthy son of mankind, we send greetings! . . . Cyrus, we have gathered here today at your eternal tomb to tell you: sleep in peace because we are awake and we will always be awake to look after our proud inheritance.[34]

As one historian was to later comment:

A joke of the period claimed that an Iranian office worker was so enraptured by reading these words of the Shah in his newspaper that he went home unexpectedly early to tell his wife; there he found his wife and his neighbour Cyrus asleep together in his bed. Overcome by the drama of the moment he raised his hand and said, 'Sleep easily Cyrus, for we are awake'.[35]

It was satire which would return to bite the Shah during the Islamic Revolution. Humour was one of the few ways ordinary Iranians could voice their objections. While the Shah was recalling and redefining memory, he also took the opportunity to ensure that future generations would not forget him with the inauguration of the 'Shahyad Aryamehr' monument on the outskirts of Tehran, significantly, in view of the desire to impress both a foreign and domestic audience, en route to the airport. Construction of this peculiar monument was initiated in 1967 – its name means 'remember the Shah Aryamehr'. It was presented as an apparent gift from a grateful nation to the Shah, and was opened on 17 October 1971 in the presence of international dignitaries, following a visit to the mausoleum of Reza Shah.[36] The young architect in charge of construction argued that the design was meant to incorporate Achaemenian, Sassanian, Safavid and modern Iranian influences, and was meant to symbolise the link between ancient and modern.[37] The lavish expense of the ceremonies had largely been dismissed by the Shah, who explained to reporters that the event was both an excellent public relations exercise and that, in any case, many infrastructural projects would be completed.[38] Subsequently, explanations were felt necessary for the extensive purchase of foreign goods and food, which seemed to contradict the essential Iranian spirit of the festivities.[39]

Indeed, while many privately condemned the expense of the festivities, the Shah ensured that the risk of disruption was eliminated by effectively banning ordinary Iranians from attending. Pervasive security meant that Iranians themselves had to watch the event on television. Ardashir Zahedi, the Shah's son-in-law, is reported to have urged the Shah to encourage the security services to be more lenient; others simply expressed private regret and refused to attend the ceremonies.[40] The most virulent public criticism came from Najaf in Iraq, where Ayatollah Khomeini used the occasion to declare his opposition to the monarchy as a whole, a significant shift in his political outlook. While the Shah was praising the virtues of kingship, Khomeini was arguing that the 'goodness' of Iranian kings was relative, and even the best had been capable of atrocities against their own people. He added that 'the title of King of Kings, which is borne by the monarchs of Iran, is the most hated of all titles in the sight of God'. He concluded by declaring the festival un-Islamic and urged people, Iranian and foreign alike, not to participate, for, 'to participate in it is to participate in the murder of the oppressed people of Iran'.[41]

These criticisms were, however, far outweighed (certainly in the Shah's eyes) by the generous praise for the Shah's achievements in the world's press. Even his critics at home had to wonder whether the Shah had not got it right all along, when they compared their own concerns with the international media's lavish compliments and congratulations. It appeared as if the Shah's narrative had been swallowed whole by foreign observers. *The Times* commented:

> To the people of Iran, the Institution of Monarchy is not a mode of government but is rather a way of life which has become an essential part of the nation's very existence. This is as it should be, for since the birth of their nationhood, the Iranians ... have always considered monarchy and nationhood to be synonymous ... the institution of monarchy has run like a connecting thread, even like a lifeline through twenty-five centuries of eventful history, and has been the most effective factor in ensuring the Iranian people's survival as a nation, with its own identity, characteristics, art and civilisation. It is often said that the Iranians owe the continuity of their nationhood ... to their ability to adapt and to adopt ... The real secret of this continuity lies in the institution of monarchy, which, since the founding of the Persian Empire, has stood for nationhood, independence and unity. This has given the Monarch a unique role in the nation's life, for he is not only the Head of State and the country's foremost citizen but also the spiritual leader, mentor and paragon of virtue. He provides guidance in all the nation's major activities and is the ultimate source of justice ... In short he is looked upon as the supreme authority for ensuring the nation a happy prosperous life.

Moreover:

> Within the short span of less than a decade, the Shahanshah has led his nation in a gigantic leap forward and created from a feudalistic society with a backward economy, a modern, thriving state that has already achieved much and seems certain to achieve even more in the immediate future ... Twenty-five centuries after Cyrus the Great, history is repeating itself through another great King, Mohammad Reza Shah Pahlavi, whose nation has given him the title of 'Aryamehr' (Light of the Aryans) for his gallantry and farsighted efforts to revive the splendour of Persia, and to uphold a tradition of humanitarianism established by the founder of the Persian Empire.[42]

Similar themes ran through the American press.[43] The Shah had arrived on the international stage, and he revelled in it.

The international statesman

The Shah had always wanted to play a greater role internationally than the realities of Iran allowed. Iranians, of course, had always had an acute if somewhat heightened appreciation of their cultural achievements, and were enthusiastic to translate this into effective political power abroad. In short, few Iranians, of any political hue, were prepared to publicly accept the consequences for Iran's international status implicit in the Treaty of Turkmenchai (1828), which essentially had signalled the end of Iran's Great Power status. The loss of political power was compensated for with a heightened sense of cultural and historical superiority, which constantly reminded Iranians of past imperial glories and demanded of her leaders a restoration of what were widely regarded as her 'natural rights'. It is this acute sensitivity and intense pride borne of political humiliation which has encouraged a succession of Iranian leaders to consistently try and punch above Iran's weight in the international ring. The Shah was no exception. While Reza Shah concentrated on domestic reconstruction, Mohammad Reza Shah was anxious to turn his attention abroad. Throughout the 1950s and 1960s he had sought to do this by integrating Iran's interests with those of the United States so that he could acquire the finance and military support which would allow him to extend Iran's armed forces. In doing so, he had incurred the wrath of a variety of critics, who regarded this expansion as little more than the pursuit of militarism, with little value to the inherent strength of the modern Iranian state. His decision to lead Iran into the Baghdad Pact (subsequently CENTO – Central Treaty Organisation) and to grant capitulatory rights offended Iranian sensibilities.

Yet by 1971, as the march past in front of the ruins of Persepolis indicated, the Shah felt that Iran's military power was such that she could reclaim her rightful place, in the very least as a regional power. He saw his opportunity with the decision by the Wilson government in 1968 to declare that Britain would no longer maintain permanent military forces 'East of Suez'. Fortunately for the Shah, this announcement coincided with the election of President Nixon. The Shah had always found it easier to get along with Republican presidents; the relationship he developed with Nixon was to be altogether more intimate and of considerable benefit to the Shah's ambitions. With Nixon's support, the Shah not only had access to increasingly sophisticated weaponry (spelled out in the 1972 Nixon Doctrine), but he also had carte blanche to pursue his ambitions as a regional hegemon following the British withdrawal. The British, departing according to some with indecent haste, were unable to leave matters in the Persian Gulf as tidy as they would have liked. Anxious to ensure the political stability and security of the Persian Gulf emirates, they had encouraged the formation of a broad-based federation, including Bahrain, Qatar and the current constituent states of the United Arab Emirates. While they succeeded in ensuring that the Shah would relinquish any claims to Bahrain, an island many Iranians continued to call Iran's fourteenth province, they were unable to persuade Bahrain to join in a wider federation. Sensitive to nationalist sentiment, the Shah had made repeated claims to Bahrain throughout his reign, often to the extreme irritation of the British, and indeed he proved reluctant to definitively relinquish these claims.[44] Ultimately, however, much to the chagrin of zealous nationalists, he conceded that the people of Bahrain could vote for independence, should they wish, in a UN-administered election. Bahrain, which had effectively been independent for many years, chose to continue to do so in 1970, and the Shah proclaimed this as a triumph of Iranian diplomacy and respect for international law.[45] While criticisms simmered, they were largely subsumed by the news in 1971 that Iran had reclaimed three of 'her' islands in the Persian Gulf – Abu Musa and the Greater and Lesser Tumbs. The British had managed to negotiate a settlement on Abu Musa with Sharjah, whereby sovereignty was left ambiguous, but no such agreement was reached on the other, even smaller islands, which were reoccupied without an agreement with Ras al Khaymah. The occupation of these islands has been a continuing source of trouble between Iran and the United Arab Emirates, but at the time, for all the consternation in Ras al Khaymah, it seemed a natural development. The Shah, after all, was now delegated the responsibility of 'Policeman of the Gulf', and he took his responsibilities seriously, expecting a certain deference from the Gulf sheikhdoms. Indeed the Shah made it clear that Iran would not recognise the formation of the United Arab Emirates if her claims to the three islands were not accepted. In the end, the British and their Arab clients relented, somewhat reluctantly, though it appears that the casting vote came from the United States.

For all the growing intimacy of the US–Iran relationship, the Shah remained, in foreign policy terms at least, an acute realist. His appreciation of the limitations of US support and protection were confirmed during the Indo-Pakistan war of 1971, when Pakistan was forced to concede independence to Bangladesh. The feeling that the US had failed to sufficiently support her ally in South Asia was acute in Tehran, and, ironically, just when relations with the US seemed to be peaking, the Shah decided to pursue an even more independent role, which coincidentally American faith in Iran as a reliable ally now allowed.[46] Not that this position was entirely new. In 1966, the Shah signed a comprehensive economic agreement with the USSR, in which Iran agreed to supply Moscow with more than $600 million worth of natural gas in return for Soviet industrial aid, including the construction of a major steel plant in Isfahan. The following year the USSR agreed to supply some $110 million worth of light armaments in return for more natural gas. The agreements, which transformed Iran's relations with the USSR, revealed the Shah's strategic vision in international affairs, a vision which he was unable to replicate in domestic politics. The Shah understood that the economic relationship forged with the Soviet Union was worth several divisions, and gained him influence among the radical Arab regimes that so irritated him. Indeed, he was later privately to admit that he never seriously considered the Soviet Union a threat to Iran's independence – this it seemed was more to placate the Americans. Rather, he recognised that threats to Iran's independence had historically come from the Western border, formerly in the guise of the Ottoman Empire and now, he presciently observed, Iraq.

The Shah's development into an international statesman impressed many of his contemporaries and, as a result, the Shah's international relations in a personal sense grew and matured, further enhancing his own sense of mission and purpose. His ability to convince his international partners was, however, not effectively translated at home. It is true that while some criticised the loss of Bahrain, many more accepted that Bahrain had in practice been independent for many years, while the acquisition of the three islands, however small, seemed to signify that the period of decline and territorial losses inaugurated by the Qajars was now at an end. Nevertheless, by agreeing to become the 'Policeman of the Gulf' (in Persian translated as 'Gendarme', a term with more servile connotations), the Shah inadvertently played into the hands of his opponents who argued that he was merely doing the West's dirty work. This charge would surface again when Iranian troops were sent to help suppress the Dhofar rebellion in Oman in 1972.

Domestic tensions

Most of the Shah's domestic problems resulted from his continuing inability, or unwillingness, to facilitate genuine political development. For all his talk of democracy, supporters and critics alike could see little evidence of this in practice. While supporters increasingly became apologists, in part to justify their own continuing and increasingly dependent relationship with the regime, opponents simply argued that their original suspicions about the Shah were being confirmed. Indeed, rather than use the elaborate celebrations of the 2,500th anniversary of the Persian monarchy to begin a genuine process of democratisation, even if incremental and gradual, the Shah seemed to be going into reverse. Whereas he had previously argued that Iran was not ready for democracy, now the emphasis shifted to argue that Iran was indeed democratic but in its own peculiarly Iranian sense. At the end of 1970, Prime Minister Hoveida argued,

> the secret of Iran's economic and social success lay in the fact that it did not follow baseless schools of thought, nor was it inspired by East or West in its revolution – the revolution was inspired by national traditions and the Shah's revolutionary ideals.

He then continued with an attack on Western conceptions of democracy, alluding to a theme which would become increasingly virulent – that such conceptions simply created social problems.

> As the Shah has said, social democracy cannot exist without economic democracy. In my view most of those who talk about democracy are still limited in their concept to the schools of thought advocated by Plato, Montesquieu and others, whereas democracy today is conditioned by mod-ern times. We do not believe democracy means anyone should be free to act against national interests and moral values and traditions. From our standpoint democracy means respecting human rights and individuals.

The interesting question is whether such democracy exists in those countries which are preaching to us on democracy.[47]

The Shah's disinterestedness in credible elections was to be seen in the extensive manipulation surrounding the 1971 elections for the Majlis, which were derided by the opposition as 'tomfooleries' and 'fabricated'.[48] Moreover, it was becoming increasingly clear that the economy was faltering and that, while growth remained on the surface impressive, targets were not being met.[49] This tangible failure was being ascribed to the lack of communication between the Shah and the implementers of the reform. Quite simply, it was argued that people either did not understand, or were unwilling to exert the effort required to maintain the momentum of the revolution. The Shah, increasingly convinced of his message, blamed the messenger. In addressing the new cabinet in September 1971, the Shah admonished them with the statement that

> Your revolutionary spirit must not flag for even one moment. All this progress or, as foreigners say, all this miracle in Iran could not have been achieved by routine work. All this has been achieved through faith and conscious belief in the charter of the revolution. This revolutionary zeal must exist with the same intensity it had during its first days.

Then, in order to deal with the unsatisfactory 'education', the Shah proceeded to argue that, 'The people should adopt the revolutionary spirit, otherwise progress will not be made. It is the job of the Information ministry to acquaint the people with their duties'.[50] This need to educate a generally receptive and willing public was combined with harsh words for those who simply would not co-operate. Thus Prime Minister Hoveida declared, 'Unless a man is patriotic there is no room for him in our society'.[51]

This growing belief in the power of exhortation and the inspiration of the Shah was also extended overseas, where foreigners were urged to learn from Iran and its great leader. As Hoveida argued,

> The great feats initiated in Iran under the Iranian leader's initiative which have now assumed a global dimension. The great feat of the campaign against illiteracy and the formation of the legion to serve mankind are among them . . . This is yet another example of the great achievements initiated in Iran and which have rapidly assumed international dimensions.[52]

Unaccustomed to being lectured by the Iranians, some foreign correspondents decided to hit back, and when the British *Daily Telegraph* questioned the validity of the 1971 elections, the retaliation was swift:

> The Conservative paper would do better to look at itself first and then try to explain democracy. The *Daily Telegraph* would see Britain as a country facing great economic, social and political difficulties. It would see the way

military force is used in preserving a type of tranquillity in Northern Ireland . . . That type of democracy naturally does not exist in Iran, and no one wants to follow blindly the British style of life. What the Conservative's paper calls democracy is of no interest to us.[53]

This dismissive attitude to critics of the regime was echoed with similar vitriol internally. At a press conference the Shah argued, 'I can tell you that the number of political prisoners in this country is exactly amounting to the number of traitors in this country'.[54] Such 'traitors' were increasingly held responsible for all the ills that befell the country and gradually domestic traitors (the red and black) were linked to foreign imperialists, the distinction having been gradually removed. Even a bank robbery was described as an exercise in colonialism:

> The colonial powers which have become accustomed to sucking the blood of nations can equip their devoted hirelings with money, as they have done. The Iranian nation, which has already seen the ugliness of colonialism reflected in the most infernal of faces and which has seen how rotten and abominable colonialism aims to mar the calm, creative and constructive atmosphere of Iranian life with disturbance and fear, no longer needs to ask why the devoted hirelings of colonialism kill two respectable Iranians for 47,000 rials. Their target and that of their masters and motivators is Iran's security and stability at this auspicious time.[55]

Or again, in responding to criticisms of Iran from abroad, Tehran Radio argued that,

> National interest is the highest priority in Iran. This should be known by both the left and right reactionaries . . . Iran has chosen to tread an extremely clear and unequivocal road . . . Any step taken outside this main line will meet certain defeat . . . The Iranian nation condemns any type of reaction and any type of colonialism, in whatever form or colour.[56]

This vitriolic language against 'traitors' both foreign and domestic was matched by an increasing use of religious terminology to describe the Shah and his mission. Having institutionalised and officially sanctioned the language of 'revolution', the Shah now proceeded to infuse Iranian political discourse with crude, often dichotomous, religious imagery – the struggle of good versus evil, light versus darkness. Indeed, by the early 1970s, it was apparent to observers that the revolutionary monarch was giving way to sacral kingship. Basking in international recognition, the Shah was becoming less tolerant of criticism at home and ideological fluidity was giving way to ruthless dogma. On a trip to Baluchestan, one of the least developed provinces in Iran, Prime Minister Hoveida hinted at the new agenda when he pointed out to the bewildered masses that, 'You young people will never see these dark and disastrous days',[57] adding for good measure that the future was full of 'brightness and hope'. The rhetoric of hope clothed in religious certainty was lambasted by opponents as an indication of how out of touch the regime was becoming:

> [Hoveida] informed the people that in the near future Iran will become a world military power and called on the people to pray for the Shah and the crown prince. Obviously all his remarks were utterly incomprehensible to the Sistan and Baluchestan people, who have never seen a factory chimney or a railway and who are being further impoverished every year by trying to put up with repeated droughts and cultivate their arid land. The first reaction of the people to Hoveida was undoubtedly the bewildered question: who is this man? Where has he come from? What is he trying to say?[58]

Similarly the Shah's increasing use of Islamic terminology was viewed as an ominous, if slightly ridiculous, development:[59]

> In touching upon internal issues the Shah truly gives himself away. The Shah . . . claims Divine inspiration. This is not the first time he has uttered such things. It is, however, the first time he openly claims to be a prophet. But is not our country a constitutional one? Then how is it that a prophet is ruling it, a prophet ruling it through Divine inspirations?[60]

The growing pomposity and intolerance of the Shah could not completely disguise the fragility of the state over which he presided. Indeed, intolerance and repression fostered the very reaction from a frustrated youth that he had sought to avoid. Disillusionment with the Shah's growing political conservatism encouraged some political activists to resort to violence and join the ranks of two organisations – the *Mojahideen-e Khalq* and *Fedayin-e Khalq* (both of which were to play pivotal roles in the Islamic Revolution). Much to the consternation of the authorities, these organisations drew members from the educated lower middle classes (as well as occasionally from higher up the socio-economic scale), young idealists, well read and determined, who had benefited most from the growth in education. The Shah was singularly unable to understand this 'ingratitude' and blamed such developments on Marxist or Islamic Marxist indoctrination, the unfortunate consequence of his magnanimous and generous welfare programme. In true patrimonial style, he dismissed them as misguided and spoilt children who needed to better appreciate his achievements.[61] The first indications of this trend, which occurred in the very year the Shah had sought to present Iran to the world, were brusquely dismissed as an anomaly. In February 1971, 13 young men attacked a Gendarmerie post in the village of Siakal, killing three Gendarmes. They fled into the forests but were captured and executed. Later that year, another 50 people accused of anti-state activities were arrested, while, most distressing for the Shah, his nephew Prince Shahram was attacked and almost kidnapped. Such activities were to continue intermittently and were largely dismissed by the authorities as inconsequential. In 1974, however, the regime blundered when it chose to parade another apologetic activist on television, ostensibly to publicly recant and acknowledge the error of his ways. Khosrow Golsorkhi, a left-wing poet and writer, refused to recant and publicly condemned the regime in front of millions of people, thereby signing his own death warrant.[62] It was a stark indication of the widening gulf between the Pahlavi state and Iranian society. Its impact as a public relations disaster was only appreciated long after the damage had been done. The Shah, for his part, was too preoccupied with international affairs to notice, let alone fully appreciate the social consequences of internal repression.

The 'Emperor of Oil'

These early indications of growing social and economic difficulties seemed to pale into insignificance when compared with the Shah's international achievements by the end of 1973, in the aftermath of the Yom Kippur War. His instrumental role in engineering the quadrupling of oil prices in December 1973 thrust him into the forefront of the international limelight. The Shah was no longer 'emerging', nor had he 'arrived' onto the international stage: he seemed by all accounts to be dictating the pace. He succeeded in confounding his critics at home and astonishing his colleagues abroad, who began to wonder aloud what Iran's newfound international status meant in practice. Domestically the Shah was once again unable to translate this international triumph into success, since the influx of revenue simply compounded the errors he had made since 1971. Rather than pursuing political reforms from a position of unparalleled economic strength, the Shah, comfortable in his financial autonomy, extended the alienation of the Pahlavi state from Iranian society, and pursued with even greater conviction his concept of sacral kingship. This confidence could be seen in his increasingly dismissive attitude towards the West and his prognostications of the imminent collapse of Western civilisation.

In his New Year message in March 1974, the Shah announced that his quadrupling of the oil price the previous December had 'introduced a new order more in line with the realities of the international community and the requirements of its development'.[63] In the aftermath of the Yom Kippur War and the Arab boycott of the West, the Shah was able to portray himself as a friend of the West, while at the same time demanding a significant change in the relationship between Iran and the oil consortium which had been operating in Iran since 1954. Yet if the commemorations for the 2,500th anniversary of the Persian monarchy had raised only a few criticisms in the Western media, this event, in so far as it led directly to economic difficulty in the Western industrialised world, resulted in a much closer scrutiny of Iranian affairs and the government of the Shah. Initially, however, the response was respectful. In the words of *Time* magazine, the Shah had become 'The Emperor of Oil'. The very real power the Shah exerted on Western economies through his control of oil prompted the Associate Editor of *Time*, Spencer Davidson, to argue that 'The Shah's power is exploding and Americans would be wise to pay attention to his dreams'.[64] Later, directly echoing the official Iranian line, he proposed that 'Mohammad Reza Pahlavi has brought Iran to a threshold of grandeur that is at least analogous to what Cyrus the Great achieved for ancient Persia'.[65] With such praise it is not hard to see why the Shah became increasingly arrogant and confident in his discussions with foreign reporters. The result was that political prudence, which may have previously disguised his more extreme views and contradictions, was left by the wayside as the Shah lectured people on his thoughts and their own inadequacies. Some of this was undoubtedly an exercise in political theatrics and helped confirm the image of the lofty imperial monarch both for foreign and domestic audiences alike. When he announced the decision to raise the price of oil at a press conference relayed by Tehran Radio, the Shah declared:

> As far as the industrial world is concerned . . . the era of extraordinary progress and income – and an even more extraordinary income – based on cheap oil has ended. They should find new energy resources and gradually tighten their belts, and eventually all the children of wealthy families who have plenty to eat, who have cars and who act almost like terrorists, planting bombs here and there, or choosing other ways will have to reconsider these aspects of this developed industrialised world. They will have to work harder.

The Shah then pointed out that since Iran would soon join the industrialised club, she did not want to deliberately hurt the industrialised world, or indeed to 'destroy' it, but simply to remove 'defects'; in other words encourage an adjustment.[66] This theme was repeated again in an interview with *Il Corriere della Serra*, when he described the move as one of 'self defence'. 'We do not wish any harm either to the developing countries or to the industrial countries, particularly since our own country will soon become an industrial nation'.[67] In an interview with *Der Spiegel*, the Shah appeared to avoid any distinction between the state of Iran and himself when he remarked: 'I shall sell *my* oil in the form of petrochemical products [my italics]'.[68]

The extra revenue made available by the price rise meant that the Fifth Development Plan had to be reviewed, and the $21 billion originally allocated leapt to over $70 billion overnight. In 1975, the Finance Minister Hushang Ansari announced that economic growth was expected to reach 41 per cent![69] In the accompanying enthusiasm there was talk of making Tehran an Asian financial centre. Central Bank Governor Yeganeh enthused 'that effective steps might be taken towards a grand [great] civilisation . . . that the constructive and critical role assigned to the Iranian economy in the international arena by the Iranian nation's great leader, the Shahanshah Aryamehr, might be achieved in the shortest possible time'.[70] As the utopian vision acquired an unprecedented air of possibility, so the belief that Iran was about to cross the frontier into the Great Civilisation, and indeed overtake the West, became voiced with increasing conviction. In an interview with *Al Ahram*, the Shah argued that

> In ten years Iran's population will be equal to that of France and Britain today. Iran's population, in other words, will not be less than 45m, but I can see Iran 25 years from now and we hope to be better off than France and Britain. Iran will have an income that will probably be more than Britain's.[71]

In a famous interview with Peter Snow, the Shah was far more emphatic in elucidating these themes and, in particular, lecturing the British, behaviour calculated to win him the support of nationalists, for whom Britain remained the villain.[72]

> In 25 years Iran will be one of the world's five flourishing and prosperous nations . . . I think that in 10 years' time our country will be as you are now. I am not the only one who says this but, according to others, during the coming 25 years Iran will become one of the five most flourishing and prosperous nations of the world.

The motivation for attacking the British not only came from a desire to play to anti-British sentiment but was also an attempt to distinguish Iran from the West, so that unfavourable comparisons over democratic rights could not be drawn. When Peter Snow asked what the Shah's views were on the sociopolitical system in the West and Britain in particular, the Shah replied:

> I do not really oppose it but I should state my opinion on it for you. If you continue this unruly and indisciplined social system, your country will explode . . . You will go bankrupt, you do not work enough, you try and receive more money than necessary for what little you do and this situation cannot continue; it can possibly continue for a few months or for a year or two but not forever.

When challenged over the issue of democratisation, the Shah was even more explicit: 'Who says the people of Iran want to have the type of democracy that you have in Britain?' When it was emphasised that economic progress might lead to political democracy, the Shah finally laid to rest any hopes for political liberalisation which might have permeated his thoughts in the early 1960s. Democracy had been definitively replaced by a paternalistic monarch who knew what was best for his people:

> This is not necessarily the case because we Iranians have a custom which is exactly the opposite of this. The people and the Shah of Iran are so close to each other that they consider themselves to be members of one family. I think that the people of Iran respect their Shah in the same way that children of Iranian families respect their fathers.[73]

Democratic centralism: the Rastakhiz (Resurrection) Party

Having tired of the illusion of multi-party politics, the Shah decided, with now characteristic arbitrariness, to establish a single governing party, which in his eyes would encourage and foster democratic participation within a carefully controlled environment. The impetus for this may have been the Shah's burgeoning relationship with China or, as some commentators have argued, a genuine desire to encourage constructive debate. Whatever his ultimate motives, it proved to be another significant political mistake.[74] With Rastakhiz the Shah essentially served notice that political ambivalence and apathy were no longer sufficient; on the contrary, the people must show *positive* loyalty to the Shah. It was in effect an experiment in 'democratic centralism' in which competing views could be aired within the ideological umbrella of Pahlavism – now renamed the 'philosophy of the revolution'. Rastakhiz was intended to become the ultimate tool of ideological dissemination and political control. Its membership would define loyalty to the Pahlavi system and members of the party could expect preferential treatment and patronage, while they would provide the raw material for the political education of the masses through lectures, rallies and the publication of a party newspaper. This forced many who would have tolerated his otherwise grandiose behaviour and rhetoric to make a decision about their political position with often negative results for the Shah. As one student activist later recalled, the Shah was not interested in partial support. Given a choice of being labelled friend or foe, many chose the latter.[75] With the foundation of Rastakhiz even apologists were hard pressed to argue that the Shah was a 'transitional authoritarian'.

His explanation and rationalisation of the decision further infuriated those who might otherwise have been sympathetic to his plans for social and economic development.

> I reached the conclusion – in view of the fact that we are again witnessing provocations with regard to oil, the country's astonishing progress on the international scene and other provocations in the country – that we should separate the ranks of Iranians clearly, properly and identifiably . . . Those who believe in the constitutional law, the monarchy regime and the 6th Bahman revolution will be on one side and those who do not believe in these on the other.

Having explained that within this umbrella organisation, or 'movement' as it was later to be characterised, opinions could be freely aired, as long as they did not contravene [dynastic] national principles, the Shah concluded with a statement that particularly insulted the sensibilities of the professional educated classes whose support he arguably most needed to cultivate:

> Two alternatives are open to those who do not join this organisation or do not believe in these principles I have already mentioned. Such individuals either belong to an illegal organisation – that is, they are Tudeh Party members, as we call them; in other words, as we say, and with the force of evidence, stateless individuals. These belong in an Iranian gaol. Alternatively, they could be given passports tomorrow with the greatest of pleasure and without charging them any exit dues, so that they can go, if they so wish, to any country they choose. This is because they cannot be regarded as Iranians; they have no home country and their activity is illegal – the penalty for their activity having been already determined by law.

He then prevaricated before confirming his initial viewpoint:

> On the other hand, those who may not be Tudeh Party supporters – or
> traitors to their country – and who, at the same time, do not believe in
> the above-mentioned principles – such individuals are free provided they
> officially and openly declare that they are not against the homeland. But
> backing both sides and wanting their cake and eat it is no longer acceptable.
> Everyone must clarify their position in this country like a man . . . So my
> point is that, from now, from tomorrow, everyone of voting age should
> establish their national position.[76]

This was a remarkably stupid statement to make and, combined with an
increasingly mystical self-perception, many intellectuals concluded that the Shah
had finally turned the corner well beyond simple delusions of grandeur and begun
the descent into insanity. It seemed that the Shah had crossed a line he had himself
warned about, 'There is nothing more dangerous for a man or for a nation than
to be a prisoner of one's personal sentiments and a captive of one's egotism'.[77]
The paternalistic and benign Shah was increasingly quoted in the party organ,
while he began to acquire a new title, that of *Farmandeh*, 'Commander', possibly
an allusion to the Islamic/Arabic *amir al-momenin* (commander of the faithful,
usually ascribed to Imam Ali). Indeed, this was not only a distinctly Iranian
revolution, but it was also quintessentially a 'spiritual' revolution which, aside
from providing industrialisation and welfare, would also inaugurate a classless
society.[78] Indeed, with the advent of Rastakhiz, the Shah's claims for his policies
simply became more extravagant. For example, in August 1975 the Shah decided
to institute share ownership for factory workers as yet another principle in the
'Shah–People Revolution' which he argued would pre-empt the development of
'industrial feudalism' transferring the myth of feudalism to industrial relations.
This 'extortionate situation', which he described as 'the exploitation of man by
man', would be eliminated by this policy.[79] He later made the extraordinary claim
'that the word exploitation no longer figures in the Iranian revolution's new
vocabulary' thereby implying that by eliminating the word, one eliminated the
problem.[80] Surrounded by sycophants, there was a palpable sense that by the end
of 1975 the Shah was becoming cocooned within a semiological chain of his own
construction, and was increasingly alienated from the social reality beyond the
boundaries of the court.

The myth of imperial authority: the apogee of sacral kingship

During a speech from the throne at the opening of the new Majlis and Senate,
the Shah made it clear that a main function of Rastakhiz was political education.

> The true purpose of education is not only to teach lessons but also to train
> even more worthy individuals, imbued with the spirit of patriotism and
> nationality, and moral and spiritual virtues; in other words, principles on

which the future of Iranian society is based . . . This is the responsibility of the Resurgence Party as the country's leader in political education.[81]

This was a task that the party newspaper *Rastakhiz* seemed to have embarked on with some vigour, more so in the Persian year 1355/2535 (1976–77) which marked the fiftieth anniversary of the dynasty. A sampling of the articles in *Rastakhiz* exemplifies the mood in 1976, the prevailing sense of spirituality and the importance of Islam.[82] There was, for example, a renewed emphasis on reinforcing the Shah's religious credentials in order to stress the sanctity and religious authority of the monarchy. There were pictures of him on pilgrimage to Mashhad, as the protector of the shrine of Imam Reza, and mourning the death of Imam Hussein. For the anniversary of the White Revolution, some 300 mullahs were drafted in to praise the Shah, and the Rastakhiz Party held a thanksgiving ceremony praying for the health of the Shah.[83] On 14 Mehr 1355/2535 (5 October 1976), it pointed out that the Shah understood the centrality of religion to the nation.[84] On 26 Bahman (14 February 1977), Dariush Homayun editorialised that the purpose of Rastakhiz was to mobilise the people for political and public life – the word he used, significantly enough, is *basij*.[85] On 12 Esfand (2 March 1977), Jamshid Amuzegar argued that the aim of the party was to create 'faith' among the people, ostensibly one would guess in the future of the country, but more probably in the person of the Shah.[86] On the inauguration of the fifteenth anniversary of the White Revolution, the centrality of the Shah was emphasised when a huge demonstration was held at the Shahyad Monument with the participation of 150,000 people. Books were published, foreign reporters invited. Newspapers hailed the 'revolution' with headlines about the millions of Iranians in celebration, and the fact that the 'sun of the 6th Bahman (the Persian date of the referendum) rises'. At a Rastakhiz Party commemoration, a huge portrait of the Shah was unveiled in the now familiar pose of the Shah in civilian clothes standing among the clouds with his arm raised.[87] The cultivation of the myth of the saviour continued throughout the year. For example on 2 Dey (22 December 1976) an article on leadership was published comparing the Shah, once again described as the *Farmandeh* (Commander), to such notables as Churchill and the leaders of the USSR.[88] Churchill's foresight was constrained by Parliament, while the Communist dictators lacked foresight altogether. The Shah, on the other hand, was farsighted and wise, and if problems arose it was only because the Iranians had misunderstood him. For the first time he is described, in a phrase which presages the Islamic Revolution, as *rahbar-e enghelab-e melli* (the leader of the national revolution). According to Ibn Saud, the Shah was 'one of the standard bearers of the Islamic movement in the twentieth-century world'.[89] The theme of Divine guidance is again stressed in his description of the decision to march on Azerbaijan, which was:

> really inspired and decided by that mystical power to which I owe my career and its direction. It is this Divine intelligence that directs my actions, as also the timing of them, and assures their success . . . The fates have so arranged

the course of events around me as to leave me in no doubt about the Divine hand guiding me to my destiny . . . this is the reason why I am more and more concerned every day with my deep belief in this mystical life of mine and the mission ordained for me by higher powers.[90]

A more illustrious genealogy was also constructed to complement this redefined monarchical mystique. In an interview with Karanjia, who flattered the Shah with the notion that he should write a new *Shahnameh* to record his own deeds, the Shah then discussed his family lineage in Mazandaran province, which he described as one of the ancient homelands of the Aryan tribes.

> It was from a traditional military family belonging to the hardy Bavand clan from the upper Mazanderan region of the Savadkuh which was part of the original homelands of the ancient Aryan races, that my father Reza Shah was happy and proud to trace his ancestry.[91]

This genealogy cannot but be a fabrication.[92] Nevertheless, for all his illustrious genealogy, the centrepiece of the Pahlavi resurrection of Iran was of course Mohammad Reza Shah himself, as detailed by a newly commissioned chronicle of the dynasty entitled *Gahnameh-ye Panjah Saleh-ye Shahanshahi-ye Pahlavi* (Chronicle of Fifty Years of the Pahlavi Monarchy).[93] The chronicle was dated in the new Imperial calendar, read in this case retrospectively into recent Iranian history.

The Shah's decision to suddenly impose a new calendar upon the country in 1976, on the fiftieth anniversary of the Pahlavi dynasty, was a blatant act of historical revisionism, changing overnight and without much consultation the historical reference point with which most Iranians were familiar. It was an explicit attack on the historical framework on which the myths sustained by Iranian popular culture were situated. This fourth calendar (the Imperial calendar) dated from the reign of Cyrus the Great. Overnight, Iranians who thought they were in the year 1355 (1976), found themselves in 2535. Hoveida congratulated the Majlis on ratifying the new calendar with the words: 'Your decision is indeed a reflection of the historic fact that during this long period, there has been only one Iran and one monarchic system and that these two are so closely interwoven that they represent one concept'.[94] The year was harder to comprehend because a mere five years earlier the Shah had triumphantly announced the 2,500th anniversary of the Persian Monarchy. The date was in actual fact correct if calculated from 559 BC, but it cannot have been lost on the Shah that this meant that the beginning of his reign coincided with the Imperial year 2500 (1941). Thus while Cyrus the Great spawned the first 2,500 years of Iranian history, Mohammad Reza Shah would define the next 2,500 years.

Towards the Great Civilisation

In an interview with the Iranian journalist Amir Taheri, the Shah was asked about the achievements of the Pahlavi dynasty during the first 50 years of their rule.

After commenting on the poor state of the country prior to his father's accession and asking the people to judge for themselves the differences that had emerged since 1921, the Shah reflected that 'to tell the truth I no longer think of the past, for my thoughts are directed towards the future'.[95] The product of his reflection on the future, the promise to which he would lead his people, was his third and arguably final book,[96] *Towards the Great Civilisation*, published in 1977 and in the Shah's words intended to deal with the future, just as the first had dealt with the past and the second with the present. Much criticised in retrospect by the intelligentsia, who mocked the simple analysis and somewhat vague if mystical self-reflection which permeated the book, it was, nonetheless, less the ramblings of a madman than a last testament with probably a more honest expression of personal belief than many would have liked. For his detractors, it was just another example of the Shah's detachment, and it is indicative of this huge divide from social reality that the book was treated with more derision than reverence. Central to the book is the concept of sacral monarchy and the fact that the Shah believes himself to be Divinely guided, though there are hints of fatalism in this statement. Characteristically, the Shah emphasises the paternal role of the Iranian monarch with respect to his people. Indeed for the first time the Shah explains what he understands by the term *Shahanshahi*:

> An important point to note is the real meaning of the word shahanshahi, which cannot be explained in ordinary historical terms. When it is necessary to translate it into a foreign language, it is normal to translate it as 'Imperial', but the meaning of the Western term Imperial is simply political and geographic, whereas from the Iranian perspective, the term shahanshahi has more than the normal meaning, it has a spiritual, philosophical, symbolic, and to a great extent, a sentimental aspect, in other words, just as it has a rational and thoughtful relevance, so too it has a moral and emotional dimension. In Iranian culture, the Iranian monarchy means the political and geographic unity of Iran in addition to the special national identity and all those unchangeable values which this national identity has brought forth. For this reason no fundamental change is possible in this country unless it is in tune with the fundamental principles of the monarchical system.[97]

Monarchy, he stresses, is central to the Iranian identity:

> Another manifestation of the eternal national values is the monarchical system of Iran. This is a system which from the very first day has been identified with the existence and identity of Iran and its durability . . . can be counted as one of the triumphs of history.[98]

In this book the Shah moves more emphatically away from the West. Criticising the immoral lifestyle of the West, the Shah also attacks, in language which seems more appropriate to Marxist writings, the unfair international system which serves the industrialised world. In light of this he warns his people against becoming

'Westoxicated', actually using the phrase *gharbzadegi* which Jalal Ale Ahmad had made famous nearly 30 years previously, though he cautions that this should not be confused with anti-Westernism.[99] Iran will avoid the mistakes of the West and head towards a glorious future which, according to the Shah, is unparalleled in Iranian history, thereby confirming his importance in Iranian history. As for the Great Civilisation itself, the Shah describes this in vague utopian terms, which he nonetheless believes are achievable:

> In Iran during the era of the Great Civilisation, there will be nothing left of such age old and destructive factors such as: poverty, ignorance, illiteracy, corruption, exploitation, discrimination and the like. The widening activities of the health service will maximise the health and fitness, up to that which research allows, for each Iranian; and the spread of education will bring the maximum mental and intellectual well-being, up to available standards.[100]

Essentially the Great Civilisation is a super welfare state combining intellectual and political well-being with religious conviction and spirituality.

> A highly humanitarian and democratic social order will prevail in Iran during the era of the Great Civilisation, with individual freedoms, social justice, economic democracy, decentralisation, informed public participation in all affairs, and productive national culture.[101]

Although in some areas the era of the Great Civilisation has already begun, the Shah appears to push the frontier further back as compared with earlier speeches. Nevertheless this frontier can be crossed:

> If all our efforts continue as at present, and if no foreseeable situation outside our control arises, we shall construct during the next 12 years a solid industrial, agricultural and technological substructure for the country's development and will reach the present level of progress of Western Europe. At that time our country will have a population of 45 to 50 million, i.e. comparable to the population of larger countries of Europe, and the era of the 'Great Civilisation' will have begun.[102]

Notes

1 Pahlavi, *Mission for My Country*, p. 322:

> One of the few mistakes my father made was to rely upon a narrowing circle of advisers. Fearing Reza Shah, they flattered him rather than telling him the truth; and I am sorry to say they were by no means always incorruptible. My system is entirely different . . . in lieu of advisers I obtain information from many quarters and then try to strike my own balance sincerely and solely in the light of the public interest. Let me add that in no way do I regard myself as the one true repository of knowledge and enlightenment.

Critics would later note that on the contrary while courtiers always feared lying to Reza Shah, they were scared to tell Mohammad Reza Shah the truth.

2 BBC SWB ME/3301/D/1 dated 10 February 1970, Tehran Radio, dated 8 February 1970. Hoveida praises the 'wise leadership' of the Shah. BBC SWB ME/4180/D/1 dated 29 December 1972, Hoveida's statements on the country's progress, Tehran Radio, dated 27 December 1972. See also BBC SWB ME/3504/D/1 dated 10 October 1970, *Keyhan* dated 8 October 1970.

3 There were 19 farm corporations in total of which only one was named after a previous king (Dariush-e Kabir); four others after other members of the royal family and two denoting 'justice'. See D.R. Denman, *The King's Vista*. Berkhamstead: Geographical Publications, p. 216.

4 BBC SWB ME/3383/D/1 dated 20 May 1970, Tehran Radio, dated 17 May 1970.

5 BBC SWB ME/2640/D/2 dated 7 December 1967, *Radio Iran Courier*, dated 4 December 1967.

6 BBC SWB ME/2596/D/1 dated 17 October 1967, excerpts from the Tudeh Party monthly *Mardom*, dated 15 October 1967.

7 *Rastakhiz* 3 Aban 2535/25 October 1977; see also F. Pahlavi, *My Thousand and One Days*. London: Allen, 1978, p. 60.

8 Interview with Sir Denis Wright, October 1996.

9 Pahlavi, *My Thousand and One Days*, p. 62.

10 BBC SWB ME/2589/D/1 dated 9 October 1967, Tehran Radio, 6 October 1967; Shah's speech from the throne on the occasion of the opening of the Fifth Senate and Twenty-second Majlis.

11 Farah recounts that 'I was very proud . . . to be the first Empress of Iran to be crowned for so many centuries of its history'. Pahlavi, *My Thousand and One Days*, p. 63.

12 O. Fallaci, *Mosahebeh ba Tarikh* (Interview with History), Tehran: Amir Kabir, 1978. The original in Italian was published earlier but was censored in Iran. The interview with the Shah was conducted in October 1973. In this interview, among other things, he argued that although women may be equal to men under the law, they were not equal to them in ability, p. 10.

13 BBC SWB ME/2580/D/1 dated 28 September 1967, Tehran Radio, dated 16 September 1967.

14 BBC SWB ME/2604/D/1 dated 26 October 1967; ME/2610/D/1 dated 2 November 1967; ME/2616/D/1 dated 9 November 1967; ME/2622/D/1 dated 16 November 1967, Tehran Radio, dates as noted. This was just the first batch!

15 BBC SWB ME/2999/D/2 dated 13 February 1969, Tehran Radio, dated 3, 4 February 1969.

16 BBC SWB ME/2713/D/1 dated 6 March 1968, Tehran Radio, dated 29 February 1968.

17 Pahlavi, *The White Revolution*, p. 1.

18 BBC SWB ME/2580/D/1 dated 28 September 1967, Tehran Radio, dated 17 September 1967.

19 BBC SWB ME/2672/D/1 dated 18 January 1968, Tehran Radio, dated 6 January 1968.

20 BBC SWB ME/2596/D/1 dated 17 October 1967, excerpts from *Mardom*, dated 15 October 1967.

21 BBC SWB ME/2596/D/1 dated 17 October 1967, excerpts from *Mardom*, dated 15 October 1967.

22 BBC SWB ME/3010/D/1 dated 26 February 1969, *Radio Iran Courier*, dated 24 February 1969.

23 BBC SWB ME/3567/D/2 dated 23 December 1970, *Peygham-e Emruz*, dated 21 December 1970.

24 FO 371 175 743 EP 1961/21 dated 21 September 1964.

25 BBC SWB ME/3619/D/1 dated 25 February 1971, Hoveida's budget speech, dated 23 February 1971. His reference to 'next year' implies the next Iranian year, which began on 21 March.

26 BBC SWB ME/3641/D/1 23 March 1971, Shah's *No-Ruz* speech, dated 21 March 1971.

27 *Facts about the Celebration of the 2500th Anniversary of the Founding of the Persian Empire by Cyrus the Great (1971)*, Committee of International Affairs, Tehran, July 1971.

28 For a sampling, see articles in the *Historical Research Magazine* for the year 1350/1971–72. Shoja ed Din Shafa's description of the cylinder as the first Bill of Rights (see note 194, pp. 219–20), a theme often reiterated, undoubtedly meant more to Americans than to Iranians.

29 BBC SWB ME/3794/D/1 dated 23 September 1971, Hoveida's speech to the Majlis, dated 19 September 1971.

30 BBC SWB ME/3818/D/3 dated 21 October 1971, press conference at Saadabad Palace, dated 18 October 1971.

31 *Facts about the Celebration*, p. 28.

32 *Rastakhiz* newspaper, dated 18 Mehr 1356/9 October 1977.

33 See W. Shawcross, *The Shah's Last Ride*. London: Chatto & Windus, 1989, p. 39. See also Pahlavi, *My Thousand and One Days*, p. 90.

34 *Rastakhiz* newspaper, dated 19 Mehr 1356/10 October 1977.

35 R. Mottahedeh, *The Mantle of the Prophet: Religion and Politics in Iran*. London: Chatto and Windus, 1986, p. 327.

36 *Facts about the Celebration*, p. 29.

37 *Rastakhiz* newspaper, dated 26 Mehr 1356/17 October 1977.

38 BBC SWB ME/3818/D/3 21 October 1971, press conference at Saadabad Palace, dated 18 October 1971. According to Charlotte Curtis of the *New York Times*, the Shah felt compelled to personally answer journalists who were questioning the wisdom of the expenditure. See W.A. Dorman and M. Farhang, *The US Press and Iran*. Berkeley, CA: University of California Press, 1987, p. 119.

39 See in particular Pahlavi, *My Thousand and One Days*, pp. 87–97, which covers the festivities in detail and responds to the criticism of foreign purchases.

40 Ardashir Zahedi, transcript of interview for BBC2 documentary *Reputations*, April 1996.

41 R. Khomeini, *Islam and Revolution* (trans. H. Algar). Berkeley, CA: Mizan Press, 1981. Declaration issued from Najaf on 31 October 1971, *The Incompatibility of Monarchy with Islam*, pp. 200–208.

42 *The Times*, special supplement, dated 25 September 1971.

43 Dorman and Farhang, *US Press and Iran*, pp. 118–19.

44 The Shah sought to maintain rights to Bahrain right up until the last minute; see BBC SWB ME/2968/D/1 dated 8 January 1969, Tehran Radio, dated 7 January 1969; ME/2975/D/1 dated 16 January 1969, Tehran Radio, dated 13 January 1969.

45 BBC SWB ME/3502/D/1 dated 8 October 1972, Shah's speech at the opening of the Majlis and Senate 6 October 1970. See also BBC SWB ME/3710/D/1 dated 16 June 1971, Tehran Radio, dated 14 June 1971.

46 Bill, *The Eagle and the Lion*, p. 199.

47 BBC SWB ME/3562/D/1 dated 17 December 1970, Hoveida's speech to the Central Committee of the Iran-Novin Party, dated 15 December 1970. The notion of 'neither east nor west' is repeated in other speeches, see BBC SWB ME/3568/D/1 dated 28 December 1970, Hoveida's statement to Iran-Novin Party meeting, dated 22 December 1970. See also Hoveida's comments to students and staff at Tehran University, dated 26 April 1972, BBC SWB ME/3975/D/1 dated 28 April 1972.

48 BBC SWB ME/3733/D/1 dated 13 July 1971, *Radio Iran Courier*, dated 9 July 1971.

49 See for example, A.K.S. Lambton, *Persian Land Reform 1962–66*. Oxford: Clarendon Press, 1969; BBC SWB ME/4419/D/1 dated 9 October 1973, Shah's speech to Majlis, dated 6 October 1973, in which he refers to more attention to raise agricultural yields and measures to deal with overpricing by 'shop-keepers'; H. Richards, 'Land Reform and Agribusiness in Iran', Middle East Research and Information Project (MERIP), September 1975.

50 BBC SWB ME/3788/D/1 dated 16 July 1971, Shah's speech to the new cabinet, dated 13 September 1971.

51 BBC SWB ME/3796/D/1 dated 25 September 1971, Hoveida's speech to the Majlis, dated 23 September 1971.

52 BBC SWB ME/3635/D/1 dated 16 March 1971, speech to 2nd Workers' Congress, dated 13 March 1971.

53 BBC SWB ME/3739/D/1 dated 20 July 1971, *Keyhan*, dated 15 July 1971.

54 BBC SWB ME/3818/D/1 dated 21 October 1971, Shah's press conference at Saadabad Palace, dated 18 October 1971.

55 BBC SWB ME/3887/D/1 dated 13 January 1972, Tehran Radio, dated 10 January 1972.

56 BBC SWB ME/3929/D/1 dated 2 March 1972, Tehran Radio, dated 27 February 1972. See also BBC SWB ME/4056/D/1 dated 2 August 1972, Tehran Radio condemns terrorism and associates it with colonialism, dated 30 July 1972.

57 BBC SWB ME/4111/D/1 dated 6 October 1972, Iran-Novin rally in Zahedan, dated 4 October 1972.

58 BBC SWB ME/4112/D/2 dated 7 October 1972, *Radio Iran Courier*, dated 5 October 1972.

59 BBC SWB ME/4203/D/1 dated 25 January 1973, Tehran Radio dated 23 January 1973. Continued in ME/4204/D/1 dated 26 January 1973.

60 BBC SWB ME/4423/D/2 dated 13 October 1973, *Radio Iran Courier*, dated 5 October 1973.

61 In this attitude, the Shah had a soulmate in Richard Nixon.

62 Bill, *The Eagle and the Lion*, pp. 191–2.

63 BBC SWB ME/4558/D/1 dated 23 March 1974, Shah's New Year Message, dated 21 March 1974.

64 *Time*, 4 November 1974, pp. 28–38. The title says it all, 'Oil, Grandeur and a Challenge to the West'. There are suggestions, as yet unverifiable, that the Shah effectively bought these articles in *Time*.

65 *Time*, 4 November 1974, p. 28.

66 BBC SWB ME/4485/D/1 dated 28 December 1973, Shah's press conference, dated 23 December 1973.

67 BBC SWB ME/4493/D/1 dated 7 January 1974, *Il Corriere della Serra*, dated 5 January 1974.

68 BBC SWB ME/4494/D/1 dated 8 January 1974, interview with *Der Spiegel*, dated 5 January 1974.

69 BBC SWB ME/4833/D/1 dated 18 February 1975, Tehran Radio, dated 15 February 1975.

70 BBC SWB ME/4498/D/1 dated 12 January 1974, Tehran Radio, dated 10 January 1974.

71 BBC SWB ME/4515/D/1 dated 1 February 1974, interview in *Al Ahram*, dated 30 January 1974.

72 That this rhetoric may have had more impact among certain domestic constituents is exemplified by the fact that during the Revolution of 1978–79, some urged the Shah to 'apologise' to the British for the harsh criticism he had unleashed.

73 BBC SWB ME/4514/D/1 dated 31 January 1974, interview with Peter Snow for ITV, dated 29 January 1974.

74 Some have argued that the impetus for the establishment of a one-party state came from technocrats in the service of the Empress Farah. See P.M. Amini, 'A Single Party State in Iran, 1975–78: The Rastakhiz Party: the Final Attempt by the Shah to Consolidate His Political Base', *Middle Eastern Studies* 38(1), 2002, pp. 132–3.

75 Abbas Abdi, transcript of interview for BBC2 documentary *Reputations*, April 1996.

76 BBC SWB ME/4845/D/1 dated 4 March 1975, Shah's press conference, dated 2 March 1975.

77 Pahlavi, *Mission for My Country*, p. 126.

78 *Falsafe-ye enghelab-e Iran* (The Philosophy of the Iranian Revolution) in *Rastakhiz* newspaper 452, Wednesday 5 Aban 2535/26 October 1976.

79 BBC SWB ME/4976/A/2 dated 8 August 1975, Tehran Radio, dated 6 August 1975.

80 BBC SWB ME/5119/A/1 dated 28 January 1976, Shah's speech at the fourteenth anniversary of the White Revolution, dated 26 January 1976.

81 BBC SWB ME/5332/A/5 dated 8 October 1976, Shah's speech at the opening of the Majlis, dated 6 October 1976. See also BBC SWB ME/5348/A/4 dated 27 October 1976, interview with Amir Taheri, dated 25 October 1976.

82 Excerpts taken from *Rastakhiz*, dated 1355–56/1976–78.

83 *Rastakhiz*, 6 Bahman 1355/2535/22 January 1977, p. 1.

84 *Rastakhiz*, 14 Mehr 1355/2535/5 October 1976, pp. 13–14. This was reportedly first said in 1968.

85 *Rastakhiz*, 26 Bahman 1355/2535/14 February 1977, p. 4. The Islamic Republic was later to mobilise the masses, the *basijis*.

86 *Rastakhiz*, 12 Esfand 1355/2535/2 March 1977, p. 1.

87 *Rastakhiz*, 6 Bahman 1355/2535/26 January 1978, p. 1.

88 *Rastakhiz*, 2 Dey 1355/2535/22 December 1976, p. 8.

89 *Rastakhiz*, 7 Mehr 1355/2535/28 September 1976. There is a complete list of admirers in this issue including Churchill, Ibn Saud, Kennedy, Pope Paul VI, Padegorni, Hirohito, Ford, Nixon, Johnson, Roosevelt and King Baudouin. US presidents predominate.

90 *Rastakhiz*, 7 Mehr 1355/2535/28 September 1976, pp. 89–90.

91 *Rastakhiz*, 7 Mehr 1355/2535/28 September 1976, p. 31.

92 Few Iranian families would have been able to trace their ancestry beyond the early Qajars. Documentation is scarce and normally non-existent, and since Reza Shah himself introduced surnames (including his own) and registration, it is difficult to see how the lineage of the lowly Cossack officer could be accurately traced for more than a couple of generations.

93 Shoja ad Din Shafa, *Gahnameh-ye Panjah Saleh-ye Shahanshahi-ye Pahlavi* (Chronicle of 50 Years of the Pahlavi Monarchy). Tehran, 1978.

94 *Keyhan International*, 15 March 1975, quoted in M. Zonis, *Majestic Failure: The Fall of the Shah*. Chicago, IL: University of Chicago Press, 1991, p. 82.

95 BBC SWB ME/5350/A/1 dated 29 October 1976, Shah's interview with Amir Taheri, Tehran Radio, dated 25 October 1976.

96 His final book was in actual fact *Answer to History* but this was written after his downfall.

97 M.R. Pahlavi, *Be Sooye Tamadun-e Bozorg*. Tehran: Markaz-e Pazhuhish va nashr-e farhamg-e Dowran-e Pahlavi, 1977, p. 244.

98 Pahlavi, *Be Sooye Tamadun-e Bozorg*, p. 243.

99 Pahlavi, *Be Sooye Tamadun-e Bozorg*, p. 231.

100 Pahlavi, *Be Sooye Tamadun-e Bozorg*, p. 258.

101 Pahlavi, *Be Sooye Tamadun-e Bozorg*, p. 279.

102 Pahlavi, *Be Sooye Tamadun-e Bozorg*, p. 265.

13 Revolution, war and 'Islamic Republic'

Then sovereigns and statesmen began to see that what they had taken for a mere every-day accident in history was an event so new, so contrary to all former experience, so widespread, so monstrous and incomprehensible, that the human mind was lost in endeavoring to examine it. Some supposed that this unknown power, whose strength nothing could enhance and nothing diminish, which could not be checked, and which could not check itself, was destined to lead human society to complete and final dissolution . . . On the other hand, others discerned the hand of God in the Revolution, and inferred a gracious design of Providence to people France and the world with a new and better species.[1]

The political framework

By the end of 1977, the Pahlavi state, centred on the person of Mohammad Reza Shah, appeared secure and well entrenched. Critics had either been silenced or co-opted, and economic growth, while erratic and occasionally showing signs of strain, appeared to provide its own justification for a continuation of Pahlavi rule. A substantial increase in oil revenues in December 1973 provided the Shah with a financial cushion his predecessors could only envy. Yet the surfeit of money which had been injected into the Iranian economy after 1974 only seemed to accentuate and exaggerate the worst excesses of the regime. Not only were income disparities growing at an exponential rate, but corruption (especially at the higher levels of the regime), normally tolerated as an accepted part of social and economic life, now grew to such proportions that even the tolerant considered it obscene. Particularly embarrassing for the regime were allegations of commissions in arms procurement, frequently involving senior army officers and tarnishing the reputation of an institution regularly heralded as the epitome of national integrity.[2] That such payments were involved in the procurement of weapons many critics of the regime considered unnecessary if not altogether harmful to the economic prosperity of the country, only confirmed the belief that such purchases were fraudulent and of more benefit to the US arms industry. While income disparities were nothing new in Iran – and monarchists complained that critics talked as if the Shah had invented poverty – it was the increasing absence of social safety valves to contain and control the poverty which resulted in heightened anger among sections of the populace and a growing belief that social justice had been sacrificed at the altar of rapid economic growth.

Before the White Revolution, the landed aristocracy, while imperfect, had often acted as important social intermediaries, mediating and managing the difficulties of their particular constituents.[3] Wealth might be unevenly distributed, but the local peasant or labourer knew where to turn for financial assistance, a loan or political mediation. What had existed was a highly decentralised and deeply personal network of social relations in which every landlord theoretically operated as the local 'king' or 'shah'. This, as noted, was certainly one way to interpret the term 'Shahanshah' or King of Kings, regarded by many in the West as highly pretentious given its associations with the divine in Christianity. This decentralised interpretation would have regarded the Shah as a sort of *primus inter pares*. Mohammad Reza Shah, of course, did not share this interpretation of his title. It is certainly true that his father introduced the ideas of the modern state and remained scathing about the idle *ayans*, but he remained resolutely patrimonial in his own approach to monarchy. In accumulating vast amounts of land, he implicitly recognised the right of others to retain land as well. The primacy of Reza Shah was established in such a way that few dared consider themselves 'equals'. As we have seen, Mohammad Reza Shah, having survived a period of uncertainty and consolidation, desired to be a revolutionary monarch. In the White Revolution, he sought to eliminate the political power of the landed aristocracy, whom he considered reactionary, and to further centralise control under his person through an ever expanding bureaucracy. In pursuing this process of centralisation and personalisation – a totalising process which he was able to carry out to much greater effect than his father – the Shah succeeded in emphasising a growing sense of alienation between state and society.[4] In seeking to embody the state, and in centralising power and authority within his person, the Shah ironically succeeded in 'impersonalising' the state.

The late Pahlavi state could therefore be characterised as a curious amalgam of traditional and modern structures, embodying the personal aspects of a traditional state by identifying the dynasty and the person of the monarch with the state, while at the same time projecting to the mass of Iranians an intensely depersonalised state in the form of a burgeoning bureaucracy. By the end of the 1970s, the Pahlavi state incorporated the worst aspects of 'tradition' and 'modernity', with its central contradiction being exemplified in the person of the Shah himself, who attempted to convince an increasingly incredulous public that he was a revolutionary dynast, guided both by God and by an interpretation of radical socialism. That he failed to convince his public reflected his growing alienation and the insularity of the court, whose preoccupation with obscure court factional rivalries blinded the Shah and his acolytes to the storm brewing beyond the palace walls. By being both willing and able, in the late 1970s, to impose his idea of the state onto society and to demand social conformity to the state, the Shah succeeded in provoking a social reaction of unprecedented force in modern Iranian history.

In many ways, the Shah was a victim of his own success. But it was a success that he could not understand, and it was this incomprehension which fatally hindered his ability to act, and thus sealed his fate and that of his dynasty. The White Revolution had altered the fabric of Iranian society in ways which the Shah and his supporters had failed to predict. It was certainly true that the country had benefited from economic growth, but this had been both uneven and erratic, and accompanied by severe social and economic tensions. These tensions, exemplified by the migration of peasants to the cities, were inadequately disguised by the dramatic increase in oil revenues. Oil revenues certainly protected the Shah from criticism in so far as they allowed the Pahlavi state a degree of autonomy which was dangerously disconnected.[5] Far from recognising the need for a measure of accountability to his ever cynical and fractious public, the Shah used the oil revenues to compound his error by further developing his image of 'Divine righteousness', a 'myth of the saviour', which his people found difficult to relate to.

This social disconnection was accentuated, as noted above, by that other key development of the White Revolution – the elimination of the landed aristocracy as a mediating class, and their replacement by a centralised bureaucracy administered by technocrats with a heightened sense of 'rationalism' and little taste for the personal networks which had so characterised local politics. These disenfranchised aristocrats, along with the *ulema*, and to some extent the *bazaar* merchants, were treated with varying degrees of contempt by the parvenu late Pahlavi state establishment, on whom they would ultimately wreak an intensely personal revenge. These 'traditionalists' were to be joined in 1978 by the new left, the successors to the National Front and the Tudeh Party, a new generation of politicised students bred on a diet of rigorous religious nationalism and revolutionary rhetoric, and influenced by the French student uprisings of 1968. These were the products not only of the White Revolution's education policies, with many having received state scholarships to study abroad, but crucially of the Shah's own brand of messianic leadership. The Shah's inability to retain the loyalty of these particular beneficiaries of the Pahlavi state remains a damning indictment of his failure to convince and a lasting testament to the essential fragility of his authority. This inability to communicate is all the more remarkable when one considers that many of his student critics came from affluent backgrounds, enjoyed a good education and were generally cosmopolitan in their outlook. They were, in many ways, his natural constituents. As de Tocqueville noted astutely, 'It is not always in going from bad to worse that one falls into revolution'.[6] The Shah simply could not understand that in raising the political consciousness of his subjects he would have to renegotiate the social contract with them. Gratitude could not be eternal.

Yet none of these material, nor indeed ideological, changes in the nature of Iranian society and politics made the revolution which erupted in 1978–79 inevitable. While they may point to the weakness of the state, they could not determine its collapse. Few 'revolutions' are anticipated and are only accorded that accolade with the benefit of hindsight, a hindsight frequently tainted by

trauma or elation. 'Inevitability' is the means by which the victors rationalise and legitimise a political upheaval, ensuring that an extraordinary event is
accepted as part of the natural order of development. For the losers, it justifies
and explains failure and crucially obviates the need for responsibility. While
the victors will often look to providence, the losers look to more malevolent
third parties. Paradoxically therefore, it is an exercise in rationalisation which
discards the need for rational (sober) analysis. In truth, the Islamic Revolution
was a product of uniquely Iranian circumstances, a coincidence of interests and
developments founded on a historical inheritance, and dependent ultimately
on the actions and inactions of the one man who, by his own volition, formed
the linchpin of the Pahlavi state. In analysing the Islamic Revolution in Iran, the
apparent inevitability of structural determination should not obscure the essential spontaneity of individual agency.

Reality bites: the fall of the Shah

On 31 December 1977, President Jimmy Carter and his wife alighted in Tehran
to spend New Year's Eve with the Shah and the Empress Farah. It was a visit
intended to signal the consolidation of a traditional relationship that had been
unusually strained since Carter's inauguration the previous January. Many considered that the advent of a Democratic president would make life more difficult
for the Shah although, Kennedy excepted, the Shah had not found his relations
significantly affected by the party affiliation of the sitting American president.
The Qarani affair had, after all, occurred during the Eisenhower administration. Nevertheless, the Shah had enjoyed an unusually empathic relationship
with the Nixon administration, which continued largely unchanged under
Ford. Observers watched with interest to see how the Shah would handle the
transition. Carter's avowed determination to pursue human rights around the
world was regarded by many opponents of the Shah as an indication that the
relationship would no longer be so intimate. Yet the view that Carter pressured
the Shah to impose reforms, in much the same way as Kennedy had apparently
done, is largely erroneous. In the first place, the Shah's perception of himself
and his role in the world, to say nothing of his relationship with the United
States, had been completely transformed since the late 1950s. Moreover, the
United States was aware of this change and was unlikely to 'dictate' policy to
the Shah. Evidence suggests that the Shah came to the conclusion that some
measure of reform would be required to secure the succession, aware as he
was that he had been diagnosed with cancer. This illness gave him a sense
of urgency and undoubtedly compounded any insecurities he possessed, but
again it is important not to exaggerate the implications of the illness. The Shah
tinkered with reform and tested the social atmosphere by allowing a measure
of political freedom. But as his decision to launch the Rastakhiz Party proved,
he intended to retain control and his abrupt imposition of the Imperial calendar simply confirmed to many observers that he was becoming lost within the
deluded wilderness of his own imagination.

For those who hoped that the new US administration would temper the Shah's ambitions, 1977 was to prove a year of mixed signals, symbolised by the Shah's visit to Washington in November of that year. Carter talked of human rights, but in fact pursued a policy very similar to that of his predecessors. The visit to Washington seemed emblematic of the consolidation of relations, although the dispersal of demonstrators with tear gas had resulted in the unintended consequence of the Shah and President Carter, along with their consorts, mopping their eyes as the gas drifted over to the podium. Broadcast in Iran, the sight of the monarch and his wife crying on the White House lawn looked not only bizarre but deeply humiliating and critics eager to over-rationalise quickly concluded that the event had been a deliberate snub to the Shah and a signal to opponents of the regime that all was not well with the US–Iran relationship. That opponents of the regime could take heart from such an occurrence was indicative of the Shah's inability to communicate with his people. In the absence of reliable news, people invented their own truths. Nevertheless, Carter's decision to spend New Year's Eve with the Shah in Tehran would seem to indicate that the key actors were oblivious to the signals they were sending. At the dinner, Carter was effusive, and used a phrase much appreciated and used by the Shah himself. Because of the great leadership of the Shah, Carter noted, Iran was 'an island of stability in one of the more troubled areas of the world'. This, the President added, was a great tribute to the Shah's leadership, 'and to the respect, admiration and love which your people give to you'.[7] Few speeches can have enjoyed worse timing. Within a week, the extent of the people's love for their Shah would be severely tested – and found wanting.

The event that was to lead to the unwinding of the Pahlavi state machinery and the flight of the Shah into exile for the second time in his reign, appears in retrospect to have been the most trivial of misjudgements. Yet it reflected the heightened insularity of the court, the narrowness of political life and its conduct beyond the reach and comprehension of ordinary Iranians. Apparently reassured by Carter's generous praise, the Shah decided to sanction the printing of an article in the newspaper *Etela'at*, ostensibly responding to the latest vitriolic commentary emanating from Ayatollah Khomeini, situated beyond his political reach in Najaf. It is not clear whether the Shah had a direct hand in dictating the response, or indeed whether he had done more than complain of his 'turbulent priest'. How this was to be achieved was not necessarily clear, and it appears that the Minister of Court, Hoveida, was anxious to please the Shah and dictated a suitably vitriolic response.[8] All that is known for certain is that an article outlining the Shah's beliefs, his conception of the historical narrative, the opposition of the 'red and the black', and the particularly wicked and reactionary role of the Ayatollah Khomeini was dispatched from the Ministry of Court to the Ministry of Information with instructions that it be published. This relatively short column, 'Iran and the Colonisation of the Red and the Black',[9] was a concise summary of the imperial myth and, apart from the attack on Ayatollah Khomeini, consisted largely of repetitions of the Shah's imperial vision. For those within the increasingly insular and isolated political establishment, including the then Minister of Information, Dariush Homayun, the publication of the article was a matter of routine,[10] so routine in fact that Homayun neglected to actually read the article before sending it on to the relevant newspapers, only one of which – *Etela'at* – actually had the courage to publish it. Nevertheless, few could have anticipated the scale of the reaction and the momentum towards revolution which would result. There had been murmurs of discontent, especially on university campuses during the last months of 1977, but nobody had considered these dangerous to the stability of the regime. At most they were regarded as natural outbursts of frustration which were to be expected from a society which had had its political freedoms suppressed for so long. Indeed some welcomed the social disturbances as healthy for the body politic, and there were certainly indications that 'protest' had been encouraged among government officials and members of the Rastakhiz Party.

That the encouragement of official dissent should have coincided with the emergence of genuine opposition on the streets was, to say the least, unfortunate timing, and explains much about the government's contradictory approach during the critical final year of the regime. In short, the Islamic Revolution gathered momentum because the political elite were divided; engrossed in their own political rivalries, they failed to recognise the consequences of their actions. The article dispatched by Hoveida to Dariush Homayun was itself indicative of this trend, but far more significant was the decision by the Shah some years earlier to allow the formation of a separate 'court' around the Empress.[11] Of all the attempts to 'liberalise', this was perhaps the most symbolic. Supporters of the regime who recognised the need for reform understood that the Empress, popular among the people, harboured more liberal thoughts than her husband (to whom she had unique access) and therefore was considered the best means by which reform could be achieved. The Shah, on the other hand, as clearly expressed in his interview with the Italian journalist Oriana Fallaci, did not take the Empress's role seriously. The Regency was a public relations exercise designed to show the Shah's respect for women's equality. He had no intention of relinquishing any real power. Whether tangible reform was ever a possibility, the establishment of a separate court, a focal point around which critics of the Shah (if not the Pahlavi state) could gather, was to have serious consequences for the development and application of policy. In the first place, the Shah's supporters became concerned at the Empress Farah's willingness to co-opt left-leaning intellectuals, some of whom harboured ambitions of displacing the Shah with the Empress as Regent until the Crown Prince could come of age. If the Shah could be encouraged to abdicate, it was thought, a transition to a more constitutional monarchy could be assured, securing the succession and ensuring the continuation of the dynasty.[12] As the decade developed, it appears that the Empress, not unlike her husband, may have succumbed to the flattering suggestions of her courtiers. It soon became apparent to some observers that the Empress's court was a government-in-waiting.[13]

One of the first serious indications of this division came with the convening of the Shiraz Arts Festival in the autumn of 1977. Since the arts and culture were the natural preserve of the Empress, her supporters were the principal architects of a festival whose chief aim was to challenge and extend the cultural horizons of ordinary Iranians. For liberally minded technocrats educated on the Parisian Left Bank, it was the natural function of art to challenge conceptions and it was entirely acceptable to achieve this end by shocking the observer.[14] The value of such strategies is vigorously debated in Western societies to this day, and the decision to apply it to a traditional Muslim society can only be regarded as a misjudgement of enormous proportions. As the British Ambassador Sir Anthony Parsons noted in his memoirs, the Shah seemed curiously ambivalent about the consequences of the festival, which raised considerable religious ire:

> The Shiraz Festival of 1977 excelled itself in its insults to Iranian moral values. For example according to an eye-witness, a play was enacted which represented, as I was told, the evils of military rule and occupation. The theatre company had booked a shop in the main shopping street of Shiraz for the performance, which was played half inside the shop and half on the pavement outside. One scene, played on the pavement, involved a rape which was performed in full (no pretence) by a man (either naked or without any trousers, I forget which) on a woman who had her dress ripped off her by her attacker. The denouement of the play, also acted on the pavement, included a scene where one of the characters dropped his trousers and inserted a stage pistol up his backside, presumably in order to add verisimilitude to his suicide. The effect of this bizarre and disgusting extravaganza on the good citizens of Shiraz, going about their evening shopping, can hardly be imagined. This grotesquerie aroused a storm of protest which reached the press and television. I remember mentioning it to the Shah, adding that, if the same play had been put on, say, in the main street of Winchester (Shiraz is the Iranian equivalent of a cathedral city), the actors and sponsors would have found themselves in trouble. The Shah laughed indulgently.[15]

While the alternative court was pursuing its own agenda, the Shah himself was faced in 1977 with the loss of the one courtier whom many considered possessed the strength of conviction to speak honestly to him – Asadollah Alam. Alam had finally succumbed to cancer in 1977, and was replaced by the sycophantic Hoveida, whose rivalry with his successor Jamshid Amuzegar the Shah, in good patrimonial style, fully encouraged. Observers noted that Hoveida's displacement could have been taken as an encouraging sign had he not immediately been appointed Minister of Court. Hoveida, a cosmopolitan, well-educated technocrat, was arguably more popular with foreign ambassadors than with the Iranians themselves, not so much because of his personal affability (which he indeed possessed in abundance) but because of his perceived ineffectiveness. It was simply inconceivable to many Iranians that anyone could survive 13 years as the Shah's prime minister without being intimately complicit in the repression associated with the regime. The article which Hoveida summarily dispatched for publication was emblematic of his style and his earnest desire to please his master.

It may have been surmised, with some justification, that in comparison with the Shiraz Arts Festival, the article would be received as a mere footnote. After all, religious agitation had failed to incite the crowds in Shiraz. Now, however, the response was more virulent, and reflected the personal loyalties Ayatollah Khomeini enjoyed despite some 14 years in exile.[16]

This loyalty had been carefully cultivated, and far from being the result of an irrational response to religious charisma – although this played a role – it was a direct consequence of Khomeini's political acumen. While his supporters like to lend an air of providence to Khomeini's imminent return to Iran, there is scant contemporary evidence that the Ayatollah himself, stubborn and determined as he was, had any inkling of the developments that were to occur around his name in the year to come. Indeed by all accounts, and despite the fact that according to the Muslim lunar calendar the faithful were approaching the year 1400 (considered auspicious by some), Khomeini was distinctly melancholy at the beginning of 1978. He had just suffered the loss of his eldest son, Mustapha, in what his supporters regarded as mysterious circumstances.[17] Nevertheless, far from being forgotten as the Shah hoped, Khomeini made sure that his messages were heard, especially among the young. One of the unforeseen consequences of the Algiers Accord, signed with Iraq in 1975, was that pilgrimage routes to Najaf and Kerbala were once again available to Iranians, some of whom took the opportunity to visit the 'Imam', as he was increasingly termed by his closest supporters. Not only did they bring news of Iran to Khomeini but they acted as a conduit to Iran for his sermons, usually via mass-produced tapes. It has already been noted that Khomeini had successfully captured the nationalist initiative in the aftermath of the 'American Capitulations' in 1964. It was a measure of his political skill, and the Shah's political myopia, that he never really lost this initiative. As the Shah secured his hold on the political life of the country, and the secular nationalists and left-wing parties were either suppressed or co-opted, the Khomeini option became increasingly attractive. This was especially true of the more idealistic young, who were eager for change and disillusioned with the leadership available to them within the country. Khomeini was extremely careful to maintain a core of support among students, acutely aware of their potential role as the vanguard of his movement.[18] That seemingly progressive young radicals should be held in thrall to the musings of a traditional aged cleric is at first glance odd, and there were many among the establishment who found the alliance on anything other than irrational ideological grounds incomprehensible. On the contrary, the alliance between the 'red' and the 'black', as the Shah liked to characterise the situation, was founded on a profound (if occasionally awkward) coincidence of interests which reflected the changing intellectual climate of Iran in this period.

Khomeini was an unusually unorthodox mullah, in many ways thoroughly modern in outlook, whose growing popularity reflected not only his determination to confront the political and ideological challenges facing Iran, but also the changing intellectual climate which witnessed the growth of religious discourse within a political environment. As with other countries in the Middle East, secular nationalism was proving an inadequate remedy for the myriad ills of the state. Eloquent intellectuals pointed to its artificial nature and its lack of authenticity in an Iranian context. As we have seen, writers such as Jalal Ale Ahmad complained bitterly about the 'Westoxication' of Iran and the cultural pollution this entailed. Drawing on the Western Marxist tradition, Ale Ahmad complained about the 'treason of the intellectuals', arguing that the modern Iranian intellectual had forsaken his political responsibilities. This was a theme taken up by other writers who began to distinguish between two types of intellectuals – those who abjured social responsibility, and the real intellectuals who pursued social and political justice.[19] This political transformation was assisted by the reintroduction of religious discourse which added a moral dimension to the struggle. Yet this new religious discourse, married as it was to politics, was practical, not theoretical. Rejecting superstitious, legalistic dogma, religious thinkers, in particular those from a lay background, argued for the revitalisation of a philosophical and spiritual Islam, which would act as a moral impetus to political action. Drawing on writers such as Franz Fanon, the popular lay religious thinker, Ali Shariati argued that a material revolution had to be predicated on a moral and ideological revolution, which in Iran's case could only be achieved through the medium of authentic Shi'ism.[20] This 'revolutionary' Islam, while often eclectic in its construction (Shariati's influence is often considered a product of the eloquence of his articulation rather than in the rigorous internal cohesion of his thought) enjoyed a prestigious intellectual pedigree in Iran, stretching back in the first instance to Jamal al Din al Afghani in the nineteenth century.

Far from being immune to these changes, Khomeini was well aware of them and, contrary to the image of turbanned austerity which he projected to great effect to his traditional constituents, his more youthful adherents saw in him a mullah who usefully transcended both the modern and the traditional. He famously taught Western philosophy, much to the indignation of his fellow ayatollahs who considered it blasphemous, if only to repudiate it,[21] and kept abreast of the writings of thinkers such as Ale Ahmad and Shariati. Indeed, until Shariati's resolute rejection of the utility of the *ulema* to religious progress, he had co-operated extensively with one of Khomeini's chief supporters and arguably the ideological architect of the Islamic Revolution, Ayatollah (*ostad*) Motahhari. Motahhari, more than any other cleric, sought to understand and deconstruct Marxist thought, incorporating those elements he thought useful, while rejecting its atheism. In this way, he attempted to draw the young away from vulgar Marxism by arguing that, within certain limits, Islam was inclusive of other ideas. He famously noted that he had more time for Marx and Engels than the average Muslim, since at least they had tried to find solutions for the ills of the world. This brand of 'Islamic Marxism' was not the contradiction in terms its critics liked to portray, however uncomfortable the marriage might have been. It was rather a complex synthesis of ideas which, while rough around the edges, possessed the immediate attraction of reconciling two traditions into an authentic whole regarded as both national and legitimate. Khomeini became the personalisation of this synthesis, symbolising and in some ways possessing both its potency and its inherent contradictions. For the traditional masses of religious Iranians, he represented all that was traditional and authentic about Shi'a Iranian culture. For the young idealistic students who were to become the ideological vanguard of the movement, he represented unorthodoxy and rebelliousness. They saw him as a champion of national independence and integrity. Khomeini did not simply think about the world, he wanted to change it. This was an immensely attractive mantra to the young. He symbolised the force of 'religious nationalism', a somewhat hybrid construction to those who grew up on a diet of rigorously 'secular' nationalism, but an entirely logical and rational development to those Iranians who believed that national resurrection could only be achieved by a return to cultural authenticity, of which Shi'ism was an integral part.

It is important to remember that the movement which resulted in the overthrow of the Shah was fundamentally nationalist in orientation, suffused with a righteous religious energy which sanctified the nation. That this intellectual symbiosis was as yet an incomplete, awkward and highly fluid dynamic was paradoxically in 1978 a source of peculiar strength. Ambiguity allowed a disparate plurality of groups to unite against the Shah. A lack of definition allowed differences to be buried in the interests of the immediate focus of discontent. The Shah was the real leader of the Islamic Revolution. His actions and inactions dictated the pace and development of the movement in 1978. The first few months of 1978 were characterised by inaction. The Shah seemed disinterested in the discontent being expressed on the streets, limited in the first instance to Qom, and the authorities were convinced that any unrest – a product of the tentative liberalisation as they saw it – was a healthy reaction which could easily be contained. The problem was that the security forces had not been trained for this new liberal environment and, far from 'containing' the demonstrators, opened fire on them. A number of deaths and injuries resulted and, while the figures are disputed, it was a qualitative rather than quantitative defining moment. It should be remembered that it took the death of one religious student in 1906 to catalyse and define the Constitutional Revolution. Moreover, as in 1906, the authorities found themselves confronted by protests from other senior members of the *ulema*, in particular Grand Ayatollah Shariatmadari (not a known firebrand), who openly condemned the shooting of demonstrators in Qom. More ominous still, and yet seemingly unnoticed by the authorities, was the subsequent decision by members of the Tehran *bazaari* to close their shops on 12 January to protest against the shootings. For the first time since 1963, the *bazaar* and the *ulema* appeared to be acting in concert. In the absence of any serious response by the authorities, the movement continued to gather momentum. Following the 40-day mourning period for the deaths of the Qom demonstrators, further riots broke out in late February and spread to Tabriz.[22] More casualties resulted in yet another cycle of protest in March and May, moving from provincial towns to finally erupt in the capital itself. Typically for a highly centralised state, it was only when the disturbances reached Tehran that the authorities decided to take firm action, and now they appeared to overreact.

Having been almost dismissive to begin with, and having allowed the movement to gather pace, the government now decided to deploy tanks on the streets of Tehran. Far from being an intimidating show of force, it convinced the most dedicated revolutionaries that the government was frightened. By summer in any case, the 'myth of heroic resistance' could only benefit and be fuelled by signs of government repression, and nothing symbolised this more than the presence of tanks on the streets of the capital.

The extreme reactions of government reflected the divisions within it. Hawks around the Shah wanted a more vigorous response, anxious not to lose the initiative and acutely aware that 'the most dangerous moment for a bad government is usually when it begins to reform itself'.[23] The real absurdity of the government's response to the demonstrations, and a salutary lesson in the proximity of the sublime to the ridiculous, was that the 'left hand' (represented by the Empress's court) was trying to convince the 'right hand' (the Shah and the hawks) that what was occurring was a natural and healthy response to 'reform'. There was nothing wrong in people letting off steam, and in fact to do otherwise might be more dangerous. The result of this persuasive argument was that one half of the political establishment was pursuing reform at the very time large segments of society were fomenting revolution. This was not so much a case of reform preceding revolution, as being coterminous with it, an extreme example of the Tocquevellian maxim. Meanwhile the hawks could not understand the Shah's inactivity, and this only increased levels of anxiety and panic. When he did decide to act, he tended to overreact. Divisions between the two sides were undoubtedly heightened by the suspicions with which each observed the other. The 'radical chic' doubted the efficacy of brute force and regarded it, not without justification, as unsustainable in the long run and damaging to the monarchy. The hawks were profoundly suspicious of the 'dangerously liberal' tendencies of the Empress and her supporters, fearing that their real intention was to seek a transfer of power to themselves.

The deployment of tanks did little to assuage popular anger, but did significantly raise the political temperature. Those who had hitherto paid little attention to developments now began to take note. It was too early to talk of 'revolution', but, by June, it was fair to say that localised disturbances were being transformed into a 'crisis'. The demonstrations became so frequent as to belie any pattern, and the least excuse was used to organise yet another anti-Shah gathering. They reached a peak in August in Isfahan, when a senior cleric called for the end of the monarchy, and martial law was declared in the city. Far worse, however, was the news on 19 August that a fire had broken out in Cinema Rex in Abadan, killing nearly 400 people. The arson attack had been launched by religious zealots determined to eradicate moral corruption, but the popular belief was that it had been caused by the state security apparatus, SAVAK. Such was the public distrust of the Pahlavi state that unsubstantiated allegations of this nature could pass as truth. The political establishment grew concerned at the apparent inability of the Shah, at the head of the 'fifth largest armed forces in the world', to stop the unravelling of his regime. By the end of August the Pahlavi elite had begun to take out insurance policies – the possibility of vacations abroad was investigated, and gradually money began to flow out of the country. The ease with which the Pahlavi elite were willing to abandon the Shah has been commented on by several observers, not least the Shah himself, who later, in response to a journalist's question over why he did not mobilise his supporters as Charles de Gaulle had done in the Champs-Elysées, pointed out that this was exactly his problem, his supporters *were* in the Champs-Elysées! Yet while the politically (and financially) unscrupulous were not few among the elite, the fact that the Shah had fled once before when faced with a crisis did not inspire confidence. What was needed at this stage was firm and decisive leadership of the uncompromising sort Khomeini was in actual fact offering his supporters. Instead, the Shah, determined to behave in a balanced and reasonable manner, appeared ambivalent and dangerously out of touch. The cautioning influence of the Empress's men was now being compounded by a growing personal realisation that there was a problem on the streets which contradicted all his meticulously constructed convictions about the 'special relationship' between himself and his people. The consequence was a mixture of denial and fatalism, neither of which was productive, especially when all looked to the Shah as the linchpin of the system.

The immediate result of the Cinema Rex fire was the dismissal of the Amuzegar government and the decision to recall an elder statesman, Jafar Sharif Emami, and instruct him to form a 'government of national reconciliation'. Sharif Emami, while personally close to the Shah, was not regarded as an obsequious technocrat, and more importantly was seen as a religious man with strong connections to the *ulema*. It was a tentative and somewhat lukewarm effort to dampen the religious momentum of the demonstrations, and the new Prime Minister responded by immediately restoring the Muslim calendar (so presumptuously dismissed by the Shah in 1976) and closing down all gambling houses and casinos. Furthermore, Sharif Emami moved to censor publications considered injurious to Islam, released a number of prominent religious leaders from internal exile and liberalised the press so that analytical discussions of events starting with the publication of the infamous article were widely aired. With the abrupt legalisation of a number of political parties (including a newly revitalised National Front), the consequence of these imaginative and somewhat liberal policies, which in retrospect should have been applied some years earlier, was to provide fuel in abundance for the revolutionary funeral pyre of the dynasty. The problem was not so much that opposition groups were able to vent their frustrations and air their views, but that this dynamic intellectual debate about the future of the country exposed the ideological vacuity of the Pahlavi state. In short, the Pahlavi inner circle had nothing to contribute to the debate. This may have had as much to do with the acute absence of credible advocates as with the paucity of material, which by any objective standards should have been substantial.

For all the apparent sincerity of the Sharif Emami government, which in any case many doubted, the concessions simply made the opposition bolder.

Students, Islamists, the left and the National Front took the opportunities afforded to reiterate their case and to stand firm on their demand which, as Khomeini articulated with uncompromising starkness, was the restoration of the Constitution. Khomeini resolutely declared that there was nothing to negotiate and that all these so-called concessions had been guaranteed by the Constitution in the first place – these were rights which should be implemented irrespective of negotiation. Khomeini's clear if ruthless logic stood in stark contrast to the ambiguity being expressed by the Shah. In practical terms, the riots continued and the Shah now decided, somewhat belatedly, that enough was enough and in early September declared martial law for a duration of six months in a number of cities including Tehran. Sharif Emami's concessionary government was juxtaposed with the reality of martial law. Unsurprisingly, people ignored martial law. Many have subsequently observed that this marked the beginning of the end for the Shah. If the threat of force no longer cowed the population, then actual force would have to be used to reassert Pahlavi authority, but the Shah, in spite of his wife's influence at this stage, simply did not possess the moral or political fibre to do this. When the Shah heard that demonstrators had been shot and killed in Jaleh Square in Tehran, apparently following the orders of the far more ruthless military governor of Tehran, General Oveissi, he was reportedly horrified, but then made the catastrophic mistake of prevaricating. This prevarication was all the worse because, as many conjectured (entirely erroneously), the Shah had been directing the shooting from a helicopter.[24] If the opposition naturally exaggerated the deaths (the government figure of 86 was remarkably close to the later conclusion that 88 had in fact been killed) the fact that blood had been spilt in significant numbers was certainly a watershed.[25] The nature of his monarchy would never be the same. But had the Shah sanctioned a ruthless suppression it is possible, even at this late stage, that the momentum could have been stalled and a measure of stability restored. The avowed revolutionaries were certainly stung by the events of Jaleh Square and paused to consider the consequences of their actions. In retrospect it was probably the last opportunity for the Shah to take back the initiative and reassert a semblance of authority. Unfortunately for his dynasty, he was the first to blink and what moral authority he retained collapsed. According to some reports, for the first time crowds began to chant 'Death to the Shah'.

The Jaleh Square 'massacre' epitomised the contradictions in the Shah's approach. Even those who tended to sympathise with the monarchy failed to see the logic of imposing two orders, one civilian and conciliatory, another military and confrontational. It was a policy which resulted in solidifying the opposition, in so far as the conciliation appeared weak, and alienating supporters, in that military government exemplified the repression so often alluded to by the opposition, and undermined any credibility the Shah may have had as an 'enlightened despot'. As the number of demonstrations mounted, the government made yet another mistake by persuading Saddam Hussein to remove

Khomeini. Saddam Hussein characteristically offered to dispose of the wayward Ayatollah altogether, but the Shah demurred and encouraged the Iraqi leader simply to remove him from Iraq. Khomeini first tried to leave for Kuwait, but the authorities there were less than enthusiastic about welcoming such a contentious visitor, and Khomeini was finally persuaded to make the fateful journey to France. In a marvellous example of the wonders of modern communication, and a prescient indication of the consequences of globalisation, Khomeini found that, with easy access to the modern mass media, he was more accessible to his Iranian followers than he had been sitting in Najaf 100 miles from the Iranian border. Established in Neauphle-le-Chateau, in the suburbs of Paris, and carefully nurtured by his largely French-educated supporters, Khomeini now indulged himself, prudently and somewhat enigmatically, in the avid attentions of the Western media, curious to understand (however simplistically) the esoteric power of a 'medieval cleric'.

Other French-educated intellectuals were having less success in determining the best course of action for the Shah. With Khomeini taking an increasingly prominent role, members of the National Front went to Paris to pay court; by the end of October it became clear that they were demanding an end to the monarchy. This marked a shift in the political temperature; not only was there now a formal link between the religious and secular nationalist leadership, but also the apparent demand for 'unconditional surrender' imposed upon the Shah. Few would have realised that this was exactly what he was about to do. Faced with a strike by oil workers in mid-October (which at a stroke deprived the regime of its autonomy,[26] and indeed exposed the real fragility of the Shah's power) and with continuing demonstrations of gathering intensity, the Shah dismissed the Sharif Emami government on 5 November. The following day he imposed a military government under the leadership of the one general many recognised as inherently incapable of ruthlessness, General Azhari, and at the same time took the fateful decision to broadcast to the nation. He began:

> Dear Iranian people, in the climate of liberalisation which gradually began two years ago, you arose against oppression and corruption. The revolution of the Iranian people cannot fail to have my support as the monarch of Iran and as an Iranian.

He continued:

> I have heard the revolutionary message of you, the people, the Iranian nation. I am the guardian of the constitutional monarchy which is a God-given gift, a gift entrusted to the Shah by the people. I guarantee the safeguarding of what has been gained through your sacrifices. I guarantee that in the future the Iranian government will be divorced from tyranny and oppression and will be run on the basis of the Constitution and social justice . . . Remember that I stand by you in your revolution against colonialism, oppression and corruption. I will be with you in safeguarding our integrity and national

unity, the protection of Islamic precepts, the establishment of fundamental freedoms, and victory and in realising the demands and aspirations of the Iranian nation.[27]

This speech – in which the Shah, with audible nervousness, not only acknowledged (to the amazement of the general public) both his mistakes *and* the 'revolution', but sought to lead it – must rank as one of the most peculiar if not singularly stupid political speeches in recent history.[28] Up until 6 November, the vast majority of the Iranian public, outside the ideological vanguard of the opposition, had been unaware they were necessarily living through a 'revolution'. Now, everyone, including staunch monarchists, confronted the unsavoury reality of imminent revolution and a Shah who, far from defending their interests, appeared intent (contrary to all political logic) on 'switching sides' and leading it. It cannot have escaped the attention of many observers (the great mass of the politically uncommitted) that now might be the time to protect themselves (and their property) by joining the ostensibly 'winning' side. The Shah surrendered his state – from now on it was a matter of procedure.

Whether the speech was a cause or consequence of the final failure of communication, it seemed to mark the moment when the Shah lost control and became to all intents and purposes a political cipher.[29] Although the precise motivation is unclear, the decision to deliver the speech appears to have been imposed on him, reportedly unwillingly, by the advisers to the Empress.[30] Perhaps, while the 'Jacobins' were plotting in Paris, the heirs of Mirabeau were urging the king to ride the crest of the revolutionary wave.[31] The myth of the French Revolution can rarely have been evoked with more catastrophic consequences. While monarchists sought to analyse the speech in favourable terms, arguing that it indicated the special relationship between the *Shahanshah* and the people, the revolutionaries recognised it for the mortal wound that it was.[32] As Khomeini announced contemptuously, 'This is the end for the Shah. The monarchy will be eradicated. Pahlavi forced himself upon the Iranian people; no one wanted him', adding for good measure, 'The Shah lives in a morbid dreamworld'.[33]

Confirmation of the regime's determination to commit political suicide was provided by the decision, on the day after the Shah's speech, to arrest a wide range of the establishment, while at the same time granting amnesties to those who had been convicted of agitating against the state.[34] The diversity of the individuals arrested served only to further unnerve and frighten members of the Pahlavi elite, whose trust in the ability of the Shah to protect them against the revolutionary onslaught was all but vanishing. Not only were the obvious candidates for arrest, such as the former head of the state security organisation (SAVAK), General Nematollah Nasiri, taken into custody, but also the hapless Minister for Information, Dariush Homayun, who had been instructed earlier that year to oversee the publication of the now notorious article against Khomeini. On 8 November, Amir Abbas Hoveyda, the originator of the article, and former prime minister, was summarily arrested.[35] Such political heavyweights were accompanied to the cells by a raft of second-tier officials, such as the former secretary of the Imperial Club and the former secretary to the Asian Games Committee.[36] The extensive nature of the arrests (in large part on allegations of corruption) and the manner in which they were conducted (Nasiri, who was Ambassador to Pakistan, was summoned home and then arrested), simply accentuated the sense of insecurity and hopelessness felt by the regime's supporters. Depending on one's definition of corruption, the net could be cast wide, although few believed it would reach the Imperial family itself. Indeed, much to general bewilderment and no little amusement, the Imperial family now took it upon itself to express its religious devotion with a much-publicised trip by the Empress to the 'holy places' in Iraq, where she was granted an awkward audience with the determinedly non-political cleric, Grand Ayatollah Khoie.[37] Homayun was later to describe, with some justification, the juxtaposition of the arrest of the regime's supporters with the release of its opponents as 'perverse'.[38] Needless to say, many members of the political elite decided that now was the time to cash in their 'insurance' policies, and rumours abounded of the immense flow of capital out of the country.[39]

While, to be sure, leaders of the National Front were also arrested, their incarceration proved short-lived, released as they were less than one month after their arrest. This was probably an attempt to diffuse tension during the holy month of Moharram, which had begun on 2 December, and would reach a climax on the Shi'a festivals of Tasu'a and Ashura, which commemorated the martyrdom of Imam Hussein, the Prophet's grandson. Fearing the worst, the government first tried to ban any commemorative marches, although given the difficulty in maintaining martial law and the accompanying curfew, this option seemed impractical. In the end the government decided to sanction organised marches, but sought to co-ordinate with the opposition to ensure that they were peaceful. The marches which were organised for 9 and 10 December proved to be the largest witnessed in Iran, or indeed in any other state, in recent times.[40] Some argued that two million people (nearly half the population of Tehran) had participated and whatever the real figures the crowds were sufficiently large to have impressed one notable foreign observer who commented on the unique expression of the 'collective will' that he had witnessed.[41] Such mass participation may have had as much to do with a desire to be seen on the winning side, as with motivation, but the message for the Shah, along with other observers, was clear. Of equal interest, certainly to outside observers, was the general peacefulness of the demonstrations. There were undoubted expressions of violence, more often than not a consequence of nervous conscripts firing into the crowds, and there is little doubt that the various 'guerrilla' organisations, such as the Marxist *Fedayin-e Khalq* (composed mainly of ideologically motivated students), went out of their way to provoke trouble.[42] Yet, on the whole, the revolutionary movement was comparatively peaceful, and the overwhelming exhortations of the lay and religious leaders were for disciplined protest with minimum violence. Given the military's reluctance, or indeed, inability, to act, there was in fact little need for violent opposition. As Khomeini had earlier noted, 'It is my wish that the national movement should not assume the form of an armed struggle'.[43] Such attitudes drew widespread sympathies from the cohorts of foreign journalists flown in to witness a revolution, leading some to consider Khomeini the 'Gandhi' of Iran.[44] It may be conjectured that both sides were deterred from using force for fear of plunging the country into civil war. The revolutionary struggle became, in the purest sense, a clash of 'wills', as one side sought to gradually demoralise and ideologically undermine the other to the point of collapse, while the other had nothing to offer but ineffectual conciliation. For those hardliners in the armed forces the situation was one of extreme frustration, and while some soldiers did begin to desert, it is erroneous to suggest that the army collapsed. If the army proved less than decisive, this had more to do with the prevarications of its political masters, in particular its commander-in-chief, who by December had himself withdrawn from the political fray.

Faced with mass demonstrations against his rule, rumours circulated of the imminent declaration of a regency under the management of the Empress. These were rigorously denied.[45] While some still believed that the monarchy could be saved by the apparent popularity of the Empress, others (in particular in the army) thought it essential that the Shah remain firmly in place, even as a figurehead. Still others felt that the army had been neutered through the intervention of the Americans, who had now decided that a smooth transition of power should be encouraged so that their interests would be protected.[46] Massive economic and military investments ensured that developments in Iran were likely to be a major preoccupation in Western capitals, and there is little doubt (given the intimate ties between the Pahlavi elite and members of the US establishment) that the behaviour of the US government would be influential. But the suggestion proposed by staunch monarchists that the US, and to a greater or lesser extent Britain, was responsible for the Shah's fall, must be dismissed as another example of the ease with which some Iranians were anxious to abdicate responsibility for their own affairs. The Shah had demanded respect and independence of action; he could hardly expect the US administration to suddenly dictate policy to him now. In any case, attitudes to the West remained ambivalent. The government continued to criticise the BBC Persian Service for its apparent interference in domestic affairs by broadcasting Khomeini's speeches, the French government felt compelled to explain its continuing hospitality,[47] while at the same time vocal statements of support for the Shah by US and British officials were viewed as counter-productive.

Indeed, in many ways, the revolutionary movement had won the ideological battle abroad as well as in Iran. Many of its leaders were educated abroad. Karim Sanjabi, for instance, the leader of the National Front, was a fluent French speaker and regularly explained developments to the French press.[48] Many of Ayatollah Khomeini's advisers, such as Abol-Hassan Bani-Sadr, were French-educated and able to communicate effectively to their hosts, while another, Ibrahim Yazdi, had lived in Texas for the previous 15 years and understood the US media machinery. In much the same way as the Shah's regime had become alienated from Iranian society, so too did it lack the ability to communicate effectively with the social representatives of even its staunchest allies abroad.[49] While there had been periodic complaints against the Western press and liberal intelligentsia for much of the previous decade, this failure to connect now became an acute handicap.[50] Sufficient numbers of the Western intelligentsia were sympathetic to the revolutionary movement to convince local governments that, while the transition might be bumpy, it could certainly be managed. A more liberal democratic Iran, albeit with an Islamic flavour, would not necessarily be antithetical to Western interests, and indeed in the long run might prove to be beneficial. Iran, it was argued, could provide the model for transition from authoritarian rule that could be copied elsewhere in the 'free world'. This sympathetic relationship was reciprocated, to the extent of reiterating the distinction between hostile governments and sympathetic 'peoples'. Khomeini himself was induced on several occasions to emphasise the fact that, for all the anti-imperialist rhetoric, the revolution was not inherently anti-foreign. In an attempt to assuage German concerns, he stressed:

> We are not hostile towards foreigners. We never said anything about foreigners. We are hostile to those governments which have applied pressure on Iran and which have forced the Shah on Iran, and to governments at whose hands we have suffered. We are not hostile towards the citizens of these governments. As regards Germany, we are not hostile towards it. Everything this country is doing there and owns there that does not conflict with the interests of our country will remain free and protected.[51]

By the end of December it was clear that the Shah would have to leave. Some monarchists retained the illusion that the Shah's departure would ease the situation and facilitate the retention of the institution of the monarchy. But this was not 1953, and it was a measure of the Shah's success in identifying himself so intimately with the institution, that people talked of his departure as signalling the end of '2,500 years' of monarchy. Certainly there were those who recognised this and urged the Shah to stay and fight to the end. From their perspective, it would be better for the long-term survival of the institution if the Shah, at the very least, became a martyr to the cause he cherished. A variety of factors, however, construed to prevent this, including the Shah's own profound disillusionment, the belief among some supporters that his absence was essential and the insistence of Shahpour Bakhtiar (the former National Front politician who had been persuaded to form a new administration). Bakhtiar had agreed to break ranks on condition that the Shah did not interfere in domestic politics. Experience suggested that this could only be achieved if the Shah was physically absent from the scene. Willingly or unwillingly therefore (and reports remain contradictory), the *Shahanshah*, Light of the Aryans, departed Iran for the last time, ostensibly for a rest holiday, on 16 January 1979.[52] It was the end of an era.

The triumph of the revolution: the premiership of Bazargan

For Iranians, the departure of the Shah was a singular moment in their history. Ecstatic expressions of jubilation were mixed with a keen sense of anxiety. Few believed that the 'omnipotent' Shah, backed by the United States, could be so easily dismissed and removed from power with relatively little violence. Indeed for all the hyperbole of the day, later assessments suggested that a total of 2,781 people had died in the year of revolution to Khomeini's return in February 1979.[53] It was in political terms a remarkable achievement and it was a psychological watershed – tangible proof of the 'miracle' of the revolution that undoubtedly lent credence to the view, held by many Iranians, that there was a messianic quality to Khomeini's leadership. For the mass of the traditional constituency who supplied the raw manpower which dominated the streets, and who were fed on a regular diet of religious imagery, it was easy to see in Khomeini a new Moses throwing out the corrupt Pharaoh. While the 'messianism', which occasionally approximated the 'religious hysteria' alleged by critics of the revolution, was indeed pervasive among sections of traditional society, it would be a mistake to exaggerate its importance. It was certainly cultivated and encouraged, often by very rational critics of the monarchy, in order to enhance Khomeini's charismatic qualities, but it formed only one aspect of the revolutionary strategy and was certainly not the most important.[54] To suggest that the revolution succeeded through mass uncontrollable religious hysteria is to both over-dramatise and oversimplify the issue, and to characterise the revolution as an anomalous, irrational occurrence. Both sides of the revolutionary divide have been guilty of supporting such an argument, one in order to emphasise the inherent 'irrationality' of the movement, the other to stress Khomeini's divinely inspired charisma. In truth, Khomeini's success had less to do with Divine Providence – although, given a population force-fed the Divine Right of Kings, it should have come as little surprise that the people were receptive to such ideas – than with a keen sense of political realities. Few modern leaders have enjoyed such levels of charismatic authority, but Khomeini's leadership can be better understood in patrimonial terms, assisted by periodic and potent doses of charisma. Each complemented and, in some measure, compensated for the flaws in the other.

For instance, while Bakhtiar struggled for credibility, Khomeini (through no authority other than his own) established an Islamic Revolutionary Council composed of his lay advisers, and essentially created the government-in-waiting.[55] At the same time, the limits of charisma were exemplified by his anxiety over his ability to control the actions of the army (now released from the restraining hand of the Shah) or indeed of his more radical supporters, who were keen to confront the armed forces. The overwhelming tenor of messages emanating from Khomeini and other religious leaders in the first few months of the revolutionary regime was an urgent appeal for calm. They were acutely aware that, in the absence of an obvious 'enemy' and a focus for its attentions, the revolutionary momentum might descend into anarchy. Even before the Shah's departure, Khomeini urged the people 'to treat the military and security forces with kindness and, should hooligans attempt to attack them, to defend their brothers'.[56] Such views were echoed by other religious leaders such as Ayatollah Shariatmadari, who urged people not to be misled by agents provocateurs intent on causing mischief,[57] or by the leadership of the National Front.[58] Even Khomeini's return to Iran on 1 February (facilitated by air force technicians who ensured that the airport was open), for which an estimated one million Iranians poured into the streets of Tehran, did not herald a return to stable government. On arrival, Khomeini asked to be taken to Beheshte Zahra cemetery, south of Tehran, where he delivered his first speech in praise of the martyrs of the revolution. Accompanied by his erstwhile ideological ally Ayatollah Motahhari, Khomeini arguably made his first political mistake by announcing, with an air of pretentiousness, that he would now convene a government. Prompted by Motahhari, he then corrected himself by inserting the important caveat that he would do this as the representative of the people. It was a political faux pas which some clearly noticed, but which the masses, overtaken by the charismatic moment, willingly overlooked. Having completed his first task as de facto leader of the revolution and country, Khomeini then departed for the Alari girls' religious school in Tehran, which he transformed into his political base.

If Khomeini was able relatively easily to dispose of the Bakhtiar government by installing Mehdi Bazargan as Prime Minister of the provisional government on 5 February, the restoration of law and order was another matter. With the paralysis of the state encouraged to ensure the removal of the Shah, local government regulation and policing duties had been taken over on an ad hoc basis by local groups of militants, often formed in revolutionary *komitehs*, in another echo of the French Revolution. These *komitehs* by and large consisted of young, idealistic radicals, empowered both by their successful overthrow of the Shah, and their possession of weapons. Eager to please their political masters, whether Marxist, Islamic Marxist or Islamic, they were more often than not willing to take the initiative on issues irrespective of the dictates of their political leaders.[59] Instructions were frequently issued via radio, with little or no way of verifying the source.[60] They also regularly disagreed with each other, not only in terms of jurisdiction, but also in the implementation of revolutionary justice. There was a wide variation in the interpretations of Islamic law and Marxist doctrine. Political life in Iran was descending into a complex network of patron–client relations, in which the client more often than not acted on behalf of an unknown leader. It was a severe societal reaction to the centralising tendencies of the late Pahlavi state and in the absence of authentic tribes people invented their own. The rush to adhere to Khomeini's every word might have given the impression of unfettered charismatic authority, but this did not necessarily translate into political control. The paradox of charisma, powerful as it might be, is that it is open to interpretation and mediation by the follower. Khomeini's difficulties, however, were as nothing compared to his technocratic, though sincere, Prime Minister, Mehdi Bazargan, who lacked both power and any semblance of authority.

On 11 February, Bakhtiar finally resigned and went into hiding. The army formally announced its decision not to interfere in the political process.[61] Khomeini's response to the completion of this first and crucial phase of the revolution encapsulates both the jubilation and anxiety felt by Iran's new leaders:

> Courageous Iranian nation, alert Tehrani sisters and brothers, now that with the will of God the victory is near, now that the army has withdrawn and announced its non-interference in political affairs and support for the nation, the dear and courageous nation, being fully alert to the situation, and while maintaining their preparedness for possible defence, must maintain peace and order. If saboteurs decide to create a tragedy by arson and destruction, they should be reminded of their legal and humane duties; they should not allow them to denigrate the nation by resorting to such acts. They must not attack embassies.[62]

That the appeal for calm and the implementation of the law was reiterated some two hours later the same day is a clear indication of how the atmosphere of triumphalism was turning towards revenge.[63] Up until now the number of casualties incurred in the overthrow of the Shah had been comparatively light.[64] However, it was becoming increasingly apparent that, while the forces of coercion had indicated their willingness to forsake their Pahlavi patrons, there were many elements in society who were not so readily convinced of their new oath of allegiance. Anxieties abounded of a dangerous descent into civil strife, a consequence some conjectured which would be of immense assistance to any impending imperial coup. As always in Iran, the spectre of Mosaddeq hung heavy in the minds of Iranian politicians. Of immediate concern were the remaining units of the Imperial Guard,[65] but these soon surrendered and were somewhat unceremoniously sent home without their uniforms. The real problem lay with individual officers and the collapse of discipline within the ranks, as accusation and counter-accusation flew, leading to outbursts of violence.[66] Such outbursts were of course facilitated by easy access to weapons, often bought and sold by the very people instructed to keep the peace, or taken home by soldiers who were now deserting their posts without fear of retribution.[67] In his message to the nation on 13 February, Khomeini urged people to hand in their weapons:

> You should take note that the sale of arms is prohibited by our religion. They belong to others. They belong to the nation. No one should either purchase or sell arms. Those who have purchased them should return them to the committee or to the mosques.

Urging calm, he continued:

> Another issue is that these disturbances and demonstrations, which are now quite inappropriate, ought to be avoided. Uproar should be avoided.

The people must not think that now they have won victory they should disturb public peace, they should do this or that. You should act with order, discipline, with humanity, in the Islamic spirit. You should make the world understand that you are a Moslem nation, that you are aware of the facts of Islam, that you adhere to the precepts of Islam. You should strictly avoid such acts as looting and unlawful occupations.[68]

That these admonitions needed repeating with such regularity must reflect their relative ineffectiveness.[69] Not only were people taking their revenge on alleged members of the former regime, but groups appeared to be intent on attacking each other. According to one report, 'counterrevolutionary elements, appearing in revolutionary uniforms, even in clerical garb, are trying to harm the revolution'.[70] Indeed frustrations soon became apparent, as the government berated 'unnecessary shooting by individuals who are using their weapons as toys', and *begged* individuals 'to refrain from telephoning and threatening individuals who have committed certain errors'.[71] The pervasiveness of violence was of course not the only means by which the revolution could be undermined. One of the most unusual warnings to be issued regarded the distribution of suspect cigarettes:

Warning to the night guards. We were informed a few minutes ago by the medical committee of the University of Tehran that a number of counter-revolutionaries are planning to penetrate your organised ranks by any means and to stop the movement reaching its final goal. Their method is this: A group of these [counter-revolutionaries] have distributed cigarettes among night guards. These cigarettes have caused an intense emotional state, lasting a few hours, among the night guards. The victims are in the medical committee of Tehran University. I beg of you to avoid accepting cigarettes . . . I personally beg of you to refrain from smoking any cigarettes, even if you need them very badly.[72]

More serious were the injunctions against 'unlawful occupations' and 'attacking embassies'. Embassies seemed, in the early stages at least, to be a favourite target of the zealous youth. Particular favourites were embassies of countries thought to be giving the Shah refuge; one of the first embassies to come under attack was that of the Kingdom of Morocco.[73] At the same time, the government began preparations to initiate extradition procedures against the Shah once he arrived in Rabat.[74] However, more enticing for the young idealists scouring the streets of Tehran, the 'diplomatic prize' was still the US embassy, which was regarded not only as the political power behind the Shah, but in more general terms as the symbol of international capitalism. In fact an assault on the US embassy was not long in coming and it suffered the indignity of occupation on 14 February. For a brief moment, Ambassador William Sullivan, 70 diplomatic staff and 20 US Marines were placed under arrest.[75] In both cases, diplomatic crises were averted following the intervention of the government with Khomeini's full authority.

In spite of the immense difficulties which the new government faced, a semblance of government nevertheless began to take shape, even if this process remained highly decentralised and pluralistic. There were many competing factions to contend with, and more often than not the government reacted to rather than dictated the pace of events. Nevertheless, as the oil workers returned to the refineries,[76] the machinery of central government began a slow return to a very imperfect operation. Government at this stage can be characterised as contested. The political groups that had united against the Shah – the left, secular and religious nationalists of various hues – had done so under a broad ambiguous banner whose lack of definition facilitated inclusivity. For all the 'Islamic' content of Khomeini's central message, the language of the early revolution reflected the views of the main groups that had forged it.[77] Not only was society to be 'classless',[78] but even Khomeini talked of an 'Iranian' revolution, while others emphasised the need for a 'national Islamic' programme of development. Moves were initiated to redistribute wealth and eliminate 'unwarranted privileges',[79] while the oil policy of the Shah was attacked as against the national interest. The language was uncompromising, but also highly revealing of the prevalent ideological views:

> World capitalism and its affiliate, the Shah's regime, were bent on finishing Iran's oil resources within the next twenty years in order to make possible their own survival. We must bear in mind that by selling independently 40,000,000 tonnes of crude oil by our national and revolutionary government we shall bring to Iran the same revenues which would have been achieved through the sale of 300,000,000 tonnes of oil by the puppet regime.[80]

All agreed, however, that the extent of the 'corruption' (both in a financial and a moral sense) of the former regime meant that a regeneration of the state could only be achieved by the ruthless transformation of institutions through (Islamic) 'revolutionisation'. Reconstruction, however, could not proceed before the 'ancien régime' had been deconstructed; in practical terms this entailed the purging of old personnel.[81] The desire for popular revenge ensured that the new government was encouraged to satiate the public appetite by implementing some well-publicised retirements, some of which proved rather too permanent for the more legalistic members of the National Front, including some members of the provisional government. For the radicals, whether Islamic or leftist in orientation, there were no such qualms about the need to 'execute' the former regime. Indeed, it is worth bearing in mind that some of the most enthusiastic 'executioners' resided within the provisional government itself, and the subsequent distinction between the hapless but genuine government and zealots in the revolutionary organisations (such as the revolutionary courts) is misleading.

For the revolution to succeed, these erstwhile 'Jacobins' concluded that blood must be shed. The government was divided on the best way to proceed. Khomeini, correctly judging the public mood, encouraged a measure of controlled bloodletting, though how much control he was ultimately to have over this process is a matter of fierce debate. Much to the consternation of the elder statesmen within the provisional government, and in stark contrast to their public calls for legalism and calm, revolutionary courts acted with some haste to sentence to death, and speedily execute, leading members of the former regime (some of whom, like Nasiri and Hoveyda, had of course been imprisoned by the Shah).[82] The sentences were carried out with a brutal rapidity that proved both embarrassing to the provisional government and shocking to much of the international community, who had never been privileged to watch a revolution unfold on television. The explanation of the executions, for both domestic and foreign consumption, was telling:

> We believe . . . that to destroy and kill evil is part of the truth and that the purging of society of these persons means paving the way for a unified society in which classes will not exist . . . To execute evildoers is the great mission of Moslems in order to realise the perfection of nature and society. We execute those such as Nasiri in order to break the chains and fetters that confined and restricted the weak in our society for many years . . . Our aim is to execute the corrupt regime. The execution of the traitor Generals is the beginning of the execution of the regime.[83]

The total number of people executed by the revolutionary government, in its various guises, during the first few months of the revolution remains a matter of intense dispute; in such a highly politicised situation, exact figures are difficult to establish with certainty. Furthermore, most of the early assessments were made with information provided by the 'victims', whose perspective, unsurprisingly, differed markedly from that of the 'victors'. In truth, the figure is unlikely to be higher than several hundred prominent members of the Pahlavi establishment, although the manner of their dispatch left no doubt as to the seriousness with which the revolution took itself. The pride with which some zealous revolutionary judges administered their duties was felt by some to be profoundly distasteful.[84] Of far more concern were the ad hoc executions which took place throughout the country, carried out by local organisations including members of the newly founded 'revolutionary guards', the *komitehs*, and individuals seeking to settle old debts. There is little doubt that many took advantage of the collapse of central authority to take revenge on rivals for a variety of revolutionary and non-revolutionary reasons. It was sufficient to be labelled a member of the former internal security service SAVAK to be dragged in front of a 'court' and summarily sentenced to death. Such excesses, whether authorised or not, did little to sustain or enhance the moral standing of the revolutionary regime. Groups of all political hues indulged in retribution, occasionally competing to be more revolutionary and hence authentic; more often than not it was the leftist organisations that sought out properties to confiscate. In this period government can best be described as a measure of controlled decentralisation.

In such a situation, connections, networks and affiliations were vital to individual and collective security. People moved quickly to reestablish, and in many cases reinvent, old ties. Networks were particularly keenly sought among the *bazaar* and the *ulema*, the two sections of traditional society the Pahlavi establishment had been eager to dismiss. Those who had not entirely forsaken their social and cultural roots were more often than not able to escape the worst excesses of revolutionary justice, although in most cases at some cost to their personal and material well being. Those who were unable or unwilling to forge new links, who may be said to have been truly alienated from their own traditional society, were considerably more vulnerable, and the cost was correspondingly higher. Still, for all the imprisonments, confiscations and executions, and the trauma which they undoubtedly caused, and continued to cause, it is worth placing these events in an historical perspective. While concerns were expressed, few people in society at large were necessarily surprised nor profoundly shocked by the retribution which followed the collapse of the Shah's regime. Political retribution and property confiscations were after all not alien to the Shah's regime and, while the revolution exuded an unprecedented righteous ferocity, in numerical terms (even following the subsequent 'civil war' with the Left) the bloodletting remained comparatively low when juxtaposed with the French or Russian revolutions. Even foreign observers tended to view the application of revolutionary justice, erratic as it might be, as a natural consequence of and reaction to the collapse of an authoritarian and repressive state apparatus. Nor was the situation generally regarded as overly anarchic. Objective observers commented that Khomeini was to some extent able to exude a positive influence by restraining the most zealous revolutionaries.[85] Indeed, comparatively speaking, the numbers fleeing abroad compare favourably with the number of 'loyalists' who left for Canada following the American Revolution. For most Iranians, the first few months of the revolution represented the 'Spring of Freedom'; the real contest for the future direction of the revolution had yet to be fought. Similarly, it is worth bearing in mind that while the US embassy took the precaution of scaling down its presence and replacing embassy staff, other Western embassies were enthusiastically pursuing their own economic interests. Some US officials noted with some irritation that their loss was turning out to be everyone else's gain. Journalists and academics were also more often than not sympathetic to the revolutionary movement, and empathised with its leftist radicalism. The antagonism with the West that was to subsequently identify the 'Islamic Revolution' had yet to materialise, although sympathy with the Palestinians on both religious and socialist grounds had led to a definitive rupture of relations with Israel. There was, to be sure, considerable 'anti-imperialist' rhetoric and, as noted above, activists had seized the US embassy. But this had been peacefully resolved with the full authority of Khomeini, leading analysts to conclude that even the US would be able to manage the transition.[86]

The nature of this transition was as yet unclear. The inclusive ambiguity of the revolutionary movement had yet to be defined. Early indications were that the new state would take the form of some type of republic, with Khomeini as the popularly acclaimed 'Leader of the Revolution', and the bestowal of the symbolic though somewhat contentious title of 'Imam',[87] performing a supervisory role.

Khomeini had indeed retired to Qom, where he pursued his teaching and research with an absence of ceremony which struck many observers. There was no obvious indication of any desire on his part to become directly involved in the political management of the country. This was the task of the provisional government and the new political establishment, whose first duty was to define a constitution for the new republic. This new establishment reflected the varied groups who had united in opposition to the Shah. In the Shah's absence, clear differences began to appear, and for some it soon became apparent that all were not equal in the political reality of revolutionary Iran. The Islamic Revolution was undoubtedly popular, with considerable mass appeal. Yet for all the pretensions to 'modernity' which the Pahlavi state presumed, society still leaned towards the traditional.[88]

Social and economic developments during the last 25 years of Pahlavi rule undoubtedly resulted in a growth in political consciousness when compared with the period following the abdication of Reza Shah, but the intellectual growth reflected the economic expansion of the period. People in general benefited, but key sectors benefited disproportionately. These key sectors reflected the traditional leading groups in society such as the landowners, *ulema* and *bazaar*, inasmuch as it was these groups that possessed either the means, desire or social preconditions necessary for further politicisation. To these groups must be added the expanding student body, which was mainly drawn from the *ulema* and *bazaar*, but also contained elements from the 'modern' middle class – the real beneficiaries of state education policies. These social groups were the target of the various political groupings' recruitment campaigns. Affiliation to a political grouping might be influenced but was not dictated by one's social affiliation, nor was a political affiliation necessarily exclusive; on the contrary it tended to be highly fluid. The *ulema* and *bazaar* might form the core of the Islamist groups, but not all harboured radical Islamist views. Many were influenced by left-wing thought. Similarly, students tended to be heavily influenced by the various strands of Marxist thought, ranging from communist to Islamic socialist. They both operated under the loose intellectual umbrella of the nationalists (both secular and religious), whose intellectual legacy and influence belied their small numbers. As ambiguity gave way to definition, however, and politics began to polarise, so 'nationalism' ceased to function as a distinct political grouping and became absorbed by the intellectually more rigorous and popular left-wing and Islamist groups. Indeed, the Left and the Islamists, in their various guises, soon came to dominate the political theatre of revolutionary Iran. Their initial political union might appear distinctly 'unholy' and paradoxical, but they shared sufficient practical common ground to hide the intellectual differences they undoubtedly harboured. Anti-imperialism was a slogan both the Left and the Islamists could claim as their own, while the nationalisation of private assets and the confiscations of property could be interpreted as socialist, nationalistic (property belongs to the people administered by the state) or Islamist (property belongs to God, administered by the Islamic state). These were particular interpretations, but they were, to a point, functional.

The one social group that singularly miscalculated the consequences of the revolution were the former landowners, whose latent grievance against the Shah's White Revolution had led many of them to morally encourage and in some cases financially support Khomeini's return. Some presumed that Khomeini would restore their estates in a 'glorious' return to tradition. They were sorely mistaken. For those scions of the aristocratic landowning families who had forsaken their roots and turned to revolutionary activism, inclusion into the new revolutionary establishment remained a possibility; otherwise the doors to political conversion were firmly barred. When one eager young aristocrat offered his services to Ayatollah Beheshti, a founding member of the newly formed Islamic Republican Party (IRP), he was curtly dismissed with the notification that the days for him and his like were over. Yet the failure of the aristocracy to correctly divine the political character of the revolution also alerts us to the essential ambiguity which was crucial to its success and which ultimately led to the domination of the Islamist groups. The revolution's success was predicated on an ambiguous inclusivity which, by leaving room for interpretation, allowed a breadth of appeal hitherto unknown in Iranian political movements, and, as noted above, permitted a tactical political union between the Left and the Islamists. As each wing of the revolutionary movement sought to define itself according to its own logic, power was likely to accrue to the group that could continue to relate to the mass of Iranians. Despite the steady immigration to urban centres in the 1960s and 1970s, the mass of Iranians remained distinctly 'traditional' in their ideological orientation, retaining a rural outlook which belied their urban relocation. They remained politically reactive rather than proactive. With such constituents, leadership was likely to fall to those traditional groups who, above all, could *communicate* with the mass of Iranians. This is not to underestimate the attraction of the Left for many (young) Iranians, although even here it was those who professed a brand of Islamic Marxism who garnered most support. Indeed, as the revolution sought to define itself in constitutional terms, the influence of the Left seemed to be in the ascendant.

The fact that Khomeini had put his authority behind the need to establish a 'republic' seemed to be indicative of this trend. His more devout followers had, in fact, been looking forward to the establishment of an 'Islamic state' according to the blueprint Khomeini himself had laid out in his earlier writings. Indeed, there had been nothing in his previous publications which pointed towards a republican settlement.[89] Yet Khomeini was nothing if not pragmatic, and with characteristic political astuteness sought to bind the two political trends together in an 'Islamic Republic'. The evidence suggests that this move was more deliberate than opportunistic, and that Khomeini had understood and recognised the political realities of modern Iran. According to Ibrahim Yazdi (who was foreign minister in Bazargan's government), when prior to the fall of the Shah he presented Khomeini with a draft constitution entitled 'Islamic State', Khomeini without hesitation struck out the word 'state' and replaced it with 'republic'.[90] Nevertheless, this phrase was sufficiently ambiguous to be open to interpretation, and hence inclusive. It reassured traditional constituents by the emphasis on Islam, while at the same time appealing to the 'modernists' by being republican and hence progressive. Dismissing other appellations, Khomeini urged an early referendum in March 1979 before any of the details of the constitution could be worked out.[91] In the absence of any clear details, therefore, the referendum, which was by any account well attended, was more a vote *against* the monarchy than *for* any specific system of government. Indeed few traditional constituents, faced with the novel situation of being told that voting was an Islamic duty, can have had much idea of the consequences of their actions, save the abolition of the monarchy, which naturally was the purpose of the revolution. The referendum, therefore, essentially confirmed a political reality by popular affirmation. In this first symbolic action of the fledgling Islamic Republic, differences of interpretation were already apparent. For authoritarian Islamists, the implication of the referendum was simply the popular affirmation of a political reality dictated from the top. For the 'republicans', many Muslim activists included, the referendum was symbolic of the popular roots of the revolution and the reconnection of the state with society. Furthermore, contrary to orthodox Islamic interpretations, women were equal participants, a reality the authoritarians took to be a temporary, transitional compromise en route to an authentic Islamic state.

Nevertheless, the first draft of the constitution after the referendum, following intense discussions, tended to support the republican view, borrowing heavily from the constitution of the French Fifth Republic, complete with an elected 'President' and 'Prime Minister', and a separation of powers between the executive, judiciary and Majlis (parliament). The Prime Minister appointed his cabinet and essentially acted as the executive, while the President acted as 'head of state', initially enjoying powers which were later to devolve upon the 'Leader'. All elected institutions sat for a fixed term of four years and, as in the United States, a president could not sit for more than two consecutive terms.[92] The rights of citizens to free speech, freedom of association and other civil rights common to Western democracies were also enshrined. Torture was unconditionally banned. The document was remarkably liberal in its basic composition and in many ways reflected an enormous intellectual debt to the Constitutional Revolution of 1906. Religion was central, in so far that Twelver Shi'ism was enshrined as the state religion and all laws had to be checked for compatibility with the Shari'a. But ensuring compatibility with Islamic law was not the same as making Shari'a the basis of the law.[93] While the 1906 Constitution had defined a body of five senior members of the *ulema*, the Constitution of the Islamic Republic defined a 'Guardian Council' of six religious and six lay lawyers.

More surprising perhaps was the deliberate nationalism which the Constitution reflected. The Majlis may have been renamed the 'Islamic Consultative Assembly', removing the word 'national', but it was nevertheless considered the 'house of the nation' and accorded great importance. Similarly, while there were changes in nomenclature (in large measure to distinguish this revolution from the many which had preceded it, including the White Revolution in its various forms), in practice national priorities were not subjected to broader Islamic ones.[94] Much has been made by opponents of the Islamic Revolution of its disdain for Iranian nationalism and its adoption of Islamic symbolism. The replacement of the distinctly national

'Lion and Sun' symbol from the flag by an Islamic motif was indicative to many critics of this trend. Yet it is erroneous to define the contest as nationalism versus Islamism. Far better to see this in terms of competing nationalisms, each trying to supplant the other as *the* authentic nationalism. For the religious nationalists of the Islamic Revolution, the Lion and Sun motif was indicative (justifiably or otherwise) of the dynastic nationalism they had discarded. In fact, historically speaking, their brand of nationalism, in which Shi'ism was seen as integral to Iranian identity, was far more authentic than the 'secular' version imported by the Pahlavis from Europe. While there were undoubtedly members of the *ulema* who supported 'Islamisation' on a radical scale, enthusiastically if naively encouraging the destruction of all symbols of monarchy (including archaeological sites) and the wholesale adoption of Arabic, this was not reflected among the leaders of the Revolution. Statues of the Pahlavi Shahs were removed, street names changed and the tomb of Reza Shah razed to the ground, but other sites, because of their 'cultural significance', were retained and protected.[95] Certainly extensive damage was done to some key sites, especially in Isfahan,[96] but this was a consequence of the failure of central government, not an aspect of policy. Khomeini himself forbade any destruction of cultural sites including Persepolis and, despite the protestation of his critics, held an altogether ambivalent attitude towards Iranian nationalism, on the one hand stressing the internationalism of his religious intellectualism, while at the same time betraying sympathies for his native country.[97] Although he urged Iranians not to practice the various New Year rituals, which drew inspiration from the country's Zoroastrian past, at the same time he stubbornly refused to speak Arabic to his Arab guests (despite his fluent Arabic), insisting instead on speaking Persian through an interpreter. Arabic was certainly to be promoted, but Persian, as the lingua franca of the 'eastern Caliphate', was to be encouraged and developed. Khomeini was himself, much to the outrage of the orthodox *ulema*, a keen poet with mystical leanings. While the Muslim calendar was used, unlike Mohammad Reza Shah, Khomeini did not attempt to abolish or modify the Iranian solar *hegri* calendar, institutionalised under Reza Shah, complete with names of months derived from Iranian mythology. The preeminence of nationalism can perhaps be best seen in Khomeini's instruction that elected officials of the new state had to have been born in Iran. One subsequent presidential candidate was vetoed by Khomeini because he had been born in Afghanistan.[98] This specific constitutional directive, perhaps more than anything, betrayed the limitations of the Revolution's universalist pretensions. This was in essence, from the beginning, an *Iranian* Islamic Revolution (the 'Gulf' of course remained resolutely 'Persian'[99]). It should be stressed that, for all its symbolic attempts to distinguish itself from the immediate past, the state defined in the Constitution of the Islamic Republic betrayed more continuity with than change from the state established by Reza Shah. In appropriating the Pahlavi state, the revolutionaries may have imposed modifications, but it was in meaning, rather than structure or architecture, that the change was most keenly felt.[100]

It was this distinguishing desire which determined the drive towards 'Islamisation', itself a highly contested policy. There were broadly two strands of thought on this matter: on the one hand, there were the republicans who understood Islamisation as an essential complement to the process of democratisation; and on the other, the authoritarians, who were more concerned with ritualisation and institutionalisation. The republicans regarded Islamisation as essential to the republican project, in the same vein as Montesquieu had argued that, for a republic to be successful, it had to be 'virtuous'. This was to be a spiritual revolution, a cultural and intellectual rejuvenation via the medium of an Islamic 'liberation'. This rejuvenation could not be imposed, it had to be educated into the body politic. For the authoritarians, this ideological project could not be a matter of choice. The people had voted for an Islamic Republic in which 'Islam' was obviously the senior partner. It needed to be introduced into society, forcibly if necessary. Their belief that the people needed to be led reflected an elitist conception of politics, which nevertheless was more in concert with the traditional tendencies of Iranian society. It was, in short, a political view which was sustained by and in large part depended on the absence of consistent political consciousness among a broad swathe of the Iranian population.

The development of the notion of an Islamic Republic and the definition of its constituent terms marked the first step towards a definition of the inclusive ambiguity the revolution had presented. In the preamble, the dynastic nationalists had been excluded – the obvious consequence of the revolution. Now it was the turn of the secular nationalists and assorted left-wing groups, who found themselves at variance with the emphasis on Islam, although in the first instance this was not a problem.[101] Even secular nationalists recognised the cultural pervasiveness of Islam, and its importance to Iranian identity, although their understanding of Islam tended to be sociological and utilitarian. It should also be remembered that in the first year of the revolution there was no imposition of Islamic strictures. Even the *hejab* (the veil) was regarded as a matter of choice for women. Khomeini certainly recommended it, but he did not impose it.[102] By the end of 1979, however, it was becoming increasingly apparent that a more rigorous interpretation of Islam was coming to the fore and groups realigned themselves for the new contest. This process of polarisation was a direct consequence of the failure of the provisional government to reestablish central government in an efficient manner. This was not entirely the fault of Bazargan and his cabinet, since the reality was that many groups had no intention of submitting to his government. Frustrations mounted, as it became apparent that Bazargan's 'legalism' was a highly ineffective tool for the re-establishment of order, and many feared (and some no doubt hoped) that the country would, once the euphoria had settled, descend into fratricidal civil war. Already some key members of the revolutionary establishment had become victims of assassination, including Ayatollah Motahhari,[103] while the country was being convulsed by demonstrations which were regularly descending into (often well-orchestrated) street brawls. Anarchy or the fear of anarchy, it is often said, is but a stepping stone to absolute power, and it was a natural consequence of this situation that the authoritarian tendencies on both left and right would gain ascendancy.

The immediate consequence of this development, however, was to begin to redraft the constitution to institutionalise Khomeini's role as the leader of the Revolution, in the form of his concept of the *velayat-e faqih*. This was another contested idea, which nevertheless served the political needs of the time, although the precise parameters of the responsibilities of the *vali-e faqih* were left vague.[104] Khomeini had developed this idea in his book *Islamic Government*. Essentially this developed from an argument raised by previous *ulema* to its logical political conclusion. In the absence of the legitimate authority of the Twelfth Imam, such authority would pass to the righteous jurists, who alone were able to understand and interpret the law. While power might lie with the temporal body, authority would naturally devolve onto the jurists. A recognition of this religious authority had in fact formed the basis of the Qajar dynasty's ascent of the Peacock throne at the end of the eighteenth century, and an increasingly uneasy partnership sustained the Qajar dynasty for over a century. The Pahlavis had been dismissive of any such dependence and had refused to define their legitimacy in Shi'a terms. Now Khomeini argued that for the authority of the jurists to become institutionalised, it had to be delegated to one supreme jurist. This fact alone was bound to cause problems, for while other members of the *ulema* were willing to accept him as the 'Leader' of the Revolution, a constitutional position which provided him with the remit to interpret and define Shari'a law struck many as a step too far. It went against the grain of Shi'a tradition and was condemned by some as a dangerous 'innovation'.

On a broader level, concern was expressed at the institutionalisation of clerical power that this represented, a fact which enthused those clerics anxious for power, as much as it horrified those who were against such a move.[105] Khomeini recognised that the inclusion of the concept of the *velayat-e faqih* would cause problems, but he was able to pursue this through his own undoubted popularity, and because of the assurances he was able to give. Ayatollah Montazeri, Khomeini's deputy, who drafted this section of the Constitution, was clear that the position would be a supervisory one, and did not, as Khomeini himself reiterated on several occasions, entail the monopoly of power by the *ulema*.[106] This was not, however, how both supporters and critics of the inclusion interpreted the development. Indeed, many critical members of the *ulema* feared that direct involvement in politics would ultimately prove destructive for the clerical class as a whole. Nevertheless, the inclusion of the concept of the *velayat-e faqih* signified the institutionalisation of ambiguity, which would serve the charismatic and patrimonial interests of the office holder, who, as was true for Khomeini, possessed the necessary charismatic authority and political astuteness to manage the implicit tensions – Islamism v nationalism, authoritarianism v democratisation, tradition v modernity. The office was Khomeini's creation. It would evolve and be defined through his practice.

Such constitutional discussions, however, did not prove sufficient to cultivate stability. On the contrary, it appeared that political volatility was now matched by vigorous debate over the future direction and definition of the new state. Anxieties over impending anarchy at both levels encouraged the view that a distinct 'third party' had to be found, if necessary invented, to focus the attentions of the competing factions. On 4 November 1979, Khomeini was provided with the perfect opportunity. The deposed Shah had spent much of his first year in exile travelling from country to country seeking sanctuary, and ultimately medical help for his cancer, which had developed rapidly. Finally he had decided to seek medical attention in the United States, and President Carter, against the advice of his senior officials and under considerable pressure from the pro-Pahlavi establishment (including former Secretary of State Henry Kissinger) decided, fatefully, to allow his erstwhile ally access to US medical help.[107] The arrival of the Shah in the United States triggered alarm bells in Iran, where there was widespread disbelief in the Shah's illness and a developing conviction that the United States was planning a repeat of the events of 1953. That said, there was little immediate indication of the consequences of development. Iranian and US officials were negotiating a settlement of outstanding matters in Algeria, and while there was some concern expressed that the US embassy might be subject to protests and even attack, this was, in the circumstances, not entirely unexpected. Previous occupations, as noted above, had been peacefully solved. Furthermore, the embassy staff, which had considerably shrunk in size since February, was largely composed of volunteers well versed in Persian and Islamic culture, who had chosen to serve in Tehran, in some cases 'to witness a revolution first hand'.[108] Few could have foreseen how intimate this observation would become.

At the beginning of November, a group of students, following the 'Line of the Imam' (*Khat-e Imam*), decided to organise a sit-in at the US embassy to protest the admission of the Shah. There is no evidence that Khomeini was aware of these plans, although it is likely that some senior revolutionary officials were briefed that something was afoot. According to the leader of the students, Asgharzadeh, the aim of the sit-in was to make a highly public point which would hopefully ingratiate them with the Imam, although they could not be certain of this.[109] In any case, with a supremely ironic sense of timing, the students decided to assault the US embassy at precisely the moment the US chargé d'affaires, Bruce Laingan, was discussing security at the Iranian Foreign Ministry. At first the US Marines greeted the vitriolic protest at the gates with some calm; even their concern at the subsequent assault over the walls was restrained, the experience of previous incursions suggesting that there should be minimal provocation. However, when the students produced weapons and began arresting staff, it gradually dawned on the American diplomats that this was an altogether different type of sit-in. Officials frantically began shredding what documents remained. Laingan was informed by phone and conveyed his concern to the Foreign Minister, Ibrahim Yazdi, who, somewhat embarrassed, struggled to find a solution.[110] The British embassy had been assaulted on the same day, but the occupation had ended peacefully so there was no substantive reason for believing that the same could not be achieved in the American case.

When Yazdi approached Khomeini on the following day for the authority to remove the students, he did not receive the answer he expected. The reason for this, according to Yazdi, was the popular euphoria which the occupation had engendered, especially in the press, which by Yazdi's reckoning convinced Khomeini that, on this occasion, he should ride the crest of the populist wave. To much popular acclamation (and student relief), Khomeini approved of the occupation, declaring the embassy to be a 'nest of spies'. In essence, and oblivious to the international and long-term consequences, Khomeini, under advice, considered the occupation too good an opportunity to forego. Of particular interest to some in the revolutionary establishment was the successful seizure by the students of the embassy archives, which had been shredded but not burned. Much to the astonishment of the embassy staff, now joined by Laingan (who had refused an offer from fellow members of the diplomatic corps to escape in disguise), enthusiastic students began the laborious process of stitching back the shredded documents. These documents were later published in an extensive series and, while much of the material was not of a sensitive nature, aspects proved of use in the subsequent power struggle as it became apparent that some members of the revolutionary leadership had been in contact with embassy staff.[111] The occupation rapidly became the central focus of the revolutionary movement. As Khomeini had hoped, fratricidal infighting was set aside in the interests of a unified posture against the greater 'evil' posed by the United States – an enemy sufficiently threatening to sustain and indeed enhance the Revolution's certainty and profound conviction of its own historical and international significance. It proved to be a defining moment. Henceforth, the Revolution would in large part be defined by its antagonistic relationship with the United States – a definition which would in time be reciprocated. Indeed, the humiliation of the occupation, and the subsequent failed rescue attempt (much publicised in Iran), also proved a pivotal moment in US self-perception, and it has served to colour US policy towards Iran ever since.

This further definition of the Revolution also served to exclude the members of the National Front, Freedom Movement and other secular nationalists from the mainstream of political life. Bazargan's provisional government resigned in disgust, and politics increasingly revolved around the 'Islamic Marxists' (coalescing under the leadership of the Mujahedeen-e Khalq Organisation, MKO), their allies and the 'Islamists' (including the Islamic Republican Party), in their various hues. Both these major wings of the Revolution, in contrast to the provisional government, fully supported the occupation of the US embassy. As for the students themselves, they cannot have foreseen how central to the Revolution's fortunes they would become, as the occupation extended over weeks and then months. Far more than the executions and confiscations, the prolonged occupation of the US embassy served to alienate the Revolution from even its most sympathetic supporters in the West, who had now come to harbour serious reservations about the Revolution's motives. Although the students argued that no physical harm was done to the hostages[112] (a claim challenged by many of the hostages themselves), no one could doubt that the act was a gross breach of international law. This simple fact was to have serious ramifications for Iran's international position in the forthcoming year. Yet in domestic terms it served a purpose. Few people appear to have appreciated the legal ramifications, viewing it essentially as another, if somewhat dramatic, part of the political theatre that was revolutionary Iran.[113] In realpolitik terms, it proved a vital if short-term expedient, although it remains the supreme irony that at the moment of rejection, Iran effectively tied herself to the international system. As future President Bani-Sadr was to complain, America was ironically restored to centre stage in Iranian life: 'We threw the Americans out of the window, and climbed in through the window'.[114]

This, in all likelihood, was a retrospective judgement, since at the time most political actors supported the seizure, and the fall of the provisional government opened the way for the implementation of the Constitution (complete with the concept of *velayat-e faqih*) and elections for the presidency. Having admitted that he had made a mistake in appointing the hapless Bazargan, observers now watched to see how Khomeini in particular, and the revolutionary leadership, would administer the first political elections of the Islamic Republic. There had been much comment as to the need for the candidates to be 'good Muslims', and people wondered what this actually might mean in practice. It was stressed that any successful candidate would have to be approved by the *vali-e faqih*, in whom authority in religious and constitutional terms ultimately lay. But the extent of these powers had yet to be tested by experience. As it happened, Khomeini initially vetoed a candidate on national rather than religious grounds, but then forced the leader of the MKO, Masud Rajavi, to withdraw because the MKO had boycotted the ratification of the new Constitution in December 1979. The first elections started with a flurry of diverse candidates and ended in a public acclamation (resounding as it was) for the eventual winner, Abol-Hassan Bani-Sadr, a French-educated technocrat who had been with Khomeini in Neauphle-le-Chateau. Bani-Sadr, drawing on his credentials as a lay religious intellectual, sought to bind together the two wings of the revolutionary movement. Neither, however, was willing to submit to the authority of the President, and Bani-Sadr found himself replicating the premiership of his predecessor as political polarisation continued and each wing sought to undermine the power of the other. The Islamists, determined to push ahead with the Islamisation of society, were a more amorphous group, but were socially entrenched, with loyalties in the rural areas and among traditional constituents. The MKO approached the pinnacle of their popularity by attracting all those who were becoming increasingly disaffected with and disconnected from the religious bent of the traditionalists. Bani-Sadr sought to consolidate his grip on the presidency and appropriate some authority by solving the hostage crisis. The Islamists, however, were determined to prolong the situation so as not to allow the President any form of political triumph, and to ensure that his attention was distracted from essential domestic matters. In the event, far more serious international matters were to overtake this depressing cycle of domestic political decay.

War

As becomes a revolution of historical importance, Iran's Islamic revolutionaries were eager to 'export' their revolutionary ideas. This was not an outcome unique to the Islamic revolution; the Shah had sought to educate foreigners about the benefits of the 'Shah–People Revolution' (White Revolution). Other revolutionary movements, from the French to the Russian, have also been internationalist in their ambitions, to say nothing of the Westernising momentum of liberal capitalism, against which the Islamic Revolution increasingly defined itself.[115] Khomeini, as with his exhortations at home (and with similar results), argued that the Revolution could not be spread by force but only through argument and persuasion, through which the truth of the movement would become self-evident.[116] The Revolution was, after all, not only for Shi'as but for all Muslims. (To stress this, the Imam banned the traditional cursing of the first three Caliphs, and the burning of the effigy of Caliph Omar, so offensive to Sunnis.) Increasingly for all the 'oppressed' of the world, this rhetoric conveniently conformed to Marxist world-views. Nevertheless it was in the Shi'a areas of the Muslim world that sensitivities were most acute, and none more so than in Iran's traditional rival in the region, Iraq. The Ba'athist strong man of Iraq, Saddam Hussein, who had made himself president in 1979, viewed events in Iran with a keen sense of anxiety and opportunism. Having been forced to concede to the Shah's demands over sovereignty of the Shatt al-Arab waterway (part of the border between the two countries) in the Algiers Accords of 1975, Saddam saw in the developing political turmoil of Iran a means by which he could both recoup his losses and divert the attention of Iraq's Shi'a majority. The Shah, for all his affectation for military hardware, had privately conceded that the real threat to Iran came not from the north, but, as history suggested, from the west: from either the Ottoman Empire or its successor states. Viewing the military buildup in Iraq, he had told the British ambassador that if Iraq acquired 500 tanks, then he would demand 1,000.[117] In this way he had successfully deterred the expansionist tendency of the Iraqi dictator. But now Iran's armed forces were in apparent disarray, suffering from purges and desertions, while the international political climate seemed eminently hospitable. There is little doubt that Iran's new ambassador to Baghdad, a firebrand mullah, took his revolutionary duties far too seriously (especially for the Ba'athist government), as witnessed by his vitriolic denunciations of his host government and his demands for a popular revolution. But the road to war was more a matter of encouraged calculated opportunism than provocation.

The Iraqis were undoubtedly justified in their complaint that the new Iranian ambassador's public denunciations were incompatible with his diplomatic status, and they cannot have been reassured by the decline in border security. However, many steps could have been taken prior to a declaration of war and, in so far as extensive preparations were made for an invasion, the decline in the political situation was not sufficient to warrant such a massive military response.

Three factors were crucial to the decision to invade: the first and most obvious was the perception of internal disarray and the belief that an Iraqi attack would meet minimal response. Not only could Iraq then dictate a peace with respect to the Shatt al-Arab waterway, but Saddam played with the idea that he would be able to occupy and indeed seize portions of Khuzestan, the south-western oil-rich province which possessed a sizeable Arab population and portions of which until the rule of Reza Shah had been referred to as 'Arabistan'. This ambition was encouraged by the apparent ambivalence of the Americans, who were preoccupied with the hostage crisis. They did little to restrain Iraqi war plans, and the ambitions of the exiled monarchist officers and politicians, in particular Shahpour Bakhtiar and the former military governor of Tehran, General Oveissi. That 'Islamic radicalism' was a serious threat to world peace and needed to be suffocated at birth was a view that was already gaining ground among some commentators. They were encouraged by monarchists who convinced themselves and the Iraqis that the establishment of a 'bridgehead' in Khuzestan would act as a rallying point for the 'oppressed' people of Iran, and provide the catalyst for the overthrow of the Revolution. Saddam Hussein was clearly not interested in establishing a bridgehead for the restoration of the monarchy, but the idea that he could assist in the 'liberation' of the Iranian people, and the Arabs of the south-west in particular, had a certain appeal. Despite these assurances a measure of orchestration was still required, and this was provided, with the help of Iraqi intelligence, by the creation of an 'Arab Liberation Front', whose requests for 'liberation' would of course be heeded by the Iraqi state. Such calls had to be heard, of course, and thus it was essential that 'an event' be managed in a place where wide publicity would be guaranteed. London was eventually chosen, not only because of its position as an international media centre, but also because it was (erroneously) argued that, as the British police were unarmed, a peaceful solution would be ensured. Such, in any case, were the arguments which led to the recruitment of a number of young (and as it turned out, naive) Iranian Arabs from Khuzestan, with the promise of rich rewards if they seized the Iranian embassy in London, and drew world attention to the plight of the oppressed Arabs of 'Arabistan'. Everything went according to plan, including extensive media attention, until one of the hostage-takers murdered an Iranian diplomat, and persuaded the new British Prime Minister, Margaret Thatcher, that radical action was necessary. The decision to dispatch the SAS (Special Air Service) transformed the Iranian embassy siege of 1980 into an aspect of British contemporary folklore. Much of the detail of the operation, from its conception to conclusion, has never been openly questioned. Every one of the hostage-takers except one (who escaped with his life by dint of good fortune) was killed in the televised assault, effectively eliminating any means of investigation.

As far as Saddam Hussein was concerned, however, the embassy siege served its purpose. In September 1980, much to the astonishment of the preoccupied factions in Tehran, Saddam publicly tore up the Algiers Accord and launched his invasion of Iran. Saddam, like many military opportunists, anticipated a short, sharp geographically limited war. He had no plans to go much further than Khuzestan,[118] but this would still be sufficient to deal a decisive political blow against the revolutionary regime. Initial reports were reassuring. There was minimal opposition. The Iranian army had clearly been caught off guard, and in reality lacked any sense of cohesion. In Tehran, disbelief and doubt were soon transformed into resolute conviction. Few Iranian politicians believed that Iraq would attack without external (i.e. American) support and encouragement. This was really an American attack, and when juxtaposed with the Soviet invasion of Afghanistan in 1979, it seemed to some that the Iranic world was under assault. This momentous event, underpinned by Khomeini's stubborn determination to resist, only fuelled the growing conviction that the Revolution was worth fighting, and if necessary dying, for. Indeed, few observers (Iranian or otherwise) anticipated the ferocity with which the Iranians would resist the Iraqi invasion, not least the Iraqis themselves.[119] While the invasion appeared to proceed with some ease, resistance began to harden in the urban centres. Most of these towns were stubbornly defended by pockets of 'Revolutionary Guards', a new and somewhat haphazard military organisation intended ultimately to replace the armed forces (regarded as the quintessential product of the Pahlavi state and thus by definition disloyal). Iraqi commanders were in fact distinctly unwilling to become involved in urban street fighting and the capture of the towns, especially Khorramshahr, was achieved only through extensive fighting.[120] Formal resistance by the armed forces took at least six weeks to organise, as President Bani-Sadr urged soldiers to return to active service and tried to stem the flow of desertions. Having spared no effort in criticising the Shah's arms purchases, many senior officials now gave thanks that both trained soldiers and weapons were available. Once the armed forces began a systematic mobilisation, the full weight of Iran's revolutionary forces fell on the unsuspecting Iraqis. Far from parading in triumph through Tehran in recently ordered ceremonial uniforms, Iraqi generals found themselves trapped in a bitter war.

In many ways, as Khomeini announced, the war proved a 'blessing'. It proved a timely focus and provided a concrete purpose for those political activists who were determined to find a 'war' to fight. At the same time, the label has often been interpreted to indicate the opportunity the war gave for further Islamisation and a marginalisation of the Left, in particular the MKO. Certainly, in the state of emergency which now existed, a far more centralised and authoritarian order could be both justified and imposed. The war against Iraq became a 'holy war', the 'motherland' became 'sacred'. The imposition of Islamic austerity at home became a natural adjunct. Internationally, it was important to reorder relations, and the first problem to be solved was the hostage crisis. Mohammad Reza Shah had died in June 1980, thereby removing the ostensible reason for the US embassy occupation, and the crisis seemed to be being needlessly prolonged by the sheer lack of political will to find a solution. With the Iraqi invasion, a solution became urgent, especially when it was discovered that diplomats at the UN Security Council were unwilling to formally condemn the invasion – a deliberate omission which simply confirmed the belief that Iran was taking on the world. Extensive discussions finally resulted in the hostages, somewhat conveniently, being released moments after President-elect Reagan's inauguration, in January 1981.[121]

With the war gaining momentum, the domestic contest became increasingly vicious. Having followed Khomeini from France, Bani-Sadr found himself being increasingly outmanoeuvred by the Islamic Republican Party, headed by wily politicians such as Ayatollah Beheshti and Hojjat-ol-Eslam Hashemi Rafsanjani. Eventually Bani-Sadr found himself unable to choose his prime minister and cabinet (Rajai became Prime Minister in September 1980 against Bani-Sadr's wishes); he looked increasingly like a lame-duck president. To counter this, he sought support from the MKO, calling along with Rajavi for mass protests against clerical power, a move which simply confirmed his dispensability as far as his opponents were concerned. With little progress in the war, they finally persuaded Khomeini to dismiss him. Bani Sadr considered it prudent to disappear, and eventually fled abroad. Faced with the possibility of uncontainable political unrest, the religious establishment and their conservative allies began to strike back with increasing ruthlessness, serving notice through executions that they were willing to contest any agitation and suppress it by whatever means. The spiralling tension was to culminate in a dramatic bomb blast at the headquarters of the Islamic Republican Party which, after some prevarication, the religious establishment blamed on the MKO. An estimated 72 people died in the blast, among them senior members of the leadership, including the pivotal Beheshti.[122] Faced with a war on two fronts, the revolutionary regime launched a reign of terror against its leftist opponents, which resulted in their decimation as a distinct political force in Iran. Again, figures are difficult to confirm, but it seems likely that in the months following the bomb blast, the number of executions reached several thousand. What was arguably more shocking than the figures themselves was the apparent enthusiasm with which the executions (many in public) were carried out.[123] The destruction of the Left was merciless, and extended into the realm of intellectual deconstruction, as religious intellectuals sought to disprove historical materialism and its associated theories.[124] In practical terms, the MKO leadership escaped abroad where it initially set up its headquarters in Paris, eventually moving in 1986 to Baghdad, where they continue to prosecute the civil war begun in 1981.[125] The success of the Islamists against the Left can be assigned to several factors: extraordinary measures were increasingly tolerated during a time of general crisis, and the reaction was regarded as justified in light of the war; the Islamists, in their various hues, enjoyed far wider support among the mass of traditional constituents, with whom they were able to communicate effectively, unlike the 'Marxist' MKO (who appealed far more to the emergent professional middle classes); but probably most important was the Islamists' ability to attract the support of other traditional socio-economic groups, such as the *bazaar* and the aristocracy, for whom the prospect of 'red revolution' was even more galling than the Islamic variety they were currently experiencing. In short, the Islamists had social roots which were deeper than the undoubtedly extensive political tentacles of the MKO and their affiliates.[126]

There is little doubt that Bani-Sadr's fall from grace was in part a product, as he argued, of his opponents' determination to have him removed.[127] However, he made their task considerably easier by his own mismanagement of the war effort.[128] The distrust between the Revolutionary Guards and the regular armed forces certainly did not facilitate success at the front. The armed forces continued to insist on well planned and well organised operations according to their training, while the Revolutionary Guards, whose defence of Khuzestan had garnered them considerable popular prestige, argued that zeal and determination were enough. The new 'Islamic' man, much like the *sans-culottes* of the French Revolution, would win through superior morale. The consequence of this was a duplication of effort, and a division of finite resources which became increasingly scarce when an international embargo on arms sales to both warring parties was imposed. While Iraq was to receive considerable support from the Arab states and ultimately Europe and the United States, Iran was faced with a steady erosion of its military capability, especially since much of it was sourced to either the United States or Great Britain, and the US in particular had no intention of coming to the aid of the Islamic Republic. After 1981, however, and the consolidation of the domestic situation, a measure of co-ordination was imposed on the war effort. The varied strengths of the Revolutionary Guards and the armed forces were welded into a unified and highly effective whole. The armed forces provided the logistical back-up, preparation (especially in the use of air power) and overall co-ordination, while the Guards provided the motivated manpower. Indeed, faced with the prospect of a shortage of equipment, Iran's military planners came to rely increasingly on a steady reservoir of poorly armed, modestly trained but highly motivated troops. The use of human waves – often cited by the Western press to denote the 'fanaticism' of the Iranians – was not only a necessary response to the available resources, but in time was applied with some tactical astuteness (for example, feigned retreats) and sophistication, which only discipline could realise. In time the government would seek to tap into Iran's manpower surplus by launching a popular mobilisation (*basij*) as a means of recruiting outside the standard age remits allowed for the Guards and the regular armed forces. These *basij* in many cases provided the basis of the zealous manpower thrown into the battlefront, and many fought with extreme bravery. That many came from age groups not normally associated with combat (either very young or very old) emphasised the social impact of the war, but also gave rise to another popular misconception, that boys were forcibly press-ganged into service. There is no evidence for this, and, while peer pressure may have played a role (much as in the First World War in Europe) a policy of forcible recruitment was never in evidence. The enthusiasm with which, initially at least, many volunteered is interpreted as a reflection of the innate fanaticism of the Iranians. Yet Iranian mobilisation and the use of human wave tactics, even the gradual dependence on a strategy of attrition, compare favourably with the experience of the British in the First World War (in which it should be remembered that Haig considered fighting not only a national but a Christian duty), or the Soviet defence of 'Holy Mother Russia' during the Great Patriotic War.

By 1982, very much to the surprise of foreign observers, Iran was in a position to launch its final offensive in order to recapture the territory occupied by Iraq. The co-ordinated operation, *Beyt ol Moqadas*, proved a spectacular success. The town of Khorramshahr was recaptured and the Iraqi troops retreated behind their own border. It is difficult to underestimate the catalytic effect which the recapture of Khorramshahr had on Iranian society. It engendered a sense of euphoric empowerment second only to the departure of the Shah. In fact its impact may have been greater since it was a military triumph Iranians of all political hues could truly share. For a nation inured to decades, if not centuries, of military defeat, the 'conquest of Khorramshahr' showed what the nation, when determined and focused, could achieve, even in the absence of international support. As far as the Islamic Revolution was concerned, it was the event which confirmed the righteousness and sanctity of the Republic. Yet for all the religious righteousness of much of the rhetoric, Khorramshahr marked the moment when the national narrative was born. For while this was a triumph for the Islamic Iranian nation, it was in essence a national achievement, and provided Iranians with a military victory, socialised and committed to collective memory, which was distinct from the annual commemoration of Karbala.[129] However, this moment of triumph was to have unfortunate consequences for the future direction of the Revolution. The Iraqi invasion of Iran had been regarded by many foreign states as a means by which the Revolution could be both weakened and contained. This ambition appeared to have been thwarted, and the apparent determination of Iran's leaders to take the war to the Iraqis (and even on to Jerusalem) only exacerbated concerns, both regionally and internationally, that the Islamic Revolution could indeed spread and undermine the stability of the pro-Western autocracies of the Middle East. The Saudi government was so concerned at the consequences of an Iranian victory that it offered to financially underwrite any settlement and recompense Iran for the damage to its territory.

The Iranian leadership, however, was not in a mood to listen. In retrospect, given the destructive prolongation of the war, there has been much debate about why it was decided to prosecute the war after Khorramshahr, given the paucity of military hardware, and against the advice of most senior generals. It was pointed out that the determination to evict the Iraqis from Iranian soil might not be replicated when the war was taken to Iraq and the Iraqis were defending their own soil. Furthermore, while Iranian logistical capability was declining, it was apparent that the Iraqis would be in receipt of considerable assistance. These arguments appear to have been persuasive as far as Imam Khomeini was concerned.[130] His priorities were domestic, and he judged, undoubtedly correctly, that much could be achieved domestically on the back of a military triumph. Unfortunately, his judgement seems to have been influenced by members of the Revolutionary Leadership, including commanders of the Revolutionary Guards and, it has been suggested, Hashemi Rafsanjani, that the Revolution must ride the momentum of military victory and extend it, thus bringing even richer rewards to the Islamic Republic.[131] Still others, sceptical of the flawed strategic vision of some of the leadership, accepted that Iraq could not go unpunished for the invasion, and that some measure of retribution had to be imposed. It proved a fateful decision, and in the following six years, much of the acquired reservoirs of heightened morale were wastefully dissipated in what became a prolonged war of attrition.

In a succession of campaigns, some of which exemplified the ingenuity and resourcefulness of the Iranian armed forces (including Guards and *basij*), over and above the seeming ineptitude of their political masters, Iran inched its way into Iraqi territory. For the next few years, however, the war ground to a stalemate as Iran, with its depleting arsenal but massive reserves of manpower, faced an entrenched Iraqi army, generously endowed, with weapons, finance and in some cases manpower, by regional and international allies. Indeed, despite the imposition of an international embargo on both sides, Iraq enjoyed a steady stream of assistance from both the regional Arab states, anxious to contain the 'destabilising' Revolution and, more controversially, from Western states, similarly determined to contain what they perceived to be the spread of Islamic fundamentalism. Fuelled by tales of oppression emanating from refugees, and somewhat bewildered by the resurgence of Islam in such a strategically vital part of the world, the West took the short-term, though some would argue expedient, view that support for a 'Western-style' dictator was the lesser of two evils. While the Americans were undoubtedly justified in their grievance with respect to the seizure of their embassy (although many Iranians would have considered this just recompense for their past misdemeanours), the decision by Western powers to support Iraq stands as an indictment of the shortsightedness of their policy, and the utter failure of intellect which could not see beyond the religious dimensions of the Revolution.[132] This indictment becomes more damning when it is considered that some policy makers actively sought the prolongation of the war as a means of both exhausting the Revolution and containing the emergence of Iraq, irrespective of the human cost.[133] This is not to argue that the West was the cause of the collapse in relations with Iran and the 'diplomatic revolution' which followed, but that it must share some of the responsibility for this breakdown. As noted above, the decision to continue the war after 1982 was Iran's, and there is little doubt that the creation of a new, self-confident republic was unlikely to have a stabilising effect on the socially insecure autocracies of the region, but these tensions were hugely exaggerated and exacerbated by an overreaction which simply compounded the problem. The decision to assign all the evils of the region to Iran was extremely shortsighted, and only fuelled the radical interpretation of international relations among the Iranian leadership who regarded the world as inherently unjust, anarchic and determined by 'might' rather than 'right'.

While the failure of the UN to condemn the Iraqi invasion might be seen as a direct consequence of Iran's failure to respect international law with respect to the US embassy, the West's support for the Iraqi chemical weapons programme, and their subsequent use against Iranian soldiers, was at the very least a dereliction of moral responsibility and reinforced the belief in Western hypocrisy. Indeed for the Iranians it appeared as if the Iraqis could do no wrong in their extension of the war into different areas of combat. For instance, chemical weapons were used soon after the Iranian decision to invade Iraq; their use was justified on the grounds of national survival. As evidence of the use of chemical weapons became apparent, the Iranians invited journalists to witness what was happening. Yet the initial official reaction was to deny any such use, and even to argue that the Iranians had concocted elaborate fictions. It took several years, and the presence of UN monitors, for it to be reluctantly accepted that Iraq had used chemical weapons, although no official condemnation was forthcoming on the dubious grounds that the Iranians were using them too. In fact it is unclear whether the Iranians retaliated at all, and Imam Khomeini was quite clear in his condemnation of the weapons as un-Islamic.[134] Similarly, it was the Iraqis who extended the war into civilian areas by launching attacks on the cities, at one stage causing panic in Tehran with the threat of a chemical attack. They extended the war into the Persian Gulf, by attacking Iranian tankers, in an effort to destroy the economic foundations of the country. Iran, without access to land-based pipelines, was determined to keep the Persian Gulf shipping lanes open. Iran attacked not only Iraqi shipping, but also ships that had been reflagged under the colours of one of the Gulf states, and was rapidly labelled the disturber of the peace. Under this dubious pretext, Western navies, in particular the US Navy, entered the Persian Gulf 'to protect shipping', but in effect launched a second front against the Islamic Republic. This role was expanded when the Kuwaitis threatened to reflag their ships under Soviet colours, forcing the Americans to pre-empt Soviet involvement by offering their own protection. The implicit bias became explicit with the attack in 1987 on the *USS Stark* by an Iraqi pilot flying a Mirage fighter bought from France, and firing an Exocet missile 'on loan' from France. The accidental attack caused at least 30 casualties and yet President Reagan, with no hesitation, somehow contrived to blame the entire incident on the 'barbarian' Iranians.

In this context, and with the lack of progress on the Iraqi front, Iran sought to extend its reach and retaliated, by pursuing a deliberate policy of destabilisation in those Arab states seen as supportive of the Iraqi war effort, by attacking those Iranians abroad who were regarded as supportive of the Iraqi position, and by obstructing US interests, most obviously in the Lebanon. The decision to support a policy of hostage-taking in the Lebanon cannot be understood without reference to the broader war and, in some ways, in bringing pressure to bear on the United States, it served its purpose. It certainly led to one of the more curious episodes of the war, the decision by the United States to pursue a parallel covert policy of support for Iran, with Israeli mediation. Both Iran and the United States portrayed the tentative relationship which was investigated as an aspect of realpolitik. Iran needed weapons, and the United States wanted Iranian pressure brought to bear on the hostage-takers in the Lebanon. Yet there is little doubt that the move also represented divisions in opinion at the highest level on both sides, with some elements investigating the possibilities of a rapprochement. Given the antagonistic rhetoric, it was an enormous risk to take and, while leaders on both sides would later feign ignorance, there is little doubt that the operation was sanctioned at the highest level (again, on both sides). The leak emerged first from Iran. America once again felt humiliated, though it is significant that the individual regarded as responsible for sabotaging the operation in Iran was the one who faced the firing squad, not those responsible for establishing the links in the first place. This is all the more surprising when the Israeli connection is considered. The failure of what became known as 'the Iran-Contra Affair' marked the last time the United States made serious approaches to the Islamic Republic, although even these showed a curious neglect in preparation, and the resulting embarrassment ensured that the US would not pursue the covert way again.[135]

With the sudden realisation that Iran was making progress in its operations against Iraq, signified by the successful capture of the Fao Peninsula in 1986, the US abandoned any pursuit of détente and put its full weight behind Iraq. Far from having fought the Iranians to a standstill, the capture of Fao revealed the considerable reserves of resourcefulness that were left. Having flooded and electrified the marshlands, the Iraqis were surprised to discover that the Iranians were involved in massive engineering works to drain the marshes largely by building canals by hand.[136] These images were provided by Western satellites, and subsequently the US was to take the unprecedented decision to provide the Iraqis with real-time satellite information so that troop movements could be carefully monitored. Moreover, while Iranian troops had become accustomed to discovering Western 'doctors' near the front line, open assistance was signalled by the stepping-up of operations against Iranian assets in the Persian Gulf. While ostensibly following strict rules of engagement, US naval ships aggressively sought to intercept the Iranian gunboats. One incident was to lead to disaster. The *USS Vincennes* accidentally shot down an Iran Air airbus en route from Shiraz to the Emirates. The loss of some 240 passengers stunned Iran, and convinced the ageing Imam that the US was about to launch a full-scale assault. Few in Iran accepted the US explanation (especially since the captain of the vessel was awarded a special medal), and initial US attempts to lay the blame at Iran's door not only proved distasteful but subsequent investigations have tended to lend weight to the Iranian view that, at the very least, the captain of the *Vincennes* was guilty of criminal neglect.[137] In any case, having refused to accept a succession of UN resolutions calling for a ceasefire (on the pretext that none allocated blame to Iraq for starting the war), a tired Imam instructed the government to accept UNSCR 598. An exhausted nation breathed a sigh of relief, as Khomeini reflected on the causes, consequences and conduct of the war.[138]

The social and political consequences of the war

By all accounts the eight-year-long Iran–Iraq War was a catastrophe for Iran. Iraq retained control of some slivers of Iranian territory, and the Shatt al-Arab waterway (the ostensible *casus belli*) was so choked with destroyed shipping that it remained inaccessible. Iran suffered substantial casualties in what was to prove its first encounter with modern warfare although the final figures were to prove lower at between 170,000 and 215,000 fatalities than initially headlined.[139] However, the damage to its material and economic infrastructure, despite the benefits of enforced self-sufficiency, proved incalculable, especially when the opportunity cost of the war was included. As the Imam's public reflections indicated, it was not long before Iranians themselves were questioning the aims and consequences of the war. Such questioning was itself a reflection of the deeper changes which had begun to thoroughly permeate Iranian society. If Iranians had entered the war as obedient subjects, they emerged from it with a keener sense of their own relationship to the state. The transformation from subjects to citizens had begun in earnest – it was by no means complete, but the foundations had been laid. The Iran–Iraq War was not only the first fought by Iran in the modern age; it was the first time Iranians had experienced anything approaching a total war. To be sure the leaders of the Islamic Republic had hesitated to fully mobilise the resources of the state, acutely aware as they were of the social implications of such a move.

As it was, the advent of war had forced an uneasy compromise between the austerity of the Islamic state and the instinctively rebellious and cosmopolitan society. As the war progressed and pressures increased, so too the balance of tensions favoured society. One of the determining factors leading to the acceptance of UNSCR 598 was the political unreliability of the populace. Indeed, by the end of the war, the tensions implicit in religious nationalism were being resolved in favour of nationalism.[140] This re-entrenchment of nationalism, albeit with a strong Islamic flavour, had been encouraged by Iraqi propaganda portraying the war against Iran as an extension of historic Persian/Arab antipathies, but it was also a recognition that for much of the Iranian population, their distinctive identity remained important. Even Revolutionary Guardsmen (some 88 per cent of whom were conscripts by the end of the war) proved scathing about the qualities of their Shi'a brethren in Iraq, whose failings were blamed openly on their ethnic roots.

Similarly, the tensions between autocracy and democratic pluralism, despite the opportunities presented by the war, had not been resolved in favour of autocracy, thus allowing a measure of openness in discussion. This in part was encouraged, consciously and unconsciously, by Khomeini himself, who, sometimes to the frustration of his supporters, was in the habit of consulting on the most trivial of political issues.[141] This tendency, which belied the criticism of his opponents that he had established a religious dictatorship, was best seen in the establishment of yet another political body (the Expediency Council in 1988) whose purpose was to arbitrate disputes between the Majlis and the Guardian Council. Incomplete as the process was, Khomeini was instrumental in seeking to transform Iranian sensibilities away from a dependence on personalities towards a more institutionalised order. This development had followed a striking decision by the Imam to announce that in an Islamic state the interests of the state took precedence over everything. Religious obligations could be suspended if the survival of the state were threatened.[142] This dramatic statement, exercised in the context of a dispute between the government of Mir-Hussein Musavi and the Guardian Council, was essentially a vote in favour of governmental prerogatives and against the often dogmatic strictures of the Guardian Council. It remained, nevertheless, immensely controversial, especially when the implications of its internal logic were acknowledged.[143] Considered opportunistic by some, and condemned by many members of the *ulema*, this statement seemed to point towards a pragmatic rationalisation, if not secularisation, of the entire order including by implication the subjection of Islamic diktats to the 'national' interest.

There were, of course, clear limitations to this process, reflecting Khomeini's own political methods, the political sophistication of the Iranian public and the ambitions of his devotees. Yet such tendencies were not entirely without historical foundation. In his early speeches, especially after the assassinations of President Rajai and Prime Minister Bahonar in the summer of 1981 at the hands of the MKO, Khomeini emphasised the vital (modern) distinction between the 'state' and its 'leaders', who he pointed out were transitory. More unintentional were the lessons drawn from the dispute between Khomeini and Ayatollah Shariatmadari, whose open rivalry with the Imam and the emergent establishment of the Islamic Republic resulted in his being associated with the MKO and unceremoniously 'demoted' from the rank of Ayatollah to that of Hojjat-ol-Eslam. This was an unprecedented act, since prior to this religious titles had been a matter of popular acclamation and were not formally awarded. This tentative rationalisation into a formal hierarchy initiated a process of demystification and made apparent to the watching masses that it was not only kings who could be overthrown.

The social impact of these political changes was not fully appreciated by all the leaders of the Islamic Republic, who emerged battered, though not crippled, from the eight-year war. In one sense, the state emerged with its self-confidence enhanced, and there is no doubt that, whatever the criticisms, Iranians surprised themselves with their ability to resist what by all accounts appeared to be insurmountable odds. In this sense, the experience of war proved empowering, not only for society but for the state, which in stark contrast to Iraq, emerged from the war with minimal debt. This self-confidence led to different convictions from those of broad bands of society whose zeal had been tempered by the brutality of war. For them, the lessons of the war were Islamic 'austerity', 'discipline', 'unity' and, by implication, autocracy.[144] Politics was less a matter of participation than acclamation, or at best a measure of populism to ensure that the social foundations of the Revolution remained intact. With the war abroad over, they eagerly turned their attentions to the war at home and their determination to create the ideal Islamic state. And in this lay the bitterest legacy of the war: the crisis of demobilisation, not only in an economic sense but also in a psychological sense. For some returning veterans, politics was the continuation of war by an admixture of other means: it was to be a seamless if profoundly problematic transition.

Rafsanjani and the ascendancy of the mercantile bourgeoisie

In many ways the most powerful man to emerge from the war was Ali Akbar Hashemi Rafsanjani, a close confidante of Imam Khomeini and Speaker of the Majlis. Regarded by many as a progressive mullah, he was also an acute political operator as well as a shrewd businessman, having made much of his money in the building boom of the 1970s. While the Prime Minister, Mir-Hussein Musavi, had successfully managed the economy during the war on broadly statist principles, and the President, Hojjat-ol-Eslam Ali Khamenei acted as a titular 'head of state', it was Hashemi Rafsanjani who orchestrated political affairs. Khomeini was at this stage exhausted and approaching 90, increasingly reflective about his achievements and failures, and the future direction of the Islamic Republic. The energy which he had enjoyed in the early years had dissipated, and if anything he became more stubborn and defensive when confronted with the undoubted corruption (moral and financial) which was emerging as he himself increasingly withdrew from political life. This new reality became apparent in his decision to replace his erstwhile heir, Ayatollah Montazeri, with Hojjat-ol-Eslam Khamenei, whom he abruptly promoted to 'ayatollah', despite the latter's lack of qualification for such a rank.[145] Montazeri had grown increasingly concerned by the behaviour of some of Khomeini's lieutenants, their manipulation of the political environment for their own interests and their extreme interpretation of the Leader's observations. He was particularly incensed by the activities of the law enforcement and prison services, and the executions which seemed to occur with an extrajudicial regularity. He protested in the strongest terms to Khomeini, who responded that such outrages were simply not possible in an Islamic Republic.[146] It was in such a state of denial that Khomeini delivered his infant creation into the hands of less scrupulous successors.

Following the end of the war, the MKO, which had since relocated to the vicinity of Baghdad, decided (with almost grotesque political naivety) that now was the time to launch their liberation of Iran. The result of this miscalculation was a massacre at the front, and a concomitant slaughter in the prisons, as the Islamic Republic responded with justifiable ferocity along the Iraqi border, and with an appalling lack of magnanimity in the prisons. In seeking to settle the score with the MKO, the Islamic Republic prolonged the enmity and the hatred, which exists to this day.[147] Another decision which added to the complex legacy Khomeini left his heirs was the response to *The Satanic Verses* by Salman Rushdie, who was born in India but educated in England. Khomeini's decision to issue a *fatwa* (or, as has more recently been argued, an edict, *hokm*), has been the subject of considerable speculation, since with a single stroke the Imam severely hampered Iran's ability to renegotiate its international position. There is little doubt that Khomeini's response resulted from advice he received, and questions remain about the validity of that advice. It was not clear whether anyone had actually read the book, and few people in Iran were particularly interested. In fact Rushdie was a popular author in Iranian literary circles, having received an award for one of his earlier books, and travelled to Iran to receive it. Now, however, *The Satanic Verses*, the implications of its title and the narrative relating to the Prophet Muhammad, caused widespread outrage in the Islamic world, finally resulting in deaths on the Indian subcontinent. It was some five months before Khomeini was persuaded to respond. He argued that anyone who insulted the sanctity of the Prophet would be automatically condemned to death. A country which to date had shown little interest in the book (there had been no riots or demonstrations in Iran) suddenly became the focus of attention and Western criticism. Both sides in Britain and Iran sought to calm the situation. Even President Khamenei pointed out that if Rushdie apologised he might be forgiven – thus earning a stern reprimand from the Imam. In the UK, the Conservative government sought to play down the implications of the *fatwa*. However, the situation rapidly descended into a battle of principles, as radicals on both sides refused to concede ground. The one man who could have solved the problem, by clarifying his comments, died in June 1989. Imam Khomeini, who had founded the Revolution and guided the country through an eight-year struggle with Iraq, and who had lived in conditions of considerable austerity, was accorded an unprecedented funeral, with an estimated turnout of some two million mourners. He was the first Iranian ruler in over 80 years not to be exiled or murdered but to die peacefully in his bed.

The Islamic Republic defined

Following the trauma of Khomeini's death, the political establishment of the Islamic Republic moved quickly to consolidate its position, and by its own reckoning the stability of the state itself. The first necessity was to ensure a smooth succession from Khomeini to Khamenei. The Assembly of Experts quickly convened to confirm a somewhat reluctant Ali Khamenei as the new Leader and *vali-e faqih*. Aware that Khamenei lacked the necessary religious qualifications for the post and the charisma of his predecessor, moves were also taken to formalise his position in the Constitution. The late Imam had in fact urged a review of the Constitution to see where refinements could be made.[148] Nevertheless, the interpretation of his legacy in favour of authoritarianism (the word 'absolute' (*motlaqe*) was inserted prior to *velayat-e faqih* in the Constitution) was viewed with some concern in more progressive quarters as a wilful misinterpretation of Khomeini's earlier comments on the primacy of the state.[149] At the same time, Rafsanjani took the opportunity to further modify the Constitution to abolish the post of prime minister and transfer his prerogatives to the presidency – a move regarded as the much-needed rationalisation of an over-cumbersome political system by many observers. It did not go unnoticed that Rafsanjani's subsequent election to the presidency (in a managed election common in the war years) made him the chief beneficiary of the change.

The state defined by Rafsanjani, however, went considerably further than constitutional modifications. In the absence of Khomeini's charisma, a new settlement had to be reached which bound the different groups in a tight network of commercial self-interest.[150] The consequence of this was an alliance of interests between the 'mercantile bourgeoisie', centred on but not exclusive to the traditional *bazaar*, and the patrimonial presidency of Rafsanjani, who proceeded to develop a loyal bureaucracy very much in his own image. Rafsanjani would govern with the interests of the merchant classes in mind, interests which coincided with his own commercial background, while the *bazaar* would help finance the presidency. Tensions undoubtedly existed between these two wings, especially with respect to the position of the Islamic authoritarians who were closely allied to the *bazaar*, but it was a potent meeting of interests. After the austerity of the war, exemplified by the Imam's lifestyle, Rafsanjani signalled that making money was a 'good thing' which should be encouraged, and the *bazaar* started to reap the rewards of the revolution it had been so central in supporting. This new mood of commercial optimism also served Rafsanjani's instinctive populism. He had ambitions to be the central figure in the political history of the maturing Islamic Republic, the architect of the new state; he craved a historical legacy as well as immediate popularity. In many ways the state defined by Rafsanjani mirrored that of the last Shah, except that the Shah had increasingly relied on a 'comprador bourgeoisie', while Rafsanjani developed a relationship with a social network of mercantile bourgeoisie which the Shah had largely ignored. Furthermore, Rafsanjani was aware that the Shah's economic successes were based on fragile political foundations through an acute social disconnection. Rafsanjani would not make the same mistake and, much to the satisfaction of the Islamic Left and pro-republicans, Rafsanjani publicly espoused the ideals of democratisation. In reality, however, Rafsanjani's chief interests lay not in the political field but in economic reconstruction, and the former was managed only in so far as it satisfied the needs of the latter.

Indeed, with the inauguration of Rafsanjani's first administration, the Islamic Republic of Iran entered the self-proclaimed 'era of reconstruction'. The President's first task was to restore a sense of centralised order. He combined the various law enforcement organisations into one formal structure through the integration of the *komitehs*, and united the hierarchy and structure of the Revolutionary Guards with the armed forces, forcing the Guards to institute military ranks. Despite huge resistance from the Guards, the armed forces henceforth possessed one logistical support structure. Much to the consternation of the *ulema*, Rafsanjani also tried to formalise and regularise the 'profession' by instituting examinations which would weed out the unqualified. Religious bodies which sat in Qom were brought to Tehran so as to be better supervised. In fact the rationalisation of the religious hierarchy was to have problematic results. Many senior ayatollahs who had objected to the concept of *velayat-e faqih* found themselves politically marginalised. When they died, the state was unwilling to recognise the qualifications of a new generation lest they challenge the authority of the Leader, whose paucity of religious authority among the *ulema* themselves proved consistently problematic. The number of 'political' ayatollahs mushroomed (thereby devaluing the title) as the state sought to elevate sympathetic mullahs, a process which effectively secularised religious authority. Political loyalty, not religious learning, was what mattered.

Crucially, Rafsanjani stated publicly that those covert units used to assassinate opponents during the war would now be terminated, having served their purpose. All these moves sounded impressive, but observers witnessed considerably more centralisation than rationalisation and, as critics would discover, much of the process remained distinctly and dangerously incomplete. Many of the ad hoc revolutionary organisations remained in place, in particular the various judicial bodies established to control wayward *ulema* and the press during the heat of the

Revolution and the war. Most obvious of the untouched legacies of the war were the large religious foundations, or *Bonyads*, in particular the Foundation of the Oppressed, whose administration was awarded to Mohsen Rafiqdoust, a former street trader who had risen rapidly through the ranks of the establishment by virtue of his having been Imam Khomeini's driver on his arrival in Tehran in 1979. Rafiqdoust had been responsible for arms procurement for the Revolutionary Guards during the war, and was not regarded as entirely scrupulous in his financial dealings. His appointment to head the largest conglomerate in the country was consequently viewed with suspicion by many observers. That said, in 1989 a war-weary population proved ready to buy into the promise of the better life Rafsanjani proclaimed.

Rafsanjani had ambitious economic plans. He had inherited an economy that had been managed largely on statist principles during the war, and proclaimed, much to the concern of the left-leaning Third Majlis, his desire to move towards a free-market economy. To much fanfare he launched the first Five Year Development Plan, drawn up by the Plan and Budget Organisation, and proceeded to reconstruct the country with the help of a highly technocratic cabinet, many of whom had been educated in the United States. The economic plans pursued by the Rafsanjani administration soon ran into problems, partly as a consequence of their ambition, but also because of the limitations of the Iranian political-economic environment and Rafsanjani's own unwillingness to enforce the changes necessary for real economic progress. In short, Rafsanjani was either unwilling or unable to tackle the variety of revolutionary organisations who obstructed economic reform, while they often insisted on reform (in particular transparency and accountability) being led by example, in other words from Rafsanjani down. The result was the implementation of halfhearted reforms, and the development of a two-tier economic system. On the one hand, the Ministry of Finance sent out auditors to inspect company accounts; on the other, the Foundation of the Oppressed (which some argued, dominated some 40 per cent of the Iranian economy) remained exempt from any such inspection. Similarly, the existence of several exchange rates, a means by which strategic industries could enjoy import subsidies during the war, were continued to the benefit, in the main, of the Foundation of the Oppressed. When the then Central Bank Governor Hussein Adeli hastily determined to unify the exchange rates, and thereby eliminate these inconsistencies, the exercise collapsed in farce as a black market rate quickly emerged and organisations used to receiving their favourable rate demanded re-establishment of their subsidies. This weakness of the Iranian rial was predicated on the perceived weakness of the economy.

In simple terms, for the Iranian economy to grow and stabilise it was in urgent need of investment, whether foreign or domestic. The oil industry, the central pillar of Iran's economy and source of all patronage, needed massive injections of capital if Iran was to fully exploit its resources; opportunities also existed within a variety of other sectors, including the mining sector. But to secure foreign investment a stable economic environment had to be created, with legal transparency and accountability, and this conflicted with Rafsanjani's personal and political leanings. Moreover, Rafsanjani completely misunderstood the transformation in Iran's international relations which had taken place since the Revolution, believing (erroneously as it happened) that self-interest was the guiding principle of Western foreign policy. Ironically, the West's ideological suspicion of Iran betrayed the ideological determinism of its own foreign policy. Rafsanjani's efforts to solve the Lebanese hostage crisis, and to moderate Iran's views on the Arab–Israeli Peace Process (or indeed the Rushdie affair) failed to dent the 'wall of mistrust' which had emerged.

The result for the economy was a populism purchased through the pursuit of loans[151] and the printing of money, both of which proved inflationary. In 1991–92, the boom following the war was finally followed by an enormous bust, and Iran found itself unable to pay its debts. Domestically, those with access to capital (in particular hard currency) flourished; those who did not, principally those payed in rials, found their financial resources plummeting. The income disparities commonly associated with the Shah had returned with a vengeance, and many observed that a new 'thousand families' were emerging to replace the old. The effective collapse of the economy proved a fatal wound for the Rafsanjani presidency, though this was not yet apparent in 1992. Rafsanjani blamed his economic woes on the intransigence of the Majlis, which, he argued, was dominated by unreconstructed Islamic leftists, enthusiastic about retaining a centralised economy. To some extent, Rafsanjani and his ministers were accurate in their depiction of the Majlis, but the Majlis members too had a point when they argued that Rafsanjani's 'free-market' policies in reality meant a market dominated by mercantile interests not open to competition and ignorant of any notion of social justice.

In any event, in 1992, the managed elections to the Fourth Majlis provided the immediate result Rafsanjani sought – the eviction of the Left and the domination of the Majlis by the right-wing deputies. However, at his moment of apparent political triumph Rafsanjani found himself being squeezed by both the Left and the Right. The Right increasingly dominated the institutions of the state, not having been targeted in Rafsanjani's 'cleansing' (*pak-sazi*) of the ministries and now, with control of the legislative body, appeared to grow weary of their saviour. Much to Rafsanjani's consternation, they began to agitate against him and in support of their own candidate. Furthermore, some on the Right began to argue for the implementation of an Islamic state as opposed to a republic, dismissing the need for a presidency and for elections of any sort. The more commercially successful the Right became, so too their political ambitions grew, and while not all on the Right supported a move away from any pretence of a republic, such moves were taken seriously not only by the marginalised Left but by Rafsanjani himself, who sought to disassociate himself from these views. Indeed the Left, while suspicious of Rafsanjani's intentions, cautiously welcomed this realignment as an indication that the Right was beginning to split.

In his settlement, Rafsanjani had sought to implement a modus vivendi which allowed the authoritarian Right considerable room to manoeuvre, allowing, for instance, through legal amendment, the Conservative Guardian Council to interpret and exercise its powers more extensively than the Constitution had arguably envisaged. In one sense, their authoritarianism appealed to his own notion of order, while he recognised the utility of religion in this form as a means of social control. They, on the other hand, agreed to justify the settlement in religious terms, but their ambitions were divided on a number of issues, and in many ways remained tense. For instance, on social issues, Rafsanjani tended to have cosmopolitan tastes, encouraging women to wear colourful veils, and, on one occasion, appeasing youthful frustrations by encouraging the practice of 'temporary marriage' without the need for any form of registration. Rafsanjani sought to ease the constant checks on religious probity conducted by the various law enforcement agencies, while the Right viewed this as a necessity to check corruption. As a result the Right increasingly revolved around the Leader Ali Khamenei, who had his own reasons for feeling marginalised from the political fray. Unwilling to be the junior partner to Rafsanjani, Khamenei saw benefits in championing the Right, who in turn pushed for a more interventionist role for the Leader. While differences of opinion between the two men were often exaggerated, there is little doubt that they grew apart as the Rafsanjani administration progressed. One of the more unsavoury aspects of this relationship related to the continued existence of right-wing hit squads who would target 'liberals' they considered harmful to the state. Exactly how much Rafsanjani knew of these developments is unclear, though at the very least he was guilty of wilful neglect. While he had probably succeeded in curtailing the activities of these shadowy groups abroad,[152] he allowed them considerable leeway at home. Nevertheless, their activities constituted a major blemish on the Islamic Republic's international reputation and made it vulnerable to continued criticism.[153]

Notes

1 Alexis de Tocqueville, *The Old Regime and the Revolution*, Vol I (trans. John Bonner). New York: Harper & Brothers, 1856. http://oll.libertyfund.org/titles/tocqueville-the-old-regime-and-the-revolution-1856.
2 See Bill, *The Eagle and the Lion*, pp. 209–10 on the scandal involving pay-offs by Grumman Aerospace to the Deputy Minister of War, General Hassan Toufanian.
3 See, as a comparison, de Tocqueville, *The Old Regime and the Revolution*, p. 180.
4 The 'paradox of sultanism' writ large.
5 The political disconnection is described well by the British Ambassador; see A. Parsons, *The Pride and the Fall: Iran 1974–79*. London: Cape, 1984, pp. 23–4.
6 de Tocqueville, *The Old Regime and the Revolution*, p. 222.
7 Quoted in Bill, *The Eagle and the Lion*, p. 233.
8 For an alternative reading of these events see A. Milani, *The Persian Sphinx: Amir Abbas Hoveyda and the Riddle of the Iranian Revolution*. London: Tauris, 2000, p. 286.
9 *Etela'at*, 8 January 1978.
10 Dariush Homayun, BBC *Reputations*, 'The Last Shah', 1996.
11 See Amini, 'A Single Party State in Iran, 1975–78', p. 132.
12 Talk of voluntary abdication certainly reached the ears of the British Ambassador; see Parsons, *The Pride and the Fall*, p. 48.
13 See interview with Dariush Homayun, BBC *Reputations*, 'The Last Shah', 1996.

14 See interview with Ghaffari, BBC *Reputations*, 'The Last Shah', 1996.

15 Parsons, *The Pride and the Fall*, pp. 54–5. The organisers had different recollections of the impact of the play.

16 See B. Moin, *Khomeini: Life of the Ayatollah*. London: I.B. Tauris, 1999, p. 136.

17 Mustapha's death was blamed on SAVAK, although alternative theories point to tuberculosis.

18 See Moin, *Khomeini*, pp. 149–50.

19 For a detailed discussion see N. Nabavi, 'The Changing Concept of the "Intellectual" in Iran of the 1960s', *Iranian Studies* 32(3), Summer 1999, pp. 333–50. There are obvious comparisons to be made to the ideas of the Italian Marxist Antonio Gramsci.

20 For an excellent discussion of Shariati see A. Rahnema, *Ali Shariati: A Political Biography*. London: I.B. Tauris, 1998.

21 See Ahmad Khomeini's comments in Moin, *Khomeini*, p. 276.

22 On the innovative nature of these protests see Charles Kurzman, *The Unthinkable Revolution in Iran*. Cambridge, MA: Harvard University Press, 2004, Kindle edition, loc: 678/3531.

23 de Tocqueville, *The Old Regime and the Revolution*, p. 222.

24 See BBC *Reputations*, 'The Last Shah', 1996.

25 C. Kadivar, 'A Question of Numbers', *Rouzegar-e Now*, 8 August 2003.

26 D. Menashri, *Iran: A Decade of War and Revolution*. London: Holmes & Meier, 1990, p. 55.

27 BBC SWB ME/5962/A/10–11 dated 7 November 1978, The Shah's 6 November speech, Tehran Home Service, dated 6 November 1978.

28 On the background to this see the memoirs of Amir Aslan Afshar, *Khaterat doctor amir aslan afshar*. Montreal: Farhang, 2012, pp. 479–82. Afshar argues that the Shah was effectively bounced into reading the speech which was drafted for him, unusually, by Reza Ghotbi and Seyyed Hossein Nasr, neither of whom would have normally been responsible for such matters.

29 The failure of communication is exemplified by an incident in which a member of the political elite phoned the palace to seek reassurance, and was told by the Empress not to worry, tanks had surrounded the palace and the Imperial family were safe! Interview with author.

30 A.A. Massoud Ansari, *Man va Khandan-e Pahlavi* (The Pahlavi Family and I). San Jose, CA: Tooka Publishing, 1997, pp. 98–9.

31 Mirabeau to Louis XVI, quoted in de Tocqueville, *The Old Regime and the Revolution*, p. 98:

> Compare the new order of things with the regime; from this comparison is born consolation and hope. Most of the acts of the National Assembly are clearly favourable to the monarchy. Is it nothing to be without parlements [sic], without pays d'états, without the assembly of the clergy, without privileges or nobility? The idea of having only one class of citizens would have pleased Richelieu; equality facilitates the exercise of power. Several reigns of absolute government would not have done as much for royal authority as this single year of revolution has done.

32 BBC SWB ME/5964/A/5 dated 9 November 1978, Comment on the Shah's 6 November speech, Tehran Home Service, dated 7 November 1978.

33 BBC SWB ME/5963/A/8 dated 8 November 1978, Ayatollah Khomeini interviewed by West German magazine, dated 6 November 1978.

34 See BBC SWB ME/5978/A/12 dated 25 November 1978, More political prisoners to be released, Tehran Home Service, dated 23 November 1978. See also, BBC SWB ME/5989/A/9 dated 8 December 1978, Pardons, Tehran Home Service, dated 7 December 1978.

35 BBC SWB ME/5965/A/8 dated 10 November 1978, Arrest of Hoveyda, Tehran Home Service, dated 8 November 1978.
36 BBC SWB ME/5964/A/6 dated 9 November 1978, Arrests in Tehran, Tehran Home Service, dated 7 November 1978.
37 BBC SWB ME/5973/A/6 dated 20 November 1978, Shahbanu's visit to Iraq, INA, dated 18 November 1978.
38 Interview with Dariush Homayun, BBC *Reputations*, 'The Last Shah', 1996.
39 BBC SWB ME/5982/A/10 dated 30 November 1978, Transfer of money abroad by Iranians, Tehran Home Service, dated 28 November 1978.
40 BBC SWB ME/5986/A/12 dated 5 December 1978, Religious holidays, Tehran Home Service, dated 3 December 1978.
41 M. Foucault, 'Iran: The Spirit of a World without Spirit', in *Politics, Philosophy and Culture: Interviews and Other Writings 1977–1984*. London: Routledge, 1988, p. 215. The figure of 2 million is undoubtedly an exaggeration, as the rounded number would suggest. G. Afkhami in his biography of the Shah has effectively questioned this extraordinary figure which was certainly given succour by Foucault's comments, see G. Afkhami, *The Shah*. Berkeley, CA: University of California Press, p. 667, note 49.
42 BBC SWB ME/5989/A/11 dated 8 December 1978, Tehran Military Governor's 6 December communique, Tehran Home Service, dated 6 December 1978.
43 BBC SWB ME/5963/A/9 dated 8 November 1978, Ayatollah Khomeini interviewed in West German magazine, DPA, dated 6 November 1978.
44 See BBC SWB ME/5986/A/12, Incident involving British and US journalists, Pars, dated 4 December 1978.
45 BBC SWB ME/5987/A/8 dated 6 December 1978, Information Ministry denial of regency rumour, Tehran Home Service, dated 4 December 1978.
46 This is the continued interpretation among supporters of the monarchy of the 'Huyser' mission which the White House dispatched in January 1979. The Shah himself gave credence to this view. See M.R. Pahlavi, *Answer to History*. New York: Stein & Day, 1980, p. 172. For alternative readings see Bill, *The Eagle and the Lion*, pp. 253–5; R.E. Huyser, *Mission to Tehran*. New York: Harper & Row, 1986. See also S. Zabih, *The Iranian Military in Revolution and War*. London: Routledge, pp. 93–115.
47 BBC SWB ME/6021/A/6 dated 20 January 1979, Ayatollah Khomeini: French and Libyan reports, Paris Home Service, dated 18 January 1979.
48 BBC SWB ME/5989/A/10 dated 8 December 1978, Iranian National Front Leader's interview for French Radio, Paris Home Service, dated 6 December 1978.
49 See Bill, *The Eagle and the Lion*, pp. 278–80.
50 See comments by Parviz Radji, BBC *Reputations*, 'The Last Shah', 1996.
51 BBC SWB ME/6017/A/7 dated 16 January 1979, Ayatollah Khomeini's interview with Hamburg Television, Hamburg Television, dated 12 January 1979.
52 BBC SWB ME/6018/A/15 dated 17 January 1979, The Shah's farewell interview, Tehran Home Service, dated 16 January 1979.
53 Kadivar, 'A Question of Numbers'.
54 Disenfranchised landowners were often crucial in encouraging such views, despite their nonsensical nature.
55 BBC SWB ME/6017/A/8 dated 16 January 1979, The Islamic Revolutionary Council members, JANA, dated, 15 January 1979.
56 BBC SWB ME/6017/A/7 dated 16 January 1979, Khomeini's 14 January message to the nation, Tehran Home Service, dated 14 January 1979.
57 BBC SWB ME/6021/A/6 dated 20 January 1979, Shariatmadari's call for calm during the 19 January demonstrations, Tehran Home Service, dated 18 January 1979.
58 BBC SWB ME/6201/A/7 dated 20 January 1979, The 19 January marches, Tehran Home Service, dated 19 January 1979.

59 See for example BBC SWB ME/6044/A/10 dated 16 February 1979, Fedayin-e Khalq message to Bani Sadr, dated 14 February 1979.
60 See for example, BBC SWB ME/6041/A/10/15 dated 13 February 1979, Developments in Iran, Tehran Home Service, dated 11 February 1979.
61 BBC SWB ME/6040/A/10 dated 12 February 1979, The security situation in Iran, dated 11 February 1979.
62 BBC SWB ME/6041/A/5 dated 13 February 1979, Developments in Iran, Tehran Home Service, dated 11 February 1979.
63 BBC SWB ME/6046/A/11 dated 19 February 1979, Developments in Iran, Tehran Home Service, dated 17 February 1979.
64 See BBC SWB ME/6043/A/9 dated 15 February 1979, Ayatollah Khomeini's 13 February message to the nation, Tehran Home Service, dated 13 February 1979.
65 BBC SWB ME/6041/A/7 dated 13 February 1979, Developments in Iran, Tehran Home Service, dated 11 February 1979.
66 BBC SWB ME/6041/A/11 dated 13 February 1979, Developments in Iran, Tehran Home Service, dated 11 February 1979. BBC SWB ME/6044/A/6 dated 16 February 1979, Developments in Iran, Tehran Home Service, dated 14 February 1979. BBC SWB ME/6046/A/10 dated 19 February 1979, Developments in Iran, dated 17 February 1979.
67 BBC SWB ME/6044/A/8 dated 16 February 1979, Khomeini's message to soldiers, Tehran Home Service, dated 14 February 1979.
68 BBC SWB ME/6043/A/10 dated 15 February 1979, Ayatollah Khomeini's 13 February message to the nation, Tehran Home Service, dated 13 February 1979.
69 BBC SWB ME/6045/A/10 dated 17 February 1979, Developments in Iran, Tehran Home Service, dated 16 February 1979. Also, BBC SWB ME/6051/A/7–8 dated 24 February 1979, Shariatmadari's 22 February statement, Tehran Home Service, dated 22 February 1979.
70 BBC SWB ME/6046/A/12 dated 19 February 1979, Developments in Iran, Tehran Home Service, dated 17 February 1979.
71 BBC SWB ME/6043/A/13 dated 15 February 1979, Developments in Iran, Tehran Home Service, dated 13 February.
72 BBC SWB ME/6045/A/9 dated 17 February 1979, Developments in Iran, Tehran Home Service, dated 15 February 1979.
73 BBC SWB ME/6045/A/7 dated 17 February 1979, Developments in Iran, Tehran Home Service, dated 15 February 1979.
74 BBC SWB ME/6046/A/12 dated 19 February 1979, Developments in Iran, Tehran Home Service, dated 17 February.
75 BBC SWB ME/6043/A/14 dated 15 February 1979, Developments in Iran, Tehran Home Service, dated 14 February 1979. Also, BBC SWB ME/6044/A/4, Developments in Iran, Tehran Home Service, dated 14 February 1979.
76 BBC SWB ME/6046/A/10 dated 19 February 1979, Developments in Iran, Tehran Home Service, dated 16 February.
77 See E. Abrahamian, *Khomeinism*. London: I.B. Tauris, 1993, pp. 13–38.
78 BBC SWB ME/6046/A/9 dated 19 February 1979, Developments in Iran, Tehran Home Service, dated 16 February.
79 BBC SWB ME/6045/A/8 dated 17 February 1979, Developments in Iran, Tehran Home Service, dated 15 February 1979.
80 BBC SWB ME/6045/A/9 dated 17 February 1979, Developments in Iran, Tehran Home Service, dated 15 February 1979. See also BBC SWB ME/6046/A/9 dated 19 February 1979, Developments in Iran, Tehran Home Service, dated 16 February.
81 BBC SWB ME/6047/A/6 dated 20 February 1979, Retirement of senior Iranian officers, Tehran Home Service, dated 18 February.
82 BBC SWB ME/6045/A/10 dated 17 February 1979, Developments in Iran, Tehran Home Service, dated 15 February.

83 BBC SWB ME/6047/A/5–6 dated 20 February 1979, Comment on the execution in Iran of Nasiri and others, Tehran Home Service, dated 16 February.

84 Hojjat-ol-Eslam Khalkhali gained notoriety for the pride and corresponding publicity he took in his work. See S. Khalkhali, *Khaterat-e Ayatollah Khalkhali* (The Memoirs of Ayatollah Khalkhali). Tehran: Nashr-e Sayeh, 1380/2001, p. 291, where Khalkhali argues, somewhat unconvincingly, that he had never wanted the position of head of the revolutionary courts, since it would be a job full of blood which would tarnish his legacy. Nevertheless, the Imam insisted.

85 Recounted to author.

86 The complexities of the US relationship are detailed in the excellent article by M. Gasiorowski, 'US Intelligence Assistance to Iran, May–October 1979', *Middle East Journal* 66(4), Autumn 2012, pp. 613–27.

87 The origins of the title are debated, although it appears as if it was acquired in Iraq, where, as in most Arab countries, it is more common and essentially denotes a *mujtahid*. The title was adopted in Iran to distinguish Khomeini from other *mujtahids* and ayatollahs, although it continues to be contentious within a Shi'a framework. See H. Algar, *Roots of the Islamic Revolution*. New York: Oneonta, 2001, p. 78. Khomeini meticulously avoided any association of this title with that of the infallible Imams of Shi'a tradition, despite the attempts of some of his followers.

88 Cf. M. Weber, 'In Traditional Societies, Charisma Is the Real Revolutionary Force', in *Economy and Society*, Vol I. Berkeley, CA: University of California Press, 1978, p. 245.

89 See Vanessa Martin's excellent account of the development of Khomeini's political ideas, *Creating an Islamic State: Khomeini and the Making of a New Iran*. London: I.B. Tauris, 2000.

90 See the interview with M. Karrubi in the Persian daily *Nowruz*, 30 Ordibehesht 1381/20 May 2002, pp. 1–2; see also Martin, *Creating an Islamic State*, p. 157.

91 See Menashri, *Iran*, p. 84.

92 See Martin, *Creating an Islamic State*, p. 158.

93 A nuance noticed by Algar, *Roots of the Islamic Revolution*.

94 An interesting example is provided by the renaming of the main thoroughfare in Tehran, first known as Khiaban-e Pahlavi; this became Khiaban-e Mosaddeq, and subsequently Vali-Asr. The pre-revolutionary name in fact remained in common usage for over a decade.

95 Some notable sites which escaped serious damage were the tomb of Shah Ismail Safavi, the Shah who brought Shi'ism to Iran in the sixteenth century, and the tomb of Nadir Shah in Mashhad. In the latter case, the statue sat atop the tomb, and soldiers were able to prevent zealots from destroying it. Similarly, in some cases the state had to concede to social determination in the restoration of some pre-revolutionary names, e.g. Kermanshah Province.

96 Zealots in some cases sought to remove the 'faces' from some paintings in key palaces.

97 Much is made for instance of Khomeini's utterance of '*hichi*' (nothing), when asked by reporters what he felt on returning to Iran after 14 years' exile. Some commentators have noted that as a religious intellectual, who strictly speaking owed his allegiance to God, an explicit national sympathy would have been inappropriate.

98 Martin, *Creating an Islamic State*, p. 166; also Menashri, *Iran*, p. 120.

99 Reportedly, when a delegation approached Khomeini for his view on what the 'Gulf' should be named, he answered that it should be named after the power which 'exploits' it, in other words, 'the American Gulf'!

100 For example, the argument of some *bazaar* merchants that they only needed to pay Islamic taxes was swiftly quashed.

101 It should be remembered that Ayatollah Taleqani, who died at the end of 1979, was regarded as sympathetic to the Left and a protector of their interests.

102 See Hasan Yusefi Eshkevari's speech on 'Law and the Women's Movement', delivered at the 'Berlin Conference', April 2000, reprinted in M.A. Zakrayi (ed.), *Conference-e*

Berlin: Khedmat ya Khiyanat? (The Berlin Conference: Service or Treason?). Tehran: Tar-e No, 1379/2000, p. 232. It should also be borne in mind that the veil remained in widespread use during the reign of Mohammad Reza Shah.

103 He, along with the Commander-in-Chief Gharebaghi, was assassinated by a group known as *Furqan*, whose origins are unclear. For a list of assassinations which convulsed the early republic see Bill, *The Eagle and the Lion*, p. 269.

104 For the extensive debates over the inclusion of the concept, see A. Schirazi, *The Constitution of Iran*. London: I.B. Tauris, 1998, pp. 45–61.

105 Criticisms came from some unexpected places. Hussein Khomeini, son of Mustapha and grandson of the Imam, reportedly berated the public in Mashhad that they should not let the *ulema* take power, since they would never relinquish it, adding for good measure that the Caliph Yazid (who killed Imam Hussein) also wore a turban.

106 During the first Presidential elections in January 1980, for instance, Khomeini made it clear that he did not want clerics to stand for the post, thereby ensuring their withdrawal. See Menashri, *Iran*, p. 120.

107 For details see Bill, *The Eagle and the Lion*, pp. 293–304.

108 See comments by Mike Metrinko, Moorhead Kennedy, *444 Days*, Antelope Films, 1998.

109 Interview with Asgharzadeh, September 1999.

110 A British diplomat, David Redaway, was passing through Yazdi's office at the time.

111 Gasiorowski, 'US Intelligence Assistance to Iran, May–October 1979'. A question remains as to how much material was suppressed.

112 One of the more surreal moments followed when Khomeini agreed to allow a priest to celebrate Christmas with the hostages in 1979. Hostages and hostage-takers held hands and prayed together in what proved a highly emotional moment for at least one of the student guards.

113 One may conjecture that even these most 'modern' of students were subsumed within the traditionalism of Iranian politics, which posited the 'personal' over the 'legal-rational'.

114 See comments by Bani-Sadr in *444 Days*.

115 'Neither East nor West', although the 'West' proved the first among equals.

116 See R. Ramazani, *Revolutionary Iran: Challenge and Response in the Middle East*. Baltimore, MD: Johns Hopkins University Press, 1986, p. 25.

117 Recounted by Sir Anthony Parsons, at the School of Oriental and African Studies.

118 The reasons for the Iraqi decision to limit their advance are disputed; see A.H. Cordesman and A.R. Wagner, *The Lessons of Modern War*, Vol II: *The Iran–Iraq War*. London: Mansell, 1990, pp. 89–90; also S. Chubin and C. Tripp, *Iran and Iraq at War*. London: I.B. Tauris, 1988, pp. 54–5.

119 It is not an exaggeration to state that the dominant view was that expressed by James Morier, 'Persians will only fight as long as nobody has to die', *Hajji Baba of Isfahan*.

120 Cordesman and Wagner, *Lessons of Modern War*, p. 93.

121 For further analysis see Gary Sick, *October Surprise: America's Hostages in Iran and the Election of Ronald Reagan*. London: I.B. Tauris, 1991. See also the interview with B. Nabavi in *Nowruz*, 4 Khordad 1381/25 May 2002, p. 9, in which he argues that he wanted the hostage crisis solved within Carter's administration.

122 The total number killed is disputed, and proved convenient in so far as it conformed to the figure martyred at Kerbala with Imam Hussein. Hashemi Rafsanjani fortunately left the building some five minutes earlier.

123 E. Abrahamian, *Radical Islam: The Iranian Mojahedin*. London: I.B. Tauris, p. 220; see Cordesman and Wagner, *Lessons of Modern War*, p. 117, where they note that the government admitted to 2,000 executions while other estimates put the figure at 3,300.

124 See, for example, Abdolkarim Sorous, *Reason, Freedom and Democracy in Islam* (trans. and ed. M. Sadri and A. Sadri). Oxford: Oxford University Press, 2000.

125 For details see E. Abrahamian, *Radical Islam*, pp. 243–63.

126 One student member of the *Fedayin-e Khalq* was struck, on his return to Iran, at how limited the reach of the Left was in comparison to the mosque. Interview with author.

127 See A.H. Bani-Sadr, *My Turn to Speak*. London: Brasseys, 1989, pp. 161–73.

128 See Cordesman and Wagner, *The Lessons of Modern War*, p. 114.

129 The battle of Karbala, in which Imam Hussein and his followers were martyred by the Caliph Yazid, had been (and indeed remains) the pre-eminent military narrative commemorated annually in the religious festivals of Tasu'a and Ashura.

130 In a Friday prayers sermon, Rafsanjani conceded that Imam Khomeini had no desire to extend the war into Iraq. See *Hayat-e No*, 4 Khordad 1381/25 May 2002, p. 2.

131 See A. Ganji, 'Rowshanfekran va Ali-jenab Sorkh-poosh' (His Red Eminence and the Intellectuals), *Fath* 6/11/1378/26 January 2000, reprinted in *Alijenab Sorkhpoosh va Ali-jenab Khakestari: asib shenasi gozar beh dowlat demokratic-e tose'ekar* (Pathology of Transition to the Developmental Democratic State). Tehran: Tar-e No, 1380/2001, p. 139.

132 See M. Mesbahi, 'The USSR and the Iran–Iraq War', in F. Rajaee (ed.), *The Iran–Iraq War*. Gainesville, FL: University of Florida Press, 1993, pp. 88–9.

133 See discussion in R. King, *The Iran–Iraq War: The Political Implications*. Adelphi Paper 219, International Institute for Strategic Studies, Spring 1987, pp. 46–59.

134 See Chubin and Tripp, *Iran and Iraq at War*, p. 50 on the tendency for the Iranians to show restraint.

135 Although covert operations are by their nature unknown!

136 See also James Woolsey's comments, BBC *Panorama*, 3 November 2002. Recounted to author.

137 See BBC *Correspondent*, 'The Other Lockerbie', 2000; this incident has led some to argue that Iran was responsible for the Lockerbie bombing.

138 See Ganji, 'Rowshanfekran va Ali-jenab Sorkh-poosh', p. 139. Khomeini noted that there were many valid questions to be asked about the war, though now was not the time.

139 In 2000, IRNA put the figure at 188,015. Figures for those wounded have not been collated but could be up to four times that figure. Much depends on the statistics being used and whether civilian casualties are included in the total. For an analysis of the figures see W. Beuttel, 'Iranian Casualties in the Iran–Iraq War (1980–1988): A Reappraisal', *The International TNDM Newsletter* 2(3), December 1997. See also C. Kurzman, https://kurzman.unc.edu/death-tolls-of-the-iran-iraq-war/. Also Batool Mousavi, Maziar Moradi-Lakeh, Mojgan Karbakhsh and Mohammadreza Soroush, 'Years of Life Lost among Iranian People Killed in the Iraq–Iran War: The 25-Year Perspective', *International Journal of Injury Control and Safety Promotion* 21(4), 2014, pp. 382–7. The authors include in their figure of 'at least' 183,623 Iranians died as a result of the war though to 2005.

140 See the revealing assessment of the reassertion of 'Persian' over Muslim names as early as 1982, N. Habibi, 'Popularity of Islamic and Persian Names in Iran before and after the Islamic Revolution', *International Journal of Middle East Studies* 24, 1992, pp. 253–60.

141 See, for example, Hasan Yusefi Eshkevari's speech on 'Law and the Women's Movement', delivered at the 'Berlin Conference', April 2000, reprinted in Zakrayi (ed.), *Conference-e Berlin*, p. 229.

142 See the full text BBC SWB ME/0043/A7–8 dated 8 January 1988, Tehran Home Service, dated 7 January 1988.

143 Moin, *Khomeini*, pp. 259–61. As Moin correctly observes, 'Despite his ideological conservatism, there was in Khomeini a rebel with a vision which at times made him act as a radical in the sphere of politics'.

144 Interesting parallels may be drawn with the return of Vietnam veterans in the US.

145 Khamenei's appointment has since become a matter of intense discussion, given that the only other person present when the nomination was reportedly made was Hashemi Rafsanjani.

146 For details, see Moin, *Khomeini*, pp. 276–92.
147 The estimate of the number of summary executions varies but certainly numbered in the thousands. It continues to haunt the Islamic Republic.
148 Moin, *Khomeini*, p. 293.
149 See in particular M. Kadivar, *Baha-ye Azadi: defa'at Mohsen Kadivar* (The Price of Freedom: The Defence of Mohsen Kadivar). Tehran: Ghazal, 1378/1999–2000, p. 200.
150 For more detail see A.M. Ansari, *Iran, Islam and Democracy: The Politics of Managing Change*. London: Royal Institute of International Affairs, 2000.
151 Rafsanjani himself commented that in securing loans he had secured investment by the back door.
152 There were a number of notable assassinations abroad including Shahpour Bakhtiar, Qasemlou, and of course the murder of the Kurds at the Mykonos restaurant in Berlin in 1992.
153 For many Iranians these activities were not unique to the Iranian state.

14 Khatami and the challenge of reform

The failure of Rafsanjani's settlement was predicated on more than a division at the top; it was founded on a social revolution from below. Iran has a highly communicative social structure and one of the strengths of the Islamic Revolution was the reciprocal osmosis which existed between state and society. Divisions at the top (characterised by some in the growing criticism emanating from the Imam's son, Ahmad Khomeini),[1] were soon replicated in society below, but what was more important was the extensive politicisation of the public that was taking place, largely unnoticed by the political rivals at the top. This was in part a consequence of Rafsanjani's tentative liberalisation of the press and his affectation for a measure of populism. A public space began to emerge. But the public which emerged to fill this space was the product of much more than Rafsanjani's patronage. These were veterans of the war and children of the Revolution who viewed with disdain the bureaucratic centralism and lack of social justice which characterised the Rafsanjani administration. Discontent was expressed in the mid-1990s in riots which shook Iranian cities, the most serious in Qazvin in 1994.[2] These malcontents were even more scathing about the President's allies. The authoritarian Islamists, or 'conservatives' as they were increasingly known, found themselves confronted not only by social discontent, but by an intellectual renaissance in Islamic thought, led by intellectuals such as Abdolkarim Soroush and Mojtahed Shabestari. This was in part galvanised by the threat posed of the possible imposition of an Islamic state. These scholars shaped the intellectual foundation of the reinvention of the Islamic Left. They forcefully argued that the Revolution was being betrayed and that its promise had been left unfulfilled. Challenging the dogma of the conservatives, the Reformists (as the Left came to be known) argued for 'Islamic democracy', adherence to the Constitution, civil rights, the rule of law and transparency in the economic activities of the country. While the political elite fought among themselves, these ideas were gradually disseminated via selected newspapers (reflecting the growing literacy of the population), lectures and the network of student associations. The test of this growth in political consciousness was to take place in May 1997.

The elections to the Fifth Majlis in 1996 had dented the dominance of the conservatives in Parliament. They still represented a majority, but they no longer held an absolute majority. What was distinctive about these elections was that within the limits on candidature imposed by the Guardian Council, they proved to be keenly contested. Moreover, the obvious vote-rigging which took place, especially the arbitrary reallocation of votes after the event, became a matter of open discussion and in many cases ridicule. Columnists such as Abbas Abdi and Saeed Hajarian (a former Deputy Minister of Intelligence) wrote forcibly about the need to emphasise the 'republican' aspect of the Constitution, and launched stinging attacks on the illogicality of the Conservatives. Forging an alliance of interests with Rafsanjani's centrists, including the influential Mayor of Tehran, the Reformists sought a suitable candidate to challenge the conservative (and very much establishment) candidate, Ali Akbar Nateq Nuri. Having failed to persuade the former Prime Minister Mir-Hussein Musavi to run, the Reformists settled on the relatively unknown Seyyid Mohammad Khatami. Khatami had been Minister for Culture and Islamic Guidance in the first Rafsanjani administration but had resigned in disgust following pressures from conservatives. Since 1992, he had occupied himself with administering the National Library. Highly educated, Khatami represented everything his rival was not, and he managed to persuade the establishment to allow him to run, with the argument that if he could raise political participation in the elections by a mere 10 per cent, it would be a triumph for the Revolution and the Islamic Republic. With the realisation that a divided establishment intended to allow a relatively free contest to take place – on the assumption that the conservative candidate would win – the Reformist press and student organisations throughout the country mobilised a sceptical public. The campaigns of Nateq Nuri (who behaved very much as if he had been President-elect) and Khatami could not have been more different, and Khatami benefited from not only his intellectual appeal but the determination of a populace eager to wrong-foot an increasingly distant and arrogant establishment. Right up until the day before the election, observers (including many in the diplomatic corps) doubted that Khatami would win. Yet much to everyone's astonishment, the appeal of the modest intellectual proved infectious, and Khatami won a landslide so decisive it proved impossible to overturn. With at least 20 million votes to Nateq Nuri's 7 million, Khatami's election triumph on 23 May (2 Khordad) began a new chapter in the political history of Iran. As a social phenomenon it was the culmination of a century of popular political agitation. Yet it did not signal the end but the beginning of an intense struggle to define the meaning of the modern Iranian state and its relationship with society.

The dramatic landslide election victory of Seyyed Mohammad Khatami on 23 May 1997 came as a surprise not only to the international community, but by all accounts to the candidate himself.[3] Having persuaded sceptics within the political establishment to allow his candidacy – with a view to increasing the level of popular participation – Khatami and his supporters discovered, to their great satisfaction, that the message of civil society and Islamic democracy had resonated far more widely within Iranian society than they had anticipated. Conversely, members of the conservative elite looked on with barely disguised trepidation. Two groups had reason to be anxious: the conservative mercantile elites; and their erstwhile political allies, the Islamic authoritarians. For both these groups, realising the dream of 'Islamic democracy' required the implementation of a system of transparency and accountability, the consequences of which were bound to adversely affect their political power, and more importantly their access to the means of accumulating wealth. Still, their initial response to this potential threat to their interests was to pretend it did not exist, and that on the contrary, Khatami was either politically ephemeral or a short-lived phenomenon. This dismissiveness was complemented by a popular fatalism which argued that the elites would simply not allow Khatami to succeed – a view which was shared by many observers abroad – with the consequence that the first few months to Khatami's inauguration in August 1997 were spent in frenzied speculation regarding his imminent political demise.[4] This was a motif which was to plague Khatami's presidency to the end of his second term, and while Khatami was to continually confound his critics with the durability of his presidency, there can be little doubt that the continued uncertainty did not help him.

Khatami's first administration

Khatami not only achieved his inauguration unharmed, he also, much to people's surprise, succeeded in securing parliamentary ratification for a cabinet, which would have left his conservative opponents in no doubt that he was serious about fulfilling his promises.[5] Two key individuals were Abdullah Nuri, who was nominated for the post of Interior Minister, and Ataollah Mohajerani, who became Minister for Culture and Islamic Guidance. The latter was charged with loosening the restrictions on the press and providing the intellectual space for the growth of civil society, while Nuri – paradoxically considered 'too revolutionary' by the conservative elites – was charged with providing the political and legal framework within which these ideas could take practical shape.[6] They were joined behind the scenes by Saeed Hajarian, a former Deputy Minister of Intelligence, who was responsible for overall strategy. Indeed as Khatami's presidency proceeded, the full extent of Hajarian's pivotal role became more apparent, and he was generally regarded as the 'brains' behind the Reformist Movement. Above all, Hajarian understood that serious, durable change could not be achieved through formal political avenues, that is, the institutions of government; but that informal pressure – through the Iranian street – would also have to be exerted if the various vested interests were to be persuaded to relinquish their tight grip on the Iranian state apparatus.[7] In this respect, he sympathised with the approach adopted by the Mayor of Tehran, Gholamhussein Karbaschi, who argued that a strategy which rigidly adhered to legal formalities was meaningless in a political culture which had scant respect for the authority of the law. Consequently, the implementation of the rule of law occasionally required the use of extra-legal measures and tactics.

Herein lay the central paradox of the Khatami presidency. The Reformist agenda was nothing less than the transformation, through rationalisation, of the Iranian state from one founded on traditional principles of authority reliant on opaque personal networks, to one founded on accountable institutions, dependent on transparent due process and the rule of law. This was to be a project which would fulfil the democratic promise of the Islamic Revolution and complete the modernisation of the state which, by their own reckoning, had begun with the Constitutional Revolution of 1906.[8] However, although the Reformists now controlled the executive, they did not control the legislature or judiciary. Nor, crucially, did they have control of the coercive tools of the state, in particular the law enforcement forces. So those who pursued the establishment of a legal state had no access to the relevant institutional tools, while those who opposed it were able to use legal institutions to prevent the establishment of a state founded on the rule of law. That they were able to do this by appearing to follow the law, while the Reformists had to resort to tactics which could be considered 'unlawful', remained the supreme irony and central contradiction of the Khatami presidency. Moreover, Khatami himself was determined to lead by example and show that the system could be transformed by working within it rather than pressure from outside. He was convinced that persuasion would be sufficient to convince his opponents to concede political ground, and his strategy was overwhelmingly institutional with a view to capturing the major organisations of the state. Sceptics considered this legalistic approach naive to the point of complicity.

While his political allies shared his aims, they recognised the shortcomings of this approach, and the new triumvirate of Nuri, Mohajerani and Hajarian set to work transforming both the political culture and landscape of the Islamic Republic. As the press became emboldened by the existence of a minister of culture who believed in aggressively supporting them, the Interior Minister Nuri engaged with university students and encouraged them to take a more active role in politics. They were after all the vanguard of the movement, and Nuri not only granted repeated licences to demonstrate, he was also outspoken in their defence when they were consistently attacked by hardline vigilantes. Conservatives for their part were shocked at what was perceived as Nuri's brusque manner, which they argued had less to do with reforming the system than with overturning it.[9] They swiftly criticised the Khatami administration's focus on political liberalisation, arguing that what was needed was economic growth. This argument was remarkably similar to that which Mohammad Reza Shah had used against his own political critics, many of whom were now sitting comfortably among the conservative establishment. The Reformists argued emphatically otherwise. Iran's problems were principally political, not economic. Bad governance was at the root of the problem, and if the government of the country could be reorganised on rational-legal grounds then the economy would fall into place. In short, the economy was a political problem, and the solution to Iran's perennial problems was to reform these areas in tandem and not in isolation.

For all their initial dismissiveness, the hardline conservatives soon moved to resist the Reformist heresy, by first exercising revenge against the Mayor of Tehran, Gholamhussein Karbaschi, whom many viewed as the chief architect of the Reformist victory in Tehran. Karbaschi was promptly put on trial; the first of many show trials that rapidly went badly wrong for the conservatives. The bombastic Karbaschi captured the public mood by berating the hapless judge for his legal ignorance, and within a matter of weeks the event, broadcast nightly, became more show than trial. Few doubted the outcome. But what mattered to Iranians was the performance, and the conservative-controlled state television unwittingly provided the Reformists with an unprecedented national platform from which to preach to a receptive public.[10] More ominous for the Reformists than the trial itself was the fact that former President Rafsanjani, who had played an important role in securing Khatami's election, did not come to the aid of the mayor he had appointed. It was an indication that this more flexible member of the mercantile elite was himself anxiously shifting towards the right. Indeed, while moderate conservatives were happy to tolerate a measure of political liberalisation, the increasing attention to the structural weaknesses of the economy, and the clear threat this posed to their financial position, encouraged the various factions on the right of the political spectrum to bury their political differences. With Karbaschi safely behind bars, the conservatives moved to impeach Interior Minister Nuri, a process which the conservative-dominated Parliament achieved with little difficulty in 1998 – although they took care to proceed when public attention was preoccupied with the football World Cup in France.[11] Khatami regarded this move as indulgent, and swiftly responded by making Nuri his Vice-President with responsibility for Interior Affairs, a move which unsurprisingly angered the conservative deputies. Nonetheless, it was also apparent that his administration would remain vulnerable if the Reformists could not secure control of the Parliament. Political strategy was therefore directed towards winning the Parliamentary elections in 2000, in the firm belief that a victory in the legislature would provide the Reformists with the legal platform for legislative reform. Nuri's reforms of the Interior Ministry and his appointment of new governors in the provinces had sufficiently prepared the electoral framework with a view to minimising corruption, but Parliament and the judiciary continued to target journalists and activists. While Mohajerani was able to issue new newspaper licences as quickly as the judiciary could close them down, it was clear to all that the press law would have to be amended. As it stood, both journalists and students were on the frontline of what was turning out to be a protracted guerrilla war between the two factions.[12]

At the end of 1998, however, a series of gruesome murders came to light which was to dramatically transform the contest. The discovery of the bodies of the four political activists, especially those of the veteran politician, Dariush Foruhar, and his wife Parvaneh, sent shock waves throughout Iranian society. The manner of their deaths had been particularly brutal, and there was little doubt that they had been murdered as a warning to others.[13] It says much for the changes within Iranian society that the intended warning proved entirely counter-productive. As conservatives scrambled to dismiss the murders as inconsequential, Khatami launched an investigation which soon had his opponents on the back foot. Far from burying bad news, the government pointed the finger squarely at the Intelligence Ministry, forcing the resignation of the minister, and drawing attention to the possible complicity of the previous Intelligence Minister, Ali Fallahian. While the murders were publicly blamed on rogue elements led by one 'Saeed Emami' (alternatively 'Islami'), the real consequence of the investigation was the purge of the ministry which followed, and the further revelations which appeared in the Iranian press.[14] In many ways, it proved a watershed moment, and if the victory was incomplete (many of the purged officers simply relocated to the judiciary), Khatami served notice to the hardline conservative establishment that it was not 'business as usual'.[15]

The reverberations continued through to 1999, as journalists exposed a far more extensive policy of extra-judicial killing than had been appreciated.[16] Indeed it was soon alleged that hardline elements within the Intelligence Ministry had been pursuing a strategy for the elimination of dissidents for some years, and that the net of complicity fell far wider within the conservative establishment than had been previously thought. It was widely speculated that *fatwas* had been issued to legitimise the murders, but just as Emami was being interrogated, and in the eyes of some, scapegoated for virtually every misdemeanour committed by the Intelligence Ministry, he committed suicide.[17] While the guilty parties might breathe a sigh of relief, Emami's untimely death did not stop the speculation, and in the summer of 1999, the reformist newspaper *Salaam* published yet another revelation, this time alleging that Emami, along with his conservative allies, had been preparing a draconian new press law, which would essentially prevent the emergence of a free press.[18] This was regarded as a precursor for the wider implementation of an authoritarian government. So outraged was the conservative establishment at these allegations that the judiciary immediately issued an order suspending the paper. This in turn infuriated Reformists, particularly among the student body, who decided to hold a demonstration in favour of *Salaam*, but their application, in light of the sensitivities surrounding the issue, was peremptorily turned down. Some students at the University of Tehran nevertheless decided that some sort of protest needed to be made. With characteristic form the hardline conservatives decided that this violation of the law had to be dealt with. However, rather than have the police deal with the matter in an ordered manner, police officials decided to delegate this particular responsibility to the hardline vigilante group known as the *Ansar-i Hizbollah* (Helpers of the Party of God). What had been intended as a routine disruption with a view to teaching recalcitrant youngsters a lesson proved to have an altogether different result. The consequences of the assault on the student dormitories was to shake the foundations of the Islamic Revolution to the core.

As members of the *Ansar* moved into the campus and through the dormitories – a violation of the sanctity of the university in the eyes of many – they began to beat and harass the students. One unfortunate army conscript visiting his student friends was caught in the melee and killed. For the students, this proved an assault too far. Enough was enough. Moreover, they had prepared a co-ordinated nationwide response. Over the following three days, student protests throughout the country – co-ordinated through email and mobile phones – caught the political establishment completely unawares.[19] Both the chancellor of Tehran University and the minister of higher education protested the vigilante intervention, with the latter resigning in disgust. Conservatives meanwhile found themselves lost for words, prompting some Reformists to question whether they had in fact sanctioned the attack on the university. Most conspicuous by his silence was the Supreme Leader Ayatollah Khamenei, who had reportedly been shaken by the increasingly bitter slogans directed against him by students who accused him of having supported the murder of Foruhar. Indeed it is unclear whether the conservative establishment were more concerned by the Leader's weakness than the demonstrations themselves, but in the absence of any decisive leadership, a group of conservatives, including key members of the Revolutionary Guards, issued a stern warning to Khatami that if he was not able to re-establish control, they would.[20] Eventually, following several days of protests, which at time bordered on the riotous, Ayatollah Khamenei finally spoke out against the protests.[21] Khatami had publicly dismissed the letter from the Revolutionary Guards, deftly quoting back at them Ayatollah Khomeini's instructions that the military should never interfere in politics. But there can be little doubt the conservative fears, and the threat of coup they harboured, affected Khatami and his allies. Iranian politicians are regularly haunted by the spectre of Mosaddeq, and while opposition parties in Iran and abroad were urging him to lead the masses as Mosaddeq had done, Khatami's legalistic demeanour was antithetical to anything which smacked of mob rule. Indeed there were indications that conservatives were infiltrating the demonstrations with agents provocateurs intent on providing the justification for a conservative coup and crackdown.[22] Why risk a coup, and the destruction of all that he hoped for, when much could be achieved in the forthcoming Parliamentary elections, less than a year away? Khatami therefore took the fateful decision to condemn any rioting while also urging the students to come off the streets. The latter, aware that support from the Reformist leadership was waning, obeyed the instructions on the promise that the guilty parties in the initial dormitory raid would be brought to account, but more importantly, that the far greater prize of the Parliament lay ahead.

It has been estimated that perhaps as many as 70,000 people were on the streets of Tehran, with many more in cities around the country. Many of these were clearly not students. But the organisation and management of the demonstrations was student-led, and there was considerable coordination with the press and the Reformist leadership. This triangular relationship was tighter than many people have recognised, and it explains why the leadership of the student movement was willing to trust the guidance of the Reformist leadership. Hajarian, in particular, was not unhappy with the demonstrations. They had ultimately not grown out of control, and crucially had had the desired effect on the conservative establishment. The latter had now clearly lost their monopoly of violence on the streets but, perhaps more importantly, were severely shaken by the experience. It is often forgotten that along with the estimated 1,500 students that were arrested, at least 113 law enforcement officers were also arrested and charged (the number may have been as high as 400), and in the subsequent government enquiry, the finger of blame was pointed squarely at the vigilantes along with their police accomplices.[23] For a population used to government cover-ups, the Khatami administration appeared refreshingly transparent. Few, especially in the press, were convinced that the judiciary would prosecute the officials with any objectivity – the chief officer in question was eventually acquitted – but immediate concerns now turned to the forthcoming Parliamentary elections.

Far from being demoralised by the experience over the summer the Reformist Movement, in particular the student activists, had been galvanised by it.[24] There was a palpable sense of empowerment and considerable energy was directed towards organising for victory in the forthcoming elections. For many control of the Parliament would seal the Reformist triumph. Conservatives looked on with trepidation, and concerns remained among Reformists that the Guardian Council would radically vet prospective candidates with a view to maintaining conservative control of the legislature. At the same time, the conservatives had clearly not learnt the lessons of the summer and continued to provide Reformists with further causes célèbres to unify around. With election fever mounting the judiciary considered it opportune to arrest Vice-President Nuri, on charges so extensive it took two hours to read to completion. In seeking to decapitate the Reform Movement, the conservatives simply fuelled the anger of its supporters. Like Karbaschi, Nuri proved an adept performer in a court which yet again served as a pulpit for Reformist ideas.[25] As if this were not enough, the increasingly unpopular Hashemi Rafsanjani decided that this would be the moment to announce his decision to run for Parliament. The fact that he sought to become Speaker – the position many felt Nuri had been poised to get – was regarded by many in the electorate to be at best distasteful, and at worst politically incompetent. The combined effect of these two manoeuvres was to focus minds among the Reformists. Anticipating the possibility of rigorous vetting by the Guardian Council, extensive lists were drawn up with many candidates held in reserve. When the Council proved unexpectedly lenient, the lists were radically streamlined to ensure that the Reformists backed a single unified candidate in each constituency.[26] The Guardian Council's decision, as Hajarian had correctly assessed, had little to do with a newly discovered altruism, and more with the barely disguised fear of the Iranian street. Much as he had hoped and planned for, organised civil society was proving to be a match for elite obstinacy.

The result was a second dramatic election victory for the Reformists, and in many ways this particular triumph was much more significant that Khatami's presidential victory some three years earlier. In the first place, Khatami and his policies were no longer an unknown quantity, yet three years on and in the face of rigid resistance from the conservatives, the people had endorsed the Reformist project. Moreover, this was a nationwide election in which local politics mattered, and the fact that Reformist candidates did well in the provinces proved that this was not an urban or indeed simply a Tehran-based phenomenon. The Khatami factor certainly remained important, but the dramatic swing against the conservatives showed that the Reformist agenda was not a political aberration. At the very least, it showed the Reform Movement to be a well organised and co-ordinated machine, and the emergence of the Islamic Participation Front (*Mosharekat*) with its slogan, 'Iran for all Iranians', held the promise of a party political system finally coming of age. Unfortunately for the Reformists, it was at this moment of triumph that the political ball began to slip from their grasp. Intoxicated by a victory which even saw the ailing patrician Rafsanjani fail to secure election within the Tehran lists, they singularly failed to consolidate their position in the months that followed. It was as if they had organised for victory but not for its consequences. Fundamental to this subsequent incoherence was the removal of the one person on whom Reformist strategy was dependent.

In March 2000, the Reformist Movement was buoyant and triumphalism was in the air. The Reformist press enthusiastically announced the new legislation which would now result and the possibilities for institutional reform which now beckoned. Not only would a new press law be submitted, but political life would be liberalised on a legal basis, and most dramatic of all, the political economy of the country would be rigorously interrogated and rationalised. In short, the Sixth Parliament would allow the Reformists to translate their ideas into definitive action. For some Reformist politicians it appeared as if the war for the soul of the Iranian state had been won. The reality was to prove somewhat different. While conservatives viewed with concern the prospect of greater political and social freedoms – with all the decadence they believed this implied – they were truly horrified at the suggestion that their sources of wealth were to be investigated. Khatami's notion that the Iranian economy needed to be funded increasingly by income tax – rather than depend on oil revenue – was bad enough. His new political disciples were arguing for a root and branch overhaul of the economic system. Their principal target was the large unaccountable religious foundations – *Bonyads* – through which many of the conservative mercantile elite allegedly laundered their money beyond the eyes of the Ministry of Finance. The threat of this proved the essential catalyst for the reunification of the conservatives – crucially, the hardliners and the moderate conservatives under the iconic leadership of Hashemi Rafsanjani, who having been humiliated in the recent elections now faced the prospect of being investigated for corruption. Unsurprisingly, he moved quickly to counter the suggestion that the *Bonyads* could be investigated at all. This should have been a warning sign to the Reformists that they would either need to make necessary compromises, or be prepared for a fight. In the event the fight came to them in the form of a bungled assassination attempt on Saeed Hajarian. Hajarian, the architect of victory, was gunned down as he left his offices in the Tehran City Council. The assassin failed to kill his target but instead the bullets, hitting Hajarian in the neck, paralysed him.[27] Hajarian's political demise was a far more serious blow to the Reformist Movement than the imprisonment of Nuri. At a critical moment, the master strategist had been disabled, and in a practical sense the Movement became rudderless. This was all the more serious because Khatami was shocked by the attack on his friend, and from then he began to question whether the costs of reform were justified. Consequently, the coherence and unity of the Reform Movement began to waver; the leadership began to compromise just when resoluteness was required; ideological discipline began to falter as the leadership failed to organise an increasingly mass movement into a recognisable whole. The idea of reform became so fashionable that it is quite apparent that those with little idea of its implications were proclaiming themselves adherents. Victory had, paradoxically, inaugurated the incoherence of reform.

The first signs of a serious reaction came with the mass closure of key sections of the Reformist press in the spring of 2000.[28] Erring on the side of caution, and still shaken by the attempt on Hajarian's life, the leadership urged patience, on a movement that was growing increasingly frustrated. No one had considered that victory in the elections would lead to more restrictions. But, it was argued, now was the time for magnanimity. Triumphalism would only encourage further reaction, and with the inauguration of the new Parliament in the August, a new legislative programme could be initiated. The press closures were merely the parting shots of a defeated foe. So the press and the student activists waited patiently. Then in November, the much vaunted press law was introduced into the Parliament, only to find that the Leader, Ayatollah Khamenei, had sent a letter to the Speaker urging that in the interests of stability and harmony the legislation be deferred to an unspecified later date.[29] It was a momentous intervention, in so far as the Leader had rarely if ever intervened so openly in the legislative programme of a Parliament. It was the definitive moment of disempowerment, made worse by the fact that the new deputies paid increasingly less heed to the wishes of their constituents, and busied themselves instead with the intricacies of parliamentary politics. Far from freeing the Reform Movement, Parliament served to cage it within the confines of a building, and to separate the leadership from the masses on whom they depended. Few election victories had been so effectively wasted, and while Khatami himself remained popular, as his re-election the following year would prove, the critical momentum had been lost.

9/11 and its consequences

If Khatami had been a reluctant president-elect in 1997, the experiences of 2000 had made him seriously consider the implications of running again. As an individual he remained popular with the electorate, and it was argued that it was better to have a reformist at the helm to shield and protect Iran's emergent civil society than to risk its reversal after four years. Indeed there was little doubt that for all the difficulties, substantial strides had been taken to liberalise Iran's political culture, to further the bounds of democratisation, and to encourage often vigorous debate. But Khatami also entered his second term without two of his key lieutenants (Nuri and Hajarian), and with a third (Mohajerani) exhausted, and on the verge of resignation. Khatami himself had lost much of the energy which had driven him in his first term, and found himself increasingly barracked by the growing polarisation of Iranian politics. Student activists were growing frustrated with the slow pace of reform, while conservatives wanted to reverse it altogether. Hardline conservatives began to articulate the view that the aim must be an Islamic state not an Islamic democracy, while students protested that the reform within the Constitution was clearly impossible and that the Constitution itself needed reviewing. These contending views resulted in considerable inaction at the centre, and it was almost with relief that Khatami found that events now dictated he turn his attention abroad.

A major platform of Khatami's strategy on entering office in 1997 had been to redefine Iran's relationship with the outside world. According to his then chief of staff, Abtahi, Khatami knew Iran, and importantly, he understood Iran's place in the world. A seemingly innocuous statement, Abtahi's comment revealed a great deal about Khatami's world view, which rejected the imperious confrontations of old, and argued instead for a new relationship founded on mutual respect and trust. For Iran to grow politically and economically, it needed regional stability and stable international relations which would encourage foreign investment. Moreover, better relations would open up markets and help win over his conservative mercantile critics. Central to this strategy was a new relationship with the West and the United States in particular. Khatami articulated these views in a series of speeches and interviews, most famously that with CNN in 1998, which were complemented by a number of highly publicised state visits to European countries. Iranians, for the first time since the Revolution, enjoyed seeing their head of state being welcomed and to some extent courted by the Europeans. For all their public relations value, Khatami's ability to communicate with the West was an enormous asset, both for himself, the movement he led, and the country as a whole. Iran's relations with the West since 1979 had been tense and riven with mutual misunderstanding and distrust, and Khatami believed he had the answer. His decision to pursue a 'Dialogue between Civilisations', a response to Huntington's 'Clash of Civilisations', was mocked and misunderstood by his critics both at home and abroad, and the Western response was certainly slow and largely disappointing to Khatami. He had been especially hopefully that the European Union would respond with a concrete trade offer with which he could placate conservative critics at home. Yet he received little more than gestures of goodwill. His most successful impact was with the United Nations, who decided to adopt his ideas and proclaim 2001 the 'Year of Dialogue between Civilisations'.

The key to his foreign policy agenda remained in many ways a redefinition of Iran's relationship with the United States. The United States had remained a central aspect of Iranian political life despite the absence of formal relations, and President Rafsanjani had made several attempts to broach the question of normalisation. Clinton had remained for the bulk of his administration resolutely deaf to any deal with Iran. But the arrival of Khatami took the US foreign policy establishment by surprise. Indeed it was soon apparent that they had no coherent response to offer and it took some time before one could be articulated. Eventually in 2000, with considerable enthusiasm in the White House itself, the message from the United States began to soften, and it was even announced that sanctions on Iranian handicrafts, along with pistachios, would be lifted. By 2000 however, Khatami was in the grip of his own domestic turmoil, and as so often in the past, when faced with a decision, it was decided to procrastinate. Not only did opposition to US relations among the conservative establishment – and the Leader in particular – remain strong, but Khatami's foreign policy advisers argued that it would be better to wait until the November Presidential elections in the US, when they added, it was likely a more sympathetic Republican administration would be in office. Rarely has Iranian assessment of US domestic political developments been so wide of the mark. Very much like their US counterparts, Iranian foreign policy analysts were basing their assessments on historical snapshots which took no account of changes over time. Consequently, when George W. Bush took over the White House in January 2001, many Iranians anticipated a return to the policies of his father: the foreign policy of realpolitik without the ideological baggage.

The reaction was not what had been expected. Indeed while Khatami prepared for his re-election campaign in the summer of 2001, Iranians reflected that there had been no reaction at all. President Bush by all accounts seemed disinterested in foreign policy. Then came 9/11. Having reassured himself that no Iranians or Iranian-backed groups had been associated with the attacks on the twin towers, Khatami moved quickly to offer his condolences to the US President. Similar messages of support were sent by the mayor of Tehran, and the head of the Tehran Fire Service, to their respective counterparts.[30] It soon transpired that the culprits, Al Qaeda, were being supported by the Taleban in Afghanistan, and the Iranians soon recognised the opportunity that now confronted them. The United States was determined to dismantle Al Qaeda, and in the face of Taleban obstinacy decided on the removal of the Taleban. Nothing could be more amenable to the Iranians, who had been waging a proxy war against the Taleban for the better part of five years. Indeed in 1998, after the murder of Iranian diplomats, Iran had come close to launching its own military strike against the Taleban. Now the Iranians had no difficulty in assisting the Americans to achieve this, and extensive cooperation was offered, including, most importantly, delivering the Afghan Northern Alliance. Only days earlier, the Iranians had been mourning the assassination of Ahmad Shah Massoud, the leader of the Northern Alliance. Now they would facilitate the overthrow of the government which had perpetrated the crime. The collaboration which took place both during and after the war against the Taleban seemed to inaugurate a period of détente between Iran and the United States, and rapprochement was undoubtedly in the air. But not all were enthusiastic about this development and tensions began to rise again with American accusations that Iran had harboured some Al Qaeda fugitives, and most glaring of all, the revelation, following the capture of the shipment by the Israelis, that Iran was supplying arms to the Palestinian Authority. Whatever the veracity of the accusations, many Iranians considered them trivial in the grand scheme of the 'global war on terror', and assured themselves that these problems could now be overcome given the coincidence of interests the two powers now shared.

It came as something of a shock therefore to discover that President Bush had decided to label Iran part of the 'Axis of Evil', along with Iraq and North Korea.[31] No one was damaged more by this particular piece of rhetoric than Khatami himself, who had staked his personal reputation on the collaboration with the US. Now it appeared that the hardliners within the regime had been correct after all; the United States could not be trusted, and Khatami, increasingly seen as ineffectual at home, was now being lampooned as ineffective abroad. More problematic as far as the West was concerned, the very faction which had been sympathetic to dialogue now felt both betrayed and distrustful. Khatami himself felt bound, through internal political pressure and personal belief, to take a tougher stance. Within Iran, politics became dominated by discussions about the United States, swamping all other political debates and in effect suspending the factional struggle.[32] Now debate tended to revolve around relative positions towards the United States, and the conservatives argued with increasing vigour that those in favour of talks were in fact fifth columnists and traitors.[33] The most obvious example of this was the arrest of pollsters who had assessed that the majority of the Iranian population, while distrustful of the US and its motives, nonetheless believed that some sort of dialogue needed to take place to diffuse tensions.[34] For the hardline conservatives, however, this foreign policy imperative was placed second to the domestic imperative of crushing the Reform Movement. Consequently, as international relations deteriorated, Iran's politicians focused on their own internecine battles. Indeed, far from seeking to build bridges, hardline conservatives argued that Iran's international difficulties had been made worse because Khatami had been too accommodating of the West. The only solution was to be robust. In light of the various rebuffs which Iranian politicians received at the hands of the West between 2002 and 2004, it was difficult not to come to the conclusion that Western hawks helped reinforce this view. Indeed in the aftermath of the Iraq invasion, Iran's relations with the West entered a deteriorating cycle of mutual mistrust, driven in the main by ideologues for whom confrontation was a matter of principle. Few events exemplified this process better than the laboured negotiations over Iran's nuclear programme.

In the summer of 2002, the National Council of Resistance of Iran (NCRI) held a press conference to announce that Iran's nuclear programme was more advanced than the country was revealing and that by implication, Iran had been in breach of its commitments under the Nuclear Non-Proliferation Treaty (NPT). Iran initially denied these allegations and it was not until some gentle encouragement from the European Union that the country conceded in early 2003 that its nuclear plants in both Natanz and Arak were well in advance of what the International Atomic Energy Agency (IAEA) and the broader international community had believed. There can be little doubt that Iran's failure to be transparent was a transgression of its international obligations. But there was likewise little doubt that the nature of the transgression was magnified by the poor state of Iran–US relations. The political nature of the dispute was unfortunately dismissed by Iranians, when it was this particular aspect which made it all the more serious. While the Europeans sought to approach the matter from a legal perspective and to persuade Iran that it needed to fulfil its international treaty obligations, the Americans were making it abundantly clear that post 9/11 the old rules no longer applied. Iranian assessments of the legal justification for the Iraq invasion further complicated the situation as conservatives argued that the obvious absence of any recourse to the law made regime survival dependent on a nuclear deterrent. Despite this, official Iranian pronouncements consistently emphasised the peaceful nature of the nuclear programme, and while the IAEA inspectors remained dissatisfied at the level of transparency offered by Iran, they failed to find any convincing proof of a weapons programme. Suspicions abounded, however, and the Iranians, for the reasons noted above, felt it prudent to remain ambiguous. In many ways they were caught between the legal imperative of the Europeans, and the threat posed by the Americans. Given the two, they feared the Americans more, and consequently the Europeans grew more frustrated at the persistent ambiguity, which in turn pushed the Europeans towards the Americans. Iran's ambitions can perhaps be best ascertained by turning to history. The country's nuclear programme had begun under the Shah with the support of the West. The Shah likewise publicly eschewed nuclear weapons, but in private he conceded that it would be good to retain the option. The Islamic Republic too wished to retain the option, hence its determination to master the technology. While Europe and the US accepted Iran's right to a civil nuclear programme (its legal right under the NPT), neither has been happy with Iran retaining the option, and while the mastery of the science is within Iran's NPT rights, the West has increasingly argued that previous transgressions constrain that right. In short, a treaty founded on mutual trust has been groaning to breaking point under the weight of mutual mistrust.

The domestic political ramifications for Iran of this crisis have in many ways been more dramatic than the international ones. In 2003, following the fall of the Ba'athist regime in Iraq, Iran was persuaded to sign an agreement with the European Union (represented in this case by Britain, France and Germany), with a view to settling the crisis through a reaffirmation of the terms of the NPT. In October 2003, Iran and the EU signed the Tehran Agreement by which each side reaffirmed its obligations under the NPT and Iran also agreed to sign and subsequently ratify the Additional Protocol. The Agreement was hailed as a triumph by both sides, though as is occasionally the case with diplomatic agreements, the flamboyance of the ceremony was expected to disguise the disagreements which remained. In this case, two terms were to enjoy different interpretations: 'temporary suspension' and 'objective guarantees'. Throughout 2004 it was to become increasingly clear that the only objective guarantee acceptable to the United States was a permanent suspension of uranium enrichment. This was quite clearly unacceptable to Iranian negotiators, for whom the nuclear programme had become a matter of national principle. Far more damaging to the prospects of a settlement, however, were the domestic political consequences which ensued.

The spectre of Mosaddeq and the coup of 1953 appeared to have affected Iran's European interlocutors in a manner wholly unexpected. Anxious not to be seen to be interfering in Iran's political affairs and aware of the sensitivities of the Iranians on this issue, the Europeans appear to have afforded their Iranian counterparts an assurance that they would not interfere in domestic political matters. Combined with the fact that the Europeans had for the best part of the negotiations ignored the elected government and instead opted to deal with conservative negotiators, it is unsurprising that conservatives rather than Reformists gained succour from the proceedings.[35] Where both the Europeans and their conservative interlocutors miscalculated however, was in correctly divining the changing shape of conservative politics in Iran. As the Reformists were increasingly marginalised, the battle for political control shifted to the Right, between the moderate and hardline conservatives. It was the latter – Iran's neo-conservatives – who were to make the greater gains in a succession of elections beginning with the municipal elections in 2003, emphasised with the Parliamentary elections in 2004, and crowned with the election of Ahmadinejad as President in 2005. The seeds of this political transformation were laid by the incoherence and indecisiveness of the Reformist leadership after 2000.[36] But they were also encouraged by the continued international crisis and the regional instability created by America's 'global war on terror'.

The neo-conservative agenda was born out of a local disillusionment with political gridlock, and an admiration for the proactive policies administered by America's neo-conservative movement. Beginning as a movement to find a 'third way' between Iran's Reformist and traditional conservative movements, Iran's neo-conservatives soon took on the ideological mantle of their bedfellows in the United States.[37] However, if America's neo-conservatives represented left-wingers who had moved to the right, Iran's neo-conservatives were hardline authoritarians who sought to appropriate the populism of the Left – without any democratic pretensions. Indeed in their radical populism and appeal to the common man, Iran's neo-conservatives were in many ways the products of the Reformist transformation of Iranian politics. They had learnt their lessons well, and if they were antithetical to the underlying philosophy of the Reform Movement, they were not shy about appropriating their ideas or tactics. The Reformists in the meantime, having created the terrain, proceeded to vacate it, ignoring their constituents, and vacillating when decisive leadership was demanded. The result was that many became disillusioned with politics while others turned to the only group that remained to offer them hope. Heavy on style but short on substance, Iran's neo-conservative movement was riven with contradictions which their bombastic rhetoric of economic populism and vulgar nationalism sought to disguise. The latter in particularly was greatly assisted by the air of international crisis. Whereas Khatami needed regional stability to encourage economic growth, the neo-conservatives thrived on the distractions of a worldwide problem. Whereas the Reformists sought to enhance civil society and the spirit of popular democracy, the neo-conservatives sought to depoliticise the public and replace it with populism. This in many ways remained the most obvious contradiction. Their rise depended on the depoliticisation of a disillusioned public, but they drew their sustenance from the belief in a strong state with popular support. Only the existence of an international crisis of sufficient magnitude could re-engage the public, though on this occasion in an act of national unity around the leader, who at the same time could use this situation to justify the further excision of the Reformist heresy. It helped if the international crisis appeared to be leaning in Iran's favour, thus further reinforcing the justice of the neo-conservative cause.

In 2003, a low turnout of voters facilitated the rise of the neo-conservatives and the emergence of the hitherto unknown Ahmadinejad as Mayor of Tehran.

In 2004 the Guardian Council ruthlessly vetted candidates for the Parliamentary elections, all but ensuring a hardline seizure of the Parliament. The triumph was made complete by the incoherent and indecisive response of the Reformist leadership, along with the disillusion of many voters. Even by Iranian standards, the election was a mockery. The absence of any criticism from the European Union only emboldened the hardliners and assured cynical Iranians that the West had in fact supported the conservative takeover.[38] Ironically, the new Parliament refused to ratify the Additional Protocol and instead criticised the negotiating team (led by a moderate conservative) for being too weak and offering too many concessions. Parliamentarians immediately moved to pass legislation which would further tie the hands of the negotiators. The European Union diplomats in the meantime found themselves renegotiating from a weaker position. Not only was time being lost but the deteriorating situation on the battlefields of Iraq and Afghanistan was strengthening Iran's hand, and her neo-conservatives were becoming even bolder. The seizure of eight British servicemen from the Shatt al-Arab waterway in the summer of 2004 was a clear indication that a more confrontational attitude was prevailing in the Iranian governing elite. Throughout 2004 the theatre of negotiations continued, but what transpired was less diplomatic than political, as trust diminished rather than grew. This ensured that the hurdle was raised higher at every turn, and each side's red line grew more distant. By 2005, the neo-conservatives had consolidated their political grip by seizing the presidency in yet another controversial election. Mahmoud Ahmadinejad secured victory after a bitterly fought contest which saw not only the marginalisation of a disorganised Reform Movement, but the dramatic defeat of the traditional conservatives. By the beginning of 2006, the nuclear negotiations were formally ended, and a period of intense confrontation with the West entered a new and daunting phase.

Notes

1 Ahmad Khomeini's somewhat sudden death in 1995 only fuelled public suspicions that he had been prematurely prevented from speaking his mind and exposing the profound ills of the developing 'Islamic Republic'.

2 These riots were pivotal in persuading many of the leadership that force alone could not tame the Iranian population.

3 See for example *Jame'eh Madani va Iran-e Emrooz* (Civil Society and Today's Iran). Tehran: Naqsh & Negar, 1377/1997, p. 259.

4 See for example H. Amirahmadi's comments in a round table discussion for *Etela'at Siyasi-Eqtesadi*, in *Jame'eh Madani va Iran-e Emrooz* (Civil Society and Today's Iran), p. 242; see also p. 256.

5 BBC SWB ME/3004 MED/2 dated 22 August 1997, IRNA news agency, dated 21 August 1997.

6 *Salaam*, 13 Esfand 1376/4 March 1998, p. 1.

7 For details of Hajarian's thinking and the development of his ideas in this regard, see the collection of his articles compiled in, S. Hajarian, *Jomhuriyyat: Afsoon-zadai az ghodrat* (Republicanism: Demystification of Power). Tehran: Tarh-e No, 1379/2000.

8 See for example S. Hajarian's comments in *Jame'eh Madani va Iran-e Emrooz* (Civil Society and Today's Iran), pp. 310–11; see also Khatami's comments, BBC SWB ME/3318 MED/17 dated 29 August 1998, IRIB radio, dated 27 August 1998.

9 *Salaam*, 14 Esfand 1376/5 March 1998, p. 1.

10 See *Tous*, 5 Mordad 1377/27 July 1998, p. 1; it was claimed at the time that the trial was the most watched and heard programme on radio and television since the Revolution, see *Jame'eh* 22 Tir 1377/13 July 1998, p. 1.

11 For Nuri's defence see BBC SWB ME/3260 MED/2 dated 23 June 1998, IRNA news agency, dated 21 June 1998. The impeachment actually took place on the day of the US–Iran encounter in the World Cup; of the 265 deputies present, 137 voted for, 117 against and 11 abstained.

12 *Salaam*, 9/4/1378 quoted in A. Ganji, *Tarik-khaneh-ye ashbah* (The Cellar of Phantoms). Tehran: Tar-e No, 1378, p. 280.

13 H. Kaviani, *Dar jostejoye mohafal jenayatkaran* (Investigating the Murderous Associations). Tehran: Negah-ye Emruz, 1378, p. 30.

14 Kaviani, *Dar jostejoye mohafal jenayatkaran*, pp. 149–53, according to a report in *Salaam*, Emami was actually recruited by Fallahian during a trip to the United States.

15 Ganji, *Tarik-khaneh-ye ashbah*, p. 17.

16 Kaviani, *Dar jostejoye mohafal jenayatkaran*, p. 38.

17 Ganji, *Tarik-khaneh-ye ashbah*, p. 250; see for example, Ba Tasveer (Saeed Emami) (With Picture [Saeed Emami]). Adineh, 139, Mordad 1378/August 1999, p. 9.

18 See Kaviani, *Dar jostejoye mohafal jenayatkaran*, p. 163.

19 BBC SWB ME/3586 MED/1 dated 14 July 1999, IRNA news agency, dated 12 July 1999; BBC SWB ME/3585 MED/4 dated 13 July 1999, IRNA news agency, dated 11 July 1999; see also M.A. Zekryai, *Hijdahom Tir Mah 78 beh raviat jenahaye siyasi* (The 18 Tir 78, from the Perspective of Political Factions). Tehran: Kavir, 1378, pp. 453–4.

20 See Ganji's comments published in *Sobh Emrooz*, Ganji, *Tarik-khaneh-ye ashbah*, pp. 302–14; see *Sobh Emrooz*, 17 Shahrivar 1378/8 September 1999, p. 1.

21 BBC SWB ME/3587 MED/1 dated 15 July 1999, IRNA news agency, dated 14 July 1999; see also the comments of the Supreme National Security Council, BBC SWB ME/3588 MED/1 dated 16 July 1999, Iranian TV, dated 14 July 1999.

22 BBC SWB ME/3586 MED/3 dated 14 July 1999, IRIB radio, dated 13 July 1999, see also the interview with students, in BBC SWB ME/3587 dated 15 July 1999, Iranian TV, dated 13 July 1999. See also comments by Reza Hojati in *Entekhab* reprinted in Zekryai, *Hijdahom Tir Mah 78 beh raviat jenahaye siyasi*, pp. 326–7.

23 See SNSC announcement, BBC SWB ME/3585 MED/6 dated 13 July 1999, Iranian TV, dated 11 July 1999; also, *Iran*, 24 Mordad 1378/15 August 1999, p. 1.

24 See Announcement no. 8, which laid the blame on the judiciary, LEF and 'pressure groups', Zekryai, *Hijdahom Tir Mah 78 beh raviat jenahaye siyasi*, pp. 442–3; this view was echoed by Karroubi, see p. 31, also pp. 303–4.

25 See for example, *Sobh Emrooz*, 16 Aban 1378/7 November 1999, pp. 2 and 11, *Sobh Emrooz*, 19 Aban 1378/10 November 1999, pp. 6–7.

26 BBC SWB ME/3767 MED/1 dated 18 February 2000, IRNA news agency, dated 16 February 2000.

27 For details, see *Akhbar-e Eqtesad* 23 Esfand 1378/13 March 2000, p. 1. Abdolkarim Soroush pointedly noted that Hajarian was a victim of Islamic 'fascism', see *Akhbar-e Eqtesad*, 15 Farvardin 1379/3 April 2000, p. 3. Hardliners unsurprisingly pinned the blame on the US, see Dehnamaki's comments quoted in M.A. Zakrayi, *Terror-e Hajarian beh ravayet-e jenahaye siyasi* (The Assassination of Hajarian from the Perspective of the Political Factions). Tehran: Kavir, 1379/2000, p. 269.

28 BBC SWB ME/3823 MED/1 dated 25 April 2000, IRNA news agency, dated 23 April 2000.

29 The catalyst for this intervention was reported to have been Emaddedin Baqi's article in the Persian daily *Neshat* on the death penalty in Islam, which some senior jurists considered offensive, although opinion was divided, see BBC SWB ME/3973 MED/16 dated 17 October 2000, ISNA, dated 15 October 2000.

30 See the interesting reflection on the attack and Iranian sympathies for Americans in M. Hajizadeh, *Aqazadeh-ha* (Aghazadeh-ha). Tehran: Jameh Daran, 1381/2002, pp. 143–6. Popular sympathy for the United States continued, see *Aftab-e Yazd*, 5 Esfand 1382/24 February 2004, p. 5.

31 See commentary in *Nowruz*, 2 February 2002, BBC SWB Mon MEPol; see Elahe Koulaee's comments in *Nowruz*, 24 Ordibehesht 1381/14 May 2002, p. 2; also *Aftab-e Yazd*, 21 Khordad 1381/11 June 2002, p. 1.

32 *Hayat-e No* website, 1 June 2002, BBC SWB Mon MEPol. See also *Nowruz*, 19 Khordad 1381/9 June 2002, p. 7; *Hayat-e No*, 11 Khordad 1381/1 June 2002, p. 1.

33 See for example, BBC SWB Mon ME1 MEPol, IRIB, dated 12 July 2002, 'Demonstrators support Khamene'i, call for trial of "fifth columnists"'; also, *Etemad*, 29 Mordad 1381/20 August 2002, p. 2.

34 See *Mardomsalari*, 18 Dey 1381/8 January 2003, pp. 4 and 9; there was some evidence of Ministry of Information collusion, see *Entekhab* website, 24 December 2002, BBC SWB Mon ME1 MEPol.

35 See 'Iran Conservatives to Ease Engagements', AFP 18 February 2004.

36 *Aftab-e Yazd* website 20 May 2003, BBC SWB Mon ME1 MEPol. Even closest advisers admitted this failure to lead, see M.R. Khatami, *Newsweek International*, 1 March 2004; A.R. Alavi-Tabar, *Yas-e No*, 20 Bahman 1382/10 February 2004, p. 2.

37 See for example, *Aftab-e Yazd*, 20 Bahman 1382/9 February 2004, p. 11.

38 See *Aftab-e Yazd*, 10 Esfand 1382/29 February 2004, p. 11.

15 Ahmadinejad, populism and the politics of confrontation

The Parliamentary and Presidential elections of 2004 and 2005 established a new template for political development in Iran, away from the tendency to cement and reinforce the republican institutions, towards those revolutionary organisations accountable directly to the Supreme Leader. That the Supreme Leader himself was, in theory at least, accountable only to God, a theory that was to be tested to excess during the Presidential election crisis of 2009, did not bode well for the democratic aspirations of the regime. The debate between an Islamic democracy and an Islamic state driven and directed by an autocratic Supreme Leader was moving emphatically in the direction of the latter, aided and abetted by a president whose understanding of democratic accountability was to be dangerously confused with populism, generated in part by his own avuncular political style, but paid for in large measure by an unprecedented injection of oil money. It is to be sure, one of the tragedies of contemporary Iran, that Ahmadinejad's ascendancy coincided with a prolonged period of high oil revenues; monies that he distributed with a largesse that bought the loyalty of key sectors of the revolutionary establishment, and an unaccountability that effectively bankrupted the government.

The economic realities of Ahmadinejad's populist politics – a heady mixture of superstition and vulgar nationalism – would come home to roost as the oil price inevitably declined and his politics of confrontation elicited the most severe sanctions ever to be imposed on the country. An already fragile political system found itself buffeted from opponents, both within and without, and has yet to recover from the enormous damage wrought to the fabric and cohesion of the state in this period. The West for its part, preoccupied and focused on matters of regional and international security – most obviously during this period, Iran's nuclear programme – failed to fully appreciate the structural changes that had been affected and remained, in large part transfixed by an Islamic Republic defined by Khatami – the very president and movement they singularly failed to support. Just as the spectre of Mosaddeq was to increasingly shape American views, most obviously during the Obama presidency, so too in a more immediate sense did the ghost of Khatami haunt the Western mindset when the opportunity arose to make amends for past sins.

The Reformists treated Ahmadinejad's victory in the Presidential election of 2005 with a mixture of shock and disbelief. He had in truth effectively come from nowhere to challenge Rafsanjani in a visceral runoff that had many members of the 'traditional' political establishment campaigning with a degree of anxiety and foreboding that has become all too familiar in Western democracies. The electorate was nonetheless in a rebellious mood, disillusioned with the status quo – the causes of which could not be agreed upon – and enthusiastic or resigned to, depending on one's political leanings, a period of 'creative destruction'. It was a political atmosphere redolent of the Revolution itself, and it was unsurprising that Ahmadinejad's supporters viewed events as an exercise in revolutionary renewal, while the new elites formed under Rafsanjani's presidency viewed developments with trepidation. Ahmadinejad was the clear outlier in the contest. He had not registered in the early opinion polls and few took him seriously, despite or indeed because of his eccentric activities as Mayor of Tehran.

He nevertheless enjoyed a number of significant advantages beyond the general contempt with which he was held by the establishment, and these were a campaigning style and organisation that were a good deal more sophisticated than his demeanour suggested, and support from both the Revolutionary Guard and *Basij* militia, who effectively maintained a national network that, crucially, paid little heed to the standard rules and regulations of electioneering. Critics of Ahmadinejad had tended to emphasise this aspect of his election-winning formula, and as important as it was, it has disguised the fact that his technologically savvy campaign and man-of-the-people approach were also to prove vote winners. One could argue that the revolutionary state ensured his advance to the second round – Mehdi Karroubi, who found himself overtaken by the upstart, was no doubt justified in protesting Ahmadinejad's curiously propitious political ascent – but that once there and in the political limelight, it was his own style and approach that ensured victory. He was helped of course by the extraordinary hubris and complacency of his opponent. Rafsanjani was attempting a comeback as the compromise candidate who would resolve the outstanding issues of the Islamic Republic, not least the debilitating relationship with the United States. The general of reconstruction would return as the latest incarnation of Iran's periodic saviours. Convinced of the destiny of his mission and dismissive of his opponent, Rafsanjani took a lackadaisical approach to campaigning, focusing his efforts on what might be termed the 'new middle class' of north Tehran, and curiously, given the extensive use of English on his campaign placards, on the many foreign journalists who paid attention to Iran at election time.

In the event the mantle of saviour was to fall on Ahmadinejad whose new 'digital' campaign proved as innovative as Khatami's televisual campaign some eight years earlier, while his accessible style contrasted favourably with Rafsanjani's somewhat aristocratic approach to the apparent tedium of campaigning. These somewhat sober and sanguine reasons for his shock victory were nonetheless insufficient for his key supporters who were keen to characterise his electoral triumph as a political miracle worthy of a Shi'a saint, an approach that Ahmadinejad was only too keen to promote and which suggests Khatami's reportedly allergic reaction to the news of Ahmadinejad's victory was grounded in a realistic anxiety of the consequences for the country. One person who could barely disguise his elation was Ayatollah Khamenei, for whom Ahmadinejad's victory was a personal triumph against his perennial critics, and a humiliation for Rafsanjani. Here was an opportunity to bury the heresy of reform once and for all, and the popularity that Khatami enjoyed could now be transferred to Ahmadinejad. Khatami for his part found himself ostracised; criticised by his own supporters for lacking political back-bone and denied the traditional offices and role of ex-presidents by Khamenei, Khatami was flung into the political wilderness presumably to reflect and in time repent. Ahmadinejad for his part proceeded to behave like the spoilt child of victory, with an abundance of oil money and a self-belief so strong that criticism only reinforced. If others had not awoken to his genius it was, his supporters argued, simply because they could not keep up with him, and it was indeed only a matter of time before even his staunchest critics recognised the innate – one might even suggest, esoteric – insights of the 'Socrates of the Age'.[1] Students of Iranian history will no doubt see parallels with earlier ages though one should add that Ahmadinejad's brand of millenarian messianism was more imbued with superstition than intellectual rigour.

Much of this reflected the nature of the man himself. While Ahmadinejad enjoyed something of a honeymoon among sections of the international media, careful scrutiny of his background and ascent revealed a man beholden to an image largely constructed from his own imagination, reinforced and embellished by supporters who were equally surprised by their hero's political success. Indeed, a central feature of the 'cult' that was emerging around him was the conviction that his abrupt rise could only be credited to Providence and therefore was confirmation of the miraculous and divinely inspired character of his achievement, which was of course projected backwards to provide further proof (if it was indeed required) of his unique qualities.[2] The reality was to prove much more mundane. The awkward absence of any photos of Ahmadinejad in battle fatigues at the front during the Iran–Iraq War – a requisite for any political career – was put down to the fact that he had spent his time in covert operations. The reality appears to have been Ahmadinejad had served in logistics well behind the front lines. Likewise, his doctorate, like many other qualifications achieved by aspiring politicians in the higher education institutions of the Islamic Republic, was less a reflection of his intellect and more of his contacts, as critics considered just how profound a dissertation on traffic management might be? While the accolade of 'international mayor of the year', far from reflecting his excellent managerial skills, was the result of a highly selective online poll which had been swamped by his supporters in the year in which he had received the award. Closer scrutiny of his career whether in IRGC logistics, or as an aspiring politician revealed a man with eccentric ideas about religion, obsessed with the return of the Hidden Imam, with whom he suggested, he had a special relationship. These peculiar ideas would come to tarnish his relationship with the man that mattered, Ayatollah Khamenei, but initially at least, there was no conflict of interest.

On the contrary, Khamenei encouraged Ahmadinejad to speak his mind, to speak if you will truth to power on the basis that the (international) order, founded on a lie, would buckle under the strain of the truth delivered unvarnished. Ahmadinejad for his part wasted no time in playing the role that had been (divinely) ordained for him replacing the tact and diplomacy of his predecessor, with a bumptious if somewhat vulgar manner of communication which horrified his critics as much as it endeared him to his devotees. Domestically Ahmadinejad pursued a policy of rolling back the 'republic', stripping it of the means and institutions of accountability, most notably the Plan and Budget Organisation which had been in existence since 1948, and transferring as much wealth and power to the revolutionary institutions who could increasingly carry on their activities without the modest scrutiny to which they had previously been subjected. He was enabled in this strategy by the unprecedented oil revenues at his disposal, in excess of anything enjoyed since 1974 at the oil price rise instigated by the Shah. It has since been estimated that between 2005 and 2013, some $800 billion of oil revenue flooded into the Iranian economy disappearing out through private accounts and revolutionary organisations for whom auditing was an alien concept. The travesty of such political decadence was that the government neither saved the money as a sovereign wealth fund to be used in emergencies, nor applied it to important infrastructure projects. Instead political expediency ensured that this strategic asset was applied for short-term political gain while those close to the centres of power insured themselves against instability by aggressively enriching themselves oblivious to the fact that such behaviour simply served to weaken the state on which they ostensibly depended. For some it appeared that the hubris and decadence of the 1970s was repeating itself though the problem was of course much deeper than that and would have been familiar to observers of Qajar Iran not least Malcolm. Short-termism and the political instability it induced was now being reinforced rather than ameliorated, though as a means of eradicating 'reformism', it appeared that this was a strategic cost worth bearing. The Revolution was no longer a means to a (Islamic) republican end. The Republic now served the Revolution and if the stability of the Republic had to be sacrificed to insure the Revolution, then so be it. In this context it is perhaps unsurprising that Khamenei described Ahmadinejad's government as the most competent since the Constitutional Revolution.[3]

These structural changes where enabled by vast oil wealth and disguised behind a welter of robust rhetoric designed to satisfy his political base but targeted in many ways abroad. If Khatami had sought regional stability and alliances in order to foster investment at home, Ahmadinejad pursued a policy of 'creative destruction', with a view to re-establishing a regional hegemony to which Iran's modern monarchs could only aspire. Promoting a neo-imperial vision that appealed to both his religious and nationalist constituencies, Ahmadinejad and his supporters promoted the idea that the US had invaded Iraq in order to hinder the return of the Hidden Imam, while justifying the expansion of Iran's regional power as both a religious duty and a national obligation. He seemed equally at home calling on Cyrus the Great as he was recounting his various mystical experiences, most famously claiming that a green halo had appeared behind him as he spoke to the UN General Assembly. Indeed, Ahmadinejad was explicit in his affectation for the ancient Persian Empire and Cyrus the Great in particular who in this post-revolutionary rendition, was presented to the public in prophetic terms, drawn in many ways from Biblical rather than Qur'anic references (though in this respect the figure of 'Zulqarnain', generally considered to refer to Alexander the Great, was presented, as Iranians tended to do, as referring in actual fact to Cyrus the Great). Ahmadinejad's historical grandstanding drew criticism from his more purist supporters, who cautiously welcomed his principal obsession with the Hidden Imam but found his preoccupation with Cyrus and the Achaemenids too close to the Shah for comfort. Ahmadinejad even organised for the loan of the Cyrus Cylinder from the British Museum, received with much pomp and emotion, and which the President pointed out had been achieved at less cost and for a greater length of time than the Shah had managed. The outpouring of eulogies for the Achaemenid, included Ahmadinejad citing from Xenophon's Cyropaedia to suggest that Iranian 'government' was welcomed everywhere. At the very least it confirmed that the Islamic Republic was just as keen as the Pahlavis and the Qajars in plundering the past for political purpose.[4]

And indeed, the association with Cyrus, and his 'good governance' sat well with Ahmadinejad's aspirations for Iran abroad. Constructive engagement and alliance building was discarded in favour of a more robust foreign policy, led in the main by the Revolutionary Guard Corps, rather than the Foreign Ministry, which found itself increasingly sidelined as far as regional issues were concerned. The first indication of a shift in policy came with policy in Iraq. While Khatami had intimated that the 'Coalition of the Willing' should remain in Iraq until they had cleared up the mess they had made, Ahmadinejad and his IRGC allies were far keener to ratchet up the political and military pressure in order to get them to vacate Iraq earlier. Ahmadinejad made no secret of the fact that he felt Iran should replace them, and this gradual reclamation of Mesopotamia to Greater Iran (or *Iranshahr*)[5] found a receptive audience among broad swathes of an Iranian population that had become bored with the repetitive sermonising of the clerical hierarchy. It was a salutary reminder that Iranian society, no less that the Iranian state, was still beholden to a certain historical impression of itself, and that this impression retained imperial pretentions that would not have been out of place in a succession of pre-revolutionary royal courts. This exploitation of national and imperial sentiment also had the added advantage of appealing to diaspora Iranians who had little affection for the religious aspects of the regime but could set aside their dislike in pursuit of a common 'national' agenda. Both Rafsanjani and Khatami had of course appealed to this sentiment, one economic and the other cultural, but Ahmadinejad now appealed to something a good deal more visceral, an emotional nationalism that allowed a generation of diaspora Iranians, long divorced from the realities of Iran, to 're-connect' with their Iranian identity from the relative safety and comfort of Europe and North America.

Few developments showed this to better effect that the ongoing crisis over Iran's nuclear programme. Talks with the Europeans had ground to a halt in 2006, in large part because the United States refused to participate, and the guarantees Iran sought could not be provided by the EU3 alone. Ahmadinejad threw diplomatic caution to the wind and rather than play the system, dismissed it as irrelevant. His aggressive and somewhat theatrical posturing about Iran's nuclear 'rights', and boasts over Iran's enrichment capacity and technological mastery, hit a nationalistic nerve that resonated with many who felt that Iran had been unjustly treated by the international community. As a public relations exercise this proved reasonably effective, and Ahmadinejad benefited from the crisis of confidence that was then afflicting US intelligence agencies that had yet to recover credibility from the debacle over the existence or otherwise of Iraq's weapons of mass destruction (WMD). Thus, just as internal pressure was mounting because of his mishandling of Iran's nuclear file which the International Atomic Energy Agency in Vienna had voted to send to the UN Security Council – effectively transforming a technical issue into a political one – the US National Intelligence Estimate (NIE) concluded in 2007 that Iran had in fact most likely ended any work on weaponisation in 2003. The apparent momentum towards a military confrontation receded and the pressure which had been mounting was abruptly lifted. Ahmadinejad's opponents within Iran found themselves wondering whether the President's self-belief did have some merit after all.

It proved, however, to be a false dawn insofar as the impending crisis over Iran's nuclear programme was deferred rather than solved, even if the NIE had signalled to Iran's rulers that the US had little stomach for any further confrontation in the Middle East. Israel of course was a different matter, and repeated threats by Israel to take action were welcomed. The measured view in Tehran was that an Israeli strike on Iran's nuclear assets could not only be contained but it would likely have the beneficial effect of increasing Iranian popularity in the Arab street, and allow Iranian politicians to point to the obvious 'double standard' with which the international community treated nuclear developments in each country – the Israeli response that it was not a signatory to the Nuclear Non-Proliferation Treaty (NPT) and therefore not subject to its strictures, while legally correct, simply ceded the moral high ground to Iran in the popular consciousness. Ahmadinejad's approach appeared to bear fruit with the enormous popularity Iran and the President himself achieved on the Arab street following the Israeli–Lebanese confrontation of 2006, when for a brief moment it looked as if Hizbollah, the Shi'a militia backed and funded by Iran, had transformed itself into an Arab 'nationalist' movement and the only effective resistance to Israeli power. But this too was to prove deceptive. Ahmadinejad's hubris, a function of his self-confidence, gradually tipped the regional balance against him and Iran. Iran's advances in Iraq and the popularity of 'Shi'a' Hizbollah was causing consternation in Arab capitals, not least Amman and Riyadh who feared the emergence of a 'Shi'a Crescent', including Syria, that would dominate the Middle East and exclude them. This ascribed to Ahmadinejad a good deal more calculation and strategic forethought than he was probably capable of, but he likewise appeared incapable of observing diplomatic norms of behaviour, relishing the notoriety which accompanied his more outrageous and provocative comments. In this he was not particularly different to populist politicians the world over, and he was not discriminating in his targets, attacking both domestic and overseas opponents. Needless to say it was his attacks on Israel and the nature of the Holocaust, that drew the most attention, fuelled his ego and encouraged him further, on the dubious basis as noted above that the controversy was clearly an indication of the veracity of his opinions.

There were two distinct attacks on Israel and Israeli identity. The first reflected the general opinion among Iranian officials that Israel was a blight on the Muslim world and would eventually vanish off the face of the earth. In his speech Ahmadinejad had used the passive voice suggesting that the injustice of Israel made such an eventuality inevitable, the consequence of its many internal contradictions. Previous Iranian administrations, while never formally recognising Israel, had concluded that they could not do more than the Palestinians themselves – then in the throes of negotiations – and for all practical purposes accepted the notion of a two-state solution. Ahmadinejad definitively ended any such idea but sought to mollify his rhetoric by suggesting that a referendum be held by all the peoples of Palestine as to their future, ending one might imagine in a single Palestinian state with both Jewish and Arab citizens. In this, it was argued, Israel as a state would vanish from the page of history, while no harm would befall the Jews themselves. This diplomatic explanation could not disguise, however, the fact that many other hardline officials had much more simple solutions in mind, and these solutions were not expressed in the passive voice. More problematic was his assertion that the Holocaust had not actually happened, and indeed had been invented in order to justify the existence of the state of Israel. Such arguments exposed the anti-Semitic roots of Ahmadinejad's thinking and at the very least his dependence on core anti-Semites within his inner circle. It showed little understanding of the origins of Zionism and a somewhat naive belief that his mere expression of this 'truth' would serve to weaken the foundations of the state of Israel. Some Western commentators sought to explain away these comments by suggesting that Ahmadinejad was using the term 'myth' in an academic social scientific sense, criticising the ideology rather the denying the validity. But in this case the evidence was against them. The Persian expression used by Ahmadinejad and his supporters could leave no doubt that he was arguing that the Holocaust was a fantasy, and Ahmadinejad was emboldened by the response to convene an 'international conference' to debate the issue, inviting a rogues gallery of Holocaust deniers to support his mission.[6] The condemnation from polite international society was to be expected and they served to further convince Ahmadinejad of the righteousness of his cause. But far from turning him into a cause célèbre, such activities along with his regional ambitions accelerated Iran's isolation and made any compromise on the nuclear issue far more difficult. It was in all probability these 'extra-curricular' activities that ensured enough votes could be garnered to send Iran's nuclear file to the UNSC – a reminder that the nuclear crisis was a symptom and not a cause of the wider malaise in relations.

The Presidential election of 2009 and the establishment of the 'paranoid' state

The tendency to read all events in Iran through the prism of international affairs, and the actions of the United States in particular, is a frequent conceit of Western policy makers – the notion in particular that it is international affairs that matter, and decisions made at this level affect and change actions at a domestic level. It is in many ways a hangover from classical realist thought in international relations and is especially pervasive in the United States where the belief in that country's decisive impact on the course of events is more widespread in policy circles than often understood. To criticise this position is not to underestimate the role of the 'Great Powers' in shaping and affecting Iranian policy, but one should neither exaggerate this impact nor diminish the reality that Iranian politicians are in the main driven by domestic considerations – that it is domestic politics that drives the international agenda and not the other way round. Iran's politicians have never been short of self-confidence, even as we have seen at the nadir of her international fortunes in 1919. Ahmadinejad's self-confidence and belief was even by Iranian standards remarkable, a conviction that was reinforced as we have seen by his astonishing rise to the presidency. But his confidence reflected a wider self-assuredness which emanated from the leadership and the revolutionary institutions, whose main policy and determination was the eradication of 'reform' and the drive towards revolutionary purity – as they understood it. Success abroad of course served to reinforce and legitimise positions at home and the seduction of the international stage was ever present and tempting, but it was domestic consolidation that was the priority and it was in the domestic arena that the first cracks in this agenda became apparent. Indeed in the pursuit of economic and political consolidation Ahmadinejad paradoxically undermined the very foundations of stability that Rafsanjani and Khatami, for all their flaws, had painstakingly attempted to construct. It is as always far easier to destroy than to build and Ahmadinejad effectively washed away what modest achievement had been made in a torrent of misspent oil money. This would in turn have a profoundly detrimental effect on Iran's ability to project its power (whether hard or soft) abroad.

It reveals much of the political mismanagement that took place that despite an embarrassment of riches Ahmadinejad succeeded in alienating key elements of political society within Iran. He was already regarded with considerable disdain by students and intellectuals, but this was not surprising given their Reformist leanings. What was perhaps more striking was his alienation of the traditional professional and bureaucratic classes, many of whom retained a lingering loyalty to the man who had done most to shape their position and world view – Hashemi Rafsanjani. Khatami and Rafsanjani became in many ways the political representatives of these two disgruntled groups, and while Ahmadinejad made a virtue of offending the former, the latter groups were more problematic insofar as their political views were broader, and many came from what might be termed the traditional conservative backgrounds. These were not liberals by any stretch of the imagination, but they were pragmatic enough to recognise that the stability of the regime, as elusive as it might be, would be enhanced by a degree of harmonisation between the various political groups. The 'heresy' of reform should be contained, but to eliminate it altogether both was unnecessary and harboured potential problems for the future, not least when it came to harnessing the youthful idealism that would be useful for the prolongation of the regime. Ahmadinejad and his supporters had no such compunctions moving instead to curtail university campuses and restrict what modest journalistic freedom had been achieved. In many ways he was simply extending a process that had begun in Khatami's second term as he contended with the hardline judiciary, but Ahmadinejad confirmed and endorsed the process, politically aligned as he was with the judiciary and the security forces. Indeed a key factor in enabling Ahmadinejad's policies was the unusual alignment with the executive and the coercive arms of the state. Rafsanjani may have been a conservative, but his pragmatism had swiftly resulted in conflicts with other more conservative elements.

With Ahmadinejad the stars were aligned and it was in this period that the IRGC received its greatest economic boost in the allocation of government contracts, in large part on the basis of dubious security concerns, justified on the further basis of domestic and international concerns which were in turn in no small part due to Ahmadinejad's own brand of confrontational politics. The IRGC, which had long been transforming itself from the 'armed wing' and guardian of the Revolution, increasingly defined its protective remit in the broadest possible terms, and became in due course a business conglomerate of far greater reach and influence than the religious foundations of old, in large part because unlike them it was armed and not averse to using coercion to get its way. In a curious twist, having trialled its brand of political and economic control in Iraq, it was bringing the model back home under the helpful eye of a president who had of course previously served in its logistical arm. With the growth of IRGC power came the emergence of the IRGC cult, which would be identified in time with the personality of Qasem Soleimani, the ubiquitous commander of the Quds force – that element of the IRGC which operated abroad – but which was initially experienced in the cultivation of the myth of the Iran–Iraq War, the emphatic and decisive role of the IRGC itself (as opposed to the army) and the celebration of martyrdom. This latter process caused a good deal of irritation among opponents when it transpired that Ahmadinejad intended to reinter war dead within university campuses, lest students forget the sacrifices that had been made.[7] Among his supporters this was not an unpopular policy. Among many veterans certainly there was a view that their sacrifice had not been fully recognised, but like much of his rhetoric, this was more about theatrics than meaningfully attending to their needs, and critics contended that Ahmadinejad was preoccupied with turning the country into a cemetery.

The sacrifice of 'rights', insofar as they existed, on the altar of populism was exemplified by Ahmadinejad's generous distribution of patronage to key supporters, many of whom received extraordinary 'pensions' and 'fees' for attending committees and meetings of little practical value and in many cases related to his obsession with the Hidden Imam. He played on popular superstitions by heavily investing in a new shrine at Jamkaran, the site of a well, where some believed the Hidden Imam had disappeared and from where he would re-emerge.[8] Ayatollah Khamenei similarly endorsed and financed this move with a view to associating himself with a religious endowment distinct from and outside of the control of the traditional clergy who viewed all these developments with a healthy scepticism, and as far as the president himself was concerned, increasing contempt. But all this was tolerated as long as the people appeared to be onside – state television spared no expense at televising Ahmadinejad's various provincial tours in an effort to cement and reinforce the popularity which certainly existed among sections of the population that had hitherto been marginalised from the Tehran-centric political process – and crucially, they were compensated by an unprecedented level of economic largesse.

But despite the theatrics, behind the curtain things were not well. And just as the country's diplomats lamented his mishandling of the nuclear file and the real and impending difficulties of it having been referred to the Security Council, so too domestically keen observers were increasingly appalled at the dismantling of both civil society and the emasculation and contempt for the republic institutions within the country. A simple if powerful example of the direction of travel was highlighted in the developments surrounding the notorious case of serial murders committed in Kerman at the latter end of Khatami's presidency. Largely ignored by domestic media – in part one suspects because it occurred outside Tehran (or any of the major cities) – the case became notorious in legal circles because of the implications of the initial judgement and the obvious corruption it revealed. A number of people, including young couples, had been found murdered, in often quite gruesome circumstances, and the local investigations pointed towards a group of *Basij* militia who were duly arrested and charged. A number of these individuals were related to senior officials in the political establishment but they also claimed that they had simply been acting on the admonishment of a senior Ayatollah (widely believed to be Ahmadinejad's mentor, Ayatollah Misbah Yazdi), known for his hardline pronouncements, who had urged religiously minded youngsters to act whenever they saw 'evil' being perpetrated. The religious injunction to forbid evil and encourage good had traditionally fallen short of actually murdering the hapless 'sinners' but in this case the members of the *Basij* took their instructions to the extreme. The individuals were convicted but then appealed to the higher court in Tehran which overturned the conviction on the astonishing legal argument that the *Basij* had only been fulfilling their religious obligations and that it was up to the deceased to prove their innocence. This extraordinary ruling effectively gave carte blanche to vigilante groups around the country and at a stroke deprived the 'modern' Iranian state of its monopoly over legitimate violence. Unsurprisingly lawyers were among the first to protest but it soon became apparent that the consequences of the ruling would make government impossible and the judgement was appealed again to the supreme court which finally restored the convictions but rather than a prison sentence, ruled that the culprits could pay the families compensation.[9] The integrity of the state was retained, and the criminals effectively let off with the most minor of punishments. This case was emblematic of the wider malaise afflicting the Islamic Republic.

This was to erupt into the public sphere in the Presidential elections of 2009. The aftermath of these elections marked the most serious crisis faced by the Islamic Republic since its inception in 1979. It tore at the fabric of the political settlement established by Rafsanjani and built on by Khatami and created the most severe civil rupture in recent Iranian history with wounds that have yet to heal. It revealed the depth and organisation of civil society and the limits of Ahmadinejad's policies. It was in many ways anticipated and planned for as a means of delivering the *coup de grâce* to the reform movement, but not only did the authorities underestimate the depth of the opposition, in ruthlessly repressing it they redoubled and reinforced the damage that Ahmadinejad had already wrought.

Hardline officials, most obviously in the judiciary and the IRGC, were not oblivious to the opposition Ahmadinejad was engendering. It was indeed part of his strategy to provoke and test the limits of loyalty through the sheer absurdity of his ideas. Only those who were willing to forgo reason could believe some of the ideas he confidently prognosticated on, and one of the policies that came to be identified with him was his tendency to divide people into 'us' and 'them', largely on the basis on whether they were like him a 'true believer'.[10] What this constituted remained vague but it gradually turned on a belief in him and his ideas but initially at least it revolved around a conviction in the Hidden Imam and the Supreme Leader. Early within Ahmadinejad's first term judiciary officials were arresting individuals, notably well-known dual nationals, who were involved in civil society organisations promoting democracy, on the basis that they were fomenting 'sedition' and encouraging 'regime change'. Seemingly borrowing from a playbook written in Russia and applied in the Ukraine, officials began warning of foreign-inspired plots with unerring regularity, justifying further securitisation but clearly also in an attempt to set the scene for a showdown. Their paranoia was not all unjustified insofar as the opposition was mobilising to fight the forthcoming Presidential election scheduled for 2009. Foreign involvement was, however, more difficult to pinpoint and matters took a surreal turn when British sailors and marines were captured in the Persian Gulf in 2007 having crossed into Iranian waters. Ahmadinejad treated the entire episode as a public relations gift of enviable proportions, but the assertion of his allies that he had foiled a British invasion was met with widespread ridicule.

As miscalculations went, however, it was as nothing compared to the domestic debacle to follow. There were reasons to be confident. Ahmadinejad appeared by all accounts popular if not in the major cities certainly in the countryside, although one suspects that the evidence for such an electoral distinction was made to fit the presupposition. Be that as it may, Ahmadinejad and his supporters had the confidence and self-assurance of individuals who controlled all the main levers of power. Previous elections had seen different political factions in control of the Ministry of Interior (tasked with running the election) and the Guardian Council (charged with oversight). On this occasion one faction was in control of the entire machinery. It was in large part because of the reality of this situation that the opposition had to organise efficiently and beneath the political radar, and the fact that they did it so well and out of sight meant that the authorities, blindsided by developments, could naturally only conclude that they had not misjudged the situation and that only foreigners could have engineered such a movement. The Shah had of course come to a similar conclusion in 1978.

So confident were the authorities in their ability to handle any eventuality that the run up to the election in the summer of 2009 took on the unusual characteristic of a US primary election as various candidates jockeyed for pole position before the formal period of campaigning began. Nevertheless so as to remove any doubt that the situation was not all that it seemed to be, Khatami's much anticipated re-emergence into the political fray was cut short when he announced that the 'pressures' of politics had persuaded him not to run. Just what these pressures were was not made clear but it became abundantly apparent that Khatami retained a popularity that had unnerved the authorities and exposed the limitations of Ahmadinejad's appeal. The opposition eventually settled on the former Prime Minister during the Iran–Iraq War, Mir-Hussein Musavi, with the former, somewhat idiosyncratic speaker of the Sixth Majlis, Mehdi Karoubi, as the back-up candidate for the Reformists. Other candidates, such as the former commander of the IRGC, Mohsen Rezai, were essentially there to make up the numbers, though Rezai proved himself a formidable debater against Ahmadinejad. Karoubi for his part was seen as too much of an outlier to have a significant impact and most of the Reformist votes were expected to go to Musavi who was widely considered to be boring enough to be safe. Musavi nonetheless drew some huge crowds at his rallies, became a passionate advocate for the principles of reformism, most obviously as it pertained to the universities, and was wrapped in a network of support that at times seemed to surprise him. His wife, Zahra Rahnavard, proved to be an especially potent political asset as she refused to let religious sensibilities get in the way of practical politics. Her experience and background suggested a first lady who would be a real asset to her husband as opposed to Ahmadinejad's wife, who clearly shunned the political limelight.

Up until the last week, everything appeared to be going to plan, but then the authorities appeared to take fright at the possibilities of what they had unleashed. Political campaigns rarely gain steam in Iran until the final weak when the general population begin to pay attention and in this case their attention was warranted because many felt that an upset might actually be on the cards. The crowds for Musavi had continued to grow – adopting the colour green and proclaiming themselves a movement (a shift in momentum that itself fuelled the paranoia of the hardline establishment preoccupied as they were with 'velvet or coloured' revolutions) – but it was also apparent that Ahmadinejad was bungling his campaign. No longer the insurgent but the incumbent, he had to stand on a record that was, for all the money, decidedly mixed. And if Musavi proved a reliably lacklustre debater, Rezai and Karoubi more than made up for it by tearing into Ahmadinejad's conceit. Even Musavi was able to make Ahmadinejad look petty and vindictive as he resorted to threats to reveal details of his wife's apparently dubious history, and in an act of apparent desperation launched into a vitriolic attack on the Rafsanjani family. Such threats were regarded as cheap by many Iranians and indicative of how base Iranian politics had become. The tension had succeeded in ensuring a high turnout – the sine qua non of any election as far as Ayatollah Khamenei was concerned – but the anxiety had clearly spread and the authorities decided to take pre-emptive action just to be sure that the correct result came out of the ballot box. The strategy proved a risky one for two reasons: first, the international press corps that had been invited to witness the glories of Iranian democracy were due to remain in place for at least another week until their visas ran out; second, the result they wanted to engineer – a landslide for Ahmadinejad that would surpass anything achieved by Khatami – was bound to provoke incredulity among the populace. Security forces poured into Tehran, communication systems were slowed and in some cases blocked, the Ministry of Interior was blockaded in seeming anticipation of trouble, and key agents of sedition – Reformist politicians – were summarily arrested as the polls closed and the counting ostensibly began. One hardline news website inadvertently put the result up on its website before the polls had closed before swiftly removing it.[11]

Aware that something was afoot, Musavi's campaign headquarters moved to pre-empt any announcement to the contrary, by declaring that he was in the lead and well on the way to victory, a gambit that risked making matters considerably worse, even if this appeared itself to be a response to a reported declaration of victory for Ahmadinejad. That said, his move in all probability accelerated and exposed a vote count that was already looking farcical as the Ministry of Interior issued periodic results with breathtaking speed and efficiency, with the percentage of votes accrued by each candidate remaining remarkably static whatever the tally.[12] Indeed Ahmadinejad's lead barely shifted throughout the night. Opposition candidates, including Rezai, protested that procedures were not being followed and that election monitors from each HQ were not being allowed access to the various counts.[13] The speed of the count was attested to the efficiency of Iranian elections, an accolade that few would have considered appropriate either politically or historically, but to avoid the charge of fraud a number of officials suggested that it was because of the 'computerised' nature of the process – implying that the vote itself had been digital and thereby collated and counted by computer.

In fact Iranian elections are and remain remarkably basic in administration if not straightforward in procedure. In the first place there is no electoral register with voters simply having to provide proof of identity – normally their identity card – resulting in the possibility of people voting outside their normal place of residence which means that in some cases, electoral districts registered more than 100 per cent turnout (in this particular election 170 constituencies enjoyed between 95 and 140 per cent turnouts).[14] Quite apart from this figure being a staggering achievement one might expect as a consequence lower turnouts elsewhere, but this rarely happened and was in the circumstances difficult to ascertain in any case. The voter was then handed a ballot within which they wrote the full name of the chosen candidate (often in full view of officials), along with their distinct electoral number – a number often confused with the listed number of the candidate. These numbers were often confusing and in this case Ahmadinejad's electoral number (44) was often confused with Musavi's list number (4). But more important was the fact that the name had to be written out in full and legibly, otherwise it risked being misread and/or discarded. These were then hand counted, various boxes being designated to various officials who then took the boxes home to be counted. It was a remarkably casual procedure, and was certainly labour intensive and open to abuse. It took one hour between the formal close of the polls at 10pm to the first announcement of results at 11pm for Ahmadinejad to be declared the winner; not on the basis of an exit poll, but of actual votes – some 5 million – having apparently already been counted (this was confirmed 50 minutes later by the Ministry of the Interior).[15] Although few people initially absorbed what was going on, by early morning all the opposition candidates had filed complaints. It took some time next morning for Iranians to digest the news but so as to leave no one in any doubt, Ayatollah Khamenei promptly pre-empted the formal procedures accompanying any vote (they had to be ratified by the Guardian Council, never in any doubt on this occasion but normally a procedure that for form's sake took a number of days) by endorsing the triumphant re-election of his protégé by such a staggering margin. He was by all accounts well pleased by the result.

It was not long after this that the protests began. All three opposition candidates, including Rezai, who had curiously been beaten by Ahmadinejad in his home village, protested the result, not least the extensive margin of victory proclaimed.[16] For them the result had been 'engineered'. All three, not least Musavi himself, were astonished at the scale of the protests that were emerging. For Ahmadinejad's supporters, these were proof, if it were ever needed, that the regime was facing an existential threat 'engineered' and directed from abroad. The following six months witnessed perhaps the most extraordinary period of political and civil unrest in the post-revolutionary period. The size of the crowds which emerged, certainly in Tehran, were unprecedented, and even accounting for the population growth since 1979, far exceeded anything that had been witnessed for the overthrow of the Shah, with crowds in Tehran at one stage estimated to have reached three million.[17] They proved to a curious amalgam of efficiency and naivete as street organisers that had been key to the mobilisation of the vote for Musavi now turned their skills to maintaining the protest against the vote and demanding a rerun of the election. But their skill at bringing the crowds out was undermined by their propensity to announce the time and place of the protest, which although they remained on the whole 'civil', were also remarkably punctual. What is perhaps surprising is that, despite the somewhat transparent process, it took the authorities so long to suppress. One of the reasons has to be that they completely misunderstood the nature of the protests, which they regarded as led from the top. Consequently the initial strategy was simply to arrest the main opposition leaders and let the protests run out of steam. Ahmadinejad's victory speech, where he notoriously referred to the protestors as mere dust and dirt, reflected this view, and the fact that it simply provoked more protest showed how little he understood the situation.

The protests were, with the odd exception, initially peaceful in the apparent expectation that Khamenei would notice the widespread disillusion, and as the 'father' of his people would provide a balanced assessment that would urge the parties to reconcile and, it was hoped, have a rerun of the election. More sober observers might have realised that precedent suggested otherwise. In 1999, when the students had protested, Khamenei initially took the abuse directed at him with an air of tired regret, appeared to publicly weep at the difficult decisions he now had to make before authorising the security forces to take all necessary action to bring the protests to an end. On this occasion he did not disappoint and indeed seemed to go much further in his condemnation of the protests. It might be possible he argued for an election to be rigged by a million votes, but surely not by the margin of victory claimed?[18] It was all told a curious position to take, but after the formality of emotion, he instructed the crowds that they had had their fun and it was time to move on. As a minor concession he instructed the Guardian Council – the very body thought to be complicit in the irregularities – to conduct a recount of 10 per cent of the ballots, the result of which unsurprisingly absolved them of any wrongdoing. The 'Emperor' may have had no clothes in 1978, but on this occasion Khamenei was determined to show a ruthlessness that indicated the lessons of that earlier confrontation had been learnt The security forces were authorised to crack down on the protests, and the contest became decidedly violent. The opposition movement split, insofar as Rezai now towed the line, arguing that constitutionally the Leader had the 'last word' and once he had made his decision, it was time for people to fall into line.[19] But a sizable section of the population were profoundly shocked at the turn of events and refused to bend the knee to developments that appeared to completely undermine the integrity of the Republic. The security forces found themselves facing unprecedented anger and violence against their own persons, while other protestors took to chanting decidedly unofficial slogans including death to Russia (who ironically the protestors felt were supporting the government) and China.

Matters became even worse when Ayatollah Misbah Yazdi pronounced, in an interview that was subsequently withdrawn, that obedience to the affirmed President was equivalent to obedience to God. Since, argued Misbah Yazdi, the Supreme Leader, as the *vali-e faqih*, was the (temporary) replacement for the absent Hidden Imam, he accrued all his divinely mandated power and authority. Moreover, belief in the 'Guardianship of the Jurist' must be accepted as one of the pillars of Islam, and an absence of belief rendered you a non-Muslim, a *kuffar*, or heretic. This was an extraordinary step to take – it signified a claim to authority far in excess anything imagined by Iranian monarchs – and was a cause of some embarrassment among loyalists, while others including some notable senior clerics spoke out against what they considered a theological travesty.[20] By any orthodox understanding of the faith such arguments had themselves crossed the boundary into blasphemy, but by defining the struggle as a religious as well as a political contest, Misbah Yazdi had effectively sanctioned the most extreme use of violence.[21]

The nature and extent of the violence used against protestors has never been adequately assessed in large part because most reporters were limited to Tehran and were in any case instructed to leave the country once their visas had run out, which was normally within weeks of the election. There can be little doubt, however, that the number of casualties lay comfortably beyond the estimates provided by the government.[22] The more immediate scandal revolved around the treatment of prisoners, and the torture and sexual abuse that was inflicted on them – a consequence no doubt of their categorisation as *kuffar*. The government's attempts to deny any such abuse was taking place was soon exposed by the ubiquity of video evidence uploaded to the web – the most famous example of this of course being the murder of Neda Agha-Soltan, a student who was ostensibly caught in the cross fire. The authorities in any case appear to have concluded that desperate times required desperate measures and in the absence of any lingering affection for the regime, fear was the only solution. Violence would be used to tame the protests but its arbitrary use would also force those sitting on the fence to come out in favour of 'order'. Meanwhile levels of paranoia were ratcheted up in order to shore up support on their own side. This reached hysterical levels when Ahmadinejad's Foreign Minister, Manouchehr Mottaki claimed, in front of bewildered foreign ambassadors, that plane loads of foreign 'spies' (mainly it would appear British) were pouring into the country to foster rebellion.

The protests interestingly peaked some six months after the elections with the sudden and unexpected death of Ayatollah Montazeri, Khomeini's one time heir and a long-time critic of the Islamic Republic, which he scathingly condemned for having lost its way. For a moment, it appeared that the 'middle-class' secular struggle might extend to the religious working class. In truth, the protests could never be so easily categorised; they ranged wide over socio-economic groups and while driven by students, journalists and other like-minded professionals, they drew on a broad range of support and crucially were socially embedded and rooted. It was this social reach that made the protests so difficult to uproot and Musavi was much more a symbol rather than a leader of the Green Movement with which he was identified. By January 2010, the protests had finally run out of steam. The protestors retreated from the fray, disillusioned and dejected. Many fled abroad. The Islamic Republic had survived. But it was a decidedly pyrrhic victory.[23]

The first and most immediate crisis was one of authority. Ahmadinejad had shown himself to be considerably less popular than his self-confidence suggested. But far more serious was the resistance that had been shown to the authority of Khamenei, who had presumed, incorrectly, that his word was in effect the law. Many people it would seem disagreed but Khamenei was in no mood to compromise on this point of revolutionary purity whatever the cost might be to the integrity of the Republic. The regime was determined to take back control of the narrative and it pursued its objective with near totalitarian ruthlessness.[24] The idea that the protest had been a great act of foreign-inspired sedition was reinforced with show trials and televised confessions, extracted on the basis of physical and more often psychological torture. At one stage government lawyers sought to ascribe blame to a range of Western academics, one of whom, the German sociologist, Max Weber, had long since died.[25] Weber's concept of 'Patrimonialism' and his arguments about how societies might transition from traditional to modern types of authority and political organisation had featured in the preamble to the constitution of the reformist Islamic Participation Front. The regime was not only determined to control the message but to take control of the messengers. Western journalists had long since been expelled from the country – less than a handful of accredited journalists remained and henceforth if foreign news agencies wanted accredited journalists on the ground, they had to select from a new group of emerging reporters many of whom had served time on the Iranian State TV English-language service, Press TV. Moreover, taking a leaf from the Russian experience, new think tanks and NGOs emerged, to replace those that had been shut down, staffed by approved researchers with sufficiently good English that they could be used as pundits and commentators for a Western media starved of information.[26]

There was a good deal of ground to make up. The experience of 2009 left many Western journalists and diplomats traumatised by what they witnessed, not necessarily by the scale of the violence but by the fact that it had happened at all. Like many Iranians themselves, most had accepted the Islamic Republic for what it was, at best an emerging democracy, with its own idiosyncrasies, but at the end of the day, with admirable conceit, marginally on the civilised side of social behaviour. The brutality that was witnessed challenged those preconceptions and in essence exposed the deep state in all its ugliness. It was not an exaggeration to say that Iranian society was scarred by the experience, and that Western observers were deeply disturbed by what they saw. Both were deeply divided in their assessments, while the authorities sought to reinforce their narrative at every available opportunity, seeking at the very least to sow doubt and at best to exploit any residual benefit of doubt that might come their way. In this they were probably more successful abroad than they were at home, in large part because time and distance was a better healer – or disguiser of wounds – than time alone. That said there is little doubt that a diplomatic community that had hitherto been open to Iranian suggestion, was now finding itself increasingly unsympathetic to Iranian pleading. The situation was not helped by an Iranian foreign minister whose diplomatic skills appeared limited to offending friend and foe alike.

Resetting the button

President Obama came into office in 2009 with the avowed intention of bringing America's Middle East entanglements to a close and breaking new ground in terms of diplomatic outreach. His personal interest appears to have been to break the Gordian knot of US–Iran relations and to this end he has sent two private letters to Ayatollah Khamenei to explore the possibility of dialogue. Khamenei's public response to the reported missives was characteristically robust but any prospect of dialogue was derailed by the debacle of the Presidential election in Iran later that year. The official narrative had determined Western-inspired sedition so there was little prospect of Iran 'unclenching' its first at this stage, and instead for all the lacklustre response to the protests, the West, broadly defined, remained the culprit of choice for the hardline political establishment. In political terms, a stalemate ensued insofar as the Iranian authorities were seeking to stabilise the situation at home, while the Obama administration bided its time preparing for an opportunity to engage should the situation arise. During Obama's first term, however, such opportunities as there might be were constrained in part by Secretary of State Hillary Clinton's more sceptical approach to Iran, and the reality that many of the mechanisms put in place by George W. Bush to increase pressure on Iran were only now beginning to bear fruit and Obama was under pressure from various agencies to keep them in place. Hawks in the administration felt these would bring Iran to heel, others, including in all probability the President, felt they would incentivise Iran to come to the negotiating table.

One of the problems they faced was not only a divided leadership within Iran – not an unusual situation to face – but a leadership that was unusually bitter in its divided recriminations. Ahmadinejad had somewhat blithely passed the responsibility for the protests onto others in the establishment, characteristic political flippancy that had once been applauded as bravado, but now, having been experienced closer to home, was greeted with barely disguised irritation. Ahmadinejad's criticism of the Rafsanjani clan, his repeated allusions to 'secret' dossiers collected on members of the political elite, and his abnegation of any responsibility ensured that his second term – traditionally the time when Iranian presidents became weaker – would be contentious and fractious. Khamenei, who had publicly backed him, felt to disown his protégé would be an admission of failure and so determined to keep him in place until the formal end of his term. But he took an increasingly hands-on approach to his 'guardianship', regularly intervening to block appointments and ensuring key portfolios were in safe hands. Moreover in a clear indication that power was moving decisively from the presidency to the leadership, key policy decisions were now being taken by the Leader over the head of, and strikingly often without the knowledge of, the President.

In 2011 two distinct political developments revealed the limitations of the presidency. The 'Arab Spring' spread throughout the region, following an uprising in Tunisia, like wildfire to Libya, Egypt and as far as the Gulf states. The Western democracies were taken by surprise and characteristically reacted with a mixture of idealism and ineptitude seeking at once to understand the nature of the uprising and to direct it, while at the same time maintaining key interests in place. It proved an irreconcilable task with obvious contradictions in policy. Members of Iran's lingering Green Movement seized the opportunity to applaud the emulation of their Arab brethren and to suggest that their own movement was part of something broader – a new wave of democratisation – a view that never successfully gained traction among weary (and wary) Western policy makers. By far the most opportunistic claim, however, came from Khamenei and his acolytes who made the bold assertion that the Arab Spring was nothing less than belated Islamic Revolutions springing up throughout the Arab world in emulation not of 2009 but of 1979.[27] Khamenei's supporters even went so far as to claim that popular movements worldwide, including, it was claimed, 'Occupy Wall Street', were a consequence of the inspirational leadership of Ayatollah Khamenei. This striking claim began to unwind when Syria too fell into the grip of a protest movement of its own. With an intellectual agility only ideologies can provide, Iran swiftly reversed its position as far as Syria was concerned, returning to the narrative of the Green Movement and foreign-inspired sedition. Syria became the new battleground in a resistance movement against the West and the Iranians would do their best to support their ally Bashar al Assad. What was striking about the assistance that was provided, piecemeal and specific to begin with but increasing with time, was that it was led by the Revolutionary Guards under the specific authority of Ayatollah Khamenei. The Iranian government, not least its Foreign Ministry, now led by the former Head of the Atomic Energy Organisation of Iran, Ali Abkar Salehi, was not fully appraised of the nature and the extent of the support being provided and widespread disagreements existed at the highest echelons of the political establishment as to the value of any such commitment to a 'dictator' whose ideas were clearly antithetical to anything to which the Islamic Republic – in an ideal world – aspired. But Khamenei, justifying the intervention on esoteric grounds, had no such qualms.

A more pragmatic if striking intervention in policy, however, came elsewhere. With the Iranian government in a heightened state of incoherence, any possible progress on the nuclear file was proving even more difficult and slow than normal. An attempt to reach a preliminary resolution in October 2009 came to naught as internal disagreements in Iran resulted in a rejection of the offer and a decision instead to ramp up enrichment capacity. It seems remarkable given the turmoil inside Iran at this time that international negotiators felt that any progress at this stage might be feasible, but in any case, the decision the following year to increase enrichment capacity ensured that the West, along with Russia and China, who were themselves finding the Ahmadinejad administration problematic, were increasingly of one mind. Indeed, Ahmadinejad's exercise in vulgar diplomacy was achieving what few other Iranian governments had managed, an unusual unity of purpose between Europe, the US, China and Russia. Consequently, when Iran revisited the original proposal some six months later with the help of Brazil and Turkey, Russia was among the first to reject it, and the process was set in place for a dramatic increase in sanctions targeting in this case all financial transactions with the Islamic Republic.[28] Less transparent measures were also apparently being applied with the development of a sophisticated computer virus – Stuxnet – to disrupt the nuclear programme and the suspicious murder of a number of nuclear scientists.[29] Matters were made considerably worse when following the imposition of further restrictions on Iran's financial transactions by the UK, the British embassy was summarily ransacked by 'students' (although most were of a mature age) in a misplaced attempt to recapture the mood of 1979. Khamenei singularly failed to apologise or condemn the attack; the British Embassy was closed and the staff withdrawn (although relations were not formally severed). Europe, already reeling from the impact of 2009, considered this breach of the Vienna Convention well beyond the pale, and set into motion its own sanctions against the purchase of Iranian oil, ratified in January 2012 and due to be implemented in July 2012.

These collected sanctions were nothing short of disastrous for Iran. A fragile political economy with a disgruntled citizenry was now confronted with a determined international coalition imposing severe sanctions now authorised by the UN Security Council. While it was true that Iran had lived with a series of sanctions since 1979, these were of a wholly different scale and were being imposed at a time when Iran had few if any international friends and a domestic situation that was far from settled. While Ahmadinejad liked to portray Iran's expanding nuclear programme as the will of the Iranian people and a matter of pride – a view too readily accepted abroad – opinion in Iran remained divided and a good deal more sanguine. Moreover nationalist rhetoric and the legitimacy it sought had proved somewhat hollow during the 2009 election and the repression that followed. Added to this was the general discomfort over Iran's involvement in regional struggles, most obviously Syria, which was absorbing resources that many felt would be better applied at home. In this febrile environment Khamenei took the unprecedented decision of authorising exploratory talks with the United States with a view to breaking the impasse on Iran's nuclear programme and relieving the pressure of sanctions. What was perhaps most remarkable from a domestic political point of view was that Khamenei authorised Ahmadinejad's Foreign Minister, Ali Akbar Salehi, without actually informing the President. If the defence of Syria was a case of policy being outsourced to the revolutionary organs of the state, this particular exercise witnessed the almost complete emasculation of the office of the presidency.

As it happened, this period, the end of 2011 and the beginning of 2012, proved propitious as far as the United States was concerned. Obama had just been elected to a second term and had replaced Hillary Clinton with John Kerry as Secretary of State. Kerry, a former Chair of the Senate Committee on Foreign Relations, was on the hunt for a legacy, and had already made his predilection for a new relationship with Iran known. As Chair of the Senate Committee he had already held meetings with Iranian officials in which he had expressed his openness to new approaches to the Iranian nuclear impasse including, according to Iranian officials, a willingness to consider uranium enrichment on Iranian soil, a recognition Iran had long sought and one that would allow them to say they had achieved what the Shah had singularly failed to. This would have been a symbolic yet significant gain for Iran, although Kerry disputed ever making the offer, and much of course depended on the scale of the enrichment that would be considered. Moreover at this stage Kerry did not hold an official post in the administration – a technicality that Iranians would have missed.

Throughout the 1970s, and despite the terms of the NPT, the main nuclear powers had always resisted the extension of enrichment capability, largely because it was an obvious means of restricting proliferation. The Shah and the then head of the Iranian Atomic Energy Organisation, Dr Akbar Etemad, had found the general resistance frustrating since Iran was keen to develop what amounted to a self-sufficient nuclear industry, which it was argued would enable Iran to leap ahead in the process of industrialisation. Like with much else in the policy making of the Islamic Republic, these ideas were essentially lifted out of the Pahlavi era and reinvigorated for the contemporary age, with little assessment of the different context in which they were operating. Iranian officials argued, somewhat ahistorically, that the treatment of Iran was different now to that which it had experienced under the Shah. This was only partially true as noted above but it likewise tended to ignore the change in international relations – for which the

Islamic Republic bore a hefty responsibility, and the general change in attitude to nuclear power. Even in the 1970s British officials argued that 'self-sufficiency' was a mirage; now with Iran's economic situation considerably worse, it made little economic sense at all.[30]

Be that as it may, it was an ambition that Iranian officials had rediscovered, and despite their initial rejection of the programme as one of the Shah's 'Western' follies, now clothed it, as noted above, in robust nationalist rhetoric, which had the advantage of serving a wider political agenda. Kerry's suggestion, however seriously it might have been taken, proved to be just the bait Iranian negotiators needed not only to satisfy critics at home but also as a means of justifying an engagement that had long been rejected but was now necessary if Iran's international predicament was to be ameliorated. It was in sum possible to suggest that the United States had changed its behaviour. Initially nevertheless Kerry sought his legacy in both the Arab–Israeli Peace Process and the ongoing Syrian conflict. He found both cases characteristically unresponsive and so turned in due course to the one place that did seem interested. Clinton had initiated secret talks in Oman as a consequence of negotiations that had resulted in the release of three US hikers who had been abducted on the Iranian–Iraqi border. Omani intermediaries believed that this would provide an opportunity for some meaningful face-to-face discussions about the possibilities that might exist for further engagement. Despite later reports to the contrary, this was not the first time Iranian and US officials had met either openly or covertly (the Algiers Accord and the subsequent Hague tribunal spring to mind, to say nothing of the Iran-Contra scandal), but the ambitions, at least on the American side were quite different, especially once Kerry took the helm of the negotiations. Indeed the discussions from 2012 through to early 2013 in many ways represented a watershed in US–Iran relations insofar as there now seemed the political will on both sides to make significant progress. Both sides seemed convinced that the other was genuine.

It was in this sympathetic context that Khamenei decided that the time was right for a relaxation of the repressive apparatus that had sat awkwardly over domestic politics since 2009. The 2012 Parliamentary elections, rigorously managed and controlled, had proved, unsurprisingly, to be a lacklustre affair and there was a clear sense that some vitality needed to be injected into the political process if some sort of meaningful healing was to take place. Moreover, Ahmadinejad remained deeply unpopular among wide sections of the political elite including some members of Khamenei's own office, notably the former Presidential candidate, Ali Akbar Nateq Nuri. There was in sum a critical mass of the elite who were opposed to Ahmadinejad's policies, saw them as destructive to the fabric of the state – not least the Republic – and were pushing for a change in tack to confront the problems that remained outstanding. At the same time, a more congenial and outward looking president in office would facilitate a deal on Iran's nuclear programme and certainly send the right signal. The Presidential election of 2013 nonetheless started as inauspiciously as many others, with intense debates on who was and was not allowed to run. Hashemi Rafsanjani re-emerged, somewhat late in life, to position himself as the saviour and there was much excitement about what the new Rafsanjani, chastened by life outside the inner circle of power, might be able to achieve. He was certainly seen by many as the man who could ultimately heal the divisions in society as well as politics at large. Regrettably for him and his supporters, Khamenei was not overly enthusiastic about welcoming back the prodigal son of the Revolution – the individual who more than anyone might pose a serious challenge to his authority. Rafsanjani was ruled unsuitable as a candidate by the Guardian Council on account of his advanced age.

The mantle thus fell on his protégé, Hasan Rouhani. Rouhani came from the traditional conservative political stable exemplified and led by Rafsanjani. He was a political insider whose career was spent within the regime's security and intelligence establishment, and was therefore regarded as a safe pair of hands. Having been in charge of Iran's nuclear negotiations until 2005, he seemed the ideal candidate to take forward the progress that had already been achieved. He was certainly a known quantity to the Europeans who by all accounts had a high appreciation of his abilities. At the same time he was fluent, congenial and reportedly open to new ideas, as he was to make clear during the brief campaigning, when he increasingly portrayed himself as the heir to the Reformist cause, even adopting for this purpose a colour of his own, purple. Khatami, the other key political player, for all his estrangement from the political establishment, urged his supporters to vote for Rouhani as the one man willing and, crucially, able to reverse the process of securitisation that had suffocated civil society over the past eight years. Khatami urged more authentic Reformist candidates to step aside in favour of a united front behind Rouhani and the latter did not disappoint in the rhetoric and ideas he now professed to support. His chief opponent was Ahmadinejad's nuclear negotiator, the incomprehensibly hardline Saeed Jalili whose professed 'unconditional' loyalty to the Supreme Leader did little to compensate for his general unpopularity. Even Ahmadinejad was unwilling to endorse him, and in the debates that followed he found himself consistently outwitted by the verbally agile Rouhani who presented himself as a man of the law. In the event Rouhani won in the first round and Iranians, as well as many keen observers around the world, breathed a heavy sigh of relief. For Khamenei, the success of the election was reflected in the relatively high turnout and, crucially, in helping to lay the ghost of 2009 to rest.[31]

Nevertheless the despair caused by Ahmadinejad was now replaced by an equally unhealthy devotion as the hopes and aspirations of millions were now placed on the shoulders of an individual whose governing prose was to be found to be far short of the poetry he expressed during the campaign. To be fair, Rouhani inherited a political landscape that had been battered and bruised by eight years of Ahmadinejad, but Iranians (within Iran) were soon to be faced with the distinct probability that behind Rouhani's soaring rhetoric lay a conservative who was pragmatic rather than moderate and far from keen to rock the political boat. Indeed having made fulsome promises during the campaign about de-securitising the political environment, along with suggestions that a resolution would be found to the continued house arrest of the leaders of the Green Movement, Mir-Hussein Musavi and Mehdi Karroubi, Rouhani proceeded on his inauguration to parrot the official line on the great sedition of 2009. His supporters ascribed such verbal acrobatics to his need to navigate the otherwise difficult waters of Iranian politics but as time wore on the enthusiasm with which his election was greeted dissipated somewhat quicker than many had anticipated. More astute observers noted wryly that he was peddling hope, and that such a strategy left unrealised would be pregnant with problems for the future.

The real 'hope' of course lay in a new settlement of Iran's international relations. Here Rouhani echoed the policies of his mentor Rafsanjani, though perhaps shorn of the acquired wisdom of experience. In sum Rouhani's strategy for Iran lay in economic development whose potential could only be released by a resetting of her foreign relations, and above all a working settlement with the United States. Unlike the 'later Rafsanjani', or indeed the Khatami administration, internal political issues were to be set to one side in the assumption that economic development would inevitably trigger the change necessary. What it ignored altogether was the possibility that political realities left unreformed would make all this difficult to achieve, and that the attraction of foreign investment depended not only on sanctions being lifted, but on Iran's opaque political economy being reformed. None of these problems were especially new but the intensity of the crisis and the urgency for a solution were much greater. But perhaps most striking was the reality that a Revolution and Republic that had prided itself on autonomous action and independence now placed its future prosperity squarely in the hands of an international negotiation and the ability of foreign powers to deliver.

Rouhani thus presented a successful conclusion to the nuclear talks and the lifting of sanctions as the *key* that would unlock all of Iran's problems. The focus of attention was henceforth to be on securing a successful conclusion to talks that Rouhani discovered to his astonishment had been proceeding for some time, in secret in Oman.[32] Government supporters duly fell into line, praising Rouhani's election and foresight as a turning point in Iranian history – one former Reformist argued with scant attention to historical detail that Rouhani's election was the single most important election in 150 years – and insisting that such was the damage inflicted by the previous administration, that this painstakingly incremental and economic approach was the only solution.[33] Indeed the one thing they all shared was a visceral dislike of Ahmadinejad, but it was notable that while the former president had been ostracised from polite revolutionary company, he was never fully banished by Ayatollah Khamenei, who duly appointed him to all the bodies former presidents normally sat on, including the Expediency Council. The contrast with Khatami was revealing.

Indeed the earliest indication that little had changed, or indeed could change domestically was the treatment meted out to both Khatami and Rafsanjani. Khatami's effective house arrest and regular harassment became increasingly oppressive such that in due course his image was banned from all public dissemination. Rafsanjani remained too important and popular a figure among key sections of the elite to be treated with such disdain, but he too found himself marginalised while key supporters and members of his family found themselves likewise regularly harassed. Rouhani enjoyed no particular electoral constituency beyond the support brought to him by these two pillars of Iranian political life. Their gradual emasculation sent a strong signal to Rouhani not to get ideas above his station. Despite this, he did move to restore the Plan and Budget Organisation, which had been so summarily abolished by Ahmadinejad, but beyond that there was little progress on the domestic front beyond presentation and Rouhani seemed unwilling, as the inclusion of hardliners in his cabinet seemed to suggest, to openly challenge the revolutionary establishment, limiting himself to the occasional rhetorical sortie.[34]

Circumstance and personal predilection therefore, forced him to face outwards, where he had real possibilities of progress and where he appeared to have the authority to at the very least get sanctions lifted and break the unity of the international coalition against Iran that Ahmadinejad had so recklessly enabled. How much further he might be able to go was a matter of some conjecture and rune reading by keen observers of Khamenei's utterances. Much was made of Khamenei's allusion to 'heroic flexibility' to suggest that the Supreme Leader was finally coming round to the idea of a détente with the United States. But this tended to read too much into a wrestling metaphor which basically argued for tactical concessions to be made in order to achieve strategic goals and there was little formal indication at least that Khamenei's strategic goals had changed substantively over the previous two decades.[35] A deep suspicion of the United States permeated his entire world view. The question for some was how rooted this was and whether Rouhani, and his newly appointed Foreign Minister, the loquacious Dr Mohammad-Javad Zarif, might in time be able to shift Khamenei from his comfort zone. Zarif was popular in the West and well known among European and American diplomats having served at the UN mission for both Khatami and Ahmadinejad, though he did not see the latter's term through and like many others appears to have found Iran's mercurial president just too much to cope with. After a few years of reflection and teaching he was now back as the country's senior diplomat, ratified by Parliament, and approved by the Supreme Leader, as were now all senior ministerial appointments. Indeed Khamenei's oversight was yet another indication of the growing management of the executive by the Leader's office.

Brought up to speed by Salehi, now transferred back to the Atomic Energy Organisation, Rouhani prepared for the annual visit to the UN General Assembly in the September of that year, where in light of international excitement that had greeted his election, anticipation was high. In the event, for all the enthusiasm and obvious relief that he had delivered a diplomatic speech shorn of references to the Hidden Imam, there was no 'impromptu' encounter between himself and Obama. But there was an engineered telephone call, apparently on the way to the airport, when Presidents Obama and Rouhani exchanged pleasantries and practised what limited Persian and English they each possessed. It was nonetheless now generally apparent what the Americans had been aware of for some time, that a page had been turned on the Ahmadinejad era and at the very least Iran's approach had changed. Formal negotiations now began in earnest and very swiftly reached a conclusion in Geneva with the Joint Plan of Action, which would see Iran suspend its nuclear activities in return for limited sanctions relief, pending a final agreement. The speed at which this was achieved surprised many who had been unaware of the previous 12 months' preparations, not least the French, who were clearly irritated at being kept in the dark, resulting in objections which delayed the announcement. All this of course served to heighten the political – and media – excitement, and the pattern became a staple of the negotiations that were to follow over the next two, somewhat tedious years.

Indeed after the initial agreement was struck, Rouhani appeared to suggest that a final agreement could be reached within months, arguing that the entire impasse had been caused by an enormous misunderstanding that could now be easily reconciled. Much was made of Ayatollah Khamenei's apparent issuance of a '*fatwa*' outlawing weapons of mass destruction. Although written evidence of this *fatwa* was hard to pin down, it was enthusiastically promoted by proponents of dialogue and unusually endorsed by the White House – despite the inviolability of this *fatwa* contradicting previous positions with regard to the *fatwa* against Salman Rushdie.[36] Even if this was a somewhat optimistic reading of the past decade and political landscape, there was a view, held by those privy to the preparatory negotiations, that the framework of the agreement had been laid out and what was left was to agree certain details. The devil of course was in those details and it would be important to get them right, but there was also a sense that the Iranians were playing for time, in the belief that the Americans were determined to get an agreement, and the longer the Iranians could hold out the better the terms would be for them. In this sense the Iranian negotiators turned the tables on their American interlocutors by recognising that the American election cycle had in fact made the urgency to get a deal agreed and bedded down an American priority rather than an Iranian one. They had turned an ostensibly weak hand into a strong one by exploiting American political vanity and effectively promoting a narrative of guilt by identifying Zarif with Mosaddeq and suggesting that current problems were fundamentally a result of American historical duplicity (it is worth noting on this point that Khamenei's view of Mosaddeq was not that of a tragic hero but of a political naïf). In so doing, however, they largely lost sight of their own vanity, began to believe much of the fawning rhetoric that presented them as expert negotiators and seemed singularly oblivious to the reality that the American election cycle affected them as well. The most serious immediate one was the US mid-term elections which saw control of Congress pass to the Republicans. This effectively ensured that any agreement would not be legally institutionalised through ratification as a Treaty in Congress, but would now have to be considered a non-binding executive agreement.

The art of procrastination, so well honed by the Iranians it was presented as a virtue, also served to amplify the theatrics of the negotiations and to ensure that any ultimate deal would be truly valued. At one stage it appeared as if the salubrious location of the negotiations, in Geneva and then Vienna, was helping to prolong them, sustaining as it was a veritable industry of journalists, commentators and various other hangers-on. For the American negotiators who had to fly on a weekly basis across the Atlantic, the process became especially wearing.

Nonetheless, despite repeated missed deadlines, the negotiations came to their final exhausting conclusion, characteristically, some two weeks after the first final deadline had been passed, for an announcement to be made on 14 July 2015. The excitement, born as much of relief that an end state had been reached, was palpable, largely drowning out, for the time being at least, the flaws in the agreement, or indeed Khamenei's initial response (15 July) and then robust speech on 18 July, which made clear his own considered limitations on what the agreement could and could not aspire to.[37]

Indeed the presentation of the agreement – the Joint Comprehensive Plan of Action (JCPOA) – as a watershed moment in US–Iran relations on a par with Nixon's opening to China in the early 1970s, served to both disguise its weaknesses and ironically to undermine its efficacy since it raised expectations beyond its ability to deliver. Rouhani himself was by far the most guilty in this respect, promising the Iranian public an economic and political dividend which far exceeded what the agreement might realistically deliver, not least because the Iranian economy itself had not been prepared for the eventuality of integration into the global economy. But he was closely followed by many observers and the occasional participant who argued that the agreement set Iran on the path not only of global integration but also liberal democracy, presumably applying a 'modernisation thesis' that took no account of internal political dynamics and simplistically assuming that economic development would naturally lead to political openness. The model was as simple as it was intoxicating and it soon established itself as the narrative of the agreement, such that a number of Western diplomats, most notably from the EU, sought to stress the limited focus of the agreement on Iran's nuclear programme. In essence the JCPOA was a confidence-building measure which prescribed strict restrictions on Iran's nuclear programme, its facilities and capacity for a set amount of time, during which time sanctions would be first suspended and then ultimately lifted. The technical parts of the agreement were clear and the obligations largely fell on the Iranians who moved with surprising alacrity to shut out aspects of their programme with a view to accessing much needed sanctions relief. In January 2016 the International Atomic Energy Agency verified that Iran had indeed complied with the requirements and key sanctions were suspended, notably those applied by the UN and the EU oil embargo. Sanctions that related to human rights and/or terrorism were not lifted and the vast majority of US sanctions also remained in place, most notably restrictions on the use of the US dollar and US financial markets. This proved to be a very serious omission on the part of the Iranian negotiators and effectively ensured that Iran remained locked out of the global financial system and all that implied for trade and investment.[38]

From the American side other problems were becoming apparent. Never a popular agreement, in the political sense, Obama struggled to ensure that Congress did not reject the agreement outright but found instead restrictions placed upon his abilities to deliver what was required in terms of sanctions relief. Essentially the survival of the JCPOA depended on the President issuing regular waivers to allow, among other things, US subsidiary companies, many of them in

Europe, to operate in Iran. As long as the President was sympathetic this would not be a problem, but it did indicate the essential political fragility of the agreement as far as the United States was concerned. It also meant that the agreement could easily be buffeted by political ill winds, if for the sake of argument Iran continued to behave in ways that were deemed provocative and contrary to US interests. This became all the more difficult because the agreement had taken so long to conclude that the United States was now entering its latest Presidential election cycle where the issue of Iran was likely as always to be a topic for debate.

There was consequently little or no time for the agreement to bed down and become part of the fabric of US politics. On the contrary, as Khamenei's 18 July speech indicated, Iran had no intention of restraining itself in other areas, extending itself in regional conflicts, most obviously Syria; engaging in extensive missile launches and bravado over the extent of its missile arsenal; and perhaps most acutely, seizing dual nationals on opaque charges of espionage (the seizure of American sailors on the cusp of the implementation of the agreement was resolved with the minimum of fuss though the Iranian authorities made the most of the humiliation over the months that followed). All these were grist to the mill of opponents of the agreement who further criticised the limitations of the inspections regime and the acceptance of 'sunset clauses', after which Iran would be allowed to pursue a nuclear programme as might any other signatory of the NPT. In truth it would have been difficult to envisage Iran agreeing to a tighter inspections regime or indeed an agreement that did not have an end point. But Iran did not make life easier for itself by making declarations of its intention to pursue an 'industrial'-scale enrichment programme once the restrictions had been lifted.[39] Even the Europeans expressed concern about this possibility and raised the prospect of further talks and an extension of the restrictions, a possibility that the Iranians categorically rejected as an infringement of the agreement.

None of this might be a problem if the 'modernisation thesis' unfolded as the more positive policy makers projected.[40] Integrated economically, and moving in the direction of a democratic settlement, an engaged Iran would have a vested interested in divesting itself of its revolutionary fervour and aspirations, with the consequence that these issues would no longer be raised or indeed be relevant. But the failure to negotiate a clear path of sanctions removal, to negotiate the complex web of financial sanctions that had been imposed, meant that the possibility of an economic dividend had in the very least been postponed. The continuing political malaise, combined with extensive diplomatic fatigue, ensured that necessary further discussions to iron out the remaining difficulties and address the problems that inevitably arise out of any diplomatic agreement were deferred. Moreover, the lack of any substantive progress on internal reform compounded an already difficult situation, ensuring that the Iranian economy remained sanctioned both at home and abroad. Indeed, some argued, with justification, that domestic problems remained by far the more serious of the obstacles to development.[41]

Far from initiating a period of economic reconstruction, optimism soon gave way to disappointment and then despair as the political and economic situation in the country grew gradually worse. For many it seemed as if nuclear security for the West had been won at the cost of human security at home. Rouhani successfully won re-election in 2017, albeit against a candidate, Ibrahim Raisi, widely considered to have been heavily implicated in the mass execution of prisoners in 1988. But Rouhani's re-election came against the backdrop of a dramatic change in the United States with the election of Donald Trump to the US presidency in 2016. Trump made no secret of his dislike of the agreement and withdrew the United States from the JCPOA in May 2018, threatening to re-impose the most draconian sanctions by the end of the year. The window of opportunity for a détente in US–Iran relations, brief as it may have been, appeared to all intents and purposes, closed.

Notes

1 'Nahad Riyasat Jumhuri: Ahmadinejad soghrat-e zaman ast' (The Office of the Presidency: Ahmadinejad Is the Socrates of the Age), Baztab.com, 28 Shahrivar 1386/19 September 2007. Critics were at pains to point out that Socrates committed suicide.

2 See Fatemeh Rajabi, *Ahmadinejad: Mojeze-ye hezare-ye sevom* (Ahmadinejad: The Miracle of the Third Millennium). Tehran: Nashr Danesh Amuz, 2005. The title is especially unusual because the dating – third millennium – is Christian.

3 See A. Ganji, 'Rafsanjani and Khamenei: The Ahmadinejad Years', *Al Jazeera*, 25 September 2013, www.aljazeera.com/indepth/opinion/2013/09/rafsanjani-khamenei-ahmadinejad-2013923732579341.html.

4 Ahmadinejad's interview relating to the cylinder can be viewed here: www.youtube.com/watch?v=eaOxn7Igs9A; at the official unveiling in Tehran in 2010, the cylinder was described by Iranian TV as the first declaration of 'human rights', a description which would not have gone amiss with the Shah, see: www.youtube.com/watch?v=qhbFrD_BpB8.

5 On the 'rediscovery' of *Iranshahr*, see Ansari, *The Politics of Nationalism in Modern Iran*, pp. 298–301.

6 See interview with Ahmadinejad: 'Defa az baz khani-e holokaust' (A Defence of Holocaust Revisionism), Baztab.com, 4 Farvardin 1386/24 March 2007; see also editorial in Iranian daily *Keyhan*, 'Een Mikh va an taboot' (This Nail and That Coffin), 28 January 2007; Interview with Mohammad Ali Ramin, 'Bazkhani-ye Holokaust dar Iran' (Holocaust Revisionism is Iran), Baztab.com, 6 Dey 1385/27 December 2006.

7 See Golnaz Esfandiari, 'Iran: Students Protest Burials of War Dead on Tehran Campuses', Radio Free Europe/Radio Liberty, 15 March 2006, www.rferl.org/featuresarticle/2006/03/6035bfe4-0e35-4807-ad4b- cdd4fce89821.html.

8 See A. Amanat, *Apocalyptic Islam and Iranian Shi'ism* (London: I.B. Tauris, 2009), p. 230.

9 See in particular, Nehmat Ahmadi, 'Negahi beh parvandeh-ye ghatl-haye mahfeli-e kerman az aghaz ta konoon' (A Look at the File of Kerman Derial Murders from the Beginning to the Present), *Etemad*, 29 Farvardin 1386/18 April 2007.

10 Hossein Shahriatmadari, the long-time hardline editor of *Keyhan* had a tripartite division of 'us-you-them'. Those among the 'you' were in the main insiders who had fallen out of favour. If you were among 'them' you were effectively outcast.

11 Fars' premature claim was captured by *Asr-Iran*: 'Khabar zood hengam Fars az natijeh-ye entekhabat' (The Early News of the Election Result from Fars), Asriran.com, 12 June 2009; the news is timed at 18:40.

12 'Sadeq Mahsuli: The People's Votes Are Similar All over the Country', Resalat, Tehran, in Persian, 27 Jun 2009, p. 2, BBC Mon ME1 MEPol ta.

13 'The Social Intelligence and Enthusiasm of the Iranian Nation Will Not Believe So Much Injustice and Violation of the Law in Its Historical Memory', Qalam news, 20 June 2009 (BBC Monitoring).

14 www.radiofarda.com 29 Khordad 1388/19 June 2009.

15 For a sequence of events see *Al Jazeera*, 'Mousavi Sees Election Hopes Dashed', 13 June 2009. According to this report, Daneshju first appeared at 11.50 to announce the results of five million votes.

16 According to Raja News on 23 Khordad 1388/13 June 2009, which sourced the figures to IRNA, Rezai won only 70 of the 900 available votes in his home village.

17 See MERIP report, dated 28 June 2009, www.merip.org/mero/mero062809.

18 The final tally claimed 24 million votes for Ahmadinejad ahead of Musavi on 13 million. Ahmadinejad later claimed that in reality he had been deprived of a further 16 million votes, making his own claim of fraud.

19 'Agar taqalob ham shode, vaghti rahbar taeed kard, eteraz maani nadarad' (Even If There Has Been Fraud, Once the Leader Confirms the Result, Protest Is Meaningless), Ayadenews.com, 20 Mordad 1388/11 August 2009.

20 The moderate Ayatollah Sanei famously spoke out against these developments and was marginalised as a consequence. See for example, www.youtube.com/watch?v=IwzG4vwi0ms, also, www.youtube.com/watch?v=ceHREFzgp10.

21 'Misbah-Yazdi: eta'at az rais jomhur, eta'at az khodast!' (Misbah Yazdi: Obedience to the President Is Obedience to God), *Tabnak*, 22 Mordad 1388/13 August 2009, www.tabnak.com/nbody.php?id=8792. Misbah Yazdi argued that it was a mistake to consider Islam a religion of moderation, 'Doshmanan migoyand Islam din-e Tasahol ast' (The Enemies Say That Islam Is a Religion of Moderation), Rooz online 28 Mehr 1388/20 October 2009. He added that maximum force should be used against opponents.

22 The government issued figures in the tens and over the six-month period, settling at around 70. Anecdotal evidence from the streets and hospitals easily placed this figure in the hundreds, though provincial accounts place the total casualties in the thousands. The truth remains that the exact figure will never be known.

23 For the context of recent elections in Iran see Ali M. Ansari, *Crisis of Authority: Iran's 2009 Presidential Election*. London: Chatham House, 2010. Also Farhad Khosrokhavar and Marie Ladier-Fouladi, *The 2009 Presidential Election in Iran: Fair or Foul?* EUI Working Papers, RSCAS 2012/29, Robert Schuman Centre for Advanced Studies, European University Institute, Florence, 2012. An initial assessment of the vote was provided in, Ali Ansari, Daniel Berman and Thomas Rintoul, *Preliminary Analysis of the Voting Figures in Iran's 2009 Presidential Election*. Chatham House Programme Paper, June 2009, www.chathamhouse.org.uk/publications/papers/view/-/id/755/; and Walter Mebane, 'Note on the Presidential Election in Iran, June 2009', www-personal.umich.edu/~wmebane/note22jun2009.pdf.

24 The key text in this regard was published by the Kayhan Research Institute, entitled *Shovalie-haye nato-ye far- hangi: yek nama az koodetah-ye makhmali* (The Cultural Knights of NATO: One Example of the Velvet Coup d'état), by Payam Fazli-nejad, with an introduction by Hossein Shariatmadari. The book was published in 1386/2007. The more absurd aspects of this development have to do with studies on the seditious effects of TV series. Hasan Abbasi, who goes by the title 'Expert on Strategic Serials', has taken aim at *24*. The political satirist Ebrahim Nabavi takes Abbasi to task in 'Hasan Abbasi: Serial Friends, aghaz fitne sabz' (Hasan Abbasi: 'Friends' and the Beginning of the Green Sedition), www.roozonline.com, 15 March 2010.

25 See in this regard Charles Kurzman, 'Reading Weber in Tehran', *The Chronicle Review*, 1 November 2009.

26 See 'How Iran Tries to Control News Coverage by Foreign-based Journalists', RSF, 6 September 2017.

27 S. Peterson, 'On the Road: Iran's Khamenei Sets Stage for a Less Democratic Future', *Christian Science Monitor*, 17 October 2011.

28 The ostensible reason was that Iran had not accounted for the increase in enriched uranium it now possessed but the more probable cause of the rejection was a mixture of diplomatic fatigue and the fact that the US was determined to take advantage of the unprecedented unity among the P5+1.

29 Both these were widely assumed to have originated in or been instigated by Israel.

30 See A.M. Ansari, 'The Curious Case of the Nuclear Company of Britain and Iran', *Iran* 55(1), 2017, pp. 73–86.

31 'Entekhab 92 Edaye taqalob dar entekhabat 88 ra be gorestan sepord' (The Election of 13 Has Sent Those Who Claimed Fraud in 09 to the Grave), Digarban.com, 28 Khordad 1392/18 June 2013. 'Rai dadan kesani ke be Nezam eteghadi nadarand, neshaneh etemad anha beh Jomhuri Eslami ast' (The Voting of Those Who Don't Believe in the System Is Indicative of Their Trust in the Islamic Republic), Digarban. com, 5 Tir 1392/26 June 2013.

32 'Salehi: mozakerati ke miyan iran va emrika dear Oman anjam shode bood, baraye rouhani bavar pazir nabood' (Salehi: The Negotiations That Had Been Conducted between Iran and America in Oman Were Unbelievable to Rouhani), BBC Persian, 5 August 2015.

33 Abbas Abdi argued, curiously, that this was the most important election in 150 years since it was the first time an opposition had been recognised. See *Mehrnameh* 29, Special issue on the Election 92, Tir 1392/June–July 2013, pp. 98–106.

34 Motafa Pourmohammadi, who was implicated in the 1988 murder of prisoners, was appointed Minister of Justice. The appointment was criticised by opponents.

35 'Ayatollah Khamenei: zaman "narmesh-e gharemani" ast' (Ayatollah Khamenei: Now Is the Age of 'Heroic Flexibility'), Khodnevis.org, 26 Shahrivar 1392/17 September 2013; 'Narmesh gharemaneh tanha yek taghir-e taktiki ast' (Heroic Flexibility Is Only a Tactical Change), Digarban.com, 28 Shahrivar 2013/19 September 2013.

36 For a summary of the debate see, G. Kessler, 'Did Iran's Supreme Leader Issue a Fatwa on the Development of Nuclear Weapons?', *Washington Post*, 27 November 2013.

37 His initial highly cautious comments were issued on 15 July 2015, 'Supreme Leader Ali Khamenei Urges "Careful Scrutiny" of Iran Deal', *New York Times*, 15 July 2015, to be followed by more explicit comments on the occasion of Eid-e Fetr, 18 July 2015, www.youtube.com/watch?v=z4qgO6dj2i4.

See also S. Lucas, 'Supreme Leader Slaps down Rouhani's "Naïve" Foreign Policy and Talks with the US', *Enduring America*, 7 October 2015.

38 R. Gladstone, 'Iran Not Seeking Entry to US Financial System, Envoy Says', *New York Times*, 20 April 2016.

39 'Salehi: 15 sal bad az barjam, tavanai 1 million soo ghani sazi uranium dareem' (Salehi: 15 Years after the JCPOA We Will Be Able to Have Enrichment of 1 Million Centrifuges), BBC Persian, 16 December 2015.

40 See G. Harris, 'Deeper Mideast Aspirations Seen in Nuclear Deal with Iran', *New York Times*, 31 July 2015.

41 Rouhani's attempts at reform have remained stillborn, partly as a result of the Supreme Leader's objections, but also due to his own inability to grasp the nettle. His 'citizen's charter' being a case in point, see, 'Jorm siyasi' (Political Crimes), *Tasnim News.com*, 31 Shahrivar 1392/22 September 2013, www.tasnimnews.com/Home/Single/146499. For legal concerns see, 'Tarh Jorm Siyasi ba didgah ye hoqoqdanan montabegh neest' (The Draft Law on Political Crimes Does Not Conform with the Views of Lawyers), Kaleme.org, 1 Mehr 1392/23 September 2013.

16 Conclusion
Iranians and their history

No country has undergone during the last 20 centuries more revolutions than the kingdom of Persia, there is perhaps none that is less altered in condition.[1]

History suggests that the Persians will insist upon surviving themselves.[2]

In 1725 a thesis was submitted for consideration at the University of Uppsala in Sweden, by one Isaac Isaacson, entitled, 'On the Current Revolutions in Persia'. The focus was on the turmoil that had afflicted the country following the fall of Isfahan in 1722 and the supremacy of the Afghan warlords. The following century witnessed further political turmoil with the dramatic ascent to power of Nader Shah and the re-establishment of an Iranian hegemony over the region, followed by an equally dramatic fall with the country economically exhausted and morally fractured by the brutalities of war. The interregnum of the Zand 'dynasty' was followed by the ruthless and bloody establishment of the Qajars by one of the most extraordinary figures ever to bestride Iranian history, the eunuch king, Agha Mohammad Khan, whose strategic foresight and brutality restored a measure of political stability to the 'imperial kingdom' of Iran. But it was a pyrrhic victory, bought at a cost that was not sustainable in the long term without the application of substantive reform to the political economy of the country. The situation was made all the more acute because Iran emerged from the turmoil of the eighteenth century into a world that had dramatically changed and where the balance of power had shifted definitively towards Europe.

Sir John Malcolm's revealing conversation with Fath Ali Shah on the differences between the British and Iranian forms of monarchy and their implications for long-term political stability went to the heart of the problem that has plagued a succession of Iranian statesmen and leaders. For Malcolm it was clear that the sort of change that Iranian leaders sought could not be applied piecemeal but had to be implemented as part of a broader package of political reforms – political reforms that would provide the firm foundations for economic and social change. These were not beyond the Iranians to achieve – most observers, including one might add Lord Curzon, had concluded that in the right political framework, there was little the Iranians might not achieve. James Morier, frequently considered contemptuous of Iranians, had little doubt of the innate ingenuity that political liberty might harness and release. Iranians too, from the earliest encounters with the West, were convinced of the veracity of the proposition and argued with increasing force that the establishment of the *rule* of law was an essential prerequisite for productive and durable development.

The Constitutional Revolution, that *pivotal* moment in modern Iranian history, anchored in the past and forcefully facing the future, was the singular moment when these ideas became part of the fabric of Iranian politics. That its immense promise could not be realised in the short order that many reformers and revolutionaries had wanted was in part a consequence of the very real structural weaknesses that existed. Mohammad Ali Foroughi, one of the leading lights of the Iranian Enlightenment reflected poignantly on the extraordinary problems faced by the Constitutionalists who sought to develop an educational and legal infrastructure for a country that had little or nothing to start from. What was the point of a code of law when one had no judges or lawyers?[3] Similarly where does one begin to construct a system of mass education when there are as yet no teachers, or accepted rules of grammar and instruction? The consequence was to take the fateful if understandable step to establish an authority and a power that could impose and develop the governmental machinery required to implement the wider social and economic reforms. Drawing from the European experience, 'Enlightened Despotism', the acceptable, and at times, necessary form of despotism, would be harnessed to push through the structural reforms for the creation of a functioning state. This 'enlightened despot' in the language of the time, would be distinct from his predecessors in being a 'national' monarch, devoted to the welfare of his people and drawing authority from his position as the first servant of the state. In time, he would be reconstituted as a constitutional monarch, the defender of the Constitution, and the guarantor of the rule of law: 'a first magistrate', as Malcolm had described to Fath Ali Shah.

But that, as Iranians have only been too acutely aware, was not how the political shape of the country developed. Reza Shah might be excused his autocracy as reflective of the realities of the time, but Mohammad Reza Shah not only failed to fulfil the promise of his father's legal reforms but decided on a wholesale adoption of the then dominant modernisation thesis which focused on economic-led development as opposed to a balanced approach that included a measure of political reform. The conflict with Abol-Hassan Ebtehaj was emblematic of this struggle to define durable development. The tensions inherent in such an approach became all the more apparent as the education reforms initiated by his father and pursued with some vigour by himself, began to yield fruit. Mohammad Reza Shah's decision to move away from the constitutional inheritance at a time of dramatic socio-economic change, and crucially at a time when the country might have absorbed the shocks inherent in any political reform, was to prove a critical mistake, not only for the future of his dynasty but the future political development of the country. The Revolution that overthrew him was much against his own particular vision than that of the Constitutionalists or indeed the state apparatus constructed by Reza Shah – which, more acute observers noted, largely survived the upheaval that followed.

Nonetheless, the establishment of the Islamic Republic was a recognition that a measure of political participation was necessary and had to be incorporated into the fabric of any state. Ironically, following the devastation of the Iran–Iraq War, a war that Iran fought and indeed survived by exploiting the resources and inheritance of the Pahlavi state, Iran's new empowered President, Ali Akbar Hashemi Rafsanjani sought to reconstruct that legacy largely on the model provided by the late Shah – that was economic-led with minimal attention to the political framework. He was soon to discover, as the Shah had done before him, that economic reform in the absence of political reform was meaningless and that the success of one depended emphatically on the achievement of the other. In handing the baton over to Mohammad Khatami, Rafsanjani not only acknowledged this reality, but the new president was perhaps more acutely aware of the veracity of the constitutional inheritance than any other occupant of that office.

This view, needless to say, conflicted heavily with the autocratic vision of those who supported and surrounded the Supreme Leader, and in the crisis of 2009, it became apparent that the charges of 'Islamic Monarchy' that were thrown against the Ayatollah Khamenei masked a much more serious deterioration in the constitutionalist inheritance. Even if, much like his Qajar predecessors, the exercise of power was a matter of continuous negotiation, the authority he now aspired to was far in excess of anything they possessed. Indeed, the Islamic Republic expressed in exaggerated form the political tensions that have characterised Iranian states: its durability is a reflection of its republican pretensions and its ability to accommodate, more or less, the political mood of the country, but its inherent fragility is a reflection of a lurch to autocracy that brooks no compromise. That senior clerics have suggested that the concept of *velayat-e faqih* be incorporated as one of the pillars of Muslim (Shi'a) belief, and that obedience to the Supreme Leader – and by extension those he appoints – is akin to obedience to God, is a measure of how far things have gone. That many devout Iranians find such suggestions objectionable is likewise a reflection of the yawning gap between state and society – a gap that some have argued has never been greater and echoes the problems faced by the later Qajar monarchs.

It is striking that a country possessed of such remarkable human and natural resources has still not been able to find a coherent and sensible way to organise itself for the exploitation of those resources for the welfare of all. During the Ahmadinejad presidency it has been estimated that such $800 billion of oil wealth was squandered,[4] and in the absence of any form of accountability, there is little chance that any of this money will be recovered. Continued political instability has fostered further corruption as individuals seek to stabilise their own positions by hoarding wealth, at the expense of the state. This depreciating cycle, with the wide disparities in wealth it encourages, is reaching breaking point. Unable or unwilling to invest in infrastructure, Iran is a country that is fast depleting its resources, be they economic, political or indeed human.[5] Iran has one of the largest brain drains of any country in the world,[6] while the shortage of water is now becoming critical.[7] In this context, it is not surprising that political discontent is on the rise, though the recent disturbances which emerged in late 2017 were of a more fundamental and critical nature than those that gripped the country in 2009. They were undeniably smaller and more localised, but their geographic spread and basic demands reflected the widespread nature of a profound economic malaise that was affecting the country at large and insofar as even Reformist activists seemed at a loss to explain the nature of the protests, they signified that the protests were now occurring outside the regular templates of political activity. The initial outburst of protest, in all its violence, was repressed but protests continue and in a remarkable testament to the power of ideas, a student pronounced in front of Ayatollah Khamenei that the solution to the ongoing problems had to be found within and that temporary or ad hoc measures were no longer an option. The critical solution, the solution that had been recognised prior to the Constitutional Revolution to this day, was the implementation of the rule of law: a return to the Constitution (in this case that of the Islamic Republic) and the law.[8]

The response to this pointed reference remains as yet unclear. The student in question was not the first to express such political clarity in front of the Supreme Leader and won't, one suspects be the last to be ignored. Indeed, the initial response that has emerged from both Khamenei and President Rouhani has been to point the finger of blame elsewhere, and to argue that the country faces no serious economic, political or indeed cultural problems, but incredibly, simply a psychological war directed from abroad with the intention of weakening the foundations of the Islamic Republic and Revolution.[9] In his response to the current situation, Rouhani added for good measure that while the West, and the United States, had always been an 'enemy' to Iran, the current Trump administration was in a class of its own. This tendency to look abroad for causes that are in reality much closer to home is one of the less satisfactory and unintended consequences of the Iranian Enlightenment of the late nineteenth century.

This Enlightenment injected two key ideas into the Iranian body politic: constitutionalism, and nationalism. The former provided the legal framework, the latter was intended to provide the virtue that would populate and propel it. A 'republic', they would have learnt from Montesquieu, cannot survive without virtue, and the national pride this inculcated would enthuse this new Iranian state with the energy it required to develop. As with all ideologies, nationalism taken to excess becomes detrimental to its original goals. Pride in one's culture and achievements tips all too easily into hubris; national distinctions and the innate brilliance of the national genius, leads inexorably to blaming others for inevitable shortcomings. Rational and objective analysis gives way all too frequently to conspiracy theories and what we might term 'political superstitions'. Indeed, the superstition that the Enlightenment railed against, while never eliminated from Iranian discourse, was reintroduced with some enthusiasm into political discourse by Ahmadinejad's 'populist' administration. The consequence has been an instinctive, emotional nationalism, more prone to manipulation and given to virtue signalling than an objective assessment of the realities facing the country.[10] Historical writing and interpretation has not escaped this pernicious tendency.

The early ideologues were only too aware of this danger, that in their anxiety to enthuse the population to a measure of self-confidence would in turn become over-confidence. That critical self-awareness and responsibility, the political maturity that Immanuel Kant argued was the signifier of real, effective enlightenment, has yet to embed itself within Iranian culture and consciousness, with the consequence that Iranians tend to blame the 'other', while remaining reliant on that 'other'. This is a problem that continues to afflict Iran's domestic politics as well as her foreign relations.[11] None of this is to suggest that foreign powers have not impacted, often detrimentally, on the country's political life but as more astute observers have noted, the responsibility and solution for this situation must be found at home. Foreign powers have engaged with what they have encountered and if Iranians are unwilling to address the deficiencies that hinder their political and economic development, they should not expect others to do this for them.[12] Only when Iranians take responsibility for their own affairs will the promise of the Iranian Enlightenment have been fulfilled.

Notes

1 Malcolm, *A History of Persia*, p. 621.
2 Curzon, *Persia and the Persian Question*, Vol II, p. 633.
3 M.A. Foroughi, 'The History of Modernization of Law', *Journal of Persianate Studies* 3, 2010, pp. 31–45.
4 'Hashemi: dar hasht sal gozashteh 800 milliard dollar az dast raft' (Hashemi: in the Last Eight Years We Have Lost $800bn), *Radiofarda.com*, 10 Mordad 1392/1 August 2013.
5 One Iranian news site, *Asr-e Iran*, published online a list of 21 greatest challenges facing Iran, in an echo perhaps of Taqizadeh's 1921 list of prescriptions, though this list does not specify solutions; see '21 abarchalesh-e jomhuri-ye Islami Iran' (21 Greatest Challenges of the Islamic Republic of Iran), *Asr-e Iran*, 21 Khordad 1397/11 June 2018.
6 'Brain Drain Continues in Iran', *Financial Tribune*, 10 November 2016.
7 'Water Shortage "Serious" Says Environment Chief', *Tehran Times*, 12 April 2018.
8 'Sokhanan saree yek daneshju dar deedar ramazani rahbari' (The Candid Speech of a Student in the Ramadan Audience with the Leader), *Ensaf news*, 7 Khordad 1397/28 May 2018, www.ensafnews.com/115469/سخنان-صریح-یک-دانشجو-در-دیدار-رمضانی-ره/.
9 'Rouhani Regrets Popularity of Foreign-Based Persian Media in Iran', Radio Farda, 15 June 2018.
10 Much of this critique would be applicable to populist nationalism elsewhere.
11 Reformists have long argued that the concept of the Guardianship of the Jurist has developed in such a manner as to extend the self-imposed political immaturity of Iranians. A good practical example of this behaviour extended abroad is the recent nuclear negotiations, the economic dividend of which has almost exclusively been laid at the door of the West to deliver.
12 See in this respect Ahmad Kasravi's comments with regard to complaints about Reza Shah as foreign imposed, E. Abrahamian, 'Kasravi: The Integrative Nationalist of Iran', *Middle East Studies* 9(3), 1973, pp. 111–12.

Guide to further research

The literature available for the study of modern Iran is extensive and growing, reflecting the increase in scholarship both in the West and in Iran itself. There are an increasing number of textbooks and historical surveys of modern and contemporary history now available to the student and interested reader of varying length and focus. These are now generously complemented by a plethora of other publications including extremely valuable detailed monographs and studies in academic journals.

In archival terms, the historians of modern Iran find themselves increasingly spoilt for choice, if not daunted by the extent of the resources being made available, both in Iran and abroad. Those in Iran are organised in a series of archives some of which are listed below. Accessibility and availability vary according to the political mood of the country and in periods of political tension, the availability of documents may be restricted, and researchers are urged to use caution when accessing these. It is increasingly common in Western archives to use all the tools that modern technology can offer in photographing and scanning documents for later scrutiny. Such techniques may be viewed with suspicion in Iran and should as a rule be avoided.

In addition to the Iranian archives, there are substantial reserves of documents in both Europe and the United States. Russian archives which offered tentative opportunities after the fall of the Soviet Union are now increasingly difficult for foreign researchers to access. The British archives (Public Record Office and the India Office [now in the British Library]) remain invaluable for studies up to 1951 with very useful material through to 1979. Restrictions do exist on the availability of documents, and while many documents are accessible there is a standard 30- to 40-year embargo on most archival sources with obvious consequences for the study of revolutionary and post-revolutionary Iran. To some extent, this shortfall is compensated for by memoirs and sources such as the BBC *Summary of World Broadcasts*, its American equivalent, Foreign Broadcast Information Services, FOIA-driven archives such as the Digital National Security Archive produced at George Washington University and newspapers. Since 1997, the Iranian press has remained a vital and essential (if neglected – few university libraries have the resources to store newspapers in their original format) resource for the study of contemporary developments.

Perhaps the most important and easily accessible sources for modern Iranian history are the published sources that are now increasingly available in Western libraries. This development is largely down to the pioneering work of Iraj Afshar who spent a lifetime collating and editing papers – not least those of his father – which have since been published in multivolume editions. These collections of newspapers, published articles and private papers provide any researcher with an immense resource much of which has yet to be systematically interrogated.

Archival sources in Iran

Only the major archives are listed. Researchers are encouraged to check accessibility before travel and to strictly adhere to any restrictions in place for the reasons noted above. In addition to the substantial resources in the National Library and the Majlis Library, there are libraries in the various ministries (such as Oil), as well as other state organisations, such as the Central Bank (www.nli.ir).

National Archives of Iran (Sazman-e asnad-e melli-e Iran)

www.nlai.ir

Founded before the Islamic Revolution in 1979, this organisation is the main centre for the collection, cataloguing and organisation of state documents. All ministries and other governmental organisations are required by law to deposit all documents over 40 years old in the archives, and most are made available to bona fide researchers. Only a fraction of the documents have been catalogued (available through http://opac.nlai.ir), and while this remains a substantial figure (over one million), there are an estimated 200 million separate documents, largely from the nineteenth and twentieth centuries, which have yet to be catalogued. Branches of the archives are located in Tehran, as well as Isfahan, Tabriz, Yazd, Kerman, Zahedan and Hamedan. The organisation is administered by the Office of the Presidency (which has merged with the National Library).

Documentation Centre of the Presidency (Markaz-e Asnad Riyasat-Jomhuri)

The Centre is host to documents from the Ministry of Court and other government bodies, such as the Prime Minister's Office, from the accession of Reza Shah to the fall of the Pahlavi dynasty. Most have been catalogued and many have been published. Also administered by the Office of the Presidency. The Centre regularly publishes parts of its archival holdings in books which are released regularly into the market and are accessible to Western library acquisition.

Documentation Centre of the Organisation for Islamic Propagation (Markaz-e Asnad-e Sazman-e Tabliqat-e Islami)

Contains private collections (books and papers) acquired or seized from private estates after the Islamic Revolution. Many of these collections have since been transferred to the Documentation Centre of the Institute for Contemporary History.

Documentation Centre of the Institute for Contemporary History (Markaz-e Asnad-e Moasseseh-ye Tarikh-e Moaser)

www.iichs.org

Private papers seized from the estates of those who left Iran in the aftermath of the Islamic Revolution. Many have been published by the Institute itself, and are available for sale through its website. Administered by the Foundation of the Oppressed.

Documentation Centre of the Foreign Ministry (Markaz-e Asnad Vezarat-e Omor-e Kharejeh)

http://cire.ir/

One of the best organised archival centres in Iran, maintaining documents on Iran's foreign relations since the Safavid era. It has sparingly published its own holdings in book format.

Documentation Centre of the Library of the Islamic Consultative Assembly (Markaz-e Asnad-e Ketabkhane-ye Majlis Shora-ye Eslami)

http://dlib.ical.ir

Host to parliamentary papers from the period of the Constitutional Revolution (1906) to the present day. Contains particularly important documents on the era of the Constitutional Revolution, which are regularly published both in book format and in journals published by the Centre, such as *Payam-e Baharestan*.

Documentation Centre of the Islamic Revolution (Markaz-e Asnad Enqelab-e Islami)

www.irdc.ir

Contains documents pertaining to the former state security agency SAVAK. Many have been published in various collections by the Centre. Administered under the supervision of the Ministry of Intelligence.

The Centre for Historical Analysis (Markaz-e Barresiha-ye Tarikhi)

www.historydocuments.ir

The main repository of SAVAK files from before 1979, which have been progressively published in a sprawling and ongoing 250+ volume series called 'Be Revayat- Asnad-e Savak'. Despite the obvious exclusionary selection process having gone into preparing the volumes, the same offer a unique and necessary insight into the workings of the Pahlavi state.

The Institute of Historical Study and Research (Moasseseh-ye Motaleat va Pazhuheshha-ye Siyasi)

www.ir-psri.com

Another body considered to be linked to the Intelligence Ministry, the Institute produces a considerable amount of studies on political parties of contemporary Iran and has recently specialised in gaining access to reserved SAVAK files on leftist groups such as the Fadaiyan-e Khalq and the Tudeh, and has published books on them which have generated considerable controversy in Iran and abroad.

Documentation Centre of the Central Library of the University of Tehran (Markaz-e Asnad-e Ketabkhane-ye Markazi-e Daneshgah-ye Tehran)

A variety of documents relating to political, cultural and social matters. Particularly important for documents relating to the foundation and development of higher education in Iran. The university libraries also maintain significant collections of Persian language newspapers and periodicals.

Select bibliography

References to specific online articles from the *Encyclopaedia Iranica* can be found in the text.

Documentary sources (Persian)

1351 – sal-e bozorgdasht dah-e-ye enghelab-e Iran: Asl-e dovom; melli shodan-e jangalha va marat'e (1351 – The Tenth Anniversary of the Iranian Revolution: The 2nd Principle: The Nationalisation of the Forests and Pasturelands). Tehran: Ministry of Agriculture, 1351/1973.

Barnameh-ye kamel-e jashnhay-e do hezar-o pansad-omeen sal-e Koroush-e Kabir va bonyad-e shahanshahi-ye Iran (The Complete Programme for the Celebrations of 2,500 Years of Cyrus the Great and the Foundation of the Monarchy of Iran). Tehran, 1340/1961.

Bazm-e Ahriman: jashnhaye do hezar va pansad sale ye shahanshahi Markaz baresi asnad tarikhi vezarat etelaat (Ahriman's Banquet, the Festivities for the 2500 Anniversary of the Monarchy – The Historical Documents Research Centre of the Ministry of Intelligence) (2 volumes). Tehran, 1377/1998.

Vaz'e Ijtema'i-ye kargaran az Koroush-e Kabir ta Shahanshah Aryamehr (The Social Condition of the Workers from Cyrus the Great to the Shahanshah Aryamehr). Tehran: Insurance Organisation, 1350/1972.

Pahlavi, M.R. *'Sokhanan-e-Shahaneh', 1328–1336* (Royal Speeches). Tehran (undated).

Pahlavi, M.R. *Barguzideh az neveshteh-ha va sokhanan-e Shahanshah Aryamehr* (Selections from the Writings and Speeches of the Shahanshah Aryamehr). Tehran (undated).

Pahlavi, M.R. *Farmayeshat-e Shahanshah* (Orders of the Shahanshah), Army Publications, Tehran, 6 Bahman 1343/25 January 1965.

Pahlavi, M.R. *Barguzideh az neveshteh-ha va sokhanan-e Shahanshah Aryamehr az aghaz-e sal-e 1347 ta payan-e sal-e 1351* (Selections from the Writings and Speeches of the Shahanshah Aryamehr from the Beginning of 1347 [1968] to the End of 1351 [1973]). Tehran (undated).

Documentary sources (English)

Foreign Office archives held at the Public Record.

FO 248 (Consular Files) 1941–62.

FO 371 (General Correspondence) 1921–66.

Published Foreign Office Archives.

BBC *Summary of World Broadcasts* (SWB), Part 4: Middle East, Africa and Latin America, 1967–78.

BBC Television (Documentaries), Texts of interviews conducted for BBC 2 *Reputations* (* indicates interview conducted by the author) Abbas Abdi*, Abbas (Magnum photographer)*, Andrew Whitley, Anne Birley, Ardeshir Zahedi, Ayatollah Zanjani*, Claire Hollinworth, Dr Dastejerdi*, Dr Ghaffari*, Farah Pahlavi, Fereidoon Hoveida, Gary Sick, Hojjatoleslam Ghaffari*, Hushang Ansary, Marvin Zonis, Mohammad Hami*, Parviz Radji, Reza Pahlavi, Richard Helms, Setareh Farmanfarmayan, Sharokh Golestan*, Shaul Bakhash, Sir Anthony Parsons, Sir Peter Ramsbotham, William Sullivan.

Bidwell, R. (ed.) *British Documents on Foreign Affairs: Reports and Papers from Foreign Confidential Print, Part 2: From the First to the Second World War, Series B, Turkey, Iran, and the Middle East, 1918–39.*

Documents from the US Embassy in Iran, *Documents from the US Espionage Den*, Muslim Students Following the Line of the Imam.

US Interventions in Iran (10), Vol 61, Tehran, 1366/1987.
US Interventions in Iran (12), Vol 63, Tehran, 1366/1987.
The US Military Advisory Mission in Iran (1), Vol 70, Tehran, 1369/1990.
The US Military Advisory Mission in Iran (2), Vol 71, Tehran, 1369/1990.
The US Military Advisory Mission in Iran (3), Vol 72, Tehran, 1370/1990.

Newspapers and journals (Persian)

Etela'at Siyasi-Eqtesadi.
Majalleh-ye Baresi-ye Tarikhi (Historical Research Magazine) published by the Armed Forces (13 volumes), 1967–78.
Tarikh Moasser Iran (Contemporary Iranian History), quarterly journal.
Adineh.
Iran-e Farda.
Ittila'at (India Office).
Kiyan.
Payame Emrooz.
Rastakhiz (organ of the Rastakhiz Party).

Newspapers and journals (English)

British Journal of Middle Eastern Studies.
Critique.
International Journal of Middle Eastern Studies.
Iranian Studies.
Middle East Journal.
Middle Eastern Studies.
Daily Telegraph.
The Economist.
Time magazine (especially 4 November 1974, 'The Emperor of Oil').
The Times.

Secondary sources (Persian)

Beem-ha va Omid-ha (Fears and Expectations). Tehran: Hamshahri, 1378.
Abdi, A. *Ghodrat, Qanun, farhang* (Power, Law, Culture). Tehran: Qiyam, 1377.
Adamiyat, F. *Andisheh-haye Mirza Fathali Akhundzadeh.* Tehran: Khwarazmi, 1349/1970.
Afshar, A.A. *Khaterat doctor amir aslan afshar.* Montreal: Farhang, 2012.

Ale Ahmad, J. *Khedmat va Kheyanat-e roshanfekran* (The Service and Treason of the Intellectuals). Behrooz, 1357/1978.

Aqoli, B. *Davar va adleyeh* (Davar and the Administration of Justice). Tehran, 1369/1990.

Ashraf, A. 'Bohran hoviat melli va qomi dar Iran' (The Crisis of National and Ethnic Identity in Iran), *Iran-Nameh* 12(3), Summer 1373/1994, pp. 521–50.

Ashraf, A. 'Hoviat Irani' (Iranian Identity), *Goftegu* 3, Farvardin 1373/1994, pp. 7–26.

Ashraf, A. 'Toham-e Tote'eh' (Imagined Conspiracies), *Goftegu* 8, Summer 1374/1995, pp. 7–45.

Atabaki, T. 'Meliat, qomiat va khod-mokhtari dar Iran-e moaser' (Nationality, Ethnicity, and Self-Sufficiency in Contemporary Iran), *Goftegu* 3, Farvardin 1373/1994, pp. 68–83.

Azudullah, Soltan Ahmad Mirza. *Tarikh-e Azudi* (The Azudi History). Tehran: Meharat, 1376/1997.

Etemad-Moghadam, A. *Shah va Sepah bar bonyad-e Shahnameh-ye Ferdowsi* (The Shah and the Army as Seen in Ferdowsi's Shahnameh). Tehran (undated).

Fallaci, O. *Mosahebeh ba Tarikh* (Interview with History). Tehran, 1357/1978–79 (Persian translation from Italian).

Fardoust, H. *Zohur va Soghut-e Saltanat-e Pahlavi* (The Emergence and Fall of the Pahlavi Monarchy). Tehran, 1371.

Ganji, A. *Ali-jenab sorkh poosh va ali-jenab khakestari* (The Red Eminence and the Grey Eminences). Tehran: Tar-e No, 2000.

Hajarian, S. *Jomhuriyat: Asunzadaee az ghodrat* (Republicanism: Demystification of Power). Tehran: Tar-e No, 2000.

Honarmand, M. *Pahlavism: Maktab-e No* (Pahlavism: The New Ideology). Tehran, 1345/1966.

Kadivar, M. *Baha-ye Azadi: defa'at Mohsen Kadivar* (The Price of Freedom: The Defence of Mohsen Kadivar). Tehran: Ghazal, 1378/1999–2000.

Kasravi, A. *Tarikhcheh-ye Shir-o Khorsheed* (The History of the Lion and Sun). Tehran, 2536/1977.

Kasravi, A. *Tarikh Mashruteh-ye Iran* (History of the Constitution in Iran). Tehran: Amir Kabir, 1378/1999 [first published 1940].

Kermani, N. *'Tarikh-e Bidari Iranian* (The History of the Iranian Awakening). Tehran: Farhang, 1349/1970 [first published 1910].

Khatami, M. *Mardomsalari* (Democracy). Tehran: Tar-e No, 1380/2001–02.

Ladjevardi, H. *Khaterat-e Ali Amini* (Memoirs of Ali Amini), Iranian Oral History Project, Centre for Middle Eastern Studies, Harvard University, 1995.

Makki, H. *Tarikh-e bist sale-ye Iran* (A Twenty Year History of Iran) (8 volumes). Tehran 1323–25/1944–46.

Makki, M. 'Goftegu ba Hossein Makki' (Interview with Hossein Makki), *Tarikh-e Moasser-e Iran* (Iranian Contemporary History) 1(1), Spring 1997, pp. 178–216.

Nowbakht. *Shahanshah-ye Pahlavi* (The Pahlavi Shahanshah). Tehran, 1342/1923–24.

Pahlavi, M.R. *Enghelab-e Sefid-e Shahanshah* (The White Revolution of the Shahanshah). Tehran (undated).

Pahlavi, M.R. *Besouyeh Tamadun-e Bozorg* (Towards the Great Civilisation). Tehran (undated).

Rajaee, F. 'Osturesazi va tarikhnegari; afsaneh va vaqe'iyat' (Myth Making and Historiography; Fiction and Fact), *Etela'at Siyassi va Eqtessadi* 53–4, Bahman/Esfand 1370 [Feb/Mar 1992], pp. 14–23.

Roostai, M. *Tarikh nokhostin farhangestan-e iran beh ravayet asnad* (A Documentary History of the First Farhangestan). Tehran: Nashreney, 1385/2006.

Salvar, A. 'Goftegu ba Abbas Salvar, rais peesheen-e sazman-e eslahat-e arzi' (Interview with Abbas Salvar: The Former Head of the Land Reform Organisation), *Tarikh-e Moasser-e Iran* (Contemporary Iranian History) 1(4), 1998, pp. 243–76.

Shafa, S. *Gah-Nameh-ye Panjah Sal-e Shahanshahi-e Pahlavi* (Chronicle of Fifty Years of the Pahlavi Monarchy). Tehran, 1978.

Taqizadeh, H. *Kaveh* (ed. I Afshar). Tehran: Asatir, 2005 [originally published 1916–22, Berlin].

Taqizadeh, H. *Maqallat Taqizadeh*, Vol 5. Tehran: Shokufan, 2535/1976.

Taqizadeh, H. *Maqallat Taqizadeh*, Vol 7. Tehran: Shokufan, 1356/1977.

Taqizadeh, H. *Maqallat Taqizadeh*, Vol 9. Tehran: Shokufan, 2536/1977.

Yazdi, K.M. *Shast Qarn-e Tarikh va Taj-gozari* (Sixty Centuries of History and Coronation). Tehran, 1967.

Zaka ol Molk, M.A. (Foroughi). *Maqallat-e Foroghi*, Vol 1. Tehran: Tus, 1384/2005.

Zaka ol Molk, M.A. (Foroughi). *Maqallat-e Foroghi*, Vol 2. Tehran: Tus, 1387/2008.

Secondary sources (English)

Journal of the Royal Central Asian Society, 'Recent Developments in Persia' 13(2), 1926, pp. 130–32.

Journal of the Royal Central Asian Society, 'Persian Affairs' 14(2), 1927, pp. 177–80.

Journal of the Royal Central Asian Society, 'The Rise and Fall of Teymourtache' 21(1), 1934, p. 93.

Abdi, K. 'Nationalism, Politics and the Development of Archaeology in Iran', *American Journal of Archaeology* 105, 2001, pp. 51–76.

Abrahamian, E. 'The Crowd in Iranian Politics, 1905–1953', *Past & Present* 41, 1968, pp. 184–210.

Abrahamian, E. 'Communism and Communalism in Iran: The Tudeh and the Firqah-i Dimukrat', *International Journal of Middle Eastern Studies* 1(4), 1970, pp. 291–316.

Abrahamian, E. 'Kasravi: The Integrative Nationalist of Iran', *Middle Eastern Studies* 9(3), 1973, pp. 271–95.

Abrahamian, E. 'Oriental Despotism: The Case of Qajar Iran', *International Journal of Middle Eastern Studies* 5, 1974, pp. 3–31.

Abrahamian, E. 'The Causes of the Constitutional Revolution in Iran', *International Journal of Middle East Studies* 10(3), 1979, pp. 381–414.

Abrahamian, E. *Iran between Two Revolutions*. Princeton, NJ: Princeton University Press, 1982.

Abrahamian, E. *Radical Islam: The Iranian Mojahedin*. London: I.B. Tauris, 1989.

Abrahamian, E. *Khomeinism*. London: I.B. Tauris, 1993.

Abrahamian, E. *Tortured Confessions*. Los Angeles, CA: University of California Press, 1999.

Abrahamian, E. 'The Islamic Left: Radicalism to Liberalism', in Stephanie Cronin (ed.), *Reformers and Revolutionaries in Modern Iran: New Perspectives on the Iranian Left*. London: Routledge, 2004, pp. 268–79.

Abrahamian, E. and Kazemi, F. 'The Non-Revolutionary Peasantry of Modern Iran', *Iranian Studies* 11(1/4), 1978, pp. 259–304.

Adelkhah, F. *Being Modern in Iran*. London: Hurst, 1999.

Afkhami, G.R. *The Iranian Revolution: Thanatos on a National Scale*. Washington, DC: Middle East Institute, 1985.

Afkhami, G.R. *The Life and Times of the Shah*. Los Angeles, CA: University of California Press, 2008.

Afshar, H. (ed.) *Iran: A Revolution in Turmoil*. Basingstoke: Macmillan, 1985.

Afshar, H. *Islam and Feminism: An Iranian Case-Study*. Basingstoke: Macmillan, 1998.

Afshari, R. 'The Historians of the Constitutional Movement and the Making of the Iranian Populist Tradition', *International Journal of Middle Eastern Studies* 25, 1993, pp. 477–94.

Al-Ahmad, J. *Plagued by the West* (*Gharbzadegi*) (trans. P. Sprachman). Delmar, NY: Caravan 1982.

Alam, A. *The Shah and I: The Confidential Diary of Iran's Royal Court, 1969–1977*. New York: St. Martin's Press, 1992.

Alexander, Y. and Nanes, A. (eds.) *The United States and Iran: A Documentary History*. Frederick, MD: University Publications of America, 1980.

Algar, H. 'An Introduction to the History of Freemansonry [*sic*] in Iran' *Middle Eastern Studies* 6(3), 1970, pp. 276–96.

Algar, H. *Mirza Malkum Khan: A Biographical Study in Iranian Modernism*. Berkeley, CA: University of California Press, 1973.

Alvandi, R. *Nixon, Kissinger, and the Shah*. Oxford: Oxford University Press, 2014.

Amanat, A. 'The Study of History in Post-Revolutionary Iran: Nostalgia, Illusion or Historical Awareness', *Iranian Studies* 22(4), 1989, pp. 3–18.

Amanat, A. *The Pivot of the Universe: Nasir al Din Shah Qajar and the Iranian Monarchy, 1831–1896*. London: I.B. Tauris, 1997.

Amanat, A. *Modern Iran*. New Haven, CT: Yale University Press, 2017.

Amin, C.A. *The Making of the Modern Iranian Woman*. Gainsville, FL: University Press of Florida, 2002.

Amini, P.M. 'A Single Party State in Iran, 1975–78: The Rastakhiz Party. The Final Attempt by the Shah to Consolidate His Political Base', *Middle Eastern Studies* 38(1), 2002, pp. 131–68.

Amnesty International. *Iran: Amnesty International Briefing*. Amnesty International, November 1976.

Amuzegar, J. 'Nationalism versus Economic Growth', *Foreign Affairs* 44(4), 1966, pp. 651–61.

Amuzegar, J. 'Adjusting to Sanctions', *Foreign Affairs* 76(3), 1997, pp. 31–41.

Aneer, G. *Imam Ruhullah Khumaini: Shah Muhammad Reza Pahlavi and the Religious Traditions of Iran*. Uppsala: S. Academiae Ubsalienois, 1985.

Ansari, A.M. 'The Role of the *Ulema* in Iranian Politics 1951–1964', in *Religion and Politics in Iran: Proceedings of the Association of Iranian Researchers Conference*. London, February 1997, pp. 61–76.

Ansari, A.M. 'Iranian Foreign Policy under Khatami: Reform and Reintegration', in A. Mohammadi and A. Ehteshami (eds.), *Iran and Eurasia*. Reading: Ithaca Press, 2000, pp. 35–58.

Ansari, A.M. 'The Myth of the White Revolution: Mohammad Reza Shah, "Modernisation" and the Consolidation of Power', *Middle Eastern Studies* 37(3), 2001, pp. 1–24.

Ansari, A.M. 'Iran and the US in the Shadow of 9/11: Persia and the Persian Question Revisited', *Iranian Studies* 39(2), June 2006, pp. 155–70.

Ansari, A.M. *Iran, Islam and Democracy: The Politics of Managing Change*, 2nd edn. London: Royal Institute of International Affairs, 2006.

Ansari, A.M. *Iran under Ahmadinejad: The Politics of Confrontation*, Adelphi Paper 393, International Institute for Strategic Studies, London, 2007.

Ansari, A.M. 'Iran under Ahmadinejad': Populism and Its Malcontents', *International Affairs*, Royal Institute of International Affairs, 84(4), July 2008, pp. 683–700.

Ansari, A.M. *Crisis of Authority: Iran's 2009 Presidential Election*. London: Royal Institute of International Affairs, 2010.

Ansari, A.M. 'Iran to 1919', in Frances Robinson (ed.), *The New Cambridge History of Islam*, Vol 5. Cambridge: Cambridge University Press, 2010, pp. 154–79.

Ansari, A.M. *The Politics of Nationalism in Modern Iran*. Cambridge, Cambridge University Press, 2012.

Ansari, A.M. '*L'Etat C'est Moi*: The Paradox of Sultanism and the Question of "Regime Change" in Modern Iran', *International Affairs* 89(2), March 2013, pp. 283–98.

Ansari, A.M. 'Myth, History and Narrative Displacement in Iranian Historiography', in A.M. Ansari (ed.), *Perceptions of Iran: History, Myths and Nationalism from Medieval Persia to the Islamic Republic*, International Library of Iranian Studies. London: I.B. Tauris, 2013, pp. 5–24.

Ansari, A.M. 'Nationalism, Myth and History in Modern Iran', in H. Chehabi, F. Khosrokhavar and C. Therme (eds.), *Iran and the Challenges of the Twenty-First Century: Essays in Honour of Mohammad Reza Jalili*. Costa Mesa, CA: Mazda, 2013, pp. 129–43.

Ansari, A.M. 'Sir John Malcolm and the Idea of Iran', in R. Hillenbrand, A.C.S. Peacock and F. Abdullaeva (eds.), *Ferdowsi, the Mongols and the History of Iran*. London: I.B. Tauris, 2013, pp. 209–17.

Ansari, A.M. 'The Myth of Perfidious Albion: Anglo-Iranian Relations in Historical Context', *Journal of Asian Affairs*, 44(3), November 2013, pp. 378–91.

Ansari, A.M. 'The Islamic Republic of Iran, and the Crisis of Legitimacy', in N. Jebnoun, M. Kia and M. Kirk (eds.), *Modern Middle East Ramifications*. London: Routledge, 2014, pp. 225–41.

Ansari, A.M. 'Mohammad Ali Foroughi and the Construction of Civic Nationalism in Early Twentieth Century Iran', in H.E. Chehabi, P. Jafari and M. Jefroudi (eds.), *Iran in the Middle East: Transnational Encounters and Social History*. London: I.B. Tauris, 2015, pp. 11–26.

Ansari, A.M. (ed.) *Iran's Constitutional Revolution of 1906: Narratives of Enlightenment*. London: Gingko Library, 2016.

Ansari, A.M. 'Taqizadeh and European Civilisation', *Iran*, 54(1), 2016, pp. 47–58.

Ansari, A.M. 'Iranian Nationalism and the Question of Race', in M. Litvak (ed.), *Constructing Nationalism in Iran: From the Qajars to the Islamic Republic*. Oxford: Routledge, 2017, pp. 101–16.

Ansari, A.M. 'The Curious Case of the Nuclear Company of Britain and Iran', *Iran*, 55(1), 2017, pp. 73–86.

Arfa, H. *Under Five Shahs*. London: Murray, 1964.

Arjomand, S. *The Shadow of God and the Hidden Imam*. Chicago, IL: University of Chicago Press, 1984.

Arjomand, S. *The Turban for the Crown*. Oxford: Oxford University Press, 1988.

Ashraf, A. 'Historical Obstacles to the Development of a Bourgeoisie in Iran', *Iranian Studies*, 2(2/3), Spring–Summer 1969, pp. 54–79.

Atabaki, T. *Iran in the 20th Century: Historiography and Political Culture*. London: I.B. Tauris, 2009.

Axworthy, M. *Sword of Persia: Nader Shah, from Tribal Warrior to Conquering Tyrant*. London: I.B. Tauris, 2009.

Axworthy, M. (ed.) *Crisis, Collapse, Militarism and Civil War: The History and Historiography of 18th Century Iran.* Oxford: Oxford University Press, 2018.

Azimi, F. *Iran: The Crisis of Democracy.* London: I.B. Tauris, 1989.

Bakhash, S. *Iran: Monarchy, Bureaucracy and Reform under the Qajars, 1858–1896.* Ithaca, NY: Cornell University Press, 1978.

Bakhash, S. 'Iran's Foreign Policy under the Islamic Republic, 1979–2000', in L. Carl Brown (ed.), *Diplomacy in the Middle East: The International Relations of Regional and Outside Powers.* London: I.B. Tauris, 2001, pp. 247–58.

Baldwin, G.B. 'The Foreign Educated Iranian', *Middle East Journal* 17(3), 1963, pp. 264–78.

Baldwin, G.B. 'The Legal System of Iran', *International Lawyer* 7(2), 1973, pp. 492–504.

Banani, A. *The Modernisation of Iran.* Stanford, CA: Stanford University Press, 1961.

Bani-Sadr, A.H. *My Turn to Speak.* London: Brasseys, 1991.

Barr, J. *Lords of the Desert.* London: Simon & Schuster, 2018.

Bayat, M. *Iran's First Revolution: Shi'ism and the Constitutional Revolution of 1905–1909.* Oxford: Oxford University Press, 1991.

Bayat Philipp, M. 'Mīrzā Āqā Khān Kirmānī: A Nineteenth Century Persian Nationalist', *Middle Eastern Studies* 10(1), 1974, pp. 36–59.

Bayne, E. *Persian Kingship in Transition: Conversations with a Monarch Whose Office Is Traditional and Whose Goal Is Modernisation.* New York: American Universities Field Staff, 1968.

Beeman, W. 'What Is Iranian National Character?', *Iranian Studies* 9, 1976, pp. 22–48.

Beeman, W. *Language, Status and Power in Iran.* Bloomington, IN: Indiana University Press, 1986.

Beeman, W. 'Double Demons: Cultural Impedance in US–Iranian Understanding', *Iranian Journal of International Affairs*, Summer–Fall 1990, pp. 319–34.

Behdad, S. 'Winners and Losers of the Iranian Revolution: A Study in Income Distribution', *International Journal of Middle Eastern Studies* 21, 1989, pp. 327–58.

Behnam, M.R. *Cultural Foundations of Iranian Politics.* Salt Lake City, UT: University of Utah Press, 1986.

Behrooz, M. *Rebels with a Cause: The Failure of the Left in Iran.* London: I.B. Tauris, 1999.

de Bellaigue, C. *The Islamic Enlightenment: The Modern Struggle between Faith and Reason.* London: The Bodley Head, 2017.

Berberian, H. *Armenians in the Constitutional Revolution of 1905–1911.* Oxford: Westview Press, 2001.

Bharier, J. 'The Growth of Towns and Villages in Iran 1900–66', *Middle Eastern Studies* 8(1), 1972, pp. 51–62.

Bill, J. 'Social and Economic Foundations of Power in Contemporary Iran', *Middle East Journal* 17(4), 1963, pp. 400–418.

Bill, J. 'The Politics of Student Alienation', *Iranian Studies* 2(1), 1969, pp. 8–26.

Bill, J. 'Modernisation and Reform from Above: The Case of Iran', *Journal of Politics* 32(1), 1970, pp. 19–40.

Bill, J. *The Politics of Iran: Groups, Classes and Modernisation.* New York: Merill, 1972.

Bill, J. 'The Plasticity in Informal Politics: The Case of Iran', *Middle East Journal* 27(2), 1973, pp. 131–51.

Bill, J. 'Power and Religion in Revolutionary Iran', *Middle East Journal* 36(1), 1982, pp. 22–47.

Bill, J. *The Eagle and the Lion: The Tragedy of American–Iranian Relations*. New Haven, CT: Yale University Press, 1988.

Binder, L. *Iran: Political Development in a Changing Society*. Berkeley, CA: University of California Press, 1962.

Bonakdarian, M. 'The Persia Committee and the Constitutional Revolution in Iran', *British Journal of Middle Eastern Studies* 18(2), 1991, pp. 186–207.

Bonakdarian, M. 'Edward G. Browne and the Iranian Constitutional Struggle: From Academic Orientalism to Political Activism', *Iranian Studies* 26(1/2), Winter–Spring 1993, pp. 7–31.

Bonakdarian, M. 'Iranian Constitutional Exiles and British Foreign-Policy Dissenters, 1908–9', *International Journal of Middle East Studies* 27(2), 1995, pp. 175–91.

Bonakdarian, M. *Britain and the Constitutional Revolution of 1906–1911*. Syracuse, NY: Syracuse University Press, 2006.

Boroujerdi, M. 'The Encounter of Post-Revolutionary Thought in Iran with Hegel, Heidegger and Popper', in S. Mardin (ed.), *Cultural Transitions in the Middle East*. Leiden: Brill, 1994, pp. 236–59.

Boroujerdi, M. *Iranian Intellectuals and the West: The Tormented Triumph of Nativism*. Syracuse, NY: Syracuse University Press, 1996.

Boroujerdi, M. 'Contesting Nationalist Constructions', *Critique*, Spring 1998, pp. 43–55.

Boroujerdi, M. and Rahimkhani, K. *Postrevolutionary Iran: A Political Handbook*. Syracuse, NY: Syracuse University Press, 2018.

Bostock, F. and Jones, G. *Planning and Power in Iran: Ebtehaj and Economic Development under the Shah*. London: Frank Cass, 1989.

Bourke-Burrowes, D. 'Changes and Development in Persia during the Pahlavi Regime', *Journal of the Royal Central Asian Society* 18(1), 1931, pp. 39–49.

Brammer, L.M. 'Problems of Iranian University Students', *Middle East Journal* 18(4), 1964, pp. 443–50.

Browne, E.G. *A Year amongst the Persians*. London: Century Publishing, 1984 [first published 1893].

Browne, E.G. *The Persian Revolution 1905–1909*. Washington, DC: Mage, 2005 [first published 1910].

Bulliet, R.W. *Islam: The View from the Edge*. New York: Columbia University Press, 1994.

Burke-Inlow, E. *Shahanshah: A Study of Monarchy in Iran*. Delhi: Motilal Banarsidass, 1979.

Burrell, R.M. 'Ruler and Subject in Iran', *Middle Eastern Studies* 25(2), 1989: pp. 253–61.

Chehabi, H.E. *Iranian Politics and Religious Modernism: The Liberation Movement of Iran under the Shah and Khomeini*. Ithaca, NY: Cornell University Press, 1990.

Chehabi, H.E. 'Staging the Emperor's New Clothes: Dress Codes and Nation Building under Reza Shah', *Iranian Studies* 26(3–4), 1993, pp. 209–33.

Chehabi, H.E. 'The Impossible Republic: Contradictions of Iran's Islamic State', *Contention* 5(3), 1996, pp. 135–54.

Chehabi, H.E. 'The Political Regime of the Islamic Republic in Comparative Perspective', *Government and Opposition* 36(1), 2001, pp. 48–70.

Chehabi, H. and Martin, V. (eds.) *Iran's Constitutional Revolution: Popular Politics, Cultural Transformations and Transnational Connections*. London: I.B. Tauris, 2010.

Chubin, S. 'Iran's Strategic Predicament', *Middle East Journal* 54(1), 2000, pp. 10–24.

Chubin, S. and Tripp, C. *Iran and Iraq at War*. London: I.B. Tauris, 1988.

Cordesman, A.H. and Wagner, A.R. *The Lessons of Modern War*, Vol 2: *The Iran–Iraq War*. San Francisco, CA: Westview Press, 1990.

Cottam, R. 'Political Party Development in Iran', *Iranian Studies* 1(3), 1968, pp. 82–95.

Cottam, R. *Nationalism in Iran*. Pittsburgh, PA: University of Pittsburgh Press, 1979.

Cronin, S. 'Opposition to Reza Khan within the Iranian Army, 1921–26', *Middle Eastern Studies* 30(4), October 1994, pp. 724–50.

Cronin, S. 'An Experiment in Revolutionary Nationalism: The Rebellion of Colonel Muhammad Taqi Khan Pasyan in Mashhad April–October 1921', *Middle Eastern Studies* 33(4), October 1997, pp. 693–750.

Cronin, S. *The Army and the Creations of the Pahlavi State in Iran, 1910–1926*. London: I.B. Tauris, 1997.

Curzon, G.N. *Persia and the Persian Question* (2 volumes). London: Frank Cass, 1966 [first published 1892].

Dabashi, H. *Theology of Discontent*. New York: New York University Press, 1993.

De Villiers, G. *The Imperial Shah: An Informal Biography*. Boston, MA: Little, Brown, 1976.

Demorgny, G. 'Discussion of Question of Using the Latin Alphabet for Persian', *Revue des Études Islamiques II*, 1928, pp. 587–90.

Denman, D.R. *The King's Vista: A Land Reform Which Has Changed the Face of Persia*. Berkhamstead: Geographical Publications, 1973.

Dorman, W.A. and Farhang, M. *The US Press and Iran*. Berkeley, CA: University of California Press, 1987.

Eastwick, E. *Journal of a Diplomate's Three Years Residence in Persia*. London: Smith and Elder, 1864.

Ehteshami, A. *After Khomeini: The Iranian Second Republic*. London: Routledge, 1995.

Ehteshami, A. *The Politics of Economic Restructuring in Post-Khomeini Iran*, Centre for Middle Eastern and Islamic Studies (CMEIS) Occasional Paper 50, Durham, July 1995.

Ehteshami, A. *Political Upheaval and Socio-economic Continuity: The Case of Iran*, Research Unit for the Study of Economic Liberalisation (RUSEL) Working Paper 6, Exeter University (undated).

Ekhtiar, M. 'An Encounter with the Russian Czar: The Image of Peter the Great in Early Qajar Historical Writings', *Iranian Studies* 29(1/2), Winter–Spring, 1996, pp. 57–70.

Elwell-Sutton, L.P. 'Political Parties in Iran', *Middle East Journal* 3(1), 1949, pp. 45–62.

Elwell-Sutton, L.P. 'Nationalism and Neutralism in Iran', *Middle East Journal* 12(1), 1958, pp. 20–32.

Elwell-Sutton, L.P. 'The Iranian Press 1941–47', *Iran* 6, 1968, pp. 65–104.

Enayat, H. *Modern Islamic Political Thought*. London: Macmillan, 1982.

Enayat, H. *Law, State, and Society in Modern Iran*. New York: Palgrave Macmillan, 2013.

Erdman, P. *The Crash of '79*. London: Secker and Warburg, 1977.

Facts about the Celebration of the 2500th Anniversary of the Founding of the Persian Empire by Cyrus the Great. Tehran, 1971.

Farmanfarma, A. 'Constitutional Law of Iran', *American Journal of Comparative Law* 3(2), 1954, pp. 241–7.

Farsoun, S.K. and Mashayekhi, M. (eds.) *Iran: Political Culture in the Islamic Republic*. London: Routledge, 1992.

Fatemi, K. 'Leadership by Distrust: The Shah's Modus Operandi', *Middle East Journal* 36, 1982, pp. 48–61.

Fawcett, L. *Iran and the Cold War: The Azerbaijan Crisis of 1946*. Cambridge: Cambridge University Press, 1992.

Ferrier, R. *The History of the British Petroleum Company.* Cambridge: Cambridge University Press, 1982.

Filmer, H. *The Pageant of Persia.* New York: Bobbs-Merrill, 1936.

Firoozi, F. 'Demographic Review: Iranian Censuses 1956 and 1966: A Comparative Analysis', *Middle East Journal* 24(2), 1970, pp. 220–28.

Fischer, J. 'The Land of Charming Anarchists: A Report from Iran', *Harpers*, March, April 1965.

Fischer, M.M.J. *Iran: From Religious Dispute to Revolution.* Madison, WI: University of Wisconsin Press, 2003.

Forbes, J.R. *Conflict: Angora to Afghanistan.* London: Cassell, 1931.

Forozan, H. *The Military in Post-Revolutionary Iran: The Evolution and Roles of the Revolutionary Guards.* London: Routledge, 2018.

Foroughi, M.A. 'The History of Modernization of Law', *Journal of Persianate Studies* 3(1), 2010, pp. 31–45.

Foucault, M. *Politics, Philosophy and Culture: Interviews and Other Writings.* London: Routledge, 1988.

Frye, R.N. 'Islam in Iran', *Muslim World* 46(1), 1956, pp. 5–12.

Frye, R.N. 'The Charisma of Kingship in Ancient Iran', *Iranica Antiqua* 4, 1964, pp. 36–54.

Frye, R.N. *The Golden Age of Persia: The Arabs in the East.* London: Weidenfeld and Nicolson, 1975.

Frye, R.N. *The Heritage of Persia.* Costa Mesa, CA: Mazda, 1993.

Furtig, H. 'Universalist Counter-Projections: Iranian Post-Revolutionary Foreign Policy and Globalisation', in K. Fullberg-Stolberg, P. Heidrich and E. Schone (eds.), *Disassociation and Appropriation: Responses to Globalisation in Asia and Africa.* Berlin: Zentrum Moderner Orient, 1999, pp. 53–74.

Gable, R.W. 'Culture and Administration in Iran', *Middle East Journal* 13(4), 1959, pp. 407–21.

Gasiorowski, M.J. *U.S. Foreign Policy and the Shah: Building a Client State in Iran.* Ithaca, NY: Cornell University Press, 1991.

Gasiorowski, M.J. 'The Qarani Affair and Iranian Politics', *International Journal of Middle Eastern Studies* 25, 1993, pp. 625–44.

Gasiorowski, M.J. 'The Nuzhih Plot and Iranian Politics', unpublished paper, 12 November 2001.

Gasiorowski, M. 'US Intelligence Assistance to Iran, May–October 1979', *Middle East Journal* 66(4), Autumn 2012, pp. 613–27.

Ghods, M.R. 'The Iranian Communist Party under Reza Shah', *Middle Eastern Studies* 26(4), 1990, pp. 506–13.

Ghods, M.R. 'Government and Society in Iran, 1926–34', *Middle Eastern Studies* 27(2), 1991, pp. 219–30.

Ghods, M.R. 'Iranian Nationalism and Reza Shah', *Middle Eastern Studies* 27(1), 1991, pp. 35–45.

Gieling, S. *Religion and War in Revolutionary Iran.* London: I.B. Tauris, 1999.

Goode, J.F. *The United States and Iran: In the Shadow of Musaddiq.* London: Macmillan, 1997.

Goodell, G.E. 'How the Shah Destabilised Himself', *Policy Review* 16, 1981, pp. 55–72.

Graham, R. *Iran: The Illusion of Power.* London: Croom Helm, 1978.

Gregory, L. *The Shah and Persia.* Orpington: Orpington Press, 1959.

Grey, W.G. 'Recent Persian History', *Journal of the Royal Central Asian Society* 13(1), 1926, pp. 29–42.

Haas, W.S. *Iran*. New York: Columbia University Press, 1946.

Habibi, N. 'Popularity of Islamic and Persian Names in Iran before and after the Islamic Revolution', *International Journal of Middle Eastern Studies* 24, 1992, pp. 253–60.

Halliday, F. *Iran: Dictatorship and Development*. London: Pelican, 1979.

Halliday, F. *Revolution and World Politics*. London: Macmillan, 1999.

Hambly, G. 'Attitudes and Aspirations of the Contemporary Iranian Intellectual', *Journal of the Royal Central Asian Society* 51(2), 1964, pp. 127–40.

Hanson, B. 'The "Westoxication" of Iran: Depictions and Reactions of Behrangi, Al-e Ahmad and Shariati', *International Journal of Middle East Studies* 15, 1983, pp. 1–23.

Harney, D. *The Priest and the King*. London: I.B. Tauris, 1998.

Harper, B. 'The Persian Regenesis', *Foreign Affairs* 13(2), 1935, pp. 295–308.

Heiss, M.A. *Empire and Nationhood: The United States, Great Britain, and Iranian Oil, 1950–54*. New York: Columbia University Press, 1997.

Holliday, S. 'Khatami's Islamist-Iranian Discourse of National Identity', *British Journal of Middle Eastern Studies* 37(1), 2010, pp. 1–13.

Hoveyda, F. *The Fall of the Shah*. London: Weidenfeld and Nicolson, 1980.

Hoyt, E. *The Shah: The Glittering Story of Iran and Its People*. New York: P.S. Eriksson, 1976.

Humphreys, R.S. *Between Memory and Desire: The Middle East in a Troubled Age*. Berkeley, CA: University of California Press, 1999.

Hunter, S. 'Iranian Perceptions and the Wider World', *Political Communication and Persuasion* 2(4), 1985, pp. 393–432.

Hunter, S. *Iran after Khomeini*, The Washington Papers 156. New York: Praeger, 1992.

Hunter, S. 'Is Iranian Perestroika Possible without Fundamental Change?', *Washington Quarterly* 21(4), 1998, pp. 23–41.

Irfani, S. *Revolutionary Islam in Iran: Popular Liberation or Religious Dictatorship?* London: Zed, 1983.

Isaawi, C. (ed.) *The Economic History of Iran, 1800–1914*. Chicago, IL: University of Chicago Press, 1971.

Islamic Propagation Council. *Islamic Revolution of Iran*. Tehran: Islamic Propagation Council, 1990.

Jamalzadeh, M.A. Once Upon a Time *(Yeki bud yeki nabud)* (trans. H. Moayyad and P. Sprachman). New York: Bibliotheca Persica, 1985.

Jazani, B. *Capitalism and Revolution in Iran*. London: Zed, 1980.

Jones, G. *Banking and Empire in Iran: The History of the British Bank of the Middle East*. Cambridge: Cambridge University Press, 1986.

Jones Brydges, H. *An Account of the Transactions of His Majesty's Mission to the Court of Persia in the Years 1807–11*, Vol I, Elibron Classics reprint, 2005 [first published in 1834].

Karanjia, R.K. *The Mind of a Monarch*. London: Allen and Unwin, 1977.

Karsh, E. *The Iran–Iraq War: A Military Analysis*, Adelphi Paper 220, International Institute for Strategic Studies, London, Spring 1987.

Karsh, E. (ed.) *The Iran–Iraq War: Impact and Implications*. London: Macmillan, 1989.

Karshenas, M. *Oil, State and Industrialisation in Iran*. Cambridge: Cambridge University Press, 1990.

Katouzian, H. 'Nationalist Trends in Iran, 1921–1926', *International Journal of Middle Eastern Studies* 10, 1979, pp. 533–51.

Katouzian, H. *The Political Economy of Modern Iran*. London: Macmillan, 1981.

Katouzian, H. 'The Aridisolatic Society: A Model of Long Term Social and Economic Development in Iran', *International Journal of Middle Eastern Studies* 15, 1983, pp. 259–81.

Katouzian, H. *Musaddiq and the Struggle for Power in Iran*. London: I.B. Tauris, 1990.

Katouzian, H. 'Sultanism and Arbitrary Government in Pahlavi Iran', Unpublished paper presented to the workshop on 'Sultanistic Regimes' at the Centre for International Affairs, Harvard University, November 1990.

Katouzian, H. 'Arbitrary Rule: A Comparative Theory of State, Politics and Society in Iran', *British Journal of Middle Eastern Studies* 24(1), 1997, pp. 49–73.

Katouzian, H. 'The Pahlavi Regime in Iran', in H. Chehabi and J. Linz (eds.), *Sultanistic Regimes*. London: Johns Hopkins University Press, 1998, pp. 182–205.

Katouzian, H. *State and Society in Iran: The Eclipse of the Qajars and the Emergence of the Pahlavis*. London: I.B. Tauris, 2000.

Kazemi, F. 'Why Iran Chose Khatami [I]', *Middle Eastern Lectures* 3, 1999, pp. 9–16.

Keddie, N. 'The Origins of the Religious-Radical Alliance in Iran', *Past & Present* 34, 1966, pp. 70–80.

Keddie, N. 'The Iranian Power Structure and Social Change 1800–1969', *International Journal of Middle Eastern Studies* 2, 1971, pp. 3–20.

Keddie, N. *Roots of Revolution: An Interpretive History of Modern Iran*. New Haven, CT: Yale University Press, 1981.

Keddie, N. *An Islamic Response to Imperialism: Political and Religious Writings of Sayyid Jamal al Din al Afghani*. Berkeley, CA: University of California Press, 1986.

Keddie, N. *Iran and the Muslim World: Resistance and Revolution*. New York: Macmillan, 1995.

Keddie, N. and Gasiorowski, M.J. (eds.) *Neither East Nor West: Iran, the Soviet Union, and the United States*. New Haven, CT: Yale University Press, 1990.

Khan, Mirza Abul Hassan. *A Persian at the Court of King George 1809–10* (trans. and ed. M.M. Cloake). London: Barrie Jenkins, 1988.

Khomeini, R. *Islam and Revolution*. Berkeley, CA: Mizan, 1981.

Kurzman, C. 'Historiography of the Iranian Revolutionary Movement, 1977–79'. *Iranian Studies* 28(1/2), Winter–Spring 1995, pp. 25–38.

Kurzman, C. *The Unthinkable Revolution in Iran*. Cambridge, MA: Harvard University Press, 2005.

Laing, M. *The Shah*. London: Sidgwick and Jackson, 1977.

Lambton, A.K.S. 'Persia', *Journal of the Royal Central Asian Society* 31, 1943, pp. 8–22.

Lambton, A.K.S. 'Islamic Society in Persia: An Inaugural Lecture', delivered on 9 March 1954, School of Oriental and African Studies.

Lambton, A.K.S. 'The Impact of the West on Persia', *International Affairs* 33(1), 1957, pp. 12–26.

Lambton, A.K.S. 'A Reconsideration of the Position of the Marja al Taqlid and the Religious Institution', *Studia Islamica* 20, 1964, pp. 115–35.

Lambton, A.K.S. *The Persian Land Reform 1962–66*. Oxford: Oxford University Press, 1969.

Lambton, A.K.S. *Landlord and Peasant in Persia*. London: I.B. Tauris, 1991.

Lenczowski, G. 'The Communist Movement in Iran', *Middle East Journal* 1(1), 1949, pp. 29–45.

Lenczowski, G. (ed.) *Iran under the Pahlavis*. Stanford, CA: Hoover Institution Press, 1978.

Lescot, R. 'Notes sur la presse Iranienne', *Revue des Études Islamiques* 2–3(12), 1938, pp. 261–77.

Lockhart, L. 'The Constitutional Laws of Persia: An Outline of Their Origin and Development', *Middle East Journal* 13(4), 1959, pp. 372–88.

Looney, R.E. 'The Role of Military Expenditures in Pre-Revolutionary Iran's Economic Decline', *Iranian Studies* 21(3–4), 1988, pp. 52–83.

Machalski, F. 'Political Parties in Iran in the Years 1941–1946', *Folia Orientalia* 3, 1961, pp. 135–70.

Malcolm, J. *History of Persia* (2 volumes). London: Murray, 1815.

Malcolm, J. *Sketches of Persia*, 1827, Elibron Classics reprint.

Manz, B.F. *The Rise and Rule of Tamerlane*. Cambridge: Cambridge University Press, 1989.

Martin, K. 'Conversation with Dr Musaddiq', *New Statesman and Nation*, 12 January 1952.

Martin, V. 'Mudarris, Republicanism and the Rise to Power of Riza Khan, Sardar-i Sipah', *British Society of Middle East Studies Journal* 21(2), 1994, pp. 199–210.

Martin, V. *Creating an Islamic State: Khomeini and the Making of a New Iran*. London: I.B. Tauris, 2000.

Martin, V. *The Qajar Pact: Bargaining, Protest and the State in 19th Century Persia*. London: I.B. Tauris, 2005.

Martin, V. *Iran between Islamic Nationalism and Secularism*. London: I.B. Tauris, 2013.

Masroori, C. 'European Thought in Nineteenth Century Iran: David Hume and Others', *Journal of the History of Ideas* 61(4), October 2000, pp. 657–74.

Masroori, C. 'French Romanticism and Persian Liberalism and Nineteenth-Century Iran: Mirza Aqa Khan Kirmani and Jacques-Henri Bernardin de Saint-Pierre', *History of Political Thought* 28(3), Autumn 2007, pp. 542–56.

Matthee, R. *Persia in Crisis: Safavid Decline and the Fall of Isfahan*. London: I.B. Tauris, 2012.

Mathee, R. and Andreeva, E. (eds.) *Russians in Iran*. London: I.B. Tauris, 2018.

Menashri, D. *Iran: A Decade of Revolution and War*. London: Holmes and Meier, 1990.

Menashri, D. *Education and the Making of Modern Iran*. Ithaca, NY: Cornell University Press, 1992.

Menashri, D. *Post-Revolutionary Politics in Iran: Religion, Society and Power*. London: Frank Cass, 2001.

Milani, A. *The Persian Sphinx: Amir Abbas Hoveyda and the Riddle of the Iranian Revolution*. London: I.B. Tauris, 2000.

Milani, A. *Lost Wisdom: Rethinking Modernity in Iran*. Washington, DC: Mage, 2004.

Milani, A. *The Shah*. New York, NY: Macmillan, 2010.

Milani, M. *The Making of Iran's Islamic Revolution: From Monarchy to Islamic Republic*, Westview Special Studies on the Middle East. Oxford: Westview Press, 1994.

Miller, W.G. 'Political Organisation in Iran: From Dowreh to Political Party', *Middle East Journal* 23(2–3), 1969, pp. 159–67, 343–50.

Mir Husseini, Z. *Islam and Gender: The Religious Debate in Contemporary Iran*. Princeton. NJ: Princeton University Press, 1999.

Mirsepassi, A. *Political Islam, Iran and the Enlightenment*. New York: Cambridge University Press, 2011.

Moaddel, M. 'Class Struggle in Post-Revolutionary Iran', *International Journal of Middle Eastern Studies* 23, 1991, pp. 317–43.

Moin, B. *Khomeini: Life of the Ayatollah*. London: I.B. Tauris, 1999.

Mohammadi, M. *Judicial Reform and Reorganisation in 20th Century Iran: State Building, Modernisation and Islamicisation*. New York: Routledge, 2010.

Motadel, D. 'Qajar Shahs in Imperial Germany', *Past & Present* 213, November 2011, pp. 191–235.

Mottahedeh, R. *Loyalty and Leadership in Early Islamic Society*. Princeton, NJ: Princeton University Press, 1980.

Mottahedeh, R. *The Mantle of the Prophet: Religion and Politics in Iran*. London: Chatto and Windus, 1986.

Musaddiq, M. *Musaddiq's Memoirs* (ed. and introd. H. Katouzian). London: JEBHE, 1988.

Nabavi, N. 'The Changing Concept of the "Intellectual" in Iran of the 1960s', *Iranian Studies* 32(3), 1999, pp. 333–50.

Naficy, H. 'Nonfiction Fiction: Documentaries on Iran', *Iranian Studies* 12(3–4), 1979, pp. 217–38.

Naficy, H. 'Cinema as a Political Instrument', in M. Bonine and N. Keddie (eds.), *Modern Iran: The Dialectics of Continuity and Change*. Albany, NY: State University of New York Press, 1981, pp. 265–83.

Newman, A. *Safavid Iran: Rebirth of a Persian Empire*. London: I.B. Tauris, 2008.

Nick-Pay, V. *Republican Islam: Power and Authority in Iran*. London: I.B. Tauris, 2016.

Ostovar, A. *Vanguard of the Imam: Religion, Politics, and Iran's Revolutionary Guards*. Oxford: Oxford University Press, 2016.

Pahlavi, A. *Faces in a Mirror: Memoirs from Exile*. Englewood Cliffs, NJ: Prentice-Hall, 1980.

Pahlavi, F. *My Thousand and One Days: An Autobiography*. London: Allen, 1978.

Pahlavi, M.R. *Mission for My Country*. London: Hutchinson, 1961.

Pahlavi, M.R. 'Address of HIM, the Shahinshah of Iran', National Press Club Speech, Washington, DC, 13 April 1962.

Pahlavi, M.R. 'Shah's Statement of Reform', *Middle East Journal* 16(1), 1962, pp. 86–92.

Pahlavi, M.R. *The White Revolution*. Tehran: Kayhan Press, 1967.

Pahlavi, M.R. *Answer to History*. New York: Stein and Day, 1980.

Pahlavi, S. *Remembrances of Soraya*. Tehran (undated).

Parsons, A. *The Pride and the Fall: Iran 1974–1979*. London: Cape, 1984.

Philipp, M.B. 'Mirza Aqa Khan Kermani: A Nineteenth-Century Persian Nationalist', *Middle Eastern Studies* 10(1), 1974, pp. 36–60.

Piscatori, J. *Islam in the Political Process*. Cambridge: Cambridge University Press, 1983.

Piscatori, J. *Islam in a World of Nation States*. Cambridge: Cambridge University Press, 1991.

Post, J. 'Narcissism and the Charismatic Leader–Follower Relationship', *Political Psychology* 7(4), 1986, pp. 675–88.

Powell, A.E. *By Camel and Car to the Peacock Throne*. Garden City, NY: Garden City Publishing, 1923.

Price, P. 'The Present Situation in Persia', *Journal of the Royal Central Asian Society* 28, 1951, pp. 102–11.

Rahnema, A. *An Islamic Utopian: A Political Biography of Ali Shariati*. London: I.B. Tauris, 1998.

Rahnema, A. and Behdad, S. (eds.) *Iran after the Revolution: Crisis of an Islamic State*. London: I.B. Tauris, 1995.

Rajaee, F. (ed.) *The Iran–Iraq War: The Politics of Aggression*. Miami, FL: University of Florida Press, 1993.

Ramazani, R. 'Intellectual Trends in the Politics and History of the Musaddiq Era', in J. Bill and W.R. Louis (eds.), *Musaddiq, Iranian Nationalism and Oil*. London: I.B. Tauris, 1988, pp. 307–29.

Randjbar-Daemi, S. *The Quest for Authority in Iran: A History of the Presidency from Revolution to Rouhani*. London: I.B. Tauris, 2017.

Razi, G.H. 'The Press and Political Institutions of Iran: A Content Analysis of Ettela'at and Keyhan', *Middle East Journal* 22(4), 1968, pp. 463–74.

Razi, G.H. 'Genesis of Party in Iran: A Case Study of the Interaction between the Political System and Political Parties', *Iranian Studies* 3(2), 1970, pp. 58–90.

Reeves, M. *Behind the Peacock Throne*. London: Sidgwick and Jackson, 1986.

Rezun, M. 'Reza Shah's Court Minister, Teymourtash', *International Journal of Middle East Studies* 12, 1980, pp. 119–37.

Richard, Y. 'Ayatollah Kashani: Precursor of the Islamic Republic?', in N. Keddie (ed.), *Religion and Politics in Iran: Shi'ism from Quietism to Revolution*. New Haven, CT: Yale University Press, 1983, pp. 101–24.

Richards, H. 'Land Reform and Agribusiness in Iran', Middle East Research and Information Project (MERIP), September 1975, pp. 3–24.

Ridgeon, L. 'Ahmad Kasravi's Criticisms of Edward Granville Browne', *Iran* 42, 2004, pp. 219–33.

Ridgeon, L. (ed.) *Religion and Politics in Modern Iran*. London: I.B. Tauris, 2005.

Ross, C.N.B., 'Lord Curzon and E.G. Browne Confront the Persian Question', *The Historical Journal* 52, 2009, pp. 385–411.

Rouleau, E. 'The Islamic Republic of Iran: Paradoxes and Contradictions in a Changing Society', *Le Monde Diplomatique*, June 1995.

Roy, O. 'The Crisis of Religious Legitimacy in Iran', *Middle East Journal* 53(2), 1999, pp. 201–16.

Roy, O. 'Why Iran Chose Khatami [II]', *Middle Eastern Lectures* 3, 1999, pp. 17–22.

Sackville-West, V. *Passenger to Tehran*. London: L.V. Woolf, 1926.

Sadeghi-Boroujerdi, E. *Revolution and Its Discontents: Political Thought and Reform in Iran*. Cambridge: Cambridge University Press, 2019.

Sanghvi, R. *Aryamehr, the Shah of Iran: A Political Biography*. London: Macmillan, 1968.

Sanjabi, M. 'Rereading the Enlightenment: Akhundzada and His Voltaire', *Iranian Studies* 28(1/2), Winter–Spring 1995, pp. 39–60.

Schayegh, C. 'Sport, Health, and the Iranian Middle Class in the 1920s and 1930s', *Iranian Studies* 35(4), Autumn 2002, pp. 341–69.

Schayegh, C. *Who Is Knowledgeable Is Strong: Science, Class, and the Formation of Modern Iranian Society, 1900–1950*. Los Angeles, CA: University of California Press, 2009.

Schirazi, A. *The Constitution of Iran*. London: I.B. Tauris, 1998.

Shafaq, S.R. 'Patriotic Poetry in Modern Iran', *Middle East Journal* 6(4), 1952, pp. 417–28.

Shariati, A. *What Is to Be Done: The Enlightened Thinkers and an Islamic Renaissance* (ed. and annotated F. Rajaee). Houston, TX: Institute for Research and Islamic Studies, 1986.

Shawcross, W. *The Shah's Last Ride*. London: Chatto and Windus, 1989.

Sheean, V. *The New Persia*. New York: Century, 1927.

Sheikholeslami, R. 'Courts and Courtiers in the Reign of Reza Shah', *Encyclopædia Iranica*, Vol 6, 1993, pp. 381–4.

Shuster, W.M. *The Strangling of Persia: Story of the European Diplomacy and Oriental Intrigue That Resulted in the Denationalization of Twelve Million Mohammedans*. Washington, DC: Mage, 1987 [first published 1912].

Siavoshi, S. 'Cultural Policies and the Islamic Republic: Cinema and Book Publication', *International Journal of Middle Eastern Studies* 29, 1997, pp. 509–30.

Skrine, C.P. 'New Trends in Iran', *Journal of the Royal Central Asian Society* 42(2), 1955, pp. 100–115.

Skrine, C.P. 'Iran Revisited', *Journal of the Royal Central Asian Society* 45(3), 1958, pp. 218–32.

Sohrabi, N. *Revolution and Constitutionalism in the Ottoman Empire and Iran*. Cambridge: Cambridge University Press, 2011.

Soroudi, S. *Persian Literature and Judeo-Persian Culture: Collected Writings of Soroud S. Soroudi* (ed. H Chehabi). Cambridge, MA: Harvard University Press, 2010.

Soroush, A. *Reason, Freedom, and Democracy in Islam* (trans. and ed. M. Sadri and A. Sadri). Oxford: Oxford University Press, 2000.

Sullivan, W. *Mission to Iran*. New York: Norton, 1981.

Sykes, P. *A History of Persia* (2 volumes). London: Taylor & Francis, 2004 [first published in 1915].

Taheri, A. *The Spirit of Allah: Khomeini and the Islamic Revolution*. London: Hutchinson, 1985.

Taheri, A. *The Unknown Life of the Shah*. London: Hutchinson, 1991.

Tapper, R. *Frontier Nomads of Iran*. Cambridge: Cambridge University Press, 1997.

Taqizadeh, S.H. *Articles and Essays*, Vol 7. Tehran: Shekufan, 1977.

Taqizadeh, S.H. *Opera Minor: Unpublished Writings in European Languages* (ed. I Afshar). Tehran: Shekufan, 1979.

ter Haar, J.G.J. 'Murtaza Mutahhari 1919–1979: An Introduction to His Life and Thought', *Persica* 14, 1990–92, pp. 1–20.

Thaiss, G. 'The Bazaar as a Case Study of Religion and Social Change', in E. Yarshater (ed.), *Iran Faces the 70s*. New York: Columbia University, Center for Iranian Studies 1971, pp. 189–216.

Thompson, W.J. 'Iran: 1939–1944', *Journal of the Royal Central Asian Society* 32, 1945, pp. 34–43.

Vaziri, M. *Iran as Imagined Nation*. New York: Paragon House, 1993.

Volkov, D. *Russia's Turn to Persia*. Cambridge: Cambridge University Press, 2018.

Waterfield, G. *Professional Diplomat: Sir Percy Loraine*. London: John Murray, 1973.

Weinbaum, M.G. 'Iran Finds a Party System: The Institutionalisation of Iran Novin', *Middle East Journal* 27(4), 1973, pp. 439–55.

Westwood, A.F. 'Elections and Politics in Iran', *Middle East Journal* 15(2), 1961 pp. 153–64.

Widengren, G. 'The Sacral Kingship of Iran', *Numen*, supplement 4, 1959.

Wilber, D. *Reza Shah Pahlavi: The Resurrection and Reconstruction of Iran*. Hicksville, NY: Exposition Press, 1975.

Wright, D. *Memoirs*, unpublished.

Wright, D. *The Persians amongst the English*. London: I.B. Tauris, 1985.

Wright, D. 'Ten Years in Iran: Some Highlights', *Journal of the Royal Central Asian Society* 3, 1991, pp. 254–71.

Wright, D. *The English amongst the Persians*. London: I.B. Tauris, 2001.

Yarshater, E. 'Persian Letters in the Last 50 Years', *Middle Eastern Affairs* 11(10), 1960, pp. 298–306.

Yarshater, E. *Iran Faces the Seventies*. New York: Praeger, 1971.

Yoshido, A. *The Texts of the Revolution: Mutaza Mutahhari and Hannah Arendt*, Working Papers Series 3, Institute of Middle Eastern Studies, International University of Japan, Tokyo, 1985.

Young, H.B. 'The Modern Press in Persia', *Moslem World* 24, 1934, pp. 20–25.

Young, T.C. 'The Problem of Westernisation in Iran', *Middle East Journal* 2(1), 1948, pp. 47–59.

Young, T.C. 'The Social Support of Current Iranian Policy', *Middle East Journal* 6(2), 1952, pp. 128–43.

Young, T.C. 'Iran in Continuing Crisis', *Foreign Affairs* 40(2), 1962, pp. 275–92.

Zabih, S. *The Communist Movement in Iran*. Berkeley, CA: University of California Press, 1966.

Zabih, S. *The Iranian Military in Revolution and War*. London: Routledge, 1988.

Zirinsky, M.P. 'Imperial Power and Dictatorship: Britain and the Rise of Reza Shah, 1921–1926', *International Journal of Middle Eastern Studies* 24, 1992, pp. 639–63.

Zonis, M. *The Political Elite of Iran*. Princeton, NJ: Princeton University Press, 1971.

Zonis, M. 'The Political Elite of Iran: A Second Stratum?', in F. Tachau (ed.), *Political Elites and Political Developments in the Middle East*. New York: Wiley, 1975, pp. 193–216.

Zonis, M. *Majestic Failure: The Fall of the Shah*. Chicago, IL: University of Chicago Press, 1991.

Zubaida, S. *Islam, the People and the State: Political Ideas and Movements in the Middle East*. London: I.B. Tauris, 1993.

Index

Page numbers with n indicates an endnote